EARLY NEW YORK
NATURALIZATIONS

EARLY NEW YORK
NATURALIZATIONS

*Abstracts of Naturalization Records
from Federal, State, and Local Courts,
1792-1840*

Compiled by
KENNETH SCOTT

INTRODUCTION

I

N THE COLONIAL PERIOD citizenship in New York was obtained either by Act of Parliament in England or by Act of the Provincial Assembly.[1] After the Revolution, however, on March 26, 1790, Congress passed the first federal naturalization law. It enabled a free white alien of good character to become a citizen after residing two years in the United States (including one year in a particular state) and taking an oath to support the Constitution. Children under 21 in the country were included in the naturalization of the parent.

On January 29, 1795, since members of Congress anticipated what they considered an undesirable influx of foreigners, the requirement of residence from two to five years, with a declaration of intent two years before admission, replaced the more liberal legislation. Renunciation of former allegiance and an oath to support the Constitution were stipulated.

Soon, the Federalists, noting the large number of Irish immigrants, who were in accord with the views of the Jeffersonian Republicans, on June 18, 1798, passed a restrictive law that specified a residence of fourteen years and the filing of a declaration of intent five years before filing of final papers.

After the election of Jefferson to the presidency in 1800, his party, then in control of Congress, on April 14, 1802, passed a law by which the requirement of residence was reduced to five years and the filing of a declaration of intent to three years before admission. Abjuration of foreign allegiance and swearing an oath of attachment to the U.S. Constitution were obligatory.

An Act of March 26, 1834 exempted from the declaration of intent requirement aliens who were residing in the United States between the Acts of 1798 and 1802. Moreover, widows and children of aliens

---

[1] See Kenneth Scott and Kenn Stryker-Rodda, *Denizations, Naturalizations and Oaths of Allegiance in Colonial New York* (Baltimore: Genealogical Publishing Co., Inc., 1975), esp. pp. v-viii of the introduction.

dying before the completion of their admission were to be deemed naturalized.[2]

II

Records, or photocopies thereof, of early New York City naturalizations are found in three places. One is the Federal Archives and Records Center Archives Branch in Bayonne, New Jersey, under the supervision of Joel Buchwald, through whose kindness the following information has been supplied:

RECORDS OF GENEALOGICAL VALUE IN THE FEDERAL ARCHIVES AND RECORDS CENTER ARCHIVES BRANCH, BAYONNE
Records Received from the Immigration and Naturalization Service, New York, New York

1. PHOTOCOPIES OF NATURALIZATION RECORDS. 1792-1906. 1,760 ft.

   The records consist of 5″ x 8″ photographic copies of naturalization documents filed in Federal, State, and local courts located in New York City. The records vary in informational content. There is less information in the earlier records than in the later ones. The earlier records usually include for each petitioner the name and former nationality of the petitioner, the name of the witness in the matter of the petition, and an oath of allegiance to the United States. The latest records usually indicate for each petitioner the name, address, country of birth, age, port and approximate date of arrival, and occupation of the petitioner, the name and address of the witness, and include an oath of allegiance and order of the court admitting the petitioner to citizenship. The records are grouped by name of court and are arranged thereunder numerically

---

[2] For an excellent treatment of the immigration laws see James H. Kettner, *The Development of American Citizenship 1608-1870* (Chapel Hill, N.C.: University of North Carolina Press, 1978), esp. pp. 236-246.

by volume or bundle number, and by page or record number. These photocopies and the original index described in the next entry were made by the Work Projects Administration.

The photocopies of naturalization documents described above are of records originally filed in the following courts during the periods shown:

Federal Courts

Circuit Court of the United States for the Southern District of New York, 1846-76

District Court of the United States for the Southern District of New York, 1824-1906

District Court of the United States for the Eastern District of New York, 1865-1906

State and Local Courts

Court of Common Pleas for the City and County of New York, 1792-1895

Superior Court of the City of New York, 1828-95

Marine Court of the City of New York, 1806-49

Supreme Court of the State of New York, First Judicial District (formerly Supreme Court, City and County of New York), 1868-1906

The City Court of Brooklyn, 1836-94

County Court, Kings County, 1856-1906

County Court, County of Queens, 1799-1906

Surrogate's Court, County of Queens, 1888-98

County Court, County of Richmond, 1869-1906

(Three items are dated prior to 1869, as follows: 1820, 1840, and 1864.)

2. CARD INDEX TO NATURALIZATION RECORDS (1792-1906). 492 ft.

A card shows the name of the individual naturalized, the name and location of the court which granted the certificate of naturalization, the volume (or bundle) number and page (or record) number of the naturalization record, and may include other information in the naturalization papers. The index is on 3" x 5" cards arranged by name of individual naturalized according to the soundex system; that is, the cards are grouped by the initial letter of the surname, arranged thereunder numerically by a code representing the sounds of certain other letters of the surname, and thereunder alphabetically by the given name.

Records of the United States District Court for the Eastern District of New York

3. NATURALIZATION RECORDS. 1865-1929. 524 vols. 208 ft.

Included are declarations of intention to become citizens (copies), petitions to be admitted to citizenship, affidavits of petitioners and witnesses, and court orders admitting petitioners. From 1865—September 1906 the records are arranged numerically by volume and page number. After September 1906 the records are arranged numerically by petition number. The soundex index to the photocopies of naturalization records described in entry number 2 covers the records dated 1865-1906.

4. CARD INDEX TO NATURALIZATION RECORDS (1865-1929). 58 ft.

The information on the cards varies. In addition to the name of the individual naturalized, a card may contain such information as the date of naturalization, volume and record or petition number, and former nationality of the person naturalized. Some cards may also have the address, date of birth, and occupation of the individual naturalized. The index is on 3" x 5" cards arranged alphabetically by name of person naturalized.

5. DECLARATIONS OF INTENTION. 1865-1929. 274 vols. 88 ft.

Declarations of intention to become citizens. Arranged numerically by volume and declaration number. For the period 1865-1916 each volume has a name index.

6. INDEX TO DECLARATIONS OF INTENTION (1909-25). 4 vols. 1 ft.

Name index in which declarants are listed by initial letter of surname and thereunder each year numerically by declaration number.

Records of the U.S. District Court
for the Southern District of New York

7. NATURALIZATION RECORDS. 1824-1906. 152 vols. 57 ft.

    Included are declarations of intention to become citizens
    (copies), petitions to be admitted to citizenship, affidavits
    of witnesses and applicants, and court orders admitting
    applicants to citizenship. Arranged numerically by volume
    and record number. Each volume has a name index. The
    soundex index to the photocopies of naturalization records
    described in entry number 2 covers these records.

8. DECLARATIONS OF INTENTION. 1842-1940. 743 vols.
    222 ft.

    Declarations of intention to become citizens. Information
    in the declarations varies. The earlier declarations include
    declarant's name and state of former allegiance and the
    date of the declaration. Later declarations usually include
    the following information: declarant's name, address, occu-
    pation, physical description, race, nationality, birthplace,
    date of birth, city or town and country of last foreign resi-
    dence, and the port and date of entry and name of vessel
    on which the individual entered the country. Arranged
    numerically by volume and declaration number. For the
    period 1842-1915 each volume has a name index.

9. CARD INDEX TO DECLARATIONS OF INTENTION
    (1917-40). 360 ft.

    Name index on 3" x 5" cards arranged alphabetically by
    name of individual.

Records of the United States Circuit Court
for the Southern District of New York

10. DECLARATIONS OF INTENTION. 1845-1911. 151 vols.
    34 ft.

    Declarations of intention to become citizens. Arranged
    numerically by volume and declaration number. Each
    volume has a name index.

Another place where naturalization documents exist is the Office of the Clerk of New York County. Records of the Court of Common Pleas and of the Superior Court of New York County have recently been microfilmed and may be consulted there. Original papers of these same two courts are to be found on the 7th floor of the Surrogates Court in Chambers St. They are under the supervision of James Van Nostrand.

The first court in New York City to grant citizenship, beginning in 1792, was the Mayor's Court (which became the Court of Common Pleas). Its early records give the name of the alien, his status, often his country of origin, and the name of the citizen who recommended him. The place of residence is New York City unless otherwise specified. Later, frequently from 1813—occasionally earlier—through 1828, very detailed information is found: place of birth, age, status, port of departure for America, name of wife, her age and birthplace, and the same for the children. Sometimes the place where the alien intended to settle is given.

Very similar information is found in the records of the District Court of the United States for the Southern District of New York from 1824 to about 1836, after which details are more limited.

Naturalization documents of the Superior Court of New York County, from 1828 through 1830, yield such items as place of birth and age of the alien, often with the date of his arrival in the United States and the place where he intended to settle.

The Marine Court of the City of New York was extremely active in naturalizing aliens. Its voluminous records, beginning in 1806, are rich in genealogical information, especially up to 1827. Records of this court, because of their extent, have not been abstracted here beyond Volume 5.

Two other courts, through 1840, have records of a few early naturalizations. The County Court of Queens County gives three between 1799 and 1839, while the County Court of Richmond County lists one in 1820 and another in 1840. On the other hand the City Court of Brooklyn had 129 naturalizations in the period 1834-1840, but the clerk recorded merely the name of the alien, his previous allegiance, and the name of the citizen who recommended him.

It should be pointed out that upon occasion the clerks misunderstood names given them orally, could not read the signatures in German script, and tended to anglicize names of immigrants who did not come from the United Kingdom. In many instances the name of a citizen who vouched for the alien reveals a family relationship.

It is hoped that the present volume, with its index of between 14,000 and 15,000 names, will facilitate genealogical research in the period after the Revolution and through 1840. The compiler wishes to express his gratitude to Joel Buchwald of the Federal Records Center in Bayonne and his staff, to Joseph C. Hipius, Chief Clerk of New York County and members of his staff, especially Esther Weinkofsky and Ann Hassel, and to Joseph Van Nostrand, all of whom greatly facilitated the preparation of this book. Special thanks are due Aurelia G. Scott, who transcribed a large part of the naturalization records of the Court of Common Pleas which are located in the Federal Records Center in Bayonne.

Bundle 1

Youle, John - 6 Mar. 1792 [1]

Paterson, Stephen, merchant - 26 Aug. 1794 [2]

Plummer, Richard; rec. by Joseph Marschalk - 16 Dec. 1794 [3]

Garniss, Thomas, cordwainer; rec. by James Teller, hatter -
6 Mar. 1792 [4]

Gibbon, John, confectioner; rec. by Peter Lacour, painter -
5 July 1794 [5]

Salazar, Peter Goncalias, subj. of Portugal; rec. by Francis
Barretto - 5 Nov. 1793 [6]

Talbot, Valentine, mariner; rec. by Thomas Milne, silversmith -
25 Sept. 1793 [7]

Taylor, Benjamin, gentleman; rec. by Thomas Service, merchant -
14 Jan. 1794 [8]

Taylor, John, merchant; rec. by John Ellis, merchant - 21 Feb.
1794 [9]

Tait/Teait, George; rec. by Hector Stevenson - 10 Mar. 1794 [10]

Thompson, John; rec. by Nehemiah Allen, of Brooklyn, innholder -
17 Dec. 1794 [11]

Allsce, William, subj. of G.B.; rec. by John Beekman, druggist -
3 Sept. 1793 [12]

Akers, William; rec. by John Ross, hairdresser - 4 Feb. 1794
[13]

Ayscough, Richard; rec. by Joshua Sands, merchant - 16 July 1794
[14]

Arnold, George, merchant; rec. by George Pollock, merchant - 3
Oct. 1794 [15]

Archer, Edmond, merchant; rec. by Ph. Dubey, merchant - 7 Nov.
1794 [16]

Aaron, Henry, merchant; rec. by James Cooper - 18 Dec. 1794 [17]

Fisher, John, grocer; rec. by John Miller - 18 Dec. 1794 [no. no.]

Ferrier, John, mariner; rec. by James R. Smith, merchant - 31
Aug. 1793 [18]

Fanton, Peter; rec. by John Brown - 6 May 1794 [19]

Fischer, Johann Bernhard, furrier, of the 7th Ward; rec. by
Jacob Appley, butcher - 3 June 1794 [20]

Flyn, Michael, mariner; rec. by George Copland, grocer - 5 Aug.
1794 [21]

Foose, George; rec. by Josiah Ogden Hoffman - 9 Aug. 1794 [22]

Mac Gregor, Coll; rec. by Hay Stevenson - 3 Sept. 1793 [23]

McFarlan, John, mariner; rec. by George Copland, grocer - 14 Jan.
1794 [24]

McDonagh, James, mariner; rec. by Barney Byrn, grocer - 19 Jan.
1795 [25]

McNab, James; rec. by John Brown - 6 May 1794 [26]

McQuinn, John; rec. by Peter Dustan - 7 May 1794 [27]

McKay, James; rec. by Peter Eltinge - 12 Aug. 1794 [28]

McDonald, Alexander; rec. by Daniel Garrison, farmer, of Richmond Co. - 16 Sept. 1794 [29]

McCall, James; rec. by Robert Lylburn, merchant - 17 Sept. 1794
[30]

"Fisher, John," see John Aaron - 10 Dec. 1794 [31]

McCammon, Mark, bricklayer; rec. by Alexander Lamb, cartman -
18 Dec. 1794 [32]

Maurice, Benjamin, merchant; rec. by Walter Buchanan, merchant -
8 Oct. 1794 [33]

Mackinnen, Daniel, gentleman; rec. by George Pollock, gentleman - 8 Oct. 1794 [34]

Snow, Robert; rec. by Barnet Mooney, hatter - 14 Jan. 1794 [35]

Masterton, Adam, mariner; rec. by Peter Masterton, attorney-at-
law - 18 Mar. 1794 [36]

Marley, John, merchant; rec. by James Watson, Jr. - 5 Nov. 1793
[37]

Mills, James, mariner; rec. by George Copland, grocer - 26 June
1794 [38]

Miller, John, mariner; rec. by Robert Mitchell, pilot - 26 June
1794 [39]

Millner, William, merchant; rec. by Joseph Byrnes, merchant, a
Quaker - 16 Dec. 1794 [40]

Maurice, William, merchant; rec. by Andrew Mitchell, merchant -
16 Dec. 1794 [41]

Morewood, Thomas, merchant; rec. by Gilbert Morewood, merchant -
17 Dec. 1794 [42]

Surtees [or Surtus?], Thomas, mariner; rec. by Andrew McNeil,
rigger - Dec. 1794 [43]

Stewart, William; rec. by George Goswell, carman - 26 June 1794
[44]

Speck, Francis, mariner; rec. by Joseph Wood, shoemaker, of the
First Ward - 5 Aug. 1794 [45]

Snow, William, mariner; rec. by James McCall, mariner - 5 Nov.
1794 [46]

Sadler, Henry, merchant; rec. by Joseph Ogden Hoffman - 25 Nov.
1794 [47]

Sadler, John; rec. by John Murray, merchant - 26 Nov. 1794 [48]

Suckley, George, merchant; rec. by Alexander Dunlap, merchant -
18 Mar, 1794 [49]

Schepts [or Schebh?], George, of the 7th Ward, butcher; rec. by
Jacob Appley, butcher - 18 Mar. 1794 [50]

Story, William W.; rec. by Cornelius Herttell - 18 Mar. 1794
[51]

Shedden, Robert, mariner; rec. by James Deas, grocer - 9 Oct.
1794 [52]

Coster, John Gerhard, merchant; rec. by John Abrams, merchant -
25 Feb. 1794 [53]

Conacheche, Joseph, merchant; rec. by John G. Brasser - 20 Mar.
1794 [53AA]

Clapp, Samuel; rec. by Charles Curtis - 26 May 1794 [54]

Carr, Joseph; rec. by John Murray - 7 Nov. 1793 [55]

La Cour, Peter, painter; rec. by John Reins, constable - 28 Nov.
1793 [56]

Cameron, John, mariner; rec. by Ebenezer Young, shipwright - 26 June 1794 [57]

Christie, James; rec. by George Copland, grocer - 26 June 1794 [58]

Crone, David; rec. by John Sullivan, grocer - 17 July 1794 [59]

Currie, John G., grocer; rec. by John Bomon - 6 Aug. 1794 [60]

Craig, William, merchant; rec. by Henry Sadler, merchant - 7 Oct. 1794 [61]

Courtney, George, plaister of Paris manufacturer; rec. by Garret B. Abeel - 16 Dec. 1794 [62]

Curre, Angus, mariner, from Scotland; rec. by Archibald Curre, grocer - 16 Dec. 1794 [63]

Carver, William; rec. by Matthew Bolmar, granary keeper - 16 Dec. 1794 [64]

Clayton, Thomas, merchant; rec. by Gilbert Morewood, merchant - 17 Dec. 1794 [65]

Copland, George, grocer; rec. by Archibald McWilliam, grocer - 18 Dec. 1794 [66]

Verolier [clerk wrote "Verdier"], Francis Jean Charles; rec. by Cart Ludlow, attorney-at-law - 5 Aug. 1794 [67]

White, Charles, cabinetmaker, from Waterford Co., Ire.; rec. by Barnet Mooney, hatter, of the 7th Ward - 31 Dec. 1793 [68]

Wyche, William; rec. by Cary Ludlow, Esq. - 8 Apr. 1794 [69]

Ward, Benjamin; rec. by Alexander Gibson, cooper - 3 June 1794 [70]

Worthy, Thomas, mariner; rec. by Harry Bruce, mariner - 2 June 1794 [71]

Willson, Sweney; rec. by Robert Provoost - 15 July 1794 [72]

Williams, Thomas; rec. by William Lawler - 16 July 1794 [73]

West, Thomas; rec. by John Anderson, auctioneer - 16 Sept. 1794 [74]

Wilson, William, merchant; rec. by Samuel Boyd - 7 Oct. 1794 [75]

Woolsey, George, merchant; rec. by Francis Panton, merchant - 4 Nov. 1794 [76]

Walker, Thomas, merchant; rec. by John L. Broome, merchant - 10 Nov. 1794 [77]

Wilson, Campbell, merchant; rec. by Gilbert Morewood, merchant, and Colin Easton, merchant - 17 Dec. 1794 [78]

Williams, Michael, mariner; rec. by Ezekiel Hubbell, of Stratford, Conn., mariner, and John Harrison, of NYC, gentleman - 25 June 1794 [79]

Bellamy, Samuel; rec. by Robert Murray - 3 Sept. 1793 [80]

Butler, Thomas; rec. by Josiah Adams - 3 Sept. 1793 [81]

Brantingham, Thomas H., merchant; rec. by Richard Underhill, a Quaker - 14 Jan. 1794 [82]

Brown, Richard, mariner; rec. by Robert Bowne, merchant, a Quaker - 18 Mar. 1794 [83]

Barnes, Robert, merchant; rec. by Richard Loines, merchant, a Quaker - 18 Mar. 1794 [84]

Brown, Daniel Obrien, Hairdresser; rec. by Jonathan Penny - 8 May 1794 [85]

Bullock, Thomas, late of Staffordshire, Eng.; rec. by Abraham H. Watson, attorney-at-law - 3 June 1794 [86]

Bradish, James, merchant; rec. by George Pollock - 4 June 1794 [87]

Bertre, Louis; rec. by Joseph L'Epine, merchant - 26 June 1794 [88]

Bryan, William, tobacconist; rec. by Robert Lylburn, merchant - 8 Oct. 1794 [89]

Buchanan, John; rec. by Arthur Chichester Beaumont - 8 Oct. 1794 [90]

Le Bon, Benedict Benjamin, merchant; rec. by Stephen Nocus, merchant, and Philip Vaché, florist [the last crossed out] - 6 Nov. 1794 [91]

Bell, William; rec. by Gilbert Morewood, merchant - 16 Dec. 1794 [92]

Berry, John, Jr., merchant; rec. by Michael D. Henry, attorney - 17 Dec. 1794 [93]

Battenbergh, John, cartman; rec. by John Binckes, house-carpenter - 17 Dec. 1794 [94]

Bush, William, shopkeeper; rec. by Thomas Philips, druggist - 18 Dec. 1794 [95]

Bryson, Robert; rec. by Thomas James - 7 Aug. 1794 [96]

Richardson, John, mariner; rec. by Thomas Fardon, tailor - 27 Feb. 1794 [97]

Rooke, John, formerly of London, Eng.; rec. by John S. Hunn, notary public - 12 Dec. 1794 [98]

Rankin, John; rec. by John Quackenbos - 8 Apr. 1794 [99]

Reynold, Rowland; rec. by James Byrne - 7 Apr. 1794 [100]

Guthrie, William; rec. by Lawrence Yates - 9 Apr. 1794 [101]

Gillender, James, mariner, late of Eng.; rec. by James Smith, merchant - 15 July 1794 [102]

Graves, Benjamin; rec. by Gerret Keteltas, merchant - 16 Dec. 1794 [103]

Gilbert, Charles; rec. by Gerret Keteltas, merchant - 16 Dec. 1794 [104]

Gourlay, Robert, shopkeeper; rec. by Cary Dunn, silversmith - 18 Dec. 1794 [105]

Rogers, Edward; rec. by Thomas Ferdon - 5 May 1794 [106]

Roy, Alexander; rec. by Peter Dunstan - 7 May 1794 [107]

Place, Paul Richards, mariner; rec. by Marinus Willett - 24 June 1794 [108]

Reid, John; rec. by Duncan Ferguson - 25 June 1794 [109]

Robins, Andrew, mariner; rec. by Bernard Byrne, shopkeeper - 25 Nov. 1794 [110]

Rommel, John Christian Frederick; rec. by John Harrison, gentleman - 26 Nov. 1794 [111]

Reilly, John, gentleman; rec. by John Byrne, innholder - 16 Dec. 1794 [112]

Renwick, William, merchant; rec. by John Hudswell, merchant - 18 Dec. 1794 [113]

Oakes, Thomas, potter; rec. by Robert Connolly, mariner - 7 Aug. 1794 [114]

Nicholson, Joseph, mariner; rec. by George Copland, grocer - 7
   Oct. 1794 [115]

Newsham, Robert; rec. by Dougall McDougall, mariner - 16 Dec.
   1794 [116]

Duchesne, Peter, subj. of France; rec. by Francis Christopher
   Mantel, merchant - 15 Jan. 1794 [117]

Da Silva, Joaã Jose, merchant; rec. by Stephen Nocus, merchant -
   3 June 1794 [118]

Dougherty, Charles; rec. by James Stewart, grocer - 5 Aug. 1794
   [119]

Drummond, James; rec. by John Kemp, Esq. - 5 Aug. 1794 [120]

Douzabre, Jean Baptiste, merchant; rec. by Henri Dubosq [or
   Dugastand?], starch- and hair-powder manufacturer - 5 Aug.
   1794 [121]

Desdoity, John Baptist; rec. by William M. Seton - 7 Aug. 1794
   [122]

Dawson, Abraham; rec. by William Lawler, tallow Chandler - 16
   Sept. 1794 [123]

Dickay, George, mariner; rec. by George Brown, grocer - 9 Oct.
   1794 [124]

Dixon, George, bookkeeper, subj. of G.B.; rec. by James Bennet,
   bookkeeper - 25 Nov. 1794 [125]

Duplex, George, mariner; rec. by William Neilson, merchant - 4
   Nov. 1794 [also numbered 125]

Deas, David, mariner; rec. by John Rankin, grocer, of the 6th
   Ward - 16 Dec. 1794 [126]

Earl, John, gentleman; rec. by John Kingsland, shopkeeper - 28
   Aug. 1794 [127]

Hobson, Jonathan; rec. by Edmund Prior, a Quaker - 26 Feb. 1794
   [128]

Harris, Alexander; rec. by Jonathan Penny - 5 May 1794 [129]

Hallyday, Henry; rec. by George Dally - 6 May 1794 [130]

Hyde, John; rec. by William Thomas - 7 May 1794 [131]

Hutchinson, John; rec. by Jedidiah Rogers - 30 Aug. 1794 [132]

Hattrick, Peter; rec. by William Wilson, merchant - 4 Nov. 1794
   [133]

Harrison, James, merchant; rec. by Henry Titus, a Quaker - 8
   Nov. 1794 [134]

Harrison, Thomas, farmer, of Columbia Co., N.Y.; rec. by Henry
   Titus, a Quaker - 7 Nov. 1794 [135]

Harrington, Matthias, mariner; rec. by Francis Barrotto - 7 Nov.
   1794 [136]

Hunt, Thomas, grocer; rec. by Thomas Beekman - 16 Dec. 1794 [137]

Hastier, John; rec. by Francis Bassett - 17 Dec. 1794 [138]

Jarvis, Mathew; rec. by James McIntosh - 27 Feb. 1794 [139]

Inness, Henry; rec. by Adrian Dow, chairmaker - 4 June 1794
   [140]

Jameson, Robert; rec. by William Willson, merchant - 4 Nov. 1794
   [141]

Jenkin, Edward, mariner; rec. by James McCall, mariner - 5 Nov.
   1794 [142]

Kelly, Andrew, mariner; rec. by James Leeson, innholder - 15
    July 1794 [143]

Knox, John, merchant; rec. by Thomas Eddy, merchant, a Quaker -
    4 Nov. 1794 [144]

Ledet, Isaiah Lewis, merchant; rec. by William Williams and
    John Baptist Desdoity - 17 Dec. 1794 [145]

Lenox, James, merchant; rec. by William Hill, merchant - 10
    Nov. 1794 [146]

Leyns, Peter; rec. by William Chevers, mariner - 15 Sept. 1794
    [147]

Leoffler, August Charles Frederic; rec. by George Scriba - 9
    Nov. 1793 [148]

Lewis, James, merchant, late of City of London; rec. by John
    Rogers - 9 Apr. 1794 [149]

Leader, Henry; rec. by Henry Sadler, merchant - 4 June 1794
    [150]

Little, Michael, innholder; rec. by Anthony L. Bleecker, mer-
    cahnt - 15 July 1794 [151]

Lowey [or Lowy?], Arthur, mariner; rec. by James Ryan, grocer -
    6 Aug. 1794 [152]

Bishop, Thomas, tavern-keeper; rec. by William Lawler, tallow
    chandler - 7 Aug. 1794 [153]

La Barre, Joseph, farmer, late of Port au Prince but now of
    Orange Co; rec. by Philip Dubey, merchant - 5 Sept. 1794 [154]

Bundle 2

Waning, Henry, gentleman; rec. by George Scriba, merchant - 31
    Jan. 1794 [1]

Landell, John, native of Scotland, mariner; rec. by Robert Aff-
    leck, merchant - 15 Apr. 1794 [2]

McEvers, Daniel, merchant, of Albany; rec. by Cornelius Rosa, of
    Albany - 8 Aug. 1794 [3]

McLeod, George; rec. by James Campbell - 31 Jan. 1794 [4]

Manly, James; rec. by Philip Parisen, goldsmith - 30 Apr. 1794
    [5]

Le Breton, Stephen, native of France; rec. by Joseph Thebaut -
    19 Apr. 1794 [6]

Van den Heuvell, Kornelis Wilhelm, physician, native of Vlaar-
    dingen, Holland; rec. by Rogier Gerard Van Polanen - 15 Apr.
    1794 [7]

Whyte, Archibald, clerk, subj. of G.B.; rec. by George Gosman,
    mason - 24 Apr. 1795 [8]

Walsh, Michael, subj. of G.B.; rec. by John Byrne - 21 Apr.
    1795 [9 and 10]

Mathews, William, merchant; rec. by Thomas Ferdon, gentleman -
    31 Jan. 1795 [11]

McDonagh, James, mariner; rec. by Bernard Byrne, grocer - 21
    Jan. 1795 [12]

Vaché, John, florist; rec. by Alexander Ogsbury, Jr., merchant -
    23 Apr. 1795 [13]

Mellis, Samuel, cabinetmaker, subj. of G.B.; rec. by Henry
    Crocheron, cabinetmaker - 24 Apr. 1795 [14]

McKay, George, grocer, subj. of G.B.; rec. by Josiah Ogden Hoffman, Esq. - 9 May 1795 [15]

Lombart, John Baptist Ann Marie; rec. by Lewis Simond - 26 Jan. 1795 [16]

Lappon, William, merchant, of Norway, Herkimer Co., N.Y.; rec. by James McGourk, of the City of Albany - 29 Oct. 1795 [17]

McEntee, Thomas, merchant, of Norway, Herkimer Co., N.Y.; rec. by William Lappon, of Norway, Herkimer Co. - 29 Oct. 1795 [18]

Mickle, James, farmer, of Montgomery Co., N.Y., subj. of G.B.; rec. by John Campbell - 1 Aug. 1795 [19]

Mackercy, George, carver & gilder, subj. of G.B.; rec. by George Gosman, mason - 24 Apr. 1795 [20]

Miller, Andrew; rec. by William Turnbull, merchant - 20 Jan. 1795 [21]

Mason, Daniel, shoemaker, subj. of G.B.; rec. by Henry Titus, innkeeper - 8 May 1795 [22]

Massias, Abraham, merchant, subj. of G.B.; rec. by Isaac Gomez, Jr., merchant - 8 May 1795 [23]

Walther, Frederick, farmer, of Cazenovia, Herkimer Co., N.Y., subj. of Elector of Saxony; rec. by Simeon Dryer, of Cazenovia, Herkimer Co., farmer - 24 Oct. 1796 [24]

Wilson, John, baker, subj. of G.B.; rec. by David Deas, gentleman - 7 May 1796 [25]

Went, Christopher, starch-maker, subj. of Elector of Hanover; rec. by Matthew Bolmer. grainer - 3 May 1796 [26]

Wuth, Charles, grocer, subj. of Prince of Orange; rec. by William Jacobs, cordwainer - 27 Apr. 1796 [27]

Werth, John Jacob, subj. of Elector Palatine of Bavaria; eec. by Abraham Van Eps, of Westmoreland, Herkimer Co., N.Y. - 20 Apr. 1796 [28]

Wishart, John, gentleman, subj. of G.B.; rec. by Cornelius Wynkoop, gentleman - 23 Jan. 1796 [29]

Worsey, William, merchant, subj. of G.B.; rec. by William Allam, merchant - 20 Jan. 1796 [30]

Walsh, Martin Tobias, mariner, subj. of G.B.; rec. by Thomas Carberry, mariner - 5 Jan. 1796 [31]

Lyons, Henry, grocer, of City of Albany, subj. of G.B.; rec. by Daniel McEvers, merchant, of Albany - 24 Oct. 1796 [32]

Le Fort, John, gentleman, subj. of France; rec. by William Hosack, student-at-law - 29 Jan. 1796 [33]

Lague, Barthelemy, subj. of France; rec. by Richard Harison - 25 Apr. 1796 [34]

Linacre, James, cabinetmaker, of Albany, subj. of G.B.; rec. by Charles R. Webster, printer, of Albany - 6 Aug. 1796 [35]

McKarr, John, tailor; rec. by John Boris, hairdresser - 30 Apr. 1794 [36]

Vass, William, cartman, subj. of G.B.; rec. by John McLean, grocer - 29 Apr. 1796 [37]

Lopes, Louis, gentleman; rec. by Simon Nathan, merchant - 22 Jan. 1796 [38]

Lintz, Frederick, grocer, subj. of Emperor of Germany; rec. by Henry Heiser, starch manufacturer - 6 May 1796 [39]

Morgan, Richard, merchant, subj. of G.B.; rec. by James Bradish, merchant - 6 May 1796 [40]

Miller, Daniel, baker, subj. of Emperor of Germany; rec. by William Jacobs, cordwainer - 27 Apr. 1796 [41]

Maurice, Thomas, grocer, of Albany; rec. by David B. Lynsen, physician, of Rensselaer Co. - 4 Aug. 1796 [42]

Millson, John, printer, subj. of G.B.; rec. by Peter Conrad, house-carpenter - 3 May 1796 [43]

MacIntyre, Malcom, subj. of G.B.; rec. by Archibald MacIntyre - 5 May 1796 [44]

McLaren, Finlay, merchant, of Albany, subj. of G.B.; rec. by William Reid, of Albany Co. - 4 Aug. 1796 [45]

McLaren, Daniel, shopkeeper, subj. of G.B.; rec. by Michael D. Henry, counsellor-at-law - 27 Apr. 1796 [46]

McDonald, Dennis, cartman, subj. of G.B.; rec. by Dennis McGahgay - 26 Apr. 1796 [47]

Moran, Edward, merchant tailor, subj. of G.B.; rec. by Jeremiah Joseph - 29 Jan. 1796 [48]

Marshall, Joseph, shipwright, subj. of G.B.; rec. by Robert Bruce, grocer - 29 Apr. 1796 [49]

McCready, Thomas, grocer, subj. of G.B.; rec. by Thomas Allen, bookseller - 26 Apr. 1796 [50]

Weyman, Abner, clothier, subj. of G.B.; rec. by John Fisher, grocer - 28 Jan. 1797 [51 and 52]

Woolf, Anthony, farmer, of Morrissania, Westchester Co., subj. of Emperor of Germany; rec. by James Anderson, shopkeeper - 27 Jan. 1797 [53]

Wortman, Robert, mariner, subj. of G.B.; rec. by Bernard Byrne, merchant - 23 Jan. 1797 [54]

Jackson, James, merchant, subj. of G.B.; rec. by John Hyde, innkeeper - 6 Apr. 1797 [55]

Heller, Abraham, grocer, subj. of France; rec. by Philip Rhine-lander, merchant - 6 Apr. 1797 [56]

Johnson, John, gentleman, of Ontario Co., subj. of G.B.; rec. by Nicholas Fish - 27 Nov. 1797 [57]

Somerville, James, farmer, of Westchester Co., subj. of G.B.; rec. by John Knox, merchant - 24 Nov. 1797 [58]

Dollet, Nicholas, of Flat Bush, Kings Co., merchant, subj. of France; rec. by Johannis E. Lott, of Flat Bush - 27 Nov. 1797 [59]

Armstrong, John Warren, merchant, subj. of G.B.; rec. by Daniel Van Voorhis, goldsmith - 2 Dec. 1797 [60]

Walker, Thomas, merchant, subj. of G.B.; rec. by Richard S. Hallett - 4 Dec. 1797 [61]

Smith, Charles, bookseller, subj. of Prince of Wirtemberg; rec. by George Gilferd - 6 Apr. 1797 [62]

Mason, James, farmer, of Queens Co., subj. of G.B.; rec. by Henry Titus, innkeeper, a Quaker - 20 Oct. 1797 [63]

Murray, William, cordwainer, subj. of G.B.; rec. by William Crawley, tinman - 18 Oct. 1797 [64]

Malingre, Lewis, merchant, subj. of France; rec. by Stephen Nocus, merchant - 19 Oct. 1797 [65]

Cheetham, James, hatter, subj. of G.B.; rec. by Edward Smith, hatter - 25 Nov. 1797 [66]

Longchamp, Ignacius P., subj. of the Pope; rec. by John Mouchon - 27 Jan. 1797 [67]

Mayell, William, hatter, subj. of G.B.; rec. by John Gilmor, cabinetmaker, member of the Baptist Church in NYC - 25 July 1797 [68]

McNab, John, grocer, subj. of G.B.; rec. by Matthew Jarvis - 25 July 1797 [69]

Metcalfe, Bernard, subj. of G.B.; rec. by John McVickar, merchant - 24 Jan. 1797 [70]

Miller, Christian, merchant, of Albany, subj. of the Emperor of Germany; rec. by John Taylor, Esq., of Albany - 21 Apr. 1797 [71]

Ledet, Joseph M., merchant, subj. of France; rec. by Isaiah Lewis Ledet, merchant - 5 Dec. 1797 [72]

Robertson, Charles, merchant, subj. of G.B.; rec. by Alexander MacKenzie - 5 Apr. 1797 [73]

Marcorelle, Anthony, subj. of France; rec. by Brockholst Livingston - 21 July 1798 [74]

Meinel, George, tanner, subj. of Emperor of Germany; rec. by Elias Beekman, blacksmith - 10 Aug. 1798 [75]

Roach, Patrick, mariner, subj. of G.B.; rec. by John O'Conner, mariner - 20 Mar. 1799 [76]

Deaves, Henry, subj. of G.B., age 25 yrs. & 6 mos. - 29 Mar. 1799 [77]

Helme, John, hairdresser, subj. of G.B., age 44 - 26 July 1800 [78]

Lauff, Philip L., innkeeper, subj. of Elector Palatine; rec. by Philip Becanon, innkeeper - 21 July 1802 [79]

Wale, Patrick, merchant, subj. of G.B.; rec. by James Cummings, merchant - 21 July 1802 [80]

La Rue, Joseph Henry, subj. of France; rec. by Gudon S. Mumford, merchant - 3 May 1803 [81]

Wilson, George, merchant, subj. of G.B.; rec. by Robert Smart, merchant - 19 Nov. 1803 [82]

Williams, William R., born Co. Surrey, Eng., age 63; emigrated from London - 29 Aug. 1804 [83]

Wallace, James, born Kilkenny, Ire., age 28, emigrated from London - 29 July 1809 [84]

Wylie, David, born Gallaugh, Ire., age about 27, emigrated from Ire. - 4 Mar. 1812 [85]

Walsh, James, clerk, born Co. Longford, Ire., age 20, emigrated from Longford - 2 Mar. 1826 [86]

Ward, Patrick, gardner & farmer, born Co. West Meath, Ire., age 25, emigrated from Ire. - 29 Mar. 1826 [87]

Watterson, William, chandler, born Co. Down, Ire., age 21, emigrated from Ire. - 29 Mar. 1826 [88]

Walsh, John Brennan, surgeon, born Dublin, Ire., age 26, emigrated from Ire. - 31 May 1827 [89]

Wilckens, Jacob Frederick, subj. of Republic of Bremen - 1 Mar. 1831 [90]

Wilson, Andrew, mariner, subj. of Sweden - 13 Oct. 1832 [91]

Whales, Richard, farmer, of North Hempstead, L.I., subj. of
G.B. - 31 Jan. 1837 [92]

Miller, Joseph, milkman, of Southfield, Richmond Co., subj. of
G.B. - 30 Oct. 1839 [93]

Wright, Ruth, merchant, subj. of G.B. - 4 Feb. 1839 [94]

White, Edward, painter, late of London - 1 Sept. 1840 [94AA]

Lennon, Patrick, labourer, late of Ire. - 4 Nov. 1844 [95]

Waters, Philip, labourer, late of Ire. - 4 Nov. 1844 [96]

Welch, John, brush [?] printer, late of Ire. - 4 Nov. 1844 [97]

Walsh, Philip, labourer, late of Co. Kilkenny, Ire. - 3 Oct.
1844 [98]

Wetton, Charles, plater, late of Eng. - 5 Nov. 1844 [99]

Williams, John, seaman, late of Londonderry, Ire. - 4 Nov. 1844
[100]

Winterhoff, Rudolph, subj. of Republic of Hamburgh - 3 Feb. 1845
[101]

Wilson, Hugh, laborer, late of Ire. - 29 July 1845 [102]

Bundle 3

Auchinvole, David, subj. of G.B.; rec. by John Taylor, merchant -
31 Dec. 1803 [1]

Aucat, Richard, of Brooklyn, painter & glazier, subj. of G.B.;
rec. by William Kidd, grocer - 15 July 1803 [2]

Alexander, Andrew, merchant, subj. of G.B.; rec. by Archibald
Phillips, merchant - 12 July 1803 [3]

Adams, William, ship master, subj. of G.B.; rec. by Robert M.
Steel, ship master - 14 June 1803 [4 & 6]

Amelung, Frederick Leopold Eberhard, merchant, subj. of Duke of
Brunswick; rec. by Frederick William Dannenbergh - 9 Aug. 1803
[5]

Brown, John, house-carpenter, subj. of G.B.; rec. by George
Durand, mason - 21 May 1803 [7]

Bowen, John, painter & glazier, subj. of G.B.; rec. by Seth
Wayland, currier - 23 Apr. 1803 [8]

Brown, Thomas, grocer, subj. of G.B.; rec. by Robert Buchan,
lumber merchant - 23 Apr. 1803 [9]

Britton, James, labourer, subj. of G.B.; rec. by Hugh Gobel,
grocer - 23 Apr. 1803 [10]

Burnet, James, gardner, subj. of G.B.; rec. by William Robertson, grocer - 23 Apr. 1803 [11]

Boyd, John, hairdresser & perfumer, subj. of France; rec. by
Nehemiah Allen, grocer - 31 Dec. 1803 [12]

Brezy, Henry, merchant, subj. of France; rec. by Gurdon S. Mumford, merchant - 31 Dec. 1803 [13]

Bogle, William H., teacher, subj. of G.B.; rec. by Robert Thomson, merchant - 20 Dec. 1803 [14]

Barras, Stephen, gentleman, & wife Marie Catherine Mesnard Barras,
subj. of France; rec. by Peter Rousseau, merchant - 1 Nov.
1803 [15]

Byrnes, Garret, mason, subj. of G.B.; rec. by Thomas Ward, cordwainer - 12 Feb. 1803 [16]

Babb, James, wire worker, subj. of G.B.; rec. by Thomas Lownes, baker - 2 Feb. 1803 [17]

Ball, Archibald, mason, subj. of G.B.; rec. by John Rodman, mason - 12 Feb. 1803 [18]

Bredin, John, grocer, subj. of G.B.; rec. by John Mathews, grocer - 21 May 1803 [19]

Brown, James, grocer, subj. of G.B.; rec. by James Richardson, distiller - 21 May 1803 [20]

Bowering, Caleb B., merchant, subj. of G.B.; rec. by Ezekiel Robins, Esq. - 21 May 1803 [21]

Bell, Abraham, merchant, a Quaker; rec. by Francis Thompson, merchant, a Quaker - 11 Jan. 1803 [22]

Beaty, John, weaver & pedlar, subj. of G.B.; rec. by David Law, cordwainer - 15 Jan. 1803 [23]

Bathgate, James, miller, of West Chester, subj. of G.B.; rec. by David King, innkeeper - 3 Dec. 1803 [24]

Boucheron, Augustus, merchant, subj. of France; rec. by Jaques Benoit Durand, merchant - 14 June 1803 [25]

Brookes, Joshua, merchant, subj. of G.B.; rec. by Samuel Mabbatt, cordwainer - 9 Aug. 1803 [26]

Bingham [signs "Bigher"], James, subj. of G.B.; rec. by Andrew Alexander, public porter - 26 Mar. 1803 [27]

Buckley, James, merchant, subj. of G.B.; rec. by Anthony Bartow & Jacob Walden, merchants - 12 July 1803 [28]

Coppin, John, house-carpenter, subj. of G.B.; rec. by Seth Wayland, currier - 23 Apr. 1803 [29]

Cardwill, James, cartman, subj. of G.B.; rec. by William Thompson, cartman - 24 Mar. 1803 [30]

Cunningham, John, lumber merchant, subj. of G.B.; rec. by Robert Buchan, lumber merchant - 23 Apr. 1803 [31]

Crown, John, shipwright, subj. of G.B.; rec. by Charles Broome, shipbuilder - 23 Apr. 1803 [32]

Cauldwell, John, merchant, subj. of G.B.; rec. by Jacob Smith, cordwainer - 23 Apr. 1803 [33]

Collier, Mathew, cartman, subj. of G.B.; rec. by Mathew Nowlin, blacksmith - 23 Apr. 1803 [34]

Cox, Charles, storekeeper, subj. of G.B.; rec. by Abraham Van Gelder, grocer - 23 Apr. 1803 [35]

Couman, John, mariner, subj. of G.B.; rec. by William Leaycraft, inspector of customs - 20 Apr. 1803 [36]

Crawley, Patrick, cartman, subj. of G.B.; rec. by Thomas Ward, cordwainer 12 Feb. 1803 [37]

Craig, John, gardner, subj. of G.B.; rec. by Alexander Fisher, grocer - 21 May 1803 [38]

Craig, Hector, merchant, subj. of G.B.; rec. by Silvanus Miller, Esq. - 15 Jan. 1803 [39]

Cairon, Peter, merchant, subj. of France; rec. by James Vidalot, merchant - 2 Nov. 1803 [40]

Cullens, Peter, mariner, subj. of G.B.; rec. by Alexander Fisher, grocer - 16 July 1803 [41]

Curtis, Robert, merchant, subj. of G.B.; rec. by Thomas Fradgley, storekeeper - 1 Mar. 1803 [42]

Deary, James, cartman, subj. of G.B.; rec. by John Browne, cartman, of the 6th Ward - 1 Mar. 1803 [43]

Duluce, Andrew, accomptant, subj. of France; rec. by Thomas
Daniel, merchant - 29 Nov. 1803 [44]

Duslan [or Duflon?], John P., subj. of Switzerland; rec. by
John Sutter, accomptant - 3 Nov. 1803 [45]

Dane, Archibald, merchant, subj. of G.B.; rec. by Robert Thomson, merchant - 31 Dec. 1803 [47]

Dudley, Charles Edward, merchant, subj. of G.B.; rec. by Oliver
Kane, merchant - 31 Dec. 1803 [48]

De Negre, John, gentleman, subj. of France; rec. by John Baptiste Dennis Le Sueur, gentleman - 31 Dec. 1803 [49]

Daly, Thomas, trader, subj. of G.B.; rec. by Gregory Donlany,
grocer - 23 Apr. 1803 [50]

Dougherty, Philip, stevedore, subj. of G.B.; rec. by James
McLoughlan, lamplighter - 23 Apr. 1803 [51]

Daly, Nicholas, grocer, subj. of G.B.; rec. by Lawrence Courtney,
drayman - 23 Apr. 1803 [52]

Eager, Henry, baker, subj. of Emperor of Germany; rec. by John
Van Gelder, grocer - 23 Apr. 1803 [53]

Eckford, Henry, shipwright, subj. of G.B.; rec. by David King,
innkeeper - 18 June 1803 [54]

Finlay, William M., subj. of G.B.; rec. by Thomas T. Gaston,
merchant - 9 Aug. 1803 [55]

Fisher, James, mason, subj. of G.B.; rec. by James Mitchell,
mason - 18 June 1803 [56]

Fisher, Daniel, merchant, subj. of G.B.; rec. by Robert Mc
Conachy, cabinetmaker - 15 Jan. 1803 [57]

Farrell, John B., merchant, subj. of G.B.; rec. by Frederick
Baker, merchant - 3 Dec. 1803 [58]

Fortun [or Forteen?], David, house-carpenter, subj. of G.B.;
rec. by James Douglass, stone cutter - 27 Dec. 1803 [59]

Fritot, Charles E., segar maker, subj. of France; rec. by Stephen
Liancourt, jeweller - 27 Dec. 1803 [60]

Fitzpatrick, Edward, blacksmith, subj. of G.B.; rec. by David
Cameron, blacksmith - 28 Dec. 1803 [61]

Fowler, Charles, mariner, subj. of G.B.; rec. by Henry Carrier,
butcher - 23 Apr. 1803 [62]

Flinn, James, pilot, subj. of G.B.; rec. by John Ming, pilot -
23 Apr. 1803 [63]

Glen, Alexander, cartman, subj. of G.B.; rec. by John Beaty,
merchant - 26 Mar. 1803 [64]

Gaudin, Francois, mariner, subj. of France; rec. by Andrew
Mathieu, innholder - 9 Aug. 1803 [65]

Godbery, James, grocer, subj. of G.B.; rec. by William Marrener,
innkeeper - 3 Dec. 1803 [66]

Godoy, Louis, confectioner, subj. of France; rec. by Stephen
Liancourt, jeweller - 15 Jan. 1803 [67]

Griffiths, Richard, blacksmith, subj. of G.B.; rec. by Evan
Thomas, tailor - 11 Jan. 1803 [68]

Grellet, Stephen, merchant, subj. of France; rec. by Thomas
Franklin, a Quaker - 19 May 1803 [69]

Gervaize, John Marie, merchant, subj. of France; rec. by James
Martin, merchant - 20 May 1803 [70]

Geraerdt, John Peter, merchant, subj. of Denmark; rec. by John
Grigg, ironmonger - 13 Feb. 1803 [71]

Godfroid, William, merchant, subj. of France; rec. by John
Hathorn, merchant - 2 Nov. 1803 [72]

Grahme, Richard, merchant, subj. of G.B.; rec. by Alphaus Dunham, merchant, of Boston, Mass. - 27 Dec. 1803 [73]

Gemmill, Matthew, watchmaker, subj. of G.B.; rec. by Robert
Thomson, merchant - 28 Dec. 1803 [74]

Giller, John E., merchant, subj. of G.B.; rec. by Alexander
Glen, cartman - 31 Dec. 1803 [75]

Gentil, Thomas, fruiterer, subj. of France; rec. by Jonathan
Penny, hairdresser - 23 Apr. 1803 [76]

Heffernan, John, merchant, subj. of G.B.; rec. by Henry Tredwell, shipmaster - 18 June 1803 [77]

Hinton, John, grocer, subj. of G.B.; rec. by Charles McCarty,
grocer - 18 June 1803 [78]

Hurtel, Peter, merchant, subj. of France; rec. by Isaac Roget,
merchant - 27 Dec. 1803 [79]

Hathorn, John, merchant, subj. of G.B.; rec. by John B. Brooks,
painter - 2 Nov. 1803 [80]

Hoggan, William, tobacconist, subj. of G.B.; rec. by Samuell
Russell, merchant - 22 Apr. 1803 [81]

Hewitt, Thomas, carpenter, subj. of G.B.; rec. by Joseph
Brotherton, a marshal of NYC - 23 Apr. 1803 [82]

Irwin, William, labourer, subj. of G.B.; rec. by John Mark, a
marshal of NYC - 26 Mar. 1803 [83]

Johnston, James, merchant, subj. of G.B.; rec. by Andrew S.
Norwood, merchant - 15 Jan. 1803 [84]

Jones, John, clerk, subj. of G.B.; rec. by Jacob Smith, cordwainer - 23 Apr. 1803 [85]

Kelly, Robert, merchant, subj. of G.B.; rec. by John Riddell,
physician - 14 June 1803 [86]

King, Joseph, farmer, of Flushing, Queens Co., subj. of G.B.;
rec. by William R. Thurston, merchant - 5 Mar. 1803 [87]

Keenan, Barnard, merchant, subj. of G.B.; rec. by John Flack,
merchant - 14 June 1803 [88]

Kelso, James, grocer, subj. of G.B.; rec. by James Sterling,
cooper - 15 Jan. 1803 [89]

Koster, John, sugar boiler, subj. of Emperor of Germany; rec.
by John Schultz, sugar boiler - 21 May 1803 [90]

Kid, William, storekeeper, subj. of G.B.; rec. by David King,
innkeeper - 8 Feb. 1803 [91]

Kursheedt, Israel B., merchant, subj. of Emperor of Germany;
rec. by Robert S. Bartow, auctioneer - 8 Feb. 1803 [92]

Kennedy, Thomas H., grocer, subj. of G.B.; rec. by John Gassner,
storekeeper - 27 Dec. 1803 [93]

Luff, John N., baker, subj. of Emperor of Germany - 15 Jan.
1803 [94]

Levy, Asher Samuel, subj. of the Batavian Republic - 14 June
1803 [95]

Lindsey, David, house-carpenter, subj. of G.B.; rec. by John Fitzpatrick, house-carpenter - 31 Dec. 1803 [96]

Le Canee, David Solomon, subj. of France; rec. by Sebastian Noth, innkeeper - 11 Aug. 1803 [97]

Le Breton, Jacques Peter, merchant, subj. of France; rec. by John Juhel - 30 Dec. 1803 [98]

Mabbatt, Samuel, cordwainer, subj. of G.B.; rec. by Peter R. Sprainger, cordwainer - 23 Apr. 1803 [99]

McEuen, James, grocer, subj. of G.B.; rec. by Thomas Freeborn, a marshal of NYC - 23 Apr. 1803 [100]

McIntire, William, bricklayer, subj. of G.B.; rec. by Thomas Riley, bricklayer - 23 Apr. 1803 [101]

McAnaley, Martin, grocer, subj. of G.B.; rec. by Edward Moran, tailor - 23 Apr. 1803 [102]

Mitchell, Robert, pilot, subj. of G.B.; rec. by Nathaniel Funk, pilot - 23 Apr. 1803 [103]

Mayo, Benjamin, teacher, subj. of G.B.; rec. by Jacob Mayo, High Constable of NYC - 23 Apr. 1803 [104]

McCullock, Hugh, grocer, subj. of G.B.; rec. by Robert Steele, tallow chandler - 23 Apr. 1803 [105]

Morris, Nicholas, mariner, subj. of Holland; rec. by Edward Small, hairdresser - 20 Apr. 1803 [106]

Mayo, John, teacher, subj. of G.B.; rec. by Francis Wayland, currier - 23 Apr. 1803 [107]

McBurney, Cad., farmer, of Montgomery Co., subj. of G.B.; rec. by Henry Adams, cartman - 19 Apr. 1803 [108]

McMahon, Michael, grocer, subj. of G.B.; rec. by Jos. Fitzpatrick, grocer - 29 Dec. 1803 [109]

Morton, John, cartman, subj. of G.B.; rec. by Walter Morton, merchant - 29 Dec. 1803 [110]

Mitchell, David, pilot, subj. of G.B.; rec. by John Fargee, silversmith - 12 Feb. 1803 [111]

Meier, Casper, merchant, subj. of Emperor of Germany; rec. by George Gilford, music seller - 12 Feb. 1803. [112]

McQueen, Robert, millwright, of Troy, subj. of G.B.; rec. by Nathaniel Negus, boatman, of Troy, Rensselaer Co. - 20 May 1803 [113]

Moffatt, John, gentleman, of Cayuga Co., subj. of G.B.; rec. by George D. Cooper, attorney-at-law - 11 Jan. 1803 [114]

Managhan, Edward, public porter, subj. of G.B.; rec. by John McCombs, paver - 15 Jan. 1803 [115]

Morgan, John, mariner, subj. of G.B.; rec. by Frederic Worth, mariner - 12 Jan. 1803 [116]

Mansel, Godfried, cordwainer, subj. of Bishop of Hildesheim; rec. by Francis Dunnenberg, farrier [or furrier?] - 18 June 1803 [117]

Magee, James, merchant, subj. of G.B.; rec. by Jabez Fowler - 9 Aug. 1803 [118]

Maule, Thomas, Jr., accomptant, subj. of G.B.; rec. by Robert Curtis, merchant tailor - 3 Mar. 1803 [119]

Melloy, Henry, cartman, subj. of G.B.; rec. by Thomas Freeborn, a marshal of NYC - 26 Mar. 1803 [120]

McKay, Patrick, grocer, subj. of G.B.; rec. by Archibald Taylor, tailor - 26 Mar. 1803 [121]

McGowan, James, cartman, subj. of G.B.; rec. by Robert Wallace, a marshal of NYC - 23 Mar. 1803 [122]

McKinley, John wood sawyer, subj. of G.B.; rec. by Joseph Whitley, saw filer - 26 Mar. 1803 [123]

Vaughan, Thomas, saw maker, subj. of G.B.; rec. by Cornelius Warner, cartman - 23 Apr. 1803 [124]

Valloo, Lewis, seaman, subj. of France; rec. by Pexel Fowler, shipmaster - 1 Nov. 1803 [125]

Van Der Sluys, Peter, carpenter, subj. of France; rec. by Peter B. Van Tuyl, merchant - 13 July 1803 [126]

Thurston, Peter, carver & gilder, subj. of G.B.; rec. by Francis Wayland, currier - 23 Apr. 1803 [127]

Thompson, Edward, subj. of G.B.; rec. by William Leaycraft, custom house officer - 5 Mar. 1903 [128]

Turcot, Peter D., upholsterer, subj. of France; rec. by Jacob Van Winkel, upholsterer - 15 Jan. 1803 [129]

Thompson, Robert, merchant, subj. of G.B.; rec. by Alexander Somerville, merchant - 9 Aug. 1803 [130]

Thompson, William, cartman, subj. of G.B.; rec. by John Simpson, a marshal of NYC - 23 Mar. 1803 [131]

Taylor, William, shipmaster, subj. of G.B., late of parish of Ballymorey, Co. Antrim, Ire.; rec. by Thomas Pearce, shipmaster - 13 July 1803 [132]

Taylor, James, grocer, subj. of G.B.; rec. by Samuel Stevenson - 21 Apr. 1803 [133]

Norris, Thomas, innholder, subj. of G.B.; rec. by James Elmes, mariner - 18 May 1803 [134]

Newman, Samuel, shipmaster, subj. of G.B.; rec. by Nicholas Roosevelt - 19 May 1803 [135]

Nevin, John, cartman, subj. of G.B.; rec. by John S. Moore, builder - 23 Mar. 1803 [136]

Orr, Arthur, cartman, subj. of G.B.; rec. by Abraham Chadwick, coal broker - 21 Apr. 1803 [137]

Pindar, Martin, cordwainer, subj. of Prince of Hesse Castle; rec. by William Brown, baker - 26 Mar. 1803 [138]

Pollock, Thomas, mariner, subj. of G.B.; rec. by Carlile Pollock, merchant - 9 Aug. 1803 [139]

Page, Benjamin, merchant, subj. of G.B.; rec. by Horace Johnson, merchant - 9 Aug. 1803 [140]

Peterson, Nicholas, merchant, subj. of Emperor of Germany; rec. by Glaud Fortin, jeweller - 10 Aug. 1803 [141]

Plaine, John F., subj. of France; rec. by William Gibson, merchant - 29 Nov. 1803 [142]

Perry, Peter, merchant, subj. of France; rec. by Isaac Van Hook - 30 Dec. 1803 [143]

Palmer, John J., clerk, subj. of G.B.; rec. by John Adams, merchant - 31 Dec. 1803 [144]

Phyfe, Duncan, cabinetmaker, subj. of G.B.; rec. by John B. Dash, Jr., merchant - 23 Apr. 1803 [145]

Richards, Thomas, watchmaker, subj. of G.B.; rec. by James Woods, attorney-at-law - 23 Apr. 1803 [146]

Rousseau, Peter, merchant, subj. of France; rec. by Jonathan
Beach, merchant - 20 Apr. 1803 [147]

Reid, John, merchant, of Albany, subj. of G.B.; rec. by James
Palmer, Jr., of Albany, merchant - 31 Dec. 1803 [148]

Rodger, William, merchant, subj. of G.B.; rec. by Walter Morton,
merchant - 28 Dec. 1803 [149]

Richardson, William H., millwright, subj. of G.B.; rec. by
Walter Morton, merchant - 28 Dec. 1803 [150]

Ruden, Jaques, merchant, subj. of Batavian Republic; rec. by
Jacob Seixas, "merchandizing" - 1 Nov. 1803 [151]

Roberts, Robert, merchant, subj. of G.B.; rec. by Alexander
Cuthill, tailor - 12 Feb. 1803 [152]

Reid, James, seaman, subj. of G.B.; rec. by Jonathan Harned,
tailor - 1 Nov. 1803 [153]

Roach, John, mariner, subj. of G.B.; rec. by Thomas J. Barry,
merchant - 3 Dec. 1803 [154]

Rohde, George, turner, subj. of Landgrave of Hesse Darmstadt;
rec. by Joseph Baker, brass founder - 3 Dec. 1803 [155]

Roland, Johan Adam, blacksmith, subj. of Elector of Bavaria;
rec. by Francis Dannenberg, furrier - 18 June 1803 [156]

Rea, Robert, merchant, subj. of G.B.; rec. by Thomas Carberry,
shipmaster - 14 June 1803 [157 & 158]

Rankin, Robert, merchant, subj. of G.B.; rec. by Horace Johnson,
merchant - 9 Aug. 1803 [159]

Richey, Thomas, cartman, subj. of G.B.; rec. by Joseph McKibbin,
cartman - 24 Mar. 1803 [160]

Roy, John, house-carpenter, subj. of G.B.; rec. by William
Cruikshank, grocer - 25 Mar. 1803 [161]

Rae, John, mariner, subj. of G.B.; rec. by Thomas Gender,
fruiterer - 12 July 1803 [162]

Slesson, John, mariner, of Suffolk Co., subj. of G.B.; rec. by
Solomon Ketcham, grocer - 8 Feb. 1803 [163]

Steele, Robert, tallow chandler, subj. of G.B.; rec. by John
Airs [?] - 26 Mar. 1803 [164]

Smith, William, cabinetmaker, subj. of G.B.; rec. by John Drennan, cotton manufacturer - 23 Apr. 1803 [165]

Soret, Martin, merchant, subj. of France; rec. by Anthony Moret,
merchant - 23 Apr. 1803 [166]

Scott, Thomas, stone cutter, subj. of G.B.; rec. by John Smith,
blacksmith - 23 Apr. 1803 [167]

Spencer, William, mason, subj. of G.B.; rec. by Jacob Smith,
cordwainer - 23 Apr. 1803 [168]

Smith, Nathaniel, perfumer, subj. of G.B.; rec. by Jacob Smith,
cordwainer - 23 Apr. 1803 [169]

Spencer, Paul, cabinetmaker, subj. of G.B.; rec. by George
Shipley, cabinetmaker - 19 Apr. 1803 [170]

Sands, George, mariner, subj. of G.B.; rec. by James Lyall,
stone cutter - 31 Dec. 1803 [171]

Somerville, Archibald, grocer, subj. of G.B.; rec. by James B.
Paterson, sadler - 28 Dec. 1803 [172]

Sedgfield, John, merchant, subj. of G.B.; rec. by Caleb B.
Bowering, merchant - 28 Dec. 1803 [173]

Scrymgeair, Alexander, jeweller; rec. by Walter Morton, merchant -
28 Dec. 1803 [174]

Swarts, Aron, ship-carpenter, subj. of Emperor of Germany; rec.
by Lewis Webb, trader - 12 Feb. 1803 [175]

Scott, David, cordwainer, subj. of G.B.; rec. by Stephen Lockwood, cordwainer - 12 Feb. 1803 [176]

Short, Francis, bricklayer, subj. of G.B.; rec. by Hugh Clarke,
grocer - 15 Jan. 1803 [177]

Soulier, John Augustus, merchant, subj. of France; rec. by James
Martin, merchant - 18 June 1803 [178]

Shanewolf, Frederick, hairdresser & dentist, subj. of Landgrave
of Hesse; rec. by Bernard Oblenis, accomptant - 15 June 1803
[179]

Stone, Robert, ropemaker, subj. of G.B.; rec. by Jonathan
Weedon, ropemaker - 14 June 1803 [180]

Stewart, Thomas, labourer, subj. of G.B.; rec. by John Wark, a
marshal of NYC - 24 Mar. 1803 [181]

Sassenberg, George A., accomptant, subj. of Prussia; rec. by
Francis Dannenberg, furrier - 18 June 1803 [182]

Sommer, Johan Samuel, shopkeeper, subj. of King of Prussia; rec.
by Frederic Arcularius, baker - 14 June 1803 [183]

Warburton, George, mariner, subj. of G.B.; rec. by William Bush,
grocer - 12 July 1803 [184]

Wille, Charles G., tailor, subj. of King of Prussia; rec. by
Sebastian Noth, innkeeper - 13 July 1803 [185]

White, James, labourer, subj. of G.B.; rec. by Philip Fulkerson,
a marshal of NYC - 23 Apr. 1803 [186]

Woodcock, John, whipmaker, subj. of G.B.; rec. by Seth Wayland,
currier - 23 Apr. 1803 [187]

Williams, John, minister of the Gospel, subj. of G.B.; rec. by
Seth Wayland, currier - 23 Apr. 1803 [188]

Warner, Jeremiah, grocer, subj. of G.B.; rec. by John Minuse,
grocer - 23 Apr. 1803 [189]

Welshman, Robert, cartman, subj. of G.B.; rec. by Samuel Stevenson, stone cutter - 21 Apr. 1803 [190]

Walker, William, bookbinder, subj. of G.B.; rec. by Robert Thomson, merchant - 31 Dec. 1803 [191]

Weir, George, merchant, subj. of G.B.; rec. by Walter Morton,
merchant - 28 Dec. 1803 [192]

Wright, James, grocer, subj. of G.B.; rec. by Walter Morton,
merchant - 28 Dec. 1803 [193]

Wirth, John H.G., merchant, subj. of King of Prussia; rec. by
George Scriba, merchant - 27 Dec. 1803 [194]

Western, Ann (wife of Thomas Western, piano forte maker), subj.
of G.B.; rec. by Thomas Ball - 8 Feb. 1803 [195]

Weldon, Peter, musician, subj. of G.B.; rec. by John C. Moller,
musician - 14 June 1803 [196]

Andrews, Joseph, gentleman, subj. of France; rec. by Benjamin
Seixas, merchant - 21 July 1802 [197]

Armon, Patrick, grocer, subj. of G.B.; rec. by Patrick Lynch,
grocer - 29 Apr. 1802 [198]

Adams, Robert, blacksmith, subj. of G.B.; rec. by John Adams,
Jr., innkeeper - 29 Apr. 1802 [199]

Adams, Henry, cartman, subj. of G.B.; rec. by John Riddell,
    physician - 29 Apr. 1802 [200]

Adams, John, Jr., innkeeper, subj. of G.B.; rec. by David Law,
    cordwainer - 29 Apr. 1802 [201]

Alexander, Andrew, public porter, subj. of G.B.; rec. by John
    Bogert, public porter - 22 July 1802 [202]

Armstrong, Robert, drayman, subj. of G.B.; rec. by Henry
    Lawther, cartman - 14 Sept. 1802 [203]

Anderson, John, mariner, subj. of G.B.; rec. by John Bogert,
    porter - 13 Oct. 1802 [204]

Backhouse, Edward, cabinetmaker, subj. of G.B.; rec. by Simeon
    Deming, cabinetmaker - 17 Aug. 1802 [205]

Bogg, John, of Newtown, Queens Co., subj. of G.B.; rec. by
    George Johnson, carpenter - 17 Aug. 1802 [206]

Banks, James, rigger, subj. of G.B.; rec. by James Davis, inn-
    keeper - 18 Aug. 1802 [207]

Beatty, William, porter, subj. of G.B.; rec. by Mark McCammon -
    21 May 1802 [208 & 209]

Beatty, William, carman, subj. of G.B.; rec. by Robert Gilcrest,
    grocer - 29 Apr. 1802 [210]

Benson, John, a marshal of NYC, subj. of G.B.; rec. by Hugh
    Goble, grocer - 12 Oct. 1802 [211]

Borgors, Christian, shopkeeper, subj. of G.B.; rec. by John
    Fawpell, hairdresser - 29 Apr. 1802 [212]

Bonner, George, sugar baker, subj. of France; rec. by John Remmey,
    potter - 21 Dec. 1802 [213]

Bourosan, Anthony, subj. of Duke of Brunswick; rec. by Joseph
    Shelburgh - 17 Aug. 1802 [214]

Braiden [clerk wrote "Bradey"], James, cartman, subj. of G.B.;
    rec. by Lewis Barcley, cordwainer - 14 Oct. 1802 [215]

Britton, Christopher, stone cutter, subj. of G.B.; rec. by
    Peter Devoe, carver & gilder - 12 Oct. 1802 [216]

Bromley, Dury, millwright, subj. of G.B.; rec. by John Muston,
    carver & gilder - 9 Nov. 1802 [217]

Brown, John, grocer, subj. of G.B.; rec. by Philip McArdle,
    baker - 15 Oct. 1802 [218]

Brown, John, cartman, subj. of G.B.; rec. by John Hatfield,
    mason - 22 July 1802 [219]

Browne, Charles, ship-carpenter, subj. of G.B.; rec. by John
    Smart, sadler - 18 Aug. 1802 [220]

Brown, John, mariner, subj. of G.B.; rec. by Joseph Quinion,
    tailor - 29 Apr. 1802 [221]

Buckland, William, subj. of G.B.; rec. by Thomas Conney, a mar-
    shal of NYC - 19 Aug. 1802 [222]

Bull, Mitchell B., carpenter, subj. of G.B.; rec. by Henry Pyke,
    storekeeper - 28 Apr. 1802 [223 & 224]

Burgess, Richard, carpenter, subj. of G.B.; rec. by John
    Withington, brewer - 17 Aug. 1802 [225]

Burns, Henry, cooper, subj. of G.B.; rec. by John Utt, cooper -
    29 Apr. 1802 [226]

Byrne, William, watchmaker, subj. of G.B.; rec. by James Farrell,
    grocer - 29 Apr. 1802 [227]

Caines, George, Esq., who came to U.S. in March or April 1797,
   subj. of G.B.; rec. by Abraham Ogier Stansbury, bookseller -
      [228]

Cainey, John, boatman, subj. of G.B.; rec. by Hugh Goble,
   grocer - 14 Oct. 1802 [229]

Cassady, Dennis, cordwainer, subj. of G.B.; rec. by John Granger, slater - 29 Apr. 1802 [230]

Cassidy, John, grocer, subj. of G.B.; rec. by Gregory Dunleavy,
   grocer - 29 Apr. 1802 [231]

Cassie, James, baker, subj. of G.B.; rec. by Ronald McIntyre,
   grocer - 29 Apr. 1802 [232]

Chapman, Benjamin, stoko plasterer, subj. of G.B.; rec. by
   David King, innkeeper - 20 July 1802 [234]

Cheetham, John, hatter, subj. of G.B.; rec. by James Cheetham,
   printer - 21 Dec. 1802 [235]

Christian, Charles, cabinetmaker, subj. of G.B.; rec. by John
   Hoes, cabinetmaker - 29 Apr. 1802 [236]

Clark, Alexander, subj. of G.B.; rec. by Henry Lowther, cartman -
   21 Dec. 1802 [237]

Clark, Hugh, grocer, subj. of G.B.; rec. by William Norman,
   stevedore - 29 Apr. 1802 [238]

Clifford, James, bricklayer, subj. of G.B.; rec. by Thomas
   Fairchild, house-carpenter - 12 Nov. 1802 [239]

Clifford, James, mason, subj. of G.B.; rec. by John Riddell,
   physician - 28 Apr. 1802 [240]

Clyde, James, cartman, subj. of G.B.; rec. by John Rodman,
   mason - 29 Apr. 1802 [241]

Cleman, George, baker, subj. of Margrave of Anspach; rec. by
   Charles Wood, innkeeper - 29 Apr. 1802 [242]

Cockran, Francis, mason, subj. of G.B.; rec. by James Thorburn,
   grocer - 29 Apr. 1802 [243]

Cole, Andrew, inspector of pot- and pearl ashes, subj. of G.B.;
   rec. by Frederick Mabie, measurer of grain - 29 Apr. 1802
   [244 & 245]

Collins, Bartholomew, mariner, subj. of G.B.; rec. by John R.
   Skidde [or Skiddy?], mariner - 12 Oct. 1802 [246]

Connolly [signs Conolly], William, merchant, subj. of G.B.; rec.
   by Thomas Tracy, grocer - 28 Apr. 1802 [247]

Conway, John, grocer, subj. of G.B.; rec. by Nevin Willson,
   cooper - 21 July 1802 [248]

Cowan, John, merchant, subj. of G.B.; rec. by John Drennan,
   cotton manufacturer - 17 Aug. 1802 [249]

Coyle, Daniel, mariner, subj. of G.B.; rec. by Dennis Herraty,
   labourer - 24 Dec. 1802 [250]

Cromwell, Samuel, mariner, subj. of G.B.; rec. by William Moore,
   butcher - 29 Apr. 1802 [251]

Crooks, Robert, grocer, subj. of G.B.; rec. by John Rodman,
   mason - 29 Apr. 1802 [252]

Cross, Alexander, boatman, subj. of G.B.; rec. by John Flower,
   labourer - 21 July 1802 [253]

Cuthill, Alexander, tailor, subj. of G.B.; rec. by Abraham
   Brown, hatter - 29 Apr. 1802 [254]

Donovan, William, tobacconist, subj. of G.B.; rec. by Edward
    Moran, merchant tailor - 12 Nov. 1802 [256]

Donovan, Richard, millstone manufacturer, subj. of G.B.; rec.
    by Edward Moran, merchant tailor - 28 Apr. 1802 [257]

Dando, Stephen, hatter, subj. of G.B.; rec. by William Mayell,
    hatter - 28 Apr. 1802 [258]

Daily, Charles, cartman, subj. of G.B.; rec. by John Rodman,
    mason - 29 Apr. 1802 [259]

Dailey, Hugh, cartman, subj. of G.B.; rec. by John Rodman,
    mason - 29 Apr. 1802 [260]

Downey, John, gardner, subj. of G.B.; rec. by Philip McArdle,
    baker - 29 Apr. 1802 [211]

Drennan, John, cotton manufacturer, subj. of G.B.; rec. by
    George Johnson, carpenter - 20 July 1802 [262]

Derose, John J., gentleman, subj. of G.B.; rec. by John Withing-
    ton, brewer - 17 Aug. 1802 [263]

Dow, Henry, cartman, subj. of G.B.; rec. by Joseph Brotherton,
    a marshal of NYC - 13 Oct. 1802 [264]

Donnen, John, farmer, subj. of G.B.; rec. by John McBride,
    cartman, 15 years in U.S. - 14 Oct. 1802 [265]

Dougherty, Charles, grocer, subj. of G.B.; rec. by Gregory Dun-
    leavy, grocer - 15 Oct. 1802 [266]

Divine, John, gentleman; rec. by Mathew Knowland, blacksmith -
    28 Apr. 1802 [267]

Eagle, Henry, storekeeper, subj. of G.B.; rec. by William Henry
    Pyke, storekeeper - 28 Apr. 1802 [268]

Egenton, Thomas, grocer, subj. of G.B.; rec. by Samuel Wilson,
    millstone maker - 29 Apr. 1802 [269]

English, Middleton, a Quaker, subj. of G.B.; rec. by William
    English, a Quaker - 1 May 1802 [270]

Donaldson, James, baker, subj. of G.B.; rec. by John Hyslop,
    baker - 13 Nov. 1802 [255]

Erwin, John, labourer, subj. of G.B.; rec. by William Ellis,
    mariner - 14 Sept. 1802 [271]

Euson, John, mariner, subj. of G.B.; rec. by Garrit Kip, grocer -
    12 Oct. 1802 [272]

Farrell, James, grocer, subj. of G.B.; rec. by Edward Moran,
    merchant tailor - 28 Apr. 1802 [273]

Foot, Thomas, mason, subj. of G.B.; rec. by Edward Moran,
    merchant tailor - 28 Apr. 1802 [274]

Ferguson, John, porter bottler, subj. of G.B.; rec. by Henry
    Rankin, grocer - 29 Apr. 1802 [275]

Farrell, Richard, custom house inspector, subj. of G.B.; rec. by
    Jonathan Perry, hairdresser - 29 Apr. 1802 [276]

Fitzpatrick, James, hairdresser, subj. of G.B.; rec. by Henry J.
    Halsey, hairdresser - 29 Apr. 1802 [277]

Fisher, Alexander, grocer, subj. of G.B.; rec, by John Henning,
    cartman - 22 July 1802 [278]

Flack, John, subj. of G.B.; rec. by George Hunter, auctioneer -
    21 Aug. 1802 [279]

Freeborn, Thomas, a marshal of NYC, subj. of G.B.; rec. by Hugh
    Goble, grocer - 12 Oct. 1802 [280]

Fox, Warren, mariner, subj. of G.B.; rec. by James Noble, mariner - 26 Oct. 1802 [281]

Flanagan, Christopher, bookseller, subj. of G.B.; rec. by
George Lord, carpenter - 24 Oct. 1802 [282]

Gunton, Mark, grocer, subj. of G.B.; rec. by John Gilmor,
cabinetmaker - 22 July 1802 [283]

Gilchrist, Robert, grocer, subj. of G.B.; rec. by John Riddell,
physician - 28 Apr. 1802 [284]

Green, William, tobacconist, subj. of G.B.; rec. by Peter Wynkoop, tobacconist - 28 Apr. 1802 [285]

Graham, Francis, grocer, subj. of G.B.; rec. by William L.
Smith, cordwainer - 29 Apr. 1802 [286]

Gibson, Thomas, printer, subj. of G.B.; rec. by David King,
tavern-keeper - 29 Apr. 1802 [287]

Gotier, Joseph, grocer, subj. of Italy; rec. by Lawrence Lazar,
shipmaster - 21 Aug. 1802 [288]

Hanrahan, James, trader, subj. of G.B.; rec. by Henry O'Neil,
boarding house keeper - 28 Apr. 1802 [289]

Herford, Henry, hatter, subj. of G.B.; rec. by Cornelius Davis,
bookseller - 28 Apr. 1802 [290]

Herford, John, merchant, subj. of G.B.; rec. by Henry M. Dobbs,
watchmaker - 28 Apr. 1802 [291]

Hooke, John, grocer, subj. of G.B.; rec. by Philip Fulkerson, a
marshal of NYC - 29 Apr. 1802 [292]

Hyland, Mark, yeoman, subj. of G.B.; rec. by James Fitzpatrick,
grocer - 29 Apr. 1802 [293 & 294]

Hanna, William, farmer, of Orange Co., subj. of G.B.; rec. by
Solomon Wright, grocer - 29 Apr. 1802 [295]

Hurley, John, composition maker, subj. of G.B.; rec. by Charles
Mahony, tailor - 29 Apr. 1802 [296]

Healy, Dennis, grocer, subj. of G.B.; rec. by James Fitzpatrick,
hairdresser - 29 Apr. 1802 [297]

Herbert, Henry, milkman, subj. of Prince of Osnaburg; rec. by
John A. Haring, merchant - 2 July 1802 [298]

Henriques, Philip, labourer, subj. of G.B.; rec. by Benjamin
Thurston, grocer - 18 Aug. 1802 [299]

Howey, Archibald N., shipmaster, subj. of G.B.; rec. by Catharine Bartlett - 14 Sept. 1802 [300]

Hassen, Mathew, labourer, subj. of G.B.; rec. by Henry Lowther,
cartman - 14 Sept. 1802 [301]

Humphreys, Thomas, fireman in Curtenius's Furnace, subj. of G.B.
rec. by Enoch McCammon, moulder - 13 Oct. 1802 [302]

Hays, Thomas, chairmaker, subj. of G.B.; rec. by Garret Peterson,
blacksmith - 16 Oct. 1802 [303]

Johnson, Nicholas, mariner, subj. of Denmark; rec. by Henry
Thorne, boatbuilder - 15 Oct. 1802 [304]

Jones, William, cordwainer, subj. of G.B.; rec. by John Grainger, cordwainer - 29 Apr. 1802 [305]

Johnston, William, merchant, subj. of G.B.; rec. by George Lord,
house-carpenter - 24 Dec. 1802 [306]

Kelly, John, painter & glazier, subj. of G.B.; rec. by William
Carver, farrier - 28 Apr. 1802 [307]

Kervann, Lawrence, grocer, subj. of G.B.; rec. by Mathew Reed, tallow chandler - 29 Apr. 1802 [308]

Kayler, Frederick, grocer, subj. of G.B.; rec. by Charles Wood, innkeeper - 29 Apr. 1802 [309]

Lovett, John, innholder, subj. of G.B.; rec. by John Low, bookseller & printer - 28 Apr. 1802 [310]

Lucy, William, printer, subj. of G.B.; rec. by Richard Crooker, printer - 29 Apr. 1802 [311 & 312]

Linehan, Dennis, grocer, subj. of G.B.; rec. by Charles McCarty, grocer - 29 Apr. 1802 [313]

Lynch, Patrick, grocer, subj. of G.B.; rec. by William Norris, innholder - 29 Apr. 1802 [314]

Lannaier/Lannsur, Augustine, subj. of France, confectioner; rec. by John Vaché, artificial flowerist - 20 May 1802 [315]

Leary, Dennis, mariner, subj. of G.B.; rec. by David Crone, grocer - 21 July 1802 [316]

Luff, Valentine, grocer, subj. of German Emperor; rec. by Jacob Evans, gardner - 21 July 1802 [317]

Logan, Adam, house-carpenter, subj. of G.B.; rec. by Daniel McLaren, clothier - 21 July 1802 [318]

Murray, Hugh R., grocer, subj. of G.B.; rec. by John Low, bookseller - 28 Apr. 1802 [319]

Mahony, Charles, tailor, subj. of G.B.; rec. by Richard Donovan, millstone manufacturer -28 Apr. 1802 [320]

Matthews, John, grocer, subj. of G.B.; rec. by John Riddell, physician - 28 Apr. 1802 [321]

Maher, Patrick, labourer, subj. of G.B.; rec. by Richard Donovan, millstone manufacturer - 29 Apr. 1802 [322]

Meeks, Thomas, mason, subj. of G.B.; rec. by John Taylor, grocer - 29 Apr. 1802 [323]

Morton, Walter, merchant, subj. of G.B.; rec. by David Law, cordwainer - 29 Apr. 1802 [324]

Miller, John, painter, subj. of G.B.; rec. by Robert McConachy, cabinetmaker - 29 Apr. 1802 [325]

Milligan, William, stone cutter, subj. of G.B.; rec. by Alexander McBeth, cartman - 29 Apr. 1802 [326]

Murray, John, mariner, subj. of G.B.; rec. by Hugh Robert Murray, grocer - 20 May 1802 [327 & 328]

Morris, Robert, merchant, subj. of G.B.; rec. by John Morris, merchant - 21 July 1802 [329 & 330]

Mitchell, Walter, boat builder, subj. of G.B.; rec. by Robert Boughn, attorney-at-law - 18 Aug. 1802 [331]

Moran, John, grocer, subj. of G.B.; rec. by James Davis, innkeeper - 18 Aug. 1802 [332]

More, Jere, merchant, subj. of G.B.; rec. by Peter McNamara, master rigger - 13 Oct. 1802 [333]

Muston [or Maston?], John carver & gilder, subj. of G.B.; rec. by James Hoferon, grocer - 15 Oct. 1802 [334]

Miller, Henry, trunkmaker, subj. of G.B.; rec. by Seth Wayland, currier - 12 Nov. 1802 [335]

Morrison, James, ship-carpenter, subj. of G.B.; rec. by Joseph Fowler, sailing master - 13 Nov. 1802 [336]

Meek, Eduard, carpenter, subj. of G.B.; rec. by William Bullock, printer - 24 Dec. 1802 [337]

McBride, James, merchant, subj. of G.B.; rec. by John Adams, merchant - 12 Oct. 1802 [338]

McBride, John, cartman, subj. of G.B.; rec. by Richard Furman, gentleman - 14 Oct. 1802 [339]

McLaghlan, James, lamplighter, subj. of G.B.; rec. by Gregory Dunleavy, grocer - 20 July 1802 [340]

McBeth, Alexander, cartman, subj. of G.B.; rec. by John Riddell, physician - 28 Apr. 1802 [341]

McConachy, Robert, cabinetmaker, subj. of G.B.; rec. by Joseph Tate, tailor - 29 Apr. 1802 [342]

McNabb, John, clothier, subj. of G.B.; rec. by Ronald McIntyre, grocer - 29 Apr. 1802 [343]

McKinley, Robert, storekeeper, subj. of G.B.; rec. by John Rodman, mason - 29 Apr. 1802 [344]

McKenna, John, merchant, subj. of G.B.; rec. by John Rodman, mason - 29 Apr. 1802 [345]

McCready, James, labourer, subj. of G.B.; rec. by Eli Knapp, cordwainer - 20 July 1802 [346]

McCormick, Hugh, labourer, subj. of G.B.; rec. by John Hatfield, mason - 22 July 1802 [347]

McGary, Richard, labourer, subj. of G.B.; rec. by Henry Rutgers, Esq. - 28 July 1802 [348]

McClaine, James, grocer, subj. of G.B.; rec. by Henry Lowther, cartman - 24 July 1802 [349]

McVickar, James, merchant, subj. of G.B.; rec. by Archibald Philips, merchant - 16 Oct. 1802 [350]

McGarry, Christopher, cartman, subj. of G.B.; rec. by Richard McGarry, labourer - 16 Oct. 1802 [351]

McNiel/McNeal, Patrick, grocer, subj. of G.B.; rec. by Hugh Gobel, a captain of the City Watch of NYC - 27 Oct. 1802 [352]

McMillin, James, rigger, subj. of G.B.; rec. by Peter McNamara, rigger - 27 Oct. 1802 [353]

McNiven, Archibald, mariner, subj. of G.B.; rec. by George Copland, grocer - 21 Dec. 1802 [354]

McKibbin, Joseph, grocer, subj. of G.B.; rec. by Hugh Gobel, a captain of the City Watch of NYC - 24 Dec. 1802 [355]

Napier, Andrew, subj. of G.B.; rec. by George Hunter, auctioneer - 21 Aug. 1802 [356]

Newton, Samuel, house-carpenter, subj. of G.B.; rec. by John King, house-carpenter - 30 Oct. 1802 [357]

Norman, William, stevedore, subj. of G.B.; rec. by Philip Mc Ardele, baker - 29 Apr. 1802 [358]

Norris, William, cooper, subj. of G.B.; rec. by Patrick Lynch, grocer - 28 Apr. 1802 [359]

Nowlin, Mathew, blacksmith, subj. of G.B.; rec. by Ross Duffy, cooper - 15 Oct. 1802 [360]

Oates, Edward, mariner, subj. of G.B.; rec. by Archibald Campbell, merchant - 26 Oct. 1802 [361]

O'Hara, Hugh, baker, subj. of G.B.; rec. by John Tuckness, baker - 29 Apr. 1802 [362]

O'Neil, Thomas, grocer, subj. of G.B.; rec. by James Ferris, merchant - 28 Apr. 1802 [363]

Palmer, William, printer, subj. of G.B.; rec. by James Cheetham, printer - 28 Apr. 1802 [364]

Paterson, Robert, blacksmith, subj. of G.B.; rec. by James Laing, grocer - 22 July 1802 [365]

Penny, Thomas, grocer, subj. of G.B.; rec. by Jonathan Penny, hairdresser, a native of New Jersey - 29 Apr. 1802 [366]

Peters, John, tailor, subj. of G.B.; rec. by James Cheetham, printer - 29 Apr. 1802 [367]

Picornell, Juan Bta. Mariano, physician, subj. of Spain; rec. by Stephen Liancourt, jeweller - 24 Dec. 1802 [368]

Platt, Ralph, grocer, subj. of G.B.; rec. by William Donovan, tobacconist - 28 Apr. & 29 Nov. 1802 [369 & 370]

Powers, Thomas, brewer, subj. of G.B.; rec. by Patrick Lynch, grocer - 29 Apr. 1802 [371]

Purcell, Dominick, gentleman, subj. of G.B.; rec. by John Riddell, physician - 29 Apr. 1802 [372]

Pye, Thomas, locksmith, subj. of G.B.; rec. by John Low, bookseller - 14 Sept. 1802 [373]

Reilly, Alexander, mariner, of New Baltimore, Green Co., subj. of G.B.; rec. by William Wiltse, mariner, of Fishkill, and also Andrew McCarty, yeoman, of Coeymans, Albany Co. - 19 May 1802 [374]

Richardson, James, labourer, subj. of G.B.; rec. by John Henning, cartman - 22 July 1802 [375]

Ridley, George, tailor, subj. of G.B.; rec. by David Law, cordwainer - 29 Mar. 1802 [376]

Ringwood, Thomas, printer, subj. of G.B.; rec. by Henry C. Southwick, printer - 28 Apr. 1802 [377]

Ross, Andrew, butcher, subj. of G.B.; rec. by Edward Watheys, tallow chandler - 21 May 1802 [378]

Rushforth, William, cordwainer, subj. of G.B.; rec. by John Grainger, cordwainer - 29 Apr. 1802 [379]

Schmitzer, George Michael, butcher, subj. of King of Prussia; rec. by Jasper Ward, grocer - 21 July 1802 [380]

Scott, Hector, merchant, subj. of G.B.; rec. by John Turnbull, merchant - 26 June 1802 [381]

Scott, Henry, merchant, subj. of G.B.; rec. by James Sterling, cooper - 24 Dec. 1802 [382]

Shapter, Thomas, Jr., accountant, subj. of G.B.; rec. by John Goodeve, merchant - 29 Apr. 1802 [383]

Shaw, Kemeys, brewer, subj. of G.B.; rec. by John Withington, brewer - 17 Aug. 1802 [384]

Shaw, William, tobacconist, subj. of G.B.; rec. by George Miller, sailmaker - 29 Apr. 1802 [385]

Sharp, James, shipmaster, subj. of G.B.; rec. by Matthew Gallaher, grocer - 18 Aug. 1802 [386]

Sharpe, John, carpenter, subj. of G.B.; rec. by Benjamin Cheetham, hatter - 12 Nov. 1802 [387]

Shields, William, cartman, subj. of G.B.; rec. by John Harrington, cartman - 14 Oct. 1802 [388]

Siemon, Walrob, fruiterer, subj. of Hesse Cassel; rec. by Francis Child, conveyancer - 12 Nov. 1802 [389]

Simpson, David, gardner, subj. of G.B.; rec. by James Thorburn - 29 Apr. 1802 [390]

Simpson, George, gardner, subj. of G.B.; rec. by James Thorburn, grocer - 29 Apr. 1802 [391]

Simpson, John, a marshal of NYC, subj. of G.B.; rec. by Joseph Brotherton, a marshal of NYC - 14 Sept. 1802 [392]

Simpson, William, gardner, subj. of G.B.; rec. by James Thorburn, grocer - 29 Apr. 1802 [393]

Singleton, John, watchmaker, subj. of G.B.; rec. by Abraham G. Forbes, silversmith - 24 Dec. 1802 [394]

Slipper, Joseph, cordwainer, subj. of G.B.; rec. by John Mills, cordwainer - 29 Apr. 1802 [395]

Small, Christian, innkeeper, subj. of Landgrave Graviter; rec. by Matthew Bolmer, grocer - 15 Oct. 1802 [396]

Smith, Jacob, cordwainer, subj. of G.B.; rec. by Seth Wayland, currier - 12 Nov. 1802 [397]

Smith, John, blacksmith, subj. of G.B.; rec. by David King, tavern-keeper - 29 Apr. 1802 [398]

Smith, William, blacksmith, subj. of G.B.; rec. by John Black, of 31 Cedar St., bookbinder - 29 Apr. 1802 [399]

Sparks, John, dairyman, subj. of G.B.; rec. by John Remmey, porter - 21 Dec. 1802 [400]

Sterling, William, cooper, subj. of G.B.; rec. by James Sterling, cooper - 29 Apr. 1802 [401 & 402]

Stevenson, James, blacksmith, subj. of G.B.; rec. by Thomas Stevenson, blacksmith - 27 Oct. 1802 [403]

Stevenson, Samuel, stone cutter, subj. of G.B.; rec. by John Riddell, physician - 29 Apr. 1802 [404]

Stuart, Daniel, labourer, subj. of G.B.; rec. by John Rodman, mason - 28 Apr. 1802 [405]

Stuart, Robert, cartman, subj. of G.B.; rec. by John Rodman, bricklayer - 29 Oct. 1802 [406]

Swan, William, merchant, subj. of G.B.; rec. by John Murray, merchant - 24 July 1802 [407]

Tate, Joseph, merchant tailor, subj. of G.B.; rec. by John Rodman, mason - 29 Apr. 1802 [408]

Taylor, John, grocer, subj. of G.B.; rec. by Philip McArdle, baker - 29 Apr. 1802 [409]

Thomas, Evan, of the 6th Ward, tailor, subj. of G.B.; rec. by John Disbrory [?], tailor - 22 May 1802 [410]

Thomson, Robert, merchant, subj. of G.B.; rec. by David Law, cordwainer - 29 Apr. 1802 [411]

Thompson, Francis, merchant, a Quaker, subj. of G.B.; rec. by Thomas Walker, merchant, a Quaker - 15 Oct. 1802 [412]

Tilford, William, grocer, subj. of G.B.; rec. by John Concklin, a marshal of NYC - 29 Apr. 1802 [413]

Tracy, Thomas, grocer, subj. of G.B.; rec. by Henry C. Southwick, printer - 28 Apr. 1802 [414]

Trivett, James, cordwainer, subj. of G.B.; rec. by John Gilmor, cabinetmaker - 22 July 1802 [415]

Twitchings, Henry, grocer, subj. of G.B.; rec. by John Sullivan, merchant - 12 Nov. 1802 [416]

Vanreynegom, Francis W., mariner, subj. of France; rec. by Charles Hall, mariner - 12 Oct. 1802 [417]

Wallace, Robert, a--marshal of NYC, subj. of G.B.; rec. by John Riddell, physician - 28 Apr. 1802 [418]

Ward, Thomas, cordwainer, subj. of G.B.; rec. by Henry Rutgers, gentleman - 21 July 1802 [419]

Wannenberg, Francis, furrier, subj. of Duke of Brunswick; rec. by Christian Baehr, merchant - 17 Aug. 1802 [420]

Wark, John, a marshal of NYC, subj. of G.B.; rec. by Cornelius Clark, mariner - 12 Oct. 1802 [421]

Watts, Robert, cartman, subj. of G.B.; rec. by Hugh Gobel, grocer - 14 Sept. 1802 [422]

Walton, George, bricklayer, subj. of G.B.; rec. by Robert Wallace, a marshal of NYC - 14 Oct. 1802 [423]

Weir, Robert, merchant, subj. of G.B.; rec. by Peter Laing, merchant - 17 Aug. 1802 [424]

Walsh, James, grocer, subj. of G.B.; rec. by Charles McCarty, grocer - 29 Apr. 1802 [425]

Weir, Edward, coachmaker, subj. of G.B.; rec. by John Black, bookbinder - 29 Apr. 1802 [426]

Wilmshurst, Richard, tailor, subj. of G.B.; rec. by John Muston, carver & gilder - 11 Nov. 1802 [427]

Bundle 4

Buckle, William, brushmaker, subj. of G.B.; rec. by John Jones - 21 Apr. 1804 [1]

Bloomfield, Isaac, tailor's salesman, subj. of G.B.; rec. by Thaddeus Smith silver plater - 23 Apr. 1804 [2]

Bonner, Cornelius, rigger, subj. of G.B.; rec. by William McIntire - 23 Apr. 1804 [3]

Boyle, Thomas, paver, subj. of G.B.; rec. by Owen O'Neill - 23 Apr. 1804 [4]

Boyle, Patrick, cartman, subj. of G.B.; rec. by William McIntire - 23 Apr. 1804 [5]

Cashman, Michael, grocer, subj. of G.B.; rec. by Robert B. Norton - 23 Apr. 1804 [6]

Cummings, John, grocer, subj. of G.B.; rec. by Hugh Clarke - 23 Apr. 1804 [7]

Connell, John, grocer, subj. of G.B.; rec. by James McGowan - 24 Apr. 1804 [8]

Devoy, Michael, cartman, subj. of G.B.; rec. by Jonah Tilley - 23 Apr. 1804 [9]

Doyle, Dennis, carpenter, subj. of G.B.; rec. by Cornelius Heeney - 23 Apr. 1804 [10]

Eloden, Benjamin, house-carpenter, subj. of G.B.; rec. by Seth Wayland - 23 Apr. 1804 [11]

English, John, innholder, subj. of G.B.; rec. by John Hacket - 23 Apr. 1804 [12]

Maloy, Edward, innkeeper, subj. of G.B.; rec. by Thomas Egenton - 23 Apr. 1804 [13]

Fenwick, Thomas, bookbinder, subj. of G.B.; rec. by Henry
  Miller - 21 Apr. 1804 [14]

Gorden, George, cartman, subj. of G.B.; rec. by James Johnson -
  24 Apr. 1804 [15]

Gordon, William, labourer, subj. of G.B.; rec. by Philip Dougherty - 23 Apr. 1804 [16]

Grice, John, grocer, subj. of G.B.; rec. by Seth Wayland - 23
  Apr. 1804 [17]

Geib, John,Jr., organ builder, subj. of G.B.; rec. by John Lemaire 23 Apr. 1804 [18]

Geib, John, organ builder, subj. of G.B.; rec. by Robert C.
  Degrove - 23 Apr. 1804 [19]

Hogan, Matthew, labourer, subj. of G.B.; rec. by Lawrence Courtney - 23 Apr. 1804 [20]

Hervig, John, yeoman, subj. of G.B.; rec. by Sands Ferris - 24
  Apr. 1804 [21]

Johnson, William, house-carpenter, subj. of G.B.; rec. by
  Joseph Tate, tailor - 24 Apr. 1804 [22]

Henney, Dennis, labourer, subj. of G.B.; rec. by Lawrence Kervan - 23 Apr. 1804 [23]

Kearney, Patrick, cartman, subj. of G.B.; rec. by George Mc
  Dermott - 24 Apr. 1804 [24]

Kyle, William, blacksmith, subj. of G.B.; rec. by Nevin Wilson -
  23 Apr. 1804 [25]

Le French, George, mariner, subj. of G.B.; rec. by Francis
  Speck - 23 Apr. 1804 [26]

Lee, Richard, Jr., chemist, subj. of G.B.; rec. by John Jones -
  21 Apr. 1804 [27]

Murphy, John, grocer, subj. of G.B.; rec. by [illegible] 24
  Apr. 1804 [28]

Anastasi, Joseph, Jr., fruiterer, subj. of King of the Two
  Sicilies; rec. by Robert Degrove - 24 Apr. 1804 [29]

Morrow, William, millstone maker, subj. of G.B.; rec. by Darby
  Kine] 24 Apr. 1804 [30]

Morton, Andrew, Dr. of Physic, subj. of G.B.; rec. by Joseph
  Tate - 24 Apr. 1804 [31]

Mullan, Stuart, merchant, subj. of G.B.; rec. by John Riddell,
  physician - 24 Apr. 1804 [32]

Miller, Henry, blacksmith, subj. of G.B.; rec. by Edward Fitzpatrick - 23 Apr. 1804 [33]

Mulheran, John, tallow chandler, subj. of G.B.; rec. by David
  McKay - 23 Apr. 1804 [34]

Moan, Patrick, cartman, subj. of G.B.; rec. by Hugh Clarke - 23
  Apr. 1804 [35]

Mulhollan, Bernard, merchant, subj. of G.B.; rec. by John Flack -
  23 Apr. 1804 [36]

Mowbray, Hugh, grocer, subj. of G.B.; rec. by John Spillard,
  grocer - 23 Apr. 1804 [37]

McArdle, Patrick, cartman, subj. of G.B.; rec. by Hugh Clarke -
  23 Apr. 1804 [38]

McGaviston, John, grocer, subj. of G.B.; rec. by Michael Smallen - 23 Apr. 1804 [39]

McFadin, John, cordwainer, subj. of G.B.; rec. by Henry Dougherty - 23 Apr. 1804 [40]

McCready, John, labourer, subj. of G.B.; rec. by John Webster - 24 Apr. 1804 [41]

McConaghy, Thomas, house-carpenter, subj. of G.B.; rec. by Joseph Tate - 24 Apr. 1804 [42]

Ridden, Martin, storekeeper, subj. of G.B.; rec. by Henry Lowther - 23 Apr. 1804 [43]

Regan, William, millstone maker, subj. of G.B.; rec. by Thomas Donovan - 24 Apr. 1804 [44]

Robinson, Thomas, innholder, subj. of G.B.; rec. by Sands Ferris - 24 Apr. 1804 [45]

Ryan, Lawrence, cooper, subj. of G.B.; rec. by Thomas Ryan - 23 Apr. 1804 [46]

Spratt, William, grocer, subj. of G.B.; rec. by Joseph Titus - 23 Apr. 1804 [47]

Slattery, Andrew, storekeeper, subj. of G.B.; rec. by Dennis Healy - 23 Apr. 1804 [48]

Tolmie, Colin, blacksmith, subj. of G.B.; rec. by Edward Fitzpatrick - 23 Apr. 1804 [49]

Thomson, Ralph, cartman, subj. of G.B. - May 1804 [50]

Shaw, William, merchant, subj. of G.B. - 21 Jan. 1804 [51]

McDonnell, William, lumber merchant, subj. of G.B. - 6 Mar. 1804 [52]

Kervan, Moses, sawyer, subj. of G.B. - 16 June 1804 [53]

Kelly, Patrick, merchant, of Troy, Rensselaer Co., subj. of G.B. - 14 June 1804 [54]

Dikins, Michael, merchant, subj. of France - 12 June 1804 [55]

Wampo, Conerad, yeoman, subj. of G.B.; rec. by Sands Ferris - 24 Apr. 1804 [56]

Wilson, James, grocer, subj. of G.B.; rec. by Edward Monaghan - 23 Apr. 1804 [57]

Whithy, Nicholas, cartman, subj. of G.B.; rec. by Jonah Tilley - 23 Apr. 1804 [58]

Ward, Hugh, hairdresser, subj. of G.B.; rec. by Hugh Duffy - 23 Apr. 1804 [59]

Ainslie, Robert, merchant, subj. of G.B.; rec. by William Donalson, boat maker - 22 Jan. 1805 [60]

Aubery, Jean Louis, merchant, subj. of France; rec. by Anthony Latour, hairdresser - 12 Nov. 1805 [61]

Bresnahan, Andrew, grocer & dealer, of Catskill, Green Co., subj. of G.B.; rec. by John Sullivan - 16 Apr. 1805 [62]

Bird, Michael, iron kuper, subj. of G.B.; rec. by John D. Bird, accomptant - 17 Apr. 1805 [63]

Barr, Robert, mariner, subj. of G.B.; rec. by James Roberts, inspector of customs - 12 Nov. 1805 [64]

Byrne, Lawrence, grocer, subj. of G.B.; rec. by Michael Sullivan, grocer - 21 May 1805 [65]

Boorman, James, merchant, subj. of G.B.; rec. by Edward Kerneys, student-at-law - 24 July 1805 [66]

Corbitt, Joseph, grocer, subj. of G.B.; rec. by John S. Taylor, grocer - 23 July 1805 [67]

Churnley, Robert, hatter, subj. of G.B.; rec. by William Rut-
ledge - 8 May 1805 [68]

Clark, Allan, grocer, subj. of G.B.; rec. by Alexander Clark,
grocer - 16 Nov. 1805 [69]

Duvan, Charles, from Nantz, France; rec. by Hyacinth Agnel - 25
Jan. 1805 [70]

Duclos, Anne Rose de Kater, widow, subj. of France; rec. by Jn.
Joseph Manradin, merchant - 3 Dec. 1805 [71]

Dalton, James, shipmaster, subj. of G.B.; rec. by William Miller,
measurer - 20 Aug. 1805 [72]

Decerf, Sebastian, hairdresser, subj. of France; rec. by John
Winniss, auctioneer - 19 Dec. 1805 [73]

Dean, Joseph, mariner, subj. of G.B.; rec. by James E. Millott,
accomptant - 19 Dec. 1805 [74]

Forbes, James, merchant, subj. of G.B.; rec. by Martin S. Wilkens, Esq. - 23 July 1805 [75]

Fairbairn, Francis, merchant, subj. of G.B.; rec. by Peter Mur-
chison, merchant - 21 Dec. 1805 [76]

Griffiths, David, mason, subj. of G.B.; rec. by John Hughes,
sawyer - 25 Apr. 1807 [77]

Gillet, Thomas W., mariner, subj. of G.B.; rec. by Richard Jennings, innkeeper - 25 Apr. 1807 [78]

Harmony, Peter, mariner, subj. of Spain; rec. by Ormond Noble,
mariner - 18 Apr. 1805 [79]

Hearsfield, William, carpenter, subj. of G.B.; rec. by Daniel
Bogerts, rigger - 16 Apr. 1805 [80]

Hill, Joseph, sailmaker, subj. of G.B.; rec. by Philip McArdle,
baker - 19 Apr. 1805 [82]

Herraty, Dennis, cartman, subj. of G.B.; rec. by Jakob Peterson,
coachmaker - 12 Nov. 1805 [83]

Jacobs, Israel B., merchant, subj. of the Batavian Republic; rec.
by Jaques Ruden, merchant - 1 Oct. 1805 [84]

Kleine, Frederick Adolphus, merchant, subj. of Elector of Hanover; rec. by Peter Perry, merchant - 21 May 1805 [85]

King, John, mariner, subj. of King of Prussia; rec. by Thomas
Norris - 12 Nov. 1805 [86]

Laforen, Hipolite, gentleman, subj. of France; rec. by John
Suckley, merchant - 19 Dec. 1805 [87]

Lee, Richard, Jr., apothecary, subj. of G.B.; rec. by John Low,
bookseller - 19 Dec. 1805 [88]

Mackaness, Thomas Thornton M., subj. of G.B.; rec. by James John
Margarum, merchant - 25 July 1805 [89]

Mills, John, Jr., merchant, subject of G.B.; rec. by William
Brown, merchant - 20 Dec. 1804 [90]

Mathew, David, shipmaster, subj. of G.B.; rec. by William
Ricketts, U.S.A. - 22 Feb. 1805 [91]

Munro, Hugh, merchant, subj. of G.B.; rec. by Peter Morison,
merchant - 22 Feb. 1805 [92]

Martin, Joseph, shipbuilder, subj. of King of Spain; rec. by
Lucretia Wills - May 1805 [93]

Nugent, Robert, mariner, subject. of G.B.; rec. by Robert Smit-
ken, innkeeper - 18 Apr. 1805 [94]

Nixon, George, merchant, subj. of G.B.; rec. by Hector Craig, merchant - 16 Apr. 1805 [95]

Olsen, Richard, mariner; rec. by Joshua Werts, house-carpenter - 19 Apr. 1805 [96]

Queen, Allan, shoemaker, subj. of G.B.; rec. by David Bryson, currier - 14 Nov. 1806 [97]

Shannon, John, cartman, subj. of G.B.; rec. by James Kelly, cartman - Apr. 1806 [98]

Sanders, William, merchant, subj. of G.B.; rec. by John Hyslop - 25 May 1805 [99]

Stollenwerk, Lewis Augustus, jeweller, subj. of France; rec. by Charles Stewart, merchant - 25 July 1805 [100]

Stollenwerk, Peter, watchmaker, subj. of France; rec. by Charles Stewart, merchant - 25 July 1805 [101]

Griffith, Thomas, shipmaster, subj. of G.B.; rec. by Hanke Lilienthal, clothier - 26 July 1805 [102]

Van Bockel, Andrew J., merchant; rec. by Samuel C. Sutton - 8 Jan. 1805 [103]

Watson, Thomas, shipmaster, subj. of G.B.; rec. by John Fitzpatrick, carpenter - 20 Dec. 1805 [104]

Wacker, Justus, labourer, subj. of Prince of Hesse; rec. by Charles Stewart - 24 Jan. 1805 [105]

Walker, John, mariner, subj. of G.B.; rec. by William Thomas, printer - 19 Feb. 1805 [106]

Whyte, William Kelly, mariner, subj. of G.B.; rec. by James E. Millett, accomptant - 19 Dec. 1805 [107]

Armstrong, James, innkeeper, subj. of G.B.; rec. by James Woods, councillor -at-law - 16 Apr. 1806 [108]

Arthur, James, mariner, subj. of G.B.; rec. by Edward Livingston, whip sawyer - 26 Aug. 1806 [109]

Adams, Thomas, accountant, subj. of G.B.; rec. by John Caldwell, merchant - 18 Aug. 1806 [110]

Barr, James, storekeeper, subj. of G.B.; rec. by William Stewart, cordwainer - 23 June 1806 [111]

Bacon, Edward, merchant, subj. of G.B.; rec. by James Mullany - 22 Sept. 1806 [112]

Christie, James, coach smith, subj. of G.B.; rec. by James Warner, coach maker - 17 Nov. 1806 [113]

Connolly, Edward, porter house keeper, subj. of G.B.; rec. by Robert Quin, clothier - 17 Nov. 1806 [114]

Courtou, George, fruiterer, subj. of France; rec. by Eliakin Ford - 15 Nov. 1806 [115]

Corgen, John, grocer, subj. of G.B.; rec. by John Ferguson - 15 Nov. 1806 [116]

Crookes, John, painter, subj. of G.B.; rec. by John Nache, artificial florist - 14 Apr. 1805 [117]

Droutwine/Troutwine, William, butcher, subj. of Prince of Saxony; rec. by George M. Schnitzer, grocer -24 June 1806 [118]

Delarue, Louis, gentleman, subj. of France; rec. by Joseph De la Croix, distiller of cordials - 30 Jan. 1806 [119]

Edwards, John, scale beam manufacturer, subj. of G.B.; rec. by Richard Bowne, druggist - 31 Jan. 1806 [120]

Francolin, Louis Robert, merchant; rec. by Patrick Callahan - 17 Sept. 1806 [121]

Grenier, Felix James, gentleman, subj. of the Emperor of France and the King of Italy; rec. by Francis James Berier, teacher of French - 24 Apr. 1806 [122]

Garr, Andrew S., attorney-at-law, subject of G.B.; at age of 3 he was brought to NYC by his parents and left the U.S. only once to go to Cuba for one week; rec. by William Keese - 29 Aug. 1806 [123]

Geib, John, organ builder, subj. of the Elector Palatine; rec. by Adam Geib, pfof. of music - 18 Aug. 1806 [124]

Gordon, George, clock- and watchmaker, of Newburgh, Orange Co., subj. of G.B.; rec. by William Clark, merchant - 30 Jan. 1806 [125]

Given, Josiah, bricklayer, subj. of G.B.; rec. by Alexander McBath/McBeath - 17 Nov. 1806 [126]

Gouin, Joseph, subj. of France; rec. by Judah Zuntz, attorney-at-law - 15 Dec. 1806 [127]

Geib, John, Jr., organ builder and music instrument maker, subj. of G.B.; rec. by Adam Geib, prof. of music - 18 Sept. 1806 [128]

Higgins, William, cartman, subj. of G.B.; rec. by Elkanah Doolittle - 17 Nov. 1806 [129]

Hitchens, Philip, mariner, subj. of G.B.; rec. by John Miles, Jr., mariner, of New Haven - 18 June 1806 [130]

Higgins, John, mason, subj. of G.B.; rec. by James Fisher, house-carpenter - 19 Aug. 1806 [131]

Hunter, Hamilton, baker, subj. of G.B.; rec. by John Hyslop, baker - 16 Sept. 1806 [132]

Hamilton, William, labourer, subj. of G.B.; rec. by James Elliot, house-carpenter - 20 Oct. 1806 [133]

Hearthe, James Thomas, hairdresser, subj. of G.B.; rec. by James W. Green, innkeeper - 19 May 1806 [134]

Jackson, John, merchant, subj. of G.B.; rec. by Jonathan Ogden - 16 Jan. 1806 [135]

Kehoe, John, grocer, subj. of G.B.; rec. by Dennis Doyle, grocer - 17 Nov. 1806 [136]

Knebel, John Jacob, mariner, subj. of King of Sweden; rec. by William Jacobs, grocer - 17 Jan. 1806 [137]

Kenny, Michael, merchant tailor, subj. of G.B.; rec. by Richard Nugent, grocer - 14 Apr. 1806 [138]

Labatut, Jean Marie Joseph, gentleman, subj. of Emperor of France and King of Italy; rec. by Francis James Berier, teacher of French - 14 Apr. 1806 [139]

Logan, David, merchant tailor, subj. of G.B.; rec. by Andrew Acheson, merchant tailor and salesman - 20 Oct. 1806 [140]

Lewis, John, mariner, subj. of Queen of Portugal; rec. by Anthony Latour, hairdresser - 21 July 1806 [141]

McBeath, James, brewer, subj. of G.B.; rec. by Alexander McBeath - 17 Nov. 1806 [142]

McEvers, John, mariner, subj. of G.B.; rec. by Stephen Young, cabinetmaker - 29 Jan. 1806 [143]

McLean, Paul, pedlar, subj. of G.B.; rec. by Thomas Rossell, grocer - 30 Aug. 1806 [144]

McCallum, Zachariah, merchant, subj. of G.B.; rec. by Richard
Scott - 21 July 1806 [145]

Midellemess, Andrew, house-carpenter, subj. of G.B.; rec. by
William Purves, of the 5th Ward, carpenter - 17 Nov. 1806
[146]

Morton, William H., accomptant, subj. of the Batavian Republic;
rec. by John L. Holthuysen, merchant - 11 Mar. 1806 [147]

Moore, James, merchant, subj. of G.B.; rec. by Robert Quin,
clothing store keeper - 14 Apr. 1806 [148]

Mark, Louis, merchant, subj. of Emperor of Germany; rec. by
Jacob Mark, merchant - 23 May 1806 [149]

Mullany, James, merchant, subj. of G.B.; rec. by Robert Dillon,
merchant - 13 Sept. 1806 [150]

Moll, Jan/John, mariner, subj. of Emperor of Russia; rec. by
George M. Schmitzer - 20 Oct. 1806 [151]

Miller, Zachariah, merchant, subj. of G.B.; rec. by William
Bailey, merchant - 26 Aug. 1806 [152]

Mooney, Thomas, grocer, subj. of G.B.; rec. by Michael Smallen,
grocer and tavern-keeper - 24 Oct. 1806 [153]

Medcalf, Henry, mariner, subj. of G.B.; rec. by Thomas Mooney,
grocer - 24 Oct. 1806 [154]

Mahony, Bartholomew, ship-carpenter, subj. of G.B.; rec. by
Mary Mahony, a widow - 30 Oct. 1806 [155]

Marks, Peter, gardener, subj. of France; rec. by Frederick
Besher, poulterer - 14 Jan. 1806 [156]

Normann, Henry H., mason, subj. of G.B.; rec. by William Brady,
grocer - 17 Nov.1806 [157]

Nicoll, George, gentleman, subj. of G.B.; rec. by John Hegeman,
flour merchant - 28 May 1806 [158]

Pienowel, Antoine, merchant, subj. of France; rec. by Claudius
Bignon, grocer - 15 Apr. 1806 [159]

Pardo, Isaac Loper, merchant, subj. of the Batavian Republic;
rec. by Louis Loper, of New Jersey, farmer - 16 Apr. 1806
[160]

Poni, Charles, merchant, subj. of King of Italy; rec. by Joseph
Dela Croix, distiller - 25 Feb. 1806 [161]

Rowe, John, nerchant, subj. of G.B.; rec. by Myles Kirkby,
merchant - 18 Jan. 1806 [162]

Ross, James, accountant, subj. of G.B.; rec. by Daniel Fisher,
grocer - 27 Feb. 1806 [163]

Reiss, John Henry, physician, subj. of G.B.; rec. by George A.
Sassenberg, grocer - 28 Feb. 1806 [164]

Rothgangel, Andrew, soap boiler, subj. of Prince of Anspach;
rec. by John Ellis - 24 Oct. 1806 [165]

Rosse, Nicholas, cooper, subj. of the Pope; rec. by Joseph Anastasi, fruiterer - 20 Oct. 1806 [166]

Rapner, Langhorne Benton, livery stable keeper, subj. of G.B.;
rec. by James Warner, coachmaker - 17 Nov. 1806 [167]

Redmond, Patrick, mariner, subj. of G.B.; rec. by Thomas Larkin,
tailor - 24 Nov. 1806 [168]

Rodman, Thomas, of town of Newburgh, subj. of G.B.; rec. by John
Rodman, bricklayer - 17 Dec. 1806 [169]

Smith, Thomas, currier, subj. of G.B.; rec. by David Bryson,
   currier - 14 Nov. 1806 [170]

Spratt, John, labourer, subj. of G.B.; rec. by John O'Neale -
   17 Nov. 1806 [171]

Sago, John, mariner, subj. of King of Sweden; rec. by William
   Downs, shipmaster - 19 Aug. 1806 [172]

Smith, Francis, merchant, subj. of G.B.; rec. by Peter Thurston - 24 Sept. 1806 [173]

Sloan, John, grocer, subj. of G.B. - 17 June 1806 [174]

Strangman, Thomas, shipmaster, subj. of G.B.; rec. by Thomas
   McCready, grocer - 14 Apr. 1806 [175]

Stokes, Thomas, dealer in medicine, subj. of G.B.; rec. by Henry
   Miller, trunk maker - 17 June 1806 [176]

Sloan, John, grocer, subj. of G.B.; rec. by Hugh Clark, grocer -
   17 June 1806 [177]

Taubman, John, mariner, subj. of G.B.; rec. by Henry Kermit -
   26 June 1806 [178]

Turley, Henry, cartman, subj. of G.B.; rec. by Saxton Palmer,
   tavern-keeper - 27 Feb. 1806 [179]

Therasson, Lewis, clerk, subj. of France; rec. by Vincent Faure -
   20 Oct. 1806 [180]

Tenet, Peter, gentleman, subj. of France; rec. by Francis
   Berier, teacher - 26 Nov. 1806 [181]

Whelan, James, cooper, subj. of G.B.; rec. by John O'Neale - 17
   Nov. 1806 [182]

Ward, Hugh, hairdresser, subj. of G.B.; rec. by John McGaviston,
   grocer - 31 Oct. 1806 [183]

Wingasson, Abraham, gardener; rec. by Benjamin Vredenburgh,
   taverner - 29 Oct. 1806 [184]

Waring, Charles R., clerk, subj. of G.B.; rec. by John P.
   Fisher, physician - 24 Jan. 1806 [185]

Watt, James, labourer, subj. of G.B.; rec. by William Hamilton -
   20 Oct. 1806 [186]

                          Bundle 5

Ackman, John, ship-carpenter, subj. of G.B.; rec. by Robert
   Speir, cooper - 29 Apr. 1807 [1]

Aitkin, John, rigger, subj. of G.B.; rec. by Joseph Chadwick,
   grocer - 21 Apr. 1807 [2]

Ahlmen, Henry, labourer, subj. of Duke of Berlenburg; rec. by
   George Shemel - 21 Apr. 1807 [3]

Anderson, Robert, stone cutter, subj. of G.B.; rec. by William
   Orr - 22 Apr. 1807 [4]

Ashwell, Samuel, rigger, subj. of G.B.; rec. by James Ewing,
   rigger - 30 Apr. 1807 [5]

Abraham, John, rigger, subj. of G.B.; rec. by Evan Thomas,
   grocer - 22 Apr. 1807 [6]

Angell, Thomas, currier, subj. of G.B.; rec. by John Crop,
   clerk - 29 Apr. 1807 [7]

Allen, John, rigger, subj. of G.B.; rec. by Henry Chase - 27
   Apr. 1807 [8]

Addison, John, stevedore, subj. of G.B.; rec. by Robert Benson, Jr., merchant - 27 Apr. 1807 [9]

Anderson, David, stone cutter, subj. of G.B.; rec. by William Cunningham - 27 Apr. 1807 [10]

Agar, William, sailmaker, subj. of G.B.; rec. by Christopher Duyckinck, sailmaker - 29 Apr. 1807 [11]

André, Abraham, accountant, subj. of Prince of Hesse Cassel; rec. by Jacob Hesh - 25 Apr. 1807 [12]

Brown, John, dyer, subj. of G.B.; rec. by Joseph Story - 22 Apr. 1807 [13]

Barfe, Thomas, of Kings Co., Brooklyn, merchant, subj. of G.B.; rec. by John Clark, Jr., merchant - 29 July 1808

Bell, William W., merchant, subj. of G.B.; rec. by Zacchaeus Swaen - 24 Dec. 1808 [15]

Bryson, Archibald, merchant, subj. of G.B.; rec. by Robert Ainsley, merchant - 24 Apr. 1807 [16]

Burchill, Arthur, fig-blue maker, subj. of G.B.; rec. by Thomas Dawson - 24 Apr. 1807 [17]

Bard, John, rigger, subj. of G.B.; rec. by Wolcott Blakely, rigger - 26 Apr. 1807 [18]

Blanchard, Andrew, rigger, subj. of G.B.; rec. by John Atkin, rigger - 25 Apr. 1807 [19]

Balen, Peter, gardener, subj. of King of Holland; rec. by Cornelius Decker, cartman - 25 Apr. 1807 [20]

Brour, John, labourer, subj. of Prince of Hesse Cassel; rec. by Jan/John Lindeman - 25 Apr. 1807 [21]

Bryan, John, innkeeper, subj. of G.B.; rec. by Isaac Lozada, cabinetmaker - 23 Apr. 1807 [22]

Bowen, John, tailor, subj. of G.B.; rec. by Mark Fein, tailor - 30 Apr. 1807 [23]

Barnston, William, of Brooklyn, Kings Co., farmer, subj. of G.B.; rec. by Ralph Patchen, of Brooklyn - 30 Apr. 1807 [24]

Barnes, William, cabinetmaker, subj. of G.B.; rec. by James Laing - 22 Apr. 1807 [25]

Brown, Thomas, innkeeper, subj. of G.B.; rec. by Peter Cruger, merchant - 21 Apr. 1807 [26]

Bell, James, watchmaker, subj. of G.B.; rec. by Stephen Young, watchmaker - 21 Apr. 1807 [27]

Beattie, William, grocer, subj. of G.B.; rec. by James Rolston - 20 Apr. 1807 [28]

Brown, John, labourer, subj. of Prince of Hesse Cassel - 25 Apr. 1807 [29]

Ball, Henry, schoolmaster, subj. of G.B.; rec. by John Millen - 23 Apr. 1807 [30]

Bruges/Bridges, William, sawyer, subj. of G.B.; rec. by James Chesterman, merchant tailor - 23 Apr. 1807 [31]

Britten, John, innkeeper, subj. of G.B.; rec. by Henry Pope - 23 Apr. 1807 [32]

Beresford, Robert H., printer, subj. of G.B.; rec. by John Thorkwin - 28 Apr. 1807 [33]

Bennett, James, accountant, subj. of G.B.; rec. by William Leffingwell - 21 Apr. 1807 [34]

Barthel, Conrad, labourer, subj. of Prince of Hesse Cassel; rec.
by Jacob Warner - 21 Apr. 1807 [35]

Black, John, gardener, subj. of Duke of Brunswick; rec. by Casper Samler - 21 Apr. 1807 [36]

Betzel, Heinrich, baker, subj. of Duke of Witgenstein; rec. by
Tobias Hoffman - 25 Apr. 1807 [37]

Bethell, William, brewer, subj. of G.B.; rec. by Henry Hyde -
27 Apr. 1807 [38]

Boston, John, slater, subj. of G.B.; rec. by John Linon, cooper -
29 Apr. 1807 [39]

Buchanan, Charles, tobacconist, subj. of G.B.; rec. by Thomas
Cox, tobacconist - 29 Apr. 1807 [40]

Bliss, David, bookseller, subj. of G.B.; rec. by Beza E. Bliss,
student-at-law - 29 Apr. 1807 [41]

Brown, John, teacher, subj. of G.B.; rec. by John McKie, lumber
merchant - 29 Apr. 1807 [42]

Brown, John, rigger, subj. of G.B.; rec. by Lawrence Humphreys -
29 Apr. 1807 [43]

Birtch, John, subj. of G.B.; rec. by John J. Johnson, of Brooklyn, Kings Co., farmer - 30 Apr. 1807 [44]

Bush, Daniel, accountant, subj. of G.B.; rec. by John Pier Groshon - 23 Apr. 1807 [45]

Byrnes, James, labourer, subj. of G.B.; rec. by Lew Bleukar,
merchant - 24 Apr. 1807 [46]

Blackburn, Richard, shoemaker, subj. of G.B.; rec. by Francis
Ogsbury, merchant - 24 Apr. 1807 [47]

Brislan, Patrick, labourer, subj. of G.B.; rec. by Washington
Morton, counsellor-at-law - 27 Apr. 1807 [48]

Booker, George, merchant, subj. of G.B.; rec. by John Bailey -
27 Apr. 1807 [49]

Bryden, William, tanner, subj. of G.B.; rec. by Thomas Stevenson,
blacksmith - 27 Apr. 1807 [50]

Biart, John Peter, merchant; rec. by John Daniel McAuliffe - 20
Apr. 1807 [51]

Bitigeman, John, yeoman, subj. of Elector of Hanover; rec. by
John Jungerich - 27 Mar. 1807 [52]

Bennet, Adam, cartman, subj. of G.B.; rec. by Alexander Doig,
teacher - 28 Apr. 1807 [53]

Bissell, Robert, cordwainer, subj. of G.B.; rec. by Samuel Smith -
28 Apr. 1807 [54]

Berry, John, smith & farrier, subj. of G.B.; rec. by William
Carver, smith & farrier - 28 Apr. 1807 [55]

Bertrand, Charles Pierre, merchant, subj. of France; rec. by
Peter Harden - 20 Nov. 1807 [56]

Burk, John, carpenter, subj. of G.B.; rec. by John Aitken - 22
Apr. 1807 [57]

Barry, John, shipmaster, subj. of G.B.; rec. by Matthew Dunnett -
24 Jan. 1807 [58]

Bowering, John, grocer, subj. of G.B.; rec. by Philip Jones,
livery stable keeper - 22 Apr. 1807 [59]

Chew, Richard, innkeeper, subj. of G.B.; rec. by John Wark - 27
Apr. 1807 [60]

Chapman, William, ropemaker, of Brooklyn, Kings Co., subj. of G.B.; rec. by Henry Stanton - 27 Apr. 1807 [61]

Chalmers, James, dyer, subj. of G.B.; rec. by Abner Curtis, a marshal of NYC - 25 Apr. 1807 [62]

Chadwick, Joseph, grocer, subj. of G.B.; rec. by Davis Blackley - 24 Apr. 1807 [63]

Cave, Thomas, ship-carpenter; rec. by Robert Elliott - 27 Apr. 1807 [64]

Church, George, labourer, subj. of Elector of Saxony; rec. by George Henry Kling - 21 Apr. 1807 [65]

Coningham, Grove, teacher; rec. by Jervis Titus - 28 Apr. 1807 [66]

Crawley, Dewsberry, subj. of G.B.; rec. by Thomas Stidell, tallow chandler - 28 Apr. 1807 [67]

Campbell, William, tailor; rec. by Thomas Stevenson, blacksmith - 28 Apr. 1807 [68]

Cunningham, James, labourer, subj. of G.B.; rec. by Martin Shanahan, labourer - 28 Apr. 1807 [69]

Cole, Benjamin, rigger, subj. of G.B.; rec. by Lawrence Humphreys, rigger - 28 Apr. 1807 [70]

Chrystie, Andrew, carpenter, subj. of G.B.; rec. by Cornelius Hoffman, painter & glazier - 27 Apr. 1807 [71]

Cassady, John, of Brooklyn, Kings Co., town boatman, subj. of G.B.; rec. by Henry Stanton, of Brooklyn, cooper - 29 Apr. 1807 [72]

Castle, Robert, boatman, subj. of G.B.; rec. by John Pritchett - 29 Apr. 1807 [73]

Calder, Peter, accountant, subj. of G.B.; rec. by John McGregor, teacher - 30 Apr. 1807 [74]

Carrigan, John, bricklayer, subj. of G.B.; rec. by Thomas Miller, merchant - 29 Apr. 1807 [75]

Campbell, John, accountant, subj. of G.B.; rec. by Peter Sutton - 30 Apr. 1807 [76]

Cooper, John, carpenter, subj. of G.B.; rec. by John Van Barcom, carpenter - 30 Apr. 1807 [77]

Cars, Thomas, mariner, subj. of G.B.; rec. by Stephen Price, attorney-at-law - 30 Apr. 1807 [78]

Coffin, Peter, mariner, subj. of G.B.; rec. by Moses Brown, tavern-keeper - 30 Apr. 1807 [79]

Currie, Archibald, rigger, subj. of G.B.; rec. by John Addison, stevedore - 27 Apr. 1807 [80]

Currant, Nicholas, rigger, subj. of G.B.; rec. by John Atkins, rigger - 24 Apr. 1807 [81]

Chesterman, James, merchant tailor, subj. of G.B.; rec. by Francis Davis, merchant tailor - 24 Apr. 1807 [82]

Cook, Thomas, cabinetmaker, subj. of G.B.; rec. by John Hardie, cabinetmaker - 24 Apr. 1807 [83]

Chalmers,Andrew, grocer, subj. of G.B.; rec. by John Linon - 24 Apr. 1807 [84]

Carr, James, shipwright, subj. of G.B.; rec. by Robert Brown - 23 Apr. 1807 [85]

Castine, John, labourer, subj. of G.B.; rec. by Robert Henry - 23 Apr. 1807 [86]

Cranstoun, Thomas, grocer, subj. of G.B.; rec. by Israel Morgan -
26 Apr. 1807 [87]

Coldwell, George, pewterer, subj. of G.B.; rec. by William Fosbrook - 24 Apr. 1807 [88]

Carrick, Robert, grocer, subj. of G.B.; rec. by William Ferguson, sawyer - 24 Apr. 1807 [89]

Carrick, John, sawyer, subj. of G.B.; rec. by William Ferguson,
sawyer - 24 Apr. 1807 [90]

Cook, John, merchant, subj. of G.B.; rec. by Robert Robinson,
merchant - 20 Apr. 1807 [91]

Calling, Hugh, husbandman, subj. of G.B.; rec. by Lawrence Carberry, cooper - 20 Apr. 1807 [92]

Child, Lewis, painter & glazier, subj. of G.B.; rec. by James
MacKevey - 21 Apr. 1807 [93]

Chisholm, Thomas, stone cutter, subj. of G.B.; rec. by Hector
Sinclair, grocer - 21 Apr. 1807 [94]

Cameron, Donald, tailor, subj. of G.B.; rec. by James McIntosh,
grocer - 27 Apr. 1807 [95]

Coger, John, rigger, subj. of G.B.; rec. by John Aitken, rigger -
28 Apr. 1807 [96]

Clapp, William, grocer, subj. of G.B.;rec. by William Hughes,
gentleman - 28 Apr. 1807 [97]

Crawford, David, subj. of G.B.; rec. by John Wark - 20 Apr.
1807 [98]

Cave, William, grocer, subj. of G.B.; rec. by David Van Gelder,
carman - 22 Apr. 1807 [99]

Cameron, Hugh, grocer, subj. of G.B.; rec. by William Ferguson -
23 Apr. 1807 [100]

Kramer/Cramer, Francis, labourer, subj. of France; rec. by Henry
Hornfield - 21 Apr. 1807 [101]

Couthard, Isaac, subj. of G.B.; rec. by Robert Bogardus - 22
Apr. 1807 [102]

Dawson, Thomas, locksmith, subj. of G.B; rec. by Isaiah Leanig-
ton - 30 Apr. 1807 [103]

Dobson, William B., grocer, subj. of G.B.; rec. by Henry B.
Moore - 20 Apr. 1807 [104]

Doolin, John, of Brooklyn, grocer & tavern-keeper, subj. of G.B.;
rec. by Thomas Donovan, gardener - 21 Apr. 1807 [105]

Del Vecchio, John, merchant, subj. of Emperor of France & King
of Italy; rec. by James Anderson - 24 Apr. 1807 [106]

Doig, Alexander, teacher, subj. of G.B.; rec. by William Guest -
22 Apr. 1807 [107]

Davies, Thomas, blacksmith, subj. of G.B.; rec. by Evan Thomas,
grocer - 22 Apr. 1807 [108]

Douglass, James, teacher, subj. of G.B.; rec. by James Mc Intosh
- 22 Apr. 1807 [109]

Donald, William, stone cutter, subj. of G.B.; rec. by John
Willey - 23 Apr. 1807 [110]

Davie, James, sawyer, subj. of G.B.; rec. by John Hughes - 24
Apr. 1807 [111]

Dyke, James, cabinetmaker, subj. of G.B.; rec. by David King,
innkeeper - 21 Apr. 1807 [112]

Dawson, Thomas, physician, subj. of G.B.; rec. by Arthur Burchill - 24 Apr. 1807 [113]

Dinnen, George, distiller, subj. of G.B.; rec. by John Barkhill - 25 Apr. 1807 [114]

David, David, malster, subj. of G.B.; rec. by David John - 27
Apr. 1807 [115]

Dougherty, James, labourer, subj. of G.B.; rec. by Peter Hoffmire, bricklayer - 27 Apr. 1807 [116]

Deal, Conrad, labourer, subj. of Prince of Hohen Solm; rec. by
Henry Scherer, gardener - 27 Apr. 1807 [117]

Dunmore, William, cooper, subj. of G.B.; rec. by John Moir,
teacher - 28 Apr. 1807 [118]

Drummond, William, tailor, subj. of G.B.; rec. by Alexander
Anderson, cabinetmaker - 29 Apr. 1807 [119]

Donaldson, William, coach maker, subj. of G.B.; rec. by Michael
Gardiner, house-carpenter - 29 Apr. 1807 [120]

Doyle, Dennis, house-carpenter, subj. of G.B.; rec. by Cornelius
Heiney - 19 Jan. 1807 [121]

Delacroix, Louis, distiller; rec. by Samuel Bowne, Jr., silversmith - 29 Apr. 1807 [122]

Downes, John, merchant, subj. of G.B.; rec. by John Bailey - 21
Apr. 1807 [123]

Dawson, Thomas, physician, subj. of G.B. - 24 Apr. 1807 [124]

Davidson, John, baker, subj. of G.B.; rec. by James Greig, shipwright - 30 Apr. 1807 [125]

English, John, merchant, member of the late firm of Baker & English, subj. of G.B.; rec. by Isaac G. Ogden and David Sullivan; Sullivan states that English travelled in Europe for the
firm - 16 Feb. 1807 [126]

Escot, John Peter, baker, subj. of Emperor of France & King of
Italy; rec. by Nicholas Remi Dupage, instrument maker - 21
Oct. 1807 [127]

Enteman, Christoph, tea waterman, subj. of Prince of Hesse
Cassel; rec. by William Fosbrook, singer and instrument
maker - 25 Apr. 1807 [128]

Evans, Robert, slater, subj. of G.B.; rec. by Evan Thomas,
grocer - 22 Apr. 1807 [129]

Edwards, George, blacksmith, subj. of G.B.; rec. by John Edwards,
Jr. - 28 Apr. 1807 [130]

Edwards, John, Jr., blacksmith, subj. of G.B.; rec. by John
Jefferies - 28 Apr. 1807 [131]

Elliot, Robert, stone cutter - subj. of G.B.; rec. by Hugh
McIntyre, stone cutter - 27 Apr. 1807 [132]

Easthum, James, merchant, subj. of G.B.; rec. by John Day,
merchant - 17 Mar. 1807 [133]

Gearey, William, labourer, subj. of G.B.; rec. by John Downey -
25 Apr. 1807 [134]

Grasset, Peter, gardener, subj. of France; rec. by Jonathan
Beach, accountant - 24 Apr. 1807 [135]

Gray, Daniel, teacher, subj. of G.B.; rec. by Thomas Wood - 25
Apr. 1807 [136]

Graham, Allen, blacksmith, subj. of G.B.; rec. by James More -
25 Apr. 1807 [137]

Godtschalk, Sebastian, cartman, subj. of Prince of Hesse Cassel; rec. by Benjamin Sands - 25 Apr. 1807 [138]

Gaertner, John Samuel, subj. of Elector of Saxony; rec. by John Cramer, tailor - 27 Apr. 1807 [139]

Gordon, Peter, rigger, subj. of G.B.; rec. by Thomas Hassam - 27 Apr. 1807 [140]

Greyson, William, grocer, subj. of G.B.; rec. by John McGowan - 27 Apr. 1807 [141]

Gates, George, labourer, subj. of G.B.; rec. by John Murray - 28 Apr. 1807 [142]

Groundwell, John, gunsmith, subj. of G.B.; rec. by John Edwards, Jr. - 28 Apr. 1807 [143]

Graham, George, yeoman, subj. of G.B.; rec. by George Walton, mason - 29 Apr. 1807 [144]

Geib, Dietrich, sugar baker, subj. of Elector of Hanover; rec. by Christian Burger, tailor - 29 Apr. 1807 [145]

Gaudin, Louis, painter, subj. of Emperor of France & King of Italy; rec. by Archibald Hall, labourer - 29 Apr. 1807 [146]

Garniss, Philip, brewer, subj. of G.B.; rec. by Jeremiah Warner, grocer - 30 Apr. 1807 [147]

Greig, James, ship-carpenter, subj. of G.B.; rec. by John Hinbeck [?], or Hartuck [?] or Hartrik [?], ship-carpenter - 30 Apr. 1807 [148]

Gibbons, James, teacher, subj. of G.B.; rec. by Wilhelm Vogell, blacksmith - 30 Apr. 1807 [149]

Gardner [Gaertner?], William, tailor, subj. of Duke of Anspach; rec. by Tobias Hoffman - 23 Apr. 1807 [150]

Gordon, William, ship stower , subj. of G.B.; rec. by John Magee, grocer - 23 Apr. 1807 [151]

Gibbs, James, of Montgomery Co., yeoman, subj. of G.B.; rec. by Samuel Jackson, of Florida in sd. county, liquor - 19 May 1807 [152]

Green, John, watchmaker, subj. of G.B.; rec. by William Sanderson, merchant - 16 Mar. 1807 [153]

Graham Peter, cabinetmaker, subj. of G.B.; rec. by Peter C. Hojier - 20 Apr. 1807 [154]

Geibel, Harman, subj. of Duke of Berlenburg; rec. by John Jungerich - 21 Apr. 1807 [155]

Gable, John, labourer, subj. of Duke of Berlenburg; rec. by Henry Sherer - 21 Apr. 1807 [156]

Hendrick, William, brass founder, subj. of G.B.; rec. by Joseph F. Hipper, cordwainer - 21 Aug. 1807 [158]

Hoy, Francis, storekeeper, subj. of G.B.; rec. by Bernard O'Connor - 25 Apr. 1807 - not to have certificate until he pays $3 - [159 & 160]

Hearn, Thomas, gentleman, subj. of G.B.; rec. by John Casenave, merchant - 21 Jan. 1807 [161]

Homeyer, John Henry, merchant, subj. of Elector of Saxony; rec. by Frederick D. Kochler, merchant - 30 Apr. 1807 [162]

Harriman, Edward, merchant, subj. of G.B.; rec. by William Cowley, merchant - 26 Mar. 1807 [163]

Hughes, John, sawyer, subj. of G.B.; rec. by Evan Thomas, grocer - 23 Apr. 1807 [164]

Hall, Joseph, labourer, subj. of G.B.; rec. by Michael Lebeth - 23 Apr. 1807 [165]

Homfeld, Henry, hatter, subj. of Elector of Hanover; rec. by James Woods - 21 Apr. 1807 [166]

Howell, Thomas, grocer, subj. of G.B.; rec. by Aaron Williams - 21 Apr. 1807 [167]

Hebert, John, stocking calender, subj. of Emperor of France & King of Italy; rec. by John W. Livingston - 20 Apr. 1807 [168]

Hall, Archibald, labourer, subj. of G.B.; rec. by James Haviland - 23 Apr. 1807 [169]

Hains, Cassen, tobacconist, subj. of Elector of Hanover; rec. by Frederick Meyer, grocer - 29 Apr. 1807 [170]

Hyslop, Charles, baker, subj. of G.B.; rec. by William Bryden, tanner - 29 Apr. 1807 [171]

Harrison, John H., weaver, subj. of G.B.; rec. by Henry Remmy, grocer - 29 Apr. 1807 [172]

Hooper, George, carpenter, subj. of G.B.; rec. by George Bruorton, gilder - 29 Apr. 1807 [173]

Hyslop, Gilbert, Jr., carpenter, subj. of G.B.; rec. by William Struthers, blacksmith - 29 Apr. 1807 [174]

Hibert, Louis, sadler, subj. of Emperor of France; rec. by Gilbert Haight, sadler - 27 Apr. 1807 [175]

Hughes, William, gentleman, subj. of G.B.; rec. by William Carver, smith & farrier - 28 Apr. 1807 [176]

Hageman, Nelson, subj. of King of Sweden; rec. by Jacob F. Shoemaker - 27 Apr. 1807 [177]

Hipper, John, boatman, subj. of Elector of Hanover; rec. by John Jungerich - 27 Apr. 1807 [178]

Houseman, Heinrich, grocer, subj. of Prince of Hesse Cassel; rec. by Alexander Doig, teacher - 27 Apr. 1807 [179]

Humphreys, Lawrence, rigger, subj. of G.B.; rec. by Thomas Turner - 27 Apr. 1807 [180]

Harris, William, subj. of G.B.; rec. by Henry Stanton - 27 Apr. 1807 [181]

Henry, Robert, labourer, subj. of G.B.; rec. by Anthony Steinbach - 23 Apr. 1807 [182]

Holliday, Arthur, grocer, subj. of G.B.; rec. by Jeremiah Culbert, boatman - 24 Apr. 1807 [183]

Hamilton, William, merchant, subj. of G.B.; rec. by William Blackstock, merchant - 30 Apr. 1807 [184]

Herknep, George, subj. of G.B.; rec. by Samuel Watt, rigger - 30 Apr. 1807 [185]

Hopkins, Benjamin, yeoman, subj. of G.B.; rec. by William Ferguson, artist - 30 Apr. 1807 [186]

Hoyland, John, dairyman, subj. of G.B.; rec. by John Sparks, grocer - 30 Apr. 1807 [187]

Hooey, John, labourer, subj. of G.B.; rec. by Adolphus Brower, of Brooklyn, Kings Co. - 29 Apr. 1807 [188]

Hays, Francis, segar manufacturer, subj. of King of Spain; rec. by Thomas Hassam, rigger - 29 Apr. 1807 [189]

Hill, John, wire worker, subj. of G.B.; rec. by John James Stewart - 24 Apr. 1807 [190]

Hall, John, wheelwright, subj. of G.B.; rec. by John Woodward - 30 Apr. 1807 [191]

Inglesby, John, merchant tailor, subj. of G.B.; rec. by Leonard Bleecker, broker - 30 Apr. 1807 [192]

Imhoff, Titus, porter, subj. of Emperor of the Germanic Empire; rec. by John Davis - 29 Apr. 1807 [193]

Irwin, Richard, tailor, subj. of G.B.; rec. by George Edwards, blacksmith - 30 Apr. 1807 [194]

Jubin, John M., mariner, subj. of Emperor of France & King of Italy; rec. by Nehemiah Allen, merchant - 26 Nov. 1807 [195]

Jonas, Philip, livery stable keeper, subj. of Neu Wurthshikon; rec. by Thomas Morris - 21 Apr. 1807 [196]

Jones, Anthony, mason, subj. of G.B.; rec. by John Farrington - 23 Apr. 1807 [197]

Jefferys, Nicholas, cooper, subj. of G.B.; rec. by Nicholas Brower, cooper - 23 Apr. 1807 [198]

Jeffers, Patrick, grocer, subj. of G.B.; rec. by James McCready, labourer - 20 Apr. 1807 [199]

Jackson, John, broker, subj. of King of Prussia; rec. by Thomas Bryan, merchant - 30 Apr. 1807 [200]

Johnson, Jacob, shipwright, subj. of King of Denmark; rec. by Robert Brown, shipwright - 29 Apr. 1807 [201]

Jenkins, David, malster, subj. of G.B.; rec. by John Hughes - 24 Apr. 1807 [202]

Jones, Hugh, sieve maker, subj. of G.B.; rec. by William Pierce, mason - 25 Apr. 1807 [203]

Jones, Ellis, tobacconist, subj. of G.B.; rec. by William Pierce, mason - 25 Apr. 1807 [204]

James, John, blacksmith, subj. of G.B.; rec. by David John - 27 Apr. 1807 [205]

Jones, William, labourer, subj. of G.B.; rec. by John Hughes - 27 Apr. 1807 [206]

Jones, Richard, ship-carpenter, subj. of G.B.; rec. by John Hughes - 24 Apr. 1807 [207]

James, William, house-carpenter, subj. of G.B.; rec. by James McPeak - 27 Apr. 1807 [208]

Jacobs, Samuel, labourer, subj. of G.B.; rec. by John Randecker, ropemaker - 28 Apr. 1807 [209]

Jones, Robert, sawyer, subj. of G.B.; rec. by John Hughes, sawyer - 28 Apr. 1807 [210]

Jacobs, Benjamin, gentleman, subj. of King of Holland; rec. by Simon Nathan, auctioneer - 17 Feb. 1807 [211]

Johnson, Amond, rigger, subj. of King of Denmark; rec. by Michael Lebeth - 22 Apr. 1807 [212]

Jugley, John, labourer, subj. of Emperor of France & King of Italy; rec. by Alexander Doig, teacher - 22 Apr. 1807 [213]

John, David, scrivener, subj. of G.B.; rec. by Evan Thomas, grocer - 22 Apr. 1807 [214]

Jacobs, Christoffer, baker, subj. of Emperor of Germany; rec. by Frederick Meyer, grocer - 29 Apr. 1807 [215]

Jackson, William, blacksmith, subj. of G.B.; rec. by John Edwards, Jr., blacksmith - 29 Apr. 1807 [216]

Jungerich, John, labourer, subj. of Duke of Berlanburg; rec. by Caspar Samler - 21 Apr. 1807 [217]

Ferrall, Matthew, farmer, subj. of G.B.; rec. by John B. Murdock - 24 Oct. 1807 [218]

Fosbrook, William, surgical instrument maker, subj. of G.B.; rec. by Philip Ebert - 24 Apr. 1807 [219]

Fowler, John, rigger, subj. of Elector of Hanover; rec. by John Adam - 27 Apr. 1807 [220]

Fricketton, Evans, brewer, subj. of G.B.; rec. by Frederick Resler, tallow chandler - 27 Apr. 1807 [221]

Fluegel, Charles, baker, subj. of King of Prussia; rec. by Tobias Hoffman - 27 Apr. 1807 [222]

Foster, John, gunsmith, subj. of G.B.; rec. by John Edwards, Jr. - 23 Apr. 1807 [223]

Freeburn, Robert, rigger, subj. of G.B.; rec. by Alexander Lamb, hairdresser - 28 Apr. 1807 [224]

Floy, Michael, gardener, subj. of G.B.; rec. by David Williamson, gardener - 28 Apr. 1807 [225]

Forster, Henry, gardener, subj. of Prince of Hohen Solm; rec. by Henry Scherer, gardener - 27 Apr. 1807 [226]

Fairley, Alexander, grocer, subj. of G.B.; rec. by John McKie - 27 Apr. 1807 [227]

Forbes, Daniel, stone cutter, subj. of G.B.; rec. by Hugh McIntyre, stone cutter - 27 Apr. 1807 [228]

Frazer, John, carpenter, subj. of G.B.; rec. by Thomas Stevenson, blacksmith - 28 Apr. 1807 [229]

Frazer, Robert, cordwainer, subj. of G.B.; rec. by John Millington - 24 Apr. 1807 [230]

Vogell, Wilhelm, blacksmith, subj. of Elector of Hanover; rec. by James Foley, lumber merchant - 21 Apr. 1807 [231]

Frazer, William, blacksmith, subj. of G.B.; rec. by Ebenezer Bassett - 21 Apr. 1807 [232]

Freeland, John, maltster, subj. of G.B.; rec. by Peter White, carpenter - 20 Apr. 1807 [233]

Forrest, William, carpenter, subj. of G.B.; rec. by Thomas Simpson, printer - 30 Apr. 1807 [234 & 236]

Ferguson, John, tinman, subj. of G.B.; rec. by Henry Hyar, innholder - 30 Apr. 1807 [235]

Frede, Christian, cordwainer, subj. of King of Prussia; rec. by Tobias Hoffman - 21 Apr. 1807

Ferguson, Charles, locksmith, subj. of G.B.; rec. by Thomas Stevenson - 21 Apr. 1807 [238]

Fairley, Hugh, sawyer, subj. of G.B.; rec. by John McKee, lumber merchant - 21 Apr. 1807 [239]

Frere, S. Ermand, of Brooklyn, Kings Co., accountant, subj. of Emperor of France & King of Italy; rec. by Henry Stanton - 27 Apr. 1807 [240]

Fitzpatrick, William, grocer, subj. of G.B.; rec. by Langhorn Burton Rayner - 25 Apr. 1807 [241]

Frazer, Arthur, founder, subj. of G.B.; rec. by Abraham Davis - 25 Apr. 1807 [242]

Fox, Thomas, mariner, subj. of G.B.; rec. by Thomas Hasam - 24 Apr. 1807 [243]

Fee, Robert, shipwright, subj. of G.B.; rec. by Garret Boon - 23
  Apr. 1807 [244]

Fritz, Conrad Aaron, tailor, subj. of Prince of Hesse Cassel;
  rec. by Matthew Bolmer - 27 Apr. 1807 [245]

Fullick, Thomas, rigger, subj. of G.B.; rec. by William Watts,
  rigger - 24 Apr. 1807 [246]

King, Thomas, grocer, subj. of G.B.; rec. by William Stinson,
  weaver - 24 Apr. 1807 [247]

Kolbun, Johan, grocer, subj. of King of Prussia; rec. by Christian Burger, tailor - 28 Apr. 1807 [248]

Klessner, John, milkman, subj. of Prince of Orange; rec. by John
  Jungerich - 27 Apr. 1807 [249]

Knapper, Jacob, labourer, subj. of Prince of Wittenburgh; rec.
  by George Riddle, livery stable keeper - 24 Apr. 1807 [250]

Koehler, Frederick Daniel, merchant, subj. of Free City of
  Frankfurt am Main; rec. by Henry Frederick Liebenau - 29 Apr.
  1807 [251]

Kilpatrick, Alexander, grocer, subj. of G.B.; rec. by George
  Roy - 20 Apr. 1807 [252]

Kelly, Patrick, grocer, subj. of G.B.; rec. by James McCready,
  labourer - 20 Apr. 1807 [253]

Kirkhaldie, David, grocer, subj. of G.B.; rec. by Hector Sinclair, grocer - 21 Apr. 1807 [254]

Kling, George Henry, labourer, subj. of Prince of Hesse Cassel;
  rec. by Henry Sherer - 21 Apr. 1807 [255]

Kinsey, Evan, porter, subj. of G.B.; rec. by Robert Evans,
  slater - 22 Apr. 1807 [256]

Knaese, Warner, stone cutter, subj. of Prince of Hesse Cassel;
  rec. by Augustus H. Lawrence - 27 Apr. 1807 [257]

Kennedy, Angus, grocer, subj. of G.B.; rec. by William Collins -
  27 Apr. 1807 [258]

Kay, William, innkeeper, subj. of G.B.; rec. by John Hughes -
  25 Apr. 1807 [259]

Kirek, John Diossy, grocer, subj. of Emperor of Germany & King
  of Hungary; rec. by Lewis Hartman, grocer - 27 Apr. 1807 [260]

Lebeth, Michael, printer, subj. of Emperor of Germany; rec. by
  Henry Homfeld - 21 Apr. 1807 [261]

Lindsay, William, grocer, subj. of G.B.; rec. by John Bennie -
  20 Apr. 1807 [262]

Leiretz, John C., sugar baker, subj. of King of Prussia; rec.
  by Walter Peck, merchant - 28 Apr. 1807 [263]

Volkman, Frederick, grocer, subj. of King of Prussia; rec. by
  Conrad Loue, grocer - 29 Apr. 1807 [264]

Lindsey, George, carpenter, subj. of G.B.; rec. by William
  Robertson, shopkeeper - 29 Apr. 1807 [265]

Lainz, Joseph, carpenter, subj. of King of Prussia; rec. by John
  Walker, mason - 30 Apr. 1807 [266]

Lyall, John, coachman, subj. of G.B.; rec. by George Rodgers -
  30 Apr. 1807 [267]

Linen, George, carpenter, subj. of G.B.; rec. by Michael Gardiner, carpenter - 30 Apr. 1807 [268]

Lavermore, John, rigger, subj. of G.B.; rec. by Benjamin Cole -
  29 Apr. 1807 [269]

Leray, Peter Lewis, mariner, subj. of Emperor of France; rec. by Benjamin Cushing, rigger - 17 Aug. 1807 [270]

Lawson, John, grocer, subj. of G.B.; rec. by Alexander Doig, teacher - 28 Apr. 1807 [271]

Lax, Thomas, town farmer, subj. of G.B.; rec. by John Bradwell, both of town of Flushing, Queens Co. - 27 Apr. 1807 [272]

Lewis, Thomas, shoemaker, subj. of G.B.; rec. by Richard Blackburn - 25 Apr. 1807 [273]

Linck, Peter/Pierre, goldsmith, subj. of Elector of Hesse; rec. by Peter Lachaise - 22 Apr. 1807 [274]

Lindeman, Jan, labourer, subj. of King of Holland; rec. by Francis Kramer - 22 Apr. 1807 [275]

Lufsky, George, labourer, subj. of Emperor of Austria; rec. by George Church - 21 Apr. 1807 [276]

Lewis, Thomas, labourer, subj. of G.B.; rec. by Aaron Williams, livery stable keeper - 21 Apr. 1807 [277]

Law, David, Jr., cordwainer, subj. of G.B.; rec. by David Law - 21 Apr. 1807 [278]

Laurie, William, currier, subj. of G.B.; rec. by Robert Paton - 24 Apr. 1807 [279]

Lewis, William, shipwright, subj. of G.B.; rec. by James Carr - 24 Apr. 1807 [280]

Lewis, John, drayman, subj. of G.B.; rec. by John Hughes - 24 Apr. 1807 [281]

Lanus, Peter, grocer, subj. of Emperor of France & King of Italy; rec. by John Jousse - 27 Apr. 1807 [282]

Leinig, Johann,. tailor, subj. of King of Prussia; rec. by Christian Burger - 27 Apr. 1807 [283]

Louther, George, labourer, subj. of G.B.; rec. by Mark McCamman - 27 Apr. 1807 [284]

Lanckeman, Dietrich, sugar refiner, subj. of Elector of Hanover; rec. by Henry Scherer, gardener - 27 Apr. 1807 [285]

Louvanna, John, hairdresser, subj. of King of Portugal; rec. by William Littlewood - 27 Apr. 1807 [286]

Lanckenau, Alexander, sugar refiner, subj. of Elector of Hanover; rec. by John Jungerich, labourer - 27 Apr. 1807 [287]

Lewis, Thomas, tailor, subj. of G.B.; rec. by David P. John - 27 Apr. 1807 [288]

Labhart, John W., watchmaker, subj. of Prince of Hesse Hanau; rec. by John Webber - 27 Apr. 1807 [289]

Morrison, William, cartman, subj. of G.B.; rec. by John Pritchet, cartman - 29 Apr. 1807 [290]

Magee, John, mason, subj. of G.B.; rec. by Anthony L. Anderson, physician - 29 Apr. 1807 [291]

Masseau, Alexander, mariner, subj. of Emperor of France & King of Italy; rec. by Antonio Canowel - 17 June 1807 [292]

Morange, James, upholsterer, subj. of Emperor of France; rec. by Anthony Latour, hairdresser - 16 Feb. 1807 [293]

Maghan, Thomas, subj. of G.B.; rec. by George Wilson - 20 Apr. 1807 [294]

Macky, Joseph, shipwright, subj. of G.B.; rec. by Robert Brown - 24 Apr. 1807 [295]

McGrath, Thomas, grocer, subj. of G.B.; rec. by Hugh McDonogh, grocer - Mar. 1807 [296]

Moses, William, rigger, subj. of G.B.; rec. by Robert Roberts, rigger - 29 Apr. 1807 [297]

Mentin, Michael, millstone manufacturer, subj. of G.B.; rec. by Cathrine Sweetman - 21 Apr. 1807 [298]

Martin, Peter, watchmaker, subj. of G.B.; rec. by Alexander Fisher, grocer - 21 Apr. 1807 [299]

Mitchell, Alexander, merchant, subj. of G.B.; rec.by William Cunningham - 22 Apr. 1807 [300]

Moir, John, teacher, subj. of G.B.; rec. by Archibald Crockett - 22 Apr. 1807 [301]

Main, James, merchant, subj. of G.B.; rec. by David Deas - 22 Apr. 1807 [302]

Morgan, Howell, mason, subj. of G.B.; rec. by Evan Thomas, grocer - 23 Apr. 1807 [303]

Martin, Samuel E., house-carpenter, subj. of G.B.; rec. by William M. Morris, goldsmith - 23 Apr. 1807 [304]

Morrison, John, labourer, subj. of G.B.; rec. by Adolph Carter - 23 Apr. 1807 [305]

McMurray, George, merchant, subj. of G.B.; rec. by Ralph B. Forbes, merchant - 30 Apr. 1807 [306]

Merry, Edward, carpenter, subj. of G.B.; rec. by William Sherman, mariner - 30 Apr. 1807 [307]

Millen, William, ship-carpenter, subj. of G.B.; rec. by Robert Brown, ship-carpenter - 30 Apr. 1807 [308]

Meldrin, James, house-carpenter, subj. of G.B.; rec. by Henry Burden, cooper - 30 Apr. 1807 [309]

Meath, Henry, rigger, subj. of town of Lubeck; rec. by Robert Roberts, rigger - 29 Apr. 1807 [310]

Miles, Evan, mariner, subj. of G.B.; rec. by James Douglas - 29 Apr. 1807 [311]

Murray, John, mariner, subj. of G.B.; rec. by John Taylor, grocer - 29 Apr. 1807 [312]

Miles, James, gardener, subj. of G.B.; rec. by Robert Brissett - 29 Apr. 1807 [313]

Mole, Zacharias, rigger, subj. of G.B.; rec. by Michael Lebath - 29 Apr. 1807 [314]

Moncrief, Robert, innkeeper, subj. of G.B.; rec. by Emma Ring - 28 Apr. 1807 [315]

Martin, George, labourer, subj. of G.B.; rec. by John Randecker - 23 Apr. 1807 [316]

Marcellin, Anthony, gentleman, subj. of Emperor of France; rec. by Washington Morton, counsellor-at-law - 27 Apr. 1807 [317]

Morgans, Morgan, shoemaker, subj. of G.B.; rec. by David John - 27 Apr. 1807 [318]

Matthewson, Patrick Murdock, labourer, subj. of G.B.; rec. by John McGrath, carpenter - 27 Apr. 1807 [319]

Morris, Cornelius, dealer, subj. of G.B.; rec. by Stephen White - 25 Apr. 1807 [320]

Marchant, Frederick, grocer, subj. of G.B.; rec. by Philip Ebert, gentleman - 25 Apr. 1807 [321]

More, James, stone cutter, subj. of G.B.; rec. by John Walker - 25 Apr. 1807 [322]

McDougal, Duncan, stone cutter, subj. of G.B.; rec. by Donald McCallum, carpenter - 29 Apr. 1807 [323]

Rispen, Matthew, subj. of G.B.; rec. by James McKittrick, marble sawyer - 24 Jan. 1807 [324]

McKenzie, Alexander, innkeeper, subj. of G.B.; rec. by Donald Cameron - 27 Apr. 1807 [325]

McDonald, Alexander, sadler, subj. of G.B.; rec. by Gilbert Haight, sadler - 27 Apr. 1807 [326]

McNamara, Peter, rigger, subj. of G.B.; rec. by Edward Fitz-gerald - 23 Apr. 1807 [327]

McFall, Robert, labourer, subj. of G.B.; rec. by Benjamin Ogden, barber surgeon - 29 Apr. 1807 [328]

McKenzie, John, sexton, subj. of G.B.; rec. by Clement Joseph Delacroix, distiller - 30 Apr. 1807 [329]

McAlpin, William, stone cutter, subj. of G.B.; rec. by James Douglass, teacher - 30 Apr. 1807 [330]

McAulley, William, mason, subj. of G.B.; rec. by George Walton - 29 Apr. 1807 [331]

McDonald, Donald, cooper, subj. of G.B.; rec. by Alexander Rose - 29 Apr. 1807 [332]

McQuaid, John, grocer, subj. of G.B.; rec. by Henry Hyde - 25 Apr. 1807 [333]

McGrath, John, carpenter, subj. of G.B.; rec. by William Style, carpenter - 21 Apr. 1807 [334]

McCall, Henry, stone cutter, subj. of G.B.; rec. by William Anderson, mason - 24 Apr. 1807 [335]

McKoy, Thomas, labourer, subj. of G.B.; rec. by James Byrne - 24 Apr. 1807 [336]

McLaughlin, Barney, grocer, subj. of G.B.; rec. by James Mc Cready - 20 Apr. 1807 [337]

McClure, John, carpenter, subj. of G.B.; rec. by Hector Sinclair, grocer - 21 Apr. 1807 [338]

McGeoch, John, carpenter, subj. of G.B.; rec. by Hector Sinclair, grocer - 21 Apr. 1807 [339]

McNaughten, Donald, sawyer, subj. of G.B.; rec. by Hector Sin-clair, grocer - 21 Apr. 1807 [340]

McDonald, Alexander, carpenter, subj. of G.B.; rec. by Robert Thompson - 22 Apr. 1807 [341]

McKenzie, Dugald, grocer, subj. of G.B.; rec. by Robert Queen - 23 Apr. 1807 [342]

McNeely, Isaac, mariner, subj. of G.B.; rec. by Andrew Gaitley, cartman - 18 Feb. 1807 [343]

McGill, Robert, grocer, subj. of G.B.; rec. by Robert Lenox, merchant - 25 Apr. 1807 [344]

McGonigal, Felix, labourer, subj. of G.B.; rec. by Joseph Benson, grocer - 25 Apr. 1807 [345]

Needham, Thomas, rigger, subj. of G.B.; rec. by James Thompson - 21 Apr. 1807 [346]

Nesbett, John, place labourer, subj. of G.B.; rec. by John Ran-decker, ropemaker, of Brooklyn, Kings Co. - 28 Apr. 1807 [347]

Nolton, Jacob, cartman, subj. of Prince of Hesse Cassel; rec. by John Waydel - 27 Apr. 1807 [348]

Newton, James, grocer, subj. of G.B.; rec. by Peter Sutton - 27 Apr. 1807 [349]

Nourse, Thomas, mariner, subj. of G.B.; rec. by Thomas Hasam - 24 Apr. 1807 [350]

Norsworthy, Samuel, merchant, subj. of G.B.; rec. by Robert Bogardus - 23 Apr. 1807 [351]

Nummo, Alexander, shoemaker, subj. of G.B.; rec. by Robert Patterson, blacksmith - 30 Apr. 1807 [352]

Neil, John, mariner, subj. of G.B.; rec. by Sarah Neil - 30 Apr. 1807 [353]

Otter, Edward, of Brooklyn, gardener, subj. of G.B.; rec. by James Souarby - 28 Apr. 1807 [354]

O'Connor, Bernard, storekeeper, subj. of G.B. - 25 Apr. 1807 [355]

Oliver, William, carpenter, subj. of G.B.; rec. by John Walker - 27 Apr. 1807 [356]

Ohl, George, baker, subj. of Hesse Darmstadt; rec. by Johann Ernst Schneider - 27 Apr. 1807 [357]

Owen, William, rigger, subj. of G.B.; rec. by Ellis Jones - 27 Apr. 1807 [358]

Orr, William, subj. of G.B.; rec. by William Robertson - 27 Apr. 1807 [359]

O'Connor, Thomas, merchant, subj. of G.B.; rec. by James McKay, dealer - 25 Apr. 1807 [360]

Pierce, William, mason, subj. of G.B.; rec. by Abraham Simmons, engraver - 23 Apr. 1807 [361]

Ponsford, James, tallow chandler, subj. of G.B.; rec. by William Wright, butcher - 27 Apr. 1807 [362]

Pestana, Manuel, tailor, subj. of King of Portugal; rec. by Francis Barretto, merchant - 27 Apr. 1807 [363]

Passfield, John ship captain, subj. of G.B.; rec. by Charles Stoudinger - 25 Apr. 1807 [364]

Paxton, James, stone cutter, subj. of G.B.; rec. by William Smith, cabinetmaker - 25 Apr. 1807 [365]

Paton, Robert, grocer, subj. of G.B.; rec. by Thomas Monilaws, grocer - 21 Apr. 1807 [366]

Pymer, David, porter house keeper, subj. of G.B.; rec. by John Ladrick, cordwainer - 22 Apr. 1807 [367]

Parks, James, grocer, subj. of G.B.; rec. by Aaron Wolff - 22 Apr. 1807 [368]

Phillips, Joseph, stone cutter, subj. of G.B.; rec. by William Rees, stone cutter - 22 Apr. 1807 [369]

Privaly, John, ship-carpenter, subj. of Emperor of France & King of Italy; rec. by James Sowarby - 23 Apr. 1807 [370]

Porterfield, Alexander, carpenter, subj. of G.B; rec. by Peter Graham - 20 Apr. 1807 [371]

Platt, Richard, shipwright, subj. of G.B.; rec. by John Burger - 30 Apr. 1807 [372]

Paul, John, tavern-keeper, subj. of King of Denmark; rec. by Moses Brown, tavern-keeper - 30 Apr. 1807 [373]

Provo, John, labourer, subj. of Prince of Hesse Cassel; rec. by
   Leonard Fisher, surgeon dentist - 30 Apr. 1807 [374]

Pallister, Thomas, cabinetmaker, subj. of G.B.; rec. by Christian Claus, cabinetmaker - 30 Apr. 1807 [375]

Pierce, Thomas, ship-carpenter, subj. of G.B.; rec. by William
   Williams - 29 Apr. 1807 [376]

Peters, John, tavern-keeper, subj. of King of Holland; rec. by
   Isaac Crandle, shoemaker - 29 Apr. 1807 [377]

Pitcarthy, Robert, stone cutter, subj. of G.B.; rec. by John
   Walker - 29 Apr. 1807 [378]

Roberts, David, cooper, subj. of G.B; rec. by David L. Daniels,
   auctioneer - 29 Apr. 1807 [379]

Roos, David, labourer, subj. of G.B.; rec. by John Castine - 23
   Apr. 1807 [380]

Ruf, Adolph, labourer, subj. of Emperor of France & King of
   Italy; rec. by James Bryar, tobacconist - 30 Apr. 1807 [381]

Reid, John, teacher, subj. of G.B.; rec. by Abraham L. Braine -
   29 Apr. 1807 [382]

Richardson, Robert, tailor, subj. of G.B.; rec. by William Mc
   Lean, house-carpenter - 29 Apr. 1807 [383]

Randal, Thomas, labourer, subj. of G.B.; rec. by Abraham Rassel -
   28 Apr. 1807 [384]

Right, Johan, rigger, subj. of King of Russia [for Prussia?];
   rec. by John Adam, rigger - 28 Apr. 1807 [385]

Reid, James, teacher, subj. of G.B.; rec. by Thomas McCready,
   grocer - 28 Apr. 1807 [386]

Rose, John, labourer, subj. of G.B; rec. by Alexander Doig,
   teacher - 24 Apr. 1807 [387]

Rouault, Joseph, musician, subj. of Emperor of France; rec. by
   Jonathan Beach - 24 Apr. 1807 [388]

Roberts, Richard, sawyer, subj. of G.B.; rec. by John Hughes -
   24 Apr. 1807 [389]

Russell, Robert, tailor, subj. of G.B.; rec. by Alexander Doig,
   teacher - 28 Apr. 1807 [390]

Rees, Thomas, slater, subj. of G.B.; rec. by David John - 27
   Apr. 1807 [391]

Richardson, John, labourer, subj. of G.B.; rec. by Alexander
   Fisher - 27 Apr. 1807 [392]

Richards, Edward, house-carpenter, subj. of G.B.; rec. by Abraham Brady, coach painter - 25 Apr. 1807 [393]

Roebelin, John, cordwainer, subj. of Prince of Hesse Cassel;
   rec. by Heinrich Windt - 25 Apr. 1807 [394]

Robertson, Joseph, grocer, subj. of G.B.; rec. by Gavin Spence -
   25 Apr. 1807 [395]

Reynolds, Daniel, grocer, subj. of G.B.; rec. by Dennis Harraty,
   cartman - 29 Apr. 1807 [396]

Robinson, William, livery stable keeper, subj. of G.B.; rec. by
   John Bogart - 20 Apr. 1807 [397]

Riddle, George, livery stable keeper, subj. of Emperor of France
   & King of Italy; rec. by Robert James Livingston - 21 Apr.
   1807 [398]

Rapp, J.B. Henry, grocer, subj. of Emperor of France & King of
   Italy; rec, by James Gardiner, boarding house keeper-4/21/o7 [399]

Robertson, Thomas, subj. of G.B.; rec. by William Robertson -
22 Apr. 1807 [400]

Rees, John, blacksmith, subj. of G.B.; rec. by Evan Thomas,
grocer - 22 Apr. 1807 [401]

Robertson, Joseph, grocer, subj. of G.B. - 25 Apr. 1807 [402]

Rees, William, stone cutter, subj. of G.B.; rec. by Evan Thomas,
grocer - 22 Apr. 1807 [403]

Roemer, David, subj. of Prince of Hesse Rheinfels; rec. by Henry
Sherer - 21 Apr. 1807 [404]

Robertson, George, merchant tailor, subj. of G.B.; rec. by
James Main - 23 Apr. 1807 [405]

Reimer, John Peter, innholder, subj. of Elector of Hanover; rec.
by James W. Green - 23 Apr. 1807 [406]

Rudd, Stephen, house-carpenter, subj. of G.B.; rec. by Philip
Ebert - 23 Apr. 1807 [407]

Silon, John, cabinetmaker, subj. of King of Portugal; rec. by
Thomas McCready, grocer - 28 July 1807 [408]

Scoles, John, engraver, subj. of G.B.; rec. by Stephen Sands,
merchant - 28 July 1807 [409]

Struck, John, coach smith, subj. of City of Hamburg; rec. by
Jacob Warner, coach maker - 24 Apr. 1807 [410]

Steele, Charles, gardener, subj. of G.B.; rec. by Marinus Willett - 27 Apr. 1807 [411]

Smith, John, grocer, subj. of G.B.; rec. by Thomas Stevenson,
blacksmith - 27 Apr. 1807 [412]

Steward, John, place labourer, subj. of G.B.; rec. by John Randicker, of Brooklyn, Kings Co., ropemaker - 28 Apr. 1807 [413]

Steward, Alexander, place labourer, subj. of G.B.; rec. by John
Randicker, of Brooklyn, Kings Co., ropemaker - 28 Apr. 1807
[414]

Sears, Samuel, carpenter, subj. of G.B.; rec. by Alexander Gifford, mason - 29 Apr. 1807 [415]

Smith, Thomas, tailor, subj. of G.B.; rec. by Robert Richardson,
tailor - 29 Apr. 1807 [416]

Scott, Alexander, grocer, subj. of G.B.; rec. by Daniel Lamoreux,
carpenter - 29 Apr. 1807 [417]

Smith, John, carpenter, subj. of G.B.; rec. by Daniel McCallum -
29 Apr. 1807 [418]

Summers, William, rigger, subj. of G.B.; rec. by Alexander Campbell, rigger - 29 Apr. 1807 [419]

Schlim, Gottlieb, baker, subj. of King of Prussia; rec. by
Frederick Meyer, grocer - 29 Apr. 1807 [420]

Stroebel, John C., physician, subj. of Prince of Schwartzenburg;
rec. by Leonard Fisher, surgeon dentist - 29 Apr. 1807 [421]

Stewart, John, Jr., of Brooklyn, labourer, subj. of G.B.; rec.
by John Randecker - 30 Apr. 1807 [422]

Simon, Joseph, tailor, subj. of Emperor of France & King of Italy;
rec. by Jacob Clark, Jr. - 30 Apr. 1807 [423]

Stevens, Thomas, brewer, subj. of G.B.; rec. by Charles Hyslop,
baker - 30 Apr. 1807 [424]

Schmoll, Ludewick, sugar baker, subj. of Prince of Hesse Cassel;
rec. by Leonard Fisher, surgeon dentist - 30 Apr. 1807 [425]

Streusel, George, labourer, subj. of Duke of Berlenburg; rec. by Leonard Fisher - 21 Apr. 1807 [426]

Simpson, Thomas, painter, subj. of G.B.; rec. by Monteath Farlane - 30 Apr. 1807 [427]

Thurkey, John, tobacconist, subj. of G.B.; rec. by Thomas Cox, tobacconist - 29 Apr. 1807 [428]

Stanley, John, labourer, subj. of G.B.; rec. by Thomas Brown - 22 Apr. 1807 [429]

Smith, John, carpenter, subj. of G.B.; rec. by Joseph Newton - 22 Apr. 1807 [430]

Sinclair, Duncan, sawyer, subj. of G.B.; rec. by Hector Sinclair, grocer - 21 Apr. 1807 [431]

Sanders, John, house-carpenter, subj. of Elector of Hanover; rec. by George Church - 21 Apr. 1807 [432]

Sherer, Henry, gardener, subj. of Prince of Hesse Cassel; rec. by Leonard Fisher, dentist - 21 Apr. 1807 [433]

Smith [Schmidt?], Anthon, subj. of Duke of Hagenburg; rec. by George Church - 21 Apr. 1807 [434]

Stoudinger, Charles, storekeeper, subj. of Emperor of Germany; rec. by John Hughes - 25 Apr. 1807 [435]

Shrauder, John, house-carpenter, subj. of Emperor of Germany; rec. by Jacob Hesch - 25 Apr. 1807 [436]

Smith, George, rigger, subj. of G.B.; rec. by William Watts - 24 Apr. 1807 [437]

Struthers, William, blacksmith, subj. of G.B.; rec. by John Walker - 25 Apr. 1807 [438]

Smith, David, drayman, subj. of G.B.; rec. by John Barkhill - 25 Apr. 1807 [439]

Schumacher, Jacob F., sugar baker, subj. of City of Hamburgh; rec. by John Jungerich - 27 Apr. 1807 [440]

Striker, Henry, tailor, subj. of Prince of Hesse Cassel; rec. by Peter C. Hojer - 27 Apr. 1807 [441]

Stewart, Alexander M., carpenter, subj. of G.B.; rec. by James MacKay - 27 Apr. 1807 [442]

Smith, John, tailor, subj. of Prince of Hesse Cassel; rec. by John Jungerich - 27 Apr. 1807 [443]

Smith, James, stone cutter, subj. of G.B.; rec. by John Willey - 23 Apr. 1807 [444]

Smith, Thomas, sawyer, subj. of G.B.; rec. by Israel Morgan - 23 Apr. 1807 [445]

Spence, Gavin, watchmaker, subj. of G.B.; rec. by James Stewart - 24 Apr. 1807 [446]

Steck, Johan, subj. of Duke of Witgenstein; rec. by Leonard Fisher - 24 Apr. 1807 [447]

Scott, Francis, carpenter, subj. of G.B.; rec. by John Burkhill - 24 Apr. 1807 [448]

Smael, William, grocer, subj. of G.B.; rec. by Samuel Mansfield - 24 Apr. 1807 [449]

Stein Bach, Johannes, labourer, subj. of Prince of Hesse Cassel; rec. by George F. Harison - 24 Apr. 1807 [450]

Sutton, Peter, tailor, subj. of G.B.; rec. by Gavin Spence - 24 Apr. 1807 [451]

Schneider, Johann Ernst, baker, subj. of Duke of Nassau Weilberg;
    rec. by Jacob Warner - 23 Apr. 1807 [452]

Stoltz, John, labourer, subj. of Bishop of Mainz; rec. by Leo-
    nard Fisher - 21 Apr. 1807 [453]

Sherlock, James, grocer, subj. of G.B.; rec. by Cornelius Du
    Bois - 21 Apr. 1807 [454]

Sänger, Hänerich, labourer, subj. of Prince of Waldeck; rec. by
    Henry Sherer - 21 Apr. 1807 [455]

Smith, John D., grocer, subj. of City of Hamburgh; rec. by Abra-
    ham M. Walton - 21 Apr. 1807 [456]

Spence, Henry, house-carpenter, subj. of G.B.; rec. by David
    Crawford - 21 Apr. 1807 [457]

Fasheira, Joseph, labourer, subj. of Prince Regent of Portugal;
    rec. by William Bryan, tobacconist - 30 Apr. 1807 [458]

Taylor, Alexander, cordwainer, subj. of G.B.; rec. by William
    F. Stewart, grocer - 24 Mar. 1807 [459]

Taylor, John, mariner, subj. of G.B.; rec. by Thomas Hassam -
    24 Apr. 1807 [460]

Taylor, Robert, grocer, subj. of G.B.; rec. by John Farrington -
    24 Apr. 1807 [461]

Taylor, Thomas, labourer, subj. of G.B.; rec. by John Ground-
    well, gunmaker - 29 Apr. 1807 [462]

Terry, George, grocer, subj. of G.B.; rec. by Jeremiah Galla-
    gher, stone cutter - 27 Apr. 1807 [463]

Teto, Manuel, mariner, subj. of King of Spain; rec. by Anthony
    Grayson, innkeeper 25 May 1807 [464]

Thomson, Alexander, grocer, subj. of G.B; rec. by Joseph Robert-
    son - 25 Apr. 1807 [465]

Thomas, David, cabinetmaker, subj. of G.B.; rec. by James Dodge,
    cabinetmaker - 23 Apr. 1807 [466]

Thompson, Jeremiah, merchant, a Quaker, subj. of G.B.; rec. by
    Francis Thompson, merchant, a Quaker - 24 Aug. 1807 [467]

Thomas, John R., marine intelligence collector, subj. of G.B.;
    rec. by John Slidell - 20 Apr. 1807 [468]

Thorburn, John, printer, subj. of G.B.; rec. by John Niven, car-
    penter - 21 Apr. 1807 [469]

Tiemann, Anthon, grocer, subj. of Prince of Hesse; rec. by Jacob
    Warner - 21 Apr. 1807 [470]

Tinehant, Joseph, merchant, subj. of Emperor of France & King
    of Italy; rec. by Nicholas Remi Duparge, instrument maker -
    21 Oct. 1807 [471]

Tomlinson, Barnard, tavern-keeper, subj. of G.B.; rec. by
    Stephen Price - 24 Apr. 1807 [472]

Imbert, Frederick, gardener, subj. of Emperor of Germany; rec.
    by John Giles, cartman - 29 Apr. 1807 [473]

Turnbull, Thomas, merchant, subj. of G.B.; rec. by James McIn-
    tosh - 27 Apr. 1807 [474 & 475]

Turner, Thomas, painter, subj. of G.B.; rec. by John Burkhill -
    24 Apr. 1807 [476]

Tyler, Joseph Philips, subj. of G.B.; rec. by Joseph Tyler,
    gentleman - 27 Apr. 1807 [477]

Tyler, Samuel, innkeeper, subj. of G.B.; rec. by Stephen Price -
    25 Apr. 1807 [478]

Van der Linden, John Jacob De Jung, physician, subj. of King of Holland; rec. by John Huyler, physician - 24 Apr. 1807 [479]

Van Ewigen, Meynart Albert, labourer, subj. of King of Prussia; rec. by Caspar Samler - 24 Apr. 1807 [480]

Vinju, Jan, mason, subj. of King of Holland; rec. by Anthony Steinbach - 23 Apr. 1807 [481]

Walker, Joseph, Jr., merchant, a Quaker, subj. of G.B.; rec. by Francis Thompson, a Quaker - 24 Aug. 1807 [482]

Weber, John, morella [?] manufacturer, subj. of Emperor of Germany; rec. by Tobias Hoffman - 24 Apr. 1807 [483]

Waesh, James, clothier, subj. of G.B.; rec. by Anthony L. Anderson - 20 Apr. 1807 [484]

Wilheran, David, labourer, subj. of G.B.; rec. by Cornelius Tyson - 20 Apr. 1807 [485]

Williams, William, tailor, subj. of G.B.; rec. by Joseph I. Dorset - 27 Apr. 1807 [486]

Wood, Thomas, labourer, subj. of G.B.; rec. by Archibald Hall - 25 Apr. 1807 [487]

Whitehead, John, grocer, subj. of G.B.; rec. by John Lawrence - 27 Apr. 1807 [488]

Wareham, Dennis, carpenter, subj. of G.B.; rec. by Matthew Valentine - 27 Apr. 1807 [489]

White, Archibald, iron founder, subj. of G.B.; rec. by Abraham Davis - 23 Apr. 1807 [490]

Wilson, George, subj. of G.B.; rec. by David Crawford - 20 Apr. 1807 [491]

White, Peter, house-carpenter, subj. of G.B.; rec. by Henry Willets - 24 Mar. 1807 [492]

Wykes, Thomas, grocer, subj. of G.B.; rec. by Robert Gunner - 23 Apr. 1807 [493]

Wilson, John, brewer, subj. of G.B.; rec. by Peter White, house-carpenter - 30 Apr. 1807 [494]

Williamson, Robert, cabinetmaker, subj. of G.B.; rec. by Fenwick Lyell - 30 Apr. 1807 [495]

White, James, porter, subj. of G.B.; rec. by John Niven, carpenter - 30 Apr. 1807 [496]

Winterton, William, subj. of G.B.; rec. by Nathan J. Smith, perfumer - 30 Apr. 1807 [497]

Wade, Edward, silk dyer, subj. of G.B.; rec. by Henry Pope, gentleman - 29 Apr. 1807 [498]

Wade, John, grocer, subj. of G.B.; rec. by Henry Pope, gentleman - 29 Apr. 1807 [499]

Wilson, Andrew, mariner, subj. of King of Sweden; rec. by Robert Brown, shipwright - 29 Apr. 1807 [500]

Wooffendale, Robert, town cartman, subj. of G.B.; rec. by Henry Stanton, of Brooklyn, storekeeper - 29 Apr. 1807 [501]

Wilkinson, William, merchant, subj. of G.B.; rec. by David Wolfe, merchant - 29 Apr. 1807 [502]

Watts, William, rigger, subj. of G.B.; rec. by George Smith - 24 Apr. 1807 [503]

Williams, Robert, mason, subj. of G.B.; rec. by John Hughes - 24 Apr. 1807 [504]

Woofendale, John, dentist, subj. of G.B.; rec. by John Slidell -
  24 Apr. 1807 [505]

Williams, William, ship-carpenter, subj. of G.B.; rec. by Elizabeth Humphrey - 29 Apr. 1807 [506]

Welch, William, watchmaker, subj. of G.B.; rec. by Gavin Spence -
  24 Apr. 1807 [507]

Wilson, Andrew, cordwainer, subj. of G.B.; rec. by John McKie -
  25 Apr. 1807 [508]

Willson, James, grocer, subj. of G.B.; rec. by William Johnston -
  25 Apr. 1807 [509]

Weydell, John, labourer, subj. of Prince of Hesse Cassel; rec.
  by Jacob Hesh - 25 Apr. 1807 [510]

Williams, John, cooper, subj. of G.B.; rec. by Charles White -
  25 Apr. 1807 [511]

Williams, Joseph, cartman, subj. of G.B.; rec. by William Hughes,
  gentleman - 28 Apr. 1807 [512]

Walker, George, labourer, subj. of G.B.; rec. by Mark McCaman,
  mason - 28 Apr. 1807 [513]

Zule, John, hairdresser, subj. of G.B.; rec. by John Graham,
  cartman -24 Apr. 1807 [514]

Zeif, Leonhard, labourer, subj. of Prince of Hesse Cassel; rec.
  by Leonard Fisher - 25 Apr. 1807 [515]

Bundle 6

Adamson, John, stone cutter, subj. of G.B.; rec. by Isaac Van
  Deuzer, grocer - 17 Aug. 1808 [1]

Beigbeder, Bertram Charles, merchant, subj. of Emperor of France;
  rec. by Manuel Ducoin, merchant - 22 Dec. 1808 [2]

Boffington, John Baptiste , gentleman, subj. of Emperor of
  France & King of Italy; rec. by Louis Hibert, gentlemqn - 25
  Jan. 1808 [3]

Brunow, Berndt John, subj. of King of Sweden; rec. by Joseph
  Hilton, mariner - 20 May 1808 [4]

Burgess, James, grocer, subj. of G.B.; rec. by George Charles
  Herford, accountant - 1 Apr. 1808 [5]

Codd, Thomas, merchant, subj. of G.B.; rec. by Myles Kirkby,
  gentleman - 1 July 1808 [6]

Cuming, George, physician, subj. of G.B.; rec. by Robert Swanton, attorney-at-law - 23 Jan. 1808; report dated 29 Oct. to
  effect that he was born in Newry, Co. Down, Ire., that his age
  is 31 and that he emigrated from Hamburgh [7]

Carter, William Morris, gentleman, subj. of G.B.; rec. by Joseph
  Dickson, distiller - 15 Aug. 1808 [8]

Coquebert, Hanibal Henri Felix, merchant, subj. of Emperor of
  France; rec. by John R. Harrington - 21 Sept. 1808 [9]

Crow,John, stone cutter, subj. of G.B.; rec. by William Anderson - 23 Apr. 1808 [10]

Dow, John, stone cutter, subj. of G.B.; rec. by John Crow - 23
  Apr. 1808 [11]

Forrester, Andrew, cordwainer, subj. of G.B.; rec. by Joseph
  Forrester, of 313 Broadway, 25th Ward, cordwainer - 30 June
  1808 [12]

Gordon, John, carpenter, subj. of G.B.; rec. by Andrew Mather,
  cartman - 23 Apr. 1808 [13]

Girard, Anthony John Charles, merchant, subj. of Emperor of France & King of Italy; rec. by Thomas De Bussy, teacher - 26 Sept. 1808 [14]

Gorman, John, distiller, subj. of G.B.; rec. by Emanuel Young, shipmaster - 27 Sept. 1808 [15]

Hall, Peter, mariner, subj. of G.B.; rec. by Thomas Hasam, of 73 James St., grocer - 23 Apr. 1808 [16]

Harris, David, mariner, subj. of G.B.; rec. by Thomas Hasam, grocer - 23 Apr. 1808 [17]

Hyslop, Gilbert, carpenter, subj. of G.B.; rec. by Alexander Walker, carpenter - 25 Apr. 1808 [18]

Jephson, John, merchant, subj. of G.B.; rec. by Anthony Latour, of the 4th Ward, hairdresser - 21 June 1808 [19]

Kneringer, John, sugar boiler, subj. of Emperor of Austria; rec. by James Roosevelt - 23 Apr. 1808 [20]

Morison, Samuel, stone cutter, subj. of G.B.; rec. by Hugh Mc Intyre - 23 Apr. 1808 [21]

McNeill, Charles, Jr., merchant, subj. of G.B.; rec. by John Yates Cebra, auctioneer - 16 May 1808 [22]

Osborn, John, cordwainer, subj. of G.B.; rec. by James Sowarby, grocer - 27 Sept. 1808 [23]

Pauler, Martial, gentleman, subj. of Emperor of France & King of Italy; rec. by Joseph Kauman - 24 Oct. 1808 [24]

Paululey, John, tailor, subj. of the Statholder of the Seven United Provinces; rec. by John Wiese, baker - 25 Apr. 1808 [25]

Rossel, Auguste, merchant, subj. of Emperor of France; rec. by John R. Harrington - 21 Sept. 1808 [26]

Redmond, James, teacher, subj. of G.B.; rec. by Dennis Kenney, sawyer - 15 Aug. 1808 [27]

Rothery, William, carpenter, subj. of G.B.; rec. by John Sparks, grainery - 23 Apr. 1808 [28]

Rusher, George, cordwainer, subj. of G.B.; rec. by John E. Parker, cordwainer - 23 Apr. 1808 [29]

Storry, John, merchant, subj. of G.B.; rec. by John Watson, baker - 18 Feb. 1808 [30]

Sherman, Amos, mariner, subj. of G.B.; rec. by Thomas Hasam, of 73 James St., grocer - 23 Apr. 1808 [31]

Stoddart, Edward, stone cutter, subj. of G.B.; rec. by Thomas Manilius, grocer - 23 Apr. 1808 [32]

Thomson, John, mariner, subj. of King of Sweden; rec. by James Dupart, grocer - 21 Sept. 1808 [33]

Teesdale, James, subj. of G.B.; rec. by Edward Kemeys, attorney - at-law - 28 Mar. 1808 [34]

Walker, John, bookbinder, subj. of G.B.; rec. by Ellis Jones, grocer - 25 Apr. 1808 [35]

Wood, John, merchant, subj. of G.B.; rec. by Richard Belden, merchant - 18 Apr. 1808 [36]

Wylie, Mark, merchant, subj. of G.B.; rec. by John Baker, porter merchant - 23 Sept. 1808 [37]

Bundle 7

Baxter, John, Jr., merchant, subj. of G.B.; rec. by John B. Morie, shipmaster - 28 Oct. 1809 [1]

Leger, Daniel, mariner, subj. of G.B.; rec. by Isaac Waite, shipmaster - 27 May 1809 [2]

Duport, Peter L., subj. of Emperor of France; rec. by Stephen Price - 21 Feb. 1809 [3]

Kyle, Thomas, of Rockland Co., nailer, subj. of G.B.; rec. by James McInnick, cordwainer - 21 Mar. 1809 [4]

Lawrence, Charles Kane, mariner, subj. of G.B.; rec. by Elias Kane, merchant - 24 Mar. 1809 [5]

Lynham, George, merchant, subj. of G.B.; rec. by Colin Tolmie, blacksmith - 28 Oct. 1809 [6]

Ricord, Alexander, accomptant, subj. of Emperor of France; rec. by Anthony Latour, hairdresser - 17 May 1809 [7]

Vose, Richard, merchant, subj. of G.B.; rec. by Robert Newby, merchant - 30 Mar. 1809 [8]

Gaudin, Francis, mariner, subj. of Republic of France - 12 Oct. 1809 - 12 Oct. 1809 [9]

Norman, William, stevedore, subj. of G.B. - 29 Apr. 1809 [10]

McCeaver, Peter, sailmaker, subj. of G.B. - 6 June 1809 [11]

Lannuier, Augustus, confectioner, subj. of Republic of France - 20 May 1809 [12]

Coats, John, fruitman, subj. of G.B.; rec. by Joshua Barker, Esq. - 26 May 1809 [13]

Balbi, John Luc Jerome Armand, merchant, subj. of Emperor of France; rec. by Aaron Sorria - 26 Aug. 1809 [14]

Bromell, Samuel, mariner, subj. of G.B.; rec. by Thomas Carpenter - 26 Aug. 1815 [15]

Coughran, John, labourer, subj. of G.B.; rec. by Walter Fisher, mason - 24 Apr. 1815 [16]

Bonaffé, Edward, merchant, subj. of Emperor of France; rec. by Eugene Ferrard, merchant - 17 June 1815 [17]

Callet, James, merchant, subj. of Emperor of France; rec. by Louis Missillier, Jr. - 26 Aug. 1815 [18]

Cleeman, Gustavus, subj. of Emperor of all the Russias; rec. by Theophilas De Mello - 18 Oct. 1815 [19]

Bailey, Thomas, carpenter, subj. of G.B.; rec. by William Potter, seaman - 24 Mar. 1815 [20]

De Mello, Theophilas, merchant, subj. of Prince Regent of Portugal; rec. by John Robinson - 16 Oct. 1815 [21]

Dufourg, John R., subj. of France; rec. by Joseph H. Gouges - 29 Aug. 1815 [22]

Domec, John, merchant, subj. of Emperor of France; rec. by John D. Kireck, money collector - 25 July 1815 [23]

Delort, Theophilus, merchant, subj. of Emperor of France; rec. by Eugene Ferrard - 19 June 1815 [24]

Fougaroly, Andrew F., merchant, subj. of Emperor of Germany; rec. by Michael Werkmeister - 19 June 1815 [25]

Ferriere, Auguste, merchant, subj. of Emperor of France; rec. by Joseph W. Gouges - 18 July 1815 [26]

Feriere, Peter, merchant, subj. of Emperor of France; rec. by Alexis Gardiere, merchant - 20 June 1815 [27]

Guillot, Joseph, mariner, subj. of Emperor of France; rec. by Auguste Ferriere - 21 July 1815 [28]

Gouges, Joseph H., merchant, subj. of Emperor of France; rec.
by Michael Repos, merchant - 18 July 1815 [29]

Hipwell, Abraham, blacksmith, subj. of G.B.; rec. by Patrick
Fitzpatrick, blacksmith - 26 Sept. 1815 [30]

Hardy, Remy, merchant, subj. of France; rec. by John L. Balbi -
21 Sept. 1815 [31]

Irish, Charles, watchmaker, subj. of G.B.; rec. by Thomas Ha-
zard, Jr. - 29 Sept. 1815 [32]

Kelly, John, of 81 Lombardy St. in 7th Ward, rigger, subj. of
G.B.; rec. by Thomas Dickinson, of 81 Lombardy St. in 7th
Ward, rigger - 29 Mar. 1815; John Williams, rigger, of 47
Market St., deposed that John Kelly served on board the U.S.
sloop of war Hornet (commanded by Capt. Lawrence) and on the
U.S. brig Sngas [?] (commanded by Capt. Allen); William
Coates deposed that Kelly served on the U.S. ship of war
President [33]

Labory, Pierre Joseph, mariner, subj. of Switzerland; rec. by
Alexis Le Roy - 27 June 1815 [34]

Le Graët, Pierre, merchant; rec. by Auguste Ferriere, merchant -
20 Sept. 1815 [35]

Milhas, John, merchant, subj. of King of France; rec. by Matthew
Repos - 16 Oct. 1815 [36]

Mathieu, Helene Fortune, widow, subj. of Emperor of France; rec.
by John J. Labouisse, merchant - 29 June 1815 [37]

Navar, Francis, mariner, subj. of King of Sicily; rec. by Richmond Davis, mariner - 29 June 1815 [38]

Mace, Thomas, merchant, subj. of King of France; rec. by Joseph
Gaillard, merchant - 30 Dec. 1815 [39]

Ottignon, Claude, umbrella maker, subj. of King of France; rec.
by Genest Martinot, umbrella maker - 18 Sept. 1815 [40]

Raby, John James, merchant, subj. of Emperor of France; rec. by
Alexis Le Roy, merchant - 18 July 1815 [41]

Sagory, Charles Constants, subj. of King of France; rec. by
Auguste Ferriere - 20 Sept. 1815 [42]

Thebaud, André Augustus, merchant, subj. of Emperor of France;
rec. by Auguste Ferriere, merchant - 18 July 1815 [43]

Wilcox, John, comb maker, subj. of G.B.; rec. by John G. Bates -
20 Nov. 1815 [44]

Buechel, Frederick, confectioner, subj. of King of Prussia; rec.
by Peter Joseph Fory, furrier - 27 Oct. 1810 [45]

Barry, Edward D., subj. of G.B.; rec. by James Swords, bookseller - 21 July 1810 [46]

Broad, Amos, subj. of G.B.; rec. by James Van Antwerp, tailor -
2 June 1810 [47]

Barton, Richard, mariner, subj. of G.B.; rec. by James Taylor,
shipmaster - 2 June 1810 [48]

Benham, John, brewer, subj. of G.B.; rec. by Robert Bogardus,
attorney-at-law - 26 Mar. 1810 [49]

Beynon, Evan, teacher, subj. of G.B.; rec. by Lefferts W. Lloyd,
of Flatbush, merchant - 21 Apr. 1810 [50]

Dyde, Robert, innkeeper, subj. of G.B.; rec. by John A. Morice,
merchant - 19 Apr. 1810 [51]

Degez, John, upholsterer, subj. of G.B.; rec. by John H. Sli-
    dell, upholsterer - 21 Apr. 1810 [52]

Feltus, Rev. Henry James, of Brooklyn, Kings Co.; rec. by
    William Palmer, chairmaker - 21 Apr. 1810 [53]

McNeill, John, merchant, subj. of G.B.; rec. by Isaac Conklin,
    merchant - 26 July 1810 [54]

Reed, George Chambers, shipmaster, subj. of G.B.; rec. by
    Daniel Deas, gentleman - 26 Sept. 1810 [55]

Stover, Joh., furrier, subj. of King of Bavaria; rec. by Fran-
    cis Wannenberg, furrier - 24 Mar. 1810 [56]

Vigers, William R., mariner, subj. of G.B.; rec. by Thomas
    Welford - 24 Oct. 1810 [57]

Graham, Duncan, subj. of G.B. - 23 Apr. 1810 [58]

Benson, Benjamin, butcher, subj. of G.B.; rec. by George Ship,
    butcher - 18 Mar. 1811 [59]

Gammack, John, labourer, subj. of G.B.; rec. by John Harvey, of
    146 Washington St., boarding house keeper - 25 May 1811 [60]

Hogan, Michael, merchant, subj. of G.B.; rec. by Jacob Stout,
    merchant - 26 Jan. 1811 [61]

Marshall, Benjamin, merchant, subj. of G.B.; rec. by Jeremiah
    Thompson, a Quaker - 2 Mar. 1811 [62]

McFall, James, mariner, subj. of G.B.; rec. by Albert Smith,
    tanner & musical instrument maker - 1 June 1811 [63]

Roden, Charles, of Newark, mariner, subj. of King of Sweden;
    rec. by Thomas Hasam, of Newark, grocer - 23 May 1811 [64]

Vancamps, Charles, accountant, subj. of Emperor of France and
    of Switzerland; rec. by John D. Kirck, translator and col-
    lector - 18 Nov. 1811 [65]

Wright, Thomas, a Quaker, subj. of G.B.;rec. by Jeremiah Thomp-
    son, a Quaker - 2 Mar. 1811 [66]

Wooldrich, George, mariner, subj. of Emperor of France; rec.
    by Sebastian Michel, fruiterer - 23 Mar. 1811 [67]

Bancroft. William. of Brooklyn, subj. of G.B.; rec. by William
    Milward, of Brooklyn - 27 Jan. 1811 [68]

Broom, William, of Cromelbow, Dutchess Co., Esq., subj. of G.B.;
    rec. by Jonathan H. Lawrence, merchant - 27 May 1811 [69]

Fleming, John B., merchant, born Hamilton, North Britain, age
    25, subj. of G.B.; emigrated from Scotland - 29 Oct. 1812
    [70 & 71]

Logan, Adam, watchmaker, subj. of G.B.; rec. by John Frier,
    brass founder - 22 June 1812 [72]

Muller, Rembertus, merchant, subj. of Emperor of France; rc.
    by Jonathan Lawrence, merchant - 24 Mar. 1812; statement of
    R.F. Muller: age 43, came to U.S. from Is. of St. Martins and
    was born in Prov. of Groningen, Holland; his wife, Catharina,
    age 34, was born on St. Martins; their children, Mary Ann
    Elizabeth (age 8), Margaret Sophia (age 6) and Adrian (age 2),
    were all born on St. Martins [73 & 74]

Tyson, Peter, rigger, subj. of King of Denmark; rec. by Peter
    Stream, rigger, Adam Logan, watchmaker, and Thomas Wallace,
    brass founder - 21 May 1812 [75]

Vilac, John, surgeon, subj. of Emperor of France; rec. by John
    D. Kirck, translator - 24 Nov. 1812 [76]

Wallace, Thomas, brass founder, subj. of G.B.; rec. by John
Frier, brass founder - 22 June 1812 [77]

Lucas, Samuel, cooper, subj. of G.B.; rec. by Aaron Lucas, shoemaker - 15 Nov. 1813 [78]

Marshall, John, subj. of G.B.; rec. by Robert Boorman - 20 Sept.
1813 [79]

Purves, William, carpenter, subj. of G.B.; rec. by George Ireland, builder - 15 Nov. 1813 [80]

Thompson, Henry, mason, subj. of G.B.; rec. by Jane Gracy - 15
Nov. 1813 [81]

Wooldridge, John, labourer, subj. of G.B.; rec. by John Benham,
brewer - 28 Aug. 1813 [82]

Waite, William, carpenter, subj. of G.B.; rec. by James Vannas-
dall/ Van Arsdall, labourer - 15 Nov. 1813 [83]

Delonguemare, James Stanislaus, merchant, subj. of Emperor of
France & King of Italy; rec. by Nicholas M. Delonguemare,
merchant - 4 Mar. 1814 [84]

Delaistre, Marianne [she signs "Marie Anne Ferrier"], widow,
subj. of Emperor of France & King of Italy; rec. by Nicholas
Delonguemare, merchant - Jan. 1814 [85]

Delmont, Luce, widow, subj. of Emperor of France & King of Italy;
rec. by Nicholas M. Delonguemare, merchant - 29 Jan. 1814 [86]

McIntosh, Allan, tailor, subj. of G.B.; rec. by Daniel Voshill,
shoemaker - 26 July 1814 [87]

Wallace, Robert, cartman, subj. of G.B.; rec. by Philip Fulkerson - 27 Jan. 1814 [88]

Armstrong, David, merchant, subj. of G.B.; rec. by John McDonald,
merchant - 24 Oct. 1816 [89]

Brun, Victor L., tobacconist, subj. of King of France and Navarre; rec. by Paul Dominge - 2 Mar. 1816 [90]

Bazin, Pierre Francois, mariner, subj. of King of France and
Navarre; rec. by Eugene Ferrard - 16 Jan. 1816 [91]

Bayand, John, confectioner, subj. of King of France and Navarre;
rec. by James Callet, fringe maker - 27 July 1816 [92]

Chiquet, Lewis, carver, subj. of King of France and Navarre; rec.
by Thomas Gardner, of Boston, baker, and Louis Yvonenet, confectioner - 31 Aug. 1816 [93]

Canet, Joseph, mariner, subj. of King of France and Navarre; rec.
by Louis C. Loisson, merchant - 24 May 1816 [94]

Cluzet, Charles, merchant, subj. of King or France and Navarre;
rec. by Eugene Ferrand - 24 Feb. 1816 [95]

Coburn, Samuel, mason, subj. of G.B.; rec. by Henry Thompson and
Thomas Carelan - 27 Apr. 1816 [96]

De Perdreanville, René Elizabeth David, merchant, subj. of King
of France and Navarre; rec. by John L.J. Balbi - 2 Nov. 1816
[97]

Del Vecchio, Charles, subj. of Emperor of Germany; rec. by
William A. Seely - 19 Aug. 1816 [98]

Evans, Joseph, physician, subj. of G.B.; rec. by James Hanna,
druggist; John B. Regnier and Samuel P. Hildreth, both of
Marietta, Ohio, state that Evans lived in Marietta and later in
Janesville; Judge Jas. Houston, John Stephen, Thos. Rather and
Philip Moon state that Evans also lived in Baltimore, Md. -
27 Sept. 1816 [99]

Elder, Stewart, grocer, subj. of G.B.; rec. by James Warner &
   John Hardcastle - 27 Apr. 1816 [100]

Elliott, John, grocer, subj. of G.B.; rec. by Philip Fulkerson -
   20 Apr. 1816 [101]

Folmar, John, watchmaker, subj. of King of France; rec. by
   George Sinclair, bookseller, and John Sidell, deputy U.S.
   marshal, who states that in 1810 Andrew Folmar, watchmaker,
   made report of himself, his wife, Louisa L., and their children, Jane, John, Francis and Mary (in 1810 all under the age
   of 21); Andrew Folmar died about 1814 without becoming a
   citizen - 26 Apr. 1816 [102]

Fleury, Berteyer, subj. of King of France; rec. by Benjamin
   Fleury, of Newark, grocer - 23 May 1816 [103]

Fauré, John P., tobacconist, subj. of King of France and Navarre; rec. by Francois Le Grand - 20 Mar. 1816 [104]

Goyou, John B., merchant, subj. of King of France; rec. by Eugene Ferrard, stocking manufacturer - 16 Dec. 1816 [105]

Hart, Samuel, merchant, subj. of the ruler of that part of
   Poland called Sticy; rec. by Daniel Addis, counsellor-at-
   law - 30 Mar. 1816 [106]

Hickingbottom, William, artist, subj. of G.B.; rec. by Lewis
   Hibert, sadler - 19 Feb. 1816 [107]

Kass, Ernest, baker, subj. of Hanover; rec. by Cornelius
   Schenck and Abraham De Lamater - 25 Apr. 1816 [108]

Kelly, Daniel, grocer, subj. of G.B; rec. by Walter L. Cure -
   15 Apr. 1816 [109]

Le Grand, Francois, hatter, subj. of King of France & Navarre;
   rec. by John Tonnele, glover - 19 Mar. 1816 [110]

Loughman, James, cartman, subj. of G.B.; rec. by Francis Arden -
   25 Apr. 1816 [111]

Lachayze, Elias V., merchant, subj. of King of France & Navarre;
   rec. by John B. Fichaux - 15 Apr. 1816 [112]

McGowan, Patrick, cartman, subj. of G.B.; rec. by Philip I.
   Fulkerson - 28 Apr. 1816 [113]

Mooney, Thomas, livery stabler, subj. of G.B.; rec. by Thomas
   Carroll and Elinor Carroll - 26 Apr. 1816 [114]

Mulvey, Roger, grocer, subj. of G.B.; rec. by James McKeon and
   Hugh O'Neil - 23 Apr. 1816 [115]

Naar, Joshua, merchant, late of Curacoa & the Netherlands, subj.
   of King of Holland & King of Denmark; Joshua, age 46, was born
   at Curacoa and his sons, David, age 15, Abraham, age 13, and
   Benjamin, age 11, were born on Is. of St. Thomas; they migrated from Jamaica; rec. by Chester Clark - 21 June 1816 [116]

Ordronan, John, mariner, subj. of King of France & Navarre; rec.
   by John Flottard - 16 Jan. 1816 [117]

Rival, Francis Dupointon, gentleman, subj. of King of France &
   Navarre; rec. by John L.S.A. Balbi - 15 Apr. 1816 [118]

Rodriguez, Vincente, merchant, subj. of King of Spain; rec. by
   Louis Hibert, sadler - 24 Sept. 1816 [119]

Reynolds, Lackey, of Newtown, farmer, subj. of G.B.; rec. by
   Roger Mulvey - 22 Aug. 1816 [120]

Rapallo, Anthony, native of Genoa, student-at-law, subj. of
   King of Sardinia; filed 1st. papers at Charleston, S.C.; rec.
   by John Lewis La Coste - 22 Oct. 1816 [121 & 122]

Saunier, Claudius Antoine, subj. of King of France & Navarre;
   rec. by Francois Saunier - 18 Dec. 1816 [123]

Saunier, Francis, merchant, subj. of King of France & Navarre;
   rec. by John G. Fardy, merchant - 16 Apr. 1816 [124]

Thomson, Richard, pilot, subj. of G.B.; rec. by Thomas Norris,
   of Newark, innkeeper - 19 Aug. 1816 [125]

Whitehead, Samuel, pilot, subj. of G.B.; rec. by George Briggs,
   plumber - 19 Apr. 1816 [126]

Cherry, John, of Brooklyn, gunsmith, subj. of G.B.; rec. by
   James Stady, of NYC, and William Berry, of Brooklyn - 24 Apr.
   1817 [127]

Carley, Casper, house-carpenter, subj. of G.B.; rec. by Joseph
   Price, gunsmith, and Richard Miller, cartman - 18 Dec. 1817
   [128]

Cortilli, Augustus, physician, subj. of Emperor of Austria and
   King of Italy; rec. by John B. Mariè - 20 Mar. 1817 [129]

Garnier, Charles, merchant, subj. of King of France & Navarre;
   rec. by Peter Le Graet, merchant, & John V. Flugrai - 31 Oct.
   1817 [130]

Jahnecke, Frederick, merchant, subj. of Emperor of Germany; rec.
   by Augustus Ferrard - 31 July 1817 [131]

Geromo, Liberato, mariner, subj. of Emperor of Austria; rec. by
   John Craulos [clerk wrote "Crowley"] - 27 June 1817 [132]

Malibran, Eugene, merchant, subj. of King of France & Navarre;
   rec. by James Edward Ray - 30 May 1817 [133]

Nichols, Thomas, merchant, subj. of G.B.; rec. by Samuel I.
   King, grocer, Joseph Wilson, brass founder, and James Mack-
   rell - 25 Oct. 1817 [134]

Turner, Peter, shipwright (who formerly lived in Washington,
   D.C.), subj. of G.B.; his age is about 20; rec. by Henry Eckford, shipwright - 22 Apr. 1817 [135]

Webb, John, of Brooklyn, shipwright, subj. of G.B.; rec. by
   Moses Bampton, shipwright - 3 May 1817 [136]

Arnoux, Anthony, merchant tailor, subj. of G.B.; rec. by John
   Rosetter, hatter, and William Wheaton, merchant - 28 July 1818
   [137]

Bylandt, Jacob, subj. of King of Holland; rec. by David Levy,
   trader, and Peter Y. Calder, shipmaster - 21 Feb. 1818 [138]

Cartmel, Robert, merchant, subj. of King of Sweden; rec. by
   John Hefferman, merchant - 19 May 1818 [139]

Coggill, George, merchant, age 30, born Leeds, near Yorkshire,
   Eng., migrated from Liverpool, subj. of G.B.; rec. by Robert
   Roberts, merchant - 25 Mar. 1818 [140]

Corly, John, chairmaker, subj. of Emperor of Germany; rec. by
   Casper Corly, house-carpenter, and Joseph Collin, house-carpenter - 24 Mar. 1818 [141]

Duffy, Philip, cartman, subj. of G.B.; rec. by Thomas Mooney,
   grocer, and Owen McCabe - 22 May 1818 [142]

McCabe, Owen, cartman, subj. of G.B.; rec. by Philip Fulkerson,
   sergeant at arms, Court of Chancery, and John McCoskee, shoemaker - 19 May 1818 [143]

Zimmerman, John Christian, merchant, who first went to Baltimore
   and then removed to N.Y., subj. of King of Holland; rec. by
   Herman Vos, merchant - 18 Mar. 1818 [144]

Strong, Thomas, brewer, age 25, born Middlesex, Eng., migrated from London, subj. of G.B.; rec. by John Sidell - 18 Mar. 1818 [145]

Buckley, James, boat builder, subj. of G.B.; rec. by Daniel Dyke & Sam Jones - 24 Apr. 1819 [146]

Coghlan, James, accountant, age 39, born Clonym, Ire., subj. of G.B.; rec. by Robert Emmet, counsellor-at-law - 17 Feb. 1819 [147]

Carter, Thomas, merchant, native of Co. of York, Eng., subj. of G.B.; 1st papers in Mayor's Court in Philadelphia; rec. by John T. Lacy - 17 Jan. 1819 [148]

Cashman, Daniel, clerk, grocer, born Ire., age 24, subj. of G.B.; rec. by Adolph L. Degrove & Thomas Hyatt - 21 Apr. 1819 [149]

Dezauche, Louis, gentleman, subj. of King of France; was in U.S. 1793-1802 and also later; rec. by William A. Hosack, attorney-at-law, and Francis Pyre Ferry, of the 5th Ward - 17 Nov. 1819 [150]

Duffy, Peter, gentleman, age 50, born Dublin, subj. of G.B.; rec. by Robert Emmet, attorney-at-law, and James Coughlan, clerk - 2 July 1819 [151]

Edmonstone, James, of town & county of Westchester, farmer, subj. of G.B.; rec. by John Higham & William Brady, of the 9th Ward - 22 Apr. 1819 [152]

Ellis, John, of Putnam Co., farmer, subj. of G.B.; rec. by Samuel Gouverneur & George Belden - 24 Mar. 1819 [153]

Howell, John, formerly in Poughkeepsie, born in Wales, subj. of G.B.; rec. by James Burgess, David Brooks and V. Santine - 19 Feb. 1819 [154]

Joughin, Margaret (wife of John Joughin), subj. of G.B.; rec. by Charles Graham, attorney-at-law, & John Mowatt, Jr., merchant - 17 Feb. 1819 [155]

Reade, Eliza, spinster, subj. of G.B.; rec. by Edward Riley & Bethiah Smith - 27 Feb. 1819 [156]

Reade, Mary Ann, spinster, subj. of G.B.; rec. by Edward Riley & Bethiah Smith - 27 Feb. 1819 [157]

Reade, Charles, merchant, subj. of G.B.; rec. by Edward Riley & Bethiah Smith - 27 Feb. 1819 [158]

Casey, Patrick, labourer, age 27, and wife, Margaret, age 24, both born Waterford, Ire., subjects of G.B.; they migrated from Halifax, N.S.. and intend to live in Brooklyn - 26 Aug. 1820 [159]

Fleming, John B., merchant, subj. of G.B.; rec. by George W. Talbot, merchant - 20 July 1820 [160]

Bundle 8

Buckley, Michael, subj. of G.B.; rec. by William Clancy, grocer - 12 Sept. 1820 [1]

Creighton, James, porter vault keeper, subj. of G.B.; rec. by James Monaghan, labourer - 24 Aug. 1822 [2]

Clark, Nathan, grocer, subj. of G.B.; rec. by Philip Fulkerson & Edward Mead - 25 Apr. 1820 [3]

Fitzpatrick, John, labourer, subj. of G.B.; rec. by Philip & William Fulkerson - 20 Nov. 1822 [4]

Golden, Felix, tailor, formerly of Phila., subj. of G.B.; rec. by Philip Fulkerson & William Fulkerson, printer - 19 Feb. 1822 [5]

Linn, Edward M., cartman, subj. of G.B.; rec. by Frederick Titus, boatman, and William Patrick, cordwainer - 22 Oct. 1822 [6]

McKeon, Hugh, cartman, subj. of G.B.; rec. by Philip Fulkerson, formerly sergeant to the Court of Chancery, & Philip Fulkerson, Jr., painter - 30 Mar. 1822 [7]

McCabe, Edward, labourer, subj. of G.B.; rec. by Philip and William Fulkerson - 22 Nov. 1822 [8]

McKernan, Patrick, grocer, subj. of G.B.; rec. by Francis Arden, cabinetmaker, & Christopher Van Alstyn, rigger - 20 Apr. 1822 [9]

McLean, Daniel M., painter, subj. of G.B.; rec. by Philip Fulkerson & Philip Fulkerson, Jr. - 20 Apr. 1822 [10]

Pignatel, John B., boarding house keeper, subj. of King of France & Navarre; rec. by James Gassin, grocer, & Francis Gariel, grocer - 27 Apr. 1822 [11]

Quail, William, age 20, mariner, born Downpatrick, Ire., subj. of G.B.; migrated from Belfast; rec. by George Duplux, shipmaster - 19 Nov. 1822 [12]

Thooft, Bernardus, born in Guilderland, Holland, subj. of King of Holland; formerly lived in South Carolina - 28 Dec. 1822 [13]

Walker, Joseph, subj. of G.B.; rec. by Thomas E. Walker - 20 Apr. 1822 [14]

Rogers, Joseph, stone cutter, age 29, born Paisley, Scotland, subj. of G.B.; migrated from Greenock, Scotland; rec.by David Christer, stone cutter - 19 Feb. 1823 [15]

Bluxome, Isaac, watchmaker, age 27 in 1823, subj. of G.B.; migrated from Liverpool, Eng.; rec. by George W. Platt & John De Camp - 27 June 1828 [16]

Barter, John, age 37, born 16 Apr. 1784 in parish of Lane [?] Bryon [?], D....[?] Co., Eng., subj. of G.B.; in 1817 he came from Is. of Guernsey to Baltimore; rec. by John Stanley - 21 Apr. 1828 [17]

Burnett, Benjamin, merchant, age 29, born in Eng. and migrated from Dublin, subj. of G.B.; rec. by Edward C. Ward, watchmaker - 20 Mar. 1828 [18 & 19]

Bernard, Antoine, merchant, subj. of Republic of Switzerland; rec. by Francis J. Berier, translator, and Francis Marriott - 31 May 1823 [20]

Bailly, Simon Marie, merchant, subj. of King of France; rec. by Francis J. Berier, translator, and Thomas Marriotte, gentleman - 21 June 1823 [21]

Combault, Pierre Estaniselas, subj. of King of France & Navarre; rec. by John Martin, brass founder - 20 May 1823 [22 & 23]

Schnip, John, grocer, sausage maker & gardener, age 41, born Wuertemburgh, subj. of King of Wuertemburgh; he migrated from Antigua; his wife, Dorothy R., age 31, born Belle Brugh [?] and their daughters, Susannah, age 7, Catharine, age 4, Maria, age 2, and Sally Ann, age 1, all born in New York; rec. by George Fullmer - 20 May 1823 [24]

Shorland, Thomas, house-painter, grocer, age 38, born Eng., subj. G.B.; rec. by Barnet Rapelye, gentleman, and George Wragg, merchant - 23 Oct. 1823 [25]

Ritchie, Alexander, dyer & weaver, born Bangor, Ire., migrated from Belfast, subj. of G.B.; rec. by Alexander Fegan, weaver - 3 May 1823 [26]

Montgomery, John B., merchant, subj. of G.B.; rec. by Elam
   Williams, cabinetmaker - 1 Mar. 1823 [27]

McBride, James, labourer, cartman, age 28, born Farmanagh, Ire.,
   migrated from Sligo, Ire., subj. of G.B.; wife, Margaret,
   age 22, and their dau. Catharine, age 3, all born at Farmanagh;
   rec. by Dennis Coman, cartman - 17 Sept. 1818 [28]

Laisné, Jean Baptiste Hypolite, merchant, subj. of King of
   France; rec. by Francis Berier, translator, and Francis Marriott - 27 June 1823 [29]

Klinck, William, cooper, subj. of King of Wuertemburgh; rec. by
   Francis Wannemaker, farrier, & Obadiah Frost, Jr., grocer -
   20 May 1823 [30]

Schovich, Paul Ralph, merchant, subj. of G.B.; rec. by Francis
   Berier, translator, and Francis Mariott - 27 May 1823 [31]

Jacquelin, John Michael, merchant, subj. of King of France;
   rec. by Francis Berier, translator, and Francis Mariott,
   gentleman - 21 June 1823 [31A]

Johnson, William Cecil, of Pittstown, Rensselaer Co., age 42,
   born in Eng., as were his wife, Hanah, age 38, and children,
   Thomas, age 19, Mary Ann, age 17, Henry, age 12, and Cecil,
   age 10, subj. of G.B.; rec. by William C. Johnson, formerly
   engraver - 26 Apr. 1823 [32]

Dias, Alexis Lopez, merchant, subj. of King of France; rec. by
   Francis Berier, translator, & F. Marriott, gentleman - 27 May
   1823 [33]

Carlau, William B., mariner, subj. of G.B.; rec. by Alexander
   Brown, of NYC but late of Baltimore, mariner, & William Clay-
   don, mariner - 17 Nov. 1823 [34]

Robinson, Benjamin, farmer, born Leicestershire, Eng., age 40,
   subj. of G.B.; rec. by John Guest, cabinetmaker - 31 May 1828
   [35]

Ronen, James, weaver, age about 29, born Co. Caven, Ire., as
   was his wife Margaret, age 23; their dau. Mary Ann, age 2 mos.,
   was born in New York; they migrated from Sligo - 30 Oct. 1828
   [36]

Shaw, William, cartman, age 40, born Co. Monaghan, Ire., migrated from Newry, subj. of G.B.; rec. by Nicholas C. Everitt -
   27 Mar. 1821 [37 & 38]

Schoals, John, type founder, age 28, born Co. Londonderry, Ire.,
   and migrated from there with his wife Elizabeth, age now 26,
   who was born in Co. Antrim; he is subj. of G.B.; rec. by
   William Robinson, type founder - 1 Nov. 1828 [39]

Theriat, Augustus R., subj. of King of France; rec. by Frederick
   Place, druggist - 25 Oct. 1828 [40]

Lyon, Joseph, merchant, age now 38, born in London, Eng., subj.
   of G.B.; he migrated from Havre de Grace - 28 Feb. 1824 [41]

Martin, Guion, sadler, age 28, born Co. Donegal, as was his wife
   Margaret, age 26; they migrated from Londonderry - 9 Nov. 1825
   [42]

Desnones, Joseph, subj. of King of France; rec. by Richard Hatfield, Esq., and Christian Brown, bookbinder - 18 June 1821
   [43]

Lender, Peter, boatman, subj. of King of Prussia; his age now
   22; born in Danzig and migrated from there; rec. by William
   Bedell, cartman - 20 Jan. 1824 [44]

Develin, Francis, baker, born Co. Tyrone, Ire.; migrated from
  Londonderry; in 1818 he was aged 21; subj. of G.B.; rec. by
  John McCoskee, cordwainer - 21 Jan. 1824 [45]

Carmant, Peter, born Bordeaux, France, age 47 in 1818, subj. of
  King of France; rec. by Anthony Bleicker & Alexander McDonald -
  19 Oct. 1824 [46]

Chappell, Thomas, baker, subj. of G.B.; rec. by Gideon Ostrander,
  alderman, & Peter Williams, accountant - 6 Mar. 1826 [47]

Wood, John, musical instrument maker, subj. of G.B.; rec. by
  David Kay, cooper - 16 Oct. 1820; another document, dated 29
  Mar, 1821, gives the following data: John Wood, born Co. Leicester, Eng., age 42; his wife Lucy, born Co. Derby, age 42;
  John's step-children as follows: Caroline Matilda Shipley,
  born London, age 16; Frederick William Shipley, born London,
  age 14; Alfred Loraine Shipley,born London, age 13; Sylvanus
  Hy. Shipley, born Bristol, age 10; Selena Penelope Shipley,
  born Bristol, age 8; the family emigrated from Dublin, Ire. [48]

Lyon,Joseph, formerly of London, subj. of G.B.; rec. by Warren
  Rogers - 28 Feb. 1824 [49]

Mortimer, Richard, woolen draper, age 26 in 1817, born in Col-
  chester, Yorkshire, Eng., subj. of G.B.; emigrated from Liverpool; rec. by Daniel Rapelje, merchant - 29 Jan. 1824 [50]

Bradley, Hugh, tailor, born in Ire., age 27 in 1825; his wife
  Catherine, age 19 in 1825, was born in Ire.; rec. by James
  Kelly, grate- and fender maker - 17 Sept. 1828 [51]

Carvill, George, bookseller, subj. of G.B.; rec. by David S. Lyon,
  deputy naval officer of port of N.Y., William A. Prince,
  merchant, William Jones, gold coater - 28 Jan. 1828 [52]

Carvill, Charles, bookseller, subj. of G.B.; rec. by David Lyon,
  deputy naval officer of port of N.Y., Benjamin Haight, counsellor-at-law, William Jones, gold beater - 25 Jan. 1828 [53]

Cleland, James, grocer, born in Co. Down, Ire., age 25 in 1822,
  emigrated from Belfast, subj. of G.B.; rec. by James Hays,
  grocer - 28 Feb. 1828 [54]

Colgan, Dominick, labourer, born Londonderry, Ire., age 26 in
  1824, subj. of G.B.; rec. by Sylvester Marius & Daniel Coughlen
  - 31 Oct. 1828 [55]

Cannon, Patrick, labourer, born parish of Kilcar, Co. of Donegal,
  age 42 in 1828, migrated from Londonderry, subj. of G.B. - 13
  Jan. 1828 [56]

De Young, Morris, merchant, subj. of G.B.; rec. by Hart Levi &
  Abraham Levy, merchants - 28 Nov. 1828 [57]

Duff, John, grocer, born Ire., age 26 in 1822, migrated from Quebec, subj. of G.B.; rec. by James Morris, coachman - 26 May 1828
  [58]

Gillespie, James, subj. of G.B.; rec. by James Oakley & Philip
  Henry - 28 Oct. 1828 [59]

Healy, James, grocer, born Co. Leitrim, Ire., age 41 in 1825, migrated from Sligo, subj. of G.B.; his wife Catharine, age about
  35 in 1825, and their children, Anne, age 12, Mary, age 10, and
  James, age 6 years and 10 mos. in 1825, were all born in Co.
  Leitrim; rec. by Bernard O'Rourke, brickmaker - 31 Oct. 1828
  [60]

Karigan, Thomas, cartman, age 45 in 1821, born Co. Cavan, Ire.,
  migrated from Dublin, subj. of G.B; rec. by Michael Donohoe,
  cartman [61]

Killin, Patrick, cartman, born in Fermanagh, Ire., age 23 in 1821, emigrated from Dublin, subj. of G.B; rec. by James Killin, cartman - 19 Feb. 1828 [62]

Kane, Thomas, grocer, born in Dublin, in 1821, when he was a rigger, his age was 33, subj. of G.B.; rec. by William Van Houten, house-carpenter - 25 Oct. 1828 [63]

Kiernan, Peter, engineer, subj. of G.B.; rec. by Bernard Ranahon, hairdresser - 1 Nov. 1828 [64]

Lasak, Francis W., furrier, subj. of Emperor of Austria & King of Bohemia; rec. by William Windle - 22 Sept. 1828 [65]

Langridge, Levi, grocer, born Eng., age 32 in 1820, subj. of G.B.; when he left London he gave occupation as miller and later as grocer; rec. by Isaac Edge, of N.J., baker - 1828 [66]

Miller, Christian, subj. of G.B.; rec. by Roger Williams, grocer - 19 May 1828 [67]

O'Mara, John, grocer, subj. of G.B.; rec. by John F. Gannon, grocer - 23 Sept. 1828 [68]

Quinn, Sarah, grocer, born Co. Antrim, Ire., age 39, migrated from Belfast, subj. of G.B.; May, her dau., age 18, was born in NYC; rec. by Mary Davis, widow - 18 May 1828 [69]

Brandon, Isaac L., merchant, born Barbados, age 33 in 1826, subj. of G.B., migrated from Barbados; rec. by Moses L. Moses, merchant - 22 Apr. 1829 [70]

Brant, Thomas, rigger, born Hanover, Germany, age 32 in 1826, subj. of G.B.; migrated from Bremen; his wife, Catharine, born in Liverpool, in 1826 was aged 25; rec. by Abraham Birdsall, produce broker - 18 Mar. 1829 [71 & 72]

Clanon, Simon, painter, born New Ross, Co. Wexford, Ire., age 24 in 1820; migrated from New Ross to U.S. via St. Johns, Newfoundland; rec. by George T. Beakey, painter - 26 Oct. 1829 [73]

Davis, John, cartman, late of Co. Tyrone, Ire., subj. of G.B.; rec. by Hugh Acheson, cartman, & George A. Harrison, chemist - 29 May 1829 [74]

Harrison, John, ship-carpenter, born Liverpool, Eng., age 42 in 1826, subj. of G.B.; his wife Mary, born in NYC, was aged 32 in 1826; rec. by David Randell, counsellor-at-law - 28 Feb. 1829 [75]

Kunz, Franz, subj. of King of Bavaria; rec. by Peter Bredell - 6 Nov. 1839 [76]

Kennedy, John, whip sawyer, subj. of G.B.; rec. by Joseph Brundege & Hugh Fairley, whip sawyers - 18 Mar. 1829 [77]

Lindmark, John, mariner, born Stockholm, Sweden, age 26 in 1818, subj. of King of Sweden; rec. by Samuel Underhill, grocer - 2 May 1839 [78]

Martin, John, labourer, late of Co. Sligo, Ire., subj. of G.B. - 21 July 1829 [79]

Masterton, Alexander, stone cutter, born Forfar, Scotland, age 27 in 1823, migrated from Forfar, then to Halifax and then to NYC, subj. of G.B.; rec. by Horace Holden, attorney-at-law - 2 May 1829 [80]

Perkins, Joshua N., attorney, subj. of G.B., from village of Ithaca, Tompkins Co., N.Y.; rec. by Charles W.E. Prescott, editor, Samuel P. Bishop, physician, & Cornelius P. Hermans, physician - 21 May 1829 [81]

Wunnenberg, Albert, sexton, subj. of Duke of Braunschweig; rec.
by Francis Wunnenberg, furrier, & Jacob Moore, hackster - 28
Oct. 1829 [82]

Webb, Edward Jackson, house-carpenter, born Co. Suffolk, Eng.,
age 51 in 1824, migrated from London, subj. of G.B.; his wife
Elizabeth, born Co. Kent, Eng., was aged 49 in 1824 and their
son George was aged 19 in 1824; rec. by John C. Brown, carpenter - 21 Mar. 1829 [83]

Bundle 9

Anderson, David, subj. of G.B.; rec. by Frederic A. Stuart,
merchant - 29 Dec. 1830 [1]

Bradley, John, cutler, born in Wath, Yorkshire, Eng., age 45 in
1824, migrated from Quebec, subj. of G.B.; his wife Bridgit,
born in Ire., was aged 37 in 1824; their children, all born in
Sheffield, Eng., were Sarah, age 21 in 1824, Sussanah, age 19
in 1824, John, age 15 in 1824 and George, age 13 in 1824; rec.
by John Sweeney, grocer - 19 May 1830 [2]

Benkard, James, merchant, born Frankfort, Germany, age 27 in
1828, subj. of Town of Frankfort, migrated from Liverpool;
rec. by David Austin, merchant - 16 Mar. 1830 [3]

Bertran, Christopher, merchant, born in Catalina, town of Villa-
nueva y Gelbe, age 32 in 1824, migrated from Matanza, Cuba,
subj. of King of Spain; rec. by Francis Al Faya, boarding house
keeper - 15 Feb. 1830 [4]

Edgson, William, shoemaker, born Norwich, Eng., age 44 in 1819,
migrated from London, subj. of G.B.; rec. by Benjamin Cooper,
shoemaker - 22 May 1830 [5]

Eastmond, John, accountant, subj. of G.B.; rec. by Willet Coles
& John Puntzins, writers - 30 Sept. 1830 [6]

Hamilton, John L., type founder, subj. of G.B.; rec. by George
Hodgson, grocer, & William McComb, type founder - 1830[7]

Henderson, Thomas, dry goods merchant, born Co. Fermanagh, Ire.,
age 46 in 1827, migrated from Belfast, subj. of G.B; rec. by
Wilson G. Hunt, dry goods merchant - 18 Nov. 1830 [8]

Ireland, Henry, coppersmith, subj. of G.B.; rec. by John Gassner
& Nicholas Cort, tinplate workers - 27 Sept. 1830 [9]

Isaac, James, house-painter, born Co. Hampshire, Eng., age 39 in
1827, migrated from Liverpool, subj. of G.B; rec. by Edward
Higgins, painter - 21 July 1830 [10 & 11]

Lowery, Samuel, grocer, subj. of G.B.; rec. by Daniel Slate,
cartman, & Henry Lowery, grocer - 21 Jan. 1830 [12]

Ludly, John, tallow chandler, formerly of London, subj. of G.B.;
rec. by George Adams, butcher - 28 June 1830 [13]

McMurray, Joseph, subj. of G.B.; rec. by John Irvine, merchant -
27 Feb. 1830 [14]

McBlain, Robert, weaver, subj. of G.B.; rec. by William Haskin,
gardener - 28 Sept. 1830 [15]

McBride, Hugh, dirt cartman, subj. of G.B.; rec. by James McBride,
grocer - 1 Oct. 1830 [16]

Mensch, Frederick Augustus, merchant, subj. of King of Saxony;
rec. by Charles De Behr, merchant - 22 May 1830 [17]

Morris, William, carpenter, subj. of G.B.; rec. by William Morris,
accountant, & Philip P. Lockwood, carpenter - 16 Feb. 1830 [18]

Pignolet, Louis, dyer, born Rheims, France, age 30 in 1825, migrated from Le Havre, subj. of King of France & Navarre; his wife Susan, born in NYC, age 22 in 1825; their children, Charlotte, age 3 in 1825, & Louis, age 3 mos. in 1825; rec. by Zadock Hedden, officer of the customs - 16 Feb. 1830 [19]

Stein, John F., mariner, subj. of King of Prussia; rec. by John H. Baker, grocer and boarding house keeper - 28 Apr. 1830 [20]

Vaupell, George F., subj. of G.B.; rec. by John Eastmond & Wm. P. Low, accountants - 2 Jan. 1830 [20A]

Ashton, Stephen, smith, subj. of G.B.; rec. by Joshua Gray, of Warwarsink, Ulster Co. - 19 Sept. 1831 [21]

Black, John, cartman, born Co. Kent, Eng., age 33 in 1828, subj. of G.B. (where he was a farmer); his wife Ann, born Co. Kent, Eng., age 35 in 1828; the family migrated from London and intended to settle in Woodbridge, N.J.; rec. by John Fisher, Jr., shoemaker - 21 Jan. 1831 [22]

Edwards, Charles (who was formerly called Charles Edwards Ellis), attorney and counsellor at law, subj. of G.B. - 27 Jan. 1831 [23]

Ficken, Martin, sugar refiner, age 29 in 1827, subj. of Kingdom of Hanover, migrated from Havre de Grace; rec. by Charles Engen - 24 Sept. 1831 [24]

Heilbronn, Adolph, subj. of King of Hanover; rec. by Edward N. Mead, Esq. - 21 Apr. 1831 [25]

O'Hern, David, cartman, subj. of G.B.; rec. by John Cummins, grocer - 23 May 1831 [26]

Keogan, James, paver, subj. of G.B.; rec. by Peter Smith and Bartholomew Keogan, pavers - 19 May 1831 [27]

Knebel, Henrick, grocer, subj. of King of Hanover; rec. by John Harken, grocer - 5 Apr. 1831 [28]

Lowery, John, merchant, subj. of G.B.; rec. by Daniel Slote, cartman, & Jacob R. Nevins, merchant - 28 Oct. 1831 [29]

Moneypenny, Mary (widow of John Moneypenny), subj. of G.B.; rec. by John McMullen, grocer, & John R. McComb, physician - 22 Mar. 1831 [30]

Parsons, Margaret, widow, subj. of G.B.; rec. by George James, inspector of customs, & Moses Coddington, gentleman - 22 May 1831 [31]

Reichard, Frederick, merchant, subj. of King of France; he was born in the Dept. of the Lower Rhine, France, in Strassburg, age 40 in 1826; his wife Aglai Constance Reichard, born in Paris, France, was aged 29 in 1826; they migrated from Havre; rec. by Felix D'Herrvilly, broker - 23 July 1831 [32]

Randall, William, late of London, subj. of G.B.; rec. by Joseph B. Nones - 26 May 1831 [33]

Schwab, Christopher, baker, born Germany, age 35 in 1823, migrated from Lisbon, Portugal, subj. of King of Wittenburgh & Emperor of Prussia; wife Maria, born in Germany, was aged 28 in 1823; their children, John, age 6 in 1823, and Frederick, age 2 mos. in 1823, were born in NYC; rec. by Nicholas Eberhard, grocer - June 1831 [34]

Woodhead, John, accountant, born Hopton, Co. York, Eng., age 27 in 1817, migrated from Liverpool, subj. of G.B.; rec. by Horace Holden, counsellor-at-law - 5 Mar. 1831 [35]

Wilson, John, seaman, born Mensel, Norway, age 24 in 1827, migr. from Antwerp; rec. by Roger Williams, grocer - 1 Oct. 1831 [36]

McManus, Redmond, subj. of G.B.; rec. by James Healy, merchant - 23 Apr. 1832 [37]

Buckham, Andrew, physician, born Scotland. age 39 in 1819, subj. of G.B.; rec. by William Robertson - 24 Apr. 1832 [38]

Birmingham, Henry, born Co. Armagh, Ire., subj. of G.B.; rec. by William King, marshal - 21 Mar. 1832 [39]

Bryan, William, Jr., dyer, born in Eng., age 38 in 1825, migrated from London, subj. of G.B.; rec. by Thomas Bryan, dyer - 18 Jan. 1832 [40]

Batornniere, Auguste, late of Brooklyn, subj. of King of France & Navarre; rec. by Francis Arnaud, wine & liquor merchant - 28 May 1832 [41]

Fay, John Francis, of West Farms, Westchester Co., subj. of King of France; rec. by John Rovinx - 29 Mar. 1832 [42]

Decasse, Cecile M. (wife of Louis Decasse, merchant, subj. of G.B.; Charles Graham acts as her attorney; rec. Eugene Jarmossy & John Labouisse, merchants - 21 Dec. 1833 [43]

Fuller, William, subj. of G.B.; rec. by James C. Stoneall, innkeeper - 15 Apr. 1833 [44]

McBurney, Alexander, slater, subj. of G.B.; rec. by Thomas Cumming, corporation contractor - 26 Nov. 1833 [45]

Speyer, Eliza, spinster, age 21 on 10 May 1826; her father, Christian Frederick Speyer is dec'd; Charles Graham acts as her attorney; she is British subj.; rec. by Christopher Heiser, grocer - 26 Oct. 1833 [46]

Stevenson, George Goude, subj. of G.B.; rec. by Samuel James Lowe, shoemaker - 27 Nov. 1833 [47]

Speyer, George William, a minor, cabinetmaker, subj. of G.B.; his attorney is Charles Graham; rec. by Christopher Heiser, grocer - 26 Oct. 1833 [48]

Tyson, Isaac, subj. of G.B.; rec. by John C. Shardlow, clerk in the post office - 28 Nov. 1833 [49]

Weatherby, Peter, tailor, subj. of G.B.; rec. by John P. Douglass - 1 Nov. 1833 [50]

Wolfe [or Wolfness?], William Leo, physician, subj. of Republic of Hamburgh; rec. by Conrad Justus Bredenkamp, merchant - 21 Sept. 1834 [51]

Pope, Charles, carpenter, subj. of G.B.; rec. by Henry Simmons, merchant - 22 Oct. 1834 [52]

Philpott, John R., subj. of G.B.; rec. by Robert B. Simms, Sr. - 5 Nov. 1834 [53]

Prudhomme, John Francis Eugene, engraver (who has lived in U.S. since 1812), subj. of King of Denmark; rec. by Augustus Gaetam, former dentist, & Augustus Halbert, engraver - 4 Sept. 1834 [54]

Wilson, Samuel D., subj. of G.B., particularly of Scotland and Wales; rec. by Lewis Webb, Jr., attorney-at-law - 22 Sept. 1834 [55]

Wilkinson, John, subj. of G.B.; rec. by Jotham Peabody, carpenter - 5 Nov. 1834 [56]

Walker, David, subj. of G.B.; rec. by George Melvill, dyer - 5 Nov. 1834 [57]

Wood, William, subj. of G.B.; rec. by Thomas Fargo - 5 Nov. 1834 [58]

Wolf, Elias, physician, age 27 in 1824, subj. of Republic of
Frankfort, emigrated from Amsterdam; rec. by Pelatrick Pirit,
merchant - 1 Nov. 1834 [59]

Walker, William, born Co. Down, Ire., age 31 in Oct. 1832, subj.
of G.B., migrated from Belfast, with intent to settle in Pa.;
rec. by John Boyd - 1 Nov. 1834 [60]

Woods, William, waterman, subj. of G.B.; rec. by Cornelius Cammeyer - 4 Nov. 1834 [61]

Wagoner, John; rec. by John Berger - 4 Nov. 1834 [62]

Watts, John, subj. of G.B.; rec. by Henry Stevens - 4 Nov. 1834
[63]

Todd, Richard J., merchant, subj. of G.B.; rec. by Louis I. Fellows - 30 Oct. 1834 [64]

Toupet, Nicholas F.(who has resided in Va., Md. and N.Y.), subj.
of King of France; rec. by James Kelly & Charles Toupet - 5
Nov. 1834 [65]

Thurston, Joshua, subj. of G.B.; rec. by Richard Ellis, 53 Elm
St., a marshal - 25 Oct. 1834 [66]

Stewart, Alexander F., subj. of G.B., formerly of Ire.; rec. by
Margaret Martin - 3 Nov. 1834 [67]

Scherf, Wolfgang, subj. of magistrates of Aschaffenberg; rec.
by George Gausmann, baker - 5 Nov. 1834 [68]

Stokes, Henry, mariner, subj. of G.B.; rec. by Palmer Darrow,
public porter, & Thomas Hewitt - 4 Nov. 1834 [69]

Schwab, Johan, subj. of King of Wittenberg; rec. by George Gaus-
man - 4 Nov. 1834 [70]

Shipman, Henry, born Schlüsselberg, Prussia, age 36 in 1821,
migrated from Bremen, subj. of King of Prussia; rec. by Barna-
bas Snell, cartman - 4 Nov. 1834 [71]

Shanks, James, subj. of G.B.; rec. by Andrew Eadie - 5 Nov. 1834
[72]

Sweeney, Eugene, subj. of G.B.; rec. by Hugh Sweeney, physician -
5 Nov. 1834 [73]

Simms, Robert B., Jr., subj. of G.B.; rec. by Robert B. Simms,
Sr. - 5 Nov. 1834 [74]

Scott, Edward, mason, subj. of G.B.; rec. by Michael Higgins -
5 Nov. 1834 [75]

Hoskin, Edward W., subj. of G.B.; rec. by John Abraham Willink &
John C. Zimmerman - 4 Nov. 1834 [76]

Holm, Hans Broun, mariner, subj. of King of Denmark; rec. by
Robert McManus, captain of the Port of Portland, Maine, & John
C. Nicholas, mariner - 20 Sept. 1834 [77]

Hannah, James L., physician, born Is. of St. Martin, age 36,
subj. of King of France & Navarre; rec. by James Macomb; his
wife Ann, born Eng., age 27; their son, James W., born Eng.,
age 11 mos. - 31 July 1834 [78]

Hughes, Patrick, weaver, subj. of G.B.; rec. by James Conroy,
weaver - 5 Nov. 1834 [79]

Higgins,Michael, labourer, subj. of G.B.; rec. by Michael Reilly,
labourer - 5 Nov. 1834 [80]

Hannon, Dominick, subj. of G.B.; rec. by James Hannon, carman -
4 Nov. 1834 [81]

Carter, Samuel, Jr., subj. of G.B.; rec. by Samuel Carter, [Sr.],
4 Nov. 1834 [82]

Cassidy, Richard, shoemaker, subj. of G.B.; rec. by James O'Neil
- 27 May 1834 [83]

Caster, George Oliver, mariner, subj. of G.B.; rec. by William
Dunlap, ship-carpenter - 11 Oct. 1834 [84]

Cox, Charles, subj. of G.B.; rec. by David Evans - 1 Nov. 1834
[85]

Coleman, Bernard, subj. of G.B.; rec. by Thomas Boyle - 5 Nov.
1834 [85A]

Cochran, Robert, subj. of G.B.; rec. by David Hornel, merchant -
5 Nov. 1834 [86]

Cunningham, Philip, born Co. of West Meath, Ire., migrated from
Dublin with intent to settle in Albany, N.Y., subj. of G.B.;
rec. by James McCort, labourer - 5 Nov. 1834 [87]

Cook, Samuel, subj. of G.B.; rec. by James D. Cook - 5 Nov. 1834
[88]

Clark, John, subj. of G.B.; rec. by Joshua W. Post, druggist -
5 Nov. 1834 [89]

Canty, William, subj. of G.B.; rec. by Albert Garnsey 5 Nov.
1834 [90]

Carlin, James, subj. of G.B.; rec. by Jotham Peabody, carpenter
- 5 Nov. 1834 [91]

Carpenter, Henry, subj. of Prince of Hesse; rec. by Jacob Carpenter, coach maker - 5 Nov. 1834 [92]

Charlton, Walter, subj. of G.B.; rec. by Robert Haggerty - 4
Nov. 1834 [93]

Clinton, William, subj. of G.B.; rec. by Philip M. Sawyer - 4
Nov. 1834 [94]

Cox, Michael, subj. of G.B.; rec. by James Ryland, waiter - 5
Nov. 1834 [95]

Bretonnier, Auguste, Jr., of Newtown, Queens Co., subj. of King
of France; rec. by Auguste Bretonnier, Sr. - 4 Nov. 1835 [96]

Bell, Rebecca H., single lady (dau. of Abraham Bell and Mary C.
Bell, his late wife), subj. of G.B.; rec. by Jacob Harvey,
merchant, & Charles Graham, Esq.; Mary C. Bell was born in
Shannon, Ire., and migrated from Belfast; when she was aged
35, her dau. Rebecca H. was aged 9, her son James C. was aged
7 and her son Thomas C. was aged 6 - 29 Apr. 1835 [97]

De Figaniere, Lewis F., merchant, subj. of Emperor of Brazil;
rec. by Charles Edward, counsellor-at-law - 29 June 1835 [98]

Drommond, William E., private waterman, subj. of King of Prussia;
rec. by Thomas Brant, cartman - 20 Apr. 1835 [99]

Graham, James, subj. of G.B.; rec. by Margaret Graham - 22 Aug.
1835 [100]

Hogg, George, bookbinder, subj. of G.B.;rec. by John Watson, bookbinder - 22 Mar. 1833 [101]

Johnson, George, subj. of G.B.; rec. by Charles Powis - 13 May
1835 [102]

Martin, Patrick, painter, subj. of G.B.; rec. by Edwin S. Grimshaw - 4 Jan. 1835 [103]

Pillow, William, Leghorn hat producer, subj. of G.B.; rec. by
Abraham Potts - 22 Dec. 1835 [104]

Polack, Nathan, saw maker; subj. of King of Holland; rec. by
William N. Polack - 8 June 1835 [105]

Schaper, Henry, clerk, subj. of Prince of Waldeck; rec. by Fred
S. Schlesinger, of Brooklyn - 25 June 1835 [106]

Von Post, Lawrence Henry, merchant, born in Bremen, age 23 in
1823, subj. of Senate of Bremen, emigrated from Bremen; rec.
by George Meyer, merchant - 28 Apr. 1835 [107]

Welch, Richard, coachman, subj. of G.B.; rec. by Charles Cowen -
28 May 1835 [108]

Anstin, Moses, broker; rec. by Lewis Evans - 7 Oct. 1835 [109]

Alcock, Charles, subj. of G.B.; rec. by Jonas Booth, Jr. - 4 Nov.
1834 [110]

Ainslie, James, J.P., of Williamsburgh, Kings Co., subj. of G.B.;
rec. by Robert Ainslie, secretary of the Phoenix Fire Insurance
Co. - 3 Nov. 1834 [111]

Moore, George, butcher, subj. of G.B.; rec. by Patrick Power -
4 Nov. 1834 [112]

Martin, Robert, subj. of G.B.; rec. by Adam Gamble, shoemaker -
5 Nov. 1834 [113]

Martin, Robert, subj. of G.B.; rec. by James Lamb - 5 Nov. 1834
[114]

Miller, George, subj. of King of Wittenberg; rec. by George Gausmann - 4 Nov. 1834 [115]

Moore, James, subj. of G.B.; rec. by Janette Jones Moore - 4
Nov. 1834 [116]

Mackell, James, whitesmith, blacksmith, subj. of G.B.; rec. by
William Tyack, bun manufacturer - 5 Nov. 1834 [117]

Muldoon, Charles, subj. of G.B.; rec. by Robert Robinson - 4
Nov. 1834 [118]

Melvill, George S., subj. of G.B.; rec. by James Melvill, Sr.,
dyer - 5 Nov. 1834 [119]

Mauger, Daniel, painter, late of Island of Guernsey, subj. of
G.B.; rec. by Henry Quirisal, painter - 4 Nov. 1834 [120]

Mauger, Charles, carpenter, late of Island of Guernsey, subj. of
G.B.; rec. by Henry Quirisal, painter - 4 Nov. 1834 [121]

Young, Alexander, subj. of G.B.; rec. by James Young, mason -
5 Nov. 1834 [122]

Frantzke, Wilhelm Friderick, native of Silesia, migrated from
London, subj. of King of Prussia; rec. by Francis W. Lasak -
3 Nov. 1834 [123]

Firth, Samuel, mason, subj. of G.B.; rec. by Richard Whitaker,
tavern-keeper - 5 Nov. 1834 [124]

Featherstone, John, subj. of G.B.; rec. by Joseph Fairclough,
mariner - 4 Nov. 1834 [125]

Kerigan, James, subj. of G.B.; rec. by Jotham Peabody, carpenter
- 5 Nov. 1834 [126]

Kerr, John, cartman, born Glasgow, Scotland, age 27 in 1827,
emigrated from Greenock, Scotland; rec. by John W. Taylor,
merchant - 31 Jan. 1834 [127]

Klinder, Henry, subj. of King of Hanover; rec. by Francis
Oerthe, jeweller - 5 Nov. 1834 [128]

Kelley, Michael, subj. of G.B.; rec. by Jotham Peabody - 5 Nov.
1834 [129]

Kirkpatrick, William, subj. of G.B.; rec. by James Blair, gilder - 5 Nov. 1834 [130]

Kennedy, Andrew, tailor, born in Ire., age 29 in 1827, emigrated from Liverpool, subj. of G.B.; his wife Margaret, born in Ire. was aged 29 in 1827; rec. by Daniel Hogan, physician - 5 Nov. 1834 [131]

O'Neil, John, subj. of G.B.; rec. by Timothy O'Neil, waiter - 5 Nov. 1834 [132]

O'Neil, Timothy, subj. of G.B.; rec. by John O'Neil, servant - 5 Nov. 1834 [133]

Newman, Lawrens, subj. of King of Holland; rec. by John Dryyer - 5 Nov. 1834 [134]

Irvin, Richard, merchant, late of Glasgow, Scotland, subj. of G.B.; rec. by William Scott, merchant - 10 Nov. 1834 [135]

Vittle, William F., subj. of G.B.; rec. by Henry Stokes, mariner - 5 Nov. 1834 [136]

Love, William, subj. of G.B.; rec. by William Johnson, stone cutter - 5 Nov. 1834 [137]

Lewis, Thomas, subj. of G.B.; rec. by Morgan Morgan, Jr., brass founder - 5 Nov. 1834 [138]

Layden, Luke, carpenter, subj. of G.B; rec. by Martin McGowan, labourer - 5 Nov. 1834 [139]

Laub, John, subj. of Emperor of Austria; rec. by Joseph Laub, pipe maker - 5 Nov. 1834 [140]

Laden, Patrick, subj. of G.B.; rec. by Patrick Mulrooney, fruiterer - 5 Nov. 1834 [141]

Laudan, Charles P., subj. of G.B.; rec. by William Johnson, stone cutter - 5 Nov. 1834 [142]

Launay, Augustus, subj. of King of France; rec. by William S. Watkins, lumber merchant - 5 Nov. 1834 [143]

Lattan, Lewis, of Rochfort, France, jeweller, subj. of King of France; rec. by Joseph Gaillard, merchant, and John Patterson, grocer - 6 Dec. 1834 [144]

Doly, John, subj. of G.B.; rec. by William Bogert, labourer - 5 Nov. 1834 [145]

Davy, Richard, subj. of G.B.; rec. by William Davy, gentleman - 5 Nov. 1834 [146]

Dunley, William, mariner, born about 28 Sept. 1798 in parish of St. Nichols, Co. of Devon, Eng., age in 1827 about 29, arrived NYC via Boston, subj. of G.B.; rec. by William Varnum, of Brooklyn - 1 Nov. 1834 [147]

Divine, Francis, labourer, subj. of G.G.; rec. by Daniel Donaghue - 5 Nov. 1834 [148]

Dinan, Patrick R., subj. of G.B.; rec. by Thomas Dune, carman - 5 Nov. 1834 [149]

Darsy, John, subj. of G.B.; rec. by John J. Etheridge, Jr., mariner - 5 Nov. 1834 [150]

Dargan, William, waiter, subj. of G.B.; rec. by Michael Fitzpatrick - 5 Nov. 1834 [151]

Dary, James, tailor, subj. of G.B.; rec. by John Greer, tailor - 4 Nov. 1834 [152]

Dolan, Patrick, cartman, subj. of G.B.; rec. by Daniel Lawson, tinman - 5 Nov. 1834 [153]

Davey, Robert P., merchant, subj. of G.B.; rec. by James B. Gascoigne, merchant - 5 Nov. 1834 [154]

Delany, James, subj. of G.B.; rec. by Daniel Rooney - 5 Nov. 1834 [155]

Donaldson, Joseph, subj. of G.B.; rec. by Robert Donnaldson, gentleman - 5 Nov. 1834 [156]

Carter, John, subj. of G.B.; rec. by Catharine Lombard 5 Nov. 1834 [157]

Eiszler,Andrew, subj. of King of Wittenberg; rec. by John Ruprecht, shoemaker - 5 Nov. 1834 [158]

Edger, Charles, grocer, born Co. Caven, Ire., age 30 in 1821 (when he was listed as "cartman"), emigrated from Dublin, subj. of G.B.; rec. by James Brady, porter - 17 May 1834 [159]

Elgo, Patrick, subj. of G.B.; rec. by Stephen McInroy - 4 Nov. 1834 [160]

Griffiths, David, rigger, subj. of G.B.; rec. by Nathaniel Hollis, rigger & stevedore - 5 Nov. 1834 [161]

Graham, Johan, subj. of King of Hanover; rec. by John A. Miller, tavern-keeper 5 Nov. 1834 [162]

Guerin, John, subj. of King of France; rec. by Constant Benoit - 5 Nov. 1834 [163]

Guerin, Peter, subj. of King of France; rec. by Constant Benoit - 5 Nov. 1834 [164]

Goggin, John, labourer, subj. of G.B.; rec. by James Walsh, milkman - 5 Nov. 1834 [165]

Gilloon, John, labourer, subj. of G.B.; rec. by William Divvens - 5 Nov. 1834 [166]

Gillon, William, labourer, subj. of G.B.; rec. by John Greer, tailor - 5 Nov. 1834 [167]

Jackson, John, Sr., subj. of G.B.; rec. by Henry Radbarg, coachman - 5 Nov. 1834 [168]

Jones, Samuel, subj. of G.B.; rec. by Dennis McMahon, merchant - 5 Nov. 1834 [169]

Morrisson, Maurice, subj. of G.B.; rec. by Jotham Peabody, carpenter - 5 Nov. 1834 [170]

Maspoole, James, of Brooklyn, subj. of King of Spain; rec. by Vincent Oliver, of Brooklyn - 5 Nov. 1834 [171]

Morton, Joseph, native of Warwickshire, Eng., subj. of G.B.; rec. by Thomas Edge, engraver - 5 Nov. 1834 [172]

Moreton, George, druggist, subj. of G.B.; rec. by John Shephard - 5 Nov. 1834 [173]

Meehan, James, labourer, subj. of G.B.; rec. by James Fitzgerald - 4 Nov. 1834 [174]

Meacher, Henry, subj. of G.B.; rec. by John Barline - 4 Nov. 1834 [174A]

Brown, John, subj. of G.B.;rec. by John Brown, printer - 5 Nov. 1834 [175]

Brown, John, glass cutter, subj. of G.B.; rec. by Thomas Brown, Sr., manufacturer - 4 Nov. 1834 [176]

Brown, John, printer, subj. of G.B.; rec. by Joseph Davis - 4 Nov. 1834 [177]

Bath, George F., subj. of G.B.; rec. by Bernard Wentz - 5 Nov. 1834 [178]

Brown, Thomas, glass cutter, subj. of G.B.; rec. by Thomas Brown, Sr., cotton manufacturer - 4 Nov. 1834 [179]

Breakey, Andrew, engineer, born Co. Monaghan, Ire., emigrated from Newry; at age 23, probably in 1828 or 1829, he was a tobacconist; rec. by William Harrison, grocer - 6 Nov. 1834 [180]

Brady, Philip, subj. of G.B.; rec. by Charles Potoin, cordwainer - 5 Nov. 1834 [181]

Beattie, John, coachman, subj. of G.B.; rec. by Henry Radbarg, coachman - 5 Nov. 1834 [182]

Berger, John, subj. of King of France; rec. by Gouha Vargond - 4 Nov. 1834 [183]

Bartley, Michael, subj. of G.B.; rec. by Edward McCarty - 5 Nov. 1834 [184]

Blackburn, George, subj. of G.B.; rec. by Richard Whitaker, tavern-keeper - 5 Nov. 1834 [185]

Betts, Charles T., subj. of G.B.; rec. by Benjamin Davis, porter - 5 Nov. 1834 [186]

Benoit, Constant, subj. of King of France; rec. by Adam Pael, blacksmith - 5 Nov. 1834 [187]

Boghick, Francis, subj. of King of Austria; rec. by John J. Etheridge, mariner - 5 Nov. 1834 [187A]

Byrne, James, subj. of G.B.; rec. by Samuel Waddell, mason - 5 Nov. 1834 [188]

Browning, Thomas Charles, subj. of G.B.; rec. by Thomas Browning, pianoforte maker - 5 Nov. 1834 [189]

Brown, Henry, subj. of G.B.; rec. by Jotham Peabody, carpenter - 5 Nov. 1834 [190]

Bell, Thomas, subj. of G.B.; rec. by John W. Jackson, Jr. - 4 Nov. 1834 [191]

McGowan, Samuel, subj. of G.B.; rec. by John Reilly - 5 Nov. 1834 [192]

McWhinnie, Peter, subj. of G.B.; rec. by James McWhinney - 4 Nov. 1834 [193]

McGuire, Peter, subj. of G.B.;rec. by William Kinams, clerk - 5 Nov. 1834 [194]

McCormick, Patrick, subj. of G.B.; rec. by Edward Lynch - 5 Nov. 1834 [195]

Maguire, Edward, subj. of G.B.; rec. by Thomas Dolan, grocer - 5 Nov. 1834 [196]

McDonought, Francis, painter & glazier, subj. of G.B.; rec. by John McDonnott - 5 Nov. 1834 [197]

Maguire, Michael, subj. of G.B.; rec. by Francis Mongan - 5 Nov. 1834 [198]

McGinty, Patrick, Jr., subj. of G.B.; rec. by Patrick McGinty, Sr. - 5 Nov. 1834 [199]

McDermott, Michael, subj. of G.B.; rec. by Rufus Greene - 4 Nov. 1834 [200]

Maginnis, William, labourer, subj. of G.B.; rec. by Walter Jolly, grocer, and James Lamb - 12 June 1834 [2o1]

Loftus, James, labourer, subj. of G.B.; rec. by Patrick Loftus, waiter - 8 Nov. 1834 [202]

Lynch, James, subj. of G.B.; rec. by John Gallagher, labourer - 5 Nov. 1834 [203]

Robinson, James, confectioner, subj. of G.B.; rec. by John Hildreth, counsellor-at-law - 8 Nov. 1834 [204]

Reeves, Charles, subj. of G.B.; rec. by Dudley Sheffield, lumber inspector - 5 Nov. 1834 [205]

Ruprecht, John, subj. of Switzerland; rec. by Francis Oerthe, jeweller - 5 Nov. 1834 [206]

Robinson, Henry, subj. of G.B.; rec. by Patrick McManus, labourer - 5 Nov. 1834 [207]

Rapelye, James R., grocer, subj. of G.B.; rec. by George Rapelye, merchant, & John Passidy, merchant, both born in N.Y. State - 20 Oct. 1834 [208]

Ryan, Thomas, subj. of G.B.; rec. by Jotham Peabody, carpenter - 5 Nov. 1834 [209]

Ross, James, subj. of G.B.; rec. by John Riley - 5 Nov. 1834 [210]

Bundle 10

Feistel, Anthony, subj. of King of Prussia; rec. by Henry Meigs & James Dill, clerk of court - 23 Feb. 1836 [1]

Heydecker, Joachim, subj. of King of Bavaria; rec. by John J. Boyd - 11 Apr. 1836 [2]

Hanlon, Bernard, subj. of G.B.; rec. by William Farrell - 9 Nov. 1836 [3]

Henriques, Abigaile (wife of Ebenezer Henriques), subj. of G.B.; rec. by Joseph Henriques - 15 Apr. 1836 [4]

Hughes, Owen, subj. of G.B.; rec. by James Clark - 9 Nov. 1836 [5]

Hanegan, James, subj. of G.B.; rec. by John Delaney - 9 Nov. 1836 [6]

Haeselbarth, Adam C., subj. of King of Saxony; rec. by John A. Stemmler, attorney-at-law - 29 July 1836 [6A]

Harrison, Henry, subj. of G.B.; rec. by Arthur Harrison - 9 Nov. [7]

Hoffman, Michael, subj. of G.B.; rec. by Samuel Taylor - 9 Nov. 1836 [8]

Hanna, William, subj. of G.B.; rec. by John Williams - 9 Nov. 1836 [9]

Henriques, David, subj. of G.B.; rec. by Joseph Shelburg - 5 Apr. 1836 [10]

Hayes, William, subj. of G.B.; rec. by Edmond Bay - 9 Nov. 1836 [11]

Rittershofer, William, subj. of Grand Duke of Baden; rec. by John A. Stemmler - 14 Apr. 1836 [12]

Reiley, John, subj. of G.B.; rec. by Godfrey Shehan - 9 Nov. 1836 [13]

Rodney, Mathew, subj. of G.B.; rec. by Michael Dempsey - 9 Nov. 1836 [14]

Rogers, William, subj. of G.B.; rec. by Michael Byrnes - 9 Nov. 1836 [15]

Rians, John, subj. of G.B.; rec. by Bernard Wood - 9 Nov. 1836 [16]

Arbogast, Frederick, subj. of King of France; rec. by John A. Stemmler, attorney-at-law - 30 June 1836 [17]

Arnold, Philip George, farmer, subj. of King of France; rec. by
John Possont - 10 Apr. 1836 [18]

Ibbotson, Henry, subj. of G.B.; rec. by Thomas Darling, Jr. - 5
Nov. 1836 [19]

Watmough, Jonathan, subj. of G.B.; rec. by John Hildreth - 8
Nov. 1836 [20]

Walsh, Michael, subj. of G.B.; rec. by Francis Hearn - 9 Nov.
1836 [21]

Watson, Alexander, accountant, subj. of G.B.; rec. by William
Mullock, counsellor-at-law - 9 May 1836 _22]

Winrow, George, of Greene Co., N.Y., hunter, subj. of G.B.; rec.
by Peter Sheridan - 9 Nov. 1836 [23]

Ward, Thomas, subj. of G.B.; rec. by William Farrell - 9 Nov.
1836 [24]

Erbin, James, subj. of G.B.; rec. by Peter Sheridan - 9 Nov.
1836 [25]

Leypoldt, Lewis, subj. of King of Bavaria; rec. by Lewis Meyer -
9 Nov. 1836 [26]

Lundberg, Jonas Augustus, from Orange Co., subj. of King of
Sweden; rec. by Abraham Crist, counsellor-at-law - 27 Aug.
1836 [27]

Laughran, Edward, subj. of G.B.; rec. by Patrick McGeough - 9
Nov. 1836 [28]

Leahy, Patrick, clerk, subj. of G.B.; rec. by James Shehan - 27
Aug. 1836 [29]

Lawson, Henry, subj. of King of Sweden; rec. by John Lindmark -
18 Aug. 1836 [30]

Black, Patrick, of Co. Caven, Ire., subj. of G.B.; rec. by Bernard Hanlon - 9 Nov. 1836 [31]

Banks, William, merchant, subj. of G.B.; rec. by Robert Lenox -
10 Oct. 1836 [32]

Byrne, Michael, subj. of G.B.; rec. by William Rogers - 9 Nov.
1836 [33]

Bell, James Christy (son of Abraham Bell and of Mary C. Bell,
late wife of said Abraham; James is brother of Rebecca H.
Bell), age 21 in 1835, subj. of G.B.; rec. by Jacob Harvey and
Charles Graham, Esq. - 23 May 1836 [34]

Bennett, John, subj. of King of France; rec. by Raymond Gascon
and Nicholas C. Everett - 18 May 1836 [35]

Byrnes, Barney, subj. of G.B.; rec. by John Dugan - 9 Nov. 1836
[36]

Brady, Michael, subj. of G.B.; rec. by Bryan McCahill - 9 Nov.
[37]

Boyle, Michael, subj. of G.B.; rec. by Peter Keenan - 9 Nov.
1836 [38]

Brady, John, subj. of G.B.; rec. by Patrick McCafferty - 9 Nov.
1836 [39]

Bage, Robert, hatter, subj. of G.B.; rec. by Edward L. Tredwell,
hatter - 25 Mar. 1836 [40]

Burgy, Henry, merchant, subj. of Switzerland; rec. by John James
Boyd - 25 June 1836 [41]

O'Keiff, Michael, subj. of G.B.; rec. by William McIntyre - 9
Nov. 1836 [42 & 43]

O'Reilly, William, shopkeeper, subj. of G.B.; rec. by Edward
O'Reilly - 7 Nov. 1836 [44]

O'Leary, John, subj. of G.B.; rec. by Robert Sullivan - 9 Nov.
1836 [45]

O'Reilly, Edward, subj. of G.B.; rec. by William O'Reilly - 7
Nov. 1836 [46]

McGuoen, Patrick, subj. of G.B.; rec. by William Dougherty - 9
Nov. 1836 [47]

McGinnis, Henry, cartman, subj. of G.B. - 21 Mar. 1836 [48]

McGuire, Thomas, subj. of G.B.; rec. by John Dolan - 9 Nov.
1836 [49]

McCormick, Andrew, subj. of G.B.; rec. by Joseph Richards, of
Brooklyn - 18 Nov. 1836 [50]

McGee, John, subj. of G.B.; rec. by Andrew Darby - 9 Nov. 1836
[51]

McCormick, Thomas, subj. of G.B.; rec. by Andrew H. McCormick -
9 Nov. 1836 [52]

McLarney, Thomas, subj. of G.B.; rec. by James Clark - 9 Nov.
1836 [53]

McCanna, John, subj. of G.B. - 9 Nov. 1836 [54]

McGeough, Patrick, subj. of G.B.; rec. by Edward Loughrin - 9
Nov. 1836 [55]

Heiffron, Patrick M., subj. of G.B.; rec. by Mary Maley - 9
Nov. 1836 [56]

McMullen, James, labourer, subj. of G.B.; rec. by Daniel McAuley
- 9 Nov. 1836 [57]

McCormick, Michael, subj. of G.B.; rec. by Joseph Richards, of
Brooklyn - 7 Nov. 1836 [58]

McCluskey, John, labourer, subj. of G.B.; rec. by Paul McCluskey - 9 Nov. 1836 [59]

McGath [clerk wrote "McGraw"], Owen, labourer, subj. of G.B.;
rec. by Bernard Wood - 9 Nov. 1836 [60]

Fletcher, Patrick, subj. of G.B.; rec. by Robert Kervan - 9 Nov.
1836 [61]

Flynn, Patrick, subj. of G.B.; rec. by James Barry - 9 Nov. 1836
[62]

Fokkes, Teunis, subj. of Senate of Hamburgh; rec. by George
Sonne - 9 Nov. 1836 [63]

Flood, Patrick, subj. of G.B.; rec. by Peter McMahon - 9 Nov.
1836 [64]

Porter, Thomas, subj. of G.B.; rec. by Neil McCoy - 9 Nov. 1836
[65]

Parr, John, subj. of G.B.; rec. by John P. Cumming, of Brooklyn
- 8 Nov. 1836 [66]

Phelan, John, Jr., subj. of G.B.; rec. by John Phelan, Sr. - 9
Nov. 1836 [67]

Neeson, James, late of Co. Antrim, Ire., subj. of G.B.; rec. by
Dennis Neeson - 9 Nov. 1836 [68]

Norrie, Adam, subj. of G.B.; rec. by Robert Johnston - 8 Sept.
1836 [69]

Neeson, Dennis, late of Co. Antrim, Ire., subj. of G.B.; rec. by
James Neeson - 9 Nov. 1836 [70]

Senft [clerk wrote "Swift"], Michael, subj. of King of Bavaria;
rec. by John Leslie - 9 Nov. 1836 [71]

Sheedy, Michael, labourer, subj. of G.B.; rec. by John Maghar,
shoemaker - 30 May 1836 [72]

Skillin, James, subj. of G.B.; rec. by Hance Skillin - 9 Nov.
1836 [73]

Sonne, George, subj. of King of Hanover; rec. by Lewis Meyer -
9 Nov. 1836 [74]

Sheridan, Peter, subj. of G.B.; rec. by George Winrow - 9 Nov.
1836 [75]

Shephard, John, subj. of G.B.; rec. by Samuel Shephard, of Kings
Co. - 7 Nov. 1836 [76]

Skivington, Patrick, subj. of G.B.; rec. by Hugh Skivington - 9
Nov. 1836 [77]

Sweeny, Daniel, subj. of G.B.; rec. by John Sweeny - 9 Nov.
1836 [78]

Skillin, William, subj. of G.B.; rec. by Hance Skillin - 9 Nov.
1836 [79]

Smith, James, teacher, born Scotland, age 28 in 1825, migrated
from Selkirk, Scotland, subj. of G.B.; wife Isabella, born in
Eng., age 30 in 1825; their daughters are Margaret Ann, born
in NYC, age 3 in 1825, and Isabella, born in NYC, age 18 mos.
in 1825; rec. by Calvin Griswald - 20 Mar. 1836 [80]

Shephard, Samuel, of Kings Co., subj. of G.B.; rec. by John
Shephard - 7 Nov. 1836 [81]

Schmidt, George, subj. of King of France; rec. by Peter Schu-
haus - 12 Jan. 1836 [82]

Dodds, Samuel, subj. of G.B.; rec. by Peter Paret - 9 Nov. 1836
[83]

Dunn, William, subj. of G.B.; rec. by Robert Cunningham - 9 Nov.
1836 [84]

Doyle, James, late of Co. Langford, Ire., subj. of G.B.; rec. by
Peter Tuit - 9 Nov. 1836 [85]

Duffy, Patrick, subj. of G.B.; rec. by Patrick Duffy - 9 Nov.
1836 [86]

Dempsey, Barney, labourer, subj. of G.B., rec. by Michael Demp-
Dempsey - 9 Nov. 1836 [87]

Dorsey, Thomas, subj. of G.B.; rec. by Michael Kearney - 9 Nov.
1836 [88]

Delany, Henry, subj. of G.B.; rec. by James Clark - 9 Nov. 1836
[89]

Tuit, Peter, late of Co. Langford, Ire., subj. of G.B.; rec. by
James Doyle - 9 Nov. 1836 [90]

Tackaberry, John, minister of the Gospel, subj. of G.B.; rec. by
Cornelius R. Detosway, counsellor-at-law - 9 May 1836 [91]; in
1826 Tackaberry stated in Greene Co., Pa., that he was born
8 Sept. 1799 in Co. Wexford, Ire.

Vauthey, Louis, born in France about 1801, age 33 in 1834, migrated from Havre and disembarked in Baltimore, subj. of King
of France; rec. by Johann Schaeffer - 9 Nov. 1836 [92]

Van Veen, Karst Jans, subj. of King of Holland; rec. by Bernard
Lamb - 9 Nov. 1836 [93]

Maze, Abraham, subj. of G.B.; rec. by Andrew Darby - 9 Nov.'36[94]

Murray, Henry, subj. of G.B.; rec. by Samuel Netherington - 9 Nov. 1836 [95]

Meenan, Daniel, subj. of G.B.; rec. by James McClean - 9 Nov. 1836 [96]

Maganty, Patrick, labourer, subj. of G.B.; rec. by William Kirk - 9 Nov. 1836 [97]

Milford, Edward, innkeeper, subj. of G.B.; rec. by Elijah Boardman - 30 May 1836 [98]

Martin, Heinrich, subj. of King of Bavaria; rec. by Peter Martin - 9 Nov. 1836 [99]

Murphy, Michael H., subj. of G.B.; rec. by Patrick Merrick - 9 Nov. 1836 [99A]

Gadd, Lewis, mariner, subj. of King of Sweden; rec. by Fernando Wood - 9 Nov. 1836 [100]

Gillespie, John, labourer, subj. of G.B.; rec. by Martin Waters - 9 Nov. 1836 [101]

Galbraith, Benjamin, student-at-law, subj. of G.B.; rec. by John B. Waistell - 20 Oct. 1836 [102]

Carroll, Thomas, subj. of G.B.; rec. by Bernard Woods - 9 Nov. 1836 [103]

Clarke, James, subj. of G.B.; rec. by Owen Hughes - 9 Nov. 1836 [104]

Clancey, Patrick, subj. of G.B.; rec. by Daniel McCafferty - 9 Nov. 1836 [105]

Cruise, Patrick, subj. of G.B.; rec. by Alexander McLean - 14 Apr. 1836 [106]

Collins, Francis, gardener, subj. of G.B.; rec. by John Kerr - 8 Nov. 1836 [107]

Colsey, Henry James Chitty, cabinetmaker, subj. of G.B.; rec. by Josiah Melvin - 7 Oct. 1836 [108]

Cunningham, Robert, subj. of G.B.; rec. by John Cunningham - 9 Nov. 1836 [109]

Kiernan, Patrick, subj. of G.B.; rec. by John Riley - 9 Nov. 1836 [110]

Kearny, Michael, subj. of G.B.; rec. by Thomas Darcy - 9 Nov. 1836 [111]

Kelly, Peter, subj. of G.B.; rec. by Michael Brown - 6 Oct. 1834 [112]

Kain, Quinton, subj. of G.B.; rec. by James Halligan - 22 Dec. 1836 [113]

Kieckhofer, Adolphus T., merchant, subj. Rep. of Hamburg - 8 Mar. 1837 [113C]

Bundle 11

Cunningham, Daniel, subj. of G.B.; rec. by Hugh Cunningham - 11 Apr. 1837 [1]

Corr, Hugh, subj. of G.B.; rec. by Robert Clark - 11 Apr. 1837 [2]

Carter, Robert, subj. of G.B.; rec. by Michael O'Neil - 11 Apr. 1837 [3]

Carroll, George, subj. of G.B.; rec. by James Taylor - 12 Apr. 1837 [4]

Curtin, John, subj. of G.B.; rec. by James Handlan - 12 Apr.
1837 [5]

Carroll, Patrick, subj. of G.B.; rec. by James Handlan - 12 Apr.
1837 [6]

Callahan, Cornelius, subj. of G.B.; rec. by James Handlan - 12
Apr. 1837 [7]

Conlan, John, subj. of G.B.; rec. by Patrick Fitzpatrick - 12
Apr. 1837 [8]

Canon/Cannon, James, subj. of G.B.; rec. by Patrick Conlan - 12
Apr. 1837 [9]

Campbell, Dennis, subj. of G.B.; rec. by James McElroy - 12 Apr.
1837 [10]

Callary, James, subj. of G.B.; rec. by John Gray - 12 Apr. 1837
[11]

Clarke, Patrick, subj. of G.B.; rec. by John Clarke - 12 Apr.
1837 [12]

Collins, William, subj. of G.B.; rec. by Lewis Parie - 12 Apr.
1837 [13]

Costello, Thomas, subj. of G.B.; rec. by Daniel Gilmartin - 12
Apr. 1837 [14]

Coyle, Owen, subj. of G.B.; rec. by Daniel Donahue - 12 Apr.
1837 [15]

Calnon, Jeremiah, subj. of G.B.; rec. by Michael Harding - 12
Apr. 1837 [16]

Clinton, Hugh, subj. of G.B.; rec. by John Murray - 12 Apr. 1837
[17]

Christmann, Adam, subj. of King of Wurtemburg; rec. by Jacob
Walter - 12 Apr. 1837 [18]

Carroll, Robert, subj. of G.B.; rec. by Joseph Keeler - 13 Apr.
1837 [19]

Corvan, Philip James, subj. of G.B.; rec. by John Barrett - 13
Apr. 1837 [20]

Carr, Edward, subj. of G.B.; rec. by Alexander McEhorter - 13
Apr. 1837 [21]

Conillan, James, subj. of G.B.; rec. by John B. Arnoux - 13 Apr.
1837 [22]

Cunningham, Michael, subj. of G.B.; rec. by James Reynolds - 13
Apr. 1837 [23]

Coggan, Bartley, subj. of G.B.; rec. by Michael McCarthy - 13
Apr. 1837 [24]

Cox, Terrence, of N.J., labourer; rec. by John Kiernan - 13 Apr.
1837 [25]

Coyle, Philip, subj. of G.B.; rec. by Hugh Lynch - 13 Apr. 1837
[26]

Conlon, Charles, subj. of G.B.; rec. by Robert Grimes - 13 Apr.
1837 [27]

Conroy, Michael, subj. of G.B.; rec. by James Handlon - 13 Apr.
1837 [28]

Harron, Thomas, subj. of G.B.; rec. by John Clark - 13 Apr. 1837
[29]

Cosgrove, Michael, subj. of G.B.; rec. by Julia Cosgrove - 13
Apr. 1837 [30]

Cavanagh, Peter, subj. of G.B.; rec. by Patrick Gaffney - 13
   Apr. 1837 [31]

Connoley, Owen, subj. of G.B.; rec. by Patrick Morris - 13 Apr.
   1837 [32]

Calegan/Calligan, Martin, subj. of G.B.; rec. by James Carolan -
   6 Nov. 1837 [33]

Chatillon, George, subj. of King of Bavaria; rec. by William
   Shimper - 6 Nov. 1837 [34]

Conlan, John, subj. of G.B.; rec. by Thomas Conlan - 6 Nov.
   1837 [35]

Conley, Patrick, subj. of G.B.; rec. by Arthur Ternan - 6 Nov.
   1837 [36]

Conlan, Mathew, subj. of G.B.; rec. by Arthur Ternan - 6 Nov.
   1837 [37]

Cross, John, subj. of G.B.; rec. by Jacob M. Burroughs - 6 Nov.
   1837 [38]

Carolan, James, subj. of G.B.; rec. by George D. Campbell - 6
   Nov. 1837 [39]

Correll, Friederich, subj. of King of Bavaria; rec. by William
   Wetteroth - 6 Nov. 1837 [40]

Cook, John H., subj. of G.B.; rec. by Joshua Knapp - 6 Nov. 1837
   [41]

Cassady, Charles, subj. of G.B.; rec. by Michael Kingan - 7 Nov.
   1837 [42]

Callaghan, Jeremiah, subj. of G.B.; rec. by Maurice Duane - 7
   Nov. 1837 [43]

Caffey, Jeremiah, subj. of G.B.; rec. by James Sullivan - 7 Nov.
   1837 [44]

Conroy, William, subj. of G.B.; rec. by Patrick Conroy - 7 Nov.
   1837 [45]

Cleaver, Matthew, subj. of G.B.; rec. by John M. McCarthy - 7
   Nov. 1837 [46]

Crantz, John, subj. of France; rec. by Heinrich Crantz - 7 Nov.
   1837 [47]

Clancy, John, subj. of G.B.; rec. by John McGrath - 7 Nov. 1837
   [48]

Costello, Peter, subj. of G.B.; rec. by John McLaughlin - 7 Nov.
   1837 [49]

Clark, James, subj. of G.B.; rec. by James Bonar - 7 Nov. 1837
   [50]

Carroll, Terrence, subj. of G.B.; rec. by Charles Kelly - 7 Nov.
   1837 [51]

Connor, James, subj. of G.B.; rec. by William Johnson - 7 Nov.
   1837 [52]

Cass, Thomas, subj. of G.B.; rec. by William Cass - 8 Nov. 1837
   [53]

Coots, John, subj. of G.B.; rec. by Elias C. Cadmus - 8 Nov.
   1837 [54]

Cass, William, subj. of G.B.; rec. by Thomas Cass - 8 Nov. 1837
   [55]

Cummeskey, John, subj. of G.B.; rec. by Henry Dalton - 8 Nov.
   1837 [56]

Clark, Malcolm, subj. of G.B.; rec. by Ebenezer Bernie - 8 Nov. 1837 [57]

Callery, John, subj. of G.B.; rec. by James Callery - 8 Nov. 1837 [58]

Carnes, Thomas, subj. of G.B.; rec. by Patrick Coyle - 8 Nov. 1837 [59]

Cahill, Sylvester, subj. of G.B.; rec. by Mary Bigelow - 8 Nov. 1837 [60]

Koch, Wendelin, subj. of Grand Duke of Baden; rec. by Ludwig Körber - 8 Nov. 1837 [61]

Campbell, Joseph, subj. of G.B.; rec. by William Campbell - 8 Nov. 1837 [62]

Costigan, Daniel, subj. of G.B.; rec. by Frances N. Carr - 8 Nov. 1837 [63]

Coleman, Michael, subj. of G.B.; rec. by Michael Burke - 8 Nov. 1837 [64]

Cole, Felix, subj. of G.B.; rec. by Thomas Rodgers - 8 Nov. 1837 [65]

Curtis, James, subj. of G.B.; rec. by Timothy Kimball - 8 Nov. 1837 [66]

Connor, James, subj. of G.B.; rec. by Richard Cunningham, of 87 Broad St. - 8 Nov. 1837 [67]

Conroy, Michael, subj. of G.B.; rec. by David Patterson - 8 Nov. 1837 [68]

Carlile, Thomas, subj. of G.B.; rec. by William Carlile - 8 Nov. 1837 [69]

Arent, Antoine, subj. of King of Bavaria; rec. by Matthew Knoell - 7 Nov. 1837 _70]

Ekerlin, Carls, subj. of Grand Duke of Baden; rec. by Albert Heyde - 7 Nov. 1837 [71]

Atkin, James, born Ire., age 26 in 1827, migrated from Cork, farmer, to reside in Flushing, subj. of G.B.; rec. by William O'Driscoll - 7 Nov. 1837 [72]

Armstrong, Caldwell, subj. of G.B.; rec. by Hugh Armstrong - 12 Apr. 1837 [73]

Alvany, James, subj. of G.B.; rec. by Patrick McCabe - 12 Apr. 1837 [73A]

Donahue, Michael, subj. of G.B.; rec. by Thomas McGuire - 7 Nov. 1837 [74]

Del Hoyo, Francis, subj. of Spein; rec. by Manuel De Puga - 2 Mar. 1837 [75]

Donnelly, Thomas, subj. of G.B.; rec. by Gerrit Byrne, Jr. - 11 Apr. 1837 [76]

Doherty, John, subj. of G.B.; rec. by Henry J. Butler - 11 Apr. 1837 [77]

Dougherty, James, subj. of G.B.; rec. by James Harron - 11 Apr. 1837 [78]

Ditchett, Richard, subj. of G.B.; rec. by Charles J. Hybbs - 11 Apr. 1837 [79]

Dromay, Simon, subj. of G.B.; rec. by James Handlan - 12 Apr. 1837 [80]

Devlin, John, subj. of G.B.; rec. by James Dounelly - 12 Apr.
  1837 [81]

Delany, Daniel, subj. of G.B.; rec. by Richard Lanagin - 13 Apr.
  1837 [82]

Donovan, Richard, subj. of G.B.; rec. by William Green - 12 Apr.
  1837 [83]

Dickinson, John, subj. of G.B.; rec. by James Martindale - 12
  Apr. 1837 [84]

Duffy, Philip, subj. of G.B.; rec. by John Byrne - 12 Apr. 1837
  [85]

Dawes, Francis, carpenter, subj. of G.B.; rec. by Elisha Kingsland - 13 Apr. 1837 [86]

Driscoll, Cornelius, subj. of G.B.; rec. by Thomas O'Brien - 13
  Apr. 1837 [87]

Dolan, James, subj. of G.B.; rec. by James Jerkin - 13 Apr. 1837
  [88]

Devin, Patrick, subj. of G.B.; rec. by James Rodgers - 13 Apr.
  1837 [89]

Donovan, Timothy, subj. of G.B.; rec. by Fergus Cosgrove - 13
  Apr. 1837 [90]

Duffy, Thomas, subj. of G.B.; rec. by Jotham Peabody - 13 Apr.
  1837 [91]

Donahoe, Patrick, subj. of G.B.; rec. by Rose Donahoe - 13 Apr.
  1837 [92]

Donovan, William, subj. of G.B.; rec. by James Black - 13 Apr.
  1837 [93]

Ducey, Thomas, subj. of G.B.; rec. by James Black - 13 Apr.
  1837 [94]

De Noielle, Peter, subj. of King of Holland; rec. by Daniel
  Lord - 6 Nov. 1837 [95]

Daly, John, city of Hudson (on 7 Nov. 1831 of Stuyvesant Co. but
  late of Danmaway, Ire., [Dunmanway, Co. Cork?], age 41, migrated from Cork), subj. of G.B.; rec. by John Swanson - 7
  Nov. 1837 [96]

Doran, Michael, subj. of G.B.; rec. by Daniel P. Ingraham - 7
  Nov. 1837 [97]

Duane, Maurice, subj. of G.B.; rec. by Jeremiah Callaghan - 7
  Nov. 1837 [98]

Dunn, Henry, subj. of G.B.; rec. by Robert Cunningham - 7 Nov.
  1837 [99]

Duncan, William, subj. of G.B.; rec. by John Bruce - 7 Nov.
  1837 [100]

Duffy, James, subj. of G.B.; rec. by Joseph Murphy - 7 Nov.
  1837 [101]

Duchmann, Stephan, subj. of France ; rec. by Teunis Fokkes - 7
  Nov. 1837 [102]

Dease, Patrick, subj. of G.B.; rec. by Daniel Primrose - 7 Nov.
  1837 [103]

Dick, Christian, subj. of France; rec. by Bernard Geiler - 7
  Nov. 1837 [104]

Dillon, John, subj. of G.B.; rec. by Patrick Evers - 7 Nov. 1837
  [105]

Devlin, Michael, teamster, subj. of G.B.; rec. by John H. Burley 7 Nov. 1837 [106]

Brown, John, subj. of G.B.; rec. by James Handlan - 12 Apr. 1837 [107]

Brown, John, subj. of G.B.; rec. by John Lancaster - 11 Apr. 1837 [108]

Bell, Michael, subj. of G.B.; rec. by James Black - 12 Apr. 1837 [109]

Barron, Patrick, subj. of G.B.; rec. by Nicholas Schloser - 12 Apr. 1837 [110]

Boot, Thomas, subj. of G.B.; rec. by Stephen Noviss - 12 Apr. 1837 [111]

Butler, John, subj. of G.B.; rec. by James Handlan - 11 Apr. 1837 [112]

Boylen, Thomas, born Co. Monaghan, Ire., age 36 in 1834, migrated from Waring's Point, planned to settle in Albany; rec. by Catharine Boylen - 13 Apr. 1837 [113]

Brerenbucher, Adam, subj. of France; rec. by Jacob Gress - 13 Apr. 1837 [114]

Brown, William, subj. of G.B.; rec. by John McEvoy - 13 Apr. 1837 [115]

Boyd, James, subj. of G.B.; rec. by Martin Waters - 13 Apr. 1837 [116]

Brady, Hugh, subj. of G.B.; rec. by Patrick Marsterson - 13 Apr. 1837 [117]

Burns, William, subj. of G.B.; rec. by Felix Boylen - 13 Apr. 1837 [118]

Bracken, Lochlin, subj. of G.B.; rec. by William Green - 13 Apr. 1837 [119]

Bradon, George, subj. of G.B.; rec. by Charles McKenna - 13 Apr. 1837 [120]

Baxter, Patrick, subj. of G.B. - 13 Apr. 1837 [121]

Burk, Thomas, subj. of G.B.; rec. by Owen McCabe - 13 Apr. 1837 [122]

Butler, Patrick, subj. of G.B.; rec. by James Black - 13 Apr. 1837 [123]

Barry, Thomas, subj. of G.B.; rec. by James Black - 13 Apr. 1837 [124]

Bradley, Miles, subj. of G.B.; rec. by John McSurley - 13 Apr. 1837 [125]

Brennan, James, subj. of G.B.; rec. by James Handlan - 13 Apr. 1837 [126]

Burk, William, subj. of G.B.; rec. by Morgan Kennedy - 13 Apr. 1837 [127]

Brannon, Daniel, subj. of G.B.; rec. by Michael Kinney - 9 June 1837 [128]

Brady, Felix, subj. of G.B.; rec. by Bernard Smith - 16 Oct. 1837 [129]

Brady, Owen, subj. of G.B.; rec. by Bernard Smith - 16 Oct. 1837 [130]

Baer/Bayer, Joseph, subj. of King of Wurtemburg; rec. by Matthaeus Knoell - 6 Nov. 1837 [131]

Buchanan, Robert, subj. of G.B.; rec. by John Daly - 6 Nov. 1837 [132]

Bremer, Frederick, subj. of King of Bavaria; rec. by Peter Beritz - 6 Nov. 1837 [133]

Bowen, John, subj. of G.B.; rec. by John Sullivan - 6 Nov. 1837 [134]

Boppert, John Peter, subj. of Prince of Hesse Darmstadt; rec. by Lewis Wilmuth - 6 Nov. 1837 [135]

Boschert, Xavier, subj. of Grand Duke of Baden; rec. by John A. Stemmler - 6 Nov. 1837 [136]

Bisher, John, subj. of Grand Duke of Baden; rec. by Heinrich Robert - 7 Nov. 1837 [137]

Bodt, Charles, subj. of King of Denmark; rec. by Thomas Kearney - 7 Nov. 1837 [138]

Brady, Philip, subj. of G.B.; rec. by John McGuire - 7 Nov. 1837 [139]

Butler, Richard, subj. of G.B.; rec. by Michael Harding - 7 Nov. 1837 [140]

Baird, Thomas, subj. of G.B.; rec. by Sandford Davidson - 7 Nov. 1837 [141]

Bullmer, Jacob, subj. of King of Bavaria; rec. by Martin Keller - 7 Nov. 1837 [142]

Brisch, Engelhart, subj. of King of Bavaria; rec. by Bernard Geiler - 7 Nov. 1837 [143]

Browne, John, subj. of G.B.; rec. by Patrick Hurley - 7 Nov. 1837 [144]

Brackin, Andrew, subj. of G.B.; rec. by John Brackin - 8 Nov. 1837 [145]

Bradley, John, subj. of G.B.; rec. by Mathew Conlan - 8 Nov. 1837 [146]

Barnett, William, subj. of G.B.; rec. by Henry Johnston - 13 Nov. 1837 [147]

Bulling, Diedrick, subj. of Duke of Oldenburg; rec. by Labbe Dohm - 8 Nov. 1837 [148]

Brunnar, John, subj. of G.B.; rec. by Daniel McGrath - 8 Nov. 1837 [149]

Bruns, Christian L., subj. of King of Bavaria; rec. by Bernard Geiler - 8 Nov. 1837 [150]

Brawn, Christian, subj. of G.B.; rec. by William Higgins - 8 Nov. 1837 [151]

Buchanan, John, subj. of G.B.; rec. by Thomas M. Collins - 8 Nov. 1837 [152]

Bell, George, subj. of G.B.; rec. by Dennis Downs - 8 Nov. 1837 [153]

Bormeth, John Valentine, subj. of Grand Duke of Hesse Darmstadt; rec. by William Murtfeldt, of 218 Church St. - 8 Nov. 1837 [153A]

Egan, James, subj. of G.B.; rec. by John Brown - 8 Nov. 1837 [154]

Eversalt, Philip Jacob, subj. of King of Bavaria; rec. by William A. Vultee - 7 Nov. 1837 [155]

Eberhard, Joseph, subj. of France; rec. by John E. Kent - 7 Nov. 1837 [156]

Early, Patrick, subj. of G.B.; rec. by James Wiley - 8 Nov. 1837 [157]

Eier, Frederick, subj. of France - 8 Nov. 1837 [158]

Ellis, David H., subj. of G.B.; rec. by William Donaldson - 13 Apr. 1837 [159]

Evard, Francois J., subj. of France; rec. by Joseph Baley - 13 Apr. 1837 [160]

Dennin, John, subj. of G.B.; rec. by Michael Dennin - 8 Nov. 1837 [161]

Dearin, Andrew, subj. of G.B.; rec. by James Handlen - 8 Nov. 1837 [162]

Doyle, Thomas, subj. of G.B.; rec. by Lawrens Mauran - 8 Nov. 1837 [163]

Devlin, Peter, subj. of G.B.; rec. by Thomas Devlin - 8 Nov. 1837 [164]

Donovan, Bartholomew, subj. of G.B.; rec. by Daniel McCarthy - 8 Nov. 1837 [165]

Doherty, Francis, subj. of G.B.; rec. by James Black - 8 Nov. 1837 [166]

Driscoll, John, subj. of G.B.; rec. by James Black - 8 Nov. 1837 [167]

Dohm, Lübbe, subj. of King of Hanover; rec. by Frederick Witte - 8 Nov. 1837 [168]

Donnelly, James, labourer, subj. of G.B.; rec. by Thomas O'Connor - 8 Nov. 1837 [169]

Donally, Francis, subj. of G.B.; rec. by William Culbert - 8 Nov. 1837 [170]

Dwyer, John, subj. of G.B.; rec. by Robert F. Fraser - 8 Nov. 1837 [171]

Dolan, James, subj. of G.B.; rec. by John Quigly - 8 Nov. 1837 [172]

Delworth, Jeremiah, subj. of G.B.; rec. by John Weldon - 8 Nov. 1837 [173]

Donegan, Thomas, subj. of G.B.; rec. by John Lawton - 8 Nov. 1837 [174]

Dark, John, subj. of G.B.; rec. by William Tilden - 8 Nov. 1837 [175]

Doyle, Bartholomew, subj. of G.B.; rec. by Michael Flinn - 8 Nov 1837 [176]

Donnally, Matthew, age 30 in 1835, subj. of G.B. - 8 Nov. 1837 [177]

Dietherich, Jacob, subj. of King of Bavaria; rec. by Teunis Fokkes - 8 Nov. [178]

Dowding, George, subj. of G.B.; rec. by Alexander Corbet - 8 Nov. 1837 [179]

Donnelly, Hugh, subj. of G.B.; rec. by John Kelch - 8 Nov. 1837 [180]

Dalton, Henry, subj. of G.B.; rec. by Patrick McBarron - 8 Nov. 1837 [181]

Dennon, Owen, subj. of G.B.; rec. by John Nowlan - 8 Nov. 1837
[182]

Dowling, Peter, subj. of G.B.; rec. by Patrick Moore - 8 Nov.
1837 [183]

Doherty, Hugh, native of Ire., age 25 in 1835 when he arrived at
Amboy; rec. by John Robinson - 8 May 1837 [184]

Burke, David, subj. of G.B.; rec. by James Handlan - 8 Nov.
1837 [185]

Burdon, James, subj. of G.B.; rec. by Michael Conway - 8 Nov.
1837 [185A]

Brady, Bernard, subj. of G.B.; rec. by Thomas Smith - 8 Nov.
1837 [186]

Bracken, John, subj. of G.B.; rec. by Andrew Bracken - 8 Nov.
1837 [187]

Blakely, Michael, subj. of G.B.; rec. by James Barry - 8 Nov.
1837 [188]

Blake, Patrick, subj. of G.B.; rec. by John Kelly - 8 Nov. 1837
[189]

Burke, James, subj. of G.B.; rec. by James Simpson - 8 Nov.
1837 [190]

Burke, Patrick K., subj. of G.B.; rec. by Henry McCaddin - 8
Nov. 1837 [191]

Bawer, Philip, subj. of Grand Duke of Baden; rec. by Michael
Kelly - 8 Nov. 1837 [192]

Buerkle, Joseph, subj. of Grand Duke of Baden; rec. by Philipp
Schmass [clerk wrote "Schmall"] - 8 Nov. 1837 [193]

Bapp, Mathias, subj. of Prince of Hesse Darmstadt; rec. by Peter
Schlosser - 8 Nov. 1837 [194]

Bentz, Jacob, subj. of Grand Duke of Baden; rec. by Wendelin
Koch - 8 Nov. 1837 [195]

Burke, Michael, subj. of G.B.; rec. by Michael Coleman - 8 Nov.
1837 [196]

Bonahue, Daniel, subj. of G.B.; rec. by Jotham Peabody - 11 Apr.
1837 [197]

Barker, Luke, physician, subj. of G.B.; rec. by Elkanah Cobb,
merchant - 7 Apr. 1837 [198]

Bundle 12

Griffith, Edward Moule, jeweller, subj. of G.B.; rec. by John N.
Speck, jeweller - 11 Mar. 1837 [1]

Griffin, James, subj. of G.B.; rec. by Morgan Kennedy - 11 Apr.
1837 [2]

Gleason, Cornelius, subj. of G.B.; rec. by Edward Grant - 12
Apr. 1837 [3]

Gaffney, Patrick, subj. of G.B.; rec. by Patrick McCabe - 12
Apr. 1837 [4]

Gittere, Joseph, subj. of France - 13 Apr. 1837 [5]

Gogin, John, subj. of G.B.; rec. by James Black - 13 Apr. 1837
[6]

Gaffney, Dennis, subj. of G.B.; rec. by James McMahon - 13 Apr.
1837 [7]

Gunn, John, subj. of G.B.; rec. by Patrick Smith - 13 Apr. 1837
[8]

Grim, Catharine (widow of Oswald Grim), subj. of G.B.; rec. by Nicholas Moran - 25 June 1837 [9]

Gilbert, Catharine A. (wife of Nicholas Gilbert), subj. of France; rec. by William Slocum & Nicholas Gilbert - 21 Oct. 1837 [10]

Grischele, John, a subj.of Grand Duke of Baden; rec. by John Hettinger - 6 Nov. 1837 [11]

Grischele, Hypolite, subj. of Grand Duke of Baden; rec. by Xavier Boschert - 7 Nov. 1837 [12]

Gerst, Adam, subj. of King of Wuertemberg; rec. by Teunis Fakkes - 7 Nov. 1837 [13]

Gallagher, Peter, subj. of G.B.; rec. by Daniel Connally - 7 Nov. 1837 [14]

Golden, Hugh, subj. of G.B.; rec. by Francis Golden - 7 Nov. 1837 [15]

Godwin, Thomas, subj. of G.B.; rec. by James S. Burnes/Beurns - 7 Nov. 1837 [16]

Giblin, Peter, subj. of G.B.; rec. by John Tiernan - 7 Nov. 1837 [17]

Graham, Hugh, subj. of G.B.; rec. by Andrew Harrison - 7 Nov. 1837 [18]

Glory, John, subj. of G.B.; rec. by Bridget Tranor - 7 Nov. 1837 [19]

Galagher, John, subj. of G.B.; rec. by Michael Conway - 8 Nov. 1837 [20]

Ganter, Peter, subj. of France; rec. by John Reinhard - 8 Nov. 1837 [21]

Gaffney, James, subj. of G.B.; rec. by Joseph Keeler - 8 Nov. 1837 [22]

Gallen, Patrick, subj. of G.B.; rec. by Patrick Quin - 8 Nov. 1837 [23]

Koebel, Michael, subj. of King of Bavaria; rec. by Philip Bawer 8 Nov. 1837 [24]

Glory, James, subj. of G.B.; rec. by John Glory - 8 Nov. 1837 [25]

Glennon, Daniel, subj. of G.B.; rec. by John Sands - 8 Nov. 1837 [26]

Griffin, Martin, subj. of G.B.; rec. by Thomas P. Fitzgerald - 8 Nov. 1837 [27]

Gallagher, Hugh, subj. of G.B.; rec. by John Hanay - 8 Nov. 1837 [28]

Goodwin, Michael, subj. of G.B.; rec. by Michael Murphy - 8 Nov. 1837 [29]

Fitzpatrick, Patrick, subj. of G.B.; rec. by John Doherty - 11 Apr. 1837 [30]

Fielding, Jeremiah, subj. of G.B.; rec. by Timothy Driscoll - 12 Apr. 1837 [31]

Fargie, John F., subj. of G.B.; rec. by Stephen Norris - 12 Apr. 1837 [32]

Feeney, Thomas, subj. of G.B.; rec. by Owen Healy - 12 Apr.
1837 [33]

Faron, John, subj. of G.B.; rec. by John Doherty - 13 Apr. 1837
[34]

Flood, Philip, subj. of G.B.; rec. by George Gallagher - 13 Apr.
1837 [35]

Flanagan, Thomas, subj. of G.B.; rec. by Thomas Flanagan - 13
Apr. 1837 [36]

Fielding, Robert, subj. of G.B.; rec. by Samuel Dunn - 13 Apr.
1837 [37]

Flemming, Thomas, subj. of G.B.; rec. by Hugh Lynch - 13 Apr.
1837 [38]

Farrell, Mathew, subj. of G.B.; rec. by Philip Riley - 13 Apr.
1837 [39]

Fishermann, John William, subj. of King of Prussia; rec. by Carl
Klauberg - 6 Nov. 1837 [40]

Fairbrother, William, bookbinder, born London, age 27 in 1832,
subj. of G.B.; his wife, Eliza Elvara, born in London, age 23
in 1832; family migrated from London - 7 Nov. 1837 [41]

Forrest, David, bookbinder, subj. of G.B.; rec. by Michael
Cowhy - 7 Nov. 1837 [42]

Falvey, Jeremiah, subj. of G.B.; rec. by Francis Kemmy - 7 Nov.
1837 [43]

Finegan, Edward, subj. of G.B.; rec. by Michel Martin - 7 Nov.
1837 [44]

Fitzsimmons, John, subj. of G.B.; rec. by James Ward - 7 Nov.
1837 [45]

Ferguson, William, subj. of G.B.; rec. by Adam Gunther - 7 Nov.
1837 [46]

Foyle, Harrison, subj. of G.B.; rec. by Hugh Graham - 7 Nov.
1837 [47]

Fox, James, subj. of G.B.; rec. by John Whelden - 7 Nov. 1837
[48]

Falk, Heinrich, subj. of Duke of Hesse-Darmstadt; rec. by Bernard Geiler - 8 Nov. 1837 [49]

Ferguson, James, subj. of G.B.; rec. by Patrick Quin - 8 Nov.
1837 [50]

Finley, John, subj. of G.B.; rec. by John Kennon - 8 Nov. 1837
[51]

Fogerty, John, subj. of G.B.; rec. by David Joyce - 8 Nov. 1837
[52]

Fitzpatrick, Thomas, subj. of G.B.; rec. by Thomas Flannery -
8 Nov. 1837 [53]

Foley, Bryan, subj. of G.B.; rec. by James Black - 8 Nov. 1837
[54]

Farrell, Lewis, subj. of G.B.; rec. by Charles Doran - 8 Nov.
1837 [55]

Fitzgerald, John, subj. of G.B.; rec. by Thomas Conner - 8 Nov.
1837 [56]

Falkner, Thomas, subj. of G.B.; rec. by John Kyle - 8 Nov.
1837 [57]

Fallon, Edward, subj. of G.B.; rec. by William Chambers - 8 Nov. 1837 [58]

Flynn, Michael, subj. of G.B.; rec. by Bartholomew Doyle - 8 Nov. 1837 [59]

Flynn, Michael, subj. of G.B.; rec. by Bernard McGuire - 8 Nov. 1837 [60]

Fraser, Robert F., subj. of G.B.; rec. by Richard H. Thompson - 8 Nov. 1837 [61]

Fischel, Frederick S., subj. of King of Prussia; rec. by John T. Howard - 20 Nov. 1837 [62]

Hassett, John, subj. of G.B.; rec. by Thomas Hassett - 11 Apr. 1837 [63]

Hunt, Bartholomew, subj. of G.B.; rec. by Michael Kent - 11 Apr. 1837 [64]

Hiller, Johannes, subj. of King of Wuertemberg; rec. by Wilhelm Maier - 10 Mar. 1837 [65]

Hynes, Daniel, subj. of G.B.; rec. by Frances Edward Power - 11 Apr. 1837 [66]

Harrigan, Daniel, subj. of G.B.; rec. by Thomas Regan - 12 Apr. 1837 [67]

Healy, John, subj. of G.B.; rec. by James McQuade - 11 Apr. 1837 [68]

Hackett, Richard, subj. of G.B.; rec. by Thomas M. Collins - 12 Apr. 1837 [69]

Hackett, William, subj. of G.B.; rec. by William O'Bryan - 12 Apr. 1837 [70]

Hands, John, subj. of G.B.; rec. by Morgan Kennedy - 12 Apr. 1837 [71]

Haghue, Patrick, subj. of G.B.; rec. by James Black - 12 Apr. 1837 [72]

Hutchison, David, subj. of G.B.; rec. by Henry C. Atwood - 12 Apr. 1837 [73]

Hughes, Edward, subj. of G.B.; rec. by John S. Woods - 12 Apr. 1837 [74]

Horn, Christian, subj. of King of Denmark; rec. by Stephen Norris - 12 Apr. 1837 [75]

Haley, Thomas, subj. of G.B.; rec. by Owen Healy - 12 Apr. 1837 [76]

Hamill, Peter, subj. of G.B.; rec. by James O'Brien - 13 Apr. 1837 [77]

Holden, Patrick, subj. of G.B.; rec. by James Black - 13 Apr. 1837 [78]

Higgins, Michael, subj. of G.B.; rec. by Patrick Chrystal - 13 Apr. 1837 [79]

Horan, James, baker, subj. of G.B.; rec. by James Tuite - 13 Apr. 1837 [80]

Hanan, Joseph, subj. of G.B.; rec. by James Black - 13 Apr. 1837 [81]

Harris, George, of Orange Co., whitesmith, subj. of G.B.; rec. by Henry Brower - 13 Apr. 1837 [82]

Harron, Thomas, subj. of G.B.; rec. by John Clark - 13 Apr. 1837 [83]

Harrison, Benjamin, subj. of G.B.; rec. by Michael Donohoe - 6
    Nov. 1837 [84]

Hetzel, Charles Francis, subj. of Grand Duke of Baden; rec. by
    Lewis Willmuth - 6 Nov. 1837 [85]

Hughes, William, subj. of G.B.; rec. by Edward Hughes - 6 Nov.
    1837 [86]

Hesser, Adam, subj. of King of Wuertemberg; rec. by Henry Met-
    zendorf - 6 Nov. 1837 [87]

Hettinger, John, subj. of King of Wuertemberg; rec. by John
    Grischele - 6 Nov. 1837 [88]

Hoefle, Johannes, subj. of Grand Duke of Beden; rec. by Carl
    Klauberg - 6 Nov. 1837 [89]

Herrlich, Engelhard, subj. of King of Bavaria; rec. by Joseph
    Wolfer - 7 Nov. 1837 [90]

Huberg, Simon, subj. of King of Bavaria; rec. by Tuenis Fokkes -
    7 Nov. 1837 [91]

Hartenstein, Michael, subj. of King of Bavaria; rec. by Valen-
    tin Koehler - 7 Nov. 1837 [92]

Heyde, Albert, subj. of King of Saxony; rec. by Carls Ekerser -
    7 Nov. 1837 [93]

Handlon, James, subj. of G.B.; rec. by James Black - 7 Nov.
    1837 [94]

Halton, Joseph, subj. of G.B.; rec. by John Connell - 7 Nov.
    1837 [95]

Harrison, Patrick, subj. of G.B.; rec. by Thomas Nealer [or Nea-
    lis?] - 7 Nov. 1837 [96]

Harrison, Joseph, minister, subj. of G.B.; rec. by David Graham,
    Jr., counsellor-at-law - 7 Nov. 1837 [97]

Hurley, Patrick, subj. of G.B.; rec. by John Browne - 7 Nov.
    1837 [98]

Haescher, Samuel, subj. of France; rec. by Jacob Haescher - 7
    Nov. 1837 [99]

Heuser, Peter, subj. of France; rec. by Frederick Pfeifer - 7
    Nov. 1837 [100]

Hargrave, George, subj. of G.B.; rec. by Nixon Samuel Cue - 7
    Nov. 1837 [101]

Hannigan, Anthony, subj. of G.B.; rec. by John Townen - 8 Nov.
    1837 [102]

Hannigan, Edward, subj. of G.B.; rec. by John Townen - 8 Nov.
    1837 [103]

Halstead, James, subj. of G.B.; rec. by Robert Williamson - 8
    Nov. 1837 [104]

Honner, James, subj. of G.B.; rec. by William Campbell - 8 Nov.
    1837 [105]

Hore, James, subj. of G.B.; rec. by James Black - 8 Nov. 1837
    [106]

Hanay, John, subj. of G.B.; rec. by Hugh Gallagher - 8 Nov.
    1837 [107]

Hodder, Charles, subj. of Prince of Hesse Cassel; rec. by Hein-
    rich Vogt - 8 Nov. 1837 [108]

Hagerty, William, subj. of G.B.; rec. by Charles McKenna - 8
    Nov. 1837 [109]

Huenmondir, John, subj. of King of Wuertemberg; rec. by Philip Small - 8 Nov. 1837 [110]

Hon, George, subj. of King of Bavaria; rec. by Peter Breitz - 12 Apr. 1837 [111]

Jabas, George William, subj. of Republic of Switzerland; rec. by Joseph Baley - 12 Apr. 1837 [112]

Jabas, Abraham Lewis, subj. of Republic of Switzerland; rec. by Joseph Baley - 12 Apr. 1837 [113]

Jones, James A., subj. of G.B.; rec. by Thomas A. Jones - 13 Apr. 1837 [114]

Johnson, Nathaniel, subj. of G.B.; rec. by William K. Stafford - 8 Nov. 1837 [115]

Jochum, Michael, subj. of King of Wuertemberg; rec. by Michael Schwartz - 6 Nov. 1837 [116]

Joyce, Patrick, subj. of G.B.; rec. by Garret Byrne - 7 Nov. 1837 [117]

Jurden, Sian, subj. of G.B.; rec. by James Vincent - 8 Nov. 1837 [118]

Johnston, Charles, subj. of G.B.; rec. by Michael McDermott - 8 Nov. 1837 [119]

Jackson, Henry, subj. of G.B.; rec. by Charles Q. Lantry - 8 Nov. 1837 [120]

Johnston, Robert, subj. of G.B.; rec. by David Evans, councillor-at-law - 11 Dec. 1837 [121]

Inch, Nathaniel, subj. of G.B.; rec. by Anthony Kelly - 13 Apr. 1837 [122]

Ingram, William, subj. of G.B.; rec. by Bernard Garland - 8 Nov. 1837 [123]

Kerigan, Dennis, subj. of G.B.; rec. by Daniel Gilmartin - 11 Apr. 1837 [124]

Kammey, Francis, subj. of G.B.; rec. by Michael Harding - 12 Apr. 1837 [125]

Kern, Friedrich, subj. of King of Wuertemberg; rec. by William A. Vultee - 12 Apr. 1837 [126]

Keiley, James, subj. of G.B.; rec. by Jotham Peabody - 12 Apr. 1837 [127]

Keenan, Michael, subj. of G.B.; rec. by Bridget Keenan - 12 Apr. 1837 [128]

Kellehor, William, subj. of G.B.; rec. by James Handlon - 12 Apr. 1837 [129]

Keating, Stephen, subj. of G.B.; rec. by Timothy Quill - 12 Apr. 1837 [130]

Kiernan, Michael, subj. of G.B.; rec. by Patrick Clark - 13 Apr. 1837 [131]

Kocher, Laurent, subj. of France; rec. by John Collyers - 13 Apr. 1837 [132]

Kiely, John, subj. of G.B.; rec. by James Black - 13 Apr. 1837 [133]

Kyle, James, subj. of G.B.; rec. by James Porter - 13 Apr. 1837 [134]

Kenny, Patrick, subj. of G.B.; rec. by Dennis Scally - 13 Apr. 1837 [135]

Keenan, Michael, subj. of G.B.; rec. by John Becker - 13 Apr. 1837 [136]

Kelly, Jeremiah, subj. of G.B.; rec. by William Culbert - 13 Apr. 1837 [137]

Keogan, Philip, subj. of G.B.; rec. by James Keogan - 13 Apr. 1837 [138]

Kelly, Patrick, subj. of G.B.; rec. by John Cain - 13 Apr. 1837 [139]

Keating, Thomas, subj. of G.B.; rec. by William Dargan - 13 Apr. 1837 [140]

Kemp, James, subj. of G.B.; rec. by James Wilson - 6 June 1837 [141]

Kiefer, Lorrenz, subj. of Grand Duke of Baden; rec. by Mathäus Knoell - 6 Nov. 1837 [142]

Kearney, Felix, subj. of G.B.; rec. by Patrick McManus - 6 Nov. 1837 [143]

Knodel, Johann George, subject of Grand Duke of Baden; rec. by Carl Klauberg - 6 Nov. 1837 [144]

Kennedy, Francis, subj. of G.B.; rec. by Mary Kennedy - 7 Nov. 1837 [145]

Cain/Kain, Peter, subj. of G.B.; rec. by James Cain - 7 Nov. 1837 [146]

Kerrigan, Michael, subj. of G.B.; rec. by Alexander Leslie - 7 Nov. 1837 [147]

Keating, Thomas, subj. of G.B.; rec. by Thomas Weir - 7 Nov. 1837 [148]

Kerby, Nicholas, subj. of G.B.; rec. by John Galran - 7 Nov. 1837 [149]

Kinlan, Henry, subj. of G.B.; rec. by Hugh Kinlin - 7 Nov. 1837 [150]

Keller, Martin, subj. of Duke of Hesse Darmstadt; rec. by Jacob Bullmer - 7 Nov. 1837 [151]

Koerber, Johann Ludwig, subj. of King of Saxony; rec. by Heinrich Renner - 7 Nov. 1837 [152]

Klein, Jacob, subj. of King of France; rec. by John Mattern - 7 Nov. 1837 [153]

Kelly, Charles, subj. of G.B.; rec. by Terrence Carroll - 7 Nov. 1837 [154]

Kert, John E., subj. of Grand Duke of Baden; rec. by Joseph Eberhart - 7 Nov. 1837 [155]

Kerr, James, subj. of G.B.; rec. by John Fitch - 8 Nov. 1837 [156]

Cavenagh, Philip, subj. of G.B.; rec. by Charles H. Corbb - 8 Nov. 1837 [157]

Kennon, John, for his son, John Kennon, Jr., subj. of G.B.; rec. by John Bennet - 8 Nov. 1837 [158]

Kiernan, Robert, subj. of G.B.; rec. by Archibald Lamont - 8 Nov. 1837 [159]

Keeler, Timothy, subj. of G.B.; rec. by James Roach - 8 Nov. 1837 [160]

Bundle 13

Lynch, John, subj. of G.B.; rec. by Robert Clark - 11 Apr. 1837 [1]

Little, Robert, subj. of G.B.; rec. by Morgan Kennedy - 12 Apr. 1837 [2]

Liddel, Thomas, subj. of G.B.; rec. by Thomas Smith - 12 Apr. 1837 [3]

Leah, Patrick, subj. of G.B.; rec. by James Handlen - 13 Apr. 1837 [4]

Leper, William, subj. of G.B.; rec. by Patrick Bagan - 13 Apr. 1837 [5]

Lithgone, James, subj. of G.B.; rec. by Daniel McGloin - 13 Apr. 1837 [6]

Lockwood, Thomas S., subj. of G.B.;rec. by Crispen Taylor - 13 Apr. 1837 [7]

Lantry, Thomas, subj. of G.B.; rec. by James Smith - 13 Apr. 1837 [8]

Lonigan/Lonagan, Patrick, subj. of G.B.; rec. by John Dickinson - 13 Apr. 1837 [9]

Leary, Michael, subj. of G.B.; rec. by James Handlen - 13 Apr. 1837 [10]

Leary, Patrick, subj. of G.B.; rec. by James Handlen - 13 Apr. 1837 [11]

Laughlen, Peter, subj. of G.B.; rec. by Charles Judge - 13 Apr. 1837 [12]

Lynch, Patrick, subj. of G.B.; rec. by James Black - 13 Apr. 1837 [13]

Lloyd, Mary B. (wife of Paul B. Lloyd), subj. of G.B.; rec. by Nicholas Moran - 23 June 1837 [14]

Luxton, George, subj. of G.B.; rec. by James McGuire - 6 Nov. 1837 [15]

Layland, William, subj. of G.B.; rec. by Joseph Rose, Jr. - 6 Nov. 1837 [16]

Larney, Michael, subj. of G.B.; rec. by James Handlen - 6 Nov. 1837 [17]

Lehanke, Joseph, subj. of Grand Duke of Baden; rec. by Peter Schleper - 6 Nov. 1837 [18]

Luetz, Stephen, subj. of King of Wuertenberg; rec. by Ludwig Schtissele - 7 Nov. 1837 [19]

Languishe, William, subj. of G.B., born Co. of Tipperary, Ire., in 1833, at age of 30, migrated from Waterford to settle in Albany; rec. by John McCarty - 7 Nov. 1837 [20]

Langen, James, subj. of G.B.; rec. by Edward Langen - 7 Nov. 1837 [21]

Landy, John, subj. of G.B.; rec. by James Black - 7 Nov. 1837 [22]

Lynam, Patrick, subj. of G.B.; rec. by James Black - 7 Nov. 1837 [23]

Love, Thomas, subj. of G.B.; rec. by Thomas Bell - 7 Nov. 1837 [24]

Lang, Michael, subj. of King of France; rec. by Godfrey Hahn - 8 Nov. 1837 [25]

Lutz, Johannes, subj. of King of France; rec. by Peter Lutz - 8 Nov. 1837 [26]

Lynch, John, subj. of G.B.; rec. by Hugh Drummond - 8 Nov. 1837 [27]

Ludwig, Philip, subj. of King of Bavaria; rec. by Andreas Weis - 8 Nov. 1837 [28]

Long, Nathaniel (who in 1837 had resided 29 years in NYC), subj. of G.B.; rec. by Alexander Robb and Joseph Kerr - 8 Nov. 1837 [29]

Langan, Thomas, subj. of G.B.; rec. by Daniel Rooney - 8 Nov. 1837 [30]

Ball, Philip, subj. of King of Bavaria; rec. by Philip Ludwig - 8 Nov. 1837 [31]

Lancaster, James, subj. of G.B.; rec. by Richard Cornwall - 8 Nov. 1837 [32]

Longue/Lonague, Thomas, subj. of G.B.; rec. by James Handlen - 8 Nov. 1837 [33]

Lynch, Hugh, subj. of G.B.; rec. by Hugh McGilligan - 7 Nov. 1837 [34]

McDonald, Richard, subj. of G.B.; rec. by Robert Clark - 11 Apr. 1837 [35]

McDermott, Thomas, subj. of G.B.; rec. by Hampton Moore - 12 Apr. 1837 [36]

McMillan, James, subj. of G.B.; rec. by John Orser - 12 Apr. 1837 [37]

McMillan, William, subj. of G.B.; rec. by John Orser - 12 Apr. 1837 [38]

McLaughlin, Arthur, subj. of G.B.; rec. by Peter Byrne - 12 Apr. 1837 [39]

McCormick, Patrick, subj. of G.B.; rec. by John McCauly - 12 Apr. 1837 [40]

McCarthy, Daniel, subj. of G.B.; rec. by James Handlen - 12 Apr. 1837 [41]

McCabe, Patrick, subj. of G.B.; rec. by James McCabe - 12 Apr. 1837 [42]

McGill, Dennis, subj. of G.B.; rec. by Hugh Clinton - 13 Apr. 1837 [43]

McCullough, Patrick, subj. of G.B.; rec. by Hugh Riley - 13 Apr. 1837 [44]

McMahon, William, subj. of G.B.; rec. by Joseph Swift - 13 Apr. 1837 [45]

McIntyre, Owen, subj. of G.B.; rec. by Catharine Kiernan - 13 Apr. 1837 [46]

O'Brien, Daniel, subj. of G.B.; rec. by Morgan Kennedy - 11 Apr. 1837 [47]

O'Reilly, Edward, subj. of G.B.; rec. by Thomas Gilfeather - 12 Apr. 1837 [48]

O'Connor, James, subj. of G.B.; rec. by James Carter - 12 Apr. 1837 [49]

O'Brien, Thomas, subj. of G.B.; rec. by Cornelius Driscoll - 13 Apr. 1837 [50]

O'Brian, Michael, subj. of G.B.; rec. by Michael Cowly - 13
Apr. 1837 [51]

Oughten, Robert, subj. of G.B.; report 16 Dec. 1826: born Eng.,
age 37, carpenter, migrated from Liverpool; wife Sarah, born
Eng., age 38; dau. Faith, born Eng., age 11; rec. by Joseph
Husson - 13 Apr. 1837 [52]

O'Heron/O'Heren, William, subj. of G.B.; rec. by James Black -
13 Apr. 1837 [53]

O'Rourke, James Francis, subj. of G.B.; rec. by Frederick H.B.
Bryan - 23 May 1837 [54]

O'Connor, Eliza W., subj. of G.B.; rec. by Eliza W. Moran - 4
Aug. 1837 [55]

Oertle, Louis, subj. of Grand Duke of Baden, born Baden 9 Aug.
1805, arrived NYC 1 Sept. 1831 with intent to settle in Pa.;
rec. by Francis Oertle - 6 Nov. 1837 [56]

O'Donnell, Robert, subj. of G.B.; rec. by John Purcell - 6 Nov.
1837 [57]

Offen, Abraham, subj. of G.B.; rec. by Benjamin Offen - 6 Nov.
1837 [58]

O'Neill, James, subj. of G.B.; rec. by Francis Murphy - 7 Nov.
1837 [59]

Oberlaender, Heinrich, subj. of Grand Duke of Baden; rec. by
Ludwig Orth - 7 Nov. 1837 [60]

O'Connor, John, subj. of G.B.; rec. by John Brown - 8 Nov. 1837
[61]

O'Neill, Francis, subj. of G.B.; rec. by William Tysch - 8 Nov.
1837 [62]

O'Dunn, Edward, subj. of G.B.; rec. by Daniel Primrose - 8 Nov.
1837 [63]

Norris, William Richard, subj. of G.B.; rec. by Stephen Norris
- 11 Apr. 1837 [64]

Neale, Charles, subj. of G.B.; rec. by James Satchell - 12 Apr.
1837 [65]

Newby, Samuel, subj. of G.B.; rec. by James M. Lowndes - 12 Apr.
1837 [66]

Nuttall, John, subj. of G.B.; rec. by John W. Thorpe - 12 Apr.
1837 [67]

Nevil, Michael, subj. of G.B.; rec. by William Boyce - 13 Apr.
1837 [68]

Nowlan, John, subj. of G.B.; rec. by Owen Dennen - 8 Nov. 1837
[69]

Nichols, James, subj. of G.B.; rec. by Patrick Burke - 8 Nov.
1837 [70]

Neary, Michael, subj. of G.B.; rec. by John Couron - 8 Nov.
1837 [71]

McBride, Patrick, subj. of G.B.; rec. by James McBride - 13
Apr. 1837 [72]

McCormick, Michael, subj. of G.B.; rec. by Walter Fornan/Farnan
- 13 Apr. 1837 [73]

McLaughlin, Henry, subj. of G.B.; rec. by Thomas McCann - 13
Apr. 1837 [74]

McConnell, Edward, subj. of G.B.; rec. by Carmack Rafferty - 13
Apr. 1837 [75]

McCarty, Michael, laborer, subj. of G.B.; rec. by Bartley Coggan - 13 Apr. 1837 [76]

McSweeny, John, subj. of G.B.; rec. by William Denman - 13 Apr.
1837 [77]

McGowan, Matthew, subj. of G.B.; rec. by Patrick Burk - 13 Apr.
1837 [78]

McGuire, Bernard/Barney, subj. of G.B.; rec. by Matthias McGuire
- 13 Apr. 1837 [79]

McCann, Patrick, subj. of G.B.; rec. by Henry J. Butler - 13
Apr. 1837 [80]

McCutchin, Robert, subj. of G.B.; rec. by John Dickinson - 13
Apr. 1837 [81]

McBride, James, subj. of G.B.; rec. by Patrick McBride - 13 Apr.
1837 [82]

McCarthy, John, subj. of G.B.; rec. by James Handlon - 13 Apr.
1837 [83]

McCartney, John, subj. of G.B.; rec. by James Handlon - 13 Apr.
1837 [84]

McGuire, Matthias, subj. of G.B.; rec. by Bernard McGuire - 13
Apr. 1837 [85]

McMahon, James, subj. of G.B.; rec. by James McBride - 13 Apr.
1837 [86]

McCrum, Alexander, subj. of G.B.; rec. by William Green - 13
Apr. 1837 [87]

McCue, Patrick, subj. of G.B.; rec. by Edward Leonard - 6 Nov.
1837 [88]

McBride, Andrew, subj. of G.B.; rec. by John Moss - 6 Nov. 1837
[89]

McCall, William, subj. of G.B.; rec. by John Daly - 6 Nov. 1837
[90]

McKay, John, subj. of G.B.; rec. by Henry D.A. Metzendorf - 7
Nov. 1837 [91]

McGowan, Francis, subj. of G.B.; rec. by Patrick Minch - 7 Nov.
1837 [92]

McManus, Patrick, subj. of G.B.; rec. by James Foley - 7 Nov.
1837 [93]

McElroy, Charles, subj. of G.B.; rec. by Daniel Connaly - 7 Nov.
1837 [94]

McGinley, Dennis, subj. of G.B.; rec. by James Hunter - 7 Nov.
1837 [95]

McLaughlin, John, subj. of G.B.; rec. by Daniel Primrose - 7
Nov. 1837 [96]

McGiven, Arthur, subj. of G.B.; rec. by Patrick Clark - 7 Nov.
1837 [97]

McWilliams, David, subj. of G.B.; rec. by Joseph Stevens - 7
Nov. 1837 [98]

McCoy, Terrence, subj. of G.B.; rec. by Thomas McGuire - 7 Nov.
1837 [99]

McAlpin, Patrick, subj. of G.B.; rec. by William Driscoll - 7
Nov. 1837 [100]

McKeever, Patrick, subj. of G.B.; rec. by Edward Langan - 7 Nov.
1837 [101]

McQuirk, James, subj. of G.B.; rec. by Mark Smith - 8 Nov. 1837
[102]

McGuire, Martin, subj. of G.B.; rec. by Bartholomew O'Reilly -
8 Nov. 1837 [103]

McGinn, Daniel, subj. of G.B.; rec. by Terrence Carroll - 8
Nov. 1837 [104]

McKeever, Thomas, subj. of G.B.; rec. by James Rile - 8 Nov.
1837 [105]

McGarraty, John, subj. of G.B.; rec. by Patrick Clark - 8 Nov.
1837 [106]

McCormick, Joseph, subj. of G.B.; rec. by Richard Cornell - 8
Nov. 1837 [107]

McNally, John, subj. of G.B.; rec. by Patrick McLaughlin - 8
Nov. 1837 [108]

McKenna, Patrick, subj. of G.B.; rec. by Charles Clohen - 8 Nov.
1837 [109]

McIntyre, Richard, subj. of G.B.; rec. by Catherine Kiernan -
8 Nov. 1837 [110]

McLaughlin, Patrick, subj. of G.B.; rec. by Patrick Quin - 8
Nov. 1837 [111]

McCrystil, Patrick, subj. of G.B.; rec. by James Dorien - 8
Nov. 1837 [112]

McConkey, John, subj. of G.B.; rec. by Joseph Fowler - 8 Nov.
1837 [113]

McGrath, Lawrence, subj. of G.B.; rec. by Edward Sherlock - 8
Nov. 1837 [114]

McLaughlin, Patrick, subj. of G.B.; rec. by John McNalley - 8
Nov. 1837 [115]

McFall, Charles, subj. of G.B.; rec. by Owen Flood - 8 Nov.
1837 [116]

McKeon, Thomas, subj. of G.B.; rec. by Hugh McKeenan - 8 Nov.
1837 [117]

McNaughton, John, subj. of G.B.; rec. by William Thomas - 8
Nov. 1837 [118]

Power, John, shoemaker, subj. of G.B. - 13 Oct. 1835 [119]

Polack, William L., dry goods dealer, subj. of King of Holland
- 8 June 1835 [120]

Moran, John, subj. of G.B.; rec. by Thomas Miehan - 8 Nov. 1837
[121]

Murtagh, Robert, subj. of G.B.; rec. by Michael Cowhy - 7 Nov.
1837 [122]

Meehan, Francis, subj. of G.B.; rec. by James Ramsay - 8 Nov.
1837 [123]

Magraw, Terrence, subj. of G.B.; rec. by John Skinner - 8 Nov.
1837 [124]

Murtfeldt, William, subj. of King of Hanover; rec. by Johann
Valentin Bormeth, of 105 Ludlow St. - 8 Nov. 1837 [125]

Mangin, James, subj. of G.B.; rec. by John McCarthy - 8 Nov. 1837 [126]

Megt, Anthony, subj. of King of France; rec. by Peter Vetter - 8 Nov. 1837 [127]

Moubrey, Thomas, subj. of G.B.; rec. by John Moubrey - 8 Nov. 1837 [128]

Mallock, John, subj. of G.B.; rec. by Alexander Gray - 8 Nov. 1837 [129]

Marfilius, Wilhelm, subj. of King of Bavaria; rec. by Wenzel Schrimpft - 8 Nov. 1837 [130]

Moran, Laurens, subj. of G.B.; rec. by Thomas Doyle - 8 Nov. 1837 [131]

Mangan, James, subj. of G.B.; rec. by John Galvan - 8 Nov. 1837 [132]

Mueller, Arthur, subj. of King of Bavaria; rec. by Valentin Keeler - 8 Nov. 1837 [133]

McGuire, Michael, subj. of G.B.; rec. by Bernard McGuire - 8 Nov. 1837 [134]

Murphy, Michael, subj. of G.B.; rec. by Richard Murphy - 8 Nov. 1837 [135]

Maxwell, Thomas, subj. of G.B.; rec. by Edward Sherlock - 8 Nov. 1837 [136]

Meehan, John, subj. of G.B.; rec. by Thomas Meehan - 8 Nov. 1837 [137]

Martin, Patrick, subj. of G.B.; rec. by Patrick Regan - 8 Nov. 1837 [138]

Moore, George, subj. of G.B.; rec. by James H. Connor - 8 Nov. 1837 [139]

Mahony, Dennis, subj. of G.B.; rec. by Francis Edward Power - 11 Apr. 1837 [140]

Marky/Markay, Patrick, subj. of G.B.; rec. by Patrick Burk - 12 Apr. 1837 [141]

Murphy, Dennis, subj. of G.B.; rec. by William Swift - 12 Apr. 1837 [142]

Moss, Thomas, subj. of G.B.; rec. by Owen Healy - 12 Apr. 1837 [143]

Mulhollands, Hugh, subj. of G.B.; rec. by James Black - 13 Apr. 1837 [144]

Murphy, Thomas, subj. of G.B.; rec. by James Handlen - 13 Apr. 1837 [145]

McGuire, Hugh, subj. of G.B.; rec. by John Macklin - 13 Apr. 1837 [146]

Mullen, Michael, subj. of G.B.; rec. by John H. Burly - 13 Apr. 1837 [147]

Miller, Jacob, subj. of King of France; rec. by Friedrich Kneshin - 13 Apr. 1837 [148]

Morrison, Nicholas, subj. of G.B.; rec. by William Culbert - 13 Apr. 1837 [149]

Morrison, Thomas, subj. of G.B.; rec. by Joseph Morrison - 7 Nov. 1837 [150]

Moran, Eliza Winifred, subj. of G.B.; rec. by Mary B. Lloyd - 23 June 1837 [151]

Mairet, Henri, merchant, subj. of Republic of Switzerland; rec. by Charles Edwards, counsellor-at-law - 8 Aug. 1837 [152]

Mahoney, Patrick, subj. of G.B.; rec. by William Johnson - 8 Nov. 1837 [153]

Meighan, Francis, subj. of G.B.; rec. by George Greiff - 6 Nov. 1837 [154]

Metzer, Michael, subj. of King of Bavaria; rec. by Xavier Beschert [or Boschert?] - 6 Nov. 1837 [155]

Metzendorff, Henry D.A., subj. of Republic of Hamburg; rec. by Teunis Fokker - 6 Nov. 1837 [155A]

Moser/Mosler, Elias, subj. of Berne, Switzerland; rec. by John A. Miller - 6 Nov. 1837 [156]

Manz, Michel, subj. of Grand Duke of Baden; rec. by Lorenz Fruch - 6 Nov. 1837 [157]

Mostler, John Christian, subj. of King of Prussia; rec. by Carl Klauberg - 6 Nov. 1837 [158]

Monsies, Herman William, subj. of City of Bremen; rec. by John Bromberger - 6 Nov. 1837 [159]

Morgan, George, subj. of G.B.; rec. by James C. Cook - 7 Nov. 1837 [160]

Michael, Jacob, subj. of King of France; rec. by George Buchholz - 7 Nov. 1837 [161]

Martin, Michel, subj. of G.B.; rec. by Edward Finegan - 7 Nov. 1837 [162]

Moore, William, subj. of G.B.; rec. by George Moore - 7 Nov. 1837 [163]

Mattern, John, subj. of King of France; rec. by Jacob Klein - 7 Nov. 1837 [164]

Mitchell, Charles, subj. of G.B.; rec. by Daniel McLaughlin - 7 Nov. 1837 [165]

Murray, James, subj. of G.B.; rec. by John Flood - 7 Nov. 1837 [166]

Mulligan, Bernard, subj. of G.B.; rec. by Gabriel Dissosnay - 7 Nov. 1837 [167]

Mahony, Peter, subj. of G.B.; rec. by Denis O'Brien - 7 Nov. 1837 [168]

Maas, Peter, subj. of King of Bavaria; rec. by Jacob Stock - 7 Nov. 1837 [169]

Peel, John A., subj. of City of Bremen; rec. by Aaron Shepard - 8 Nov. 1837 [170]

Parfitt, Charles, subj. of G.B.; rec. by Hugh Reilly - 8 Nov. 1837 [171]

Pickett, Patrick, of Stamford, Conn., wire-thrower, subj. of G.B.; rec. by Edward Foley - 8 Nov. 1837 [172]

Petry, Johann Michael, subj. of Grand Duke of Baden; rec. by William A. Vultee - 8 Nov. 1837 [173]

Plummer, Joseph, subj. of G.B.; rec. by William Hatfield - 8 Nov. 1837 [174]

Pflukus [clerk wrote "Pfeiffer"], Friedrich; rec. by Winndelin Koch [clerk wrote "Caack"] - 8 Nov. 1837 [175]

Purcell, John, subj. of G.B.; rec. by Thomas O'Brien - 6 Nov. 1837 [176]

Pfeifer, George, subj. of Prince of Hesse Cassel; rec. by Heinrich Weimar - 6 Nov. 1837 [177]

Plunket, Oliver, subj. of G.B.; rec. by Peter Riley - 6 Nov. 1837 [178]

Pettigrew, James, subj. of G.B.; rec. by John Pettigrew - 13 Apr. 1837 [179]

Pickett, Thomas, subj. of G.B.; rec. by William Culbert - 13 Apr. 1837 [180]

Powers, Pierre, subj. of G.B.; rec. by James Handlen - 13 Apr. 1837 [181]

Pendan, Nicholas, subj. of G.B.; rec. by Walter Lambert - 13 Apr. 1837 [182]

Peterson, Robert, subj. of G.B.; rec. by Charles Colladay - 12 Apr. 1837 [183]

Patton, John, subj. of G.B.; rec. by Robert Patton - 12 Apr. 1837 [184]

Patton, Robert, subj. of G.B.; rec. by John Patton - 12 Apr. 1837 [185]

Pinheiro, Joaquim, subj. of Queen of Portugal; rec. by Daniel R. Franklin - 11 Apr. 1837 [186]

Paul, Michael, native of Saverne, France, subj. of King of France; rec. by George Volt - 1 Apr. 1837 [187]

Polo, Casimiro, subj. of Queen of Spain - 13 Dec. 1837 [188]

Pelham, Jabez Clinton, subj. of G.B. - 20 July 1837 [188A]

Pollak, Simon, physician, subj. of Emperor of Austria - 29 Nov. 1837 [189]

Potts, William I., of village of Brooklyn, subj. of G.B. - 8 Nov. 1837 [189A]

Bundle 14

Reed, Joseph, subj. of King of Naples; rec. by Richard Baker - 11 Apr. 1837 [1]

Riley, John, subj. of G.B.; rec. by William McDevet - 12 Apr. 1837 [2]

Regan, Thomas, subj. of G.B.; rec. by Daniel Harigan - 12 Apr. 1837 [3]

Ryan, Richard, subj. of G.B.; rec. by James Handlon - 12 Apr. 1837 [4]

Reilly, Joseph, subj. of G.B.; rec. by Owen Healy - 12 Apr. 1837 [5]

Reilly, Thomas, subj. of G.B.; rec. by John Reilly - 12 Apr. 1837 [6]

Reed, Joseph, subj. of G.B.; rec. by Michael Dermott - 12 Apr. 1837 [7]

Rosselot, Peter A., subj. of King of France; rec. by Joseph Baley - 13 Apr. 1837 [8]

Rock, James, subj. of G.B.; rec. by William Culbert - 13 Apr. 1837 [9]

Rock, Michael, subj. of G.B.; rec. by William Culbert - 13 Apr. 1837 [10]

Reynolds, William, subj. of G.B.; rec. by James Reynolds - 13 Apr. 1837 [11]

Rafferty, Patrick, subj. of G.B.; rec. by Peter Hughes - 13 Apr. 1837 [12]

Rose, Henry, subj. of G.B.; rec. by Friederich Reichle - 13 Apr. 1837 [13]

Rooney, Patrick, subj. of G.B.; rec. by Daniel Rooney - 13 Apr. 1837 [14]

Rollwagen, Philippe, subj. of King of France; rec. by C. Louis Meyer - 15 May 1837 [15]

Robinson, John, subj. of G.B.; rec. by Joseph G. Robinson - 1 Oct. 1837 [16]

Richl, Peter, subj. of King of France; rec. by Peter Britz - 6 Nov. 1837 [17]

Rohr, Augustus William, subj. of Republic of Hamburg; rec. by Teunis Fokker - 6 Nov. 1837 [18]

Reel, Andrew, subj. of G.B.; rec. by James Rhatigan - 6 Nov. 1837 [19]

Rigney, Michael, subj. of G.B.; rec. by Patrick Lanthrey - 7 Nov. 1837 [20]

Renner, Henry, subj. of Grand Duke of Baden; rec. by Johannes Ludwig Roerber - 7 Nov. 1837 [21]

Robert, Henrich, subj. of King of Prussia; rec. by Johann Besser - 7 Nov. 1837 [22]

Ruhl, Charles, subj. of King of France; rec. by Karl Weinstein - 7 Nov. 1837 [23]

Rapp, Matthias, subj. of Emperor of Austria; rec. by Matthias Knoell - 7 Nov. 1837 [24]

Reeve, Thomas, subj. of G.B.; rec. by Isaac Wilson - 7 Nov. 1837 [25]

Reiley, James, subj. of G.B.; rec. by Edward Binns - 7 Nov. 1837 [26]

Rinn, Francis, subj. of G.B; rec. by John P. Baddy - 7 Nov. 1837 [27]

Ryan, Thomas, subj. of G.B.; rec. by Michael Berningham - 8 Nov. 1837 [28]

Reilly, Patrick, subj. of G.B.; rec. by John Huys - 8 Nov. 1837 [29]

Roach, James, subj. of G.B.; rec. by Timothy Keeler 8 Nov. 1837 [30]

Riley, Philip, subj. of G.B.; rec. by Edward Reily - 8 Nov. 1837 [31]

Rendell, Abraham, subj. of G.B.; rec. by Richard Cornwall - 8 Nov. 1837 [32] - Note: Rendell was not a subject of G.B. but of Germany. He "left Germany 6 July 1832 on board the Edith Schoener, Captain Oakes, arrived in Havre de Grace on the 7th. Left Havre July 19th at 2 P.M., arrived at Staten Island Sunday morn Aug. 25, '32 at 7 o'clock A.M., discharged from quarantine grounds Wed. 29, and came in a lighter up to N. York."

Raide, Anthony, subj. of King of Prussia; rec. by Berenthard Raide - 8 Nov. 1837 [33]

Real, Levy [clerk wrote "Lewis" and so did Real later], subj. of King of France; rec. by Andreas Schilling - 8 Nov. 1837 [34]

Reinhard, John, subj. of King of France; rec. by Bernard Geiler - 8 Nov. 1837 [35]

Renet, Hypolite, subj. of King of France; rec. by Joseph Campbell - 8 Nov. 1837 [36]

Reis, Joseph, subj. of King of Bavaria; rec. by Lorenz Wahl - 8 Nov. 1837 [37]

Reis, Andreas, subj. of King of Bavaria; rec. by Philipp Ludwig - 8 Nov. 1837 [38]

Rourke, Patrick, subj. of G.B.; rec. by James Black - 8 Nov. 1837 [39]

Reilly, Andrew, subj. of G.B.; rec. by Patrick Ellis - 8 Nov. 1837 [40]

Riely, Patrick, subj. of G.B.; rec. by Mathew Armstrong - 9 Nov. 1837 [41]

Welsh, Richard, subj. of G.B.; rec. by James Handlan - 12 Apr. 1837 [42]

Wuerth, Christian, subj. of King of Wuertemberg; rec. by Xavier Steinwenter - 12 Apr. 1837 [43]

Wardlow, James, subj. of G.B.; rec. by Alexander Forbes - 12 Apr. 1837 [44]

White, James, subj. of G.B.; rec. by Francis White - 13 Apr. 1837 [45]

Wheaton, Michael, subj. of G.B.; rec. by Dennis Whelan - 13 Apr. 1837 [46] - Note: State of Pa., Lehigh Co., Nov. '29: Michael Wheaton born in barony of Fulla [?] in the co. of Clan [for Clare?] Ireland on Aug. - 1806, and now, at age of 25 yrs. emigr. fr. Ireland June 18, 1826, landed N.Y. Aug.; intent to settle in Silver Lake, Susquehanna Co., Pa."

Westall [double l crossed out by clerk], William, subj. of G.B.; rec. by Benjamin Owen - 13 Apr. 1837 [47]

Woore, Thomas, subj. of G.B.; rec. by Thomas Yates - 13 Apr. 1837 [48]

Wicks, John, subj. of G.B.; rec. by Elizabeth Wicks - 13 Apr. 1837 [49]

Wenham, Thomas Smith, of Brooklyn, subj. of G.B.; rec. by James Teiss - 10 June 1837 [50]

Wightman, Charles, subj. of G.B.; rec. by John Hagan - 6 Nov. 1837 [51]

Werner, Philip, subj. of Grand Duke of Baden; rec. by Carl Klauberg - 6 Nov. 1837 [52]

Weisman, Augustus, subj. of King of Wuertemberg; rec. by Joseph Bayer - 6 Nov. 1837 [53]

Weimar, Heinrich, subj. of Prince of Hesse Cassel; rec. by Peter Schlosser - 6 Nov. 1837 [54]

Wagner, John, subj. of King of Bavaria; rec. by Joseph Ramé - 7 Nov. 1837 [55]

Walter, Christopher Friederich, subj. of King of Wuertemberg; rec. by William A. Vultee - 7 Nov. 1837 [56]

Wode, George L., subj. of King of Hanover; rec. by George Sonne - 7 Nov. 1837 [57]

Walter, Michel, subj. of King of France; rec. by Joseph Trier - 1 Nov. 1837 [58]

Whitehead, George, subj. of G.B.; rec. by Richard Curtis - 7 Nov. 1837 [59]

Walsh, John, subj. of G.B.; rec. by Patrick Mangan - 7 Nov. 1837 [60]

Weldon, John, subj. of G.B.; rec. by James Black - 7 Nov. 1837 [61]

Weibens, Frederick, subj. of City of Bremen; rec. by Peter Heney - 8 Nov. 1837 [62]

Walton, John, subj. of G.B.; rec. by William Adamson - 8 Nov. 1837 [63]

Wood, John, subj. of G.B.; rec. by Hiram F. Frost - 8 Nov. 1837 [64]

Witte, Friederick, subj. of King of Hanover; rec. by Diederick Buliene - 8 Nov. 1837 [65]

Wharty, Bernard, subj. of G.B.; rec. by James Black - 8 Nov. 1837 [66]

Welch, Christopher, subj. of G.B.; rec. by Joseph Towill - 7 Nov. 1837 [67]

Woods, Thomas, subj. of G.B.; rec. by Michael McKenny - 8 Nov. 1837 [68]

Walker, Henry, labourer, according to decl. of intent 30 July 1827 born Ire., age 38, migrated from Dublin; rec. by Michael Conway - 8 Nov. 1837 [69]

Quigg, Edward, subj. of G.B.; rec. by John H. Burley - 7 Nov. 1837 [70]

Quill, Timothy, subj. of G.B.; rec. by Stephen Keating - 12 Apr. 1837 [71]

Quin, Thomas, subj. of G.B.; rec. by Michael Birmingham - 13 Apr. 1837 [72]

Quinlan, Denis, subj. of G.B.; rec. by Patrick McBaron - 7 Nov. 1837 [73]

Vogt, Heinrich, subj. of Prince of Hesse Cassell; rec. by Charles Hoddes - 8 Nov. 1837 [74]

Vanstan, John, subj. of G.B.; rec. by John McCarthy - 7 Nov. 1837 [75]

Travers, John, subj. of G.B.; rec. by John O'Brien - 13 Apr. 1837 [76]

Ternan, Arthur, subj. of G.B.; rec. by Patrick Conlan - 12 Apr. 1837 [77]

Toyle, James, subj. of G.B.; rec. by John Gallagher - 12 Apr. 1837 [78]

Taylor, Crispin, subj. of G.B.; rec. by Thomas S. Lockwood - 13 Apr. 1837 [79]

Tevlin, James, subj. of G.B.; rec. by James Dolan - 13 Apr. 1837 [80]

Toole, Michael, subj. of G.B.; rec. by William Toole - 6 Nov. 1837 [81]

Toole, William, subj. of G.B.; rec. by Michael Toole - 6 Nov. 1837 [82]

Trier, Joseph, subj. of King of France; rec. by Michael Walter - 7 Nov. 1837 [83]

Thompson, James, subj. of G.B.; rec. by John Salmon - 8 Nov. 1837 [84]

Timony, Daniel, subj. of G.B.; rec. by Joseph Kieler - 8 Nov. 1837 [85]

Taylor, William, subj. of G.B.; rec. by James Grant - 8 Nov. 1837 [86]

Tief, William, subj. of G.B.; rec. by Daniel Primrose - 8 Nov. 1837 [87]

Thompson, Henry, subj. of G.B.; rec. by Edward Seymour - 8 Nov. 1837 [88]

Turner, William, subj. of G.B.; rec. by Stephen Harris - 8 Nov. 1837 [89]

Tremayne, Edward, subj. of G.B.; rec. by George Ackerly - 8 Nov. 1837 [90]

Smith, Thomas, subj. of G.B.; rec. by Daniel Primrose - 8 Nov. 1837 [91]

Shloser, Nicholas, subj. of King of France; rec. by Patrick Barron - 12 Apr. 1837 [92]

Smith, Thomas, subj. of G.B.; rec. by Thomas Liddell - 12 Apr. 1837 [93]

Sheridan, James, subj. of G.B.; rec. by Charles Keanney - 12 Apr. 1837 [94]

Scott, Andrew, subj. of G.B.; rec. by John Miller - 13 Apr. 1837

Scholtenburg, Leon A.C., subj. of King of Holland; rec. by Johan Henschel - 13 Apr. 1837 [96]

Sommer, Christoph, subj. of King of Wuertemberg; rec. by Wilhelm Maier 13 Apr. 1837 [97]

Schrimpf, Wenzel, subj. of Duke of Hesse Darmstadt; rec. by Wilhelm Marfilius - 8 Nov. 1837 [98]

Struckmann, Henry Christian, subj. of Prince of Schaumberg Lippe; rec. by Friedrich Witte - 8 Nov. 1837 [99]

Schnatterbeck, Sebastian, subj. of Grand Duke of Baden; rec. by Peter Gantry - 8 Nov. 1837 [100]

Segmueller, Nicholas, subj. of King of Bavaria; rec. by Wendelin Koch - 8 Nov. 1837 [101]

Seith, Michael, shoemaker, subj. of Grand Duke of Baden; rec. by Anthony H.L. Rahm/Rehm - 8 Nov. 1837 [102]

Schneider, Adam, subj. of King of Bavaria; rec. by Engelhardt Brisch - 1 Nov. 1837 [103]

Schurk, Balthazar, subj. of King of Bavaria; rec. by Philipp Ball - 8 Nov. 1837 [104]

Schwal/Schwab, Friedrich, subj. of King of Bavaria; rec. by Peter Britz - 8 Nov. 1837 [104A]

Sculley, Daniel, subj. of G.B.; rec. by Patrick Cashman - 8 Nov. 1837 [105]

Simons, James, subj. of G.B.; rec. by Patrick Simons - 8 Nov. 1837 [106]

Sweeney, John, subj. of G.B.; rec. by Hugh Smith - 8 Nov. 1837 [107]

Scanlan, Denis, subj. of G.B.; rec. by Hugh Hart - 8 Nov. 1837 [108]

Sweeny, Patrick, subj. of G.B.; rec. by Patrick Burke - 8 Nov. 1837 [109]

Sullivan, John, subj. of G.B.; rec. by James Bowen - 8 Nov. 1837 [110]

Sachsenheimer, George, subj. of King of Wuertemberg; rec. by Johan Bromberger - 6 Nov. 1837 [111]

Schmidt, Philip W., subj. of King of Prussia; rec. by James Fokkes - 6 Nov. 1837 [112]

Sende, Peter, subj. of King of Prussia; rec. by Henry Scully - 6 Nov. 1837 [113]

Schurck, Moris, subj. of King of France; rec. by William Schimper - 6 Nov. 1837 [114]

Stoltz, Peter, subj. of King of Bavaria; rec. by Lewis Willmuth - 6 Nov. 1837 [115]

Sackmeister, Bernard, subj. of King of Bavaria; rec. by Charles Francis Hetzel - 6 Nov. 1837 [116]

Siebert, Henry, subj. of King of Bavaria; rec. by Elias Moslar - 6 Nov. 1837 [117]

Smith, Patrick, subj. of G.B.; rec. by Bernard Smith - 16 Oct. 1837 [118]

Smith, Bernard, subj. of G.B.; rec. by Felix Brady - 16 Oct. 1837 [119]

Schaeffer, Alphonse, subj. of King of France; rec. by Louis Nessel - 21 Sept. 1837 [120]

Stokes, Thomas, of Cazenovia, Madison Co., N.Y., subj. of G.B.; rec. by William Stokes - 5 May 1837 [121]

Smith, Alexander, subj. of G.B.; rec. by James W. Sorley - 13 Apr. 1837 [122]

Stinson, William, subj. of G.B.; rec. by William Reilly - 13 Apr. 1837 [123]

Smith, William, subj. of G.B.; rec. by Jonathan Nash - 10 Apr. 1837 [124]

Smith, Thomas, weaver, subj. of G.B.; rec. by Charles Keanney - 12 Apr. 1837 [125]

Staff, James, subj. of G.B.; rec. by Robert Clark - 11 Apr. 1837 [126]

Sheridan, Michael, subj. of G.B.; rec. by Daniel Primrose - 8 - Nov. 1837 [127]

Sullivan, Daniel, subj. of G.B.; rec. by Patrick Lane - 8 Nov. 1837 [128]

Swan, William, subj. of G.B.; rec. by Abraham Clark - 8 Nov. 1837 [129]

Sopel, Michael, subj. of G.B.; rec. by Peter Kulles - 8 Nov. 1837 [130]

Steel, Allen, subj. of G.B.; rec. by Thomas Devlin - 8 Nov. 1837 [131]

Simpson, William, subj. of G.B.; rec. by James Simpson - 8 Nov. 1837 [132]

Salonen, Richard, subj. of G.B.; rec. by William Culbert - 7 Nov. 1837 [133]

Satchell, James, subj. of G.B.; rec. by Charles Neale - 7 Nov. 1837 [134]

Simpson, James, subj. of G.B.; rec. by William O'Driscoll - 7 Nov. 1837 [135]

Saghorn, Henry, subj. of King of Hanover; rec. by Teunis Fokkes - 13 Apr. 1837 [136]

Langsten, Archibald, C., Jr., subj. of G.B.; rec. by Joseph
    Hindes - 13 Apr. 1837 [137]

Smith, James, subj. of G.B.; rec. by Edward Fitzsimmons - 13
    Apr. 1837 [138]

Savage, Daniel, subj. of G.B.; rec. by James Handlen - 13 Apr.
    1837 [139]

Smith, Peter, subj. of G.B.; rec. by Thomas McDermott - 13 Apr.
    1837 [140]

Scheurmin, John, subj. of King of Bavaria; rec. by John Hens-
    chen - 13 Apr. 1837 [141]

Sullivan, Denis, subj. of G.B.; rec. by Archibald McClan Tre-
    bout - 13 Apr. 1837 [142]

Schipp, Konrad, subj. of Prince of Hesse Cassell; rec. by Peter
    Schlosser - 7 Nov. 1837 [143]

Strodthoff, Diedrich, subj. of King of Hanover; rec. by John
    Skinner - 7 Nov. 1837 [144]

Stoltz, Peter, subj. of King of Bavaria; rec. by Heiterich
    Kranz - 7 Nov. 1837 [145]

Siebert, John, subj. of King of France; rec. by Jacob Heschar -
    7 Nov. 1837 [146]

Spies, John, subj. of King of Holland; rec. by Bernard Geiler -
    7 Nov. 1837 [147]

Smith, Philip, subj. of G.B.; rec. by Jacob Haslan - 7 Nov.
    1837 [148]

Seymour, Edward, subj. of G.B.; rec. by Charles Wake - 7 Nov.
    1837 [149]

Schmidt, Johann Georg, subj. of King of Wuertemberg; rec. by
    Christian Zoller - 7 Nov. 1837 [150]

Smith, James, subj. of G.B.; rec. by Cornelius Smith - 7 Nov.
    1837 [151]

Smith, James, Jr., subj. of G.B.; rec. by Cornelius Smith - 7
    Nov. 1837 [152]

Bundle 15

Delluc, Francis, subj. of King of France; rec. by Bernard Gouil-
    lard - 8 Feb. 1838 [1]

Daly, Thomas, subj. of G.B.; rec. by Dennis McKiernan - 9 Apr.
    1838 [2]

Daenzler, Frederick, subj. of King of Saxony; rec. by John
    Gassner Daenzler - 10 Apr. 1837 [3]

Daffee, Niel, subj. of G.B.; rec. by William Swift - 11 Apr.
    1838 [4]

Donnelly, Michael, subj. of G.B.; rec. by Joseph Donigan - 10
    Apr. 1837 [5]

Dowd, John, subj. of G.B.; rec. by Francis Dowd - 10 Apr. 1838
    [6]

Donovan, Edward, subj. of G.B.; rec. by Denis O'Brien - 11 Apr.
    1837 [7]

Dare, Samuel, subj. of G.B.; rec. by Titus Webb - 11 Apr. 1837
    [8]

Dougherty, Cornelius, subj. of G.B.; rec. by William McCoy - 11
    Apr. 1837 [9]

Dodsworth, Timothy, subj. of G.B.; rec. by Thomas Ogden - 12 Apr. 1838 [10]

Devlin, Francis, subj. of G.B.; rec. by John Thacker - 12 Apr. 1838 [11]

Daly, James, subj. of G.B.; rec. by Samuel Beilby - 12 Apr. 1838 [12]

Ditter, Joseph, subj. of Grand Duke of Baden; rec. by Jacob Koch - 12 Apr. 1838 [13]

Dinnen, James, subj. of G.B.; rec. by James Black - 12 Apr. 1838 [14]

Davis, Evan Jones, subj. of G.B.; rec. by David Evans - 1 Aug. 1838 [15]

Dicks, Thomas, subj. of G.B.; rec. by John Dicks - 18 Oct. 1838 [16]

Dicks, John, subj. of G.B.; rec. by Thomas Dicks - 18 Oct. 1838 [17]

Deraismes, John Francis Joseph, subj. of King of France; rec. by Nathaniel S. Burt - 30 Oct. 1838 [18]

Dyson, John, subj. of G.B.; rec. by Thomas Tudor - 1 Nov. 1838 [19]

Duckers, Henry, subj. of G.B.; rec. by William E. French - 1 Nov. 1838 [20]

Dwyer, John, subj. of G.B.; rec. by Daniel Leary - 3 Nov. 1838 [21]

Dasey, Cornelius, subj. of G.B.; rec. by William Murphy - 3 Nov. 1838 [22]

Dwyer, James, subj. of G.B.; rec. by Henry Haddaway - 3 Nov. 1838 [23]

Drake, Charles, subj. of G.B.; rec. by Francis Drake - 5 Nov. 1838 [24]

Daley, Richard, mariner, subj. of G.B.; rec. by Joseph Spencer - 5 Nov. 1838 [25]

Denison, Joseph, subj. of G.B.; rec. by Charles T. Carlbaum - 7 Nov. 1838 [26]

Divine, Thomas, subj. of G.B.; rec. by Andrew Divine - 7 Nov. 1838 [27]

Dunbar, David M., subj. of G.B.; rec. by John Brown - 7 Nov. 1838 [27A]

Dockweiler, Peter, subj. of King of Bavaria; rec. by Johan Adam Haag - 7 Nov. 1838 [28]

Delaney, James, subj. of G.B.; rec. by Gideon Freeborn - 7 Nov. 1838 [29]

Duke, David, subj. of G.B.; rec. by Samuel Grier - 7 Nov. 1838 [30]

De Loynes, George, subj. of King of France; rec. by John A. Tardy - 7 Nov. 1838 [31]

Decker, John, subj. of Prince of Hesse Cassel; rec. by John McCollis - 6 Nov. 1838 [32]

Dalziel, James, subj. of G.B.; rec. by Charles Blondell - 6 Nov. 1838 [33]

Delauney, Pierre A., subj. of G.B.; rec. by Augustus Laurent - 6 Nov. 1838 [33A]

Dillon, John, subj. of G.B.; rec. by Jacob Gragg - 6 Nov. 1838 [34]

Deraismes, Hippolite, subj. of G.B.; rec. by John Colvill - 6 Nov. 1838 [35]

Donelson, George, subj. of G.B.; rec. by Thomas Moneypenny - 6 Nov. 1838 [36]

Auld, Samuel, subj. of G.B.; rec. by Adam Miller - 11 Apr. 1838 [37]

Andrae, Christoph, subj. of Prince of Hesse Cassel; rec. by Jacob Koch - 12 Apr. 1838 [38]

Aitkin, John, subj. of G.B.; rec. by John Crawford - 12 Apr. 1838 [39]

Anthony, Lucy, single woman, subj. of G.B.; rec. by John J. Anthony - 17 Oct. 1838 [40]

Atkins, Herbert, subj. of G.B.; rec. by Bryan Ward - 5 Nov. 1838 [41]

Alleyn, James, subj. of G.B.; rec. by John J. Herrick - 5 Nov. 1838 [41A]

Ash, John, subj. of G.B.; rec. by Matthew W. King - 5 Nov. 1838 [42]

Aitchson, Robert, subj. of G.B.; rec. by John Chisholm - 6 Nov. 1838 [43]

Abry, Auguste, Jr., importer of watches, subj. of King of France; rec. by Auguste Abry, Sr. - 6 Nov. 1838 [44]

Aylard, John, subj. of G.B.; rec. by Joseph W. Stent - 6 Nov. 1838 [45]

Alcorn, George, subj. of G.B.; rec. by Joseph Pugirma - 7 Nov. 1838 [46]

Anderson, Robert, subj. of G.B.; report 23 June 1825 in Marine Court: born Scotland, age 21 years and 10 months, migrated from Liverpool, merchant, resident of U.S. since 17 Sept. 1822; rec. by James Allen - 7 Nov. 1838 [47]

Ahrens, Frederick, subj. of King of Prussia; rec. by William Williams - 7 Nov. 1838 [48]

Ahrens, George M., subj. of President of Bremen; rec. by Nathan C. Platt - 7 Nov. 1838 [49]

Assler, Johan, subj. of King of Bavaria; rec. by Maschricot Deobald - 7 Nov. 1838 [50]

De Bussey, Thomas, of Newark, N.J., subj. of G.B.; rec. by John Marsland - 30 Jan. 1838 [51]

Blackstone, James, subj. of G.B.; rec. by Effingham H. Warner - 7 Feb. 1838 [52]

Buckham, Andrew, Jr., subj. of G.B.; rec. by Thomas S. Jaycox - 7 Apr. 1838 [53]

Brown, Andrew, subj. of G.B.; rec. by Joseph Hoxie - 7 Apr. 1838 [54]

Bower [or Bauer?], Peter, subj. of King of Bavaria; rec. by Wilhelm Meier - 10 Apr. 1838 [55]

Barry, John, subj. of G.B.; rec. by James Hortney - 10 Apr. 1838 [56]

Biehy, John, subj. of King of France; rec. by Jacob Zehringer - 11 Apr. 1838 [57]

Baker, Ashley Charles, subj. of G.B.; rec. by John B. Gassner - 11 Apr. 1838 [58]

Beck, Michael, subj. of Grand Duke of Baden; rec. by John Koch - 11 Apr. 1838 [59]

Briody, Nicholas, subj. of G.B.; rec. by John Flood - 11 Apr. 1838 [60]

Bassett, John, subj. of G.B.; rec. by Edward Sanderson - 12 Apr. 1838 [61]

Pecher, Anton, subj. of King of Prussia; rec. by Johan Muller - 12 Apr. 1838 [62]

Baker, Benjamin, subj. of G.B.; rec. by Samuel Toppin - 12 Apr. 1838 [63]

Berneholtz, Conrad, subj. of King of Prussia; rec. by A. Bleakeley, Jr. - 12 Apr. 1838 [64]

Bosano, George, subj. of G.B.; rec. by John Abben - 12 Apr. 1838 [65]

Brown, James, subj. of G.B.; rec. by Andrew Bleakley, Jr. - 12 Apr. 1838 [66]

Buchanan, George, subj. of G.B.; rec. by John Buchanan - 12 Apr. 1838 [67]

Benter, Jacob, subj. of King of Bavaria; rec. by Johan Koch - 12 Apr. 1838 [68]

Barabine, Niccolas, subj. of King of Spain; rec. by Augustus Cavanna [or Caranna?] - 23 Sept. 1838 [69]

Bradford, William, Jr., subj. of G.B.; rec. by James Lindley - 8 Oct. 1838 [70]

Boynes, George, subj. of G.B.; rec. by Charles Feldwick - 26 Oct. 1838 [71]

Black, Robert, subj. of G.B.; rec. by William Robb - 1 Nov. 1838 [72]

Bowen, Thomas, subj. of G.B.; rec. by John Jones - 1 Nov. 1838 [73]

Bolton, James, subj. of G.B.; rec. by Ephraim Smith - 3 Nov. 1838 [74]

Bromily, James, subj. of G.B.; rec. by Henry Ward, of West Farms - 3 Nov. 1838 [75]

Bremer, Henry, subj. of ·City of Frankfort; rec. by William Williams - 5 Nov. 1838 [76]

Bader, John, subj. of Republic of Switzerland; rec. by George Peter - 5 Nov. 1838 [77]

Bensly, Clement B., subj. of G.B.; rec. by David R. Caswell - 5 Nov. 1838 [78]

Baker, William, subj. of G.B.; rec. by James Beggs - 5 Nov. 1838 [79]

Brown, Charles, subj. of G.B.; rec. by Jonathan Lovejoy - 5 Nov. 1838 [80]

Brissel, Philip, subj. of Duchy of Darmstadt; rec. by Engelhart Brisch - 5 Nov. 1838 [80A]

Barber, Joseph, subj. of G.B.; rec. by John Barber - 5 Nov. 1838 [81]

Blakelock, John, subj. of G.B.; rec. by Samuel W. Palmer - 6 Nov. 1838 [82]

Blakelock, Richard A., subj. of G.B.; rec. by Samuel W. Palmer
- 6 Nov. 1838 [83]

Brich/Brish, Adam, subj. of King of Bavaria; rec. by Peter
Schappert - 6 Nov. 1838 [84]

Bollinger, George, subj. of Grand Duke of Wuertemberg; rec. by
John Cook [Koch] - 6 Nov. 1838 [85]

Bennett, John, subj. of G.B.; rec. by Mark Selmes - 6 Nov. 1838
[86]

Brownlee, William, subj. of G.B.; rec. by Daniel McKay - 6 Nov.
1838 [87]

Boyle, John, subj. of G.B.; rec. by Dennis Cairns - 6 Nov. 1838
[88]

Barron, John, subj. of G.B.; rec. by Peter Crosbie - 6 Nov.
1838 [89]

Barnsby/Barnsley, Edward, subj. of G.B.; rec. by Frederick Boyce
- 6 Nov. 1838 [90]

Barry, David, subj. of G.B.; rec. by Patrick Murphy - 6 Nov.
1838 [91]

Blackwell, John, subj. of G.B.; rec. by John Bilbrough - 7 Nov.
1838 [92]

Barnes, James, subj. of G.B.; rec. by William E. Barnes - 7 Nov.
1838 [93]

Bloch, Samuel, subj. of Republic of Switzerland; rec. by Johannes Stocky - 7 Nov. 1838 [94]

Brooks, Thomas, subj. of G.B.; rec. by Charles Brooks - 7 Nov.
1838 [95]

Bridgens, William H., subj. of G.B.; rec. by Alex Patterson - 7
Nov. 1838 [96]

Brenner, John, subj. of Duke of Baden; rec. by Edward Myers - 7
Nov. 1838 [97]

Brett, James L.; rec. by James M. Smith - 7 Nov. 1838 [98]

Branndes, August, subj. of King of Prussia; rec. by Friedrich
Ahrens - 7 Nov. 1838 [99]

Boyd, William, subj. of G.B.; rec. by James Allen - 7 Nov. 1838
[100]

Boysen, Andrew F., subj. of King of Denmark; rec. by Frederick
Mang - 7 Nov. 1838 [101]

Boker, Edward, subj. of King of Prussia; rec. by James J. Hoyt
- 7 Nov. 1838 [102]

Braitmayer, Imanuel F., subj. of King of Wuertemburg; rec. by
John F. Wolf - 7 Nov. 1838 [103]

Bateman, Stephen, subj. of G.B.; rec. by William Rogers - 7 Nov.
1838 [103A]

Clay, Richard, subj. of G.B.; rec. by Robert Clay - 7 Nov. 1838
[104]

Clay, Robert, subj. of G.B.; rec. by William Briggs - 7 Nov.
1838 [105]

Clay, John, subj. of G.B.; rec. by Robert Clay - 7 Nov. 1838
[106]

Calderhead, John, aubj. of G.B.; rec. by James Graham - 6 Nov.
1838 [107]

Chambers, Thomas, subj. of G.B.; rec. by Joseph Britton - 7 Nov. 1838 [108]

Chapman, James Holmes, subj. of G.B.; rec. by Thomas Minns - 7 Nov. 1838 [109]

Connillen, Peter Patrick, subj. of G.B.; rec. by Nathaniel B. Blunt - 7 Nov. 1838 [110]

Carlbaum, Charles T., subj. of G.B.; rec. by Joseph Dennison - 7 Nov. 1838 [111]

Clarson, Frederick, subj. of King of Sweden; rec. by F.W. Estling - 7 Nov. 1838 [112]

Coyle, Peter, subj. of G.B.; rec. by Daniel Donaho - 7 Nov. 1838 [112A]

Colyer, George, subj. of G.B.; rec. by George W. Riblet - 7 Nov. 1838 [113]

Cadigan, Denis T., subj. of G.B.; rec. by Ithamer Smith - 7 Nov. 1838 [114]

Carter, William, subj. of G.B.; rec. by John Billbrough - 7 Nov. 1838 [115]

Cogan, Peter, subj. of G.B.; rec. by William Love - 6 Nov. 1838 [116]

Clark, William, subj. of G.B.; rec. by Timothy G. Sellew - 6 Nov. 1838 [117]

Cook, Andrew, subj. of G.B.; rec. by Michel Brenan - 6 Nov. 1838 [118]

Conway, Patrick, subj. of G.B.; rec. by Isaac Anderson - 6 Nov. 1838 [119]

Clements, John, subj. of G.B.; rec. by John J. Williamson - 6 Nov. 1838 [120]

Chivers, Robert, subj. of G.B.; rec. by Samuel Perley - 6 Nov. 1838 [121]

Cash, Daniel, subj. of G.B.; rec. by Andrew Bleakly, Jr. - 6 Nov. 1838 [122]

Canavan, Thomas, subj. of G.B.; rec. by John Durken - 5 Nov. 1838 [123]

Coghlan, John D., subj. of G.B.; rec. by Michael Gaffney - 5 Nov. 1838 [124]

Calday, Timothy, subj. of G.B.; rec. by James Calday - 5 Nov. 1838 [125]

Coghlan, James, subj. of G.B.; rec. by Jeremiah Coghlan - 5 Nov. 1838 [126]

Coulon, Frederick, subj. of King of France; rec. by Francois Monnier - 5 Nov. 1838 [126A]

Clark, William, subj. of G.B.; rec. by Walter Brady - 5 Nov. 1838 [127]

Crea, Samuel, subj. of G.B.; rec. by Walter McRoberts - 5 Nov. 1838 [128]

Cumasky/Cumusky, Cornelius, subj. of G.B.; rec. by James Nugent - 5 Nov. 1838 [129]

Cairns, George, subj. of G.B.; rec. by Henry Johnson - 5 Nov. 1838 [130]

Cully, Thomas, subj. of G.B.; rec. by Daniel Kerivan - 5 Nov. 1838 [131]

Cassidy, John, subj. of G.B.; rec. by Francis Cassidy - 3 Nov. 1838 [132]

Campbell, John, subj. of G.B.; report Jan. 1824: born Ire., age 19, accountant, arrived Charleston, S.C., 29 Dec. 1822, migrated from Belfast; rec. by Charles W. Norwerck - 3 Nov. 1838 [133]

Cuendet, Eugene, subj. of Republic of Switzerland; rec. by James Fellows - 1 Nov. 1838 [134]

Conway, James, subj. of G.B.; rec. by Jotham Peabody - 29 Aug. 1838 [135]

Conner, Peter, subj. of G.B.; rec. by John Lambert - 10 Aug. 1838 [136]

Coughlin, Daniel, subj. of G.B.; rec. by Maurice Fitzgerald - 3 July 1838 [137]

Curl, John, subj. of G.B.; rec. by Jacob Wirtz - 1 June 1838 [138]

Curling, Saunders, of Thomastown, Maine, subj. of G.B.; rec. by Samuel York, of Warren, Maine - 5 June 1838 [139]

Correa, Sarah, widow, subj. of G.B.; rec. by Joseph Brandon - 13 Apr. 1838 [140]

Campbell, John, subj. of G.B.; rec. by Owen McKenne - 12 Apr. 1838 [141]

Chasmar, Thomas, subj. of G.B.; rec. by Charles Chasmar - 12 Apr. 1838 [142]

Church, William, subj. of G.B.; rec. by Andrew Bleakley, Jr. - 12 Apr. 1838 [143]

Cornish, John, miner, subj. of G.B.; rec. by Richard Westlake - 12 Apr. 1838 [144]

Cooley, Patrick, subj. of G.B.; rec. by Denis Derrig - 12 Apr. 1838 [145]

Calighan, Bernard/Barney, subj. of G.B.; rec. by Patrick Dening - 12 Apr. 1838 [146]

Connolly, James, subj. of G.B.; rec. by Robert Underwood - 11 Apr. 1838 [147]

Crevier, Julien, subj. of King of France; rec. by Joseph Alker - 11 Apr. 1838 [148]

Karcher, Matthias, subj. of Grand Duke of Baden; rec. by Amos Brigg - 11 Apr. 1838 [149]

Couray, Richard, subj. of G.B.; rec. by Edward Donovan - 11 Apr. 1838 [150]

Connolly, Patrick, subj. of G.B.; rec. by Stephen McImoy - 11 Apr. 1838 [151]

Crown, Anthony, subj. of G.B.; rec. by Daniel Gilmartin - 10 Apr. 1838 [152]

Cullen, John, subj. of G.B.; rec. by James Hughes - 10 Apr. 1838 [153]

Galles, Joseph, subj. of King of Bavaria; rec. by Jacob Keiffer - 10 Apr. 1838 [154]

Crowe, John, subj. of G.B.; rec. by Charles McCarthy - 10 Apr. 1838 [155]

Cristadoro, Joseph, subj. of King of the Two Sicilies; rec. by Joseph Attinelli - 9 Apr. 1838 [156]

Crowley, Edwin Hubert, subj. of G.B.; rec. by Robert Crowley - 23 Jan 1838 [157]

Bundle 16

Gormley, John, subj. of G.B.; rec. by Bernard Gallagher - 10 Apr. 1838 [1]

Giambony, Lionzio, subj. of King of France; rec. by Natal Giambony - 13 Apr. 1838 [2]

Ganter, John, Jr., subj. of King of Bavaria; rec. by Joseph Ganter - 9 Apr. 1838 [3]

Galligan, Dennis, subj. of G.B.; rec. by Patrick Riley - 10 Apr. 1838 [4]

Graf, George, subj. of King of Wuertemburg; rec. by Johan Georg Lenxman - 17 Mar. 1838 [5]

Grant, John, merchant, subj. of G.B.; rec. by Alexander McDonald - 17 Mar. 1838 [6]

Golden, Patrick, subj. of G.B.; rec. by Edward Ward - 24 Jan. 1838 [7]

Girdler, James, subj. of G.B.; rec. by Samuel White - 11 Apr. 1838 [8]

Gerraty, Thomas, subj. of G.B.; rec. by Patrick Christal - 12 Apr. 1838 [9]

Ganly, William, subj. of G.B.; rec. by William Moore - 12 Apr. 1838 [10]

Goldschmidt, John Meyer, accountant, subj. of Govt. of Hamburg; rec. by William Collins - 8 May 1838 [11]

Graham, George, subj. of G.B.; decl. of intent in 1832; rec. by Robert Steele - 8 May 1838 [12]

Graham, Ben, subj. of G.B.; decl. of intent 1835; rec. by Henry McDonogh - 23 Oct. 1838 [13]

Granger, John, subj. of G.B.; rec. by Philip Grandin - 31 Oct. 1838 [14]

Gallot, John, subj. of G.B.; rec. by William Henry Macklin - 1 Nov. 1838 [15]

Gent, William, subj. of G.B.; decl. of intent 1836; rec. by Benjamin Pettit - 1 Nov. 1838 [16]

Greenfield, George, subj. of G.B.; rec. by John Cook - 2 Noc. 1838 [17]

Gee, John, subj. of G.B.; decl. of intent 1836; rec. by John Witts - 3 Nov. 1838 [18]

Greig, William, subj. of G.B.; decl. of intent 1834; rec. by Alexander Tully - 10 Apr. 1838 [19]

Gregg, William T., subj. of G.B.; rec. by George W. Blunt - 3 Nov. 1838 [20]

Gibbs, Henry, subj. of G.B.; decl. of intent 1834; rec. by John Gibbs - 3 Nov. 1838 [21]

Grimm, Charles A., shoemaker, subj. of Prince of Schaumburgh; decl. of intent 1832; rec. by Charles Haarstrich - 5 Nov. 1838 [22]

Gaffney, Michael, subj. of G.B.; decl. of intent 1836; rec. by John Wilkinson - 5 Nov. 1838 [23]

Garvin, Thomas, subj. of G.B.; rec. by Patrick Garvin - 5 Nov. 1838 [24]

Garvin, Patrick, subj. of G.B.; rec. by Thomas Garvin - 5 Nov. 1838 [25]

Guy, Thomas, subj. of G.B.; decl. of intent 1836; rec. by John Peckwell - 5 Nov. 1838 [26]

Goodwin, Michael L., subj. of G.B.; decl. of intent 1834; rec. by Benjamin G. Wells - 5 Nov. 1838 [27]

Gillespie, Dominick, subj. of G.B.; decl. of intent 1835; rec. by John Gallagher - 6 Nov. 1838 [28]

Gethen, Thomas, subj. of G.B.; decl. of intent 1835; rec. by Alexander Douglass - 6 Nov. 1838 [29]

Grant, Adam, subj. of G.B.; decl. of intent 1836; rec. by Daniel McKay - 6 Nov. 1838 [30]

Glass, Hugh, subj. of G.B.; decl. of intent 1835; rec. by James Beck - 6 Nov. 1838 [31]

Ganglof, Joseph, subj. of King of France; rec. by James R. Westerveldt - 6 Nov. 1838 [32]

Gloss, Andrew, subj. of King of Bavaria; rec. by Engelbart Brisch - 6 Nov. 1838 [33]

Groff, Stepen, subj. of Grand Duke of Baden; rec. by Martin Green - 6 Nov. 1838 [34]

Gardner, Thomas, subj. of G.B.; rec. by John Palmer - 6 Nov. 1838 [35]

Grist, David, subj. of King of Bavaria; decl. of intent in 1836 calls him subj. of King of Wuertembergh; rec. by George Iselen - 6 Nov. 1838 [36]

Grice, Charles, subj. of G.B.; rec. by Albert J. Fontaine - 7 Nov. 1838 [37]

Gelbraith, Robert, subj. of G.B.; decl. of intent 1835; rec. by Hugh Stinson - 7 Nov. 1838 [38]

Gallaher, John, subj. of G.B.; rec. by Daniel Leary - 19 Nov. 1838 [38A]

Engelman, Frederick, subj. of King of Saxony; rec. by John Kramer - 11 Apr. 1838 [39]

Egan, Daniel, subj. of G.B.; decl. of intent 1834; rec. by William Farrell - 12 Apr. 1838 [40]

Emmert, Francis, subj. of King of Bavaria; decl. of intent 1836; rec. by Joseph Retls - 5 Nov. 1838 [41]

Early, Charles, subj. of G.B.; decl. of intent 1833; rec. by Thomas Early - 5 Nov. 1838 [42]

Ergatt, George F., subj. of King of Bavaria; rec. by Peter T. Thompson - 5 Nov. 1838 [43]

Eckert, Valrin, subj. of King of France; rec. by Johannes Mag - 7 Nov. 1838 [44]

Hodge, William, subj. of G.B.; decl. of intent 1829; rec. by John H. Fadden - 4 Oct. 1838 [45]

Hornby, Frederick, subj. of G.B.; rec. by Benjamin Pettit - 31 Oct. 1838 [46]

Hornby, James, subj. of G.B.; rec. by Benjamin Pettit - 30 Oct. 1838 [47]

Hegel, Frederick, of Harsimus, N.J., subj. of King of Wuertemburgh; decl. of intent 1827; rec. by Richard McCollick - 14 July 1838; born Weiblingen, Wuertemburg, age 34 in 1827, migrated from Amsterdam, gardener [48]

Henriques, Abigail (wife of Joseph Henriques), subj. of G.B.; decl. of intent 1836; rec. by Joseph Brandon - 28 May 1838 [49]

Henriques, Sarah (widow of Jacob Henriques), subj. of G.B.;decl. of intent 1836; rec. by Joseph Brandon - 28 May 1838 [50]

Higgins, Thomas, subj. of G.B.; decl. of intent 1835; rec, by Barney Chrystal - 12 Apr. 1838 [51]

Holden, Edward Henry Strange, druggist, subj. of G.B.; rec. by James W. Dominick - 12 Apr. 1838; report in 1826: born in Eng., age 25, migrated from London; wife Ann Margaret, age 25 [52]

Hamilton, Owen, subj. of G.B.; rec. by Hugh McCarthy - 12 Apr. 1838 [53]

Hildwein, John Christoph, subj. of King of Wuertemberg; rec. by Christoph Sommer - 12 Apr. 1838 [53A]

Hall, James, subj. of G.B.; rec. by John Wylie - 12 Apr. 1838 [54]

Hazelton, Charles, subj. of G.B.; rec. by Samuel Hazelton - 12 Apr. 1838 [55]

Hazelton. Henry, subj. of G.B.; rec. by Samuel Hazelton - 12 Apr. 1838 [56]

Holbarg, Reyer, subj. of King of Sweden and Norway; decl. of intent 1833; rec. by Reynolds Jones - 12 Apr. 1838 [57]

Hind, Thomas, subj. of G.B.; decl. of intent 1833; rec. by John J. Perry - 12 Apr. 1838 [58]

Heis, Michael, subj. of Grand Duke of Baden; dec. of intent 1836; rec. by John A. Wolfer - 10 Apr. 1838 [59]

Hays, Edmund, subj. of G.B.; recl. of intent 1835; rec. by Thomas Holahan - 10 Apr. 1838 [60]

Hansler, John, subj. of King of Wuertemberg; decl. of intent 1836; rec. by Johann Rathgeber - 10 Apr. 1838 [61]

Hughes, James, native of Ire., subj. of G.B.; decl. of intent 1834; rec. by Andrew Bleakley - 11 Apr. 1838 [62]

Haug, Frederick, subj. of King of Wuertemberg; rec. by James Mc Cully - 12 Apr. 1838 [63]

Hall, David, subj. of G.B.; decl. of intent 1834; rec. by Thomas Hall - 12 Apr. 1838 [64]

Harman, Andrew, subj. of King of France; rec. by Peter Skopp - 9 Apr. 1838 [65]

Harris, Nicholas, subj. of King of Sweden and Norway; decl. of intent 1836; rec. by Wilhelm Meier - 10 Apr. 1838 [65A]

Hawes, John, baker, subj. of G.B.; rec. by Samuel Espie, baker - 16 Jan. 1838 [66]

Harold, James, subj. of G.B.; rec. by Andrew B. Hodges - 1 Nov. 1838 [67]

Hill [or Holl?], John, subj. of G.B.; rec. by Richard Y. Holl - 2 Nov. 1838 [68]

Hughes, Ferdinand, subj. of G.B.; report at decl. of intent 1833: born 1808 Co. of Mark [for Meath or Mayo?], Ire., arrived Portland, Maine 9 June 1828, lived in Dover, N.H., until Sept. 1830, went to Pa. and remained there until 1832 and then returned to Dover; rec. by John Hughes - 2 Nov. 1838 [69]

Hunter, Robert, subj. of G.B.; decl. of intent 1836; rec. by Elisha S. Mott - 2 Nov. 1838 [70]

Hall, Richard Y., subj. of G.B.; rec. by George Hall - 2 Nov. 1838 [71]

Haysman, William, subj. of G.B.; rec. by Samuel Gillot - 3 Nov.
   1838 [72]

Hagen, Archibald, subj. of G.B.; decl. of intent 1835; rec. by
   Riley M. Winslow - 3 Nov. 1838 [73]

Hatchman, John, subj. of G.B.; rec. by James Hatchman - 3 Nov.
   1838 [74]

Hatchman, James, subj. of G.B.; decl. of intent 1834; rec. by
   Nathaniel Smith - 3 Nov. 1838 [75]

Hoch, John, subj. of King of Wuertemberg; rec. by Christian Soll
   - 3 Nov. 1838 [76]

Hintz, Alexander, subj. of King of France; rec. by Alexander Heineman - 3 Nov. 1838 [76A]

Horbelt, John L., subj. of King of Bavaria; rec. by George Dietrich Horbelt - 3 Nov. 1838 [77]

Horbelt, George Dietrich, subj. of King of Bavaria; decl. of intent 1834; rec. by Alexander Heineman - 3 Nov. 1838 [78]

Hunter, Andrew, subj. of G.B.; decl. of intent 1836; rec. by
   George A. Fuerst - 5 Nov. 1838 [79]

Hawksworth, John, subj. of G.B.; rec. by John A. Mackell - 5 Nov.
   1838 [80]

Hammer, Joseph, subj. of Republic of Switzerland; rec. by George
   Peter - 5 Nov. 1838 [81]

Herzog, Christian, subj. of Grand Duke of Baden; rec. by Engelhart Brisch - 5 Nov. 1838 [82]

Hinritz, John, subj. of King of Wuertemburg; rec. by Jacob Rie-
   ber - 5 Nov. 1838 [83]

Hammer, Johann, subj. of Republic of Switzerland; rec. by George
   Peter - 5 Nov. 1838 [84]

Homer, Joseph, subj. of G.B.; decl. of intent 1834; rec. by Bryan
   Ward - 5 Nov. 1838 [85]

Hamilton, William, subj. of G.B.; decl. of intent 1836; rec. by
   William Brownlee - 6 Nov. 1838 [86]

Henry, Felix, subj. of G.B.; decl. of intent 1831; rec. by James
   Quinn - 6 Nov. 1838 [87]

Holford, James, subj. of G.B.; decl. of intent 1833; rec. by John
   Palmer - 6 Nov. 1838 [88]

Herman, Jacob, subj. of King of Bavaria; decl. of intent 1834;
   rec. by Engelhart Brisch - 6 Nov. 1838 [89]

Hodgson, Thomas, subj. of G.B.; rec. by Augustus Laurent - 6 Nov.
   1838 [90]

Heaney, Thomas, subj. of G.B.; rec. by F.O. Hallerin - 6 Nov.
   1838 [91]

Howard, William, subj. of G.B.; rec. by Patrick Madden - 6 Nov.
   1838 [92]

Haag, Johann Adam, subj. of King of Bavaria; rec. by Peter Schap-
   part - 6 Nov. 1838 [93]

Haggerty, Barney, subj. of G.B.; rec. by Thomas Chase - 6 Nov.
   1838 [94]

Hanning, William, subj. of G.B.; decl. of intent 1836; rec. by
   Harold Geer - 7 Nov. 1838 [95]

Harrison, George, subj. of G.B.; rec. by James Harrison - 7 Nov.
   1838 [96]

Hislop, Andrew, gardener, subj. of G.B.; rec. by D.P. Ingraham
- 7 Nov. 1838 [97]

Hoguet, Anthony, subj. of G.B.; decl. of intent 1832; rec. by
James Van Norden - 7 Nov. 1838 [98]

Hilber, George, subj. of King of France; rec. by Cilest Miller -
7 Nov. 1838 [99]

Henschen, William C., subj. of G.B.; rec. by Gabriel Weaks - 7
Nov. 1838 [100]

Haas, Martin, subj. of King of France; rec. by Christopher Decker - 7 Nov. 1838 [101]

Heineman, Alexander, subj. of King of Hanover; rec. by Henry
Rodenmond - 7 Nov. 1838 [101A]

Furlong, Philip, subj. of G.B.; decl. of intent 1836; rec. by
John Miller - 7 Nov. 1838 [102]

Hansell, John A.; rec. by Francis Smith - 7 Nov. 1838 [102A]

Finley, Richard, subj. of G.B.; decl. of intent 1834; rec. by
William McCullough - 12 Apr. 1838 [103]

Friedrichs, Claus Rickmer, subj. of G.B.; decl. of intent 1835;
rec. by William Johnson - 12 Apr. 1838 [104]

Fitz Randolph, James, subj. of G.B.; rec. by William W. Clay -
12 Apr. 1838 [104A]

Falon, Bernard, subj. of G.B.; decl. of intent 1835; rec. by
Michael Moan [105]

Finn, Hugh, subj. of G.B.; decl. of intent 1835; rec. by Michael
McManus - 11 Apr. 1838 [106]

Flammer, Jacob, subj. of King of Wuertemburg; decl. of intent
1834; rec. by John G. Flammer - 11 Apr. 1838 [107]

Fitzgerald, John, subj. of G.B.; rec. by Charles E. Johnson - 11
Apr. 1838 [108]

Flets, Johannes, subj. of King of Bavaria; rec. by Peter Flets;
his passport of 1835 bears notation "Saarbruck, Nov. 1, 1834,
Polizamt Passport" and then Hudson, New York" - 11 Apr. 1838
[109]

Fox, Michael, subj. of G.B.; rec. by James Regan - 10 Apr. 1838
[110]

Fitch, John, subj. of G.B.; rec. by James Kerr - 10 Apr. 1838
[110A]

Finnegan, Thomas, subj. of G.B.; decl. of intent 1834; rec. by
Edmund Power - 5 Apr. 1838 [111]

Fischer, Johann, subj. of Grand Duke of Baden; decl. of intent
1836; rec. by Martin Liebig - 6 Nov. 1835 [112]

Fish, Alexander, subj. of G.B.; rec. by Samuel S. Barry - 12 Apr.
1838 [113]

Flinn, Edward, subj. of G.B.; decl. of intent 1836; rec. by James
H. Kellan - 12 Apr. 1838 [114]

Fitzpatrick, Edward, subj. of G.B.; rec. by Jotham Peabody - 12
Apr. 1838 [115]

Farmer, Edward, subj. of G.B.; rec. by Margaret Byrnes - 12 Apr.
1838 [116]

Flynn, John Patrick, butcher, subj. of G.B.; rec. by James Hickey; decl. of intent 18 Nov. 1835 - 4 June 1838 [117]

Francis, Jane (wife of Isaac Francis, surgeon-dentist), subj.
   of G.B.; decl. of intent 1833; rec. by Edward S. Derry - 3 Aug.
   1838 [118]

Ferara, Vicenzo Francisco, subj. of Emperor of Austria; rec. by
   Benedict De Angelis - 6 Sept. 1838 [119]

Fenner, William, subj. of G.B.; rec. by Stephen W. West - 18
   Oct. 1838 [120]

Farrell, Bryan, subj. of G.B.; rec. by James Nugent - 31 Oct.
   1838 [121]

Foster, Henry, subj. of G.B.; rec. by James Irwin - 3 Nov. 1838
   [122]

Fitzpatrick, John, subj. of G.B.; decl. of intent 7 Apr. 1835;
   rec. by Edward Noonan - 3 Nov. 1838 [123]

Fitzpatrick, John, subj. of G.B.; decl. of intent 2 July 1835;
   rec. by Patrick McIlvany - 3 Nov. 1838 [124]

Fraser, William, subj. of G.B.; decl. of intent 30 July 1835;
   rec. by William Jones - 5 Nov. 1838 [125]

Farrell, Mathew, subj. of G.B.; decl. of intent 27 May 1833; rec.
   by John Gallagher - 5 Nov. 1838 [126]

Fatscher, Peter, subj. of King of Bavaria; rec. by Engelhart
   Brisch - 5 Nov. 1838 [127]

Foley, Patrick, subj. of G.B.; decl. of inent 15 Apr. 1835; rec.
   by John McGough - 5 Nov. 1838 [128]

Farrell, James, subj. of G.B.; decl. of intent 30 July 1836; rec.
   by William McCan - 6 Nov. 1838 [129]

Foy, Benjamin, subj. of G.B.; decl. of intent 5 May 1834; rec.
   by Isaac Morris - 6 Nov. 1838 [130]

Farley, James, subj. of G.B.; rec. by William B. Jacobs - 6 Nov.
   1838 [131]

Fish, James, subj. of G.B.; rec. by David Cation - 7 Nov. 1838
   [132]

Fohet, Augustus, subj. of Prince of Hesse Cassel; rec. by Wilhelm Krausz - 7 Nov. 1838 [133]

Friand, Louis, subj. of King of France; rec. by Florent Gourdier
   - 7 Nov. 1838 [134]

Fisher, Henry N., subj. of King of France; rec. by John Kraft -
   7 Nov. 1838 [134A]

Farrell, Bryan, subj. of G.B.; rec. by James Nugent - 7 Nov.
   1838 [135]

Fraind, Lauro, subj. of King of France; rec. by Florent Gourdier
   - 7 Nov. 1838 [135A]

Bundle 17

McGuire, James, subj. of G.B.; decl. of intent 3 Mar. 1833; rec.
   by James McSarley - 12 Apr. 1838 [135]

McCort, James, subj. of G.B.; decl. of intent 12 Sept. 1833; rec.
   by Martin McGovern - 12 Apr. 1838 [136]

McCann, Andrew, subj. of G.B.; decl. of intent 30 Oct. 1834; rec.
   by Roger Treanor - 12 Apr. 1838 [137]

McCabe, Hugh, subj. of G.B.; rec. by John James Brown - 12 Apr.
   1838 [138]

McHugh, Edward, subj. of G.B.; decl. of intent 6 July 1835; rec.
   by Hugh Doyle - 5 Oct. 1838 [139]

McKenna, John, subj. of G.B.; decl. of intent 30 Oct. 1833; rec.
by Edward D. West - 31 Oct. 1838 [140]

McCullough, James, subj. of G.B.; rec. by Andrew McCullough - 3
Nov. 1838 [141]

McGill, Robert, subj. of G.B.; decl. of intent 14 Sept. 1835;
rec. by Nathaniel Smith - 3 Nov. 1838 [142]

McNamarra, Darby, subj. of G.B.; rec. by Daniel Leary - 3 Nov.
1838 [143]

McVey, John, shoemaker, subj. of G.B., arrived Boston about 10
June 1835; born Cranne, Co. Tyrone, Ire., 29 June 1812; age
in 1836 was 24; rec. by Patrick McCaffray - 5 Nov. 1838 [144]

McVey, Patrick, subj. of G.B.; decl. of intent 6 Nov. 1834; rec.
by Thomas Verty - 5 Nov. 1838 [145]

McNamara, Patrick, subj. of G.B.; rec. by Daniel Leary - 5 Nov.
1838 [146]

Kiernan, Cornelius, subj. of G.B.; rec. by James R. Irwin - 6
Nov. 1838 [147]

McKenna, Tole, subj. of G.B.; decl. of intent 19 Oct. 1836; rec.
by William Haysman - 6 Nov. 1838 [148]

McClure, John, subj. of G.B.; decl. of intent 7 Oct. 1836; rec.
by John Maltman - 6 Nov. 1838 [149]

McNaughton, Peter Edward, subj. of G.B.; decl. of intent 7 Nov.
1836; rec. by Daniel McKay - 6 Nov. 1838 [150]

McAlarny, Bernard, ostler, subj. of G.B.; decl. of intent 26 Jan.
1836; rec. by James Kough - 6 Nov. 1838 [151]

Eugen, Paul, subj. of King of Wuertemburg; rec. by Johan Kouk [?]
- 12 Apr. 1838 [1]

Jones, John, subj. of G.B.; decl. of intent 22 Sept. 1835; rec.
by Robert McGee - 9 Apr. 1838 [2]

Jones, Thomas, subj. of G.B.; rec. by Charles Monroe - 12 Apr.
1838 [3]

Jones, Henry, subj. of King of Bavaria; rec. by Isaac Drucker -
11 Apr. 1838 [4]

Jolly [or Joller?], John, subj. of G.B.; decl. of intent 25 Oct.
1833; rec. by Henry Wilkinson - 12 Apr. 1838 [5]

Johnson, James, labourer, subj. of G.B.; decl. of intent 14 Nov.
1831; rec. by John Healy - 3 Nov. 1838 [6]

Jones, Richard S., subj. of G.B.; rec. by John R. Jones - 3 Nov.
1838 [7]

Jarvis, Thomas, subj. of G.B.; rec. by Frederick Wang - 3 Nov.
1838 [8]

Jordan, John, subj. of G.B.; rec. by Joseph Pergamin - 5 Nov.
1838; Wm. V. Heermance, clerk of court for Greene Co., N.Y.,
writes that John Jordan, of Hunter, Greene Co., made decl. of
intent 1 Sept. 1834 [9]

Johnson, Martin, subj. of King of Sweden; rec. by John Brown - 6
Nov. 1838 [10]

Johnson, John, subj. of King of Sweden - 6 Nov. 1838 [11]

Jordan, Patrick, subj. of G.B.; decl. of intent 9 Oct. 1834: born
Ire., age 32; rec. by John Durkin - 7 Nov. 1838 [11A]

Jaclard, Sebastian, wig maker, subj. of King of France; decl. of
intent 28 Jan. 1834; rec. by Lewis Phillips - 7 Nov. 1838 [12]

Jones, John M. , subj. of G.B.; decl. of intent 22 Sept. 1834;
   rec. by John E. Kendall - 7 Nov. 1838 [13]

Keiffer, Jacob, subj. of King of Bavaria; rec. by Joseph Gallas
   - 11 Apr. 1838 [14]

Kelly, Patrick, subj. of G.B.; rec. by James Kelly - 10 Apr.
   1838 [15]

Kearny, James, subj. of G.B.; decl. of intent 23 Sept. 1833;
   rec. by Patrick Fitzpatrick - 11 Apr. 1838 [16]

Kelly, John, labourer, subj. of G.B.; decl. of intent 10 Sept.
   1831; rec. by Charles Cassidy - 10 Apr. 1838 [17]

Kennedy, Edward, shoemaker, subj. of G.B.; decl. of intent 29
   Mar. 1830; rec. by John Kennedy - 11 Apr. 1838 [18]

Kramer, John, subj. of Prince of Hesse Cassel; rec. by Frederick
   Engelman - 11 Apr. 1838 [19]

Kelly, Morris, subj. of G.B.; rec. by James Kelly - 12 Apr. 1838
   [20]

Krier, Martin, subj. of King of Prussia; decl. of intent 21 Mar.
   1836; rec. by Barbara Krier - 12 Apr. 1838 [21]

Krumm, Konrad, subj. of King of Wuertemburg; rec. by Christian
   Wirth - 6 Aug. 1838 [22]

Kelly, John, subj. of G.B.; decl. of intent 29 Dec. 1833; born
   Ire., age 22 in 1834; embarked 15 Nov. 1832 at Quebec in the
   steamboat Chamberlin for U.S.; arrived Whitehall 22 Nov. 1832
   and arrived Savannah 29 Dec. 1833; rec. by John Cochlan - 31
   Oct. 1838 [23]

Kuhn, Martin, subj. of King of France; rec. by Michael Kuhn - 31
   Oct. 1838 [24]

King, Anthony, subj. of G.B.; rec. by George Feitner - 1 Nov.
   1838 [25]

Kraft, John, subj. of King of Wuertemburg; rec. by Jacob Kaemmerle - 3 Nov. 1838 [26]

Kolb, Jacob, subj. of Grand Duke of Baden; rec. by Christian
   Soll - 3 Nov. 1838 [27]

Kirkman, Robert, subj. of G.B.; decl. of intent 10 Nov. 1834;
   rec. by William Nattall - 3 Nov. 1838 [28]

Kaemmerle, Jacob, subj. of King of Wuertemburg; rec. by John
   Kraft - 3 Nov. 1838 [29]

Kochler, John, subj. of King of the Netherlands; rec. by John
   Cole - 5 Nov. 1838 [30]

Kiefer, Jacob, subj. of King of Bavaria; decl. of intent 17 Oct.
   1836; rec. by George F. Ergott - 5 Nov. 1838 [31]

Kearney, Lawrence, subj. of G.B.; decl. of intent 9 Apr. 1834;
   rec. by Thomas Fisher - 6 Nov. 1838 [32]

Klingler, George Michael Christian, subj. of King of Wuertemburg;
   decl. of intent 9 Apr. 1834; rec. by Peter Schlosser - 6 Nov.
   1838 [33]

Kassel, Adam, subj. of King of France; decl. of intent 8 June
   1837; rec. by Jacob Beuler - 6 Nov. 1838 [34]

Kersting, Johann, subj. of King of Prussia; rec. by John G. Weise
   - 6 Nov. 1838 [35]

Knight, William, subj. of G.B.; rec. by Richard Whitaker - 6 Nov.
   1838 [36]

Kirk, John G., subj. of G.B.; decl. of intent 22 Oct. 1833; rec. by Dunbar S. Dyson - 6 Nov. 1838 [37]

Kellock, George, subj. of G.B.; rec. by John Wintringham - 6 Nov. 1838 [38]

Keys, Edward, subj. of G.B.; rec. by James E. Wood - 6 Nov. 1838 [39]

Klenen, Henry, subj. of King of Hanover; rec. by Hermann Kothe - 7 Nov. 1838 [40]

Krauss, Wilzum, subj. of Prince of Hesse Cassel; rec. by Faschus Vogt - 7 Nov. 1838 [41]

Knox, Robert, subj. of G.B.; decl. of intent 3 Nov. 1834; rec. by George Ross - 7 Nov. 1838 [42]

Kelly, Richard, subj. of G.B.; decl. of intent 20 Apr. 1836; rec. by Richard T. Holmes - 7 Nov. 1838 [43]

Lambert, Robert, subj. of G.B.; rec. by David Holmes - 9 Apr. 1838 [44]

Leonard, Terrence, subj. of G.B.; rec. by John Leonard - 10 Apr. 1838 [45]

Lanxman, Johann Georg, subj. of King of Wuertemburg; rec. by Georg Graf - 10 Apr. 1838 [46]

Lamb, Thomas, subj. of G.B.; rec. by Michael Lamb - 10 Apr. 1838 [47]

Laughlin, Timothy, subj. of G.B.; decl. of intent 8 Oct. 1835; rec. by Patrick Laughlin - 11 Apr. 1838 [48]

Laughlin, George, porter, subj. of G.B.; decl. of intent 25 Jan. 1831; rec. by William Brown - 11 Apr. 1838 [49]

Lowrey, John, subj. of G.B.; rec. by James Patchill - 11 Apr. 1838 [50]

Leeman, William, subj. of G.B.; rec. by Cornelius B. Raven - 11 Apr. 1838 [51]

Lelong, Martin, subj. of King of France; rec. by Julien Crevier - 12 Apr. 1838 [52]

Larinan, Michael, subj. of G.B.; rec. by Daniel Rooney - 12 Apr. 1838 [53]

Leclerc, Fortune, subj. of King of France; decl. of intent 21 Dec. 1833; rec. by James Chesterman - 12 Apr. 1838 [54]

Levy, John, subj. of G.B.; rec. by Joseph Newmark - 12 Apr. 1838 [55]

Levi, Sylvester, subj. of G.B.; rec. by Joseph Newmark - 12 Apr. 1838 [56]

Long, William, subj. of G.B.; decl. of intent 5 Nov. 1834; rec. by Adam Long - 11 Jan. 1838 [57]

Lynch, John, subj. of G.B.; decl. of intent 30 Mar. 1833; rec. by Michael Cochlan - 3 July 1838 [58]

Lewis, Thomas, subj. of G.B.; decl. of intent 8 Sept. 1835; rec. by Robert Batten - 6 Aug. 1838 [59]

Lentz, Tobias, subj. of King of Wuertemburg; rec. by George Fullmer - 24 Oct. 1838 [60]

Lentz, David, subj. of King of Wuertemburg; rec. by George Fullmer - 1 Nov. 1838 [61]

Lestrange, Peter, subj. of G.B.; decl. of intent 21 Sept. 1836; rec. by Elias C. Taylor - 1 Nov. 1838 [62]

Latta, Robert, subj. of G.B.; rec. by Henry Farrell - 1 Nov. 1838 [63]

Lutter, Jacob, subj. of King of Bavaria; rec. by Anthony Lambrecht - 6 Nov. 1838 [64]

Lutz, Peter, subj. of King of France; decl. of intent 2 July 1836; rec. by Alexander Heinemann - 6 Nov. 1838 [65]

Lewis, William, subj. of G.B.; decl. of intent 27 July 1835; rec. by Rees Hughes - 6 Nov. 1838 [66]

Leenwarden, Moses Jacob, subj. of King of the Netherlands; decl. of intent 5 Sept. 1835; rec. by John J. Shedel - 6 Nov. 1838 [67]

Ledwith, Richard F., subj. of G.B.; rec. by Charles B. Mease - 6 Nov. 1838 [68]

Law, George N., subj. of G.B.; rec. by John Syms - 7 Nov. 1838 [69]

Lynch, Guy, subj. of G.B.; rec. by James Murray - 7 Nov. 1838 [70]

Leitch, William Trotter, subj. of G.B.; decl. of intent 3 Nov. 1834; rec. by Ralph Wise - 7 Nov. 1838 [71]

Love [or Lew?], James, subj. of G.B.; decl. of intent 25 Oct. 1836; rec. by Nehemiah P. Anderson [72]

Lockyer, Thomas, subj. of G.B.; decl. of intent 26 Sept. 1836; rec. by John Neil - 7 Nov. 1838 [73]

Liftchild, Timothy, subj. of G.B.; rec. by Samuel Goodwin - 7 Nov. 1838 [74]

Links, Georg, subj. of King of Bavaria; rec. by Christopher Decker - 7 Nov. 1838 [75]

Lowry, William, subj. of G.B.; rec. by Alexander Christie - 7 Nov. 1838 [76]

Lynch, Hugh, subj. of G.B.; decl. of intent 22 Apr. 1834; rec. by Hugh Reilly - 11 Apr. 1838 [77]

Monnier, Francois, subj. of King of France; rec. by Frederic Coulon - 5 Bov. 1838 [78]

Monypenny, James, subj. of G.B.; rec. by William Sharon - 5 Nov. 1838[79]

Miltone, Alfred, subj. of G.B.; rec. by Esther Milton - 2 Nov. 1838 [80]

Maguire, James, subj. of G.B.; decl. of intent 20 June 1836; rec. by Thomas Coyle - 5 Nov. 1838 [81]

Martin, Peter, subj. of G.B.; rec. by Heinrich Martin - 5 Nov. 1838 [82]

Martin, William, subj. of G.B.; decl. of intent 26 July 1836; rec. by Caleb M. Angevine - 6 Nov. 1838 [83]

Mitchell, David, subj. of G.B.; decl. of intent 20 Nov. 1835; rec. by Moses Collyer - 6 Nov. 1838 [84]

Martin, Thomas, subj. of G.B.; decl. of intent 4 Aug. 1836; rec. by Andrew B. Hodges - 6 Nov. 1838 [85]

Marley, Thomas, subj. of G.B.; rec. by James Roarer [as clerk wrote] - 6 Nov. 1838 [86]

Molloy, Patrick, subj. of G.B.; rec. by Bernard Sweeney - 6 Nov. 1838 [87]

Martin, Jacob, subj. of King of Bavaria; rec. by Alexander Effray - 6 Nov. 1838 [88]

Mahaffy, Francis, druggist, subj. of G.B.; rec. by Ansel Parker - 7 Nov. 1838 [89]

Matheus [or Matthews], William A., subj. of King of France; rec. by Emanuel A. White - 7 Nov. 1838 [90]

Miller, Cilest, subj. of King of France; rec. by John B. Geiler - 7 Nov. 1838 [91]

Marler, Casper, subj. of Grand Duke of Baden; rec. by Nicholas Welty - 7 Nov. 1838 [92]

Müller, Frederick, subj. of King of Denmark; rec. by Frederick Wang - 7 Nov. 1838 [93]

Monaghan, William, subj. of G.B.; rec. by John Lewis - 7 Nov. 1838 [94]

Miller, Jacob, subj. of King of Wurtemberg; rec. by Matthias Knoell - 7 Nov. 1838 [95]

Menzar, Henry, subj. of King of France; rec. by Lambert Rulay - 7 Nov. 1838 [96]

Means, Thomas, subj. of G.B.; rec. by James Bellis - 7 Nov. 1838 [97]

Maltman, John, subj. of G.B.; rec. by Joseph F. Lippit - 2 Nov. 1838 [98]

Moss, Henry, subj. of G.B.; rec. by Robert M. Malcolm - 17 Oct. 1838 [99]

Martin, John, subj. of G.B.; rec. by George Feitner - 31 Oct. 1838 [100]

Munn, Thomas [report 20 Mar. 1828: b. Co. of Kent, Eng., age 33, migr. from London, farmer, residence at Woodbridge, N.J.; rec. by William Stuart - 8 Oct. 1838 [101]

Murphy, John [report Jan. 1834]: b. Co. Kildare, Ire., 1 Aug. 1812, age now about 22, arrived Boston 6 July 1833; rec. by Patrick Moore - 28 July 1838 [102]

Murphy, John, aubj. of G.B., who sailed from Dublin in 1826 with Walter Roe; rec. by Bridget Murphy - 6 July 1838 [103]

Mulligan, John, sub. G.B.; rec. by John Kelly - 22 June 1838 [104]

Mayher, Richard, subj. of G.B.; rec. by James Black - 12 Apr. 1838 [105]

Marriott, John, subj. of G.B.; rec. by Henry F. Beldin - 12 Apr. 1838 [106]

Murphy, William, subj. of G.B.; rec. by Charles Delvecchio - 12 Apr. 1838 [107]

Martin, James, subj. of G.B.; rec. by John B. Parker - 12 Apr. 1838 [108]

Menck, William, baker, subj. of King of Prussia; rec. by Richard Coddington - 11 Apr. 1838 [109]

Martin, Thomas, subj. of G.B.; rec. by Ann Martin - 12 Apr. 1838 [110]

Madden, Patrick, subj. of G.B.; rec. by Timothy Halloran - 11 Apr. 1838 [111]

Markstein, David, subj. of King of Bavaria; rec. by Peter Sickhouse - 11 Apr. 1838 [112]

Milburn, John, subj. of G.B.; rec. by Leonard Milburn - 11 Apr.
1838 [112A]

Mitchell, Charles, subj. of Prince of Hesse Cassel; rec. by
Frederick Engleman - 10 Apr. 1838 [113]

Matthews, William, subj. of G.B.; rec. by Humphrey Miller - 10
Apr. 1838 [114]

Mawbey, William, subj. of G.B.; rec. by John Hill - 12 Apr.
1838 [115]

McKernon, Robert T., subj. of G.B.; rec. by Bernard McAnnally -
10 Mar. 1838 [116]

McCorry, Joseph, subj. of G.B.; rec. by John Brady - 9 Apr.
1838 [117]

McCready, Joseph, subj. of G.B.; rec. by William Stoutenburgh -
9 Apr. 1838 [118]

McCluskey, Richard, subj. of G.B.; rec. by Robert Friel - 10
Apr. 1838 [119]

McKenzie, James, subj. of G.B.; rec. by Moses Jackson - 10 Apr.
1838 [120]

McManus, John, subj. of G.B.; rec. by David Holmes - 10 Apr.
1838 [121]

McCormick, William, subj. of G.B.; rec. by Matthew Conlan - 11
Apr. 1838 [122]

McLaughlin, Patrick, subj. of G.B.; rec. by Timothy Laughlin -
11 Apr. 1838 [123]

McNeil, James, subj. of G.B.; rec. by James Hazlet - 11 Apr.
1838 [124]

McCready, William, subj. of G.B.; rec. by Bernard Burns - 11
Apr. 1838 [125]

McCausland, John, subj. of G.B.; rec. by Hugh Reilly - 11 Apr.
1838 [126]

McCarthy, Patrick, subj. of G.B.; rec. by Thomas Morgan - 11
Apr. 1838 [127]

McEntee/McEntie, Owen, subj. of G.B.; rec. by Peter Mahon - 11
Apr. 1838 [128]

McKnight, Michael, subj. of G.B.; rec. by William Swift - 11
Apr. 1838 [130]

McMahon, Patrick, subj. of G.B.; rec. by Patrick McNany; [re-
port 14 Dec. 1824]: b. Co. Monaghan, Ire., age 24, migr. from
Newry, weaver; wife Alice, b. Co. Monaghan, age 23 - 11 Apr.
1838 [129]

McKinley, John [report Phila. 2 Oct. 1833]: b. Ire. on 16 July
1808, age now 25, migr. from Belfast, arrived Port of N.Y. 16
July 1826; rec. by John Newman - 11 Apr. 1838 [131]

McCarthy, Daniel, aubj. of G.B.; rec. by Jeremiah McCarthy - 11
Apr. 1838 [132]

McManus, Michael, subj. of G.B.; rec. by Patrick Chrystal - 12
Apr. 1838 [133]

McDermott, Patrick, subj. of G.B.; rec. by Michael Moran - 12
Apr. 1838

McGuire, James, subj. of G.B.; rec. by James McSorley - 12 Apr.
1838 [135]

McCourt, James, subj. of G.B.; rec. by Martin McGovern - 12 Apr. 1838 [136]

McCann, Andrew, subj. of G.B.; rec. by Roger Treanor - 12 Apr. 1838 [137]

McCabe, Hugh, subj. of G.B.; rec. by John James Brown - 12 Apr. 1838 [138]

McHugh, Edward, of Paterson, N.J., subj. of G.B.; rec. by Hugh Doyle - 5 Oct. 1838 [139]

McKenna, John, subj. of G.B.; rec. by Edward D. West - 31 Oct. 1838 [140]

McCullough, James, subj. of G.B.; rec. by Andrew McCullough - 3 Nov. 1838 [141]

McGill, Robert, subj. of G.B.; rec. by Nathaniel Smith - 3 Nov. 1838 [142]

McNamara, Darby, subj. of G.B.; rec. by Daniel Leary - 3 Nov. 1838 [143]

McVey, John, subj. of G.B.; rec. by Patrick McCaffry; [report Boston May 1830]: b. Cranney [Cranagh?], Co. Tyrone, Ire., on 29 June 1812, age now 24, arrived Boston 10 June 1832, shoe-maker- 5 Nov. 1838 [144]

Mc Vey, Patrick, subj. of G.B.; rec. by Thomas Virty - 5 Nov. 1838 [145]

McNamara, Patrick, subj. of G.B.; rec. by Daniel Leary - 5 Nov. 1838 [146]

McKiernan, Cornelius, subj. of G.B.; rec. by James R. Irwin - 6 Nov. 1838 [147]

McKenna, Jole, subj. of G.B.; rec. by William Haysman - 6 Nov. 1838 [148]

McClure, John, subj. of G.B.; rec. by John Maltman - 6 Nov. 1838 [149]

McNaughton, Peter Edward, subj. of G.B.; rec. by Daniel McKay - 6 Nov. 1838 [150]

McAlarney, Bernard, ostler, subj. of G.B.; rec. by James Kough [clerk wrote Cahough] - 6 Nov. 1838 [151]

McClinin, John, subj. of G.B.; rec. by Enoch Morgan - 7 Nov. 1838 [152]

McAlister, Alexander, subj. of G.B.; rec. by James Bellis - 7 Nov. 1838 [no number]

McCormick, Patrick, subj. of G.B.; rec. by Patrick Maddan - 7 Nov. 1838 [153]

McCormick, William, subj. of G.B.; rec. by Hugh O'Donnell - 7 Nov. 1838 [154]

McDowell, Hugh, subj. of G.B.; rec. by St. Clair Lithgow - 7 Nov. 1838 [155]

Nowlan, Bernard, subj. of G.B.; rec. by John McCarthy - 10 Apr. 1838 [156]

Nugent, William, subj. of G.B.; rec. by William White - 11 Apr. 1838 [147]

Nuttall, William, subj. of G.B.; rec. by Robert Kirkman - 3 Nov. 1838 [158]

Nolan, Thomas Flood, subj. of G.B.; rec. by William L. Shardlow - 5 Nov. 1838 [159]

Neill, Thomas, subj. of G.B.; rec. by Henry Guyschard - 5 Nov. 1838 [160]

Nevills/Nevilles, James, labourer, subj. of G.B.; rec. by John Foley - 5 Nov. 1838 [161]

Neal, George, subj. of G.B.; rec. by Alexander Murray - 5 Nov. 1838 [162]

Nichols, John, subj. of G.B.; rec. by William Peterson - 5 Nov. 1838 [163]

Niblo, William, subj. of G.B.; rec. by J. Philip Phoenix - 6 Nov. 1838 [164]

Newman, Charles [report 26 Nov. 1835]: b. in Prussia, age 28, labourer, emigr. from Neurnberg [?] in June 1829 and arrived NYC 24 Aug. 1829, intending to reside in Cincinnati, Ohio; rec. by William H. Brown - 7 Nov. 1838 [165]

Priest, Francis, subj. of G.B.; rec. by Peter Gilhooley - 10 Apr. 1838 [166]

Porter, John, subj. of G.B.; rec. by Edward J. Godfrey - 7 Apr. 1838 [167]

Price, John, accountant, subj. of G.B.; rec. by Daniel Wayland - 10 Apr. 1839 [168]

Price, Joseph B., subj. of G.B.; rec. by Daniel Wayland - 10 Apr. 1838 [169]

Parry, William, subj. of G.B.; rec. by John Jesse Spemers - 10 Apr. 1838 [170]

Phillips, Solomon, subj. of King of Bavaria; rec. by Peter Sickhouse - 11 Apr. 1838 [171]

Paytin, John, subj. of G.B.; rec. by James McIntyre - 11 Oct. 1838 [172]

Pestiaux, Amedee, subj. of King of France; rec. by Eugene Ferrard - 11 Oct. 1838 [173]

Bundle 19

Bruck, Daniel, subj. of G.B.; rec. by John Bowrosan - 8 Apr. 1839 [1]

Baumer, Frantz, subj. of Republic of Switzerland; rec. by Georg Fullmer - 25 Feb. 1839 [no number]

Brett, Thomas P., subj. of G.B.; rec. by Richard F. Sause - 9 Apr. 1839 [2]

Burnett, Robert, subj. of G.B.; rec. by William Burnett - 9 Apr. 1839 [3]

Brassal, John, subj. of G.B.; rec. by Patrick Madden - 8 Apr. 1839 [4]

Beck, Richard, subj. of G.B.; rec. by Michael Calhoun - 9 Apr. 1839 [5]

Black, Hugh, subj. of G.B.; rec. by John Black - 9 Apr. 1839 [6]

Barrington, Edward A., subj. of G.B.; rec. by Elias Roberts - 9 Apr. 1839 [7]

Bonniwell, James, subj. of G.B.; rec. by Francis Marion Devoe [report in Court of Oyer and Terminer, Ulster Co., N.Y., 4 Oct. 1836]: formerly of Co. of Kent, Eng., now of Esopus,Ulster Co. - 9 Apr. 1839 [8]

Bauer, Godfrey, subj. of King of Bavaria; rec. by Christian Soll - 10 Apr. 1839 [9]

Barber, Jesse, subj. of G.B.; rec. by Thomas Gethen - 10 Apr. 1839 [10]

Burns, John, subj. of G.B.; rec. by David Owens - 10 Apr. 1839 [11]

Bauckle, John, subj. of G.B.; rec. by Philip Batz - 10 Apr. 1839 [no number]

Burns, Patrick, subj. of G.B.; rec. by Dennis Brislen [clerk wrote "Brasle"] - 11 Apr. 1839 [12]

Barry, Francis, subj. of G.B.; rec. by John Dearborn - 11 Apr. 1839 [13]

Brittain, Alfred, subj. of G.B.; rec. by Andrew Little - 11 Apr. 1839 [14]

Bessling, Henry, subj. of G.B.; rec. by Frederick Smith - 11 Apr. 1839 [15]

Berleur, Eugene, subj. of King of Belgium; rec. by Prosper Douglas - 11 Apr. 1839 [16]

Browning, George F., subj. of G.B.; rec. by Thomas Browning - 11 Apr. 1839 [17]

Browning, John, subj. of G.B.; rec. by George F. Browning] 11 Apr. 1839 [18]

Bush, Roger, subj. of Free City of Hamburgh; rec. by Georg Fullmer - 11 Apr. 1839 [19]

Bliss, Theodore E. [certificate of intent in NYC 18 Aug. 1836]: arrived in U.S. in ship Columbia at New Haven in Nov. 1819 and resided there from Nov. 1819 to 18 Aug. 1836 except when from 24 Apr. to 19 Aug. 1835 he made a voyage to Eng. and back; a merchant, subj. of G.B.; rec. by Andrew Warner - 20 June 1839 [20]

Birnie, William, subj. of G.B.; rec. by Alexander Lawrence - 10 July 1839 [21]

Biller, Nicholas [report in township of Washington, Franklin Co., Pa. 3 Oct. 1837]: b. 9 Jan. 1815 in dominions of France, age 22 in June last, migr. to U.S. in March 1833, arrived Baltimore in June 1833 and removed to Franklin Co.; rec. by Nicholas Martin - 4 Nov. 1839 [22]

Blake, Peter, subj. of G.B.; rec. by Catharine Blake - 4 Nov. 1839 [23]

Barnes, Samuel C., of Brooklyn, teacher, subj. of G.B.; rec. by Martin Ryerson - 4 Nov. 1839 [24]

Bruce, John, subj. of G.B.; rec. by Allen C. Hallock - 5 Nov. 1839 [25]

Beiser/Beisher, Andrew, subj. of Grand Duke of Baden; rec. by Jacob Foster - 5 Nov. 1839 [26]

Beach, William, subj. of G.B.; rec. by Israel W. Raymond - 5 Nov. 1839 [27]

Betz, Adam, subj. of Grand Duke of Baden; rec. by John Hettinger - 5 Nov. 1839 [28]

Brettlell, Edmund, subj. of G.B.; rec. by John A. Jackson - 6 Nov. 1839 [29]

Baker, Thomas, subj. of G.B.; rec. by Joseph William Hyne - 6 Nov. 1839 [30]

Beck, Andrew, subj. of King of Bavaria; rec. by John George Beck - 6 Nov. 1839 [31]

Baker, Martin, subj. of Emperor of Austria‾[report 19 Apr. 1821]:
b. Bremen, Germany, age (illegible)4, migr. from Liverpool,
grocer; rec. by Henry M. Stone - 6 Nov. 1839 [32]

Brady, Edward, subj. of G.B.; rec. by James Brady - 6 Nov. 1839
[33]

Bawer, Michael, subj. of King of Bavaria; rec. by William Meyer
- 6 Nov. 1839 [34]

Batson, James, subj. of G.B.; rec. by Abraham Cozzens - 6 Nov.
1839 [35]

Bennett, William, subj. of G.B.; rec. by Samuel H. Dewint - 6
Nov. 1839 [36]

Benken, Christian, subj. of City of Bremen; rec. by Charles Fon-
yer [?] - 9 Nov. 1839 [37]

Barnes, John, comedian, subj. of G.B.; rec. by Joseph H. McCann
- 14 Dec. 1839 [38]

Dury, William, subj. of G.B.; rec. by Patrick Fitzgerald - 8
Apr. 1839 [39]

Dierr [Dürr?], Augustus, subj. of King of Wurtemberg; rec. by
Gottlieb Dierr [Dürr?] - 8 Apr. 1839 [40]

Dierr [Dürr?], Johannes, subj. of King of Wurtemberg; rec. by
Gottlieb Dürr - 8 Apr. 1839 [41]

Doharty, David, subj. of G.B.; rec. by Patrick Madden - 9 Apr.
1839 [42]

Drysdale, Andrew, subj. of G.B.; rec. by Henry Walters - 10 Apr.
1839 [43]

Danger, Lewis, subj. of King of Bavaria; rec. by Peter Behler -
10 Apr. 1839 [44]

Devlin, Charles, subj. of G.B.; rec. by Anthony O'Donnell - 10
Apr. 1839 [45]

Donnellon, James, labourer, subj. of G.B.; rec. by Edmund Hurry
- 10 Apr. 1839 [46]

Day, John P., subj. of G.B.; rec. by James McCully - 11 Apr.
1839 [47]

Dunshee, Robert, subj. of G.B.; rec. by James Gray - 11 Apr.
1839 [48]

Darlington, John, subj. of G.B.; rec. by Lewis Jones - 4 Nov.
1839 [49]

Dalton, John, subj. of G.B.; rec. by N. Norris Halsted - 4 Nov.
1839 [50]

Danaher, Timothy L., subj. of G.B.; rec. by Eugene Lavielle - 4
Nov. 1839 [51]

Divenger, Gerard Henry, subj. of King of Hanover; rec. by George
W. Rose - 5 Nov. 1839 [52]

Dalrymple, Alexander, subj. of G.B.; rec. by John Brown - 6 Nov.
1839 [53]

Dixon, Edward, subj. of G.B.; rec. by John Faulkner - 6 Nov.
1839 [54]

Ellis, James, subj. of G.B.; rec. by Abraham Tipping - 11 Apr.
1839 [55]

Engelke, John, subj. of King of Hanover; rec. by Nicholas Kunz
- 10 Apr. 1839 [56]

Eckert, John, subj. of Grand Duke of Baden; rec. by John B. Geiler - 9 Apr. 1839 [57]

Eagles, Richard, subj. of G.B.; rec. by Truman B. Dickerson - 5 Nov. 1839 [no number]

Espie, James, late of Scotland, subj. of G.B.; rec. by Robert Smith - 6 Nov. 1839 [58]

Edey, Matthew, subj. of G.B.; rec. by Francis D. Marshall - 6 Nov. 1839 [59]

Elliott, Samuel M., late of Inverness, Scotland, subj. of G.B.; rec. by Allan Gold Smith - 6 Nov. 1839 [60]

Eberle, John, subj. of King of Wurtemberg; rec. by Jacob Foster - 6 Nov. 1839 [61]

Fendi, Joseph Gustave, subj. of Emperor of Austria; rec. by Andrew S. Cooke - 8 Apr. 1839 [62]

Fritz, George, subj. of King of France; rec. by Englehart Brisch - 9 Apr. 1839 [63]

Fritz, Jacob, subj. of King of France; rec. by Englehart Brisch - 9 Apr. 1839 [64]

Fullerton, Arthur, subj. of G.B.; rec. by William Robb - 11 Apr. 1839 [65]

Farley, Philip, subj. of G.B.; rec. by James Pettit - 11 Apr. 1839 [66]

Fitzpatrick. Peter, subj. of G.B.; rec. by James Kehoe - 11 Apr. 1839 [67]

Fürst, Martin J., late of Prussia, subj. of King of Prussia; rec. by George A. Fürst - 4 Nov. 1839 [68]

Gollward, Thomas, subj. of G.B.; rec. by James H. Kellam - 8 Apr. 1839 [69]

Glass, John, subj. of G.B.; rec. by Patrick Madden - 8 Apr. 1839 [70]

Gallagher, John, subj. of G.B.; rec. by Daniel Conner - 8 Apr. 1839 [71]

Griffiths, William, subj. of G.B.; rec. by Robert D. Walker - 9 Apr. 1839 [72]

Griffiths, John, subj. of G.B.; rec. by Robert D. Walker - 9 Apr. 1839 [73]

Gerhart, Valentine, subj. of King of Bavaria; rec. by Englehart Brisch - 9 Apr. 1839 [74]

Greville, James, subj. of G.B.; rec. by James Adams - 10 Apr. 1839 [75]

Gardner, John, subj. of G.B.; rec. by George Brown - 10 Apr. 1839 [76]

Gore, Francis, subj. of G.B.; rec. by Samuel McMinn - 10 Apr. 1839 [77]

Gibson, James, subj. of G.B.; rec. by James Stuart - 11 Apr. 1839 [78]

Gaarthuis, Hendrick, subj. of King of Holland; rec. by Christian Barnes - 11 Apr. 1839 [79]

Gallaghan, Bernard, subj. of G.B.; rec. by Philip McHugh - 11 Apr. 1839 [80]

Gomez, Raphael M., subj. of Queen of Spain; rec. by John Wallis, Jr. - 21 Sept. 1839 [81]

Gethen, Thomas, Jr., subj. of G.B.; rec. by Thomas Gethen, Sr. - 6 Nov. 1839 [82]

Gilbert, Jesse, subj. of G.B.; rec. by Charles E. Southard - 6
Nov. 1839 [83]

Garvey, Patrick, subj. of G.B.; rec. by Michael Smith - 5 Nov.
1839 [84]

Greene, Michael, subj. of G.B.; rec. by Henry Moore - 5 Nov.
1839 [85]

Garety, Thomas, subj. of G.B.; rec. by Abel T. Anderson - 4 Nov.
1839 [86]

Garapee, John, of town of Conwacki, Greene Co., N.Y., subj. of
G.B.; rec. by Ambrose Baker - 2 Nov. 1839 [87]

Heney, William Henry, subj. of G.B.; rec. by Christopher Heney -
1 Apr. 1839 [88]

Haas, Gottlob, subj. of Grand Duke of Baden; rec. by Christopher
Gortz - 20 Mar. 1839 [89]

Hat, Baptist, subj. of G.B.; rec. by Henry Guischard - 2 Apr.
1839 [90]

Hogg, Thomas, subj. of G.B.; rec. by William Edmonds - 4 Apr.
1839 [91]

Hollands, Walter, subj. of G.B.; rec. by Benjamin Pettit - 8
Apr. 1839 [92]

Hatfield, William, subj. of King of Bavaria; rec. by Jacob Hartmann - 8 Apr. 1839 [93]

Hendrick, John, subj. of King of Prussia; rec. by Jacob Hartmann - 8 Apr. 1839 [94]

Henrich, Peter, subj. of King of France; rec. by Thomas J. Vel-
dran - 8 Apr. 1839 [95]

Halley, Robert, subj. of G.B.; rec. by Peter Hay - 9 Apr. 1839
[96]

Holford, James, subj. of G.B.; rec. by John Palmer - 9 Apr.
1839 [97]

Heltberg, Charles, subj. of King of Prussia; rec. by Georg Fullmer - 9 Apr. 1839 [98]

Hay, Peter, subj. of G.B.; rec. by Robert Halley - 9 Apr. 1839
[99]

Haarstrich, Carl, subj. of King of Hanover; rec. by Charles
Grimme - 10 Apr. 1839 [100]

Hull, Michael, subj. of Grand Duke of Baden; rec. by Jacob F.
Pubser - 10 Apr. 1839 [101]

Hollidge, Thomas [report Phila. 7 July 1835]: native of Eng.,
age 66, arrived Port of New York 6 May 1802; rec. by Eli Hollidge - 10 Apr. 1839 [102]

Haeffile, Moritz, subj. of Grand Duke of Baden; rec. by Philip
Finey - 11 Apr. 1839 [103]

Hunter, James, subj. of G.B.; rec. by William Robb - 25 Apr.
1839 [104]

Hurley, John S., subj. of G.B.; rec. by Humphrey Moynahan [re-
port Boston Nov. 1837]: b. Co. Kerry, Ire. on 3 June 1807, age
now 30, labourer, arrived Boston 13 June 1833 - 3 Nov. 1839
[105]

Hyne, Joseph William, subj. of G.B.; rec. by Samuel Perley - 5
Nov. 1839 [106]

Hyde, Thomas W., subj. of G.B.; rec. by John Bellamy - 5 Nov.
1839 [107]

Hoyer, Jacob, subj. of King of Holland; rec. by William C. Lemon - 6 Nov. 1839 [108]

Hopkins, Matthew, subj. of G.B.; rec. by Michael Long - 6 Nov. 1839 [109]

Harvey, William, subj. of G.B.; rec. by Robert Tanner - 6 Nov. 1839 [110]

Heath, William, subj. of G.B.; rec. by Henry Cutbill - 6 Nov. 1839 [111]

Cronin, John, subj. of G.B.; rec. by David Anderson - 14 Mar. 1839 [112]

Clement, William, native of Scotland; rec. by Robert Honey - 4 Apr. 1839 [113]

Coles, Charles, subj. of G.B.; rec. by John McConnell - 5 Apr. 1839 [114]

Carmody, Thomas, subj. of G.B.; rec. by Patrick Madden - 8 Apr. 1839 [115]

Cole, William, late of London, Eng., subj. of G.B.; rec. by Henry Cole - 8 Apr. 1839 [116]

Child, Lewis, subj. of G.B.; rec. by William T. Child - 8 Apr. 1839 [117]

Curtis, Henry, subj. of King of Hanover; rec. by James A. Pearsall - 8 Apr. 1839 [118]

Cowan, Robert, subj. of G.B.; rec. by Micajah M. Staniels - 9 Apr. 1839 [119]

Carroll, James, subj. of G.B.; rec. by Benjamin Okell - 9 Apr. 1839 [no number]

Coote, Richard, subj. of G.B.; rec. by Walter Farrell - 10 Apr. 1839 [120]

Carlisle, Benjamin, subj. of G.B.; rec. by William McGarvey - 10 Apr. 1839 [121]

Carlin, James, subj. of G.B.; rec. by Laughlin Rush - 10 Apr. 1839 [122]

Carlin, Thomas, subj. of G.B.; rec. by William Pickett - 10 Apr. 1839 [123]

Cantrell, Samuel, subj. of G.B.; rec. by John Cantrell - 10 Apr. 1839 [124]

Crossley, William, subj. of G.B.; rec. by John Crossley - 10 Apr. 1839 [125]

Cowten, Charles, subj. of G.B.; rec. by William A. Haywek - 10 Apr. 1839 [126]

Carry, John, subj. of G.B.; rec. by Myrtel B. Hitchcock - 11 Apr. 1839 [127]

Colquhoun, John, subj. of G.B.; rec. by William Cartier - 11 Apr. 1839 [128]

Cardwell, Samuel, subj. of G.B.; rec. by James Birmingham - 11 Apr. 1839 [129]

Crossingham, George, subj. of G.B.; rec. by Richard Mott - 11 Apr. 1839 [130]

Campbell, Andrew, subj. of G.B.; rec. by John Wiley - 11 Apr. 1839 [131]

Cross, Henry, subj. of King of Belgium; rec. by Jane Cross - 19 June 1839 [no number]

Castles, Michael, subj. of G.B., made decl. intent 11 July 1834; rec. by John King [132]

Clark, Robert C., subj. of G.B.; rec. by John Cooper - 29 July 1839 [133]

Clark, David, subj. of G.B.; rec. by Samuel Martin - 20 Sept. 1839 [134]

Craig, Hugh, subj. of G.B; rec. by Jonathan Holbrook - 4 Nov. 1839 [135]

Carter, Charles, subj. of G.B.; rec. by Jeremiah Milbank - 4 Nov. 1839 [136]

Cowles, Joseph B., subj. of G.B.; rec. by Jacob Outwater - 5 Nov. 1839 [137]

Cowley, William, subj. of G.B.; rec. by John Evans - 5 Nov. 1839 [138]

Cumberland, William, subj. of G.B.; rec. by William Rollinson - 6 Nov. 1839 [139]

Cantrell, Peter, subj. of G.B.; rec. by John Cantrell - 6 Nov. 1839 [140]

Chartre, Michael, subj. of G.B.; rec. by Dennison Williams - 6 Nov. 1839 [141]

Carmichael, Archibald, labourer, subj. of G.B.; rec. by John Adkins [report 16 July 1833]: b. at Strade, Co. Antrim, Ire., on 8 Aug. [date gone], arrived U.S. 10 Oct. 1829 - 6 Nov. 1839 [142]

Callender, George, subj. of G.B.; rec. by Joseph Ward - 6 Nov. 1839 [143]

Clous/Klaus, Joseph, subj. of King of France; rec. by Joseph Leon - 6 Nov. 1839 [144]

Isaacs, Jonas, subj. of G.B.; rec. by Samuel M. Solomons - 6 Nov. 1839 [145]

Ithamer, William, subj. of Republic of Hamburgh; rec. by Alexander McKenzie - 29 Mar. 1839 [146]

Jones, John J., subj. of G.B.; rec. by Calvin Case - 4 Nov. 1839 [147]

Jones, John, subj. of G.B.; rec. by Thomas Furney - 6 Nov. 1839 [148]

Jeans, John, subj. of G.B.; rec. by William Witberg - 10 Apr. 1839 [149]

Jones, Abraham, subj. of G.B.; rec. by James Pilling - 9 Apr. 1839 [no number]

Jackson, Samuel, subj. of G.B.; rec, by James Jackson - 14 Mar. 1839 [150]

Johnstone, John, subj. of G.B.; rec. by Augustus W.O. Spooner - 10 Apr. 1839 [151]

Johnson, Thomas, subj. of G.B.; rec. by John Balfour - 11 Apr. 1839 [152]

Johnston, Samuel, subj. of G.B.; rec. by William Johnston - 11 Apr. 1839 [153]

Jones, Joseph, subj. of G.B.; rec. by John Gee - 11 Apr. 1839 [AA 153]

Johnston, Alexander, subj. of G.B.; rec. by Ralph R. Wise - 26 Aug. 1839 [154]; born in Scotland acc. to report 1 July 1836 in Hustings Court, Petersburg, Va.

Jevens, William A., subj. of G.B.; rec. by Thomas Goadby - 4 Nov. 1839 [155]

Jones, Samuel B., subj. of G.B.; rec. by Anthony Baptist, Jr. - 5 Nov. 1839 [156]

Jarvis, Walter, subj. of G.B.; rec. by John Henry - 6 Nov. 1839 [157]

Achren, Otto, subj. of King of Sweden; rec. by John Brown - 7 Feb. 1839 [no number]

Andrews, Charles, subj. of G.B.; rec. by George Biddulph - 1 Nov. 1839 [158]

Allen, Edward Frederick, subj. of G.B.; rec. by James D. Champlin - 9 Apr. 1839 [159]

Appleyard, William, subj. of G.B.; rec. by William K. Northall, of Brooklyn - 5 Nov. 1839

Bundle 20

Rogers, Benjamin H., subj. of G.B.; rec. by John Parker - 2 Apr. 1839 [1]

Ryley, John, subj. of G.B.; rec. by John Evans - 9 Apr. 1839 [2]

Rowe, John, subj. of G.B.; rec. by Richard Beck - 9 Apr. 1839 [3]

Rice, Edward, subj. of G.B.; rec. by James Hannan - 9 Apr. 1839 [4]

Rush, Laughlin, subj. of G.B.; rec. by James Carlin - 10 Apr. 1839 [5]

Rebrasius, Joseph, subj. of King of France; rec. by Michel Lefoulon - 10 Apr. 1839 [6]

Rohr, Augustus Wm., subj. of Republic of Hamburgh; rec. by George Peter - 10 Apr. 1839 [7]

Rozenfeld, Julian, subj. of Emperor of Russia; rec. by Charles Jurgenski - 10 Apr. 1839 [8]

Raphael, Solomon, subj. of Emperor of Russia; rec. by Lewis M. Morrison - 11 Apr. 1839 [9]

Riley, Charles, subj. of G.B.; rec. by Benjamin J. Hunt - 11 Apr. 1839 [10]

Rooney, William, subj. of G.B.; rec. by Daniel Rooney - 11 Apr. 1839 [11]

Roe, Charles S., student-at-law, subj. of G.B.; rec. by John W. Merritt - 21 May 1839 [12]

Revill, Richard, of Brooklyn, subj. of G.B.; rec. by Thomas Faye, of Brooklyn - 1 Nov. 1839 [13]

Rupp, Michael, subj. of King of France; rec. by Anthony Lambrecht - 4 Nov. 1839 [14]

Rice, Lazarus, subj. of King of Bavaria; rec. by Josiah Kittery - 5 Nov. 1839 [15]

Rankin, William, subj. of G.B.; rec. by Joseph Brooks - 5 Nov. 1839 [16]

Richards, Joseph, subj. of G.B.; rec. by William H. Guischard - 5 Nov. 1839 [17]

Reilly, James, subj. of G.B.; rec. by Owen Cassidy - 6 Nov. 1839 [18]

Rieck, Arend Hinrich , subj. of King of Hanover; rec. by Charles
   Tonjes - 9 Nov. 1839 [19]

Rapp, Mary Catharine Martha Berard (widow of John B.N. Rapp),
   subj. of King of France; rec. by Andrew Surre and Samuel Dunshee - 14 Nov. 1839 [20]

Williams, John, subj. of King of Sweden; rec. by William Witberg
   - 11 Apr. 1839 [21]

Weil, Henry, cabinetmaker, subj. of Grand Duke of Nassau; rec.
   by Arthur Eggleso - 9 Apr. 1839 [22]

Walters, Lewis, subj. of King of Prussia; rec. by George Wode -
   9 Apr. 1839 [23]

Wode, Francis, subj. of King of Hanover; rec. by George Wode -
   9 Apr. 1839 [24]

Williams, William, subj. of G.B.; rec. by David Owens - 9 Apr.
   1839 [25]

Wode, Frederick, subj. of King of Hanover; rec. by George Wode
   - 9 Apr. 1839 [26]

Wischler, Michael, subj. of King of Bavaria; rec. by Englehart
   Brisch - 9 Apr. 1839 [27]

Whearty, Andrew, subj. of G.B.; rec. by Benjamin Odell - 9 Apr.
   1839 [28]

Wilshausen, Diederich, subj. of King of Hanover; rec. by Georg
   Fullmer- 10 Apr. 1839 [29]

Williams, Martin, subj. of King of Prussia; rec. by James A.
   Pearsall - 10 Apr. 1839

Wiley, John, subj. of G.B.; rec. by William Robb - 10 Apr. 1839
   [31]

Wallis, John, Jr., subj. of Queen of Spain; rec. by Raphael M.
   Gomez - 21 Sept. 1839 [32]

Wilkinson, James, subj. of G.B.; rec. by Jotham Peabody - 8 Oct.
   1839 [33]

Walton, Alexander D., subj. of G.B.; rec. by Philip Grandin - 4
   Nov. 1839 [34]

Wareham, James, subj. of G.B.; rec. by Richard Y. Hull - 4 Nov.
   1839 [35]

Wray, Charles, subj. of G.B.; rec. by Joseph Brooks - 5 Nov.
   1839 [36]

Waterson, Benjamin Joseph, subj. of G.B.; rec. by John Anderson
   [report 17 Jan. 1827]: b. Eng., age 28, migr. from London,
   currier, intending to settle in Norwich, Conn. - 5 Nov. 1839
   [37]

Watkins, John L., subj. of G.B.; rec. by Henry W. Scott - 5 Nov.
   1839 [38]

Wray, John, subj. of G.B.; rec, by Joseph Brooks - 5 Nov. 1839
   [39]

Watts, James, subj. of G.B.; rec. by John Watts - 6 Nov. 1839
   [40]

Wheret, John Gamlin, subj. of G.B.; rec. by James H. Noe - 6
   Nov. 1839 [no number]

Wedekind, Henry, subj. of King of Hanover; rec. by Charles Tonjes - 9 Nov. 1839 [41]

Woodhead, Thomas, subj. of G.B.; rec. by John Woodhead - 8 Nov.
   1839 [no number]

Little, James, subj. of G.B.; rec. by Andrew Little - 11 Apr. 1839 [42]

Latimer, John, subj. of G.B.; rec. by Stephen B. Olmstead - 3 Apr. 1839 [43]

Lodge, William, subj. of G.B.; rec. by John Whitton - 8 Apr. 1839 [44]

Le Grand, Peter, subj. of King of France; rec. by Ceprean Lewis Tailland - 8 Apr. 1839 [45]

Longking, Joseph, subj. of G.B.; rec. by William Gent - 9 Apr. 1839 [46]

Lockwood, William, subj. of G.B.; rec. by James Lockwood - 9 Apr. 1839 [47]

Latham, Samuel, subj. of G.B.; rec. by Vincent Le Count - 10 Apr. 1839 [48]

Laughorn, Charles Frederick, subj. of King of Prussia; rec. by Georg Fullmer - 10 Apr. 1839 [49]

Lombart, Nicholas, subj. of King of Bavaria; rec. by Anthony Lambert - 10 Apr. 1839 [50]

Levy, John, Jr., subj. of G.B.; rec. by Richard Winthrop - 10 Apr. 1839 [51]

Long, James Page, clerk, subj. of G.B.; rec. by D. Randolph Martin - 16 Apr. 1839 [52]

Lynch, Jeremiah, subj. of G.B.; rec. by Edmond Fitzgerald - 3 Nov. 1839 [53]

Leary, Andrew, subj. of G.B.; rec. by William Covert - 4 Nov. 1839 [54]

Le Clair, Thomas, subj. of G.B.; rec. by Desire N. Morange - 5 Nov. 1839 [AA 54]

Leckie, William, subj. of G.B.; rec. by Peter Smith - 6 Nov. 1839 [55]

Lundy, Thomas, subj. of G.B.; rec. by John Williamson - 6 Nov. 1839 [56]

Levenstyn, Jacob, subj. of King of Holland; rec. by James Church - 6 Nov. 1839 [57]

Lecon, Richard, subj. of G.B.; rec. by Richard F. Sause - 6 Nov. 1839 [58]

Nelas, Francis, subj. of G.B.; rec. by Hugh Nelas - 8 Apr. 1839 [59]

Newson, Eli, subj. of G.B.; rec. by George A. Hood - 11 Apr. 1839 [60]

Noble, Robert, subj. of G.B.; rec. by Floyd D. Archer - 11 Apr. 1839 [61]

O'Connor, Richard, subj. of G.B.; rec. by Alfred M. Weed - 8 Apr. 1839 [62]

Oliver, John W., subj. of G.B.; rec. by Isaac J. Oliver - 1 Nov. 1839 [63]

O'Brien, Bryan, subj. of G.B.; rec. by John Regan - 9 Apr. 1839 [64]

O'Brien, Charles, late of Co. Tyrone, Ire.; rec. by Ogden Haggerty - 6 Nov. 1839 [65]

O'Brien, Denis, subj. of G.B.; rec. by Maurice O'Brien - 11 Apr. 1839 [66]

O'Donnell, Anthony [report in Phila. Co. 14 July 1834]: b. Co.
Mayo, Ire., on 17 Mar. 1799, age now 35, migr. from Liverpool,
arrived Port of New York 19 Nov. 1820, intending to settle in
Pa.; rec. by John Durkin - 10 Apr. 1839 [67]

O'Hanlon, Martin, subj. of G.B.; rec. by Charles Coffin - 21
Dec. 1839 [68]

Thomson, William S., subj. of G.B.;rec. by George Smith - 11
Apr. 1839 [69]

Towne [or Toun?], John, subj. of Queen of Portugal; rec. by
Manuel Joseph - 5 Jan. 1839 [70]

Thompson, William A. subj. of G.B.; rec. by John Stripp, rigger
- 12 Jan. 1839 [71]

Trumber, Ludwig, subj. of King of Hanover; rec. by Patrick Madden - 3 Apr. 1839 [72]

Tree, John Philip, subj. of G.B.; rec. by David Higgins - 4 Apr.
1839 [73]

Turk, William, subj. of G.B.; rec. by Robert Thompson - 8 Apr.
1839 [74]

Tuft, Joseph, subj. of King of France; rec. by John Snyder - 8
Apr. 1839 [75]

Tod, James, subj. of G.B.; rec. by John Palmer - 9 Apr. 1839
[76]

Toy, Dennis, subj. of G.B.; rec. by David Owens - 10 Apr. 1839
[77]

Turzenska, Charles, subj. of Emperor of Russia; rec. by Julian
Rozenfeld - 10 Apr. 1839 [78]

Troutman, John Jacob, subj. of King of Bavaria; rec. by Philip
Brissel - 10 Apr. 1839 [79]

Tolle, Henry, subj. of King of Prussia; rec. by Henry Klenen -
10 Apr. 1839 [80]

Tayler, John Henry, subj. of G.B.; rec. by Thomas Tayler - 2
Sept. 1839 [81]

Tease, William, subj. of G.B.; rec. by Bernard Sweeney - 4 Nov.
1839 [82]

Tilly, Samuel, subj. of G.B.; rec. by Henry Guischard, of Bushwick, Kings Co. - 4 Mar. 1839 [83]

Prindle, Timothy F., of Rahway, N.J., formerly known as Timothy
O'Brien, subj. of G.B.; rec. by Jonas Gurnee - 12 Mar. 1839
[84]

Parker, John, subj. of G.B.; rec. by Benjamin H. Rogers - 2 Apr.
1839 [85]

Pilkington, William, subj. of G.B.; rec. by Henry R. Shanklin -
6 Apr. 1839 [86]

Power, Nicholas, subj. of G.B.; rec. by Patrick Maloney - 8 Apr.
1839 [87]

Pritchard, Richard, carpenter, subj. of G.B.; rec. by Isaac Anderson - 9 Apr. 1839 [88]

Paisley, William J., cartman, subj. of G.B.; rec. by Michael
Calhoun - 9 Apr. 1839 [89]

Paton, James, subj. of G.B.; rec. by Peter Morton - 11 Apr. 1839
[90]

Pearn, Samuel, subj. of G.B.; rec. by William Steer [report Wayne Co., Pa., 27 Jan. 1834]: b. Cornwall about 1790, migr. Aug. 1830 - 11 Apr. 1839 [91]

Pedon, Robert [report 13 Apr. 1821]; b. Co. Down, Ire., age 32, migr. from Belfast, stone cutter; rec. by William Moore - 22 Oct. 1839 [92]

Pashley, Samuel, subj. of G.B.; rec. by John Pashley - 4 Nov. 1839 [93]

Pashley, John, subj. of G.B.; rec. by Samuel Pashley - 4 Nov. 1839 [94]

Pratt, Robert, tailor, subj. of G.B.; rec. by Henry A. Shanklin - 4 Nov. 1839 [95]

Phyfe, Laughlin, subj. of G.B.; rec. by John Morrison - 5 Nov. 1839 [96]

Pate, Wm. McDowell, subj. of G.B.; rec. by James Houner - 6 Nov. 1839 [97]

Peterson, George, subj. of G.B.; rec. by John Peterkin - 6 Nov. 1839 [98]

Paulus, Gustavus Ludwig Henry, druggist, subj. of Elector of Hesse Cassel; rec. by Jay Lasher - 6 Nov. 1839 [99]

Phillips, Henry, subj. of G.B.; rec. by George Cripps - 6 Nov. 1839 [100]

Phillips, Thomas, subj. of G.B.; rec. by David Evans - 14 Dec. 1839 [101]

McKenna, Thomas, subj. of G.B.; rec. by Daniel Hughes - 22 Mar. 1839 [102]

McDonnell, Terrence, subj. of G.B.; rec. by Henry Guischard - 2 Apr. 1836 [103]

McCullough, John, subj. of G.B.; rec. by Murtagh Devlin - 9 Apr. 1839 [104]

McElroy, William, subj. of G.B.; rec. by La Fayette Hammons - 9 Apr. 1839 [105]

McLaughlin, Charles, subj. of G.B.; rec. by Samuel McConnell - 10 Apr. 1839 [106]

McAnnally, James, subj. of G.B.; rec. by John Brinkley - 11 Apr. 1839 [107]

McGee, Thomas, chandler and soap boiler, subj. of G.B.; rec. by William Moffat - 10 Apr. 1839 [108]

McNulty, Patrick, subj. of G.B.; rec. by Timothy O'Hallaran - 10 Apr. 1839 [109]

McArdle, Joseph, subj. of G.B.; rec. by Henry J. Sanford - 11 Apr. 1839 [110]

McGuire, James, subj. of G.B.; rec. by Jotham Peabody - 30 Apr. 1839 [111]

McDevitt, Charles, subj. of G.B.; rec. by William H. Clayton - 4 June 1839 [111AA]

McKenzie, Alexander, subj. of G.B.; rec. by Oliver Johnston - 10 June 1839 [112]

McLaughlin, Michael, subj. of G.B.; rec. by Daniel Sweeny - 4 Nov. 1839 [113]

McCarthy, Timothy, subj. of G.B.; rec. by John Wall - 5 Nov. 1839 [114]

McGrain, James, subj. of G.B.; rec. by Joseph Wark - 6 Nov.
1839 [115]

McLeay, Richard, subj. of G.B.; rec. by Thomas Watson McLeay -
6 Nov. 1839 [116]

McCandless, John, subj. of G.B.; rec. by Alexander Christie - 6
Nov. 1839 [117]

King, James, subj. of G.B.; rec. by John King - 22 Mar. 1839
[118]

Kunz, John George, subj. of G.B.; rec. by Henry Guischard - 2
Apr. 1839 [119]

Kelly, John, subj. of G.B.; rec. by George S. Howland - 6 Apr.
1839 [120]

Kussmanl, Johannes, subj. of King of Wurtemberg; rec. by Gottlieb Dürr - 8 Apr. 1839 [121]

Kern, John, subj. of King of Bavaria; rec. by Jacob Klein - 9
Apr. 1839 [122]

Kieckhoefer, Adolphus T., subj. of Republic of Hamburgh; rec. by
Jonathan Amory - 9 Apr. 1839 [123]

Knaus, Godfrey, subj. of King of Wurtemberg; rec. by John Henry
Hand - 10 Apr. 1839 [124]

Killick,Wickens, subj. of G.B.; rec. by Jeremiah L. Knapp - 10
Apr. 1839 [AA 124]

Kennedy, Patrick, subj. of G.B.; rec. by Michael Cochran - 10
Apr. 1839 [125]

Kinnen, John, subj. of G.B.; rec. by Richard Kinnen - 10 Apr.
1839 [126]

Kirkham, John, subj. of G.B.; rec. by Thomas Curran - 10 Apr.
1839 [127]

Kind, George, subj. of King of Saxony; rec. by Alexander Lawrence - 11 Apr. 1839 [128]

Kinstry, Thomas, subj. of G.B.; rec. by Isaac Anderson - 5 Nov.
1839 [129]

Knight, John, subj. of G.B.; rec. by William Mason - 5 Nov. 1839
[130]

Knipe, James, subj. of G.B.; rec. by William Knipe - 5 Nov. 1839
[131]

King, Mark Joseph, subj. of King of Prussia; rec. by W. Mooney
- 6 Nov. 1839 [132]

King, Manheim, subj. of King of Prussia; rec. by Mark J. King -
6 Nov. 1839 [133]

Young, Robert, subj. of G.B.; rec. by James Morrison - 6 Nov.
1839 [134]

Young, Louis, subj. of King of Prussia; rec. by Englehart Brisch
- 9 Apr. 1839 [135]

Sannemann, Diedrick, subj. of Grand Duke of Oldenburgh; rec. by
Richard Yates - 22 Feb. 1839 [136]

Spackehker, Lear, subj. of King of Hanover; rec. by Bernard Ot-
ten - 27 Feb. 1839 [137]

Smith, John, subj. of G.B.; rec. by James Nicol - 30 Mar. 1839
[138]

Stent, Joseph W., subj. of G.B.; rec. by Caleb Cridland - 5 Apr.
1839 [139]

Stevenson, John, subj. of G.B.; rec. by William Stevenson - 8
Apr. 1839 [140]

Stevenson, William, subj. of G.B.; rec. by John Stevenson - 8
Apr. 1839 [141]

Smith, John, subj. of King of Denmark; rec. by John Brown - 9
Apr. 1839 [142]

Seidler, Ferdinand, subj. of King of Prussia; rec. by William
Rittershofer [report Phila. 12 Oct. 1830]: b. Berne, Prussia
in 1799, age now 31, migr. from Rotterdam, arrived Baltimore
20 Aug. 1828 - 9 Apr. 1839 [143]

Schafer, Theobald, subj. of King of Bavaria; rec. by Englehart
Brisch - 9 Apr. 1839 [144]

Smith, James, subj. of G.B.; rec. by Henry Le Britton - 10 Apr.
1839 [145]

Silva, Manuel, formerly of Oporto, confectioner, subj. of Queen
of Portugal; rec. by Francis Favereau - 10 Apr. 1839 [146]

Simpson, William, cabinetmaker, subj. of G.B.; rec. by Theodore
Dregg - 10 Apr. 1839 [147]

Strong, John, subj. of G.B.; rec. by Richard F. Sause - 10 Apr.
1839 [148]

Shauts, Thomas, subj. of King of France; rec. by John Reinhard -
10 Apr. 1839 [149]

Scobie, John G.M., subj. of G.B.; rec. by William Potter - 9
Apr. 1839 [150]

Stein, Diederick, subj. of King of Hanover; rec. by Georg Fullmer - 10 Apr. 1839 [151]

Schmidt, Jacob, subj. of King of Wurtemberg; rec. by William
Meyers - 10 Apr. 1839 [152]

Scoble, John, subj. of G.B.; rec. by William Knight - 11 Apr.
1839 [AA 152]

Search, Henry H., subj. of G.B.; rec. by Thomas B. Donnell - 11
Apr. 1839 [153]

Smith, George, subj. of G.B.; rec. by Philip Roberts - 11 Apr.
1839 [154]

Spadony, John, subj. of King of Sardinia; rec. by Prosper Douglas - 11 Apr. 1839 [155]

Summers, Thomas, subj. of G.B.; rec. by Jonas Gurnee - 11 Apr.
1839 [156]

Steneck, Johann Henry, subj. of King of Hanover; rec. by Frederick Steneck - 11 Apr. 1839 [157]

Santwaak/Santwack, Johanis [report 13 Aug. 1836]: mariner, subj.
of King of Holland; rec. by John Haase - 8 Aug. 1839

Sefton, John [report Phila. 26 Jan. 1835]: b. Liverpool, Eng., on
15 Jan. 1805, migr. from Liverpool, arrived Port of New York
20 June 1827; rec. by Abraham Fisher - 24 Aug. 1839 [159]

Steiniger, August, subj. of Grand Duke of Saxe Weimar; rec. by
Lewis Cugler - 5 Nov. 1839 [160]

Smithson, George, subj. of G.B.; rec. by John Bland - 5 Nov.
1839 [161]

Sargent, William Clark, subj. of G.B.; rec. by William Lyon
[report 4 May 1836]: b. Lincolnshire, Eng., age 30, migr. from
Hull, intending to settle in Albany - 5 Nov. 1839 [162]

Stuart, Richard, subj. of G.B.; rec. by Jacob Solomon - 5 Nov. 1839 [163]

Stone, Charles, subj. of G.B.; rec. by John D. Brown - 6 Nov. 1839 [164]

Smith, John, subj. of G.B.; rec. by Moses H. Grinnell - 6 Nov. 1839 [165]

Wolf, George Leo, subj. of Govt. of Hamburgh; rec. by Gustavus Paulus, physician - 13 Feb. 1839 [166]

Monti, Giuseppe, subj. of Switzerland; rec. by Benedict De Angelis/De Angeli - 4 Feb. 1839 [167]

Major, Richard, subj. of G.B.; rec. by Caleb Cridland - 4 Feb. 1839 [168]

Mulvey, John, subj. of G.B.; rec. by John Quin - 2 Apr. 1839 [169]

Metzinger, Peter, subj. of King of France; rec. by Emmanuel Hauser - 8 Apr. 1839 [170]

Macfarlane, John, subj. of G.B.; rec. by Joseph Macfarlane - 9 Apr. 1839 [171]

Mulvey, Peter, subj. of G.B.; rec. by Bryan McDermott - 9 Apr. 1839 [172]

Monahan, Patrick, subj. of G.B.; rec. by Patrick Maddan - 9 Apr. 1839 [173]

Marsters, Silas W., subj. of G.B.; rec. by John J. Hart - 9 Apr. 1839 [174]

Montague, Henry, subj. of G.B.; rec. by John Price - 9 Apr. 1839 [175]

Morgan, Griffith, subj. of G.B.; rec. by John Evans - 10 Apr. 1839 [176]

Mann, Godfrey, subj. of G.B.; rec. by Joseph Smith - 9 Apr. 1839 [177]

Montgomery, Hugh, subj. of G.B.; rec. by William Smith - 11 Apr. 1839 [178]

Mott, Richard, subj. of G.B. ;rec. by George Cunningham - 11 Apr. 1839 [179]

Micholls, James, subj. of King of Prussia; rec. by Moses Samson - 4 Nov. 1839 [180]

Meekes, William, subj. of G.B.; rec. by Lewis Jones - 4 Nov. 1839 [no number]

Mackin, Henry, subj. of G.B.; rec. by John Kelly - 4 Nov. 1839 [181]

Morrow, Andrew, subj. of G.B.; rec. by Hugh Craig - 4 Nov. 1839 [182]

Meyer, John Jacob, subj. of King of Wurtemburgh; rec. by John H. Hess - 4 Nov. 1839 [183]

Macartney, William, subj. of G.B.; rec. by Joseph McMurray - 4 Nov. 1839 [184]

Moylan, James, subj. of G.B.; rec. by David Moylan - 4 Nov. 1839 [185]

Martin, Edward, subj. of G.B.; rec. by Henry R. Shanklin - 4 Nov. 1839 [186]

Meyer, Lewis, subj. of King of France; rec. by Michael Andrew - 4 Nov. 1839 [187]

Mannering, George, subj. of G.B.; rec. by George Joy - 5 Nov. 1839 [188]

Milns, Henry, subj. of G.B.; rec. by Henry Wilkins - 6 Nov. 1839 [189]

Monnin, Francois, subj. of King of France; rec. by Joseph Feusier - 6 Nov. 1839

Mulholland, Richard, subj. of G.B.; rec. by William Samuel Johnson - 6 Nov. 1839 [191]

Melvill, Alexander, subj. of G.B.; rec. by James Melvill - 6 Nov. 1839 [192]

Marpe, Augustus, subj. of King of Prussia; rec. by Charles Frederick Langhorn - 6 Nov. 1839 [193]

Moffat, John, subj. of G.B.; rec. by Agnes M. Finkill - 20 Nov. 1839 [194]

Vogel, John, subj. of Grand Duke of Baden; rec. by John Hettinger - 5 Nov. 1839 [195]

Vaun, Roger, subj. of G.B.; rec. by David Owens - 9 Apr. 1839 [196]

Quirk, Edmund, subj. of G.B.; rec. by Patrick Dun - 5 Nov. 1839 [197]

Quayle, John, subj. of G.B.; rec. by William Cottier - 11 Apr. 1839 [198]

Quelet, George, subj. of King of France; rec. by Nathan C. Platt - 4 Nov. 1839 [199]

Bundle 21

Ahrens, Albert, subj. of King of Hanover; rec. by Patrick Madden - 7 Apr. 1840 [1]

Austin, Thomas, subj. of G.B.; rec. by Jonathan Amory - 11 Apr. 1840 [2]

Atkinson, Robert, subj. of G.B.; rec. by Frederick T. Perkins - 11 Apr. 1840 [3]

Aitkin, William, subj. of G.B.; rec. by William Scott - 11 Sept. 1840 [4]

Allen, John [report 13 Oct. 1824]: b. Scotland, age 32, migr. from Greenock, ship-carpenter; rec. by Gilbert Giles - 25 Sept. 1840 [5]

Austin, Richard, subj. of G.B.; rec. by John Galvin - 28 Sept. 1840 [6]

Alberts, William, subj. of King of France; rec. by John Brown - 29 Sept. 1840 [7]

Ashwell, Geo., subj. of G.B.; rec. by Wm. R. Teasdale, of Long Island - 3 Oct. 1840 [8]

Aught, Henry, subj. of G.B.; rec. by Wm. Parker - 5 Oct. 1840 [9]

Anz, Frantz, subj. of Duke of Hesse Darmstadt; rec. by Johann Groh - 5 Oct. 1840 [10]

Adcock, James, subj. of G.B.; rec. by John Williams, of 270 Bleecker St. - 6 Oct. 1840 [11]

Ash, John, subj. of G.B.; rec. by Dennis Downs, of Brooklyn - 7 Oct. 1840 [12]

Atteridge, James, subj. of G.B.; rec. by Thomas Atteridge - 8 Oct. 1840 [AA 12]

Allen, John, subj. of G.B.; rec. by Gilbert Fowler - 8 Oct. 1840 [13]

Anderson, Thomas, subj. of G.B.; rec. by Jane Anderson - 9 Oct. 1840 [14]

Ayres, Solomon, subj. of G.B.; rec. by Isaac Golden - 9 Oct. 1840 [15]

Armstrong, John, subj. of G.B.; rec. by Patrick Dolan - 10 Oct. 1840 [16]

Armstrong, Bartley, subj. of G.B.; rec. by Edward McCabe, of 117 Washington St. - 10 Oct. 1840 [17]

Atkinson, Charles, subj. of G.B.; rec. by William Atkinson - 13 Oct. 1840 [18]

Anketell, James, subj. of G.B.; rec. by John Skiffington - 13 Oct. 1840 [19]

Ash, Michael, subj. of G.B.; rec. by John Ash - 19 Oct. 1840 [20]

Ash, Simon, of Brooklyn, subj. of G.B.; rec. by John Ash, of Brooklyn - 19 Oct. 1840 [21]

Alcorn, William, subj. of G.B.; rec. by John Cowley - 21 Oct. 1840 [22]

Alexander, Alexander, subj. of G.B.; rec. by Alexander Bennett - 21 Oct. 1840 [23]

Allan, William, subj. of G.B.; rec. by William Curr, of 107 Troy [St.] - 28 Oct. 1840 [24]

Alman, Charles, subj. of G.B.; rec. by John McDougall - 29 Oct. 1840 [25]

Anderson, James, subj. of G.B.; rec. by Joseph McCracken - 30 Oct. 1840 [26]

Archard, Thomas, of Westchester Co., subj. of G.B.; rec. by John Axford - 31 Oct. 1840 [27]

Auld, Henry Alexander, subj. of G.B.; rec. by John Calvin Smith - 3 Nov. 1840 [28]

Aylward, John, subj. of G.B.; rec. by Thomas Holohan, of 58 C (illegible) St. - 3 Nov. 1840 [29]

Apted, Richard, subj. of G.B.; rec. by T. Apted, of 9 Thompson St. - 2 Nov. 1840 [30]

Archer, Thomas, subj. of G.B.; rec. by William Bennil - 3 Nov. 1840 [31]

Adley/Addley, John, subj. of G.B.; rec. by Nathaniel Underhill - 3 Nov. 1840 [32]

Ashmead, Alfred, subj. of G.B.; rec. by Dennis Harris, of 168 Duane St. [also rec. 31 Oct. 1840 in Baltimore by John F. Towner, of Baltimore] - 4 Nov. 1840 [33]

Ash, Harry, subj. of King of Prussia; rec. by Mark J. King - 4 Nov. 1840 [34]

Blanchard, Gustave, subj. of King of France; rec. by Edward Burk, of Charleston, S.C. - 21 Feb. 1840 [35]

Black, William F., subj. of G.B.; rec. by William Nealy - 7 Apr. 1840 [36]

Beam, John G., subj. of City of Bremen; rec. by George H. Arens - 11 Apr. 1840 [37]

Boyle, James, subj. of G.B.; rec. by Thomas Scanlan - 11 Apr. 1840 [38]

Bleidorn, Louis, subj. of Grand Duke of Baden; rec. by Benjamin Drake - 11 Apr. 1840 [39]

Brock, Rebecca (wife of John Brock), subj. of G.B.; rec. by Isaac Francis, dentist - 1 July 1840 [40]

Boehnken, Henry, subj. of City of Bremen; rec. by Johann Jacob Boehnken - 22 July 1840 [41]

Boehnken, Johann Jacob, subj. of Free City of Bremen; rec. by Heinrich Boehnken - 22 July 1840 [42]

Buchan, James, subj. of G.B.; rec. by Thomas B. Rich - 3 Sept. 1840 [43]

Burckholster, John, subj. of King of France; rec. by Peter Bickler - 9 Sept. 1840 [44]

Bickler, Peter, subj. of King of France; rec. by John Burckholster 9 Sept. 1840 [45]

Butters, John H. [report Monmouth, N.J., 17 Sept. 1838]: b. Co. of Fifeshire, Scotland, on 22 Apr. 1798, migr. from Scotland, arrived New York 28 Aug. 1829; rec. by John Richmond - 26 Sept. 1840 [46]

Bruerton, George, subj. of G.B.; rec. by John Bruerton - 28 Sept. 1840 [47]

Brown, Archibald, subj. of G.B.; rec. by Cornelius W. Hebberd - 28 Sept. 1840 [48]

Bruerton, John, subj. of G.B.; rec. by George Bruerton - 28 Sept. 1840 [49]

Baucke, Erdmann Ferdinand, subj. of City of Hamburgh; rec. by Teunis Fokkes - 28 Sept. 1840 [50]

Breen, Moses, subj. of G.B.; rec. by Edward Condren - 28 Sept. 1840 [51]

Bodt, Henry, subj. of King of Prussia; rec. by John Brown - 28 Sept. 1840 [52]

Bryant, John, subj. of G.B.; rec. by John Mason - 28 Sept. 1840 [53]

Bentley, Thomas, subj. of G.B.; rec. by Samuel Hazelton - 29 Sept. 1840 [54]

Bier, Charles, subj. of King of Bavaria; rec. by Jacob Haschar - 29 Sept. 1840 [55]

Brown, Hamilton, subj. of G.B.; rec. by James Nicol - 30 Sept. 1840 [56]

Butler, Samuel, subj. of G.B.; rec. by Henry Nowlan, of 28th St. and 1st. Ave. - 1 Oct. 1840 [57]

Betts, George, subj. of G.B.; rec. by Wm. O. Webb - 2 Oct. 1840 [58]

Briggs, John R., of 133 Thirteenth St., subj. of G.B.; rec. by Joseph Kennedy, of West Broadway and 9th Ave. - 3 Oct. 1840 [59]

Burk, John, subj. of G.B.; rec. by James Quarry, of 207 Mercer St. - 5 Oct. 1840 [60]

Boyland, James, subj. of G.B.; rec. by James McKenna and also Henry Williams, of Apalachicola, West Florida - 6 Oct. 1840 [61]

Bouer, Jacob, subj. of Grand Duke of Baden; rec. by Elias Hatfield - 6 Oct. 1840 [62]

Ballasteen, John, subj. of King of Sardinia; rec. by Josiah Mann; on 7 Oct. 1840 Ebenezer Foster swears that Ballasteen arrived in the U.S. in 1831 - 6 Oct. 1840 [63]

Brennan, Peter, subj. of G.B.; rec. by John Moran - 6 Oct. 1840 [64]

Bird, Philip, subj. of G.B.; rec. by Isaac H. Knowlton, of 118 Suffolk St. - 7 Oct. 1840 [65]

Burlin, Richard, subj. of G.B.; rec. by William Church, Jr. - 8 Oct. 1840 [66]

Baird, Thomas W., subj. of G.B.; rec. by David A. Baird - 7 Oct. 1840 [67]

Bale, Charles, subj. of G.B.; rec. by Frederick W. Shipley - 8 Oct. 1840 [68]

Boylan, Patrick, native of Ire.; rec. by John Trainer, of 37 Allen St. - 8 Oct. 1840 [69]

Biltis, William, subj. of King of Prussia; rec. by Frederick Adz, of 7th Ave. and 25th St. - 8 Oct. 1840 [70]

Bale, Thomas, of 52 Grand St., subj. of G.B.; rec. by Frederick W. Shipley - 8 Oct. 1840 [71]

Brown, James, subj. of G.B.; rec. by Alonzo D. Wood - 8 Oct. 1840 [72]

Butner, John P., subj. of King of Holland; rec. by John W. Cramer - 9 Oct. 1840

Beeching, John, subj. of G.B.; rec. by Robert Beeching - 9 Oct. 1840 [74]

Beeching, Robert, subj. of G.B.; rec. by John Beeching - 9 Oct. 1840 [75]

Brady, Thomas R., subj. of G.B.; rec. by Solomon Brower - 9 Oct. 1840 [76]

Besch, Jacob, subj. of King of Prussia; rec. by George W. Simmons, of 78 Nassau St. - 9 Oct. 1840 [77]

Brady, Sampson, subj. of G.B.; rec. by·Patrick Ryan, of 107 Roosevelt St. - 9 Oct. 1840 [78]

Brookman, Casper, subj. of King of Bavaria; rec. by William Hellibolt, of 260 Stant ... St. - 9 Oct. 1840 [79]

Beisinger, Augustin, of Poughkeepsie, subj. of Prince of Hesse Cassel; rec. by Leopold Beisinger, of 23 Pell St. - 29 Oct. 1840 [80]

Beucker, George, subj. of King of France; rec. by George Quelet, of 31 Brownell [?] St. - 9 Oct. 1840 [81]

Brady, Thomas R. - 9 Oct. 1840 [not completed] [82]

Bradford, Richard, subj. of G.B.; rec. by William Savidge - 9 Oct. 1840 [83]

Bacon, William, subj. of G.B.; rec. by Michael Conroy - 10 Oct. 1840 [84]

Booth, John, subj. of G.B.; rec. by Richard Whitaker - 10 Oct. 1840 [85]

Banner, Thomas, subj. of G.B.; rec. by Thomas Glinn - 9 Oct. 1840 [86]

Bundle 17 (cont'd)

Polack, William N., dry goods dealer, subj. of King of Holland; rec. by Joseph Hoxie - 12 Apr. 1838 [174]

Page, Charles Read, subj. of G.B.; rec. by George Frederick Glessing - 23 Oct. 1838 [175]

Piper, George, subj. of G.B.; rec. by Ebenezer Haywood - 25 Oct. 1838 [176]

Parker, George, subj. of G.B.; rec. by Richard M. Cary - 3 Nov. 1838 [177]

Pettit, Thomas, subj. of G.B.; rec. by Elias C. Taylor - 2 Nov. 1838 [178]

Pine, Peter, subj. of G.B.; rec. by Sally Pine - 3 Nov. 1838 [179]

Preaut, Henry, subj. of King of France; rec. by William W. Snowden - 3 Nov. 1838 [180]

Peck, Richard Denny (a minor), subj. of G.B.; rec. by Wm. Smith - 5 Nov. 1838 [181]

Patten, William, subj. of G.B.; rec. by James Riley - 5 Nov. 1838 [182]

Parry, Samuel, subj. of G.B.; rec. by Wm. J. Romer - 5 Nov. 1838 [183]

Powers, James, subj. of G.B.; rec. by Charles Chambers - 5 Nov. 1838 [184]

Platz, John, subj. of King of Wurtemberg; rec. by Englehart Brish - 5 Nov. 1838 [185]; made decl. of intent 3 Apr. 1835 in Essex Co., N.J.

Purcell, Thomas, subj. of G.B.; rec. by Isaac Anderson - 6 Nov. 1838 [186]

Pemberton, Jacob, subj. of G.B.; rec. by Henry Shellard - 6 Nov. 1838 [187]

Parker, William T., subj. of G.B.; rec. by Clinton Brownell - 6 Nov. 1838 [188]

Palmer, George T., subj. of G.B. rec. by Frederick A. Munden - 6 Nov. 1838 [189]

Polegreen, Wallace, subj. of G.B.; rec. by William A. Waterbury 7 Nov. 1838 [190]

Peyton, Henry, subj. of G.B.; rec. by Daniel T. Williams - 7 Nov. 1838 [191]

Paulsen, John Christian, subj. of King of Denmark; rec. by James Walters - 7 Nov. 1838 [192]

O'Rielly, Patrick C., subj. of G.B.; rec. by Dennis Foley - 11 Apr. 1838 [193]

Owen, William, subj. of G.B.; rec. by Morgan Morgans - 12 Apr. 1838 [194]

O'Neil, William, subj. of G.B.; rec. by Nancy Docherty - 12 Apr. 1838 [195]

O'Neil, Patrick H., subj. of G.B.; rec. by Patrick Gilmartin - 12 Apr. 1838 [AA-195]

Ottignon, Joseph, subj. of King of France; rec. by Peter Ottignon - 31 Oct. 1838 [196]

O'Connor, Patrick [report 24 Nov. 1834]: b. Co. Louth, Ire., age 34, migr. from Liverpool, intending to settle in Bethlehem, Albany Co., subj. of G.B.; rec. by Hugh McCurdy - 2 Nov. 1838 [197]

Olsen, Andrew Julius, subj. of King of Denmark; rec. by Frederick Wang - 6 Nov. 1838 [198]

O'Grady, John, subj. of G.B.; rec. by Daniel O'Grady - 6 Nov. 1838 [199]

O'Brian, John, labourer, subj. of G.B.; rec. by Abraham M. Cozzens - 7 Nov. 1838 [200]

O'Brien, Lewis, subj. of G.B.; rec. by Washington Lynch - 7 Nov. 1838 [201]

Orpen, Edward, subj. of G.B.; rec. by William Allen - 7 Nov. 1838 [202]

Bundle 18

Richter, Margaret, subj. of G.B.; rec. by John J. Anthony - 7 Oct. 1838 [1]

Rasines, Anthony, subj. of Queen of Spain; rec. by William W. Clay - 12 Apr. 1838 [2]

Raven, Cornelius B., subj. of G.B.; rec. by William Leeman - 11 Apr. 1838 [3]

Rigbey, Thomas, subj. of G.B.; rec. by John Riggs - 11 Apr. 1838 [4]

Richards, John, subj. of G.B.; red, by James Tompson - 10 Apr. 1838 [5]

Rothgaven [or Rathgaren?], John, subj. of King of Wurtemberg; rec. by Johan Hansler - 10 Apr. 1838 [6]

Riley, Patrick, subj. of G.B.; rec. by Dennis Galligan - 11 Apr. 1838 [7]

Reilly, Hugh [report Aug. 1834]: late of town of Ballinamore, Co. Leitrim, Ire.; rec. by Thomas Reilly - 1 Nov. 1838 [8]

Rae, John, subj. of G.B.; rec. by Benjamin Andrews - 3 Nov. 1838 [9]

Riley, James, subj. of G.B.; rec. by William Patten - 5 Nov. 1838 [10]

Raabe, Andrew, subj. of Prince of Hesse Cassel; rec. by George H. Arcularius - 5 Nov. 1838 [11]

Reeves, Thomas, subj. of G.B.; rec. by John Sanderson - 5 Nov. 1838 [12]

Roberts, John, subj. of G.B.; rec. by Hannah Griffiths - 5 Nov. 1838 [13]

Robertson, Alexander, subj. of G.B.; rec. by John Turnbull and Thomas McKie - 6 Nov. 1838 [14]

Rinseland, Ditmar, subj. of Prince of Hesse Cassel; rec. by Peter Kocky [?] - 6 Nov. 1838 [15]

Rogers, Patrick, subj. of G.B.; rec. by Peter Barry - 6 Nov. 1838 [16]

Ratican, Bernard, subj. of G.B.; rec. by Hugh Maguire - 6 Nov. 1838 [17]

Robertson, William, subj. of G.B.; rec. by William Knipe - 7 Nov. 1838 [18]

Rommel, Christian Bernard, subj. of King of Wurtemberg; made declaration of intent in Phila. 13 Oct. 1834; rec. by Georg Grusemeyer - 7 Nov. 1838 [19]

Rosenlor, Charles A., subj. of King of Denmark; rec. by Frederick Wang - 7 Nov. 1838 [AA - 19]

Stanton, James, subj. of G.B.; rec. by Daniel McCarthy - 11 Apr. 1838 [20]

Sullivan, Jeremiah M., subj. of G.B.; rec. by Andrew Sullivan - 11 Apr. 1838 [21]

Schmidt, George, subj. of King of Bavaria; rec. by Ernest L. Freudenberger - 11 Apr. 1838 [22]

Stolz/Stultz, Johannes, subj. of King of Bavaria; rec. by Peter Stolz - 11 Apr. 1838 [AA-22]

Sullivan, Timothy, subj. of G.B.; rec. by Ellen Sullivan - 11 Apr. 1838 [23]

Sullivan, Timothy, subj. of G.B.; rec. by Henry Brown - 11 Apr. 1838 [24]

Scott, James, subj. of King of France; rec. by William Gould - 10 Apr. 1838 [25]

Simpson, Andrew, subj. of G.B.; rec. by Robert Simpson - 9 Apr. 1838 [26]

Stooke, Thomas S., subj. of G.B.; rec. by Sidney Stooke - 4 Jan. 1838 [27]

Smith, John, of borough of Elizabeth, N.J. [report 1 Mar. 1836]: b. town of Market Bosworth, Leicestershire, Eng., age about 27; rec. by Joseph T. Jenney - 5 Oct. 1838 [28]

Seaman, John, subj. of G.B.;rec. by Charles Simpson - 4 Oct. 1838 [29]

St. Jurjo, Joseph de Rivera, subj. of Queen of Spain; rec. by Henry W. McCobb - 17 Oct. 1838 [30]

Smith, John, subj. of G.B.; rec. by Isaac Caryl, Jr. - 1 Nov. 1838 [31]

Stoppelkam, John, subj. of Prince of Hesse Cassel; rec. by Joseph Landwehr [?] - 11 Apr. 1838 [32]

Simon, Leopold, subj. of King of France; rec. by Peter Sickhouse - 11 Apr. 1838 [33]

Stinson, Hugh, subj. of G.B.; rec. by John Boyd - 11 Apr. 1838 [34]

Seath, James, subj. of G.B.; rec. by Thomas Smith - 11 Apr. 1838 [35]

Simon, George, subj. of King of France; rec. by Peter Sickhouse - 11 Apr. 1838 [36]

Schutz/Shutz, John, subj. of King of Bavaria; rec. by Englehart Brisch - 12 Apr. 1838 [37]

Smith, William, subj. of G.B.; rec. by Abraham Jackson - 12 Apr. 1838 [38]

Schneider, Francis, subj. of Duke of Baden; rec. by John Cook - 12 Apr. 1838 [39]

Schaeffer, Nicholas, subj. of King of France; rec. by John Cook - 12 Apr. 1838 [40]

Small, James, subj. of G.B.; rec. by Robert Honey - 12 Apr. 1838 [41]

Schaeffer/Schaffer. Francis C., subj. of King of Holland; rec. by Nye Hall - 12 Apr. 1838 [AA-41]

Sinclair, William T., subj. of G.B.;rec. by John Sturtevant - 12 Apr. 1838 [42]

Sherlock, James, subj. of G.B.;rec. by Thomas Rogers - 12 Apr. 1838 [43]

Sheridan, John, subj. of G.B.; rec. by James Black - 12 Apr. 1838 [44]

Stephenson, Charles, subj. of G.B.; rec. by Samuel Mann - 12 Apr. 1838 [45]

Slattery, Timothy, subj. of G.B.; rec. by Patrick Slattery - 3 July 1838 [46]

Strasburger, Bernard, subj. of Grand Duke of Baden; rec. by George Fullmer - 1 Nov. 1838 [47]

Smith, Thomas D., subj. of G.B.; rec. by Enoch Morgan - 1 Nov. 1838 [48]

Sullivan, Michael, subj. of G.B.; rec. by Henry Fudge - 2 Nov. 1838 [49]

Smith, George, subj. of King of Wurtemberg; rec. by Christian Soll - 3 Nov. 1838 [50]

Seal, James, subj. of G.B.; rec. by Abel H. Rogers - 3 Nov. 1838 [AA-50]

Simms, Robert B., Sr., gunmaker, subj. of G.B.; rec. by Joseph Pearson - 3 Nov. 1838 [51]

Smith, Ephraim, subj. of G.B.; rec. by Nathaniel Smith - 3 Nov. 1838 [52]

Smith, Job, subj. of G.B.; rec. by Nathaniel Smith - 3 Nov. 1838 [53]

Smith, James, subj. of G.B.; rec. by Michael Smith - 5 Nov. 1838 [54]

Shaughness, James, of Westchester Co., subj. of G.B.; rec. by John Shaughnessy - 3 Nov. 1838 [55]

Schmidt, Jacob, subj. of King of Wurtemberg; rec. by Christian Soll - 5 Nov. 1838 [56]

Speers, William S., subj. of G.B.; rec. by John P. Cumming - 5 Nov. 1838 [57]

Stevens, Michael, subj. of King of France; rec. by Cornelius W. Thomas - 5 Nov. 1838 [58]

Simpson, William, subj. of G.B.; rec. by Alexander Heineman - 6 Nov. 1838 [59]

Sachs, Alexander, subj. of King of Bavaria; rec. by Daniel T. Williams - 6 Nov. 1838 [60]

Stockey, Peter, subj. of King of Bavaria; rec. by Ditmar Rinsland - 6 Nov. 1838 [61]

Stultz/Stulz, George, of village of Williamsburgh, ropemaker, subj. of Grand Duke of Baden; rec. by George Carroll - 6 Nov. 1838 [62]

Stewart, John, subj. of G.B.; rec. by John Sanderson - 6 Nov. 1838 [63]

Sinclair, Daniel, subj. of G.B.; rec. by Joseph Riddock - 6 Nov. 1838 [64]

Sampson, Moses, subj. of King of Prussia; rec. by Anthony Luken - 6 Nov. 1838 [65]

Silva, Francis J., subj. of Queen of Portugal; rec. by Timothy Coffin - 7 Nov. 1838 [66]

Schwartzwalder, Christian, subj. of Grand Duke of Baden; rec. by Christian F. Buhler - 7 Nov. 1838 [67]

Stocks, Henry, subj. of King of Prussia; rec. by Hermann Kothe - 7 Nov. 1838 [68]

Schifer, Nicholas, subj. of King of Bavaria; rec. by Anthony Lambert - 7 Nov. 1838 [69]

Stockey, James, subj. of Republic of Switzerland; rec. by Samuel Block - 7 Nov. 1838 [70]

Salloway, Henry, subj. of G.B.;rec.by Samuel Palmer - 7 Nov. 1838 [71]

Swan, William, subj. of G.B.; rec. by James Kinlock - 7 Nov. 1838 [72]

Sanderson, Thomas, subj. of G.B.; rec. by Alexander L. Shaw - 7 Nov. 1838 [73]

Sharpcross, Richard, subj. of G.B.; rec. by John Bagley - 7 Nov. 1838 [74]

Smale, William, subj. of G.B.; rec. by John J. Williamson - 7 Nov. 1838 [75]

Stese/Stisi, Joseph, subj. of King of Bavaria; rec. by George Hilber - 7 Nov. 1838 [76]

Taber, James, subj. of G.B.; rec. by Thomas Taber - 6 Nov. 1838 [77]

Verelle, Hypollite, subj. of King of France; rec. by Peter M. Ottignon - 2 Nov. 1838 [78]

Vanners/Veners, Francis, subj. of King of Prussia; rec. by John C. Ritter, Jr. - 3 Nov. 1838 [79]

Vorwerck, Charles W., subj. of King of Prussia; rec. by John Campbell - 3 Nov. 1838 [80]

Verty, Thomas, subj. of G.B.; rec. by Patrick McVey - 5 Nov. 1838 [81]

Vowels, George, subj. of G.B.; rec. by Samuel Brown - 6 Nov. 1838 [82]

Videl, Eli, subj. of G.B.; rec. by James Videl - 6 Nov. 1838 [83]

Videl, James, subj. of G.B.; rec. by Eli Videl - 6 Nov. 1838 [84]

Vuuren [or Vuuven?], Cornelius, subj. of King of Holland; rec. by Karst Jan Van Veen - 6 Nov. 1838 [85]

Vienz, Jacob, subj. of King of France; rec. by John B. Geiler - 7 Nov. 1838 [86]

Valentine, Theophilus, subj. of Switzerland; rec. by Charles B. Collins - 7 Nov. 1838 [87]

Tulley, Alexander, subj. of G.B.; rec. by John Briggs - 10 Apr. 1838 [88]

Turney, John, subj. of G.B.; rec. by James Black - 11 Apr. 1838 [89]

Taylor, Charles K., subj. of G.B.; rec. by John O. Rorrbach - 11 Apr. 1838 [90]

Thorp, Zephaniah, subj. of G.B.; rec. by James Bryson - 11 Apr. 1838 [91]

Tyson, John, subj. of G.B., migr. from Liverpool 24 May 1831; decl. intent Venango Co., Pa.; rec. by Isaac M. Tyson -11Sept. [9

Terrell, James, subj. of G.B.; rec. by James McLarney - 18 Sept. 1838 [93]

Tyler, Thomas, subj. of G.B.; rec. by Ellen Tyler - 31 Oct. 1838 [94]

Tudor, Thomas [decl. of intent 9 June 1836]; formerly of Staffordshire, Eng.; rec. by John Dryson - 1 Nov. 1838 [95]

Thomas, Jonathan, subj. of G.B.; rec. by James D. Waters - 2 Nov. 1838 [96]

Thomas, Richard, subj. of G.B.; rec. by Josiah Morgan - 6 Nov. 1838 [97]

Teasdale, William Robert, subj. of G.B.; rec. by George Ashwood - 5 Nov. 1838 [98]

Troy, Nicholas, subj. of G.B.; rec. by Michael Cochran - 3 Nov. 1838 [99]

Tisdall, Fitzgerald, subj. of G.B.; rec. by Joseph Hoxie - 5 Nov. 1838 [100]

Tritheway, Robert (a minor), subj. of G.B.; rec. by Thomas R. Holden, Jr. - 5 Nov. 1838 [101]

Tichenor, Henry, subj. of G.B.; rec. by Charles Benson - 7 Nov. 1838 [102]

Tickner, William, subj. of G.B.; rec. by Thomas Armstrong - 7 Nov. 1838 [103]

Tattenall, William R., subj. of G.B.; rec. by Elias Haviland - 7 Nov. 1838 [104]

Tompson, Alfred, subj. of G.B.; rec. by Peter Le Count - 7 Nov. 1838 [105]

Thomson, Alexander, subj. of G.B.; rec. by George Pirnie - 7 Nov. 1838 [106]

Walsh, Edward, subj. of G.B.; rec. by Charles Short - 11 Apr. 1838 [107]

Waters, John, subj. of G.B.; rec. by James Waters - 11 Apr. 1838 [108]

Willersdorf, Michael, subj. of King of Prussia; rec. by William Hyde - 12 Apr. 1838 [109]

Welsh, Thomas, subj. of G.B.; rec. by James Black - 12 Apr. 1838 [110]

Welsh, Patrick, subj. of G.B.; rec. by Peter McLaughlin - 21 May 1838 [111]

Wirtz, Jacob, subj. of Switzerland; rec. by John Curl - 13 June 1838 [112]

Ward, George, subj. of G.B.; rec. by Josiah L. Wilson - 13 Sept. 1838 [113]

Wolff, George Augustus, subj. of G.B.; rec. by James French - 1 Nov. 1838 [114]

White, Thomas, of Brooklyn, subj. of G.B.; rec. by Robert Anderson - 2 Nov. 1838 [115]

White, John, subj. of G.B.; rec. by Alexander Lawrence - 2 Nov. 1838 [116]

Wymbs, Martin D., subj. of G.B.; rec. by Patrick Harrison - 3 Nov. 1838 [117]

Wheeler, Henry, subj. of G.B.; rec. by Samuel G. Bacon - 3 Nov. 1838 [118]

Whitehouse, Joseph, subj. of G.B.; rec. by John Jones - 5 Nov. 1838 [119]

Wilson, Stafford, late of London, subj. of G.B.; rec. by John C. Ritter, Jr. - 5 Nov. 1838 [120]

Walton, George, subj. of G.B.; rec. by James Adams - 6 Nov. 1838 [121]

Walters, Charles Theodore, subj. of G.B.; rec. by Frederick Wang - 6 Nov. 1838 [122]

Walker, John, subj. of King of Wurtemberg; rec. by Gottlieb Appfelbach - 6 Nov. 1838 [123]

Westlake, Richard, subj. of G.B.; rec. by John Rutter - 6 Nov. 1838 [124]

Walleson, Edward, subj. of Republic of Hamburgh; rec. by Martin Thompson - 6 Nov. 1838 [125]

Wrapson, William, subj. of G.B.; rec. by John Palmer - 6 Nov. 1838 [126]

Webb, Alexander F.W., subj. of G.B.; rec. by Franklin H. Delano - 6 Nov. 1838 [127]

Wallin, Samuel, Jr., subj. of G.B.; rec. by Bezaleel Howe - 6 Nov. 1838 [128]

West, Beal, subj. of G.B.; rec. by William C. Arthur - 7 Nov. 1838 [129]

Wagenmacher, Christian, subj. of Grand Duke of Baden; rec. by Henry N. Fistie - 7 Nov. 1838 [AA 129]

Weber, George [decl. of intent 10 Dec. 1835 in D.C.]: native of Hessen Darmstadt, age 22, migr. from Bremen, arrived Baltimore 8 Aug. 1832; rec. by John Kraft - 7 Nov. 1838 [130]

Walker, Joseph James, storekeeper, subj. of G.B.; rec. by Abraham Hatfield - 7 Nov. 1838 [131]

Williams, Peter, subj. of City of Hamburgh; rec. by Andrew Johnson - 7 Nov. 1838 [132]

Woolley, William J., subj. of G.B.; rec. by Alden J. Spooner, of Brooklyn - 7 Nov. 1838 [133]

Welti, Benedict, subj. of Republic of Switzerland; rec. by Caspar Martin - 7 Nov. 1838 [134]

Welty, Nicholas, subj. of Republic of Switzerland; rec. by Caspar Martin - 7 Nov. 1838 [135]

Webb, William, subj. of G.B.; rec. by Elisha Foot - 7 Nov. 1838 [136]

Wetz, Daniel, subj. of Grand Duke of Wurtemberg; rec. by John Cock - 6 Nov. 1838 [137]

Young, John C., subj. of G.B.; rec. by David McKinley - 5 Nov. 1838 [138]

Yohe [or Yoke?], Paul F., subj. of King of Bavaria; rec. by Balthazar Shurk - 10 Apr. 1838 [139]

Zahringer, Jacob, subj. of Grand Duke of Baden; rec. by John Biekn - 11 Apr. 1838 [140]

Bundle 21 (cont'd)

Bruce, William, subj. of G.B.; rec. by James Biggs, of 92 Eighteenth St. - 10 Oct. 1840 [87]

Bruns, Behrent, subj. of King of Hanover; rec. by Frederick Wm. Harmann - 10 Oct. 1840 [88]

Bonner, Patrick, subj. of G.B.; rec. by James McGinnis and Patrick Balfour - 10 Oct. 1840 [89]

Brady, Joseph, subj. of G.B.; rec. by Patrick Brady - 12 Oct. 1840 [90]

Byrnes, Andrew, subj. of G.B.; rec. by Mary Cass - 12 Oct. 1840 [91]

Burk, John, of Williamsburgh, subj. of G.B.; rec. by Alexander Land, of Bushwick - 12 Oct. 1840 [92]

Burg, Henry, subj. of G.B.; rec. by James Bird - 12 Oct. 1840 [93]

Barringer, Paul, subj. of King of Bavaria; rec. by Adam C, Hazelworth, of 288 Bleecker St. - 12 Oct. 1840 [94]

Ballentine, George, subj. of G.B.; rec. by William Cantrell - 13 Oct. 1840

Burns, Francis, subj. of G.B.; rec. by Michael McLaughlin, of 49 Allen St. - 14 Oct. 1840 [96]

Bernhardt, Gustav, subj. of King of Bavaria; rec. by Gustavus A. Nieuman, of 7 Frankfort St. - 14 Oct. 1840 [97]

Bell, William [report Phila. Co., Pa., 6 Oct. 1834]: b. Co. Down, Ire., on 17 Jan. 1810, srrived Port of New York 29 Dec. 1831, with intent to settle in Pa.; rec. by James Bright - 14 Oct. 1840 [98]

Bull, William, subj. of G.B.; rec. by John Sawkins, of Flatbush - 14 Oct. 1840 [99]

Bryon, John, subj. of G.B.; rec. by Henry Palmer, Jr., of 15 Wall St. - 15 Oct. 1840 [100]

Bain, James, subj. of G.B.; rec. by Robert Noble, of 33 Hudson St. - 15 Oct. 1840 [101]

Beeny, Stephen, subj. of G.B.; rec. by Edward Beeny, of 308 Cortland St. - 15 Oct. 1840 [102]

Beeny, Edward, subj. of G.B.; rec. by Stephen Beeny - 15 Oct. 1840 [103]

Benceno, Jacob, subj. of King of Bavaria; rec. by Samuel J. Farnum, of Newburgh - 15 Oct. 1840 [104]

Baistow, Richard, Jr. [report when admitted cit. 10 Sept. 1832 in N.J.]: b. Boveytressey [Bow Tracey?], Devonshire, Eng.; rec. by John Syms, of 57 Chatham St. - 19 Oct. 1840 [105]

Beck, John, subj. of G.B.; rec. by John Thorn, of Yonkers, Westchester Co. - 15 Oct. 1840 [106]

Brady, Richard, subj. of G.B.; rec. by Edward Riley, of 49 Lewis St. - 16 Oct. 1840 [107]

Brady, Thomas, subj. of G.B.; rec. by Richard Mulroony, of 45 Elm St. - 16 Oct. 1840 [108]

Burke, John [report 5 Mar. 1838 in Carroll Co., Indiana]: b. parish of Killae [?] [for Killeagh?], province of Munster, Co. of Cork, age 25; has blue eyes, light hair and fair Complex.; landed in NYC in summer of 1835; rec. by Patrick Burke - 19 Oct. 1840 [109]

Burk, Patrick, subj. of G.B.; rec. by John Burk, of Westchester
Co. - 19 Oct. 1840 [110]

Boyle, James, subj. of G.B.; rec. by Patrick McCabe, of 54 Pitt
[?] St. - 19 Oct. 1840 [111]

Beatty, Samuel, subj. of G.B.; rec. by Thomas C. Doyle, of 306
Water St. - 20 Oct. 1840 [112]

Brown, Richard, subj. of G.B.; rec. by Wm. H. Ferris, of 61
Eldridge St. - 19 Oct. 1840 [113]

Briden [alias Brighton], Barney/Behrend, subj. of King of Hanover; rec. by James De Groot - 21 Oct. 1840 [114]

Boyce, Francis, of Williamsburgh, subj. of G.B.; rec. by Nathaniel Parish, of Williamsburgh - 22 Oct. 1840 [115]

Birck, Mathias, subj. of King of Denmark; rec. by Wm. Raddy, of
325 Broadway - 22 Oct. 1840 [116]

Brannaghan, John, of Rockland Co., late of Ire., subj. of G.B.;
rec. by Michael York, of 153 Leonard St. - 23 Oct. 1840 [117]

Bird, Launcelot, subj. of G.B.; rec. by Thomas Hanna, of Staten
Island - 23 Oct. 1840 [118]

Bell, William, subj. of G.B.; rec. by Wm. Oram - 23 Oct. 1840
[119]

Billey [or Bilby?], John., of 182 Twentieth St., subj. of G.B.;
rec. by Samuel Billey [or Bilby?] and Hannah Hotchkiss - 24
Oct. 1840 [120]

Bradbrook, Robert, of 13 Ridge St., subj. of G.B.; rec. by Francis Le Count, of 111 Eighth St. - 26 Oct. 1840 [121]

Burk, John, of Queens Co. [report 7 Apr. 1821]: age 26, subj. of
G.B.; rec. by Owen Flood, of Kings Co. - 26 Oct. 1840 [122]

Brymer, John, subj. of G.B.; rec. by Maria Brymer, of Essex Co.
- 27 Oct. 1840 [123]

Brohert [or Brobert or Broheil?], Kolumban, subj. of Grand Duke
of Baden; rec. by George Sonne and Samuel Willett, of Flushing
- 26 Oct. 1840 [124]

Balten [or Batten?], Frederick, subj. of G.B.; rec. by William
Hagan [Gagan?], of 10 Marin - 26 Oct. 1840 [125]

Beurbaum [for Birnbaum?], Simon, of Poughkeepsie, Dutchess Co.,
subj. of King of Bavaria; rec. by Albert Van Kleeck - 29 Oct.
1840 [126]

Brady, Thomas, subj. of G.B.; rec. by Francis Ultz - 29 Oct.
1840 [127]

Brigham, John Harker [report 22 Aug. 1835 in Albany]: b. Yorkshire, Eng., age 40, migr. from Liverpool; rec. by Andrew
O'Connor, of 109 Cortland St. - 29 Oct. 1840 [128]

Burkhard, Peter, of 67 Vesey St., coppersmith, subj. of Grand
Duke of Baden; rec. by Matthias Scheurmann, of 215 Washington
St., porter house - 30 Oct. 1840 [129]

Beatty, Samuel, subj. of G.B.; rec. by James J. Wyckoff - 30
Oct. 1840 [130]

Boyle, Patrick, subj. of G.B.; rec. by John Dougherty, of Brooklyn - 30 Oct. 1840 [131]

Burns, Robert, of Poughkeepsie, formerly of Eng., subj. of G.B.;
rec. by Elisha Knight, of Poughkeepsie - 31 Oct. 1840 [132]

Beck, James, formerly of Ire., now of Poughkeepsie; rec. by Wm.
Mulholland - 31 Oct. 1840 [133]

Bates, Robert, of 23 Columbia St., subj. of G.B.; rec. by Samuel
    Matthews and Robert Pattison - 31 Oct. 1840 [134]

Begins, John [report Sept. 1836]: mariner, b. North Yarmouth,
    Eng., on 15 Mar. 1808, age now 28, arrived New York, removed
    to New Haven and then to Boston; arrived in U.S. 10 May 1826;
    rec. by Henry Munson - 31 Oct. 1840 [135]

Burkhart, Peter, subj. of King of Bavaria; rec. by John Michael
    - 31 Oct. 1840 [136]

Brennan, John, subj. of G.B.; rec. by James Teran - 2 Nov. 1840
    [137]

Boyle, Dennis, of Laurens St., subj. of G.B.; rec. by Patrick
    Byrns and John McGill - 2 Nov. 1840 [138]

Baker, George, of Westchester Co., subj. of G.B.; rec. by Fran-
    cis Baker, of Westchester Co. - 2 Nov. 1840 [139]

Bates, Joseph [report 5 Nov. 1834]: b. Co. Tyrone, Ire., age 22,
    migr. from Londonderry, intending to settle in Schenectady;
    rec. by Samuel Matthews - 2 Nov. 1840 [140]

Brannan, Patrick, subj. of G.B.; rec. by Peter Brannan - 2 Nov.
    1840 [141]

Babear, John T., subj. of G.B.; rec. by James Moore - 2 Nov.
    1840 [142]

Backus, Oscar, of Long Island, subj. of Saxe Coburg; rec. by
    Gustavus Backus, of 42nd St. and Eight Ave. - 2 Nov. 1840
    [143]

Brissel, John, subj. of Duke of Hesse Darmstadt; rec. by William
    Tilden - 2 Nov. 1840 [144]

Byrne, David, of Saugerties, Ulster Co., subj. of G.B., native
    of Ire.; rec. by John Kearney, of Christopher St. - 2 Nov.
    1840 [145]

Byrd, John, subj. of G.B.; rec. by Isaac Tucker, of 124 McDou-
    gal St. - 2 Nov. 1840 [146]

Barres, Cars/Charles, subj. of Emperor of Russia; rec. by Fran-
    cis Jacobuski - 3 Nov. 1840 [147]

Bird, John, subj. of G.B.; rec. by George Bird - 3 Nov. 1840
    [148]

Brady, Thomas, of 3rd Ave. and 20th St., subj. of G.B.; rec. by
    William Hand, of 21st St., between 5th and 6th Avenues - 3
    Nov. 1840 [149]

Bishop, William, subj. of G.B.; rec. by John Bills - 3 Nov. 1840
    [150]

Burns, Thomas, of 58 Hamersley St., native of Ire., carpenter;
    rec. by James B. Wallace (who knew him in Lansingburgh) and
    William Burns, of 47 Carmine [?] St., and John B. Colegrove -
    3 Nov. 1840 [151]

Baptiste, Anthony, subj. of Queen of Portugal; rec. by Benjamin
    G. Minturn and Cornelius Du Bois, Jr. - 3 Nov. 1840 [152]

Bensen, John, subj. of King of Hanover; rec. by John A. May - 3
    Nov. 1840 [153]

Brennan, Wm., subj. of G.B.; rec. by James Kiernan, of 216 Centre
    St. - 4 Nov. 1840 [154]

Burnish, Joseph, subj. of G.B.; rec. by William Burnish - 4 Nov.
    1840 [155]

Bonner, Manus, of 256 Sixteenth St., subj. of G.B.; rec. by
    Francis Tiebout, of 256 Sixteenth St. - 4 Nov. 1840 [156]

Burton, Charles, subj. of G.B.; rec. by Wm. H. Hyatt - 4 Nov. 1840 [157]

Burdon, Wm., subj. of G.B.; rec. by John Degraw - 4 Nov. 1840 [158]

Beck, Michael, subj. of King of Bavaria; rec. by John Schneider, of 10 Dominick St. - 28 Oct. 1840 [159]

Bellue, James, subj. of G.B.; rec. by Joseph Donaldson, of 219 Division [?] St. - 28 Oct. 1840 [160]

Brymer, Wm., of Essex Co., subj. of G.B.; rec. by Maria Brymer, of N.J. - 27 Oct. 1840 [161]

Brown, William, subj. of G.B.; rec. by Thomas S. Ford, of 149 Grand St. - 29 Oct. 1840 [162]

Brown, William, subj. of G.B.; rec. by Hugh McCabe, of 193 Mulberry St. - 16 Oct. 1840 [163]

Brown, William, subj. of G.B.; rec. by Thomas Burnett - 3 Nov. 1840 [164]

Bollerman, Charles, subj. of Grand Duke of Hesse Darmstadt; rec. by Dennis Mullins, of 317 Pearl St. - 2 Oct. 1840 [165]

Bundle 22

Dorgan, Morty, subj. of G.B.; rec. by John Brown - 28 Sept. 1840 [1]

Dwyer, Thomas E., subj. of G.B.; rec. by Richard Clifford - 28 Sept. 1840 [2]

Derham, James, subj. of G.B.; rec. by John Creswell - 29 Sept. 1840 [3]

Denecke, George Joseph, subj. of Duke of Brunswick; rec. by Wm. Denecke - 29 Sept. 1840 [4]

Doyle, Timothy, subj. of G.B.; rec. by Patrick McGuire - 29 Sept. 1840 [5]

Doherty, Patrick, subj. of G.B.; rec. by James Huey - 29 Sept. 1840 [6]

Daske [or Dakse?], Ludwig, subj. of Duke of Macklenburgh; rec. by Harman Antoine Martens, of 43 Rivington St. - 2 Oct. 1840 [7]

Dreyfelcher, Carl, subj. of Emperor of Russia; rec. by Henry Durgens, of 177 Forsyth St. - 2 Oct. 1840 [8]

Delany, Thomas, subj. of G.B.; rec. by John Delany, of 7 Orange St. - 3 Oct. 1840 [9]

Dotterer, Johannes, subj. of Grand Duke of Baden; rec. by Peter Schlosser - 5 Oct. 1840 [10]

Dempster, James, subj. of G.B.; rec. by Richard M. Carey - 5 Oct. 1840 [11]

Davis, Richard (who had resided in Mamakating, Sullivan Co.), subj. of G.B.; rec. by John Drake, Walter Fisher and Abraham Cadmus - 7 Oct. 1840 [12]

Dietterich, Michael, subj. of King of Wurtemberg; rec. by Urs Remsen, of Forsyth St. - 8 Oct. 1840 [13]

Dolan, John, subj. of G.B.; rec. by Edward Munson - 9 Oct. 1840 [14]

Davany, James, subj. of G.B.; rec. by Thomas Butler, of 37 Cross St. - 9 Oct. 1840 [15]

Dwyer, Martin, subj. of G.B.; rec. by John Thomas, of 70 Christopher St. - 9 Oct. 1840 [16]

Dekins, James, subj. of G.B.; rec. by James R. Hughes, of 84 Catherine St. - 9 Oct. 1840 [17]

Dugan, Thomas, subj. of G.B.; rec. by Caleb S. Fordham - 9 Oct. 1840 [18]

Dolan, James, subj. of G.B.; rec. by John Mitchell, of 59 Cross St. - 9 Oct. 1840 [19]

Dudley, Joshua, subj. of G.B.; rec. by Margaret Merrick - 9 Oct. 1840 [20]

Donnelly, James, labourer, subj. of G.B.; rec. by Cornelius W. Hibberd - 9 Oct. 1840 [21]

Dennis, Richard, subj. of G.B.; rec. by William N. Blakeman - 10 Oct. 1840 [22]

Doyle, Patrick, subj. of G.B.; rec. by Michael Kerrigan, of 2 Center St. - 10 Oct. 1840 [23]

Dunlop/Dunlap, James, clerk, subj. of G.B.; rec. by Samuel Dunlop/Dunlap - 10 Oct. 1840 [24]

Dax, John, subj. of G.B.; rec. by Thomas Kinnersley - 10 Oct. 1840 [25]

Douglas, Wm., subj. of G.B.; rec. by Alexander Douglas - 10 Oct. 1840 [26]

Douglas, Alexander, subj. of G.B.; rec. by William Douglas, of 405 Fourth St. - 10 Oct. 1840 [27]

Dunn, William, subj. of G.B.; rec. by Jacob Dunn, of 144 Fourth St. - 10 Oct. 1840 [28]

Russea, Richard D., subj. of G.B.; rec. by Francis Russea, of 283 Washington St. - 10 Oct. 1840 [29]

Duffy, Patrick, subj. of G.B.; rec. by Dominick Fenick - 10 Oct. 1840 [30]

Daniel, Charles, subj. of Duke of Brunswick; rec. by Jacob Hartman - 10 Oct. 1840 [31]

Dufour, Paul, subj. of G.B.; rec. by Lawrence Dufour, of 94 Reed St. - 10 Oct. 1840 [32]

Dufour, Thomas, subj. of G.B.; rec. by Lawrence Dufour - 10 Oct. 1840 [33]

Dufour, Lawrence, subj. of G.B.; rec. by James Litton, of 12 Wooster St. - 10 Oct. 1840 [34]

Donovan, Dennis [report 29 Oct. 1834]: b. at Bindin [?] or Buidin [?], Co. Cork, Ire., age 39, migr. from Cork, arrived town of Whitehall in 1832 and resides in Pittstown, Rensselaer Co.; rec. by Rosannah McCleary - 13 Oct. 1840 [35]

Devlin, Arthur, subj. of G.B.; rec. by Edward Teague - 14 Oct. 1840 [36]

Durant, William, subj. of G.B.; rec. by William Durant, Sr. - 19 Oct. 1840 [37]

Daly, Owen, subj. of G.B.; rec. by Philip McKiernan, of 36 Lawrence St. - 21 Oct. 1840 [38]

Dykes, Francis, subj. of G.B.; rec. by Alexander Gray, of 7th Ave. and 17th St. - 23 Oct. 1840 [39]

De Jong, Roedolph, Jr., subj. of King of Holland; rec. by Roedolph Jacob De Jong, Sr. - 23 Oct. 1840 [40]

Dougherty, John, of Throggs Neck, subj. of G.B.; rec. by James Keegan, of Throggs Neck - 24 Oct. 1840 [41]

Doherty, John [decl. of intent 22 Sept. 1829], then of New Utrecht, Kings Co., stone cutter; later of Throggs Neck, subj. of G.B.; rec. by Thomas Ryan, of corner of Whitehall & Bridge St. - 24 Oct. 1840 [42]

Dillon, Matthew, of 275 Water St., subj. of G.B.; rec. by Wm. Baird, of 313 Water St. - 26 Oct. 1840 [43]

Dummick, Henry, of No. 4 Bulls Head, now Third Ave., subj. of Grand Duke of Baden; rec. by Frederick Ahrens, of 18 Ann St. - 26 Oct. 1840 [44]

Davis, John, of N.W. corner of Hammond & Washington Sts., subj. of G.B.; rec. by Edward C. Marsh - 28 Oct. 1840 [45]

Deary/Dery, Bernard/Barney, of 231 (illegible) St., subj. of G.B.; rec. by John Hannigan, of 189 Hester St. - 29 Oct. 1840 [46]

Drawyer, John, of Putnam Co., subj. of G.B.; rec. by Robert Wright, of Putnam Co. - 30 Oct. 1840 [47]

Dawsett/Dowsett, George, of Albany Co., subj. of G.B.; rec. by Charles H. Hochkin [or Hotchkin?], of 29th St., stage driver - 31 Oct. 1840 [48]

Devery, Kearn, of Long Island, subj. of G.B.; rec. by Patrick Goldan (also by James Slivin on 3 Nov. 1834) - 30 Oct. 1840 [49]

Dekins, William, subj. of G.B.; rec. by James Smith, of 70 Cherry St. - 30 Oct. 1840 [50]

Duncan, John, labourer, of 158 Sixteenth St.; rec. by John Cochlin - 30 Oct. 1840 [51]

Ditton, Robert, subj. of G.B.; rec. by James Simpson, of Staten Island - 31 Oct. 1840 [52]

Dilke, Thomas, of Ulster Co. (who was residing in NYC on 20 Oct. 1831), surgeon, subj. of G.B.; rec. by John Sankey, of 385 Broome St. - 31 Oct. 1840 [53]

Dennon/Dennan, Thomas, subj. of G.B.; rec. by John Crawford - 2 Nov. 1840 [54]

Dolan, Maurice, of 12th St. & 6th Ave., subj. of G.B.; rec. by Nicholas Heydinger, of 12th St. and 6th Ave. - 2 Nov. 1840 [55]

Drennan, James, of Newburgh, subj. of G.B.; rec. by Robert Hamilton, of Newburgh, Orange Co. - 2 Nov. 1840 [56]

Donovan, Michael, subj. of G.B.; rec. by Ellen Donovan, of Staten Island - 2 Nov. 1840 [57]

Drespack, Henry, subj. of King of Prussia; rec. by John Wiegand, of 92 James St., and Peter Wentzel, of 5th Ave. and 19th St. - 3 Nov. 1840 [58]

Davidson, Charles, subj. of G.B.; rec. by John Wylie - 3 Nov. 1840 [59]

Darby, William G., subj. of G.B.; rec. by Aug. Thomas - 3 Nov. 1840 [60]

Downey, John, subj. of G.B.; rec. by Enoch Davis, of Brooklyn - 3 Nov. 1840 [61]

Dalton, Patrick, subj. of G.B.; rec. by Gilbert Gahagan, of 95 Mulberry St. - 3 Nov. 1840 [62]

Duff, Thomas, subj. of G.B.; rec. by William Ferguson - 4 Nov. 1840 [63]

Daily, Peter, subj. of G.B.; rec. by Barbara Daily, of Manhattanville - 4 Nov. 1840 [64]

Dow, Edward, subj. of G.B.; rec. by John Grey - 4 Nov. 1840 [65]

Dunn, David, subj. of G.B.; rec. by Benjamin S. Many - 4 Nov.
1840 [66]

Demer, John, subj. of G.B.; rec. by George Richmond, of 113
Charlton St. - 4 Nov. 1840 [67]

Dunn, Michael, subj. of G.B.; rec. by James W. Barnes, of Brooklyn, L.I. - 4 Nov. 1840 [68]

Donaldson, James, subj. of G.B.; rec. by William McElroy - 3
Dec. 1840 [69]

Cohen, Moses, quill manufacturer, subj. of G.B.; rec. by William
N. Polack - 17 Feb. 1840 [70]

Capurro, Luiz (who on 13 June 1834 was residing in Baltimore),
subj. of King of Sardinia; rec. by Jose Nunez - 24 Feb. 1840
[71]

Clonney, James G., subj. of G.B.; rec. by Abraham R. Mesier - 19
Mar. 1840 [72]

Cumming, John, subj. of G.B.; rec. by James Nicol - 11 Apr. 1840
[73]

Clark, John [report 12 Mar. 1839]: native of Co. of Kent, Eng.,
now resident of Marlborough, Ulster Co.; rec. by John Richen-
den - 21 Apr. 1840 [74]

Crowther, William, of Westchester Co., subj. of G.B.; rec. by
Richard Crowther, of West Farms - 11 Aug. 1840 [75]

Cummings/Cummins, Patrick, subj. of G.B.; rec. by Michael Waters
of Brooklyn - 28 Sept. 1840 [76]

Cocks, Henry, subj. of G.B.; rec. by John Dawson - 28 Sept. 1840
[77]

Clark, Thomas H., subj. of G.B.; rec. by Stephen Pettifer - 28
Sept. 1840 [AA 77]

Connor, Cornelius, subj. of G.B.; rec. by Thomas Griffin - 28
Sept. 1840 [78]

Coyne, Lawrence, subj. of G.B.; rec. by Michael Lynch - 28 Sept.
1840 [79]

Cahill, Robert, subj. of G.B.; rec. by John Ennis - 29 Sept.
1840 [80]

Casey, James, subj. of G.B.; rec. by Thomas Casey - 29 Sept.
1840 [81]

Clark, Daniel W., subj. of G.B.; rec. by James D. Yates - 30
Sept. 1840 [82]

Cronekin, Francis, of Yorkville, subj. of G.B.; rec. by John
Fick, of 8th Ave. & 49th St. - 30 Sept. 1840

Carroll, William, of Brooklyn, subj. of G.B.; rec. by Patrick
Murphy, of Brooklyn - 30 Sept. 1840 [84]

Coupland, Richard, subj. of G.B.; rec. by Charles Mears, of 24
White St. - 1 Oct. 1840 [85]

Carroll, John F., subj. of G.B.; rec. by Wm. R. Carroll - 1 Oct.
1840 [86]

Comb, John, subj. of Grand Duke of Baden; rec. by Leonard Comb
- 2 Oct. 1840 [87]

Craig, John, subj. of G.B.; rec. by Richard Fogarty, of 21st St.
- 2 Oct. 1840 [88]

Cohen, Mordecai, subj. of G.B.; rec. by Isaac E. Woolley, of 26 St. - 2 Oct. 1840 [89]

Carpenter, Lawrence, subj. of King of Bavaria; rec. by Mary Eveleth - 3 Oct. 1840 [90]

Chappell, William, subj. of G.B.; rec. by Michael McGrath, of 266 Broom St. - 3 Oct. 1840 [91]

Connor, William, native of Ire.; rec. by Isaac Ford, of 17th St. - 5 Oct. 1840 [92]

Coates, James, subj. of G.B.; rec. by Patrick Karney - 5 Oct. 1840 [93]

Crow, John, subj. of G.B.; rec. by John Phelan, of 40 Laurens St. - 6 Oct. 1840 [94]

Crawford, John, subj. of G.B.; rec. by David Pollack, of 24 Gold St. - 6 Oct. 1840 [95]

Cheesman, Maurice, subj. of G.B.; rec. by Washington Thurman - 6 Oct. 1840 [96]

Coulter, William, subj. of G.B.; rec. by James Phillips, of Olive & Heinz - 7 Oct. 1840 [97]

Cray, John [report 5 May 1826]: b. Ire., age 26, migr. from Belfast, tallow chandler; wife Janice, age 27, b. State of New York; rec. by John Hunt - 8 Oct. 1840 [98]

Coleman, Denis, subj. of G.B.; rec. by Simon Riley - 8 Oct. 1840 [99]

Collyer, Richard, subj. of G.B.; rec. by Andrew McPherson - 8 Oct. 1840 [100]

Cooke, Henry J., subj. of G.B.; rec. by G.A. Cooke - 8 Oct. 1840 [101]

Curtis, Robert, subj. of G.B.; rec. by George Darragh - 8 Oct. 1840 [102]

Connolly, Edward, subj. of G.B.; rec. by John W. Graydon - 9 Oct. 1840 [103]

Cook, William, subj. of G.B.; rec. by William Savidge - 9 Oct. 1840 [104]

Caldwell, David, subj. of G.B.; rec. by Thomas Geraty - 9 Oct. 1840 [105]

Cook, William, subj. of King of Bavaria; rec. by Francis H. Mumpton - 9 Oct. 1840 [106]

Callan, James, subj. of G.B.; rec. by Francis Callan - 9 Oct. 1840 [107]

Campbell, Charles [report 9 Nov. 1836 in Albany]: b. Co. Antrim, Ire., age 26, migr. from Belfast, resident of Albany; rec. by Jonathan Traphagen - 9 Oct. 1840 [108]

Carney, James, subj. of G.B.; rec. by James Sheridan - 9 Oct. 1840 [109]

Connolly, Thomas, subj. of G.B.; rec. by Edward Connolly - 9 Oct. 1840 [110]

Culin, Louis A., subj. of King of France; rec. by Antoine Gicquet - 9 Oct. 1840 [111]

Campbell, John, subj. of G.B.; rec. by Adam Miller, of 436 Houston St. - 9 Oct. 1840 [112]

Cooper, John, subj. of G.B.; rec. by Wm. Cooper, of 90 Charles St. - 10 Oct. 1840 [113]

Cross, Samuel, subj. of G.B.; rec. by Joseph Kilpatrick - 10 Oct. 1840 [114]

Connolly, John, b. Co. Galway, Ire.; rec. by Michael O'Brien - 10 Oct. 1840 [115]

Cook, John, subj. of G.B.; rec. by Horace E. Ketcham - 10 Oct. 1840 [116]

Campbell, Wm., subj. of G.B.;rec. by Wm. Grady, of 15th St. - 10 Oct. 1840 [117]

Cook, Samuel C., subj. of G.B.; rec. by Alexander Slater, of 11th St. - 10 Oct. 1840 [118]

Costello, Michael, subj. of G.B.; rec. by Patrick Costello - 10 Oct. 1840 [119]

Casey, John, subj. of G.B.; rec. by John Mahar, of 168 Leonard St. - 10 Oct. 1840 [120]

Cuthbert, Thomas, subj. of G.B.; rec. by John Horspool - 10 Oct. 1840 [121]

Carstens, Gerhard Herman, subj. of King of Hanover; rec. by Christian Benken, of Pearl & Cross Sts. - 12 Oct. 1840 [122]

Closey, William, subj. of G.B.; rec. by Richard Hennessy, of 113 Walker St. - 12 Oct. 1840 [123]

Cullen, Daniel, subj. of G.B.; rec. by Thomas Martin - 12 Oct. 1840 [124]

Curchin, Jacob, subj. of G.B.; rec. by Charles Neale - 13 Oct. 1840 [125]

Cantrell, Wm., subj. of G.B.; rec. by George Bellantine - 13 Oct. 1840 [126]

Carter, Henry, subj. of G.B.; rec. by Thomas Layman, of 537 Pearl St. - 13 Oct. 1840 [127]

Conaten, James, subj. of G.B.; rec. by Thomas Conaten, of 78 Eighteenth St. - 14 Oct. 1840 [128]

Collins, Jeremiah, native of Ire.; rec. by James Moriarty - 14 Oct. 1840 [129]

Charles, Anthony, subj. of King of France; rec. by John Brunner - 15 Oct. 1840 [130]

Caden/Cadin, Hugh [report 4 July 1836 in Boston]: b. Co. Fermanagh, Ire., on 1 Feb. 1807, age now 29, arrived East Port on 10 July 1832, now of Lowell, Mass., mason; rec. by Patrick Caden, of 39th St. - 16 Oct. 1840 [131]

Cook, Peter, subj. of G.B.; rec. by James Nicholl, of 8th Ave. - 19 Oct. 1840 [132]

Cunningham, Patrick, subj. of G.B.; rec. by Michael Canfield - 19 Oct. 1840 [133]

Cox, Charles, subj. of G.B.;rec. by Thomas Cox - 19 Oct. 1840 [134]

Cheevers, Samuel, subj. of G.B.; rec. by Thomas Cheevers, of 35 Pitt St. - 19 Oct. 1840 [135]

Connolly, Bartholomew, subj. of G.B.; rec. by Patrick Egan, of 112 Elizabeth St. - 20 Oct. 1840 [136]

Cope, William, of 69 Walnut St., subj. of G.B.; rec. by Wm. Elmore, of 429 Cherry St. - 20 Oct. 1840 [137]

Clement, Joseph, of 96 Warner St., subj. of King of France; rec. by Henry L. Dodey, of 172 Eighteenth St. - 20 Oct. 1840 [138]

Connoly, Michael, subj. of G.B.; rec. by Terrence Farmer, of
Brooklyn - 21 Oct. 1840 [139]

Cowley, John, subj. of G.B.; rec. by William Alcorn, of Brooklyn - 21 Oct. 1840 [140]

Conlan, James, subj. of G.B.; rec. by James Mortimer, of Brooklyn - 23 Oct. 1840 [141]

Condon, William, subj. of G.B.; rec. by Daniel Galvan, of 6
Marin St. - 23 Oct. 1840 [142]

Cuff, John, of Queens Co., subj. of G.B.; rec. by Edward Hall,
of 8 Marin St. - 23 Oct. 1840 [143]

Carew, Joseph, subj. of G.B.; rec. by Robert W. Higgs, of 198
Varick St. - 23 Oct. 1840 [144]

Carmody, Michael, of Williamsburgh, Kings Co., subj. of G.B.;
rec. by Timothy Foley, of 60 Ridge St. - 24 Oct. 1840 [145]

Corbett, Patrick, of West Chester, subj. of G.B.; rec. by Patrick Cherry, of 16 Vandewater St. - 26 Oct. 1840 [146]

Casey, Michael, of 43 Little St., Brooklyn, subj. of G.B.; rec.
by Patrick Casey, of 43 Little St., Brooklyn - 26 Oct. 1840
[147]

Clover, Edward, of 141½ Christopher St., subj. of G.B.; rec. by
Thomas E. Brickley, of 278 Bleecker St. - 26 Oct. 1840 [148]

Callet, Eugene P., of 256 - 19th St., subj. of King of France;
rec. by Owen Donahue, corner of Cherry St. - 29 Oct. 1840
[149]

Casserty, Peter, of corner of Bridge and Tillary Sts., subj. of
G.B.; rec. by Michael Farrell, of 79 Jackson St., Brooklyn -
27 Oct. 1840 [150]

Clark, Richard W., subj. of G.B.; rec. by John A. Weeks, of 666
Water St. - 29 Oct. 1840 [151]

Cooper, George, of Williamsburgh, subj. of Emperor of Germany;
rec. by George Wiebelt, of Brooklyn - 29 Oct. 1840 [152]

Crump, Francis Robert, subj. of G.B.; rec. by Wm. W. Young, of
135 Franklin St. - 29 Oct. 1840 [153]

Cook, William, of 360 Sixth St., subj. of G.B.; rec. by Thomas
Southington, of Task [?] and Lewis Sts. - 29 Oct. 1840 [154]

Carmichael, James, subj. of G.B.; rec. by Bernard O'Neile, of
Cold Spring, Putnam Co. - 31 Oct. 1840 [155]

Cunningham, Owen, of Bloomingdale Village, subj. of G.B.; rec.
by David O'Keefe, corner of 69th St. and Bloomingdale Road -
31 Oct. 1840 [156]

Conlan, Francis, subj. of G.B.; rec. by David Conlan - 31 Oct.
1840 [157]

Cook, William John, subj. of G.B.; rec. by Sarah Cook, of Brooklyn - 31 Oct. 1840 [158]

Crone, Julius L., of 42nd St., native of Berlin, Prussia; rec.
by Louis L. Backlman [clerk wrote "Bolman"], of 11 Leonard
St. - 2 Nov. 1840 [159]

Casey, James, of 125th St., Manhattanville, subj. of G.B.; rec.
by Jeremiah Casey, of Jersey City - 2 Nov. 1840 [160]

Curchin, Abraham J., of Williamsburgh, subj. of G.B.; rec. by
Jacob Curchin, of Williamsburgh - 2 Nov. 1840 [161]

Connaty, Charles [report Sept. 1835 in Taunton, Mass.]: b. town of Porticlow [?], Co. Cavan, Ire., age 35, migr. from Balliwan [?], Co. Cavan, arrived U.S. Feb. 1834 , arrived NYC Apr. 1834 and since May has been in Taunton; rec. by Matthew Boylan, of corner of Myrtle and Stanton Sts., Brooklyn - 2 Nov. 1840 [162]

Carr, Thomas, of Brooklyn, subj. of G.B.; rec. by Margaret Carr, of Brooklyn - 2 Nov. 1840 [163]

Conway, Patrick, subj. of G.B.; rec. by Sarah Conway, of 168 Greene St. - 2 Nov. 1840 [164]

Donohue, John A., subj. of G.B.; rec. by Michael Donnelly, of 77 Orange St. - 2 Nov. 1840 [165]

Coleman, Thomas, of 37 Willett St., subj. of G.B.; rec. by Patrick Smith, of 98 Cherry St. - 2 Nov. 1840 [166]

Collins, Jeremiah, of 299 Pearl St., subj. of G.B.; rec. by George Moran, of 432 Greenwich St. - 2 Nov. 1840 [167]

Cavanagh, Mathew, subj. of G.B.; rec. by Thomas Plunket, of 6 Center Market Place - 3 Nov. 1840 [168]

Campbell, James, of 227 - 21st. St., subj. of G.B.; rec. by Christopher Freman, of 41 Orange St. - 3 Nov. 1840 [169]

Cox, William A., subj. of G.B.; rec. by Peter Bissell - 3 Nov. 1840 [170]

Carroll, Daniel [report 2 Oct. 1834 in Albany Co.]: b. Co. Kilkenny, Ire., age 22, migr. from New Ross, settled in Albany; rec. by John Nash - 3 Nov. 1840 [171]

Curran, Patrick, of Brooklyn, subj. of G.B.; rec. by Hugh Mulligan, of Brooklyn - 3 Nov. 1840 [172]

Clough, Jesse, of 8th Ave. at 37th and 38th Sts., subj. of G.B.; rec. by Christian Worth, of 8th Ave. at 37th and 38th Sts. - 3 Nov. 1840 [173]

Clark, Thomas, of Staten Island, subj. of G.B.; rec. by Patrick Henry, of Staten Island - 3 Nov. 1840 [174]

Clark, Thomas W., of 9 Hague St., subj. of G.B.; rec. by John Dunshee, of 93 Chrystie St. - 3 Nov. 1840 [175]

Coombs/Combs, Thomas, subj. of G.B.; rec. by Philip H. Jonas, of 205 Broome St. - 3 Nov. 1840 [176]

Carran, Thomas, of 5 Chatham Sq. [report Phila. 7 Oct. 1833]: b. Ire. in 1807, age now 26, migr. from Liverpool, arrived Eastport in Nov. 1827, intending to settle in Pa.; rec. by Hugh Murray, of 193 Elizabeth St. - 3 Nov. 1840 [177]

Costello, John, of Brooklyn, subj. of G.B.; rec. by Patrick Gill, of Nyack - 3 Nov. 1840 [178]

Clarke, Edward, subj. of G.B.; rec. by Joseph G. Clarke - 4 Nov. 1840 [179]

Clancy, Thomas, subj. of G.B.; rec. by George M. Dimpsey - 4 Nov. 1840 [180]

Claffey, James, of Brooklyn, subj. of G.B.; rec. by John Claffey, of Brooklyn - 4 Nov. 1840 [181]

Cosgrove, Henry, subj. of G.B.; rec. by Thomas Johnson - 4 Mar. 1840 [182]

Cunningham, James, subj. of G.B.; rec. by George Guy - 4 Nov. 1840 [183]

Chasemere, Edward, subj. of G.B.; rec. by Thomas Chasemere - 4 Nov. 1840 [184]

Cromelin, Rowland, of 649 Bowry, subj. of G.B.; rec. by Rowland Davies, of 195 Bowry - 4 Nov. 1840 [185]

Campion, Catharine [report 4 Apr. 1836]: late of Queens Co., Ire., widow of Patrick Campion; rec. by David Pray - 11 Nov. 1840 [186]

Bundle 23

John T. Fisher, subj. of G.B.; rec. by Charles K. Taylor - 26 June 1840 [1]

Fleth, John Christoph, subj. of King of Denmark; rec. by Friedrick Gustof Rode - 28 May 1840 [2]

Flynn, Daniel, subj. of G.B.; rec. by Patrick Hays - 5 Mar. 1840 [3]

Ferris, Eugene, of 23 Jacob St., subj. of G.B.; rec. by John H. Bowie - 6 Oct. 1840 [4]

Fagan, Peter [report 11 June 1838]: late of West Meath, Ire.; rec. by Edward Rowe, of 56 Elm St. - 6 Oct. 1840 [5]

Flynn, William, subj. of G.B.; rec. by John McLear - 5 Oct. 1840 [6]

Frost, John, subj. of G.B.; rec. by John Knowles, of ..... and 2nd. Sts. - 5 Oct. 1840 [7]

Fagan, James, subj. of G.B.; rec. by Edward Rowe, of 56 Elm St. - 5 Oct. 1840 [8]

Fagan, Simon, subj. of G.B.; rec. by Ann Fagan, of 11 Ave. B. - 5 Oct. 1840 [9]

Fagan, Edward, subj. of G.B.; rec. by Richard Gregg, of Bellvue - 5 Oct. 1840 [10]

Fenwick, Cornelius C., subj. of G.B.; rec. by Frederick Wallace - 5 Oct. 1840 [11]

Flood, Robert, subj. of G.B.; rec. by James Grogan, of Brooklyn - 3 Oct. 1840 [12]

Felton, Eli, Jr., subj. of G.B.; rec. by W.H. Kearns - 2 Oct. 1840 [13]

Felton, George, subj. of G.B.; rec. by W.H. Kearns - 2 Oct. 1840 [14]

Free, William, subj. of G.B.; rec. by Albert G. Smith, of 55 Elm St. - 2 Oct. 1840 [15]

Flood, Mathew, subj. of G.B.; rec. by Philip Flood, of 4 Amity Lane - 2 Oct. 1840 [16]

Funk, Aaron, of 70 . . . . .[?] St., subj. of G.B.; rec. by Nathaniel T. Hicks, of 1st. St. - 31 Oct. 1840 [17]

Fox, James, of Kings Co., subj. of G.B.; rec. by John Ewing, of 153 Leonard St. - 31 Oct. 1840 [18]

Farrell, Bernard, subj. of G.B.; rec. by Peter McCormick, of 66 Allen St. - 30 Oct. 1840 [19]

Fleming, James [report Apr. 1834]: b. town of Clemel [?], Ire.; rec. by Edward L. [?] Fleming - 30 Oct. 1840 [20]

Friedle, Christian, subj. of King of Wurtemberg; rec. by John Friedle - 29 Oct. 1840 [21]

Friedle, John, of Queens Co., subj. of King of Wurtemberg; rec. by Christian Friedle, of Queens Co. - 29 Oct. 1840 [22]

Faulhaber, Michael, of 42nd St., subj. of King of Bavaria; rec. by Baltazar Hamel, tailor, of 20th St. - 29 Oct. 1840 [23]

Farr, William, subj. of G.B.; rec. by John Redmond, of 296 Pearl St. - 28 Oct. 1840 [24]

Flood, Arthur, of the 10th Ward [report 25 Oct. 1838 in Hudson, N.Y. when residing in Stockport, Columbia Co.]: b. Dublin, Ire., age 37, migr. from Dublin; rec. by William Hutchinson - 28 Oct. 1840 [25]

Flicker, John Adam, of 3rd St., subj. of Grand Duke of Baden; rec. by John L. Horbelt, of 76 Pitt St. - 27 Oct. 1840 [AA 25]

Foord, Stephen, of Cortlandt St., Westchester Co., subj. of G.B.; rec. by Henry V. Clearman, of 33 Christopher St. - 27 Oct. 1840 [26]

Farrell, Michael, of 79 Jackson St., Brooklyn, subj. of G.B.; rec. by Peter Cassirly, of Brooklyn - 27 Oct. 1840 [27]

Fleming, Thomas, subj. of G.B.; rec. by John Clark - 26 Oct. 1840 [28]

Feeney, John, of Stanton St., Brooklyn, subj. of G.B.; rec. by Edward Feeney - 26 Oct. 1840 [29]

Feeney, Edward [report 4 Nov. 1833 in Albany]: b. Co. Longford, Ire., age 36, migr. from Dublin, intending to settle in Albany; rec. by John Feeney, of Stanton St., Brooklyn - 26 Oct. 1840 [30]

Farrell, Christopher, subj. of G.B.; rec. by Jeremiah Wells, of Brooklyn - 23 Oct. 1840 [31]

Ferguson, John, who resided 5 years in Schoharie Co., subj. of G.B.; rec. by James Geery and Archibald Watterson - 23 Oct. 1840 [32]

Finn, William, of Brooklyn, subj. of G.B.; rec. by Andrew Warner - 22 Oct. 1840 [33]

Frisard, Victor L., subj. of Berne, Switzerland; rec. by Wm. W. Young, of 135 Franklin St. - 22 Oct. 1840 [34]

Fair, Adam, subj. of Prince of Hesse Cassel; rec. by Michael Hamer, of 16th St. - 20 Oct. 1840 [35]

Flinn, David, subj. of G.B.; rec. by Patrick Riley, of 16th Ward - 20 Oct. 1840 [36]

Farrell, Thomas, subj. of G.B.; rec. by John Ash, of Brooklyn - 17 Oct. 1840 [37]

Faul, Friedrich, subj. of King of Bavaria; rec. by Eberhart Bender - 15 Oct. 1840 [38]

Feder, George Simon, subj. of King of Bavaria; rec. by David Haas, of 39th St. - 13 Oct. 1840 [39]

Flewelling, Samuel, subj. of G.B.; rec. by Frederick A. Tallmadge and Thomas J. Oakley - 12 Oct. 1840 [40]

Faulkner, Thomas W., subj. of G.B.; rec. by William Kidder - 10 Oct. 1840 [41]

Fagan, James, subj. of G.B.; rec. by Michael Kiernan, of 33rd St. - 10 Oct. 1840 [42]

Fisher, John George, subj. of G.B.; rec. by Peter Skopp - 10 Oct. 1840 [43]

Freeborn, Andrew, subj. of G.B.; rec. by Alexander Cuscaden and Edward Thurston - 10 Oct. 1840 [44]

Frelech, William, subj. of Prince of Hesse Cassel; rec. by Lewis Koerber - 9 Oct. 1840 [45]

Fairbairn, William, subj. of G.B.; rec. by Henry Fairbairn Lewis Corduan - 9 Oct. 1840 [46]

Ferrier, Walter, subj. of G.B.; rec. by William Cook - 9 Oct. 1840 [47]

Fitzgerald, Garrett, subj. of G.B.; rec. by Andrew Sullivan - 9 Oct. 1840 [48]

Fitzpatrick, William, subj. of G.B.; rec. by John Ryan - 8 Oct. 1840 [49]

Firth, George, subj. of G.B.; rec. by Patrick O'Connor - 8 Oct. 1840 [50]

Fairclough, Henry, subj. of G.B.; rec. by Thomas Whybrew - 8 Oct. 1840 [51]

Farrell, Patrick, subj. of G.B.; rec. by William Brown - 8 Oct. 1840 [52]

Felloon, Arthur, subj. of G.B.; rec. by Richard Boyce, of 102 East Broadway - 7 Oct. 1840 [53]

Fitzgerald, James, subj. of G.B.; rec. by Richard Harrold, of 65 Lewis St. - 7 Oct. 1840 [54]

Fitzpatrick, John, Jr., subj. of G.B.; rec. by John Fitzpatrick, Sr., of 20 Roosevelt St. - 7 Oct. 1840 [55]

Farrell, Richard, subj. of G.B.; rec. by James Victor, of Brooklyn - 7 Oct. 1840 [56]

Fury, Patrick, of Brooklyn, subj. of G.B.; rec. by John Fury, of Brooklyn - 2 Nov. 1840 [57]

French, Henry, subj. of G.B.; rec. by William Bishop, of Brooklyn - 2 Nov. 1840 [58]

Fox, John G., subj. of G.B.; rec. by David Daniel, of Queens Co. - 2 Nov. 1840 [59]

France, Robert, of Dutchess Co., subj. of G.B.; rec. by William Morrison, of Dutchess Co. - 2 Nov. 1840 [60]

Fitzgerald, Andrew, subj. of G.B.; rec. by William Fitzgerald - 2 Nov. 1840 [61]

Fiedler, Armistead, subj. of G.B.; rec. by Abiel W. Botsford, of 171 Wooster St. - 2 Nov. 1840 [62]

Fitch, Michael, subj. of G.B.; rec. by Patrick Brady, of 195 Franklin St. - 2 Nov. 1840 [63]

Fury, Robert, subj. of G.B.; rec. by John Fury, of Brooklyn - 2 Nov. 1840 [64]

Fletcher, Andrew, subj. of G.B.; rec. by Henry McKee, of 213 Mulberry St. - 2 Nov. 1840 [65]

Furlong, Robert, subj. of G.B.; rec. by Moses Breen, of 93 Anthony St. - 3 Nov. 1840 [66]

French, James, of Brooklyn, subj. of G.B.; rec. by Timothy Baxter, of Brooklyn - 3 Nov. 1840 [67]

Ferrier, Thornton, subj. of G.B.; rec. by Thomas Ferrier, of 126 Clinton St. - 3 Nov. 1840 [68]

Frazer, John, subj. of G.B.; rec. by Robert Frazer - 3 Nov. 1840 [69]

William French, subj. of G.B.; rec. by Emma French - 3 Nov. 1840 [70]

Fenn, John, subj. of G.B.; rec. by Alexander Robinson - 3 Nov. 1840 [71]

Featherstonehaff, Thomas, subj. of G.B.; rec. by Henry Guischard - 3 Nov. 1840 [72]

Friory, Barnard, subj. of G.B.; rec. by James Kernan - 4 Nov. 1840 [74]

Fortenback, Wenselaus, druggist, of 14 Hudson St., subj. of King of Bavaria; rec. by T.W. Thorne, Jr., of 16 Hudson St. - 30 Sept. 1840 [75]

Flood, Patrick, subj. of G.B.; rec. by Philip Flood - 28 Sept. 1840 [76]

Frazer, John, subj. of G.B.; rec. by James Graham - 28 Sept. 1840 [77]

Fagan, John, subj. of G.B.; rec. by Peter Cane - 26 Sept. 1840 [78]

Focke, Charles A., subj. of Free City of Bremen; rec. by George F. Thomas, of Brooklyn - 11 Sept. 1840 [79]

Finn, Henry, subj. of G.B.; rec. by David Beatty - 26 Sept. 1840 [80]

Enckteller, Michael, subj. of King of France; rec. by Peter Bickler - 9 Sept. 1840 [81]

Edwards, John, subj. of King of Sweden; rec. by William D. Murphy - 24 Sept. 1840 [82]

Edey, Henry, subj. of G.B.; rec. by M.C. Edey - 28 Sept. 1840 [AA82]

Etheredge, Thomas, subj. of G.B.; rec. by Augustus Craft and George Green - 30 Sept. 1840 [83]

England, Edwin, subj. of G.B.; rec. by John England - 2 Oct. 1840 [84]

Evans, Robert, subj. of G.B.; rec. by John Belden - 8 Oct. 1840 [AA84]

Earle, William, subj. of G.B.; rec. by Adam Grant - 8 Oct. 1840 [85]

Evatt, Humphrey, subj. of G.B.; rec. by William McDonnell - 8 Oct. 1840 [86]

Egan, Michael, subj. of G.B.; rec. by Henry Owens, of 3rd St. - 9 Oct. 1840 [87]

England, Edward, subj. of G.B.; rec. by Edwin England, of 60 Dey St. - 10 Oct. 1840 [88]

Entwisle, Henry, subj. of G.B.; rec. by Peter Cock - 26 Oct. 1840 [89]

Ellis, William, of Cortlandt St., subj. of G.B.; rec. by John G. Brookwood, of 55 East Broadway - 29 Oct. 1840 [90]

Early, Thomas, of 342 Greenwich St., subj. of G.B.; rec. by Patrick Early, of 122 Warren St. - 2 Nov. 1840 [91]

Early, Patrick, subj. of G.B.; rec. by Thomas Early - 2 Nov. 1840 [92]

Ellis, Henry, subj. of G.B.; rec. by James Hunt, of Flatbush - 3 Nov. 1840 [93]

Gormley, James, subj. of G.B.; rec. by Hugh Lynch - 9 Oct. 1840 [94]

Graham, David, subj. of G.B.; rec. by John Patten, of Cedar St. - 9 Oct. 1840 [95]

Gulden, Jacob, subj. of King of Bavaria; rec. by Anthony Arent, of 128 Delancey St. - 9 Oct. 1840 [96]

Gorman, John, subj. of G.B.; rec. by Lewis Dempsey, of 60 Water [?] St. - 9 Oct. 1840 [97]

Gibb, Alexander, subj. of G.B.; rec. by Andrew Wheeler - 10 Oct. 1840 [98]

Gilhooly, Michael J., subj. of G.B.; rec. by Daniel Costigan, of 215 Center St. - 10 Oct. 1840 [99]

Gaunt, Samuel, subj. of G.B.; rec. by John Murphy - 10 Oct. 1840 [100]

Green, William Alexander, subj. of King of Sweden; rec. by Henry Jenkins - 10 Oct. 1840 [101]

Graham, James L., subj. of G.B.; rec. by Lewis Katen - 10 Oct. 1840 [102]

Grosclaude, Frederick, subj. of Canton of Neufchatel, Switzerland; rec. by Julian Droz - 10 Oct. 1840 [103]

Graydon, Samuel, subj. of G.B.; rec. by John Graydon - 10 Sept. 1840 [104]

Goeller, John M., subj. of King of Wurtemberg; rec. by Christian Klingler - 22 July 1840 [105]

Gordon, John, subj. of G.B.; rec. by David Patterson - 2 Nov. 1840 [106]

Gibson, Robert [report 29 Oct. 183- in Albany]: b. Co. Armagh, Ire., age 42, migr. from Belfast, settled in Albany; rec. by Francis Blair - 3 Nov. 1840 [107]

Goebel, Conrad, of 40 Beekman St., subj. of Grand Duke of Hesse; rec. by Louis Schwartz, of 44 Chatham St. - 3 Nov. 1840 [108]

Gordon, Joseph, of Yorkville, subj. of G.B.; rec. by Andrew Gordon - 3 Nov. 1840 [109]

Gallagher, John, subj. of G.B.; rec. by Lawrence Murtaugh - 28 Sept. 1840 [110]

Gilgan, John, subj. of G.B.; rec. by Robert A. Read - 28 Sept. 1840 [AA110]

Galvin, John, subj. of G.B.; rec. by Richard Austin - 28 Sept. 1840 [111]

Gactins, Thomas, subj. of G.B.; rec. by John Meldrum - 29 Sept. 1840 [112]

Gray, James [report 3 Nov. 1832 in Albany]: b. Co. Monaghan, Ire., age 60, migr. from Newry, settled in Albany; rec. by Theophilus Luckey - 29 Sept. 1840 [113]

Gaff, John, subj. of G.B.; rec. by Robert Thornton - 28 Sept. 1840 [114]

Gunn, James, of 5 Monroe St., subj. of G.B.; rec. by Charles Toal, of 90 Catharine St. - 30 Sept. 1840 [115]

Gray, John A., subj. of G.B.; rec. by Robert H. Gray, of 173 Monroe St. - 2 Oct. 1840 [116]

Gore, Frederick, subj. of G.B.; rec. by Henry Titus, of Westchester - 2 Oct. 1840 [117]

Gannon, Thomas, of 77 Chatham St., subj. of G.B.; rec. by Anthony O'Donnell, of 77 Chatham St. - 2 Oct. 1840 [118]

Griffin, Thomas, subj. of G.B.; rec. by Cornelius O'Connor, of 24 Water St. - 5 Oct. 1840 [119]

Gait, Sydenham, subj. of G.B.; rec. by John Simpson - 5 Oct. 1840 [120]

Goldsmith, William [report Nov. 1835 in Stark Co., Ohio]: b. in Bavaria, age 25, migr. from Havre de Grace in June 1834, arrived Baltimore Aug. 1834, merchant, resident of Stark Co.; rec. by Benjamin Wiseberg, of Pitt St. at corner of Rivington - 5 Oct. 1840 [121]

Goodwin, Benjamin, subj. of G.B.; rec. by Mary Ann Devlin - 5 Oct. 1840 [122]

Godfrey, James, subj. of G.B.; rec. by Joseph Rose, Jr., of 80 Catharine St. - 6 Oct. 1840 [123]

Graham, William, subj. of G.B.; rec. by Peter Graham, of 60 Clarkson St. - 6 Oct. 1840 [124]

Grady, James H., subj. of G.B.; rec. by Hugh McCabe - 7 Oct. 1840 [125]

Gillin, John, of 121 Charles St., subj. of G.B.; rec. by Cox Keane - 7 Oct. 1840 [126]

Givney, Peter S., subj. of G.B.; rec. by William McAlan [signed "McElene"], of 40 Laurens St. - 8 Oct. 1840 [127]

Goodman, Samuel, subj. of G.B.; rec. by Joseph R. Deming, of 26 Doner [?] St. - 8 Oct. 1840 [128]

Grocer, Thomas W., subj. of G.B.; rec. by David Ogden - 8 Oct. 1840 [129]

Glaser, Gottlieb, subj. of King of Wurtemberg; rec. by Dennis Mullins, of 327 Pearl St. - 8 Oct. 1840 [130]

Guier, John, subj. of King of Bavaria; rec. by William Miller, of 175 - 21st. St. - 13 Oct. 1840 [AA130]

Green, Michael J., subj. of G.B.; rec. by William Gelsehenen - 8 Oct. 1840 [131]

Giraud, Jacques Joseph, subj. of King of France; rec. by Anthony Jicquel, of 76 James St. - 9 Oct. 1840 [132]

Greeve, Archibald, subj. of G.B.; rec. by James Virtue - 9 Oct. 1840 [133]

Goodwin, William, subj. of G.B.; rec. by William Russell, of 53 Clinton St. - 9 Oct. 1840 [134]

Gow, David, subj. of G.B.; rec. by John McGuire - 10 Oct. 1840 [135]

Gilhooly, John, subj. of G.B.; rec. by Mathew Connolly - 10 Oct. 1840 [136]

Grisch, Anthony, subj. of King of France; rec. by John Boissoud - 10 Oct. 1840 [137]

Grape, Henry H., subj. of King of Bavaria; rec. by Peter Stocky - 10 Oct. 1840 [138]. There is no No. 139.

Gore, William, subj. of G.B.; rec. by C.W. Thomas - 10 Oct. 1840 [140]

Grew, Ludwell Dampier, subj. of G.B.; rec. by Thomas Farrington - 14 Oct. 1840 [141]

Goll, Frederick P., Jr., subj. of King of France; rec. by Frederick P. Goll, of 37 Frankfort St. - 15 Oct. 1840 [142]

Granahan, Edward, subj. of G.B.; rec. by James Freel, of Brooklyn - 15 Oct. 1840 [143]

Gardener, John M., subj. of G.B.; rec. by Alfred Webb, of 115 Green St. - 16 Oct. 1840 [144]

Gannon, Thomas, subj. of G.B.; rec. by Patrick Muldoon - 19 Oct. 1840 [145]

Garraghty, John, subj. of G.B.; rec. by Edward Carroll - 19 Oct. 1840 [146]

Garden, Robert, subj. of G.B.; rec. by James Anderson, of 430 Greenwich St. - 20 Oct. 1840 [147]

Gauley, Thomas, of 102 Eldridge St., subj. of G.B.; rec. by Joseph H. Emmons, of 130 Division St. - 23 Oct. 1840 [148]

Gillick, James, labourer, of Warham, Mass., subj. of G.B.; rec. by James Simons, of 129 Cherry St., 9th Ward - 20 Oct. 1840 [149]

Gordon, William, of Sing Sing, subj. of G.B.; rec. by George Sherwood, of Sing Sing - 23 Oct. 1840 [150]

Greasley, Thomas Taft, subj. of G.B.; rec. by Charles D. Lewis - 27 Oct. 1840 [151]

Griffin, Michael, subj. of G.B.; rec. by Edward Ward - 28 Oct. 1840 [152]

Gowdey, John, Jr., of Fishkill Landing, subj. of G.B.; rec. by Alexander Gowdey, of New Windsor - 28 Oct. 1840 [153]

Gowdey, Adam, of Orange Co., subj. of G.B.; rec. by Alexander Gowdey, of New Windsor - 28 Oct. 1840 [154]

Gescheidt, Lewis Anthony, subj. of King of Saxony; rec. by John A. Stemmler, attorney - 28 Oct. 1840 [155]

Given, John, of 224 Sixteenth St., subj. of G.B.;rec by Miles Broadby, of 7th Ave. between 12th & 13th Sts. - 29 Oct. 1840 [156]

Gilligan, Michael, of Fishkill, subj. of G.B. [report 30 Oct. 1838 in Dutchess Co.]: formerly of Ire., now of Poughkeepsie; rec. by William Golden, of 125 Anthony St. - 30 Oct. 1840 [157]

Griffin, John, of 38 Division St., subj. of G.B.; rec. by Joseph Griffin, of 38 Division St. - 30 Oct. 1840 [158]

Granger, William, of 106 York St., Brooklyn, subj. of G.B.; rec. by Thomas L. Demke, of Charles St,, Brooklyn - 30 Oct. 1840 [159]

Goldberg, Heres Lyon, subj. of Emperor of Russia; rec. by Joseph Cassel, of 152 Allen St. - 30 Oct. 1840 [160]

Glynn, John, of Brooklyn, subj. of G.B.; rec. by William Glynn, of Brooklyn - 31 Oct. 1840 [161]

Gay, Thomas, of Ulster Co., subj. of G.B.; rec. by John Johnson, of 95 Hardin [?] St. - 2 Nov. 1840 [162]

Granger, Early, subj. of G.B.; rec. by Thomas Baldwin, of Queens Co. - 2 Nov. 1840 [163]

Garvey, John, of 102 Pitt St., subj. of G.B.; rec. by Dennis Garvey - 2 Nov. 1840 [164]

Galoway, James, subj. of G.B.; rec. by Wm. Harker, of Brooklyn - 2 Nov. 1840 [165]

Grimshaw, John, subj. of G.B.; rec. by Richard Raynor - 2 Oct. 1840 [166]

Golder, Joseph, subj. of G.B.; rec. by James Wilkinson - 3 Nov. 1840 [167]

Granger, Early, of Brooklyn, subj. of G.B.; rec. by William Granger - 3 Nov. 1840 [168]

Guental, Charles, subj. of King of France; rec. by Napoleon Lauried [?] - 3 Nov. 1840 [169]

Guest, Edwin, subj. of G.B.; rec. by Bernard Covert, of Brooklyn, and David R. Huson, of 91 First St. - 3 Nov. 1840 [170]

Garner, James, farmer, subj. of G.B.; rec. by John Tryon, of 76 Bayard St. - 4 Nov. 1840 [171]

Gilbert, John, subj. of G.B.; rec. by Jos. Gilbert - 4 Nov. 1840 [172]

George, John, subj. of G.B.; rec. by James L. Montgomery - 4 Nov. 1840 [173]

Gore, John, subj. of G.B.; rec. by Elias B. Howell - 4 Nov. 1840 [174]

Gomez, Francis, subj. of Portugal; rec. by John B. Serveira [?], of the 4th Ward - 4 Nov. 1840 [175]

Goldsmith, John Thomas, subj. of G.B.; rec. by John Stiles - 4 Nov. 1840 [176]

Bundle 24

Hanson, Henry C., subj. of King of France; rec. by Henry Bremer - 28 July 1840 [1]

Hacke, Christian, subj. of Elector of Hesse Cassel; rec. by Patrick Hadden - 7 Apr. 1840 [2]

Hayes, Thomas, subj. of G.B.; rec. by John Conway - 12 June 1840 [3]

Hedrick, Conrad, subj. of King of France; rec. by John Burkholster - 9 Sept. 1840 [4]

Hayes, Lawrence, subj. of G.B.; rec. by Lovland Paddock - 12 Sept. 1840 [AA4]

Halloran, Patrick, subj. of G.B.; rec. by Charles Monahan - 29 Sept. 1840 [5]

Hughes, John, subj. of G.B.; rec. by Barney Slevan - 28 Sept. 1840 [6]

Hallebread, Daniel, subj. of G.B.; rec. by Wm. H. Brayton - 29 Sept. 1840 [7]

Halbert, Rene, subj. of King of France; rec. by Louis Halbert and Augustus Halbert - 30 Sept. 1840 [8]

Hannen, Michael, of 65 Mulberry St., subj. of G.B.; rec. by John Flynn, of 716 Anthony St. - 1 Oct. 1840 [9]

Hafard, Anthony, subj. of King of Bavaria; rec. by John Haas, of 26 Du...[?] St. - 2 Oct. 1840 [10]

Hughes, John, subj. of G.B.; rec. by James Rees, of 21 Spruce St. - 4 Nov. 1840 [11]

Higgins, David, subj. of G.B.; rec. by Thomas Howley, of Flushing - 5 Oct. 1840 [12]

Hazlet, William, subj. of G.B.; rec. by Patrick Kearney - 5 Oct. 1840 [13]

Hogan, Thomas, of 158 Madison St., subj. of G.B.; rec. by Patrick McGivney, of 2 Ferry St. - 5 Oct. 1840 [14]

Hanley, Dennis [report 13 Oct. 1834 in Albany]: b. Co. Longford, Ire., age 24, migr. from Dublin, settled in Albany; rec. by James Malone - 5 Oct. 1840 [15]

Hargrave, Michael, subj. of G.B.; rec. by Thomas Maloney - 5 Oct. 1840 [16]

Herlemann, George, butcher, subj. of King of France; rec. by Frederick Rollwagen - 6 Oct. 1840 [17]

Hoople, Charles M. [report March 1837], of Buffalo, late of Upper Canada, subj. of G.B.; rec. by Otis Field, of 35 West Broadway - 6 Oct. 1840 [18]

Humphries, Thomas, subj. of G.B.; rec. by John Thomas, of 148 Walker - 7 Oct. 1840 [19]

Hughes, Richard W., subj. of G.B.; rec. by John Hughes - 7 Oct. 1840 [AA19]

Hagan, Michael, subj. of G.B.; rec. by John Hagan - 8 Oct. 1840 [20]

Hamilton, James, subj. of G.B.; rec. by Joseph Hamilton - 8 Oct. 1840 [21]

Hayward, George, subj. of G.B.; rec. by William H. Smith, of 4 [?] Maiden Lane - 8 Oct. 1840 [22]

Hancock, George, subj. of G.B.; rec. by Walter Costello, of 44 Washington St. - 8 Oct. 1840 [23]

Hudson, Henry, subj. of G.B.; rec. by Peter Cassidy - 8 Oct. 1840 [24]

Hunter, Septimus Howgill, subj. of G.B.; rec. by Samuel Carter, of Lewis St. - 9 Oct. 1840 [25]

Herrman, Christopher Frederick, subj. of King of Wurtemberg; rec. by Casper Glastder [?], of Essex St. - 9 Oct. 1840 [26]

Hartnagle, Philip, subj. of King of France; rec. by Jacob Lux - 9 Oct. 1840 [27]

Haldane, John, subj. of G.B.; rec. by James Douglass - 10 Oct. 1840 [28]

Hearty, Thomas, subj. of G.B.; rec. by James Moylan, of 182 West Broadway - 10 Oct. 1840 [29]

Hall, Isaac, subj. of G.B.; rec. by James G. Stafford - 10 Oct. 1840 [30]

Hare, John, subj. of G.B.; rec. by Robert Fair - 10 Oct. 1840 [31]

Holmes, William C., subj. of G.B.; rec. by Wm. A. Freeborn - 10 Oct. 1840 [32]

Hickenbottom, David, subj. of G.B.; rec. by Robert Hickenbottom - 10 Oct. 1840 [33]

Harris, John, subj. of G.B.; rec. by Abr. S. Van Deuser - 10 Oct. 1840 [34]

Hickenbottom, Robert, subj. of G.B.; rec. by David Hickenbottom - 10 Oct. 1840 [35]

Hunter, Robert, subj. of G.B.; rec. by Joseph Boyce - 10 Oct. 1840 [36]

Heugham, William, subj. of G.B.; rec. by Hugh McGuire - 10 Oct. 1840 [37]

Hattaff, John H., subj. of King of Hanover; rec. by Christian Busch, of 134 Carroll [?] St. - 10 Oct. 1840 [38]

Hutton, John, subj. of G.B.; rec. by Noah Tompkins - 10 Oct. 1840 [39]

Hancock, Edward, subj. of G.B.; rec. by Patrick Dougher, of 127 Washington St. - 12 Oct. 1840 [40]

Haas, David, subj. of King of Bavaria; rec. by Conrad Linden,
of 6th Ave. between 43rd and 44th Sts. - 13 Oct. 1840 [41]

Hollis, John, Jr., subj. of G.B.; rec. by John Hollis, Sr. - 15
Oct. 1840 [42]

Harned, Patrick, subj. of G.B.; rec. by John Gearen, of 99 Beekman St. - 15 Oct. 1840 [43]

Haggerty, John, subj. of G.B.; rec. by John Kelland, of 88 Mulberry St. - 16 Oct. 1840 [44]

Hope, Frederick, of Peekskill, subj. of G.B.; rec. by David E.
Price, of Elizabeth St. - 20 Oct. 1840 [45]

Hazlett, John [report Phila. Co. 7 Oct. 1833]: native of Ire.,
age 28, residing in Phila. Co.; rec. by John Quinn, of Saugerties, Ulster Co. - 20 Oct. 1840 [46]

Harrington, Richard, of 228 William St., subj. of G.B.; rec. by
Charles Griffin, of 255 Hudson St. - 22 Oct. 1840 [47]

Harvey, Edward, subj. of G.B.; rec. by James Fury - 22 Oct.
1840 [48]

Hanna, James [report Dutchess Co. 1 Oct. 1835]: native of Co.
Monaghan, Ire., now resident of Fishkill; rec. by Peter Campbell, of Haverstraw - 23 Oct. 1840 [49]

Hanna, James, subj. of G.B.; rec. by James Connolly, of 301 Madison St. - 24 Oct. 1840 [50]

Hoffman, Charles Frederick, subj. of King of Prussia; rec. by
Frantz C. Sonneborn, of 12 Clinton St. - 24 Oct. 1840 [51]

Horrocks, James, native of Eng.; rec. by Thomas Guillan/Gillan,
of 179 Hudson St. - 24 Oct. 1840 [52]

Holder, William, of Mamaroneck, Westchester Co., subj. of G.B.;
rec. by John Holder - 26 Oct. 1840 [53]

Harris, Abraham, of 43 Clarkson St., subj. of G.B.; rec. by
George Saphar, of 6 Clarkson St. - 26 Oct. 1840 [54]

Holder, John, of West Chester, subj. of G.B.; rec. by William
Holder, of West Chester - 26 Oct. 1840 [55]

Hannan, James, subj. of G.B.; rec. by Wm. Lee, of Brooklyn - 26
Oct. 1840 [56]

Holmquist, Cornelius, subj. of King of Sweden; rec. by Martin
Murphy - 27 Oct. 1840 [57]

Hardwick, Joseph, subj. of G.B.; rec. by Joseph Thornton, of
Ulster Co. - 28 Oct. 1840 [58]

Hanigan, Henry, of 231 Sullivan St., subj. of G.B.; rec. by
Barney Deary [?], of 189 Hester St. - 29 Oct. 1840 [59]

Harrison, Richard W., of 227 Spring St., subj. of G.B.; rec. by
Wm. H. House, of 31 Anne St. - 29 Oct. 1840 [60]

Holland, Cornelius, subj. of G.B.; rec. by John Donovan, of 8
Pelham [?] - 29 Oct. 1840 [61]

Hayes, John, of Wappingers Creek [report Dutchess Co. 28 Oct.
1838]: formerly of Lancashire, Eng., but now of Fishkill; rec.
by William Scott, of 82 Center St. - 29 Oct. 1840 [62]

Hendricks, John, corner King & Hudson, subj. of King of Holland;
rec. by Abm. Franklin - 29 Oct. 1840 [63]

Horty, James, of Westchester Co., subj. of G.B.; rec. by John
Malarky, of Westchester Co. - 31 Oct. 1840 [64]

Howrth, George, of Throgs Point, subj. of G.B.; rec. by Francis
Kelly, of 230 - 12th St. - 31 Oct. 1840 [65]

Harrison, Richard, of Delaware co., subj. of G.B.; rec. by Arthur Harrison, his father - 2 Nov. 1840 [66]

Hutchins, Thomas, subj. of G.B.; rec. by Lewis Moore - 2 Nov. 1840 [67]

Hilton, William, subj. of G.B.; rec. by J. Mathew Walch - 2 Nov. 1840 [68]

Harrold, Thomas, of Bushwick, subj. of G.B.; rec. by Nicholas Rowe, of Williamsburgh - 2 Nov. 1840 [69]

Haas, Michael, subj. of King of France; rec. by John B. Geiler - 2 Nov. 1840 [70]

Hitchcock, James, subj. of G.B.; rec. by James Cernehan - 2 Nov. 1840 [71]

Hickton, John George, subj. of G.B.; rec. by George Pine, of 94 Laurens St. - 2 Nov. 1840 [72]

Hagarty, Joseph, of Staten Island, subj. of G.B.; rec. by John Ritchie, of 9 Dutch St. - 2 Nov. 1840 [73]

Hughes, David, of Rahway, subj. of G.B.; rec. by Hugh Hughes, of. 1 -12th St. - 2 Nov. 1840 [74]

Hudson, John, of Brooklyn, subj. of G.B.; rec. by Thomas S. Woodcock, of Brooklyn - 3 Nov. 1840 [75]

Hanlon, Michael, subj. of G.B.; rec. by Hugh McCabe - 3 Nov. 1840 [76]

Hickey, Bernard, subj. of G.B.; rec. by Francis Kilkenny - 3 Nov. 1840 [77]

Harney, Joseph, of Brooklyn, subj. of G.B.; rec. by John McGroot, of Brooklyn - 3 Nov. 1840 [78]

Heuston, Alexander, subj. of G.B.; rec. by William Heuston - 3 Nov. 1840 [79]

Hogan, Thomas, subj. of G.B.; rec. by Edward Crowly, of 42 Beach St. - 3 Nov. 1840 [80]

Harries, Thomas, of Varick St., corner of Vandam, subj. of G.B.; rec. by Henry R. Piercy, of 25 Ridge St. - 3 Nov. 1840 [81]

Heidegger, Gustave, of Brooklyn, subj. of King of Baden; rec. by Jacob Hartman, of 20 Bayard St. - 3 Nov. 1840 [82]

Hudson, Thomas, subj. of G.B.; rec. by Charles Hending [?] - 3 Nov. 1840 [83]

Hending, Charles, subj. of G.B.; rec. by Thomas Hudson - 3 Nov. 1840 [84]

Hanna, Henry Nelson, subj. of G.B.; rec. by John Hanna - 4 Nov. 1840 [85]

Howard, Patrick, subj. of G.B.; rec. by John Leslie, of 150 Fulton St. - 4 Nov. 1840 [86]

Hearn, Patrick, subj. of G.B.; rec. by John Hearn - 4 Nov. 1840 [87]

Holland, William P., of 144 Norfolk St. [Bernard Murphy deposed that Holland was born in Co. Down, Ire., in 1815 and came to U.S. in 1831; rec. by George H. Hinchman - 4 Nov. 1840 [88]

Hayes, Henry H., subj. of G.B.; rec. by Peter Hill - 4 Nov. 1840 [89]

Haupert, Frederick, subj. of King of Bavaria; rec. by Jacob Marx, of 58 Henry St. - 4 Nov. 1840 [90]

Hughes, John, subj. of G.B.; rec. by James Daley - 26 Sept. 1840 [91]

Jeannotat, Francis Xavier, subj. of Republic of Switzerland;
rec. by Harman King - 11 Apr. 1840 [92]

Johnson, Nicholas, subj. of King of Denmark; rec. by John Jacobs
- 29 Apr. 1840 [93]

Johnston, James, subj. of G.B.; rec. by Mark Russell - 12 Sept.
1840 [94]

Johnson, John, subj. of King of Sweden; rec. by Peter Johnson -
28 Sept. 1840 [95]

Jackson, Joseph Condon, subj. of G.B.; rec. by Samuel Leak - 22
Sept. 1840 [96]

Jefert [signature looks like "Eifert"], John, subj. of Duke of
Hesse Darmstadt; rec. by Johan Kolh [?] - 29 Sept. 1840 [97]

Johnson, Francis, subj. of G.B.; rec. by Michael Johnson, of 4
Pine St. - 5 Oct. 1840 [98]

Jackson, James, subj. of G.B.; rec. by John McCoy, of 316 Monroe St. - 5 Oct. 1840 [AA98]

Jones, Thomas, subj. of G.B.; rec. by Peter Hull and John G.
Gottsberger - 6 Oct. 1840 [99]

Johnson, Edward, subj. of G.B.; rec. by Gilbert Johnson - 7 Oct.
1840 [100]

Jones, William, subj. of G.B.; rec. by Hugh Morrison, of Broadway - 8 Oct. 1840 [101]

Johnston, Samuel, subj. of G.B.; rec. by Robert Johnston - 8
Oct. 1840 [102]

Johnson, Samuel, carpenter, subj. of G.B.; rec. by William Smith
- 8 Oct. 1840 [103]

Jenkins, William, subj. of G.B.; rec. by Joseph Meade - 9 Oct.
1840 [104]

Jenkins, Edward O., subj. of G.B.; rec. by Charles Jenkins, of
172 Forsyth St. - 10 Oct. 1840 [105]

Johnson, Thomas, of 189 Cherry St., subj. of G.B.; rec. by John
Johnson - 10 Oct. 1840 [106]

Johnson, Edward, subj. of G.B.; rec. by Edward Ward, of 94 Ridge
St. - 10 Oct. 1840 [107]

Joyce, John, subj. of G.B.; rec. by John W. Hunt - 10 Oct. 1840
[108]

Jost [clerk wrote "Just"], Andreas, subj. of Duke of Darmstadt;
rec. by Louis Schwartz - 14 Oct. 1840 [109]

Jacobs, John, subj. of Grand Duke of Baden; rec. by George Peter,
of 107 Washington St. - 14 Oct. 1840 [110]

Johnson, Henry, subj. of G.B.; rec. by Edward Johnson - 19 Oct.
1840 [111]

James, Anthony, of Richmond Co., subj. of G.B.; rec. by Ralph
James, of Richmond Co. - 28 Oct. 1840 [112]

Jones, William, of Queens Co., subj. of G.B.; rec. by James Smith,
of 257 Madison St. - 30 Oct. 1840 [113]

Jacobus, Julius, subj. of King of Prussia; rec. by Mark J. King,
of 46 Chatham St. - 31 Oct. 1840 [114]

Jackson, James, native of Eng.; rec. by Stephen Thurston - 4
Nov. 1840 [115]

Jeffers, William, of Brooklyn, subj. of G.B.; rec. by John Jeffers, of Brooklyn - 12 Oct. 1840 [116]

Isaac, Simon, subj. of Emperor of Russia; rec. by John Lyon - 14 Oct. 1840 [117]

Ingles, James, stone carver [?], subj. of G.B.; rec. by James McClane, of 746 Washington St. - 27 Oct. 1840 [118]

Krewet, Conrad, subj. of King of Prussia; rec. by Joseph Hartmann, of 139 Monroe St. - 9 Oct. 1840 [119]

Keam, John, subj. of Grand Duke of Hesse Darmstadt; rec. by Gottlieb Apffelbach - 27 Mar. 1840 [120]

Kester, Lawrence, subj. of King of France; rec. by Jacob Burras - 11 Mar. 1840 [121]

Kerigan, Patrick, subj. of G.B.; rec. by John Gaff - 29 Sept. 1840 [122]

Kiefer, Francis, subj. of Duke of Baden; rec. by John F. Jakle - 29 Sept. 1840 [123]

Kolf [or Kolb?], Johan, subj. of Duke of Hesse Cassel; rec. by Peter Scheppert - 29 Sept. 1840 [124]

Kiernan, Francis, of corner of Jay & West Sts.; rec. by Patrick McGuire, of Green Co. - 30 Sept. 1840 [125]

Kelly, John H., subj. of G.B.; rec. by Wm. P. Lane - 5 Oct. 1840 [126]

King, Joseph, subj. of King of Portugal; rec. by Joseph Wise, John Lockard, Abraham Sheridan and Philip Milspaugh - 6 Oct. 1840 [127]

Kessler, Jacob, subj. of King of Prussia; rec. by Peter Lutz - 30 Sept. 1840 [128]

Kennedy, Thomas, subj. of G.B.; rec. by Lawrence Kennedy - 7 Oct. 1840 [129]

Kiernan, Joseph, subj. of G.B.; rec. by John R. Kiernan, of 195 Mulberry St. - 6 Oct. 1840 [130]

Knox, Edward, subj. of G.B.; rec. by Thomas J. McComb, of 60 Th...[?] St. - 7 Oct. 1840 [131]

Kuhlke, Casper H., subj. of King of Hanover; rec. by William M. Smith - 8 Oct. 1840 [132]

Keyrnes, Michael, native of Ire.; made decl. of intent 8 Oct. 1838 in Utica, Oneida Co.; rec. by John Condran - 8 Oct. 1840 [133]

Koen, George [clerk wrote "Kuhn"], subj. of King of Prussia; rec. by John Charles Roessler - 8 Oct. 1840 [134]

Knox, Thomas, subj. of G.B.; rec. by Patrick Bagan, of 147 Stanton St. - 8 Oct. 1840 [135]

King, Thomas Long, subj. of G.B.; rec. by Wade B. Worall, of 26 Elm St. - 9 Oct. 1840 [136]

Kerscht, John [report Phila. Co. 9 Oct. 1838]: native of Bavaria, age 31; rec. by George Kremer - 9 Oct. 1840 [137]

Kelly, Thomas, late of Ire.; rec. by Michael Maloney - 10 Oct. 1840 [138]

King, Thomas, subj. of G.B.; rec. by Jacob Lavall - 10 Oct. 1840 [139]

Kealey, James, subj. of G.B.; rec. by Bartley McGovern - 10 Oct. 1840 [140]

Kearsley, James, subj. of G.B.; rec. by Jonathan Sykes, of 134 Barrow St. - 1o Oct. 1840 [141]

Kalz, John, subj. of King of Bavaria; rec. by Martin Stubinger - 9 Oct. 1840 [142]

Kilfoil, William, subj. of G.B.; rec. by James Freel, of Brook- lyn - 15 Oct. 1840 [143]

Keefe, Patrick, subj. of G.B.; rec. by George Taylor, of Mount Pleasant - 15 Oct. 1840 [144]

Keregan, Daniel, subj. of G.B.; rec. by John Ling - 19 Oct. 1840 [145]

King, George W., subj. of G.B.; rec. by William Gray - 19 Oct. 1840 [146]

Kelly, John [report Albany Co. 17 Feb. 1831]: b. Co. Longford, Ire., age 25, migr. from Liverpool, settled in Albany; rec. by John Nowlan - 20 Oct. 1840 [147]

Keanan, William, of Brooklyn, subj. of G.B.; rec. by Patrick Coligan, of Brooklyn, Sand Lt & Green Lane - 21 Oct. 1840 [148]

Kelly, Patrick, of Westchester Co., subj. of G.B.; rec. by Fran- cis Kelly, of 230 - 12th St. - 22 Oct. 1840 [149]

Kaough, Edward, of 454 Broadway, subj. of G.B.; rec. by Patrick Dolan, of 53 Barclay St. - 24 Oct. 1840 [150]

Keegan, James, of Throggs Neck, subj. of G.B.; rec. by John Dougherty, of Throggs Neck - 24 Oct. 1840 [151]

Kech, John Wendling, subj. of Grand Duke of Baden; rec. by John Keppell, of 101 Broome St., shoemaker - 26 Oct. 1840 [152]

Kitson, Daniel, subj. of G.B.; rec. by Peter Cock, of Oyster Bay - 26 Oct. 1840 [153]

Kenworthy, John, of Poughkeepsie, subj. of G.B.; rec. by Richard P. Pease, of Poughkeepsie - 30 Oct. 1840 [154]

Keaveny, John, of 78 Roosevelt St., subj. of G.B.; rec. by John McQuade, of 96 Catharine St. - 30 Oct. 1840 [155]

Kopp, Otto H., subj. of G.B.; rec. by Frederick H. Singer, of 120 Wooster St. - 31 Oct. 1840 [156]

Kevlan, Michael, of Kings Co., subj. of G.B.; rec. by Patrick McCollum, of 74 Orange St. - 31 Oct. 1840 [157]

Kennedy, Dominick, subj. of G.B.; rec. by Michael Gillen, of 19 City Hall Place - 31 Oct. 1840 [158]

Keckeissen, Francis, of 6 Ave. G., subj. Bavaria; rec. by Peter Stults, laborer, of 188 -2nd St. - 31 Oct. 1840 [159]

Kendall, Thomas, subj. of G.B.; rec. by Abiel W. [?] Bostford [report on Kendall in Phila. 2 Oct. 1833]: b. London 24 May 1805, age now 28, migr. from Hull, arrived NYC 29 Sept. 1829 to settle in Pa. - 2 Nov. 1840 [160]

Keyogh, Thomas, of Staten Island, subj. of G.B.; rec. by David N.V. Mersereau, of Staten Island - 2 Nov. 1840 [161]

Kemp, John, of Williamsburgh, subj. of G.B.; rec. by James Cle- wen, of Williamsburgh - 3 Nov. 1840 [162]

Kobbe, Henry, subj. of Duke of Bremen [?]; rec. by Mangel Crece, of 226 Stanton St. - 3 Nov. 1840 [163]

Kippax, William, subj. of G.B.; rec. by Samuel Kippax, of 117 Orchard St. - 4 Nov. 1840 [164]

Kelly, Henry, subj. of G.B.; rec. by John Pitts - 4 Nov. 1840 [165]

Murphy, Peter, labourer, subj. of G.B.; rec. by Barney McGuire, of 215 Elizabeth St. - 7 Oct. 1840 [1]

Murphy, Patrick, of Brooklyn, native of Ire.; rec. by William Croll, of Brooklyn - 30 Sept. 1840 [2]

Mayberry, Henry, subj. of G.B.; rec. by James Sullivan, of 45 Amity St. - 30 Sept. 1840 [3]

Muir, Ebenezer, subj. of G.B.; rec. by James Muir - 29 Sept. 1840 [4]

Mercier, Francis, subj. of Canton of Neufchatel, Switzerland; rec. by Friederich Hadike - 29 Sept. 1840 [5]

Marache, Napoleon, of Brooklyn, subj. of King of France; rec. by Meigs D. Benjamin - 23 Mar. 1840 [6]

Mackay, Joseph, subj. of G.B.; rec. by Israel Dean and Nicholas Dean - 20 Jan. 1840 [7]

Moran, Andrew, pedlar, subj. of G.B.; rec. by John Higgins - 28 Sept. 1840 [8]

Maroney/Moroney, James, subj. of G.B.; rec. by Christopher Fair - 28 Sept. 1840 [9]

Martin, John, subj. of G.B.; rec. by Richard B. Butler - 28 Sept. 1840 [10]

Monas, John, subj. of G.B.; rec. by Jotham Peabody - 28 Sept. 1840 [11]

Mook, George, subj. of King of France; rec. by Peter Bickler - 9 Sept. 1840 [12]

Magle, John, subj. of King of France; rec. by Peter Bickler - 9 Sept. 1840 [13]

Mills, George, subj. of G.B.; rec. by Isaac Robb - 8 Sept. 1840 [14]

Malone, Lawrence, subj. of G.B.; rec. by Peter Boney - 29 Sept. 1840 [15]

Murray, George, subj. of G.B.; rec. by Patrick Murray - 11 Apr. 1840 [16]

Macauley, Thomas James, subj. of G.B.; rec. by Robert Sinclair - 11 Apr. 1840 [17]

Marchant, John, subj. of G.B.; rec. by James McGee - 11 Apr. 1840 [18]

Maxwell, Thomas, subj. of G.B.; rec. by John Rorke, of Willett & ....[?] Sts. - 7 Oct. 1840 [19]

Murphy, Bartley, subj. of G.B.; rec. by James Murphy - 6 Oct. 1840 [20]

Morgan, David B., subj. of G.B.; rec. by Edward Morgan, of 56 Broadway - 6 Oct. 1840 [21]

Merrall, Richard, subj. of G.B.; rec. by Richard J. Rowe, of 168 Spring St. - 6 Oct. 1840 [22]

Moran, Peter, subj. of G.B.; rec. by Michael Hart, of 79 Morton St. - 6 Oct. 1840 [23]

McMullen, Luke, subj. of G.B.; rec. by Thomas Plunkett, of 6 Center St. - 6 Oct. 1840 [24]

Metsinger, Henry, subj. of King of France; rec. by Peter Heiser, of 236 - 3rd St. - 5 Oct. 1840 [25]

Morris, John, subj. of G.B.; rec. by Thomas G. Morris - 5 Oct. 1840 [26]

Muir, William, baker, subj. of G.B.; rec. by James Terit [?], of
121 Columbia - 5 Oct. 1840 [27]

Moran, James, native of Ire., according to decl. of intent 23
Sept. 1835 in Essex Co., N.J.; rec. by John Jones, of Greenwich St. - 5 Oct. 1840 [28]

Magrath, George, subj. of G.B.; rec. by Michael Magrath, of 166
Broome St. - 3 Oct. 1840 [29]

Magrath, Michael, subj. of G.B.; rec. by William Chappell, of
37 Hamilton St. - 3 Oct. 1840 [30]

Mechin, Rene, subj. of King of France; rec. by Nicholas Schel-
teme, of Warren St. - 2 Oct. 1840 [31]

Malloy, John, of 112 Elizabeth St. [report 17 Feb. 1838 in Bibb
Co., Ga.]: b. Co. Longford, Ire., age 23, arrived New York
Apr. 1834; rec. by John Riley, of 26 Prince St. - 2 Oct. 1840
[32]

Moncrieff, Alexander, subj. of G.B.; rec. by George Pirnie - 1
Oct. 1840 [33]

Mays, John, subj. of G.B.; rec. by George Mays - 1 Oct. 1840
[34]

Moir, William, subj. of G.B.; rec. by John Moir, of 294 Washington St. - 7 Oct. 1840 [AA34]

Mehan, Charles, subj. of G.B.; rec. by David Callaghan, of Monroe St. - 9 Oct. 1840 [35]

Morley, Timothy, subj. of G.B.; rec. by Cornelius Cronin - 9
Oct. 1840 [36]

Marston, Robert, subj. of G.B.; rec. by Otis M. Blunt - 9 Oct.
1840 [37]

Murphy, John, subj. of G.B.; rec. by Timothy Murray, of 32 Ave.
B - 9 Oct. 1840 [38]

Maxwell, William H., subj. of G.B.; rec. by James Maxwell, of
259 Bowery - 9 Oct. 1840 [39]

Most, John, subj. of King of Bavaria; rec. by Andrew L. Boehme
- 9 Oct. 1840 [40]

Murphy, Michael, subj. of G.B.; rec. by John Heuratty, of 107
Columbia St. - 9 Oct. 1840 [41]

Myers, John, subj. of G.B.; rec. by William Kinny - 9 Oct. 1840
[42]

Moore, Patrick, subj. of G.B.; rec. by John Ash - 9 Oct. 1840
[43]

Mally/Melloy, Daniel, subj. of G.B.; rec. by Owen McKernan - 9
Oct. 1840 [44]

Mills, Henry, subj. of G.B.; rec. by Laughlin Heydon [or Haydon]
- 9 Oct. 1840 [45]

Murray, Thomas, subj. of G.B.; rec. by Read Peck - 10 Oct. 1840
[46]

Myers, Henry, of 652 Greenwich St., subj. of G.B.;rec. by Daniel
Rhoades - 10 Oct. 1840 [47]

Manning, Daniel, subj. of G.B.; rec. by Dennis Meehan, of 169
Leonard St. - 10 Oct. 1840 [48]

Murphy, Michael, subj. of G.B.; rec. by James Murphy, of 196
Mott St. - 9 Oct. 1840 [49]

Moylan, Patrick, subj. of G.B.;rec. by Thomas McNamara - 10 Oct.
1840 [50]

Meakin, George, subj. of G.B.; rec. by Joseph Lewis - 10 Oct. 1840 [51]

Murphy, Daniel, subj. of G.B.; rec. by Jeremiah Collins, of 21 Dey St. - 10 Oct. 1840 [52]

Mitchell, Wm., subj, of King of Hanover; rec. by David L. Sasseen - 10 Oct. 1840 [53]

Murray, James, subj. of G.B.; rec. by John Sheridan, of 36 Broome St. - 12 Oct. 1840 [54]

Miller, Valentine, subj. of King of Wurtemberg; rec. by Wendel Saili, of Saugerties, Ulster Co. - 12 Oct. 1840 [55]

Maher, Patrick, subj. of G.B.; rec. by Andrew Thompson - 12 Oct. 1840 [56]

Murtfeld, Wm., subj. of Emperor of Germany; rec. by Wm. Murtfeld, Sr. - 14 Oct. 1840 [57]

Moore, Charles, subj. of King of Bavaria; rec. by Mark Heyman, of 64 Essex St. - 14 Oct. 1840 [58]

Mathieu, Joseph, subj. of King of France; rec. by Francis Clement - 15 Oct. 1840 [59]

Maxwell, Thomas [report St. Louis 3 Dec. 1834]: b. Ire., age 41; rec. by Bedille Maxwell - 17 Oct. 1840 [60]

Moore, John, subj. of King of Bavaria; rec. by Peter Denig - 19 Oct. 1840 [61]

Murphy, Patrick, subj. of G.B.; rec. by Michael Canfield - 19 Oct. 1840 [62]

Miles, George, subj. of G.B.; rec. by Abraham Bradbury - 19 Oct. 1840 [63]

Moore, Peter, subj. of G.B.; rec. by John Moore - 21 Oct. 1840 [64]

Metcalfe, John, subj. of G.B.; rec. by William B. Townsend - 22 Oct. 1840 [65]

Mulligan, James, of 88 Mulberry St., subj. of G.B.; rec. by James H. Sally - 23 Oct. 1840 [66]

Morris, John, of 230 Water St., subj. of G.B.; rec. by Henry Purcell, of 41 Orange St. - 23 Oct. 1840 [67]

Murphy, Patrick, subj. of G.B.; rec. by Jeremiah Scanlan, of 3 Oak St. - 24 Oct. 1840 [68]

Mulholland, James, of Poughkeepsie, late of Ire., subj. of G.B.; rec. by William D. Scally - 26 Oct. 1840 [69]

Morgantholler, Mordart, subj. of King of France; rec. by Amand Miller, of 142 Suffolk St. - 26 Oct. 1840 [70]

Miller, Frederick, subj. of King of Wurtemberg; rec. by Jacob Miller - 26 Oct. 1840 [71]

Murphy, James, subj. of G.B.; rec. by Patrick Lynch, of 47 Marine [?] St. - 26 Oct. 1840 [72]

Mayr, Christian Frederick, subj. of King of Bavaria; rec. by Otto Torp, of Boney [?] & Haverton [?] - 27 Oct. 1840 [73]

Morand, Francis, of 221 Fulton St., subj. of Emperor of Russia; rec. by John L. Augaud [?], of 133 ..... St. - 26 Oct. 1840 [74]

Moody, William, of 6 Commerce St., subj. of G.B.; rec. by Thomas Moody, of 30 ...... St. - 28 Oct. 1840 [75]

Mooring, William, of Williamsburgh, subj. of G.B.; rec. by John J. Vanderbilt, of Willimsburgh - 30 Oct. 1840 [76]

Moen, A.R., of Brooklyn, subj. of King of France; rec. by John Constantine, of 154 Fulton St. - 30 Oct. 1840 [77]

Mallam, Joseph, of 754 Greenwich St., subj. of G.B.; rec. by John Mallam, of 144 Perry St. - 30 Oct. 1840 [78]

Maxwell, George T., of 67 Eldridge St., subj. of G.B.; rec. by Charles K. Taylor - 31 Oct. 1840 [79]

Mulholland, William, formerly of Ire., now of Poughkeepsie, subj. of G.B.; rec. by James Beck - 31 Oct. 1840 [80]

Mackie, John, subj. of G.B.; rec. by Wm. Somerville, of 20th St. - 31 Oct. 1840 [81]

Magraugh/Magrath, Owen, subj. of G.B.; rec. by Edward J. Drummond - 2 Nov. 1840 [82]

Manzanedo, Jose, subj. of Queen of Spain; rec. by R.M. Bicabia - 2 Nov. 1840 [83]

Muller, Valentine [report 11 Oct. 1836 in Fairfield Co., Conn., when name is given as "Phallender Moeller"]: subj. of King of Bavaria, age 36; rec. by Frederick Oehne - 2 Nov. 1840 [84]

Mackin, Charles, of 179 Greenwich St., subj. of G.B.; rec. by Margaret Donnelly, of 152 Chambers St. - 2 Nov. 1840 [85]

Merian, John J., merchant, subj. of Switzerland; rec. by Daniel Stansbury - 2 Nov. 1840 [86]

Marsden, Thomas, subj. of G.B.; rec. by William N. Marsden, of 28 Church St. - 2 Nov. 1840 [87]

Morrison, William, subj. of G.B.; rec. by Robert France, of Dutchess Co. - 2 Nov. 1840 [88]

Marsden, William Normanton, of 28 Clarke St., subj. of G.B.; rec. by Thomas Marsden, of 28 Clarke St. - 2 Nov. 1840 [89]

Morland, Michael, subj. of G.B.; deposition on 26 Oct. in Plattsburgh, Clinton Co., by Wm. H. Morgan to effect that Michael Morland has been in U.S. since 1833 and that his age was then about 17; rec. by Nathaniel B. Lan, of 32 Mulberry St. - 2 Nov. 1840 [90]

Moore, John, subj. of G.B.; rec. by John Blair - 3 Nov. 1840 [91]

Müller/Miller, John, subj. of King of Bavaria; rec. by Godfrey Halsm - 3 Nov. 1840 [92]

Manning, Mitchell, of 248 Seventh St., subj. of G.B.; rec. by David B. Lyman, of 8 Carlile St. - 3 Nov. 1840 [93]

Malloy, Edward A., of Brooklyn, subj. of G.B.; rec. by Michael Malloy, of Brooklyn - 3 Nov. 1840 [94]

Mallisson, Mathew, subj. of G.B.; rec. by Daniel Mallisson - 3 Nov. 1840 [95]

Mallisson, Daniel, of Oyster Bay, subj. of G.B.; rec. by Mathew Mallisson, of Oyster Bay - 3 Nov. 1840 [96]

Manning, John, of 595 Greenwich St., subj. of G.B.; rec. by Wm. Dorlan, of 371 Washington St. - 3 Nov. 1840 [97]

Mullen, Edward, subj. of G.B.; rec. by Robert Gannon, of 283 Broome St. - 3 Nov. 1840 [98]

Murphy, Martin, subj. of G.B.; rec. by Dennis Dempsey, of 292 Madison St. - 3 Nov. 1840 [99]

Mullin, John, subj. of G.B.;rec. by Andrew Gordon - 3 Nov. 1840 [100]

Martin, Charles, subj. of King of France [?]; rec. by M.H. Underhill, of 118 Eldridge St. - 4 Nov. 1840 [101]

Marley, Charles, subj. of G.B.; rec. by Obadiah Higgins, of 154 West Broadway - 4 Nov. 1840 [102]

Martin, John, subj. of G.B.; rec. by Patrick Coligan, of Brooklyn - 4 Nov. 1840 [103]

Murray, Hugh, of 111 Broome St. in 13th Ward, subj. of G.B.; rec. by John Gallaher, of 111 Broome St. - 4 Nov. 1840 [104]

Mulrady, Thomas, subj. of G.B.; rec. by John Moran, of 290 - 16th St. - 4 Nov. 1840 [105]

Mackey, John, subj. of G.B.; rec. by Walter Walsh - 4 Nov. 1840 [106]

Meyer, Christian E., subj. of G.B.; rec. by Thomas Battelle - 4 Nov. 1840 [107]

Martin, Henry, of 74 Henry St., subj. of King of Sweden; rec. by Emanuel Swanson - 4 Nov. 1840 [108]

Monroe, Hugh, subj. of G.B.; rec. by Hiram Trust, of 75 Broome St. - 4 Nov. 1840 [109]

Molineux, Wm., subj. of G.B.; rec. by Edward Bush, of 23 Pell St. - 4 Nov. 1840 [110]

Minerabi, Samuel, merchant, subj. of Emperor of Austria; rec.by James Bach - 9 Nov. 1840 [111]

McKenna, Patrick, subj. of G.B.; rec. by Patrick Gannon - 38 Sept. 1840 [112]

McPherson, Andrew, subj. of G.B.; rec. by Samuel Vandyne - 26 Sept. 1840 [113]

McVey, James, of 191 Bowery, subj. of G.B.; rec. by John McVey, of 189 Bowery - 29 Sept. 1840 [114]

McLaughlin, Patrick, subj. of G.B.; rec. by Richard Fitzpatrick - 29 Sept. 1840 [115]

McGuire, Patrick, subj. of G.B.; rec. by Timothy G. Doyle - 29 Sept. 1840 [116]

McKinna, Michael, of Bedford St., subj. of G.B.; rec. by Michael Robinson, of 21 Carmine St. - 30 Sept. 1840 [117]

McCall, John, subj. of G.B.; rec. by John Gallagher - 29 Sept. 1840 [118]

McGeoy, Timothy, subj. of G.B.; rec. by John Mehan - 8 Oct. 1840 [119]

McNamara, Dennis, subj. of G.B.; rec. by Daniel McGrath, of 20th St. - 4 Nov. 1840 [120]

McLaughlin, Thomas, subj. of G.B.; rec. by James Haughey, of 21st St. - 4 Nov. 1840 [121]

McAllister, Archibald, of 147 - 15th St., subj. of G.B.; rec. by William McAllister - 4 Nov. 1840 [122]

McCracken, Samuel, subj. of G.B.; rec. by Thomas Watson - 4 Nov. 1840 [123]

McGrath, John, subj. of G.B.; rec. by William McGrath - 3 Nov. 1840 [124]

McCleester, John, of 16 G.... St., subj. of G.B.; rec. by Samuel Wandell, of 393 Bowery - 3 Nov. 1840 [125]

McGarrigal, James, of 266 Greenwich St., subj. of G.B.; rec. by Erasmus B. Derby, of 246 Spring St. - 3 Nov. 1840 [126]

McLaughlin, Daniel, subj. of G.B.; rec. by Hugh McCabe - 3 Nov. 1840 [127]

McGee, James [report Albany 1 Nov. 1832]: b. Co. Longford, Ire., age 35, migr. from Dublin, residing in Albany; rec. by Edward Feinay [?], of Brooklyn - 3 Nov. 1840 [128]

McMahon, John, Jr., subj. of G.B.; rec. by John McMahon, Sr. - 3 Nov. 1840 [129]

McDermott, Joseph, of 30 Grand St., subj. of G.B.; rec. by John McDermott, of 30 Grand St. - 3 Nov. 1840 [130]

McDermott, John, subj. of G.B.; rec. by Bridget McDermott, of Newark - 4 Nov. 1840 [131]

McSorley, Patrick, of Staten Island, subj. of G.B.; rec. by David V.N. Mersereau, of Staten Island - 2 Nov. 1840 [132]

McArdle, Owen, subj. of G.B.; rec. by Charles Kelly, of Brooklyn - 2 Nov. 1840 [133]

McCool, Denis, of Newburgh, subj. of G.B.; rec. by David Sands, of Newburgh - 2 Nov. 1840 [134]

McCarton, James, of Brooklyn, subj. of G.B.; rec. by Edward Wrenches, of 136 Stanton - 2 Nov. 1840 [135]

McEvers, Christopher, subj. of G.B.; rec. by John Murphy, of 53 Oak St. - 2 Nov. 1840 [136]

McFaul, Andrew, late of Ire.; rec. by Edward J. Fleming - 31 Oct. 1840 [137]

McFilley/McFilly, William, subj. of G.B.; rec. by Daniel McMullen, of 72 Winter St., Brooklyn - 31 Sept. 1840 [138]

McNally, Michael, subj. of G.B.; rec. by Peter Sweeny, of 24 James St. - 31 Oct. 1840 [139]

McGarvey, Bernard, of Westchester Co., subj. of G.B.; rec. by Patrick McGee, of 36 Henry St., and also by Wm. Ward, of Westchester Co. - 31 Oct. 1840 [140]

McGehan, James, subj. of G.B.; rec. by Barney McLeary, of Brooklyn - 30 Oct. 1840 [141]

McKnight, John, of Yorktown, Westchester Co., subj. of G.B.; rec. by John Sweeny, lamplighter, of 18 Roosevelt St. - 30 Oct. 1840 [142]

McCrosson, John, subj. of G.B.; rec. by James Howard, of East Chester, and John O'Connor, of 79 Crosby St. - 30 Oct. 1840 [143]

McKay, John, of Rye, Westchester Co., subj. of G.B.; rec. by John Roach, of 32 Marion St. - 30 Oct. 1840 [144]

McGrath, John, of Brooklyn, subj. of G.B.; rec. by John Ures, of Brooklyn - 29 Oct. 1840 [145]

McLaughlin, Stewart, of Hester & Suffolk Sts., subj. of G.B.; rec. by Charles Hodgetts, tinsmith, of Williamsburgh - 29 Oct. 1840 [146]

McPack, Patrick, of 13th St. and Avenue A, subj. of G.B.; rec. by Francis McPack, of 48 Christie St. - 29 Oct. 1840 [147]

McCawley, John, of Brooklyn, subj. of G.B.; rec. by James McTeague, of Brooklyn - 28 Oct. 1840 [148]

McCarthy, John, carpenter, of 48 Cherry St., subj. of G.B.; rec. by Thomas McCarthy - 27 Oct. 1840 [149]

McEvoy, Patrick, subj. of G.B.; rec. by Michael Burns and Lambert Blouk [?] - 27 Oct. 1840 [150]

McDonald, James, subj. of G.B.; rec. by Daniel Kelly, of Brooklyn - 27 Oct. 1840 [151]

McColgan, Patrick, subj. of G.B.; rec. by George McColgan, of Tillary St., Brooklyn - 23 Oct. 1840 [152]

McConnell, James, subj. of G.B.; rec. by Richard McDonald, of 267 Stanton St. - 21 Oct. 1840 [153]

McGrath, Michael, subj. of G.B.; rec. by Patrick McGrath, of Brooklyn - 20 Oct. 1840 [154]

McGeehin [or McGechin?], William, subj. of G.B.; rec. by Daniel Duffy, of 90 Crosby St. - 20 Oct. 1840 [155]

McConnell, Alexander, subj. of G.B.; rec. by John McConnell - 19 Oct. 1840 [156]

McElvay, James, subj. of G.B.; decl. of intent in Pittsburgh, Pa., 6 Oct. 1838; rec. by Dennis McFalls, of Adam St., Brooklyn - 19 Oct. 1840 [157]

McNamee, Michael, of Main St., Brooklyn, subj. of G.B.; rec. by John Ash, of 341 Prospect St., Brooklyn - 19 Oct. 1840 [158]

McConologue, Henry, subj. of G.B.; rec. by Hugh McCabe, of 193 Mulberry St. - 16 Oct. 1840 [159]

McLellan, Charles, subj. of G.B.; rec. by Benjamin Brown, of Yonkers, Westchester Co. - 14 Oct. 1840 [160]

McCue, Thomas, subj. of G.B.; rec. by Edward Langstaff, of 59 Orange St. - 13 Oct. 1840 [161]

McGill, William, of Bushwick, subj. of G.B.; rec. by Alexander Land, of Bushwick - 12 Oct. 1840 [162]

McLeod, David, subj. of G.B.; rec. by John Perkine [?] Myers and John McPherson - 12 Oct. 1840 [163]

McGram, John, subj. of G.B.; rec. by Daniel Dollen - 10 Oct. 1840 [164]

McElvoy, Patrick [report 4 Nov. 1834 in Albany]: b. Co. Fermanagh, Ire., age 40, migr. from Belfast, settled in Albany; rec. by William O'Donnell, of Centre St. - 10 Oct. 1840 [165]

McIntyre, James, subj. of G.B.; rec. by Stephen White and James McGowan - 9 Oct. 1840 [166]

McCracken, Francis, subj. of G.B.; rec. by Mary McCracken - 10 Oct. 1840 [167]

McGuire, Joseph, subj. of G.B.; rec. by John McGuire - 10 Oct. 1840 [168]

McPhun [clerk wrote "McPhin], Matthew, subj. of G.B.; rec. by John Sinclair - 10 Oct. 1840 [169]

McDade/McDeade, Robert, subj. of G.B.; rec. by Richard Griffith - 10 Oct. 1840 [170]

McAllister, William, subj. of G.B.; rec. by Samuel McKechnie - 10 Oct. 1840 [171]

McColly, John, subj. of G.B.; rec. by Mary McColly - 10 Oct. 1840 [172]

McBride, Robert, subj. of G.B.; rec. by William Finley - 10 Oct. 1840 [173]

McMahon, John, Jr., subj. of G.B.; rec. by Elizabeth Donnelly, of 13th St. - 9 Oct. 1840 [174]

McCabe, Francis, subj. of G.B.; rec. by Patrick McDermott, of 50 3rd St. - 9 Oct. 1840 [175]

McLeod, Daniel, subj. of G.B.; rec. by Stephen T. Wilson, of 40
    Greenwich St. - 9 Oct. 1840 [176]

McKernan, Owen, subj. of G.B.; rec. by Daniel Kelly - 9 Oct.
    1840 [177]

McConaghy, Alexander, of 139 - 15th St., subj. of G.B.; rec. by
    James Wilson, of 139 - 15th St. - 1 Oct. 1840 [178]

McAnally, Lawrence, of 85 Ridge St., subj. of G.B.; rec. by
    Ellen Farley, of 13 Mott St. - 1 Oct. 1840 [179]

McCall, Francis, of 68 Knight St., subj. of G.B.; rec. by Hugh
    McCann, of 60 King St. - 2 Oct. 1840 [180]

McConnell, Francis, subj. of G.B.; rec. by William Cawlin/ Caw-
    line, of 571 Grand St. - 2 Oct. 1840 [181]

McManus, Henry, of 20 William St., morocco dresser, subj. of
    G.B.; rec. by Patrick Mason, of 81 Mulberry St. - 2 Oct. 1840
    [182]

McElvany, James, subj. of G.B.; rec. by Patrick Kelly, of 7th
    St. - 5 Oct. 1840 [183]

McCormick, Robert, subj. of G.B.; rec. by Francis Quin, of cor-
    ner of University Place & 12th St. - 6 Oct. 1840 [184]

McGrain, John [report 24 Sept. 1833 in Albany]: b. Co. Longford,
    Ire., age 22, migr. from Dublin, settled in Albany ; rec. by
    James McCoy, of Brooklyn - 6 Oct. 1840 [185]

McGrath, Michael, subj. of G.B.; rec. by James McGrath, of Brook-
    lyn - 6 Oct. 1840 [186]

McCann, Hugh, subj. of G.B.; rec. by James Evans and Daniel Wor-
    den, of 111 - 12th St. - 6 Oct. 1840 [187]

McArdell, Francis, subj. of G.B.; rec. by James McArdell - 8
    Oct. 1840 [188]

McCormick, Michael, subj. of G.B.; rec. by Michael Donohue, of
    77 Bank St. - 6 Oct. 1840 [189]

Lessing, Meyer, subj. of King of Hanover; rec. by Gabriel Schif-
    fer [clerk wrote "Schaffer"] - 25 Nov. 1840 [190]

Lutz, John George, subj. of King of Wurtembergh; rec. by John A.
    Vollmer - 3 Nov. 1840 [191]

Lockwood, Thomas R., subj. of G.B.; rec. by James Libbey, of
    Brooklyn - 4 Nov. 1840 [192]

Larkin, Peter, of Manhattanville, subj. of G.B.; rec. by Martin
    Gallagher, of Manhattanville - 3 Nov. 1840 [193]

Lush, John, subj. of G.B.; rec. by Joseph Whitaker, of Williams-
    burgh - 2 Nov. 1840 [194]

Lehmann, Jacob, of 28 Orchard St., subj. of King of Bavaria;
    rec. by Philip Lauer, of 107 Essex St. - 2 Nov. 1840 [195]

Laughry, Matthew, subj. of G.B.; rec. by William Laughry, of 22
    Ave. ....? - 2 Nov. 1840 [196]

Leehinger, George, subj. of King of France; rec. by John Smith,
    of 19th St. & 8th Ave. - 3 Nov. 1840 [197]

Lucy, Robert V., subj. of G.B.; rec. by James Kettell - 3 Nov.
    1840 [198]

Lennon, James, subj. of G.B.; rec. by George H. Purser, of 70
    Wall St. - 15 Oct. 1840 [199]

Logue, Owen [report 10 Oct. 1828 in Essex Co., N.J.]: b. Co.
    Tyrone, Ire.; rec. by Arthur McCready, of 11th St. - 19 Oct.
    1840 [200]

Lavender, George, of Tarrytown, subj. [probably of Emperor of Germany]; rec. by William Lavender, of Tarrytown - 19 Oct. 1840 [201]

Lindy, Nicholas [report 15 Sept. 1832 in Phila.]: b. Ire., age 25], of Throgs Neck, Westchester Co.; rec, by Patrick Kelly, of Throgs Neck, and John Britt, of Rutgers St. - 22 Oct. 1840 [202]

Lee, William, of Sing Sing, subj. of G.B.; rec. by George Sherwood, of Sing Sing - 23 Oct. 1840 [203]

Lindsay, John, subj. of G.B.; rec. by Isabella Lindsay - 26 Oct. 1840 [204]

Leask, Henry G., of 166 Canal St., subj. of G.B.; rec. by William Graham, of 46 Hester St. - 26 Oct. 1840 [205]

Lombard, James, subj. of G.B.; rec. by James McDonald, of Brooklyn - 27 Oct. 1840 [206]

Lavender, John, subj. of Emperor of Germany; rec. by Andrew Lavender, of Kings Co. - 28 Oct. 1840 [207]

Linnehan/Linehan, Daniel, of Brooklyn, subj. of G.B.; rec. by Thomas Silk, of Brooklyn - 30 Oct. 1840 [208]

Larkin, Patrick, of 690 Washington St., subj. of G.B.; rec. by Edward Cox, of 720 Washington St. - 30 Oct. 1840 [209]

Lewis, Martin, subj. of G.B.; rec. by James H. Kellam - 31 Oct. 1840 [210]

Long, William, of 140 Walker St., subj. of G.B.; rec. by John Boyce, of 202 Elm St. - 31 Oct. 1840 [211]

Lein, John Ludowick, of 28 Crystie St., subj. of Duke of Hesse Darmstadt; rec. by John Fritz, of 47 Allen St. - 2 Nov. 1840 [212]

Lockwood, William, subj. of G.B.; rec. by David Cunningham - 2 Nov. 1840 [213]

Laughlin, James [report 5 Nov. 1836 in Albany]: b. Co. Antrim, Ire., age 21, migr. from Belfast, settled in Albany; rec. by Dennis McLaughlin, of 11 James St. - 7 Oct. 1840 [214]

Lewis, William, subj. of G.B.; rec. by Alfred T. Serrell, of Forsyth St. - 8 Oct. 1840 [215]

Leslie, Alexander, subj. of G.B.; rec. by Richard Harold, of 65 Lewis St. - 8 Oct. 1840 [216]

Lister, Emmanuel, subj. of G.B.; rec. by George W. Phyfe - 8 Oct. 1840 [217]

Lagas, Franz Henry, subj. of city of Bremen; rec. by Bartle Fanti [?] - 8 Oct. 1840 [218]

Law, John, subj. of G.B.; rec. by George M. Law, of 41 Chatham St. - 9 Oct. 1840 [219]

Lawler, James, subj. of G.B.; rec. by Dennis Tracy - 9 Oct. 1840 [220]

Larkin, Michael, subj. of G.B.; rec. by Patrick Molloy, of 255-16th St. - 10 Oct. 1840 [221]

Lercher, Gottfred, subj. of King of Prussia; rec. by Martin Kinchartz [?], of 286 Bowery - 10 Oct. 1840 [222]

Logan, George, subj. of G.B.; rec. by Patrick Bawn, of 247 Stanton St., cartman - 10 Oct. 1840 [223]

Levins, Thomas C., subj. of G.B.; rec. by John Ahern - 10 Oct. 1840 [224]

Leddy, John, subj. of G.B.; rec. by Michael Waters, of 40 John St. - 10 Oct. 1840 [225]

Lennart, John, subj. of G.B.; rec. by Daniel Lennart - 10 Oct. 1840 [226]

Ladds, Joseph, subj. of G.B.; rec. by John Roach - 10 Oct. 1840 [227]

Lewis, William [report 27 Nov. 1835]: late of Liverpool; rec. by Jane Bryan, of 142 Fulton St. - 10 Oct. 1840 [228]

Lefebre, John, subj. of King of France; rec. by Caleb Barstow - 10 Oct. 1840 [229]

Lewis, Henry T., subj. of G.B.; rec. by William Lewis - 10 Oct. 1840 [230]

Lynch, William, subj. of G.B.; rec. by Jacob Voorhees, of Brooklyn - 10 Oct. 1840 [231]

Linden, Conrad, subj. of King of Bavaria; rec. by David Haas, of 39th St. - 13 Oct. 1840 [232]

Lockyer, Cornelius C., subj. of G.B.; rec. by Henry J. Hoyt - 16 Oct. 1840 [233]

Little, Thomas Patrick, subj. of G.B.; rec. by Thomas Wellington - 11 Apr. 1840 [234]

Leech, John, subj. of G.B.; rec. by Garret Stock, of Brooklyn, and William Patterson, of Brooklyn - 27 Mar. 1840 [235]

Linn, Charles, late of Finland, subj. of Emperor of Russia; rec. by Christian Barnes - 28 May 1840 [236]

Lawler, Michael [report 5 Jan. 1824]: b. Co. Carlow, Ire., age 33, migr. from Dublin, waiter; rec. by Brian McKenna - 25 Aug. 1840 [237]

Liddle, John, subj. of G.B.; rec. by John Pomeroy - 23 Sept. 1840 [238]

Lynch, James, subj. of G.B.; rec. by Michael Lynch - 28 Sept. 1840 [239]

Leonard, Francis J., subj. of G.B.; rec. by Patrick Leonard, of 603 Water St. - 6 Oct. 1840 [240]

Larkin, James, subj. of G.B.; rec. by John Brooker, of Richmond Co. - 28 Sept. 1840 [241]

Lynch, Dennis, subj. of G.B.; rec. by Jotham Peabody - 28 Sept. 1840 [242]

Lush, Thomas Ryall, subj. of G.B.; rec. by Henry Britton - 28 Sept. 1840 [243]

Loughery, Michael, subj. of G.B.; rec. by Neal McCauley, of Brooklyn - 5 Oct. 1840 [244]

Lynch, Alexander, subj. of G.B.; rec. by William McAleway, of 40 Lauren [?] St. - 6 Oct. 1840 [245]

Lucas, John, of Belleville, N.J., subj. of G.B.; rec. by Thomas Lloyd, of 85 Perry St. - 6 Oct. 1840 [246]

Lemaire, John, subj. of King of France; rec. by Christopher Lemaire, of 111 Anthony St. - 7 Oct. 1840 [247]

Bundle 26

Quinn, James, subj. of G.B.; rec. by William Quinn - 29 Sept. 1840 [1]

Quigg, Bernard, subj. of G.B.; rec. by Peter Cain/Kain, of 302 3rd St. - 6 Oct. 1840 [2]

Quinn, Timothy, subj. of G.B.; rec. by Andrew O'Connor - 8 Oct. 1840 [3]

Quigg, William, subj. of G.B.; rec. by Bernard Quigg, of 80 Avenue D - 9 Oct. 1840 [4]

Quin, John, subj. of G.B.; rec. by Thomas Carlow, of the 11th Ward - 10 Oct. 1840 [5]

Quin, John, subj. of G.B.; rec. by Joseph Goldia [Goldin?] - 13 Oct. 1840 [6]

Quis, Anthony, of 188 Second St., subj. of King of France; rec. by Peter Dennig, of 456 Fourth St. - 2 Nov. 1840 [7]

Quinn, Patrick, subj. of G.B.; rec. by John Byrnes, of 9 Centre Market - 4 Nov. 1840 [8]

Rozynkowski, Julian K., subj. of Emperor of Russia; rec. by Thaddeus M.H. Lyon - 21 Mar. 1840 [9]

Rutzler, Frederick, subj. of Grand Duke of Baden; rec. by Franz Hartz - 11 Apr. 1840 [10]

Ruben, George, subj. of Free City of Hamburgh; rec. by Joseph Gutman - 26 Aug. 1840 [11]

Radars, Frederick, subj. of King of Prussia; rec. by John Brown - 26 Sept. 1840 [12]

Riley, Patrick, subj. of G.B.; rec. by Philip Riley - 28 Sept. 1840 [13]

Raeber, Jacob, subj. of Emperor of Germany; rec. by Johannes Simler - 28 Sept. 1840 [14]

Reilly, Thomas, subj. of G.B.; rec. by Felix McGlinn - 28 Sept. 1840 [15]

Riley, Owen, of 265 Madison St., subj. of G.B.; rec. by Edwin Chapin, of 622 Water St. - 30 Sept. 1840 [16]

Rickard, Thomas, subj. of G.B.; rec. by Thomas Maxwell, of 440 Grand St. - 1 Oct. 1840 [17]

Robinson, Morris, subj. of G.B.; rec. by John Duer and Beverley Robinson - 1 Oct. 1840 [18]

Rice, John, subj. of King of Bavaria; rec. by Joseph Rice, of 64 Sheriff St. - 2 Oct. 1840 [19]

Russ, Christian, subj. of G.B.; rec. by John Maerz, of 369 Pearl St. - 5 Oct. 1840 [20]

Reilly, Richard, subj. of G.B.; rec. by Alexander Wisely, of 8th Ave. & 125th St. - 6 Oct. 1840 [21]

Robinson, Thomas, subj. of G.B.; rec. by James Graham and Ellen Hall - 6 Oct. 1840 [22]

Reilly, Francis, subj. of G.B.; rec. by Edward Kiernan, of 12 Marion St. - 7 Oct. 1840 [23]

Roeff, Augustus [report Phila. Co. 10 Oct. 1836]: b. Wertemberg on 10 May 1807, age now 29, migr. from Hamburgh, arrived New York 2 July 1835; rec. by Francis H. Baumer, of 1360 Leonard St. - 8 Oct. 1840 [24]

Raveret, Augustus, subj. of King of France; rec. by Judith Raveret - 9 Oct. 1840 [25]

Roy, Xavier, subj. of King of France; rec. by George Quelet - 9 Oct. 1840 [26]

Russell, William, subj. of G.B.; rec. by William Goodwin, of 52 Cliff St. - 9 Oct. 1840 [27]

Robinson, Henry, subj. of G.B.; rec. by Samuel Johnson, of 28 Cortlandt St. - 9 Oct. 1840 [28]

Ritter, George, subj. of King of Wertemberg; rec. by Elizabeth Ritter - 10 Oct. 1840 [29]

Rosenfeld, Samuel, subj. of King of Bavaria; rec. by Samuel Hymen - 10 Oct. 1840 [30]

Roberts, Edwin, subj. of G.B.; rec. by Edward George Figuet [?], of Brooklyn - 10 Oct. 1840 [31]

Reid, George, subj. of G.B.; rec. by Edward Connolly - 10 Oct. 1840 [32]

Rodie, William, subj. of G.B.; rec. by William Finlay - 10 Oct. 1840 [33]

Runcie, John T., subj. of G.B.; rec. by Joseph M. Brown, of Williamsburgh - 12 Oct. 1840 [34]

Rathbone, Joseph, tailor, subj. of G.B.; rec. by John Cook - 12 Oct. 1840 [35]

Roach, David, of Westchester Co., subj. of G.B.; rec. by John Roach, of 17 Water St. - 12 Oct. 1840 [36]

Ray, George, subj. of G.B.; rec. by James Orr, of 45 Clarkson St. - 12 Oct. 1840 [37]

Regan, Patrick, of Brooklyn, subj. of G.B.; rec. by Patrick Cavanagh, of Grand St. - 13 Oct. 1840 [38]

Ryan, Patrick [report Rensselaer Co., N.Y., 4 Nov. 1834]: b. at Tollow, Co. Carlow, Ire., age 22, migr. from Dublin, arrived town of Whitehall 1 Dec. 1833, now residing in Troy; rec. by Sampson Brady - 13 Oct. 1840 [39]

Rosenburger, Jacob, subj. of King of Bavaria; rec. by Marks Heyman, of 64 Essex St. - 14 Oct. 1840 [40]

Rooney, Bernard, subj. of G.B.; rec. by Hugh McGinnis - 14 Oct. 1840 [41]

Rose, Michael, subj. of G.B.; rec. by James Freel, of Brooklyn - 15 Oct. 1840 [42]

Riley, Francis, of 119 Grand St., subj. of G.B.; rec. by Timothy Smith, of corner of Anthony and Centre Sts. - 21 Oct. 1840 [43]

Roach, Mathew, subj. of G.B.; rec. by John Taggart, of Westchester Co. - 22 Oct. 1840 [44]

Ritchie, James C., subj. of G.B.; rec. by David Mooran - 23 Oct. 1840 [45]

Ross, William J., subj. of G.B.; rec. by Nicholas Walsh, of 14 Clarkson St. - 23 Oct. 1840 [46]

Russell, James, subj. of G.B.; rec. by John Harper, of 583 -4th St. - 23 Oct. 1840 [47]

Ross, John G., subj. of King of Bavaria; rec. by Frederica Ross, of 94 Clinton St. - 26 Oct. 1840 [48]

Riley, Thomas, of 148 Varick St, age about 30, resident of N.Y. State for 11 years, subj. of G.B.; rec. by Margaret Marston, of 148 Varick St. - 27 Oct. 1840 [49]

Rice, Peter, subj. of King of Bavaria; rec. by Andrew Weber, of corner of 9th Avenue & 13th St. - 28 Oct. 1840 [50]

Rauer, Augustus, of Poughkeepsie, subj. of King of Saxony; rec. by Simon Bierbour, of Poughkeepsie - 29 Oct. 1840 [51]

Reilly, Michael, of Queens Co., subj. of G.B.; rec. by Patrick Clark, of 36 Sheriff St. - 30 Oct. 1840 [52]

Riley, William, subj. of G.B.; rec. by George Thuesen, of 208 Division St. - 31 Oct. 1840 [53]

Redlich, August Charles, subj. of King of Bavaria; rec. by John Cross, of 117 Canal St. - 2 Nov. 1840 [54]

Riley, Phillip, subj. of G.B.; rec. by Andrew Riley - 2 Nov. 1840 [55]

Rafferty, John, of Westchester Co., subj. of G.B.; rec. by John Kelly, of 36 Orange St. - 2 Nov. 1840 [56]

Reynolds, John, of Brooklyn, subj. of G.B.; rec. by Daniel Mc Mullan, of 9 Elm St. - 2 Nov. 1840 [57]

Riley, James, of 2 Centre Market Place, subj. of G.B.; rec. by Bernard Riley, of 12 Marion St. - 2 Nov. 1840 [58]

Ryne, John, subj. of G.B.; rec. by John Kinnery - 2 Nov. 1840 [59]

Read, James, weaver, subj. of G.B.; rec. by George Brikbeck - 3 Nov. 1840 [60]

Reed, Joshua, subj. of G.B.; rec. by James Reed - 3 Nov. 1840 [61]

Reubel, John, subj. of King of Bavaria; rec. by John Willing - 3 Nov. 1840 [62]

Remmergen, John, subj. of King of France; rec. by Frederick Coornby [?], of 448 Cherry St. - 3 Nov. 1840 [63]

Redman, Jeremiah, subj. of G.B.; rec. by Isaac Kull, of Brooklyn - 3 Nov. 1840 [64]

Robinson, Alexander, subj. of G.B.; rec. by John Fenn - 3 Nov. 1840 [65]

Rogers, Joseph, of Williamsburgh, subj. of G.B.; rec. by Samuel Hays, of Williamsburgh - 3 Nov. 1840 [66]

Richmond, George, subj. of G.B.; rec. by John Gatten - 3 Nov. 1840 [67]

Rae, Robert, subj. of G.B.; rec. by John Calvin Smith - 3 Nov. 1840 [68]

Renwick, James, subj. of G.B.; rec. by Charles M. Nanry, of 86 Pine St. - 3 Nov. 1840 [69]

Richardson, Joseph, subj. of G.B.; rec. by John W. Beattie, of 121 Sullivan St. - 4 Nov. 1840 [70]

Reanier, George, subj. of G.B.; rec. by James Reanier - 4 Nov. 1840 [71]

Ryan, Michael, subj. of G.B.; rec. by Thomas Ryan, of 44 Chambers St. - 4 Nov. 1840 [72]

Rees, Thomas A., subj. of G.B.; rec. by Peter Wood - 4 Nov. 1840 [73]

Nowlan, Henry, subj. of G.B.; rec. by Samuel Butler - 1 Oct. 1840 [74]

Newton, Robert, subj. of G.B.; rec. by William Farrell, of 171 Elizabeth St. - 5 Oct. 1840 [75]

Nash, Michael, subj. of G.B.; rec. by Thomas Hogan, of 4 Montgomery St. - 5 Oct. 1840 [76]

Nealis, Peter, subj. of G.B.; rec. by John McCormick, of Brooklyn - 8 Oct. 1840 [77]

Nowill, James D., subj. of G.B.; rec. by Wm. R. Wheaton, of 32 Norfolk St. - 8 Oct. 1840 [78]

William Stobbs Newham, subj. of G.B.; rec. by Richard Timms, of Newburgh - 9 Oct. 1840 [79]

Nordblad, Gustav, subj. of King of Sweden; rec. by Joseph Reynolds - 9 Oct. 1840 [80]

Nevin, John B., subj. of G.B.; rec. by William Nevin - 10 Oct. 1840 [81]

Neats, William, subj. of G.B.; rec. by Edward W. Bishop - 19 Oct. 1840 [82]

Nowlan, John [report Albany Co. 3 Nov. 1834]: b. Co. Longford, Ire., age 26, migr. from Dublin, residing in Albany; rec. by John Kelly, of Brooklyn - 20 Oct. 1840 [83]

Nicholson, James, subj. of G.B.; rec. by John Foley, of 109 Anthony St. - 24 Oct. 1840 [84]

Nelson, Samuel, of Yorkville, subj. of G.B.; rec. by Andrew Gordon, of Yorkville - 26 Oct. 1840 [85]

Nation, James, of Sullivan Co., subj. of G.B.; rec. by Joseph Swanell, of 415 Grand St. - 27 Oct. 1840 [86]

Neely, Francis, of Woodstock, Ulster Co., subj. of G.B.; rec. by Patrick Burns and Patrick McLaughlin - 27 Oct. 1840 [87]

Nicholson, Robert, of West Chester, subj. of G.B.; rec. by Frederick H. Fisher, of West Chester - 28 Oct. 1840 [88]

Nelson, John, subj. of G.B.; rec. by John Moore, of 74 Grand St., and also by James Burges, of 119 Suffolk St. - 31 Oct. 1840 [89]

Nowlen, Charles, subj. of G.B.; rec. by James Nowlen - 2 Nov. 1840 [90]

Noonan, James, of Manhattanville [report Rensselaer Co. 9 May 1837]: b. at Temple Braden, Co. Limerick, Ire., age 37, migr. from Limerick, arrived NYC 1827, now residing in Troy; rec. by Thomas Noonan, of Albany - 3 Nov. 1840 [91]

Oelricks, Hermann, subj. of City of Bremen; rec. by George F. Gerding - 21 Mar. 1840 [92]

Orth, Lawrence, subj. of Grand Duke of Hesse Darmstadt; rec. by Christian Hucke - 7 Apr. 1840 [93]

Oppenheimer, David, subj. of King of Hanover; rec. by Joseph Barrencher - 11 Sept. 1840 [94]

O'Neil, James, subj. of G.B.; rec. by Michael Glennon - 28 Sept. 1840 [95]

O'Hare, James, subj. of G.B.; rec. by Patrick Kinny - 28 Sept. 1840 [96]

Oettly, George, of 81 Forsyth St., subj. of Switzerland; rec. by Conrad Wellauer, of 24 Canal St. - 29 Sept. 1840 [97]

O'Connor, Daniel, of Brooklyn, subj. of G.B.; rec. by Michael Curtain, of 372 Pearl St. - 30 Sept. 1840 [98]

O'Brien, Daniel, subj. of G.B.; rec. by James Talbot - 1 Oct. 1840 [99]

O'Connor, William, subj. of G.B.; rec. by John Hagan, of 146 Essex St. - 3 Oct. 1840 [100]

O'Brien, William, subj. of G.B.; rec. by John Conway, of Centre St. - 6 Oct. 1840 [101]

O'Neill, John, subj. of G.B.; rec. by Constantine McCosker, of 13th & Hudson Sts. - 6 Oct. 1840 [102]

Owens, Henry, subj. of G.B.; rec. by William Roberts - 9 Oct. 1840 [103]

Owens, James, subj. of G.B.; rec. by Elias D. Brower, of 66 King St. - 13 Oct. 1840 [104]

O'Donnell, John, subj. of G.B.; rec. by James Gilmore, of 33 Marion St. - 16 Oct. 1840 [105]

Owens, John, of 41st St., subj. of G.B.; rec. by John Barth, of 50th St. - 20 Oct. 1840 [106]

O'Neile, Thomas, subj. of G.B.; rec. by Timothy O'Neile, of 26 Rosevelt St. - 26 Oct. 1840 [107]

O'Brien, Nicholas, subj. of G.B.; rec. by Hugh O'Neil, public porter - 31 Oct. 1840 [108]

O'Connor, Patrick, of 183 William St., subj. of G.B.; rec. by Nicholas Fitzgerald, of 1 Water St. - 2 Nov. 1840 [109]

Petrie, John, late of Orkney, Scotland, subj. of G.B.; rec. by Thomas Moore - 19 Mar. 1840 [110]

Pew, George, subj. of G.B.; rec. by George Boyd - 25 Sept. 1840 [111]

Pollock, Hugh, of corner of Robinson & Greenwich Sts., subj. of G.B.; rec. by Stephen S. Chamberlin, of 76 Forsyth St. - 29 Sept. [112]

Pentlow, William B., subj. of G.B.; rec. by Daniel T. Conger - 29 Sept. 1840 [113]

Patton, Thomas, of 283 Mulberry St., subj. of G.B.; rec. by Wm. Hemma, of 149 Spring St. - 30 Sept. 1840 [114]

Prior, John, subj. of G.B.; rec. by Patrick John Brady, of 332 Broome St. - 3 Oct. 1840 [115]

Pape, Carls, subj. of King of Hanover; rec. by Francis Wode, of 14 Spring St. - 3 Oct. 1840 [116]

Patterson, James, subj. of G.B.; rec. by George Ross, of 42 Franklin St. - 3 Oct. 1840 [117]

Plunkett, Edward, labourer, subj. of G.B.; rec. by Farrell Keogan, of 34 Montgomery St. - 5 Oct. 1840 [118]

Phealan, Michael, subj. of G.B.; rec. by Michael Donohue, of 88 Hester St. - 6 Oct. 1840 [119]

Pican, James, subj. of Republic of Columbia; rec. by Hezekiah W. Bennell, of 25 Sheriff St. - 6 Oct. 1840 [120]

Pearson, Thomas, subj. of G.B.; rec. by Maltby G. Lane, of Bowery - 6 Oct. 1840 [121]

Prehal, John, late of Poland, subj. of Emperor of Russia; rec. by Andrew Nessel, of 76 Ludlow St. - 6 Oct. 1840 [122]

Parker, Michael, subj. of G.B.; rec. by Francis McCadden, of Essex & Delancy Sts. - 7 Oct. 1840 [123]

Percival, James, Jr., subj. of G.B.; rec. by James Percival, Sr. - 7 Oct. 1840 [124]

Percival, James, Sr., subj. of G.B.; rec. by James Percival, Jr. - 7 Oct. 1840 [125]

Pike, Thomas, subj. of G.B.; rec. by James Charlesworth, of 59 Chambers St. - 7 Oct. 1840 [126]

Plat, Carsten, subj. of King of Hanover; rec. by Henry Plat - 8 Oct. 1840 [127]

Plat, Henry, subj. of King of Hanover; rec. by Carsten Plat - 8 Oct. 1840 [128]

Paul, Alexander, subj. of G.B.; rec. by Samuel Bennett, of Hudson St. - 9 Oct. 1840 [129]

Pinkerton, Henry, subj. of G.B.; rec. by James Pinkerton, of 719 Grand St. - 9 Oct. 1840 [130]

Phillips, George, subj. of G.B.; rec. by Thomas Bell, of Fulton St. - 9 Oct. 1840 [131]

Phelan, Owen, subj. of G.B.; rec. by Michael Kerrigan - 10 Oct. 1840 [132]

Pritchard, George, subj. of G.B.; rec. by Henry Sherwood - 10 Oct. 1840 [133]

Pappi, Luigi, subj. of Switzerland; rec. by Francis Steffani, of 4 Crosby St., glazier - 10 Oct. 1840 [134]

Peno, Andrew, late of Brussells, subj. of King of Belgium; rec. by John F. Bailey - 9 Oct. 1840 [135]

Pitt, John, subj. of G.B.; rec. by Jacob Voorhees, of Brooklyn - 12 Oct. 1840 [136]

Pentony, Michael, subj. of G.B.; rec. by James Patterson - 13 Oct. 1840 [137]

Porteous, Robert, subj. of G.B.; rec. by William Findley, of 145 Laurens [?] St. - 14 Oct. 1840 [138]

Patterson, Arthur, subj. of G.B.; rec. by Samuel Shields and Leonard D. Howse - 23 Oct. 1840 [139]

Phillips, William, of 13 Jacob St., subj. of G.B.; rec. by Charles H. Colladay, of 8 Vandewater St. - 24 Oct. 1840 [139AA]

Pashley, John, Jr., subj. of G.B.; rec. by John Pashley, Sr., of Williamsburgh - 26 Oct. 1840 [140]

Pidgeon, James, of 209 Elizabeth St., subj. of G.B.; rec. by Louis Levestre, of 113 Pitt St. - 27 Oct. 1840 [141]

Paulsen, George O. Peter, subj. of Republic of Hamburgh; rec. by George Henry Paulsen - 27 Oct. 1840 [142]

Powers, James, of Queens Co., subj. of G.B.; rec. by Foster Hendrickson, of Queens Co. - 31 Oct. 1840 [143]

Pollock, Samuel, of corner of 19th St. & 8th Ave. - 31 Oct. 1840 [144]

Pink, William, of Williamsburgh, subj. of G.B.; rec. by Benjamin Doxey, of Williamsburgh - 31 Oct. 1840 [145]

Plowright, Samuel, of West Farms, subj. of G.B.; rec. by John P. Descaso - 2 Nov. 1840 [146]

Pelham, Jabez Clinton, subj. of G.B.; rec. by Alexander Watson 2 Nov. 1840 [147]

Pessinger, Wuenafeld [?], of 23 Pell St., subj. of King of Wertemberg; rec. by Leopold Pessinger, of 23 Pell St. - 2 Nov. 1840 [148]

Philben, Martin, subj. of G.B.; rec. by Patrick Burke - 3 Nov. 1840 [149]

Parker, William H., subj. of G.B.; rec, by Thomas Withington - 2 Nov. 1840 [150]

Partridge, Stephen, subj. of G.B.; rec. by John Speir - 3 Nov. 1840 [151]

Porter, James, subj. of G.B.; rec. by William Porter - 3 Nov.
1840 [152]

Polwarth, James, subj. of G.B.; rec. by William McLean - 3 Nov.
1840 [153]

Pazolt, Thomas, subj. of Emperor of Austria; rec. by Samuel
Mails, of 393 Broadway - 3 Nov. 1840 [154]

Pyatt, Francis, of Brooklyn, subj. of G.B.; rec. by William
McDonnell - 3 Nov. 1840 [155]

Parkinson, Christopher, subj. of G.B.; rec. by Thomas Bradley,
of 103 Delancy St. - 4 Nov. 1840 [156]

Palmer, William, subj. of G.B.; rec. by Abner Toppan, of 71
James St. - 4 Nov. 1840 [157]

Phillips, Thomas, subj. of G.B.; rec. by Timothy Baxter - 4 Nov.
1840 [158]

Bundle 27

Xavier, John W., of Schenectady, subj. of King of Portugal; rec.
by John B. Bonny, of Schenectady, and Francis J. Silva, of 95
Chrystie St. - 28 Oct. 1840 [1]

Yates, James D., subj. of G.B.; rec. by Daniel W. Clark - 30
Sept. 1840 [2]

Young, George, subj. of G.B.; rec. by Wm. Cascaden, of 427 Monroe St. - 10 Oct. 1840 [3]

Young, Moses, who has residen on Long Island, subj. of G.B.;
rec. by John McCord and Benjamin Reed - 26 Oct. 1840 [4]

Yanni/Yanna, John Jacob, of 26 Thompson St., subj. of Canton of
Basle, Switzerland; rec. by Peter Burkhard, of 67 Vesey St. -
2 Nov. 1840 [5]

Yeager/Jager, Peter, of 194 Second St., subj. of King of Bavaria; rec. by David Bungert/Bumgart, of 194 Leonard St. - 3
Nov. 1840 [6]

Yochill, James, subj. of G.B.; rec. by William Husson, of 129
Bevar St. - 3 Nov. 1840 [7]

Zink, Philipp, subj. of Grand Duke of Baden; rec. by Frederick
Jung - 8 Oct. 1840 [8]

Shea, John A. [report 29 Dec. 1835 in Washington, D.C.]: b. Ire.,
age 32, migr. from Liverpool, arrived NYC in Sept. 1828, intending to reside in Washington; rec. by John F. Gannon, of
Pearl St. - 9 Oct. 1840 [9]

Stanton, James, subj. of G.B.; rec. by Patrick Stanton and also
by John Winn, of 3rd Ave. - 9 Oct. 1840 [10]

Slaven, Patrick, subj. of G.B.; rec. by Ann McQuiggin, of Jersey City - 9 Oct. 1840 [11]

Shearer, Alexander, subj. of G.B.; rec. by Elijah Withington, of
Williamsburgh - 9 Oct. 1840 [12]

Schwartz, John George, subj. of Duke of Bavaria; rec. by Adam
Schwartz - 9 Oct. 1840 [13]

Schaible, John, subj. of King of Bavaria; rec. by Michael Harmann [?] - 10 Oct. 1840 [14]

Steele, Peter W., subj. of G.B.; rec. by George Blackburn - 10
Oct. 1840 [15]

Smith, Ebenezer, subj. of G.B.; rec. by Robert Marshall - 10
Oct. 1840 [16]

Studds, Frederick, subj. of G.B.; rec. by Pearce Percival - 10 Oct. 1840 [17]

Serian, George, subj. of King of Greece; rec. by Charles Cobb - 10 Oct. 1840 [18]

Stopp, Charles, subj. of Emperor of Germany; rec. by John G. Wiese [?] - 7 Oct. 1840 [19]

Sassan/Sasseen, David L., subj. of King of Prussia; rec. by Wm. Mitchell - 10 Oct. 1840 [20]

Stobo, Alexander, subj. of G.B.; rec. by Richard Whittaker- 10 Oct. 1840 [21]

Schaffer, Caspar, subj. of Prince of Hesse Cassel; rec. by Henry Schaffer, of 12 James St. - 10 Oct. 1840 [22]

Solomon, Daniel B., subj. of King of Holland; rec. by Abraham J. Jackson - 10 Oct. 1840 [23]

Shaw, Alexander L., subj. of G.B.; rec. by Merrit Smith - 10 Oct. 1840 [24]

Samuels, Charles, of Brooklyn, subj. of G.B., and his wife Anna; rec. by John H. Bowie - 9 Oct. 1840 [25]

Soldner, John, subj. of King of Prussia; rec. by Jacob Hahn - 8 Oct. 1840 [26]

Stephenson, John, subj. of G.B.; rec. by Charles Young and John A. Jackson - 8 Oct. 1840 [27]

Shields/Shiels, Daniel, subj. of G.B.; rec. by Edward Clark, of 108 Bleecker St. - 8 Oct. 1840 [28]

Shea, Andrew, subj. of G.B.; rec. by Ellen Shea - 8 Oct. 1840 [29]

Smyth, Paul, subj. of G.B.; rec. by Bernard Lynch - 8 Oct. 1840 [30]

Swanton, Matthew [report Albany Co. 13 Apr. 1836]: b. Somerset-shire, Eng., age 26, migr. from Bristol, intending to settle in Albany; rec. by Anthony Carter - 8 Oct. 1840 [31]

Schmidt, George, subj. of King of Wertemberg; rec. by Henry Woerz, of Staten Island - 7 Oct. 1840 [32]

Stack, John, subj. of G.B.; rec. by John O'Neil, of 153 Lewis St. - 6 Oct. 1840 [33]

Sutter, James, subj. of G.B.; rec. by Alen Gray, of 7th Ave. & 17th St. - 6 Oct. 1840 [34]

Stewart, James, subj. of G.B.; rec. by Charles S. Macfarlane, of 148 - 16th St. - 5 Oct. 1840 [35]

Stahl, Georg, subj. of Germany; rec. by Valentin Schmidt, of 527 Pearl St. - 5 Oct. 1840 [36]

Stoney, Henry, subj. of G.B.; rec. by George Stoney - 5 Oct. 1840 [37]

Smith, James, subj. of G.B.; rec. by Richard Cary - 5 Oct. 1840 [38]

Stuart, William, subj. of G.B.; rec. by Griffin Green, of 438 Pearl St. - 2 Oct. 1840 [39]

Shinnick, James, subj. of G.B.; rec. by William Stokelen - 1 Oct. 1840 [40]

Small, John, subj. of G.B.; rec. by William Boyd - 1 Oct. 1840 [41]

Scullon, Hugh, of Manhattanville, subj. of G.B.; rec. by John Canning, of 8 Birmingham St. - 1 Oct. 1840 [42]

Steen, John, of 3rd Ave. & 43rd St., subj. of G.B.; rec. by George G. Barber, of 84th St. & 3rd Ave. - 30 Sept. 1840 [43]

Stumpf, Charles, subj. of Duke of Hessen; rec. by Peter Scheppert - 31 Sept. 1840 [44]

Schumpff, Anthony, of 196 Houstoun St., subj. of King of France; rec. by Joseph Vogel, of 796 Houstoun St. - 30 Sept. 1840 [45]

Sloan, Samuel, of 14 Leonard St., subj. of G.B.; rec. by Matthew Maxwell, of New Orleans - 30 Sept. 1840 [46]

Stelter, Frederick, subj. of King of Bavaria; rec. by John Eifert - 29 Sept. 1840 [47]

Schaffer, Jacob, subj. of King of Bavaria; rec. by Martin Levy - 29 Sept. 1840 [48]

Bartley Scanlin, subj. of G.B.; rec. by James McCadden - 29 Sept. 1840 [49]

Snaith, Isaac [report 8 May 1832 in New Hampshire]: b. Nottinghamshire, Eng., 19 Nov. 1796, migr. from Eng. 3 Apr. 1818, arrived NYC 20 May 1818, has resided various places and last 10 years in New Hampshire, intending to reside in Portsmouth; rec. by William Scott - 29 Sept. 1840 [50]

Straham, Thomas, subj. of G.B.; rec. by Thomas Ryan - 29 Sept. 1840 [51]

Schwartz, Michael, subj. of King of France; rec. by George Orser - 28 Sept. 1840 [52]

Spence, Andrew, subj. of G.B.; rec. by John McManus - 28 Sept. 1840 [53]

Schneider, Jacob, subj. of King of Bavaria; rec. by Martin Livey - 28 Sept. 1840 [54]

Starck, Henry, subj. of King of Bavaria; rec. by Peter Bretz - 28 Sept. 1840 [55]

Stainer, Edward, merchant, subj. of G.B.; rec. by N. Daniel Ellingwood - 28 Sept. 1840 [56]

Scheif, John Jacob, subj. of Grand Duke of Baden; rec. by Washington Smith - 26 Sept. 1840 [57]

Stevens, James, subj. of G.B.; rec. by Daniel Stevens - 26 Sept. 1840 [58]

Schwarzwaelder, Charles, subj. of Grand Duke of Baden; rec. by Christian Schwarzwaelder - 11 Sept. 1840 [59]

Seaton, Henry, ship chandler, subj. of G.B.; rec. by William Stebbins - 11 Sept. 1840 [60]

Sargeant, Thomas, subj. of G.B.; rec. by William M. Pemberton - 22 July 1840 [61]

Schreiner, Lawrence, subj. of King of Bavaria; rec. by Peter Brate/Brete - 6 Apr. 1840 [62]

Semcken, John, subj. of King of Hanover; rec. by Henry Semcken - 11 Apr. 1840 [63]

Shearer, Archibald, of Westchester Co., farmer, subj. of G.B.; rec. by Hugh Smith, of Westchester Co. - 29 May 1840 [64]

Saunders, William Edward, late of London, student-at-law, subj. of G.B.; rec. by Charles G. Havens, counsellor-at-law - 7 Jan. 1840 [65]

Sippet, Albert, mariner, subj. of Queen of Portugal; rec. by Marshall J. Brady, of Hudson, N.Y. - 23 Apr. 1840 [66]

Stone, William W., subj. of G.B.; rec. by William Corbett, of
16 Oak St. - 2 Nov. 1840 [67]

Simmons, John, subj. of G.B.; rec. by Wm. Simmons - 2 Nov. 1840
[68]

Spence, George, subj. of G.B.; rec. by John Howell - 2 Nov.
1840 [69]

Silva, Lewis B., subj. of King of Portugal; rec. by Wm. Steele,
of Brooklyn - 2 Nov. 1840 [70]

Strole, Nicholas, of Mamaroneck, subj. of King of Bavaria; rec.
by Jacob Hofarer - 2 Nov. 1840 [71]

Stevenson, James, of Factoryville, Staten Island; rec. by David
V.N. Mersereau, of Factoryville, Staten Island - 2 Nov. 1840
[72]

Sladen, Charles, of Flatbush, subj. of G.B.; rec. by James
Hunt, of Flatbush, L.I. - 2 Nov. 1840 [73]

Smith, Henry, of Williamsburgh, subj. of G.B.; rec. by John
Hassel, of 17th St. - 2 Nov. 1840 [74]

Smith, Thomas J., subj. of G.B.; rec. by Patrick Smith, of 98
Sheriff St. - 2 Nov. 1840 [75]

Sheppard, Jacob, subj. of G.B.; rec. by Charles Wadlow - 2 Nov.
1840 [76]

Senner, John, of 682 Grier St., subj. of G.B.; rec. by William
A. Watson - 3 Nov. 1840 [77]

Sullivan, Morris, subj. of G.B.; rec. by John Kennedy, labourer,
of 38 Lawrence - 3 Nov. 1840 [78]

Sirrey, William, Sr., subj. of G.B.; rec. by William Surrey -
31 Oct. 1840 [79]

Spencer, John, merchant, subj. of G.B.; rec. by Charles Rad-
cliff - 3 Nov. 1840 [80]

Snyder, Frederick, subj. of King of Bavaria; rec. by Frederick
Wallis - 3 Nov. 1840 [81]

Sands, Joseph, subj. of G.B.; rec. by Romeo Friganza - 3 Nov.
1840 [82]

Smith, Thomas Shaw, subj. of G.B.; rec. by Henry Pluca - 4 Nov.
1840 [83]

Stewart, Robert, subj. of G.B.; rec. by Elisha Van Brunt - 4
Nov. 1840 [84]

Swan, William J., subj. of G.B.; rec. by Francis McIlvain - 4
Nov. 4 Nov. 1840 [85]

Smithson, Henry, subj. of G.B.; rec. by Henry J. Brissenden -
4 Nov. 1840 [86]

Stratford, Thomas, subj. of G.B.; rec. by William Hand, of 22nd
St. - 4 Nov. 1840 [87]

Sargant, Thomas, Jr., subj. of G.B.; rec. by Thomas Sargant -
4 Nov. 1840 [89]

Shields, George, subj. of G.B.; rec. by John Sheridan - 4 Nov.
1840 [90]

Sheridan, John, of 13th Ward, subj. of G.B.; rec. by George
Shields - 4 Nov. 1840 [91]

Scott, James, who has resided in Newark, New York and Brooklyn,
subj. of G.B.; rec. by Carlisle McKee and John Jamison - 4
Nov. 1840 [92]

Scanlan, John, of 61 Madison St., subj. of G.B.; rec. by Morgan
Scanlan, of 35 Water St. - 4 Nov. 1840 [93]

Simpson, John, subj. of G.B.; rec. by George Ware - 4 Nov. 1840
[94]

Smith, John, of 40 Prince St., subj. of G.B.; rec. by James
Roach, of 206 Elizabeth St. - 4 Nov. 1840 [95]

Smith, John N., subj. of G.B.; rec. by John Smith - 4 Nov. 1840
[96]

Scobie, George [report 11 Oct. 1834 in Bergen Co., N.J.]: b.
Renfrewshire, Scotland; rec. by Frederick Stinard, of Westchester - 31 Oct. 1840 [97]

Swift, Joseph, of 84 Walnut St., subj. of G.B.; rec. by Stephen
Webb - 31 Oct. 1840 [98]

Simpson, James, subj. of G.B.; rec. by Robert Ditton, of Staten
Island - 31 Oct. 1840 [99]

Smith, Stewart J., subj. of G.B.; rec. by William R. Smith - 31
Oct. 1840 [100]

Stuckfield, Joseph, of Columbia St., subj. of G.B.; rec. by John
Hughes, of Chatham & Duane Sts. - 31 Oct. 1840 [101]

Simson, Robert, subj. of G.B.; rec. by Thomas Wallace, of Anns-
ville - 31 Oct. 1840 [102]

Swift, John, of 86 Walnut St., subj. of G.B.; rec. by Stephen
Webb - 31 Oct. 1840 [103]

Swift, William, subj. of G.B.; rec. by Stephen Webb - 31 Oct.
1840 [104]

Scott, George Penman [report NYC 20 May 1822]: b. Newcastle upon
Tyne, Eng., age 27, migr. from Liverpool, printer, resident of
NYC; rec. by George C. Thorburn - 30 Oct. 1840 [105]

Smith, George, of 40 Lispenard St., subj. of G.B.; rec. by Joseph Orr - 30 Oct. 1840 [106]

Spiller, Joel M., subj. of G.B.; rec. by John L. Sharpe, of 13th
Ward - 30 Oct. 1840 [107]

Sullivan, John, of 268 Stanton St., subj. of G.B.; rec. by
Daniel Sullivan, of 268 Stanton St. - 30 Oct. 1840 [108]

Smith, William R., of 331 Broadway, subj. of G.B.; rec. by Stewart J. Smith, of 331 Broadway - 29 Oct. 1840 [109]

Sims, George, of Sing Sing, subj. of G.B.; rec. by James Bell,
of Sing Sing - 28 Oct. 1840 [110]

Skeffington/Skiffington, Bernard, of 124 Greenwich Lane [report
20 Oct. 1830 in Perry Co.]: shoemaker, resident of Bloomfield,
Perry Co., Pa., age 26, b. Co. Antrim, Ire., migr. from Warren's Point, Ire., on 1 Apr. 1827; rec. by William Dickson, of
116 Mulberry St. [111]

Stirling, William, of Newtown, subj. of G.B.; rec. by Alexander
Ames, of Richmond Co. - 17 Oct. 1840 [112]

Smith, Henry, of Ulster Co., subj. of G.B.; rec. by Michael
Smith, of Yonkers - 26 Oct. 1840 [113]

Stirling, John, porter, subj. of G.B.; rec. by James O'Connor,
of 109 Rivington St. - 26 Oct. 1840 [114]

Schall, Frederick Edwin, subj. of G.B.; rec. by Johan Hammer,
of 107 Washington St. - 26 Oct. 1840 [115]

Schack, Otto W.C., subj. of King of Denmark; rec. by John D.
Jones - 24 Oct. 1840 [116]

Smith, Thomas [report Washington, D.C., 27 Dec. 1819]: B. Lincolnshire, Eng., age 22, migr. from Liverpool, arrived Phila. 23 June 1819, intending to reside in D.C.; rec. by Peter Milne - 21 Oct. 1840 [117]

Seery, Peter, of Brooklyn, subj. of G.B.; rec. by Patrick Coligan, of Brooklyn - 21 Oct. 1840 [118]

Smithson, George, of 3 Hoboken St., subj. of G.B.; rec. by Edward Smithson, of 3 Hoboken St. - 20 Oct. 1840 [119]

Savage, Patrick, of Flushing, Queens Co., subj. of G.B.; rec. by Michael Penton, of 8 Washington St. - 20 Oct. 1840 [120]

Sullivan, Michael, subj. of G.B.; rec. by John Wolf, of corner of 5th Ave. & 9th St. - 20 Oct. 1840 [121]

Shea, Timothy, subj. of G.B.; rec. by Patrick Shea - 19 Oct. 1840 [122]

Shaddell, Francis, subj. of G.B.; rec. by Peter Pye, of Caroline [?] St. - 19 Oct. 1840 [123]

Shaddock, William, subj. of G.B.; rec. by John Geren, of 99 Beekman St. - 16 Oct. 1840 [124]

Slevin, James, subj. of G.B.; rec. by John Williams - 15 Oct. 1840 [125]

Stell, Ezekiel, subj. of G.B.; rec. by Thomas Carlisle, of 46 Marion St. - 14 Oct. 1840 [126]

Shaieb, Fidel, subj. of Duke of Ba[den?]; rec. by Carll Cullen, of 92 Willet St. - 12 Oct. 1840 [127]

Smith, William, subj. of G.B.; rec. by Charles Hodgetts, of Williamsburgh - 13 Oct. 1840 [128]

Schwab, Rudolph, subj. of Republic of Switzerland; rec. by Abraham Martey - 13 Oct. 1840 [129]

Saili, Wendel, subj. of King of Wurtemburg; rec. by Valentine Miller, of Saugerties, Ulster Co. - 12 Oct. 1840 [130]

Siebert, John, subj. of King of Hanover; rec. by Jacob Siebert, of 115½ Willet St. - 12 Oct. 1840 [131]

Siebert, Jacob, subj. of King of Hanover; rec. by John Siebert, of 115½ Willet St. - 12 Oct. 1840 [132]

Schmidt, Philip, subj. of King of Bavaria; rec. by John W. Cramer - 9 Oct. 1840 [133]

Thamann, Antoine, subj. of King of France; rec. by Ira Campbell - 11 Apr. 1840 [134]

Traynor, Hugh, subj. of G.B.; rec. by Thomas McCosker - 29 Sept. 1840 [135]

Townhover, Adam, of 17th St., at 7th & 8th Ave., subj. King of Bavaria; rec. by Francis Dolly, of 24 Second St. - 30 Sept. 1840 [136]

Trimble, James N., subj. of G.B.; rec. by Daniel Staniford - 1 Oct. 1840 [137]

Turner, Thomas, subj. of G.B.; rec. by Leonard Wright, of 97 Murray St. - 2 Oct. 1840 [138]

Tilman, Peter, subj. of Germany; rec. by Joseph Bayer, of 84 Essex St. - 5 Oct. 1840 [139]

Terriere, Edward, subj. of G.B.; rec. by Alfred H. Mallon - 5 Oct. 1840 [140]

Tanner, Joseph, subj. of G.B.; rec. by John Owen, of 90 ? St. - 5 Oct. 1840 [141]

Tennent, Joseph, subj. of G.B.; rec. by William Forshay, of 22 Miretta [?] St. - 6 Oct. 1840 [142]

Finnen, James, subj. of G.B.; rec. by Owen Flood, of Tillary St. - 6 Oct. 1840 [143]

Toony, John, subj. of G.B.; rec. by Andrew Galligan - 8 Oct. 1840 [144]

Torpay, Edward, of Yonkers, subj. of G.B.; rec. by William Green - 9 Oct. 1840 [145]

Tongue, Herbert, subj. of G.B.; rec. by Sophia Tongue - 9 Oct. 1840 [146]

Trainer/Treiner, Peter, subj. of G.B.; rec. by John Trainer, of 7 Allen St. - 9 Oct. 1840 [147]

Twaddel, Samuel, subj. of G.B.; rec. by Samuel S. Wandell - 9 Oct. 1840 [148]

Talent, James, subj. of G.B.; rec. by John O'Connor - 10 Oct. 1840 [149]

Titien, Benjamin, subj. of King of Hanover; rec. by James Wilson - 10 Oct. 1840 [150]

Toussaint, Louis, subj. of King of Bavaria; rec. by Francis Mickel - 13 Oct. 1840 [151]

Tomlins, George, subj. of G.B.; rec. by Henry J. Youngs - 13 Oct. 1840 [152]

Thomson, John, subj. of G.B.; rec. by Cecelia Fay, of West Farms, Westchester Co. - 14 Oct. 1840 [153]

Tampkins, John, of Fishkill, Dutchess Co.; rec. by William A. Leonard, of Pine & William Sts. - 18 Oct. 1840 [154]

Teal, Thomas G., of 416 Hudson St., subj. of G.B.; rec. by John R. Smith, of 413 Greenwich St. - 28 Oct. 1840 [155]

Tobin, John, of 152 Suffolk St., subj. of G.B.; rec. by Walter Smith, of 200 Houston St. [report 8 Nov. 1830 in Huntingdon Co., Pa.]: b. Parish of Edermine, Co. of Wexford, Ire. - 29 Oct. 1840 [156]

Terriere, Daniel, subj. of G.B.; rec. by Wm. Terriere, of Williamsburgh - 30 Oct. 1840 [157]

Travers, Patrick, of Rockland Co., subj. of G.B.; rec. by Peter McCann, of 101 Bayard St. - 31 Oct. 1840 [158]

Thorn, Isaac J., subj. of G.B.; rec. by Fleming Duncan - 2 Nov. 1840 [159]

Thickett, William, subj. of G.B.; rec. by John Owen, of Brooklyn - 2 Nov. 1840 [160]

Thompson, John, subj. of G.B.; rec. by Abraham Van Orden, Jr., of 54 12th St. - 2 Nov. 1840 [161]

Trolan, William, subj. of G.B.; rec. by Daniel Parks - 3 Nov. 1840 [162]

Turner, William G., subj. of G.B.; rec. by John Cary - 4 Nov. 1840 [163]

Thorn, Richard, of 655 Washington St., subj. of G.B.; rec. by Isaac Garrison, of 147 Perry St. - 4 Nov. 1840 [164]

Ulrich, Jacob, subj. of Duke of Baden; rec. by William A. Vultee - 2 Oct. 1840 [165]

Uglow, James, subj. of G.B.; rec. by William McLean, Jr. - 10 Oct. 1840 [166]

Volz, William [report 14 Feb. 1838 in Phila. Co.]: native of Wertemberg, age 42, arrived Port of New York 5 Sept. 1831; rec. by Eberhard F. Bauer - 9 Apr. 1840 [167]

Vance, Thomas [report in Marine Court in NYC on 15 Oct. 1832]: subj. of G.B.; rec. by James Vance - 1 Oct. 1840 [168]

Voigt, Leonard, subj. of King of Saxony; rec. by Henry Kiessel, of 251½ Broadway - 3 Nov. 1840 [169]

Wilson, Robert, of 34 Roosevelt St., subj. of G.B.; rec. by Quincy Stowell, of 32 Roosevelt St. - 30 Mar. 1841 [170]

Wolfe, John, subj. of G.B.; rec. by Thomas P. Fitzgerald - 7 Apr. 1840 [171]

Wesemann, Henry, of 8 Elm St., subj. of King of Hanover; rec. by Martin Levy, of 259 Broome St. - 12 Oct. 1840 [172]

Wendell, John, subj. of King of Bavaria; rec. by Jacob F. Frey-fogel, of 166 Delancy St. - 12 Oct. 1840 [173]

Welsh, James, subj. of G.B.; rec. by Nicholas Troy, of 26 Anthony St. - 12 Oct. 1840 [174]

Wolff, Frederick, subj. of Prince of Hesse Cassel; rec. by Ferdinand Leuchte - 15 Oct. 1840 [175]

White, Robert N., subj. of G.B.; rec. by Levi Chapman - 16 Oct. 1840 [176]

Wilson, Richard, subj. of G.B.; rec. by Constantine Donohue - 17 Oct. 1840 [177]

Wotherspoon, Abraham, subj. of G.B.; rec. by George Sims, of Sing Sing - 19 Oct. 1840 [178]

Walsh, Thomas, subj. of G.B.; rec. by John Swenarton, of 133 Christie St. - 21 Oct. 1840 [179]

Waters, Bernard, subj. of G.B.; rec. by Mathew Roach, of Westchester Co. - 22 Oct. 1840 [180]

Wall, James, subj. of G.B.; rec. by John Carroll - 23 Oct. 1840 [181]

Walker, William J., of Poughkeepsie, subj. of G.B.; rec. by Wm. Sloan, of 11 Howard St. - 23 Oct. 1840 [182]

Wellman, Thomas, subj. of G.B.; rec. by Lucy Wellman, of 11 Front St. - 24 Oct. 1840 [183]

Whitehead, John, of West Chester, subj. of G.B.; rec. by Robert F. Fraser, of 322 Broadway - 26 Oct. 1840 [184]

Weinz/Wintz, Christian, of Monroe, Orange Co., subj. of Duke of Hesse Darmstadt; rec. by John Weinz [clerk wrote "Weintz"], of 34 Avenue B; when he made decl. of intent on 12 Feb. 1838 he was a resident of town of Cornwall, Orange Co. - 27 Oct. 1840 [185]

Wark, Isaac, of Albany Co., subj. of G.B.; rec. by Joseph Wark, of 26 Clark St. - 27 Oct. 1840 [186]

Wallace, Thomas, of Plainfield, subj. of G.B.; rec. by Isaac V. Austin, of 49 Sheriff St. - 27 Oct. 1840 [187]

Williams, Charles, of Bloomingdale, between 109th & 110th Sts., subj. of G.B.; rec. by Humphrey Murray, of Bloomingdale Road, near 94th St. - 27 Oct. 1840 [188]

Ward, Edward, subj. of G.B.; rec. by Michael Griffin, of Putnam Co. - 28 Oct. 1840 [189]

Whitaker, Joseph, subj. of G.B.; rec. by William Whitaker - 30 Oct. 1840 [190]

Ward, William, subj. of G.B.; rec. by John Leonard, of 60 James St. - 30 Oct. 1840 [191]

Wright, John S., subj. of G.B.; rec. by James G. Wright - 31 Oct. 1840 [192]

Wilkins, James M., subj. of G.B.; rec. by Gilbert A. Wilkins, of 434 Broome St. - 31 Oct. 1840 [193]

Watson, James, of Brooklyn, subj. of G.B.; rec. by Thomas B. Smith, of Brooklyn - 31 Oct. 1840 [194]

Waring, Edmund, of 81 Broome St., subj. of G.B.; rec. by Isaac K. Joseph - 2 Nov. 1840 [195]

Wortman, Henry, of 45 Oliver St., subj. of King of Denmark; rec. by Gamaliel L. Leaycraft - 2 Nov. 1840 [196]

Ward, John, Sr., subj. of G.B.; rec. by John Ward, Jr. - 2 Nov. 1840 [197]

Webb, John, of 21 Spring St., subj. of G.B.; rec. by Henry McKee, of 218 Mulberry St. - 3 Nov. 1840 [198]

Walters, Thomas, subj. of G.B.; rec. by Samuel D. Walters, of 26 Gaerck St. - 3 Nov. 1840 [199]

Williams, Samuel, subj. of G.B.; rec. by Thomas P. Fitzgerald - 3 Nov. 1840 [200]

Wentzel, Peter, of 5th Ave. and 19th St., subj. of King of Prussia; rec. by John Wiegand - 3 Nov. 1840 [201]

Wilson, Joseph, subj. of G.B.; rec. by Mary Wilson - 3 Nov. 1840 [202]

Weeks, Thomas, subj. of G.B.; rec. by John B. Murray - 3 Nov. 1840 [203]

Wollatt, Thomas, subj. of G.B.; rec. by John Beatty - 3 Nov. 1840 [204]

Warren, William, of Brooklyn, subj. of G.B.; rec. by William C. Smith, of Brooklyn - 2 Nov. 1840 [205]

Wilby, John, subj. of King of Bavaria; rec. by John Reubel - 3 Nov. 1840 [206]

Warner, John, of 174 Houston St., subj. of King of Wirtemburgh; rec. by Leonard Schorr, of 40 Avenue B. - 3 Nov. 1840 [207]

Wood, Thomas, of 46 Greenwich St., subj. of G.B.; rec. by Charles Wood, of 120 Liberty St. - 3 Nov. 1840 [208]

Wood, Charles, of 120 Liberty St., subj. of G.B.; rec. by Thomas Wood, of 46 Greenwich St. - 3 Nov. 1840 [209]

Westcott, Ernest August Steven, of Williamsburgh, subj. of G.B.; rec. by James Westcott - 3 Nov. 1840 [210]

Wilkinson, William [report 27 May 1833 in Westchester Co.]: b. Parish of Frodsham, Co. of Chester, Eng., age 58 on 24 Aug. last, migr. from Liverpool, res. of White Plains, Westchester Co.; rec. by Archibald M. Oakley - 3 Nov. 1840 [211]

Welch, James, subj. of G.B.; rec. by Edward Welch - 3 Nov. 1840 [212]

Womersley, William, subj. of G.B.; rec. by Nathan Gifford - 3 Nov. 1840 [213]

Wilson, Charles, of New Rochelle, Westchester Co., subj. of G.B.; rec. by John T. Gilchrist and Robert Gilchrist - 4 Nov. 1840 [214]

Wallace, Thomas, subj. of G.B.; rec. by John Riley - 9 Oct. 1840 [215]

Walsh, Robert, subj. of G.B.; rec. by Lewis Mather - 9 Oct.
  1840 [216]

Waite, Robert, subj. of G.B.; rec. by James Waite, of 10 King
  St. - 9 Oct. 1840 [217]

Winterbottom, Cicero, subj. of G.B.; rec. by John Chenoweth -
  10 Oct. 1840 [218]

Windsor, William H., subj. of G.B.; rec. by Aaron Dunham, of 19
  Cherry St. - 10 Oct. 1840 [219]

Westfall, Diederich, subj. of King of Hanover; rec. by James
  Wilson, of 2 Pelham St. - 10 Oct. 1840 [220]

Warner, John T., subj. of G.B.; rec. by William Stevenson - 10
  Oct. 1840 [221]

Weburgh, William, subj. of King of Denmark; rec. by Wm. O'Connor, of 127 Delancey St. - 12 Oct. 1840 [222]

Watson, Thomas, subj. of G.B.; rec. by William Scott, of 101
  Gold St. - 8 Oct. 1840 [223]

Welsh, James, subj. of G.B.; rec. by Luke Malone - 8 Oct. 1840
  [224]

Wallace, James, subj. of G.B.; rec. by Peter Duffield, of 31
  Cross St. - 7 Oct. 1840 [225]

Wise, Martin, of Brooklyn, subj. of G.B.; rec. by Joseph Wise,
  of Brooklyn 8 Oct. 1840 [226]

Wilson, Philip, subj. of G.B.; rec. by Thomas Cogan, of 10
  Orange St. - 9 Oct. 1840 [227]

Wolf, Michael, subj. of King of France; rec. by Joseph Winkler,
  of Rivington St. - 9 Oct. 1840 [228]

Wilson, John, subj. of G.B.; rec. by Benjamin S. Hatfield, of
  Jay St. - 6 Oct. 1840 [229]

Wheatcroft, Edward, subj. of G.B.; rec. by William Belcher, of
  Brooklyn - 6 Oct. 1840 [230]

Weintz, John, of town of Cornwall, Orange Co., subj. of Duke of
  Hesse Darmstadt; rec. by Jacob Washmann, of 92 Reed St. - 6
  Oct. 1840 [231]

Walford, William, subj. of G.B.; rec. by William B. Rodda. of
  499 Washington St. - 6 Oct. 1840 [232]

Waters, Dominick, subj. of G.B.; rec. by Griffin Green, of 438
  Pearl St. [233]

Woerz, Henry, late of Germany; rec. by Georg William Pfarrer,
  of 479 Pearl St. - 7 Oct. 1840 [234]

Watkins, Frederick, subj. of G.B.; rec. by Mary S. Watkins - 8
  Oct. 1840 [235]

Wilson, John, subj. of G.B.; rec. by John Johnson, of 33 Pell
  St. - 5 Oct. 1840 [236]

Warburgh, Adolph Rudolph, merchant, subj. of Republic of Hamburgh; rec. by Joseph Gutman - 3 Oct. 1840 [237]

Walter, Nicholas, subj. of King of France; rec. by John Montz,
  of 168 Rivington St. - 6 Oct. 1840 [238]

Ward, Patrick, subj. of G.B.; rec. by Edward Langstaff, of 59
  Orange St. - 2 Oct. 1840 [239]

Whittaker, Joseph, of 31 Catharine St., subj. of G.B.; rec. by
  John Kirkman, of 31 Catharine St. - 30 Sept. 1840 [240]

Weil, Ferdinand, subj. of Duke of Baden; rec. by Henry Wise -
28 Sept. 1840 [241]

Williams, John [report in Boston, Mass., March term 1834]:
boarding house keeper, b. London, Eng., on 4 Sept. 1796, age
now 38, arrived U.S. 5 June 1834; rec. by John Liddle - 24
Sept. 1840 [242]

Walter, Israel D., subj. of King of Bavaria; rec. by William N.
Polack - 23 Sept. 1840 [243]Wagner, Goodhart, subj. of Grand
Duke of Hesse Darmstadt; rec. by John G. Weise - 8 Apr. 1840
[244]

Wentworth, William S., subj. of G.B.; rec. by George Barnes, of
Richmond Co. - 2 Mar. 1840 [245]

A

Armstrong, David S., subj. of G.B. - 15 Jan. 1810

Angus, John, subj. of G.B. - 27 June 1812

Armstrong, Wm., merchant, subj. of G.B. - 21 Jan. 1817

Ardrion, Wm., b. Isle of Wight, age 36, migr. from Yarmouth, a
  rigger - 4 June 1819

Armstrong, Luke, b. Co. Sligo, Ire., age 25, migr. from Sligo,
  grocer; wife Jane, b. Co. Sligo, age 20 - 23 July 1819

Appleton, Etherington, b. Yorkshire, Eng., age 37, migr. from
  London, physician; wife Ann, b. Yorkshire, age 29; daughters
  (all born in London): Mary Ann, age 11; Matilda, age 6; Lydia,
  age 5; Priscilla, age 3; Susannah, age 2 - 29 May 1821

Atkinson, Thomas, b. Yorkshire, Eng., age 30, migr. from Liverpool, cartman - 31 Mar. 1821

Arnold, Francis, b. Gap, Dept. of the High Alps, France, age 36,
  migr. from Marseilles, France, grocer - 16 Apr. 1821

Alexander, Robert(report 19 Apr. 1821): b. Co. Donegal, Ire.,
  age 26, migr. from Londonderry, grocer - 20 Apr. 1821

Anderson, Robert (report 13 Apr. 1821): b. Dumfriesshire, Scotland, age 36, migr. from Belfast, grocer - 23 Apr. 1821

Althus, Conrad, b. Althous, Prussia, age 28, migr. from Antwerp,
  druggist - 18 Dec. 1821

Armour, Paul, b. Donegal, Ire., age 22, migr. from Londonderry,
  milkman - 17 Mar. 1823

Alverty, Raymond, b. village of Senollorge, Dept. of the Eastern
  Pyrenees, France, age 30, migr. from Is. of St. Thomas, grocer;
  wife Rose, b. St. Domingo, age 36, subj. of King of Denmark;
  son Dominique, b. Is. of St. Thomas, age 3; dau. Marie Louise,
  b. Is. of St. Thomas, age 1 - 17 July 1822

Anderson, John, b. Lanark, Scotland, age 38, migr. from Greenock,
  weaver - 27 Nov. 1822

Albaret, Louis, merchant, subj. of Switzerland - 18 Sept. 1828

Ashton,Smith , subj. of G.B. - 20 July 1829

Alphonse, Alexis (under age of 21, approved by his guardian, Wm.,
  Phiquepal), subj. of King of France - 2 Oct. 1829

Alexander, Robert, merchant, subj. of G.B. - 21 Jan. 1830

Anderson, David, native of Scotland, residing in Phila.(report
  25 Jan. 1823): b. Kilmarnock, Co. of Ayr, Scotland, on 1 July
  1801, age now 23, migr. from Liverpool, arrived NYC 12 Sept.
  1821, with intent to settle in Phila. - 15 Dec. 1830

Abecacis, Salvador, merchant, subj. of Emperor of Morocco - 16
  Mar. 1835

Armstrong, George, subj. of G.B., student-at-law - 21 May 1834

Avoy, James, blacksmith, subj. of G.B. - 11 Mar. 1837

Abbott, Richard, subj. of G.B. - 27 July 1836

Asche, Henry, subj. of King of Hanover - 9 Nov. 1837

Ashby, John, subj. of G.B. - 6 Apr. 1837

Ashby, John, subj. of G.B. - 6 Apr. 1838

Archer, Thomas, subj. of G.B. - 4 June 1838

Alexandrè, Francis, shipmaster, subj. of G.B. - 12 June 1838

Atherden, George, subj. of G.B. - 5 Nov. 1838

Avery, John, subj. of G.B. - 7 Nov. 1838

Adriansen, Bartel, subj. of King of Denmark - 16 Feb. 1839

Anderson, John, subj. of G.B. - 13 Mar. 1839

Austin, Thomas, subj. of G.B. - 22 Mar. 1839

Andren, Pedro A., subj. of King of Spain - 6 Apr. 1839

Arneth, Christopher, subj. of King of Denmark - 4 Nov. 1839

Aitchison, James, subj. of G.B. - 9 Apr. 1840

Appleton, Robert, subj. of G.B. - 13 Apr. 1840

Arnold, Aldous Henshaw, subj. of G.B. - 24 Apr. 1840

Ambroise, Gard Pierre, subj. of King of France - 10 June 1840

Anz, Philip, subj. of Prince of Hesse Darmstadt - 3 Aug. 1840

Abbott, William, subj. of G.B. - 8 Sept. 1840

Allispach, John C., subj. of Republic of Switzerland - 13 Oct. 1840

Ayres, Edward J., subj. of G.B. - 22 Oct. 1840

Adley, Thomas, subj. of G.B. - 29 Dec. 1840

Armstrong, William, subj. of G.B. - 4 Nov. 1840

B

Bryson, Andrew, late of parish of Bangor, Co. of Down, Ire., grocer - 24 Dec. 1802

Barry, James, b. Kinsale, migr. from Prov. of Munster, Ire. - 23 July 1812

Butts, William, of Bergen Co., N.J., subj. of G.B. - 29 Sept. 1812

Bates, Joseph, merchant, b. Halifax, Yorkshire, Eng., age 24, migr. from Liverpool; wife Mary, b. New York, age 22; dau. Ann, b. New York, age 2 - 2 July 1813

Byrne, Edward, b. Co. of Wicklow, Ire., age 33, migr. from Dublin, merchant; wife Sarah, b. Dublin, age 28; dau. Hannah, b. Dublin, age 2 years & 6 months - 25 Oct. 1816

Bashford, James, b. Carrick Macross, Ire., age 31, migr. from Liverpool, butcher; wife Margaret, b. Castlehill, Ire., age 25; dau. Ann, b. Carrick Macross, age 8; son Arthur, b. Carrick Macross, age 6; son James, b. Carrick Macross, age 3; son Henry, b. Carrick Macross, age 2 - 3 Oct. 1817

Bowyer, Robert, b. Kidderminster, Co. of Worcester, Eng., age 21, migr. from London, merchant - 10 Nov. 1817

Burton, Charles, b. London, age 36, migr. from Liverpool - 16 June 1818

Boulger, John, b. Ire., age 48, clothier; wife Ann; dau. Mary; dau. Jane; dau. Margaret; dau. Othelia - 19 June 1818

Barr, Matthew, b. parish of Lochwinnoch, Scotland, age 22, migr. from Greenock, Scotland, baker - 29 Sept. 1818

Browne, John [report 5 Aug. 1818]: b. Co. Tyrone, Ire., age 38, migr. from Londonderry, grocer; wife Mary, b. Co. Donegal, age 29 - 3 Oct. 1818

Breittmayer, Gaspard Andre Louis, b. Geneva, Switzerland, age 21, migr. from Havre de Grace, merchant - 20 Oct. 1818

Benison, William Lloyd [report 28 Oct. 1818]: b. Co. Cavan, Ire., age 26, migr. from Londonderry, mariner, formerly an officer of the British Navy - 29 Oct. 1818

Bates, William Davis, b. Wolverhampton, Staffordshire, Eng., ornamental painter, migr. from Dover - 9 Nov. 1818

Basso, Jean, b. Bordeaux, France, age 39, migr. from Cape Francois, speculator - 30 Dec. 1818

Briggs, David, b. Yorkshire, Eng., age 37, migr. from Liverpool, arrived U.S. 10 Nov. 1815 - 21 Feb. 1820

Baker, William, b. Portsmouth, Eng., age 34, migr. from Havre de Grace, ropemaker; wife Sophia, b. Portsmouth, Eng., age 26; son William Henry, born New York - 1 May 1820

Bletsoe, John Morgan [report 1 July 1820]: b. Daventry, Northhamptonshire, Eng., age 44, migr. from Liverpool, doctor of law, resident of Kings Co - 17 July 1820

Bingley, George, b. Warwickshire, Eng., age 25, migr. from Liverpool, merchant - 28 Aug. 1820

Bradshaw, Robert, b. Manchester, Eng., age 25, migr. from Dover, victual house; wife Allice, b. Bilpau [or Bilpen?], Devonshire, Eng., age 33; dau. Sarah, b. Manchester, age 5 - 3 Nov. 1820

Boyle, William F., b. London, age 40, migr. from Greenock, a teacher; wife Mary; stepson James Moncrief - 20 Jan. 1819

Burke, Robert, subj. of G.B. - 26 May 1819

Ballagh, William (by his guardian, James Ballagh) [report 18 Sept. 1819]: b. town of DrumLongfield, Co. Monaghan, Ire., age 15, migr. from Belfast, grocer - 31 Dec. 1819

Brodie, John [report 1 Nov. 1819]: b. Perthshire, Scotland, age 52, migr. from Liverpool, slater; wife Elizabeth Archibald; dau. Lindsey Brodie, age 21; son John, age 19; son James, age 17 - 15 Nov. 1819

Braithwaite, William, b. Leeds, Yorkshire, Eng., age 24, migr. from Liverpool, merchant - 30 Sept. 1819

Benedict, Martin, b. village of Ellwold, Prussia, age 29, migr. from Danzig, gardner - 21 Mar. 1821

Brown, James, b. Co. of West Meath, Ire., age 38, migr. from Londonderry, cartman - 27 Mar. 1821

Burns, Patrick, b. Co. Monaghan, Ire., age 51, migr. from Newry, cartman - 28 Mar. 1821

Brown, John, b. Co. Donegal, Ire., age 41, migr. from Londonderry, cartman - 31 Mar. 1821

Boyd, David [report 30 Mar. 1821]: b. Co. Armagh, Ire., age 36, migr. from Belfast, cartman - 31 Mar. 1821

Beatty, David, b. Co. Tyrone, Ire., age 30, migr. from Belfast, cartman - 31 Mar. 1821

Boyd, Samuel, b. Co. Armagh, Ire., age 28, migr. from Belfast, cartman - 2 Apr. 1821

Boyd, William, b. Co. Armagh, Ire., age 41, migr. from Newry, cartman; wife Margaret, b. Co. Armagh, as all the children, age 40; son John, age 17; son Mathew, age 15; son William, age 11; dau. Mary, age 19 - 4 Apr. 1821

Bryanes, Mick, b. Co. Mayde [for "Meath"?], Ire., age 28, migr. from Dublin, grocer; wife Margaret, b. Co. Cavan, age 28; son John, b. Co. Cavan, age 9; son David, b. New York, age 3 - 16 Apr. 1821

Baker, William, subj. of G.B. - 16 Apr. 1821

Brenan, Edward [report 14 Apr. 1821]: b. Co. Tipperary, Ire., age 32, migr. from Dublin, brewer - 16 Apr. 1821

Bell, Robert [report 9 Apr. 1821]: b. Cumberland Co., Eng., age 46, migr. from Liverpool, tavern-keeper; son Robert, b. Co. of Cumberland, age 13 - 16 Apr. 1821

Blanke, Sierich [report 16 Apr. 1821]: b. Hanover Town, Lower Saxony, migr. from Bremen, grocer - 17 Apr. 1821

Bruce, Alexander, b. Aberdeen, Scotland, age 32, migr. from Greensmcuth, Scotland, grocer - 18 Apr. 1821

Baker, Martin, b. Bremen, Germany, age 34, migr. from Liverpool, grocer - 19 Apr. 1821

Boyle, John [report 7 Apr. 1821]: b. Co. Armagh, Ire., age 37, migr. from Liverpool, porter - 19 Apr. 1821

Bard, Joseph [report 7 Apr. 1821]: b. Co. of Hampshire, Eng., age 47, migr. from Portsmouth, Eng., porter - 19 Apr. 1821

Bisset, Samuel [report: 10 Apr. 1821]: b. Co. of Aberdeen, Scotland, age 28, migr. from Aberdeen, saddler; wife Ann, b. Banffordshire, Scotland, age 28 - 20 Apr. 1821

Benson, Paul [report 19 Apr. 1821]: b. Co. Roscommon, Ire., age 30, migr. from Sligo, grocer - 20 Apr. 1821

Baker, Henry [report 12 Apr. 1821]: b. Oldenburg, Westphalia, age 39, migr. from Hull, grocer; wife Margaret, b. Coln on the Rhine, Germany, age 36 - 21 Apr. 1821

Brown, John, b. Co. Cavan, Ire., age 38, migr. from Newry, grocer - 21 Apr. 1821

Bishop, John [report 13 Apr. 1821]: b. Co. of Dublin, Ire., age 33, migr. from Dublin, grocer; wife Margaret, b. City of Dublin, age 30 - 21 Apr. 1821

Bordas, Eli [report 25 Apr. 1821]: b. town of Yriox, Dept. of the Haute Vienne, France, age 45, migrated from Bordeaux, a tavern-keeper; sons, both b. in town of Limoges, Dept. of the Haute Vienne, Jean Baptiste, age 19, and Simon Joseph Napoleon, age 11 - 28 Apr. 1821

Blakley, William [report 27 Apr. 1821]: b. Co. Armagh, Ire., age 36, migr. from Newry, grocer; wife Isabella, b. Co. Londonderry, Ire., age 35; son Daniel, b. Co. Armagh, age 7 or 8; his stepdau., Mary Richarson, b. Co. Armagh, age 7 or 8; his stepson, Joseph Richarson, b. Co. Armagh, age 6 - 28 Apr. 1821

Booth, Benjamin [report 9 May 1820]: b. Kellygonland, Co. Tyrone, Ire., age 22, migr. from Belfast, grocer - 16 Apr. 1821

Blair, Andrew, b. Sterlingshire, Scotland, age 34, migr. from Liverpool, tavern-keeper; wife Janet, b. Glasgow, age 28; son Thomas R., born Glasgow, age 6 - 11 May 1821

Banigan, Terrence [report 5 May 1821]: b. Co. Monaghan, Ire., age 30, migr. from Belfast, pedlar - 21 May 1821

Bradley, John [report 8 May 1821]: b. Co. Meath, Ire., age 42, migr. from Dublin, tavern-keeper; wife Ann, b. Co. Meathe, age 30 - 29 May 1821

Biddle, John, b. Devonshire, Eng., age 31; migr. from Island of Guernsey, butcher; wife Mary, born Dorsetshire, age 27; dau. Mary Ann, born. Is. of Guernsey, age 6 - 1 June 1821

Bishop, Thomas, b. London, Eng., age 44, migr. from London, farmer, res. Ohio; wife Elizabeth, b. Guernsey, age 36; son Edward Greentree, b. Surrey, Eng., age 2 - 5 June 1821

Burne, Dennis [report 11 June 1821]: b. Co. Wicklow, Ire., age
35, migr. from Dublin, coachman - 18 June 1821

Blondel, Peter [report 20 June 1821]: b., as all his family,
Dublin, Ire., age 44, migr. from Dublin, farmer, residing in
Rockland Co., N.Y.; wife Elizabeth, age 40; son William, age
16; son Joshua, age 10, son Charles, age 7; son Jacob, age 4;
son Joseph, age 1; dau. Susannah, age 15; dau. Jane, age 13 -
22 June 1821

Blair, Andrew, subj. of G.B. - 29 June 1821

Beatty, Joseph [report 14 July 1821]: b. Co. Tyrone, Ire., age
24, migr. from Belfast, soap boiler; wife Jane, b. Co. Down,
Ire., age 18 - 19 July 1821

Banks, William, b. Birmingham, Eng., age 22, migr. from Liverpool, pocketbook & fancy case maker - 27 Dec. 1821

Bray, John, b. Rathdowny, Ire., age 30, migr. from Dublin - 17
Feb. 1823

Brewer, Nicholas R., b. Falmouth, Co. of Cornwall, Eng., migr.
from Falmouth, mariner - 21 May 1823

Brennan, Thomas [report 9 May 1823]: b. Co. Kilkenny, Ire., age
35, migr. from town of Ross, Ire., labourer; wife Elizabeth,
b. Co. Kilkenny, age 20 - 24 Nov. 1823

Bluxome, Isaac, b. Liverpool, Eng., age 27, migr. from Liverpool, watchmaker - 23 Oct. 1823

Bolland, Henry, b. Birmingham, Eng., age 44, migr. from London,
merchant - 22 Nov. 1823

Barker, Frederick Henry, b. Nottinghamshire, Eng., age 22, migr.
from London, merchant - 22 Nov. 1823

Brannon, Christopher, b. Co. Donegal, Ire., age 40, migr. from
Londonderry, mason; wife Margaret, b. Co. Donegal, age 37 -
19 Apr. 1824

Burns, John [report 12 Apr. 1824]: b. Co. Sligo, Ire., age 38,
migr. from Sligo, cartman - 19 Apr. 1824

Burns, William, b. Co. Down, Ire. age 24, migr. from Belfast,
storekeeper - 26 Apr. 1824

Bordan, Henry, b. Co. Down, Ire., as were all of his family,
age 33, migr. from Newry, labourer; wife Ann, age 33; son
Samuel, age 7; dau. Margaret, age 11 - 20 Sept. 1824

Bécar, Noel J. [report 16 Oct. 1824]: b. Montrecourt, France,
age 21, migr. from Havre, merchant - 18 Oct. 1824

Belcher, Thomas [report 17 Nov. 1824]: b. Sheffield, Eng., age
29, migr. from Liverpool, rule maker; wife Martha, b. Sheffield, age 22; dau. Mary Louisa, b. New York, age 2 - 20 Nov.
1824

Belcher, William, b. Sheffield, Eng., age 26, migr. from Liverpool, rule maker - 17 Nov. 1824

Belcher, Charles, b. Sheffield, Eng., age 21, migr. from Liverpool, rule maker - 19 Nov. 1824

Brunt, Robert, b. Co. Tyrone, Ire., age 25, migr. from Londonderry, labourer; wife Eliza, b. Donegal, Ire., age 26 - 21
Feb. 1825

Brindley, John [report Feb. 1825]: b. Staffordshire, Eng., age
28, migr. from London, cordwainer; wife Hester, b. Co. of
Kent, Eng., age 28; son Frederick, b. Co. of Middlesex, Eng.,
age 8 - 7 Mar. 1825

Bradley, John, b. Wath, Yorkshire, Eng., age 45, migr. from Quebec, cutler; wife, Bridget, b. Ire., age 37; dau. Sarah, b.
Sheffield, age 21; dau. Susannah, b. Sheffield, age 19; son
John, b. Sheffield, age 15; son George, b. Sheffield, age 13 -
16 May 1825

Bradford, James, b. Eng., age 71, migr. from Bristol, pedlar -
17 May 1825

Bryan, Thomas, b. Eng., age 39, migr. from London, dyer; dau.
Louisa, b. Eng., age 10 - 23 May 1825

Bryan, William, Sr., b. Eng., age 70, migr. from Liverpool, dyer
- 23 May 1825

Berndtson, Eric (by his guardian, John A. Sidelr), b. Stockholm,
Sweden, age 20, migr. from Goteborg, mariner - 13 Aug. 1825

Brunsen, Christopher William [report 9 Dec. 1824]: b. Bremen, age
38 years, 9 months, 17 days, migr. Bremen to London and London
to NYC, labourer, subj. of Confed. of Hanseatic Towns - 15 Aug.
1825

Boothman, John, b. Manchester, Eng., age 27, migr. from Liverpool, baker, arr. U.S. 24 Apr. 1822 - 24 Oct. 1825

Blake, John [report 9 Nov. 1825]: b. (as all his family) Co. Cork,
Ire., age 37, migr. Port of Kinsale, Cork, Ire., sawyer; wife
Ellen, age 37; son Michael, age 13; son William, age 9; dau.
Catharine, age 8; dau. Mary Ann, age 6 - 21 Nov. 1825

Bradley, John [report 7 Nov. 1825]: b. Co. Tyrone, Ire., age 22,
migr. from Londonderry via St. Johns, N.S., labourer - 21 Nov.
1825

Brant, Thomas, b. Hanover, Germany, age 32, migr. from Bremen,
rigger; wife Catharine, b. Liverpool, age 25 - 21 Feb. 1826

Buchanan, John, b. Glasgow, Scotland, age 40, migr. from Greenock, Scotland, tallow chandler - 4 Mar. 1826

Breakey, Andrew [report 6 Apr. 1826]: b. Co. Monaghan, Ire., age
23, migr. from Newry, tobacconist - 20 Apr. 1826

Bruns, Martin, b. Kingdom of Hanover, age 21, migr. from Bremen,
brass founder - 19 Apr. 1826

Burns, John [report 8 May 1826]: b. Co. West Meath, Ire., age 32,
migr. from Liverpool, labourer - 15 May 1826

Brandon, Isaac L., b. Is. of Barbadoes, age 33, migr. from Barbadoes, merchant - 27 June 1826

Brady, Patrick, b. Co. Cavan, Ire., age 21, migr. from Belfast,
labourer - 19 Sept. 1826

Bosch, Jacob [report 30 Oct. 1826]: b. Gluckstadt, Denmark, age
24, migr. from Hamburgh, via Boston, mariner - 22 Jan. 1827

Bolton, Richard, b. Co. Wexford, Ire., age 30, migr. from Waterford, via Liverpool, farmer - 18 Dec. 1826

Barnsdall, John, b. Bedfordshire, Eng., age 21, migr. from London, tailor - 19 Dec. 1826

Boell, Frederick Charles, b. Wissemburg, France, age 22, migr.
from Havre, merchant - 19 Feb. 1827

Burgert [or Boorgert], Henry, b. Waldorf, Germany, age 32, migr.
from Amsterdam, baker - 21 May 1827

Brady, James, b. Co. Cavan, Ire., age 44, migr. from Dublin,
drayman; wife Margaret, b. Co. Cavan, age 36 - 1 June 1827

Bubear, Wm., b. Devonshire, Eng., age 41; migr. from Tinemouth,
Eng., labourer - 18 Sept. 1827

Broadbent, Ben. (by his guardian, William Price), b. Yorkshire, Eng., age 19, migr. from Liverpool, merchant - 20 Nov. 1827

Barry, Lackey, b. Co. Sligo, Ire., age 28, migr. from Belfast, labourer - 29 Dec. 1827

Bowen, Charles [report 29 Jan. 1828]: b. Co. Tyrone, Ire., age 38, migr. from Belfast, livery stable keeper; wife Rose, b. Co. Antrim, Ire., age 38; son William, b. Co. Antrim, age 17; son John, b. Co. Cavan, age 12; son Charles, b. Co. Down, age 8; dau. Ann, b. Co. Meath, age 15; dau. Matilda, b. Co. Down, age 10; dau. Mary, b. Co. Down, age 6 - 25 Feb. 1828

Borner, Johannes Theodorus [report 11 Feb. 1828]: b. Emden, East Friesland, Germany, age 30, subj. of King of Hanover, migr. from Emden, mariner - 19 Feb. 1828

Benkard, James, b. Frankfort, Germany, age 27, migr. from Liverpool, merchant - 28 Feb. 1828

Black, John, b. Co. of Kent, Eng., age 33, migr. from London, farmer, residing Woodbridge, N.J.; wife Ann, b. Co. of Kent, age 35 - 17 Mar. 1828

Blake, Thomas [report 24 Mar. 1828]: b. Co. Tipperary, Ire., age 21, migr. from Cork, painter - 26 Mar. 1828

Bruns, John [report 7 Apr. 1828]: b. Bremen, age 29, migr. from London, sugar baker - 21 Apr. 1828

Brown, John, b. Stavanger, Norway, age 47, migr. from Christiansand, Norway, labourer - 9 June 1828

Bredall, Rasmus Christian [report 18 June 1828]: b. town of Tromsoe, Norway, age 34, migr. from Copenhagen, mariner - 20 June 1828

Barton, William [report 9 June 1828]: b. Co. Kilkenny, Ire., age 30, migr. from Waterford, Ire., hatter - 21 July 1828

Brown, John, subj. of King of Sweden - 17 Nov. 1828

Bolger, Thomas, subj. of G.B. - 15 Dec. 1828

Black, Frederick Christian, subj. of King of Denmark - 20 May 1829

Bryson, James, late of Co. Antrim, Ire., cartman - 30 May 1829

Bonnell, George, formerly of St. Lawrence, Newfoundland - 28 Dec. 1830

Blair, George, tailor, subj. of G.B. - 27 May 1830

Burgess, John, of Bushwick, Kings Co., N.Y., farmer, subj. of G.B. - 22 Dec. 1830

Button, John, mahogany sawyer, subj. of G.B. - 2 Apr. 1831

Berry, Charles, mariner, subj. of King of Sweden - 17 Oct. 1831

Blair, Robert, mariner, subj. of G.B. - 26 Oct. 1831

Bazajou, Marie Antoine, late of village of Lisigny, Dept. of Seine et Marne, France, slater - 25 Apr. 1831

Boell, Frederick W., merchant, subj. of King of France - 28 Jan. 1832

Boell, Paul Joseph, clerk, subj. of King of France - 28 Jan. 1832

Booth, William, cotton manufacturer, subj. of G.B. - 26 June 1832

Bunch, Robert H., merchant, subj. of G.B. - 20 Nov. 1832

Brady, James, labourer, subj. of G.B. - 15 June 1833

Banks, William, merchant, subj. of G.B. - 20 Oct. 1834

Brown, Robert, baker, subj. of G.B. - 4 Nov. 1834

Birkinshaw, Joseph, grocer, subj. of G.B. - 20 Aug. 1834

Brady, John, stage-driver, subj. of G.B. - 18 Feb. 1835

Bloss, Joh. Frederick, cabinetmaker, subj. of King of Wuertemberg - 19 Feb. 1835

Baronnet, Jean, baker, subj. of King of France - 23 Feb. 1835

Beindar, Pantalron [?], butcher, subj. of Duke of Baden - 30
Mar. 1835

Buchanan, Alexander, dyer, subj. of G.B. - 3 Apr. 1835

Bresselan [or Bresselau?], Isaac, late of Hamburg, Germany - 28
Sept. 1829

Brumm, Adam, shoemaker, subj. of King of France - 6 Jan. 1836

Brandon, Rachel (wife of Joseph Brandon), subj. of G.B. - 12
Apr. 1836

Bates, Robert, farmer, subj. of G.B. - 3 May 1836

Barnes, Samuel C., of City of Brooklyn, teacher, subj. of G.B.
- 21 May 1836

Bliss, Theodore E., merchant, subj. of G.B. - 18 Aug. 1836

Brady, Richard, subj. of G.B. - 10 June 1837

Barker, Frederick, merchant, subj. of G.B. - 17 July 1837

Barnes, John, comedian, subj. of G.B. - 11 Oct. 1837

Barnes, Mary (wife of John Barnes, comedian), subj. of G.B. -
21 Oct. 1837

Benken, Christian, subj. of City of Bremen - 9 Nov. 1837

Bieck, Arend Hinrich, subj. of King of Hanover - 9 Nov. 1837

Berryman, Michael, subj. of King of France - 20 Nov. 1837

Buggy, James, subj. of G.B. - 27 Nov. 1837

Browne, Eliza (wife of Jesse Browne), subj. of G.B. - 1 Mar.
1838

Bingener, Lewis, subj. of King of Hanover - 9 Apr. 1838

Benzer, Johannes, subj. of Grand Duke of Baden - 10 Apr. 1838

Braem, Rudolph, subj. of King of Denmark - 2 May 1838

Bachman, Isaack, subj. of King of Bavaria - 8 Nov. 1838

Baker, Edwin D., subj. of G.B. - 11 June 1839

Burckholster, John, subj. of King of France - 2 July 1838

Briggs, John R., subj. of G.B. - 5 July 1838

Biehler, Peter, subj. of King of France - 5 July 1838

Bennett, George, subj. of Grand Duke of Baden - 8 Oct. 1838

Bottomley, William subj. of G.B. - 12 Oct. 1838

Benceno, Jacob, subj. of King of Bavaria - 15 Oct. 1838

Barumler, John, subj. of King of France - 15 Oct. 1838

Bell, Thomas, subj. of G.B. - 3 Nov. 1838

Bishop, William, subj. of G.B. - 3 Nov. 1838

Baack, Henry E., subj. of Republic of Hamburgh - 5 Nov. 1838

Brooks, William, subj. of G.B. - 6 Nov. 1838

Briggs, William, subj. of G.B. - 7 Nov. 1838

Brady, Michael, subj. of G.B. - 30 Nov. 1838

Brodrick, Dennis, subj. of G.B. - 5 Feb. 1839

Brierly, Thomas, subj. of G.B. - 25 Mar. 1839

Bird, James, subj. of G.B. - 5 Feb. 1839

Bihlharz, John Baptist, subj. of Grand Duke of Baden - 2 Apr. 1839

Behn, Johan, subj. of King of Hanover - 9 Apr. 1839

Béer, Cerf, subj. of King of France - 20 Apr. 1839

Byron, Henry, subj. of G.B. - 24 May 1839

Baker, John, subj. of Prince of Hesse Cassel - 24 June 1839

Browning, John, subj. of G.B. - 7 June 1839

Bornefeld, William, subj. of King of Prussia - 18 June 1839

Black, James, subj. of G.B. - 9 July 1839

Berry, Thomas, subj. of G.B. - 1 Aug. 1839

Bailey, Rishton Robbinson, subj. of G.B. - 11 Sept. 1839

Behnken, Jacob, subj. of City of Bremen - 17 Sept. 1839

Behnken, Henry, subj. of City of Bremen - 17 Sept. 1839

Boucher, Alfred, subj. of King of France - 31 Oct. 1839

Blackford, Edward, subj. of G.B. - 4 Nov. 1839

Bakman, John N., subj. of King of Sweden - 6 Nov. 1839

Bourne, Henry Blake, subj. of G.B. - 18 Feb. 1840

Bowden, John, subj. of G.B. - 8 Apr. 1840

Brown, William E., subj. of G.B. - 13 Apr. 1840

Bollwinkal, Karl Ludwig, subj. of Grand Duke of Oldenburgh - 14 Apr. 1840

Blick, William, subj. of G.B. - 14 Apr. 1840

Beaver, John, subj. of G.B. - 4 May 1840

Bleifuhs, Francis, subj. of King of Bavaria - 11 May 1840

Beesley, George, subj. of G.B. - 4 June 1840

Biabot, Pierre, subj. of King of France - 10 June 1840

Bontemps, Louis Claude, subj. of King of France - 10 June 1840

Bonnefond, John Baptist, subj. of King of France - 10 July 1840

Breymeyer, George William, subj. of G.B. - 3 Aug. 1840

Bennet, William, subj. of G.B. - 28 Sept. 1840

Boulger, Daniel, subj. of G.B. - 5 Oct. 1840

Brown, Francis, subj. of Emperor of Germany - 6 Oct. 1840

Berry, John, subj. of G.B. - 7 Oct. 1840

Borchers, Jobst, subj. of King of Hanover - 8 Oct. 1840

Brewer, John, subj. of King of France - 12 Oct. 1840

Bourke, John, subj. of G.B. - 16 Oct. 1840

Brodie, Peter, subj. of G.B. - 16 Oct. 1840

Burns, Charles, subj. of G.B. - 29 Oct. 1840

Bassett, John, subj. of Emperor of Austria - 30 Oct. 1840

Brinkworth, Samuel, subj. of G.B. - 30 Oct. 1840

Benson, John, subj. of G.B. - 31 Oct. 1840

Brown, Matthew, subj. of G.B. - 2 Nov. 1840

Bishop, William, subj. of G.B. - 2 Nov. 1840

Bohrer, Carl, subj. of King of Prussia - 3 Nov. 1840

Eraunhcld, Albert, subj. of King of Hanover - 6 Nov. 1840

Broun, Georg, subj. of Grand Duke of Baden - 25 Nov. 1840

Byrns, Patrick, subj. of G.B. - 9 Dec. 1840

Brittain, William, subj. of G.B. - 19 Dec. 1840

C

Clarke, George, hairdresser, subj. of G.B. - 16 Apr. 1810 - incomplete

Chapman, William, merchant, late of Eng. - 28 July 1810

Coates, Edward, b. North Shields, Eng., age 31, migr. from Greenock, Scotland, rigger; wife Dorothy, b. North Shields, age
30; dau. Dorothy, b. North Shields, age 10; son John, b. N.Y.
State, age 5; dau. Jane, b. N.Y. State, age 3; dau. Elizabeth,
b. N.Y. State, age 1 - 28 Dec. 1813

Collin, Joseph, house-carpenter (res. of U.S. between 18 June
1798 and 14 Apr. 1802); rec. by Joseph Price, sunsmith, and
Richard Miller, cartman - 18 Dec. 1817

Clements, James [report 28 Nov. 1817]: b. Oxfordshire, Eng.,
age 42, migrated from London, veterinary surgeon - 29 Nov.
1817

Christian, William, late of Ire., merchant - 11 Jan. 1803

Chambers, Charles, stationer, subj. of G.B. - 22 Sept. 1808

Combault, Peter Estaniselas [report 20 May 1818]: b. France,
distiller, age 42, migr. from Havana, subj. of King of France
- 20 May 1818

Chadwin, William [report 5 Aug. 1818]: b. Blidworth, Nottinghamshire, Enc., age 27, migr. from Liverpool, intending to reside in Ohio or Indiana Territory - 17 Aug. 1818

Collins, Peter, b. London, age 47, migr. from Hull, farmer, intends to reside in Ulster Co., N.Y.; wife Faith; son Henry
Savage Collins, age 16; son Edward, age 14; dau. Mary Ann,
age 12; son Peter, age 11; son James, age 9; son John Soulby,
age 7; son Charles Westley, age 4 - 31 Oct. 1818

Coghlan, James, age 41, subj. of G.B. - 10 Apr. 1815

Chartres, William, b. Dublin, Ire., age 18 years and 3 months,
migr. from Dublin, merchant - 19 Oct. 1816

Calhoon, James [report 13 Jan. 1819]: b. Co. Tyrone, Ire., age
39, migr. from Londonderry, leather dresser; wife Martha, b.
Co. Tyrone, age 38; dau. Catharine, b. Co. Tyrone, age 11 - 25
Jan. 1819

Cooper, Edward [report 16 Jan. 1819]: b. Kings Co., Ire., age
34, migr. from Newry, gentleman; wife Mary; dau. Harriet, age
11 - 19 Jan. 1819

Clark, Smith [report 19 Apr. 1819]: b. parish cf Tynan, Co. of
Armagh, Ire., age 34, migr. from Liverpool, grocer - 18 Jan.
1820

Cowley, Richard B. [report 7 May 1819]: b. Gloucestershire, age
50, migr. from Guernsey, storekeeper - 19 May 1819

Carey, Michael [report 26 May 1819]: b. City & Co. of Cork, Ire.,
    age 29, migr. from London on ship *Percions*, mason; wife Jane,
    b. town cf Kinsale, Co. of Cork, age 27 - 28 May 1819

Corris, John, b. Isle of Man, age 33, migr. from Liverpool, tai-
    lor; wife Martha, b. town of Wakefield, Yorkshire, Eng., age
    32; dau. Maria, b. Manchester, age 2 - 4 June 1819

Callaghan, Launcelot, b. Dublin, Ire., age 23, migr. from London,
    builder - 13 July 1819

Carleton, Richard, b. Co. Cavan, Ire, age 36, migr. from Cork,
    glazier, painter and grocer; wife Margaret, b. Co. Cavan, age
    29; son James, b. Co. Cavan, age 11; dau. Margaret, b. Co. Ca-
    van, age 9; son Alexander, b. Co. Cavan, age 7; son Richard, b.
    City and Co. of Cork, age 6; dau. Eliza, b. City and Co. of
    Cork, age 2 - 27 July 1819

Chatard, Peter H., b. Bordeaux, France, age 21, migr. from France
    - 25 Sept. 1819

Cunningham, John [repcrt 11 Dec. 1819]: b. Co. of Louth, Ire.,
    age 31, migr. from Dublin, farmer, intends to settle in State
    of N.J. - 23 Dec. 1819

Cunningham, Peter, b. Co. of Louth, Ire., age 21, farmer, migr.
    from Dublin, intends to settle in State of N.J. - 23 Dec. 1819

Clanon, Simcn [report 6 Jan. 1820]: b. town of New Ross, Co. of
    Wexford, Ire., age 24, painter, migr. from New Ross via St.
    Johns, Newfoundland - 18 Jan. 1820

Cacace, Orestes, b. Naples, Kingdom of Sicily, migr. from Naples,
    advocate, age 23, subj. of King of the Two Sicilies - 29 Jan.
    1820

Chubb, Jeremiah [report 24 July 1820]: b. Somersetshire, Eng.,
    age 30, migr. from Havre, France, whitesmith - 24 July 1820

Chazournes, Felix, b. Lyons, France, age 26, migr. from Bordeaux,
    merchant - 16 Jan. 1821

Capp, Thomas [report 10 Sept. 1821]: b. Yarmouth, Norfolk, Eng.,
    age 29, migr. from Carnarvon, Wales, mariner; wife Elizabeth,
    b. Pwetthewley, Wales, age 29 - 17 Sept. 1821

Claringburn, Charles [report 6 July 1821]: b. Nottingham, Eng.,
    age 47, migr. from Liverpool, silk stocking weaver and lace
    manufacturer - 17 July 1821

Carney, James, b., as all his family, Co. Monaghan, Ire., age 34,
    migr. from Belfast, farmer; wife Nancy, age 35; son Patrick,
    age 10; son Michael, age 7; dau. Ellen, age 5 - 9 June 1821

Carney, James, subj. of G.B. - 24 Apr. 1824

Cochran, William[report 7 May 1821]: b. Co. Mayo, Ire., age 35,
    migr. from Belfast, grocer; wife Mary, b. Co. Mayo, age 24; son
    Samuel W., b. Co. Mayo, age 9; son Edward, b. NYC, age 1 - 26
    May 1821

Cassidy, James [report 18 May 1821]: b. Co. Monaghan, Ire., age
    24, migr. from Dublin, brewer; wife Catherine, b. Co. Monaghan,
    age 20; son Hugh, b. Co. Monaghan, age 3; son John, born NYC,
    age 1 - 24 May 1821

Conolly, Patrick [report 16 Apr. 1821]: b. Co. Monaghan, Ire.,
    age 26, migr. from Londonderry, grocer - 21 May 1821

Chalmers, Thomas H., b. Fifeshire, Scotland, age 28, migr. from
    Greenock, Scotland, grocer - 7 May 1821

Cary, Robert, b. Co. Donegal, Ire., age 28, migr. from London-
    derry, tavern-keeper - 3 May 1821

Clark, Mathew, b. Co. Londonderry, Ire., age 29, migr. from Belfast, tavern-keeper; wife Margaret, b. Co. Londonderry, age 28; dau. Jane, b. Co. Antrim, age 6 - 28 Apr. 1821

Chipp, Isaac [report 13 Apr. 1821]: b. Somersetshire, Eng., age 26, migr. from Bristol, Eng., grocer and tavern-keeper - 23 Apr. 1821

Clements, Nicholas [report 13 Apr. 1821]: b. Island of Malta, age 28, migr. from Dublin, boarding house keeper - 21 Apr. 1821

Clark, William, b. Co. Antrim, Ire., age 24; son Robert, b. Co. Antrim, age 6 - 19 Apr. 1821

Cockran, Michael [report 7 Apr. 1821]: b. Co. Wexford, Ire., age 51, migr. from Dublin, hand cartman - 19 Apr. 1821

Cosgrove, John [report 3 Apr. 1821]: b. Co. Tyrone, Ire., age 33, migr. from Londonderry, cartman - 18 Apr. 1821

Conway, Francis [report 2 Apr. 1821]: b. Co. Tyrone, Ire., age 30, migr. from Londonderry, cartman - 18 Apr. 1821

Corbiere, William [report 14 Apr. 1821]: b. Montpelier, France, age 28, migr. from Cette, France, grocer - 18 Apr. 1821

Conolly, James [report 14 Apr. 1821]: b. Co. Monaghan, Ire., age 43, migr. from Dublin, tavern-keeper - 18 Apr. 1821

Cunningham, Thomas, b. Devonshire, Eng., age 42, migr. from Bristol, hatter; wife Elizabeth, b. Co. Cornwall, age 42 - 17 Apr. 1821

Carroll, Edward [report 11 Apr. 1821]: b. Co. Louth, Ire., age 45, migr. from Liverpool, grocer; wife Mary Ann, b. Dublin, age 34; dau. Ann, b. Dublin, age 12; son Anthony, b. Dublin, age 10; dau. Theresa, b. Dublin, age 8 - 17 Apr. 1821

Clegg, Isaac [report 10 Apr. 1821]: b. Lancashire, Eng., age 35, migr. from Portsmouth, Eng., grocer and tavern-keeper; wife Fanny, b. Glasgow, Scotland, age 30 - 16 Apr. 1821

Carlaw, Alexander, b. Lothashire [?], Scotland, age 36, migr. from Liverpool, truckman - 10 Apr. 1821

Curran, Charles, b. Co. Londonderry, Ire., as all of family, age 46, migr. from Belfast, cartman; wife Eliza, age 32; son Henry, age 5 - 30 Mar. 1821

Cassidy, Charles, b. Co. Cavan, Ire., age 31, migr. from Sligo, cartman - 29 Mar. 1821

Caffrey, Morgan, b. Co. Fermanagh, Ire., age 33, migr. from Londonderry, cartman - 28 Mar. 1821

Callaghan, Barney, b. Co. Cavan, Ire., age 39, migr. from Londonderry, cartman - 28 Mar. 1821

Cheney, Christopher, b. Co. Fermanagh, Ire., age 43, migr. from Londonderry, cartman - 28 Mar. 1821

Campbell, James, b. Co. Armagh, Ire., age 42, migr. from Belfast, cartman - 27 Mar. 1821

Cole, Charles, b. city of Londonderry, Ire., age 45, migr. from Londonderry, cartman - 27 Mar. 1821

Corr, Peter, b. Co. Roscommon, Ire., age 24, migr. from Sligo, labourer - 27 Mar. 1821

Claridge, James, age 27, b. London, migr. from London, blacksmith - 12 Feb. 1821

Coffy, John [report 20 Mar. 1822]: b. Kings Co., Ire., age 28, migr. from Dublin, coachman; wife Bridget, b. Co. Sligo, age 25 - 21 Mar. 1822

Coghlan, Daniel, b. Clonmacnoise, age 46, migr. from Ire. - 28 Mar. 1822

Corrigan, Andrew, b. Co. Tyrone, Ire., age 39, migr. from Londonderry, weaver - 29 July 1822

Cleland, James, b. Co. Down, age 25, migr. from Belfast, grocer - 22 Aug. 1822

Cox, James [report 12 Nov. 1822]: b. Yorkshire, Eng., age 30, migr. from Hull, rigger; wife Mary, born N.Y., age 25; son William, b. N.Y., age 7; son Edward, b. N.Y., age 10 months - 18 Nov. 1822

Clifford, John [report 13 Jan. 1823]: b. Co. Tipperary, Ire., age 45, migr. from St. Johns, Newfoundland, labourer; wife Johanna, b. Co. Tipperary, age 40 - 31 Jan. 1823

Colgan, Edward, b. Co. Cavan, Ire., age 31, migr. from Newry, waiter; wife Eliza, b. Derbyshire, Eng., age 26 - 17 Mar. 1823

Cook, Richard [report 2 Apr. 1823]: b. Somersetshire, Eng., age 38, migr. from London, umbrella maker; dau. Rebecca, b. London, age 14; son Norman, b. London, age 12; dau. Vashti, b. London, age 10 - 1 May 1823

Coyle, Charles [report 13 Apr. 1823]: b. Co. Tyrone, Ire., age 32, migr. from Londonderry, hack driver - 14 Apr. 1823

Christman, Charles G., subj. of King of Prussia - 23 May 1823

Cannon, Daniel [report 26 Jan. 1824]: b. Londonderry, Ire., age 25, migr. from Londonderry, labourer - 31 Jan. 1824

Collins, Henry, b. Co. Wicklow, Ire., age 29, migr. from Dublin, blacksmith - 20 Mar. 1824

Colgan, Dominick [report 26 Apr. 1824]: b. Co. Londonderry, Ire., age 26, labourer - 27 Apr. 1824

Cudlipp, David [report 25 Jan. 1820]: b. Portsmouth, Eng., age 29, migr. from Portsmouth, hatter; wife Sarah, b. Portsmouth, age 26; dau. Ema, b. Portsmouth, age 5 - 29 Aug. 1824

Curtius, John, b. Cologne, Germany, age 60, migr. from London, tailor; wife Mary, b. Cologne, age 47 - 20 Sept. 1824

Callan, Francis, b., as all the family, Co. Monaghan, Ire., age 37, migr. from Newry, weaver; wife Rosmond, age 34; dau. Jane, age 8; son James, age 6; dau. Mary, age 3 - 20 Dec. 1824

Crocket, William, b. Co. Donegal, Ire., age 34, migr. from Londonderry, labourer; wife Grace, b. near Newry, Ire., age 30, migr. from Belfast - 7 Jan. 1825

Connell, Michael, b. Co. Longford, Ire., age 26, migr. from Dublin, millstone maker - 20 Jan. 1825

Carl, Luke [report 4 Apr. 1825]: b. Co. Monaghan, Ire., age 31, migr. from Belfast, labourer; wife Sarah, b. Co. Monaghan, age 30 - Apr. 1825

Colton, Edward, b. Co. Tyrone, Ire., age 30, migr. from Londonderry, via St. Johns, N.B., labourer; wife Catharine, b. Co. Tyrone, age 30; son Francis, b. Co. Tyrone, age 10; dau. Biddy, b. Co. Tyrone, age 7; dau. Margaret, b. NYC, age 4; son Andrew, b. NYC, age 2 - 20 Aug. 1825

Caffrey, Charles [report 29 Aug. 1825]: b. Co. Cavan, age 23, migr. from Dublin, labourer - 26 Sept. 1825

Clarry, John, b. Co. Monaghan, Ire., age 35, migr. from Belfast, labourer; wife Mary, b. Co. Monaghan, age 30; dau. Margaret, b. Co. Monaghan, age 5; son Hugh, b. Co. Monaghan, age 4; dau. Mary Ann, b. Co. Monaghan, age 3; son John, b. NYC, age 1 mo. - 21 Sept. 1825

Cannon, Henry (by his guardian, Dennis Patten), b. Co. Donegal, Ire., age 19 years and 8 months, migr. from town of Kelly-beggs, mason - 3 Oct. 1825

Callaghan, Patrick [report 7 Oct. 1825]: b. Co. Cork, Ire., age 26, migr. from Cork, labourer - 17 Oct. 1825

Connolly, Edward [report 14 Oct. 1825]: b. Co. Monaghan, Ire., age 46, migr. from Belfast, via St. Andrew, Nova Scotia, labourer; wife Briget, b. Co. Fermanagh, age 38; dau. Catharine, b. Co. Monaghan, age 4; son James, b. Charleston, S.C., age 9 months - 17 Oct. 1825

Callaghan, Patrick [report 9 Nov. 1825]: b. Co. Waterford, Ire., age 26, migr. from Cork, sawyer - 21 Nov. 1825

Comasky, James, b. Co. Cavan, Ire., age 23, migr. from Dublin, labourer; wife Catharine, b. parish of Mahone [?], age 34; son Thomas, b. parish of Mahone [?] - 19 Oct. 1826

Crey, Thomas, b. Co. Down, age 23, migr. from Belfast, via Quebec, labourer - 20 Jan. 1827

Cunneen, John [report 31 Jan. 1827]: b., as all the family, Co. Tipperary, age 43, migr. from Liverpool, cordwainer; wife France, age 42; son Timothy, age 16; son Michael, age 14 years and 3 months; son John, age 13 years and 3 months; dau. Judith, age 11; son Carl, age 9; dau. Elidue, age 8; dau. Maria, age between 3 and 4 - 19 Feb. 1827

Colligan, James, b. Co. Londonderry, age 33, migr. from Londonderry, house-carpenter - 24 July 1827

Caldwell, Andrew, subj. of G.B. - 29 Dec. 1827

Carson, Johnson [report 11 Feb. 1828]: b. Co. Tyrone, Ire., age 21, migr. from Belfast, dirt cartman - 22 Feb. 1828

Claassen, Gerhard [report 16 Apr. 1828]: b. Danzig, Prussia, age 28, migr. from Danzig, via St. Johns, N.B., distiller - 22 Apr. 1828

Costigan, John D., b. Monasterevan, Co. Kildare, Ire., as also the rest of the family, age 29, migr. from Dublin, accountant; wife Mary Ann, age 26; dau. Alicia, age 3 - 25 Apr. 1828

Chapman, William B., b. London, Eng., age 29, migr. from London, comedian - 28 June 1828

Cowley, Richard B., brewer, subj. of G.B. - 24 Dec. 1828

Crux, Thomas, miller, subj. of G.B. - 21 Dec. 1829

Callagyn, Michael, subj. of G.B. - 21 Sept. 1829

Carlisle, John H., merchant, subj. of G.B. - 18 Mar. 1830

Charras, James, accountant, late of the Dept. D'Herrault, France - 16 Aug. 1830

Cruise, Patrick Russel, subj. of G.B. - 30 Sept. 1830

Correa, Sarah, b. Island of Jamaica, age 57, migr. from Jamaica, gentlewoman; dau. Rachel, b. Island of Jamaica, age 19 - 19 Jan. 1826

Coleman, Patrick [report 17 Feb. 1826]: b. Sligo, Ire., age 21, migr. from Sligo, labourer - 20 Feb. 1826

Cassidy, Michael (by his guardian, Hugh Cassidy), b. Co. Monaghan, age 19, migr. from Belfast, labourer - 3 Mar. 1826

Cassidy, Hugh, b. Co. Monaghan, age 22, migr. from Belfast, labourer - 3 Mar. 1826

Collet, Gabriel [report 28 Mar. 1826]: b. village of St. Gamand de la Cundu [?], Dept. de la Sarthe, France, age 35, migr. from Havre de Grace, merchant; wife Maria, b. England, age 21 - 29 Mar. 1826

Craton, David [report 1 May 1826]: b. Co. Donegal, Ire., age 27, migr. from Londonderry, labourer - 6 May 1826

Cassidy, John, b. Co. Donegal, Ire., age 25, migr. from town of Kellybeggs, Ire., cartman - 14 Sept. 1826

Cunaughan, James, b. Co. Donegal, Ire., age 22, migr. from Londonderry, labourer - 14 Sept. 1826

Cramer, John, subj. of Emperor of Austria and City Govt. of Frankfort - 20 Nov. 1826

Croston, Alice, widow, subj. of G.B. - 18 July 1831

Cassidy, Richard, shoemaker, subj. of G.B. - 18 July 1831

Callery, John, waiter, subj. of G.B. - 17 Oct. 1831

Cohen, Cleomenes Charles Colman, subj. of G.B. - 21 Oct. 1831

Carter, John, arrived U.S. 1 Jan. 1830, subj. of G.B.; rec. by Matthew Smith - 13 Apr. 1837

Compton, John, farmer, subj. of G.B. - 21 Mar. 1837

Cluff, John, professor in the university, subj. of G.B. - 25 Mar. 1837

Crockett, William, apothecary, subj. of G.B. - 3 July 1837

Correa, Emanuel Alvares, subj. of King of Denmark - 31 July 1837

Cosgrove, Henry, subj. of G.B. - 23 Nov. 1837

Cochran, Robert, subj. of G.B. - 23 Jan. 1832

Cronly, Michael, subj. of G.B. - 29 Mar. 1832

Cummins, Hugh, labourer, subj. of G.B. - 28 Sept. 1832

Cox, Charles, merchant tailor, subj. of G.B. - 27 Oct. 1832

Calmann, Bernhard, musician, subj. of Republic of Hamburgh - 29 Oct. 1833

Cohn, Hirsch Casper, bandbox maker, subj. of Republic of Hamburgh - 29 Oct. 1833

Clark, Frederick, late of Northhamptonshire, Eng., carpenter - 23 Apr. 1833

Cluff, Joseph, late of Dublin, Ire., student-at-law - 27 Apr. 1833

Clifford, Thomas, labourer, subj. of G.B. - 15 July 1833

Canovan, John, subj. of G.B. - 20 June 1834

Clarke, Richard, of Hallett's Cove, L.I., subj. of G.B. - 21 June 1834

Cramer, Charles, late of St. Petersburg, Russia, merchant, subj. of Emperor of Russia - 3 July 1834

Castles, Michael, subj. of G.B. - 11 July 1834

Cumming, William, subj. of G.B. - 5 Nov. 1834

Cary, Patrick, of Newtown, L.I., subj. of G.B. - 22 Nov. 1834

Carroll, John, labourer, subj. of G.B. - 24 Dec. 1834

Cobham, George Ashworth, subj. of G.B. - 19 Mar. 1835

Callaghan, James, printer, subj. of G.B. - 8 Sept. 1835

Cornish, John, miner, subj. of G.B. - 23 Mar. 1836

Canning, Edward Wm., merchant, subj. of G.B. - 18 Aug. 1836

Clapham, Samuel, merchant, subj. of G.B. - 17 Aug. 1836

Campbell, James Lawrence, residing in Jersey City, aubj. of G.B. - 19 Sept. 1836

Considine, Carroll, mason, subj. of G.B. - 8 Nov. 1836

Connolly, Christopher, of City of Brooklyn, carpenter, subj. of G.B. - 9 Nov. 1836

Crowley, Robert, subj. of G.B. - 22 Jan. 1838

Crowther, William, of Westchester Co., N.Y., subj. of G.B. - 29 Jan. 1838

Crowther, Richard, of West Farms, Westchester Co., subj. of G.B. - 7 Feb. 1838

Cape, John, subj. of King of Prussia - 11 Apr. 1838

Curran, Martin, subj. of G.B. - 12 Apr. 1838

Cunningham, James, subj. of G.B. - 12 Apr. 1838

Connolly, Edward, subj. of G.B. - 12 Apr. 1838

Conroy, Patrick, subj. of G.B. - 5 May 1838

Campbell, John, subj. of G.B. - 15 June 1838

Carmelick, Marco, subj. of Emperor of Austria - 28 Sept. 1838

Christ, George, subj. of Prince of Hesse Cassel - 3 Oct. 1838

Clough, Jesse, subj. of G.B. - 5 Sept. 1838

Clapham, Glover, subj. of G.B. - 8 Nov. 1838

Cludius, Charles, subj. of King of Hanover - 14 Nov. 1838

Currie, Michael, collier, subj. of G.B. - 26 Sept. 1838

Coleman, George, subj. of G.B. - 5 Feb. 1839

Cox, William, subj. of G.B. - 8 Apr. 1839

Clarke, Andrew, subj. of G.B. - 11 Apr. 1839

Cluff, William, subj. of G.B. - 24 June 1839

Clanny [clerk wrote "Claney"], James, subj. of G.B. - 27 June 1839

Clyde, George, subj. of G.B. - 9 Aug. 1839

Campbell, John, subj. of G.B. - 24 Aug. 1839

Corley, Michael, of Richmond Co., subj. of G.B. - 2 Nov. 1839

Carman, Nicholas, subj. of Emperor of Austria - 4 Nov. 1839

Champion, Francis, subj. of King of France - 6 Nov. 1839

Caragher, James, subj. of G.B. - 11 Mar. 1840

Connor, Matthew, subj. of G.B. - 30 Mar. 1840

Cartlidge, Charles, subj. of G.B. - 3 Apr. 1840

Campbell, Harman T., subj. of G.B. - 8 Apr. 1840

Cain, Robert, subj. of G.B. - 13 Apr. 1840

Campbell, James, subj. of G.B. - 14 Apr. 1840

Connaughton, Patrick, subj. of G.B. - 15 Aug. 1840

Chutkowski, Ignatius, subj. of Emperor of Russia - 29 May 1840

Courtenay, Charles, subj. of G.B. - 30 May 1840

Coyle, Edward, subj. of G.B. - 11 July 1840

Coyne, James, subj. of G.B. - 13 July 1840

Croydon, Glanville Henry, subj. of G.B. - 18 Sept. 1840

Conway, Cormack, subj. of G.B. - 22 Sept. 1840

Coghlin, Thomas, subj. of G.B. - 26 Sept. 1840

Carroll, John, subj. of G.B. - 1 Oct. 1840

Callaghan, Philip, subj. of G.B. - 7 Oct. 1840

Cauley, James, subj. of G.B. - 7 Oct. 1840

Cammeyer, Charles, subj. of King of the Netherlands - 9 Oct. 1840

Cammeyer, John C., subj. of King of the Netherlands - 9 Oct. 1840

Connor, Michael, subj. of G.B. - 10 Oct. 1840

Collins, John, subj. of G.B. - 22 Oct. 1840

Campbell, Peter, subj. of G.B. - 23 Oct. 1840

Cronin, Denis, subj. of G.B. - 26 Oct. 1840

Cleary, Michael, subj. of G.B. - 27 Oct. 1840

Connellan, James, subj. of G.B. - 28 Oct. 1840

Coast, John, subj. of G.B. - 30 Oct. 1840

Collin, Morris, subj. of G.B. - 31 Oct. 1840

Cunningham, Patrick, subj. of G.B. - 2 Nov. 1840

Colahan, James J., subj. of G.B. - 3 Nov. 1840

Colehan, John Hughes, subj. of G.B. - 2 Nov. 1840

Condon, Michael James, subj. of G.B. - 4 Nov. 1840

Cosgriff, Andrew, subj. of G.B. - 10 Nov. 1840

Carswell, Robert Scott, subj. of G.B. - 21 Nov. 1840

Crawford, William, subj. of G.B. - 18 Dec. 1840
  Cudlipp, Joseph (by guardian, David Cudlipp), b. Portsmouth, 20,
  migr. Havre, milkman - 25 Jan. 1820

Donaldson, Robert, gentleman, subj. of G.B. - 20 Oct. 1807

Daley, George W., b. Ire., age 23, migr. from Dublin, morocco
  finisher - 27 Feb. 1816

Dexter, William A., of Richmond Co., N.Y. [report 9 Apr. 1816]:
  b. Clonmell, Co. Tipperary, Ire., age 30, migr. from Dublin,
  tavern- and innkeeper; wife Sarah, b. Queens Co., Ire., age 26
  - 29 Apr. 1816

Doyle, Robert, living at corner of Elizabeth and Prince Sts. in
  the 8th Ward in NYC, b. Co. Wexford, Ire., age 30, migr. Dublin, cartman; dau. Catharine, b. New Town Barry, Ire., age 8 -
  4 May 1816

Doyle, Edward, cartman, subj. of G.B. - 23 Nov. 1816

Darcey, Thomas [report 5 Sept. 1817]: b. Gorey, Co. Wexford, Ire.,
  age 41, migr. from Dublin, grocer; wife Hannah, born Eng., age
  40; son Thomas, b. Dublin, age 20 - 5 Nov. 1817

Doyle, Dennis, Jr., b. Co. Wexford, Ire., age 21, migr. from Dublin, mariner - 16 Feb. 1818

De Brot, Henry, b. L'Orient, France, age 23, migr. from L'Orient, mariner - 23 Jan. 1818

De La Cadena, Mariano Velazquez, b. Mexico, age 40, migr. from Madrid, Spain, translator of languages - 23 Nov. 1818

Dehanne, Jean Vilodorez [report 25 Dec. 1818]: b. France, age 21, migr. from Havre de Grace, teacher - 26 Dec. 1818

Drake, David [report 9 Sept. 1825]: b. Norwich, Eng., age 29, migr. from London, merchant; wife Margaret, b. Norwich, age 29; son George K., b. Sudbury, Co. of Suffolk, Eng., age 3; son David C., b. fortress of Gibraltar, age 1 - 26 Sept. 1825

Duffy, Patrick, b. Co. Monaghan, Ire., age 22, migr. from Liverpool, cartman - 30 Aug. 1825

Davis, Zadock Abraham [report 10 Dec. 1825]: b. Amsterdam, age 26, migr. from Rotterdam, via Bristol, merchant - 19 Dec. 1825

Drew, Edward [report 15 Apr. 1819]: b. Dublin, Ire., age 21, migr. from Dublin, merchant - 30 Mar. 1821

Dexter, William A., subj. of G.B. - 26 Apr. 1819

Donaldson, Thomas [report 5 Aug. 1819]: b. Co. Armagh, Ire., age 32, migr. from Newry, weaver; wife Elizabeth, b. Co. Armagh, age 27

Donaldson, Thomas, cartman, subj. of G.B. - 21 Aug. 1819

Despard, Green, b. Queens Co., Ire., age 30, migr. from Dublin, merchant - 29 Sept. 1819

Daly, Bryan [report 29 Dec. 1819]: b. Queens Co., Ire., age 44, migr. from Dublin, shoemaker and labourer; wife and children (all born in Co. Kilkenny); wife, age 35; son Patrick, age 17; son Andrew, age 11; son John, age 9; son Edward, age 5; dau. Sarah, age 6 - 30 Dec. 1819 ; wife is named Elenor.

Dunlop, William, b. Manchester, Lancashire, Eng., age 30; migr. from Liverpool, merchant - 26 Jan. 1820

Drisler, Henry [report 1 Sept. 1820]: b. Abenheim near River Rein, Germany, age 40, migr. from Amsterdam, Holland, baker, residing Richmond Co., N.Y. - 24 May 1823

Donnelly, Patrick, b. Co. Longford, Ire., age 30, migr. from Dublin, labourer - 11 Sept. 1820

Douglass, John C., subj. of G.B. - 20 Jan. 1821

Duff, Fintan, b. Queens Co., Ire., age 37, migr. from Galway, labourer - 27 Mar. 1821

Dickson, William, b. Co. Monaghan, Ire., age 51, migr. from Newry, cartman - 29 Mar. 1821

Doyle, Thomas, b. Co. Wexford, age 42, migr. from Dublin, grocer - 30 Mar. 1821

Douglass, Robert, b. Bowmore, Scotland, age 27, migr. from Belfast, cartman - 31 Mar. 1821

Dey, Andrew, b. Queens Co., Ire., age 45, migr. from Dublin, cartman - 31 Mar. 1821

Dillon, Alexander [report 3 Apr. 1821]: b. Co. Antrim, Ire., age 31, migr. from Belfast, labourer; wife Ann, b. Co. Antrim, age 30 - 16 Apr. 1821

Duff, Thomas [report 3 Apr. 1821]: b. Co. of Dublin, as were all his family, age 62, migr. from Dublin, labourer; wife Mary, age 35; son Thomas, age 5; dau. Jane, age 22; dau. Mary, age 18; dau. Margaret, age 15; dau. Bridget, age 7; dau. Frances, age 6 - 16 Apr. 1821

Dougherty, Didly [report 11 Apr. 1821]: b. Co. Donegal, age 32, migr. from Londonderry, grocer - 17 Apr. 1821

Dunn, Patrick [report 5 Apr. 1821]: b. Co. Kilkenny, Ire., age 32, migr. from Dublin, porter - 17 Apr. 1821

Donnelly, Patrick, subj. of G.B. - 18 Apr. 1821

Dresel, Friederich [report 11 Apr. 1821]: b. village of Viten, Russia, age 35, migr. from Amsterdam, grocer - 18 Apr. 1821

Driscoll, Jeremiah [report 10 Apr. 1821]: b. Co. Cork, Ire., age 32, migr. from London, grocer; wife Ann, b. Co. Down, age 27 - 20 Apr. 1821

Doyle, John [report 18 Apr. 1821]: b. Co. Wexford, Ire., age 26, migr. from Dublin, tavern-keeper - 20 Apr. 1821

Darby, Michael [report 10 Apr. 1821]: b. Co. Monaghan, Ire., age 34, migr. from town of Monaghan, grocer; wife Dorothy, b. Co. Monaghan, age 29; son Owen, b. Co. Monaghan, age 9; dau. Mary Ann, b. Co. Monaghan, age 7; dau. Ellen, b. Co. Monaghan, age 4; son Michael, b. New York, age 2 - 20 Apr. 1821

Daly, Mathew A. [clerk wrote "A."] [report 13 Apr. 1821]: b. Co. Tyrone, Ire., age 29, migr. from Londonderry, grocer; son Patrick, b. Co. Tyrone, age 7 - 20 Apr. 1821

Della Torre, Joseph, b. Isola Madrè in Lake Superior, age 39, subj. of King of Sardinia, migr. from Liverpool, tavern-keeper - 21 Apr. 1821

Donahoe, Michael [report 3 Apr. 1821]: b. Queens Co., Ire., age 33, migr. from Galway, cartman - 21 Apr. 1821

Dodey, Augustine [report 20 Apr. 1821]: b. Genoa, Italy, age 31, subj. of King of Sardinia, migr. from Havanna, W.I., grocer - 27 Apr. 1821

Douglass, John, b. Dunfermlineshire, Scotland, age 40, migr. from Greenock, storekeeper - 2 May 1821

Demeiere, Philippe, b. city of Charden [?], Dept. of the Seine, France, age 33, migr. from Bayonne, tanner - 10 May 1821

Decevee, Pierre T., subj. of King of France - 22 May 1821

Delany, Nicholas, b. Co. Kilkenny, age 25 - 23 May 1821

Donahoe, Patrick, b. Co. Longford, Ire., age 26, migr. from Dublin, wheelwright and turner; wife Mary, b. Co. Longford, age 24 - 24 May 1821

Devlin, Barnard, b. Co. Londonderry, age 28, migr. from Belfast, cartman - 28 May 1821

Dempsey, John, b. Kings Co., Ire., age 33, migr. from London, gentleman; wife Elizabeth, b. Kings Co., age 45 - 2 July 1821

Decouses, Peter [report 11 Aug. 1821]: b. Varenne, Lower Canada, age 55, migr. from Montreal, victualling house and tavern-keeper - 20 Aug. 1821

Deckener, Augustus William, b. Peterborough, Northamptonshire, Eng., age 29, migr. from Liverpool, merchant - 18 Dec. 1821

De Cousse, Philip, subj. of G.B. - 17 Apr. 1822

Dunlop, Nathaniel, b. Co. Down, Ide., age 30, migr. from Hollywood, Ire., distiller; wife Maria, b. Co. Down, age 30; dau. Margaret, b. Co. Down, age 8; dau. Maria Jane, b. New York, age 5; son Hugh Graham, b. City of Jersey, age 3 - 22 July 1822

Donnellan, Thomas T., b. Connaught, Ire., age 36; migr. from Limerick, servant - 30 Oct. 1822

Dillon, John, b. Co. Longford, Ire., age 40, migr. from Dublin, farmer - 23 Dec. 1822

Duncan, John, b. Perthshire, Scotland, age 33, migr. from Greenock, merchant; wife Jane. b. Dundee, Scotland, age 37; dau. Ann, b. Fifeshire, Scotland, age 7; dau. Ellen, b. Fifeshire, age 5; son David, b. Fifeshire, age 3; dau. Jane, b. NYC, age 1 - 20 Feb. 1823

Dixon, John [report 2 June 1823]: b. Northumberland, Eng., age 29, migr. from New Castle, marble cutter; wife Elizabeth, b. Wales, age 28 - 17 June 1823

Doyle, Philip [report 8 Sept. 1823]: b. Co. Wexford, Ire., age 32, migr. from St. Johns, Newfoundland, sailmaker; wife Sarah, b. St. Johns, age 28; son Thomas, b. St. Johns, age 8; son Philip, b. St. Johns, age 6 - 15 Sept. q823

Dunn, Fintan, b. Mountrath, Queens Co., Ire., age 21, migr. from Dublin, mariner - 7 Oct. 1823

Delisle, Enemmond, b. Grenoble, France, age 62, migr. from Belfast, boarding house keeper - 20 Dec. 1823

Dunn, Michael [report 21 June 1824]: b. Co. Fermanagh, Ire., age 22, migr. from Belfast, cartman; wife Rose, b. Co. Fermanagh, age 22 - 19 July 1824

Dominguez, Manuel, b. Cadiz, Spain, age 30, migr. from Havana, Cuba, teacher and translator of languages - 21 Aug. 1824

Dobie, William, b. Lanarkshire, Scotland, age 28, migr. from Greenock, farmer, residing in Westchester Co., N.Y. 24 Nov. 1824

McDuffy, Patrick (by his guardian, Patrick McNeany), b. Co. Monaghan, Ire., age 18, migr. from Liverpool, weaver - 20 Dec. 1824

Davis, Henry, b. Gloucestershire, Eng., age 21, migr. from Liverpool, labourer - 17 Oct. 1826

Devine, Thomas, b. Co. Louth, Ire., age 26, migr. from Liverpool, labourer; wife Anne, b. Co. Louth, age 22; dau. Mary, b. Co. Louth, age 3 - 21 Mar. 1826

Damerel, George, b. London, age 30, migr. from Liverpool, iron founder; wife Mary, b. London, age 26 - 23 Mar. 1826

Donohoe, Peter [report 10 June 1826]: b. Queens Co., Ire., age 28, migr. from Dublin, labourer - 27 June 1826

Duttenhofer, Augustus, b. Wirtemberg, Germany, age 32, migr. from Rotterdam, Holland, civil engineer - 20 Nov. 1826

Davis, John [report 4 Jan. 1827]: b. Co. Worcester, Eng., age 40, migr. from Liverpool, grocer; wife Elizabeth, b. Co. Salop [Shropshire], age 29; dau. Elizabeth Ann, b. New York, age 2 - 15 Jan. 1827

Durand, Benjamin, b. Lyons, France, age 36, migr. from Havre, merchant; wife Celestine, b. Paris, age 22 - 30 Jan. 1827

Dougherty, George [report 5 Feb. 1827]: b. Co. Sligo, age 27, migr. from Liverpool, labourer - 27 Feb. 1827

Deguerre, Joseph F., b. Paris, France, age 45, migr. from Havre, jeweller - 19 Feb. 1827

Douglas, John C., b. parish of Dunfermline, Co. of Fife, Scotland, age 46, migr. from Greenock, merchant - 1 June 1827

Daly, Cornelius [report 1 May 1827]: b. Co. Cavan, Ire., age 30, migr. from Belfast, stone cutter; wife Briget, b. Co. Cavan, age 31 - 21 June 1827

Delolme, John Charles, b. Brunswick, Germany, age 40, subj. of
King of Saxony, migr. from Hamburgh, merchant - 26 July 1827

Dowdney, John, b. Devonshire, Eng., age 67, migr. from Liverpool,
gentelman, residing in Williamsburgh, Kings Co., L.I.; wife
Ada, b. Shropshire, age 55; dau. Elizabeth, b. Coventry, age
26; son John, b. Manchester, age 21; dau. Susannah, b. Manchester, age 17 - 22 Oct. 1827

Durant, Thomas, b. Devonshire, Eng., age 27, migr. from Plymouth,
printing ink manufacturer; wife Ann, b. Devonshire, age 24;
dau. Elizabeth, b. New York, age 5; son Thomas, b. New York,
age 1 year and 4 months - 17 Dec. 1827

Douglass, William, of Jersey City, N,J,, subj. of G.B. - 23 Dec.
1828

Deal, John, cartman, subj. of G.B. - 26 July 1828

Dunn, Maria, subj. of G.B. - 22 May 1834

Grubb, Janet (wife of George Grubb), b. Fifeshire, Scotland, age
40, migr. from Leith, Scotland; her son, John Thornton Mel-
ville Dow, age 15 - 20 May 1828

Donahoe, Michael, b. Co. Longford, Ire., age 24, migr. from Belfast, labourer - 2 Feb. 1828

Duffour, Amédeé (by his guardian, Wm. Phiquepal), subj. of King
of France - 2 Oct. 1829

Durant, John, silversmith, subj. of G.B. - 22 Dec. 1829

Davies, Emanuel, clerk, subj. of G.B. - 18 Aug. 1830

Duck, Daniel, surgeon, subj. of G.B. - 21 Dec. 1830

Davis, James, bookseller, subj. of G.B. - 23 Oct. 1830

Delaney, John, stone cutter, subj. of G.B. - 27 Oct. 1831

Dumastier, Anne, subj. of King of France - 22 Feb. 1831

Dixon, Joshua, merchant, subj. of G.B. - 23 Nov. 1831

Drommond, William E., private watchman, subj. of King of Prussia
- 27 Nov. 1832

De Loynes, George, subj. of King of France - 23 Apr. 1835

Dinckel, Conrad, subj. of Republic of Switzerland, weaver - 6
Oct. 1835

Davenport, William A.F., merchant, subj. of G.B. - 24 Dec. 1835

Dien, Gottlieb, carpenter, subj. of King of Wurtemberg - 17 June
1835

Dewing, Thomas Derisley, merchant, subj. of G.B. - 18 May 1836

Darby, John Lewis, late of Monteviedo, subj. of Grand Duke of
Tuscany - 5 Oct. 1836

Daly, Richard, mariner, subj. of G.B. - 1 Nov. 1836

Donnelly, John, subj. of G.B. - 11 Apr. 1837

Dortic, Sebastien C., subj. of King of France - 5 May 1837

Damainville, Denis Auguste, of Erie Co., Pa., subj. of King of
France - 30 Oct. 1837

Davis, Evan Jones, subj. of G.B. - 9 Nov. 1837

De Castro, Emanuel, subj. of Free City of Hamburgh - 20 Jan. 1838

Donnelly, John, subj. of G.B. - 2 Apr. 1838

Dürr, Jakob Simon, subj. of King of Wurtemburg - 9 Apr. 1838

Duncan, William, subj. of G.B. - 9 Apr. 1838

Dolton, Patrick, subj. of G.B. - 10 Apr. 1838

Dierker, Henry, subj. of King of Hanover - 12 Apr. 1838

Drenan, James, of Newburgh, subj. of G.B. - 19 Oct. 1838

Daley, James, subj. of G.B. - 5 Nov. 1838

Dieffenbach, John Henry, subj. of Prince of Hesse Cassel - 7 Nov. 1838

De Strzelecki, Paul Edmond, subj. of King of Prussia - 26 July 1834

Dohrmann, Otto, subj. of King of Hanover - 4 Mar. 1839

De Voss, Edward William, subj. of Free City of Bremen - 19 Mar. 1839

Delaney, John, subj. of G.B. - 19 Mar. 1839

Deniard [clerk wrote "Deniord"], Richard S., subj. of G.B. - 30 Mar. 1839

Daly, John, subj. of G.B. - 8 Apr. 1839

Dillon, James, subj. of G.B. - 11 Apr. 1839

Donovan, Timothy, subj. of G.B. - 11 Apr. 1839

Dunlop, John [clerk wrote "Dunlap"], subj. of G.B. - 11 Apr. 1839

Denniston [clerk wrote "Deuniston"], John Alexander, subj. of G.B. - 10 May 1839

D'Owleans, Albert M., subj. of Emperor of Austria - 6 June 1839

Donoho, Barney, subj. of G.B. - 13 July 1839

Dawson, Elizabeth, single woman, subj. of G.B. - 2 Oct. 1839

Delancy [clerk wrote "Delaney"], Patrick, subj. of G.B. - 4 Oct. 1839

Davis, Ann, subj. of G.B. - 9 Oct. 1839

Davis, John Joseph, subj. of G.B. - 6 Nov. 1839

Dorman, James, subj. of G.B. - 16 Nov. 1839

Dugan, John, subj. of G.B. - 5 Mar. 1840

Dowd, Patrick, subj. of G.B. - 21 Mar. 1840

Dawson, Timothy, subj. of G.B. - 14 Apr. 1840

Dewald, Alois [clerk wrote "Alvis"], subj. of King of Bavaria - 11 May 1840

Dugan, Neil, subj. of G.B. - 30 Sept. 1840

Dohrmann, Neclaus [clerk wrote "Nicholas"], subj. of King of Prussia - 16 Oct. 1840

Demont, Joseph, subj. of Emperor of Austria - 17 Oct. 1840

De Jong, Roedolph Jacob, Sr., subj. of King of Holland - 23 Oct. 1840

Deigan [clerk wrote "Degan"], Patrick, subj. of G.B. - 26 Oct. 1840

Drinkwater, Matthew, subj. of Emperor of Austria - 31 Oct. 1840

Dwane, James, subj. of G.B. - 31 Oct. 1840

Dunn, Dennis, subj. of G.B. - 31 Oct. 1840

Durning, James, subj. of G.B. - 4 Nov. 1840

E

Eyton, Edward, b. Bodfari, Co. of Flint, Wales, age 21, migr. from Liverpool - 20 Sept. 1817

Eaton, Charles G., born town of Whitehaven, Cumberland Co., Eng., age 27, migr. from Liverpool, mariner - 18 Nov. 1818

Evans, John, b. Co. Wexford, Ire., age 35, migr. from Waterford, merchant, intending to reside in Illinois Territory; wife Ann, age 40; son John, Jr., age 18; son Thomas, age 15; son William, age 13 - 7 Nov. 1818

Ellis, Alexander, b. town of Belladugh, parish of Kilkap, Co. Donegal, age 30, migr. from Londonderry, cartman - 14 Sept. 1818

Espada, Joseph M., b. Campeachy, Prov. of Yucatan, Subj. King of Spain, age 19, migr. from Campeachy, merchant - 17 Aug. 1818

English, Thomas, b. Queens Co., Ire., age 34, migr. from Dublin, carpenter, intending to settle in Illinois Territory; wife Matilda, b. Dublin, age 23; son Andrew, b. Dublin, age 1 - 27 Apr. 1818

Elliott, Robert, b. Co. Cavan, Ire., age 37, migr. from London, tavern-keeper; wife Bridget, b. Co. Meath, age 40; son Frederick, b. London, age 9; son Hugh, b. London, age 7; son James, b. London, age 5 - 1 May 1821

Earl, John, b. Birmingham, Eng., age 37, migr. from Birmingham, arrived Port of New York in Aug. 1819, merchant; wife Frances, b. Birmingham, age 28 - 22 Dec. 1823

Eccleston, Edward, b. Dublin, Ire., age 27, migr. from Dublin, merchant - 21 June 1824

Eames, Thomas [report 13 July 1824]: b. Co. Donegal, Ire., age 26, migr. from Killybegs, Ire., labourer - 19 July 1824

Ewing, William, b. Co. Antrim, Ire., age 30, migr. from Belfast, labourer - 20 July 1825

Edgar, Alexander [report 12 Dec. 1825]: b. Co. Down, as were all his family, age 36, migr. from Belfast, farmer, intending to settle in Ulster Co., N.Y.; wife Barbara, age 29; dau. Mary, age 13 years and 6 months; dau. Barbara, age 6 years - 24 Dec. 1825

Edgar, Robert [report 12 Dec. 1825]: b. Co. Down, age 26, migr. from Newry, boatman, intending to settle in Ulster Co., N.Y.; wife Margaret, b. Co. Down, age 30 - 24 Dec. 1825

Ellis, Charles Edward, b. Cambridge, Eng., age 28, migr. from Liverpool, attorney - 20 Jan. 1826

Eccleston, Edward, subj. of G.B. - 19 Jan. 1826

Eck, Johan Daniel, tailor, native of Strasburg, France - 21 Sept. 1829

Elliot, Thomas, smith, subj. of G.B. - 20 July 1829

Evans, William [report 7 Feb. 1828]: b. Co. Gloucester, Eng., age 50, migr. from Bristol, labourer - 16 Feb. 1828

Elwell, William, accountant, subj. of G.B. - 15 June 1835

Easton, Thomas [report 4 Aug. 1827]: b. Fayal, age 30, subj. of King of Portugal, migr. from Fayal, mariner - 22 Apr. 1828

Engler, Charles, merchant, subj. of Republic of Switzerland - 16 Feb. 1836

Evans, Thomas, of Jamaica, Queens Co., N.Y., carpenter, subj. of G.B. - 28 June 1836

Ernenputsch, John C., subj. of King of Prussia - 6 Aug. 1836

Elsse, Edward, subj. of G.B. - 3 July 1838

Engisch, John, subj. of King of Prussia - 6 Nov. 1838

Eichaker, Daniel, subj. of King of Bavaria - 8 Nov. 1838

Evans, David, subj. of G.B. - 26 Dec. 1838

Ettlinger, George, subj. of Grand Duke of Baden - 25 July 1839

Eschwege, Herz, subj. of Prince of Hesse Cassel - 8 Nov. 1838

Escher, Henry, subj. of Govt. of Zurich, Switzerland - 5 Feb. 1838

Egan, Thomas, subj. of G.B. - 9 Apr. 1839

Erath, Heinrich, subj. of King of Wurtemberg - 2 Dec. 1840

Erath, Aloys, subj. of King of Wurtemberg - 2 Dec. 1840

F

Friell, James, late of parish of Clandavodog, Co. Donegal, Ire., grocer - 4 Dec. 1802

Fitz Gerald, Edmond, late of the South Liberties of city of Cork, grocer - 29 Dec. 1803

Farrel, Edward [report 10 May 1816]: b. town of Kinvarra, Co. of Galway, Ire., age 31, migr. from Dublin, accountant; wife Catherine, b. Woodbridge, N.J., age 26; son Paul, b. New York, age 14 months - 11 May 1816

Fanshawe, John [report 7 Oct. 1817]: b. London, Eng., merchant, age 23, migr. from London - 22 Oct. 1817

Finlay, James, b. town of Belturbett, Co. Cavan, Ire., age 28, migr. from Cork - 10 Oct. 1817

Fabian, William, b. Bristol, Eng., age 24, migr. from Leith, Scotland, baker - 29 Oct. 1817

Floyd, Ebenezer, b. town of Minehead, Somersetshire, Eng., age 27, migr. from Liverpool, mariner - 29 Oct. 1817

Ferguson, John [report 9 July 1818]: b. town of Newtown Ards, Co. Down, age 27, migr. from Belfast - 23 July 1818

Fenan, Felix, b. Co. Armagh, age 25, migr. from Dublin, labourer - 12 Nov. 1818

Fox, James, b. Sheffield, Eng., age 22, migr. from Liverpool, merchant - 24 Dec. 1818

Fell, James, b. London, age 18, migr. from London, ship-carpenter and joiner - 20 Nov. 1818

Franks, Charles, b. Plumtree, Nottinghamshire, Eng., age 24, migr. from Liverpool, farmer, intending to settle in State of Ohio or Indiana Territory - 5 Aug. 1818

Fay, William, b. Dublin, Ire., age 21 - 22 Feb. 1819

Ferguson, Hugh [report 7 Mar. 1820]: b. town of Belfast, Co. Antrim, Ire., age 20, migr. from Belfast, marble cutter - 22 Mar. 1820

Ferguson, Michael [report 7 Mar. 1820]: b. town of Belfast, Co. Antrim, Ire., age 24, migr. from Belfast, house-carpenter - 22 Mar. 1820

Fox, James, subj. of G.B. - 30 Dec. 1820

Farley, James, b. Co. Armagh, Ire., age 44, migr. from Londonderry, cartman - 27 Mar. 1821

Fagan, James [report 12 Apr. 1821]: b. Co. Armagh, age 24, migr. from Newry, farmer - 16 Apr. 1821

Foley, David, b. Co. Waterford, Ire., age 24, migr. from Liverpool, grocer - 16 Apr. 1821

Flanagan, Edward, b. Co. Monaghan, age 30, migr. from Newry, grocer - 16 Apr. 1821

Fagan, Barnard [report 12 Apr. 1821]: b. Co. Armagh, Ire., age 24, migr. from Newry, farmer - 16 Apr. 1821

Fagan, Edward [report 10 Apr. 1821]: b. Co. Down, age 26, migr. from Newry, grocer - 18 Apr. 1821

Friel, Hugh [report 16 May 1820]: b. Newtown Cunningham, Co. Donegal, age 23, migr. from Londonderry, grocer - 28 Apr. 1821

Fitzgerald, Garret [report 7 Apr. 1821]: b. Co. Waterford, Ire., age 41, migr. from Waterford, porter; wife Catherine, b. Co. Waterford, age 30 - 21 May 1821

Fay, Luke [report 16 Apr. 1821]: b. Co. Meath, Ire., age 23, migr. from Dublin, grocer - 24 May 1821

Fitzgerald, James, b. Co. Kilkenny, age 33, migr. from Waterford, bargeman, custom house; wife Margaret, b. Co. Kilkenny, age 29 - 28 May 1821

Farrelly, Bernard, b. Co. Cavan, Ire., age 23, migr. from Dublin, cartman - 29 June 1821

Fechtman, Henry [report 14 May 1821]: b. Bremen, age 34, migr. from London, sugar refiner, subj. of Hanseatic Towns - 22 May 1821

Flynn, Joseph, b. Co. Leitrim, Ire., age 27, migr. from Sligo, merchant - 10 Nov. 1823

Feuillet, Alexander, b. Havre, France, age 34, migr. from Havre, merchant - 20 Feb. 1823

Finnil, Michael [report 6 Jan. 1823]: b. Co. Limerick, Ire., age 21, migr. from Liverpool, labourer - 21 Jan. 1823

Fitzgerald, Garret, b. Youghal, Co. Cork, age 35, migr. from London, grocer - 21 July 1823

Frankpitt, James, b. Cornwall, age 36, migr. from London, mariner; wife Phoebe, b. Yarmouth, Eng., age 37; son Thomas, b. Yarmouth, age 16 - 18 Mar. 1825

Fall, John, b. Co. Roxburgh, Scotland, age 48, migr. from London, caroenter; wife Margaret, b. Co. Norfolk, Eng., age 38; dau. Elleanna, b. Co. Middlesex, Eng., age 16 years and 5 mos.; son William, b. Co. Middlesex, age 13 years and 5 months; dau. Margaret, b. Co. Middlesex, age 9 years and 8 months - 16 June 1825

Fisher, John, b. Dublin, age 44, migr. from Liverpool, butcher; son Thomas, b. Dublin, age 19 - 20 Feb. 1826

Flanley, Hugh, b. Co. Sligo, Ire., as were all his family, ahe 41, migr. from Sligo, cartman; wife Catharine, age 29; son William, age 9; dau. Bridget, age 3 - 27 May 1826

Furey, Patrick, b. Co. Longford, Ire., age 30, migr. from Dublin, gardner - 20 June 1826

Ferreira, Jonquini Ignacio, b. Fayall, Is. of Madeira, age 21, subj. of King of Portugal, gentleman - 21 Aug. 1826

Feany, Cormick [report 5 Feb. 1827]: b. parish of Drumcliff, Co. Sligo, age 33, migr. from Sligo, labourer - 27 Feb. 1827

Fitzsimons, Lawrence [report 6 Aug. 1827]: b. Co. Longford, age 21, migr. from Dublin, labourer - 8 Aug. 1827

Finigin/Finigine, John [report 23 Aug. 1827]: b. Co. Loud [Louth], age 30, migr. from Liverpool, blacksmith - 25 Aug. 1827

Fuller, William, b. Norwich, Eng., age 36, migr. from London, gentleman - 22 Nov. 1827

Friel, John, b. Co. Sligo, age 46, migr. from Sligo, cartman; wife Hannah, b. Co. Sligo, age 44 - 18 Dec. 1827

Ficken, Martin, b. Hanover, age 29, subj. of King of Hanover, migr. from Havre de Grace, sugar refiner - 26 Dec. 1827

Feil, Peter Hinrich [report 11 Feb. 1828]: b. Stode, Hanover, age 31, migr. from Hamburgh, mariner - 19 Feb. 1828

Finnemor, Joseph, b. Co. Fermanagh, Ire., age 29, migr. from Sligo, labourer; wife Elizabeth, b. Eng., age 31; John Holmes, b. Co. Sligo, age 11, son of Elizabeth by a former husband - 21 Feb. 1828

Finin, Roger [report 13 May 1828]: b. Co. Sligo, Ire., age 22, migr. from Belfast, labourer - 19 May 1828

Fannon, Thomas, subj. of G.B. - 31 Oct. 1828

Fay, John Francis [report 14 June 1828]: b. Montloue [?], France, age 44, migr. from Havre, varnish maker - 20 Oct. 1829

Franks, John, grocer, subj. of Govt. of Hamburgh - 24 Mar. 1829

Farrell, Robert, subj. of G.B. - 21 Sept. 1829

Falque, Charles (by his guardian, Wm. Phiquepal), subj. of King of France - 2 Oct. 1829

Fabri, Dolovico, late of Tuscany, subj. of Duke of Tuscany, a designer in plaister - 15 Nov. 1830

Furney, James, of town of Castile, Genesee Co., N.Y., farmer, subj. of G.B. - 21 July 1831

Fiedler, Ernest, merchant, subj. of Hanseatic City of Lubec, Germany - 18 Apr. 1831

Feurst, Daniel Hermann, carpenter, subj. of Republic of Hamburgh - 29 Mar. 1833

Ferrier, James, merchant, subj. of G.B. - 22 July 1833

Fallon, James, labourer, subj. of G.B. - 28 Aug. 1833

Flaherty, John, labourer, subj. of G.B. - 16 Sept. 1833

Flukiger, John, subj. of Canton of Bern, Switzerland - 21 Nov. 1834

Furber, William Thomas Brown, of town of Great Egg Harbor, Gloucester Co., N.J., subj. of G.B. - 5 Dec. 1834

Fustel, Anthony [report 23 Sept. 1826]: b. Coblenz, Prussia, age 32, migr. from London, accountant - 23 Feb. 1836

Fitzsimmons, James, oil cloth manufacturer, subj. of G.B. - 24 Mar. 1836

Fulton, John, subj. of G.B. - 23 Feb. 1836

Flynn, John, shoemaker, subj. of G.B. - 30 June 1837

Fitzgerald, John, of Westchester Co., N.Y., subj. of G.B. - 20 Nov. 1837

Frosh, Anthony Lawrence, subj. of City of Frankfort, Germany - 23 Dec. 1837

Fassall, Christopher, subj. of King of Bavaria - 9 Apr. 1838

Farley, Andrew, subj. of G.B. - 10 Apr. 1838

Flynn, Patrick, subj. of G.B. - 12 Apr. 1838

Friday, Philip Lawrence, subj. of Grand Duke of Hesse Darmstadt
- 28 May 1838

Fierrier, John Peter, subj. of King of France - 28 May 1838

Fraser, John, subj. of G.B. - 11 July 1838

Fenner, Joseph, subj. of Prince of Hesse Cassel - 1 Nov. 1838

Fuller, William, subj. of G.B. - 6 Nov. 1838

Furness, Robert, subj. of G.B. - 7 Nov. 1838

Fecher, Adam, subj. of King of Bavaria - 7 Nov. 1838

Flynn, Augustus, subj. of G.B. - 7 Nov. 1838

Foost, Caspar, subj. of King of Wurtemberg - 14 Nov. 1838

Frank, Peter, subj. of King of Bavaria - 16 Mar. 1839

Farrell, Edward, subj. of G.B. - 9 Apr. 1839

Ford, Elijah, subj. of G.B. - 11 Apr. 1839

Fenelly, Nicholas, subj. of G.B. - 16 Apr. 1839

Fairback, Christian, subj. of Grand Duke of Baden - 6 Nov. 1839

Feist, Michael Charles, subj. of Free City of Frankfort on the
Main - 25 July 1839

Fletcher, James H., subj. of G.B. - 25 Mar. 1840

Farrell, James, subj. of G.B. - 6 Apr. 1840

Finn, John, subj. of G.B. - 15 Sept. 1840

Fadagan, John, subj. of G.B. - 1 Oct. 1840

Fisher, William, subj. of G.B. - 10 Oct. 1840

Faber, John H., subj. of King of Denmark - 12 Oct. 1840

Faber, Adamine, subj. of King of Denmark - 13 Oct. 1840

Finegan, John, printer, subj. of G.B. - 15 Oct. 1840

Freel, James, subj. of G.B. - 26 Oct. 1840

Forsyth, William, subj. of G.B. - 2 Nov. 1840

Folan, Thomas Edward, subj. of G.B. - 2 Nov. 1840

Fishermann, John, subj. of King of Prussia - 24 Dec. 1840

Furlong, Edward, subj. of G.B. - 28 Dec. 1840

Friedmann, Solomon, subj. of King of Bavaria - 20 Oct. 1840

Freyfogel, Jacob F., subj. of King of Prussia - 30 Sept. 1840

G

Gray, John, merchant, subj. of G.B. - 23 July 1802

Gordon, George, late of the parish of Ballymoney, Co. Antrim,
Ire. - 14 Jan. 1803

Grantham, Peter, b. Dublin, age 28, migr. from Ire. - 30 Oct.
1807

Gray, Nicholas, b. Co. Wexford, Ire., age 33, migr. from Ireland
- 25 Oct. 1809 -- same but dated 16 Jan. 1810

Gentil, Pierre Francois, b. Caudebec, France, age 32, migr. from
Martinique - 24 Apr. 1810

Graham, David, b. b. Ballywcki [?], Ire., age 29, migr. from Eng.
24 July 1812

Gildemeister [clerk wrote "Gildermerscher"], Charles A., b. in
Bremen, age 25, subj. of Emperor of France, migr. from Bordeaux - 19 Aug. 1813

Gordon, Hugh Kirk [report 30 Jan. 1816], b. Carrickfergus, [Co.
Antrim], Ire., age 29, migr. from Belfast, printer - 20 Jan.
1817

Geery, James, subj. of G.B. - 24 Apr. 1820

Ginn, John, b. Co. Fermanagh, Ire., as were all others of the
family, age 59, migr. from Londonderry, cartman; wife Elizabeth, age 42; son Arthur, age 24; son James, age 21; son William, age 22; dau. Rose, age 13 - 26 Mar. 1821

Greete, Conrad, b. town of Utrechausen, Germany, age 31, subj.
of King of Germany or Emperor of Austria, migr. from Hamburgh,
cartman - 26 Mar. 1821

Gibson, Wood [report 24 Apr. 1821]: b. Co. Cork, Ire., age 28,
migr. from London, harness maker and tavern-keeper; wife Margaret, b. near Belfast, age 22 - 28 Apr. 1821

Gaffney, Philip, b. Co. Leitrim, Ire., age 24, migr. from Dublin, grocer - 2 May 1821

Gartlan, Thomas, b. Co. Monaghan, age 22, migr. from Liverpool,
grocer - 21 May 1821

Graham, William [report 4 Apr. 1821]: b. Co. Tyrone, Ire., age
27, migr. from Londonderry, cartman - 21 May 1821

Graham, John [report 7 May 1821]: b. Co. Wicklow, Ire., as were
all his family, age 48, migr. from Dublin, grocer; son James,
age 11; dau. Margaret, age 6 - 26 May 1821

Galway, Michael [report 15 May 1821]: b. Co. Wexford, Ire., age
35, migr. from Dublin, labourer; wife Mary, b. Co. Wexford,
age 36 - 26 May 1821

Grogen, Bernard, b. Co. Cavan, Ire., age 37, migr. from Liverpool, wheelwright; wife Ellenor, b. Co. Fermanagh, age 37;
son James, b. Co. Mead [Meath], age 10; dau. Bridget, b. Co.
Cavan, age 8 - 29 June 1821

Gibbons, Francis [report 6 Aug. 1818]: b. parish of St. Andrews,
Holborn, London, age 37, migr. from London, merchant - 17 Aug.
1818

Giesz, Anthony [report 5 Dec. 1821]: b. Dept. of the Lower Rhine,
France, age 34, migr. from Amsterdam, cooper - 17 Dec. 1821

Grimshaw, John, b. Harton, Eng., age 21, migr. from Harton,
merchant - 18 Dec. 1821

Goodwin, John C., b. Derbyshire, Eng., age 27, migr. from Liverpool, butcher; wife Ann, b. Shropshire, age 26; son George
Orion, b. township of Huntington, L.I., age 2 years and 4
months; dau. Maria, b. Huntington, L.I., age 1 year and 4
days - 26 Dec. 1821

Garsed, Edward, b. Leeds, Eng., age 24, migr. from Liverpool,
flax spinner - 26 Mar. 1822

Gamble, Robert, b. Co. Londonderry, Ire., age 28, migr from
Liverpool, sadler; wife Sarah, b. Shropshire, age 37; dau.
Ellen, b. New York, age 4 - 26 Mar. 1822

Garsed, Joshua, b. near Halifax, Yorkshire, Eng., age 51, migr.
from Liverpool, flax spinner; son Joshua, Jr., b. Leeds, age
18 - 26 Mar. 1822

Gilroy, Patrick, b. Co. Leitrim, age 30, migr. Sligo, pedler;
wife Ellena, b. Co. Fermanagh, age 28; son Hugh, Co. Fermanagh, age 8; son James, b. Co. Leitrim, age 5 - 10 July 1822

Grant, William Draper, b. town of Froome [Frome], Somersetshire, Eng., age 40, migr. from Portsmouth, agriculturist, residing in Newburgh, Orange Co., N.Y.; wife Anne, b. Chichester, Sussex, age 38; dau. Esther Jane, b. Co. Cork, Ire., age 14 - 30 Aug. 1822

Gilmartin, John [report 24 Sept. 1822]: b. Co. Sligo, age 41, migr. from Sligo, fruiterer; wife Nancy, b. Co. Sligo, age 30; son Daniel, b. Co. Sligo, age 7; son Thomas, b. New York, age 3; son John, b. New York, age 2; dau. Mary, b. New York, age 5 - 20 Aug. 1825

Gannon, John F., b. Dublin, age 31, migr. from Lisbon, Portugal, grocer - 6 May 1823

Gallivan, James [report 10 Dec. 1823]: b. Co. Waterford, Ire., age 29, migr. from Cork, blacksmith and porter - 10 Dec. 1823

Gorman, Charles, b. Co. Donegal, age 45, migr. from Londonderry, grocer - 8 May 1823

Grace, Henry Jonathan, b. Buckinghamshire, Eng., age 28, migr. from London, farmer, residing in Genessee Co., N.Y. - 23 Jan. 1824

Galles, Jacob Frederick [report 30 May 1825]: b. city of Hamburg, Germany, age 21 years and 5 months, migr. from Hamburg, mariner - 20 June 1825

Galligan, Patrick, b. Co. Cavan, age 20 years and 6 months, migr. from Dublin, labourer (by his guardian, Charles Caffrey) - 29 Aug. 1825

Griffiths, John [report 16 Nov. 1825]: b. North Wales, age 27, migr. from Bangor, brass founder; wife Margaret, b. North Wales, age 35, migr. from Carnavon - 28 Nov. 1825

Grojean, Alexander Jonas (by Francis Arnaud, his guardian) [report 20 Jan. 1826]: b. village of Orvin, Canton of Berne in Switzerland, age 23 years, 3 months and 18 days, migr. from Havre de Grace, cooper - 23 Jan. 1826 - same 30 Oct. 1828

Garden, Anthony A., b. Island of Madeira, age 31, subj. of King of Portugal, migr. from Madeira, waiter - 20 Apr. 1826

Gormley, William, b. Ire., age 27, migr. from Dublin, labourer; wife Catherine, b. Ire., age 25 - 15 May 1826

Gormley, John, b. Ire., age 25, migr. from Dublin, labourer; wife Ann, b. Ire., age 25; son Edward, b. Ire., age 18 months - 15 May 1826

Gaynor, Dennis, b. Kings Co., Ire., age 28, migr. from Dublin, grocer; wife Mary, b. Ire., age 28 - 20 June 1826

Gallagher, Daniel [report 31 May 1826]: b. Co. Donegal, Ire., age 25, migr. from Londonderry, teacher - 28 June 1826

Gräsle, Gottlieb, b. village of Grosgartach, Wertemberg, age 33, migr. from Amsterdam, butcher - 25 July 1826

Goodall, James, b. Co. Wexford, Ire., age 26, migr. from Dublin, via Liverpool, farmer - 18 Dec. 1826

Green, John, b. Co. Tipperary, Ire., age 30, migr. from Waterford, labourer - 18 Dec. 1826

Gilles, Narie Pierre, b. Paris, France, age 44, migr. from Havre, professor of music - 28 Apr. 1827

Gariahan, Peter, b. Co. Longford, Ire., age 29, migr. from Ire., labourer; dau. Catharin, b. Ulster Co., N.Y., age 7 months - 22 May 1827

Gaffney, Dennis B., b. City of Dublin, Ire., age 26, migr. from Dublin, student-at-law - 27 May 1827

Gilgan, John, subj. of G.B. - 17 Mar. 1829

Gleeson [clerk wrote "Glaason"], John, b. Lower Ormond, Co. Tipperary, Ire., age 21, migr. from Dublin, cartman - 18 Mar. 1828

Greenleaf, John, b. Stockholm, Sweden, age 37, migr. from Stockholm, mariner - 30 Apr. 1828

Gravillon, Jean Claude Auguste, subj. of King of France - 27 Apr. 1830

Gaffney, Charles, labourer, subj. of G.B. - 23 May 1831

Gormlay, James, subj. of G.B. - 7 June 1831

Gooch, John, subj. of G.B. - 19 Sept. 1831

Goodall, John, subj. of G.B. - 17 Sept. 1831

Gildemeester, Hugo C., merchant, subj. of King of the Netherlands - 19 Sept. 1831

Goodin, William, subj. of G.B. - 26 Apr. 1832

Griffith, John, subj. of G.B.; rec. by James M. Tuthill - 20 July 1832

Grimme, Charles A., shoemaker, subj. of Prince of Schaumburgh - 8 Oct. 1832

Guinan, Lack, subj. of G.B. - 2 Nov. 1832

Gutmann, Joseph, subj. of Leopold, Grand Duke of Baden - 4 Dec. 1832

Glästein, Berend [clerk wrote "Bernard"], starch maker, subj. of King of Hanover - 18 June 1833

Graham, William, labourer, subj. of G.B. - 10 Apr. 1834

Greenacre, James, subj. of G.B. - 1 July 1834

Griffin, Thomas, subj. of G.B., mariner - 4 Aug. 1834

Goep, Philip Henry, late of Prussia - 25 Sept. 1834

Gignoux, Claudius, merchant, subj. of King of France - 27 Dec. 1834

Grunenthal, William Theodore, merchant, subj. of King of Prussia - 24 Feb. 1835

Gentner, Philip, subj. of King of Wurtemberg - 1 Apr. 1836

Gillick, James, labourer, subj. of G.B. - 5 Apr. 1836

Goodman, William, subj. of G.B.; rec. by Samuel Thompson, of Brooklyn, merchant - 22 Sept. 1836

Galbraith, James, gardiner, subj. of G.B. - 8 Aug. 1836

Gillan, William, miller, subj. of G.B. - 6 Nov. 1837

Gallwey, James, subj. of G.B. - 15 Dec. 1837

Gilmartin, Felix, subj. of G.B. - 31 Mar. 1838

Gorgens, Charles, subj. of Duke of Brunswick - 9 Apr. 1838

Gorman, William, subj. of G.B. - 11 Apr. 1838

Goodman, Samuel, subj. of G.B. - 12 Apr. 1838

Green, Isaac, subj. of G.B. - 23 Apr. 1838

Gaunt, James, subj. of G.B. - 4 Oct. 1838

Gow, David, subj. of G.B. - 10 Oct. 1838

Gniewkoski, Anthony, subj. of Emperor of Russia - 18 Oct. 1838

Giles, Edward, subj. of G.B. - 3 Nov. 1838

Gibbs, John, subj. of G.B. - 3 Nov. 1838

Graham, James, subj. of G.B. - 5 Nov. 1838

Gaffney, Patrick, subj. of G.B. - 6 Nov. 1838

Garnel, Michael, subj. of G.B. - 6 Nov. 1838

Gelshenen, William, subj. of G.B. - 7 Nov. 1838

Grusemeyer, George, subj. of King of France - 7 Nov. 1838

Gerken, Hermann, subj. of King of Hanover - 7 Nov. 1838

Grant, Thomas, subj. of G.B. - 30 Nov. 1838

Graham, John, subj. of G.B. - 10 Dec. 1838

Geller, Peter, subj. of King of Prussia - 6 Feb. 1839

Grimme, Henry Augustus, subj. of Prince of Schaumburgh - 13 Feb. 1839

Graham, James, subj. of G.B. - 7 Mar. 1839

Gibson, John, subj. of G.B. - 12 Mar. 1839

Gilbert, Charles, subj. of G.B. - 3 Apr. 1839

Gray, William, subj. of G.B. - 11 Apr. 1839

Graham, James, subj. of G.B. - 14 May 1839

Girod, Abraham Louis, subj. of Republic of Switzerland - 25 May 1839

Galvin, Dennis, subj. of G.B. - 12 June 1839

Gillen, Dennis, subj. of G.B. - 27 June 1839

Gaze, John C., subj. of G.B. - 8 July 1839

Gillin, Daniel, subj. of G.B. - 18 July 1839

Gavin, Thomas, subj. of G.B. - 25 July 1839

Gibney, Patrick, subj. of G.B. - 31 July 1839

Goodwin, Thomas, subj. of G.B. - 12 Aug. 1839

Garrard, William H., subj. of G.B. - 5 Nov. 1839

Gross, Lewis, subj. of King of Bavaria - 5 Nov. 1839

Gillick, Joseph, of East Wareham, Mass., subj. of G.B. - 9 Mar. 1840

Gwinner, John A., subj. of G.B. - 3 Apr. 1840

Gerhardt, Frederick, subj. of King of Saxony - 13 Apr. 1840

Gastman, Eilt Jansen, subj. of King of Hanover - 13 Apr. 1840

Gawronski, Leon, subj. of Emperor of Russia - 29 May 1840

Grandgerard, Joseph, subj. of King of France - 2 July 1840

Gerst, Henry P., subj. of King of Bavaria - 11 Aug. 1840

Germer, Ludolph, cabinetmaker, subj. of King of Hanover - 16 Sept. 1840

Gait, Sydenham, subj. of G.B. - 3 Oct. 1840

Greenwood, William, subj. of G.B. - 6 Oct. 1840

Glynn, Patrick, subj. of G.B. - 6 Oct. 1840

Garrigan, Patrick, subj. of G.B. - 10 Oct. 1840

Goehl, Henry, subj. of Prince of Hesse Cassel - 10 Oct. 1840

Gaffney, Thomas, subj. of G.B. - 12 Oct. 1840

Gensler, Lewis, subj. of King of Prussia - 12 Oct. 1840

Greene, Edward, subj. of G.B. - 13 Oct. 1840

Gray, Richard K., subj. of G.B. - 16 Oct. 1840

Gillen, Ambrose, subj. of G.B. - 17 Oct. 1840

Green, James, subj. of G.B. - 26 Oct. 1840

Green, John, subj. of G.B. - 26 Oct. 1840

Geary, James, subj. of G.B. - 2 Nov. 1840

Gallagher, John, subj. of G.B. - 3 Nov. 1840

Gottlieb, Frederick William, subj. of King of Prussia - 3 Nov.
  1840

Gibbs, Joseph, subj. of G.B. - 3 Nov. 1840

Gormley, Philip, subj. of G.B. - 3 Nov. 1840

Gibbs, John Jones, subj. of G.B. - 3 Nov. 1840

Gos, Henry, subj. of Duke of Hesse Castle [sic!] - 11 Nov. 1840

Gannon, John, subj. of G.B. - 4 Dec. 1840

H

Hogan, Michael, subj. of G.B. - 29 Jan. 1808

Hewett, Josephus, subj. of G.B. - 27 June 1812

Hill, Isaac, of Onondaga Co., N.Y., subj. of G.B. - 25 May 1815

Hornblower, Ebenezer, b. Braintree, Essex Co., Eng., age 27,
  migr. from Canada, merchant - 18 July 1815

Howell, David [report 26 Aug. 1817]: b. Pambrook [Pembroke],
  South Wales, age 47, migr. from London, cabinetmaker, intending
  to remove to Western Territory of U.S. - 30 Aug. 1817

Harrison, William [report 6 Feb. 1818]: b. Church Hill, Co. Monaghan, age 55, migr. from Cork, steamboat steward - 16 Feb.
  1818

Harley, Thomas [report 16 Mar. 1818]: b. Co. of Leicester, Eng.,
  age 30; migr. from Liverpool, cabinetmaker; wife Elizabeth, b.
  Co. Leicester, age 22; son Frederick, b. Co. Leicester, age 2
  - 17 Mar. 1818

Humphreys, Humphrey [report 16 Mar. 1818]: b. Manchester, Lancaster Co., Eng., age 32, migr. from Liverpool, age 33 - 17 Mar.
  1818

Hurley, William, b. parish of Tiverton, Devonshire, age 38, migr.
  from London, morocco finisher; wife Rebecca, b. city of West-
  minster, Devonshire, age 41; dau. Elizabeth, p. parish of St.
  Olives, Surrey, age 12; son Samuel, b. parish of Bermondsey,
  Surrey, age 2 - 27 Apr. 1818

Hayward, James, b. town of Watlington, Co. of Oxford, Eng., age
  21, migr. from Liverpool, gentleman, intending to settle in
  Illinois Territory - 8 June 1818

Hackett, James [report 6 July 1818]: b. Co. Kildare, Ire., age
  42, migr. from Liverpool, tobacconist - 21 Oct. 1818

Hardey, George Newman, b. parish of Bowdon, Chester Co., Eng.,
  age 38, migr. from London, merchant - 23 July 1818

Hume, James [report 9 Oct. 1818]: b. Sligo, Ire., age 23, migr.
  from Sligo, merchant - 23 Oct. 1818

Harrison, Andrew, b. Co. Monaghan, Ire., age 26, migr. from
   Newry, waterman - 6 Nov. 1818

Hughes, Philip, b. Co. Armagh, Ire., age 27, migr. from Liverpool, porter; wife Ann, b. Co. Armagh, age 21, migr. from
   Newry; dau. Maria, b. Liverpool, age 3, migr. from Newry; son
   Patrick, b. Co. Armagh, age 5, migr. from Newry - 12 Nov.
   1818

Husson, Joseph [report 10 Mar. 1819: b. France, age 46, migr.
   from France, grocer - 15 Mar. 1819

Hancock, Thomas John, b. London, age 33, migr. from London, sadler, harness and Collar maker - 5 Oct. 1819

Hupeden, Augustus William [report 8 Oct. 1819]: b. Hoya, Hanover, age 21, migr. from Bremen, merchant - 18 Oct. 1819

Higginson, John Henry (by his guardian, George Hodgson, grocer),
   b. town of Lisburn, Co. Antrim, age 20, migr. from Belfast,
   sadler - 2 July 1816

Hazleton, Edward [report 10 Apr. 1821]: b. Co. Tyrone, age 30,
   migr. from Belfast, grocer; wife Rachel, b. Co. Armagh, age
   25 - 20 Apr. 1821

Henrietty, Bernard, b. Co. Monaghan, age 35, migr. from Newry,
   grocer - 20 Apr. 1821

Hurford, John, b. Devonshire, Eng., age 30, migr. from Bristol,
   labourer; wife Elizabeth, b. Somersetshire, age 30; dau. Sarah
   Ellen, b. city of Bristol, Eng., age 5 - 23 Apr. 1821

Haren [or Harer?], Andrew, b. Co. Donegal, age 72, migr. from
   Londonderry, grocer - 23 Apr. 1821

Hylen, Nicholas, b. Co. Tipperary, Ire., age 37, migr. from
   Waterford, sawyer; wife Elizabeth, b. Co. Down, age 30 - 25
   Apr. 1821

Hope, Cornelius, b. Sheppy Island, Co. of Kent, Eng., age 44,
   migr. from London, seaman; wife Elizabeth, b. Liverpool, age
   43; son Cornelius, b. Sheppy Island, age 20; son John, b. Sheppy Island, age 14; son James, b. Sheppy Island, age 10; dau.
   Sarah Jane, b. Sheppy Island, age 17 - 28 Apr. 1821

Hunt, Joseph, b. city of Dublin, age 34, migr. from Dublin, grocer - 4 May 1821

Henrietta, Peter, b. Co. Monaghan, Ire., age 31, migr. from
   Newry, grocer; wife Bridget, b. Co. Armagh, age 28 - 9 May
   1821

Heffernan, John [report 8 May 1821]: b. Co. Tipperary, age 27,
   migr. from Limerick, grocer - 22 May 1821

Hall, Richard, b. Daventry, North Hampton, Eng., age 29, migr.
   from London, husbandman - 14 Nov. 1816

Hall, Frederick [report 14 Nov. 1816]: b. parish of Braunston,
   Co. of North Hampshire, age 31, migr. from London, husbandman
   - 18 Nov. 1816

Hall, Henry Long [report 14 Nov. 1816]: b. parish of Braunston,
   Co. of North Hampshire, age 26, migr. from London, linen draper - 18 Nov. 1816

Hall, Thomas [report 14 Nov. 1816]: b. parish of Braunston, Co.
   of North Hamptonshire, age 33, migr. from London, husbandman
   - 18 Nov. 1816

Hardy, Thomas [report 12 June 1821]: b. Co. Kilkenny, age 24,
   migr. from Ire., quarryman - 24 May 1827

Herne, Patrick, b. Co. Cork, Ire., age 32, migr. from Cork, porter - 27 Mar. 1821

Hardy, William [report 10 Apr. 1821]: b. Co. of Durham, Eng.,
age 44, migr. from London, grocer - 20 Apr. 1821

Hanan, Henry, b. Co. Cork, age 37, migr. from Cork, grocer - 16
Apr. 1821

Hamilton, Henry [report 2 Apr. 1821]: b. Co. Wexford, Ire., age
47, migr. from Dublin, cartman - 17 Apr. 1821

Hanley, Henry [report 2 Apr. 1821]: b. Co. Roscommon, Ire., age
38, migr. from Cork, porter - 16 Apr. 1821

Hopkins, John, b. Bremen, age 35, migr. from London, sugar baker
- 22 May 1821

Harrison, William [report 11 June 1821]: b. Co. Monaghan, age 23,
migr. from Liverpool, accountant - 22 June 1821

Hughes, Philip, subj. of G.B. - 17 Sept. 1821

Hart, Abraham [report 12 May 1821]: b. town of Wesel, Germany,
age 43, migr. from Amsterdam, grocer - 22 May 1821

Harr, John M. [report 12 Oct. 1821]: b. "Whertembergh" in Germany, age 46, migr. from Amsterdam, storekeeper; wife Henrietta,
b. Belleburgh, Germany, age 35 - 15 Oct. 1821

Hunt, Mathew, b. Co. Kilkenny, Ire., age 36, migr. from Waterford, waterman; wife Margaret, b. Co. Wexford, Ire., age 33;
son John, b. New York, age 10; dau. Mary, b. New York, age 8;
dau. Emily Cornelia, b. New York, age 6; Ann Henrietta, b. New
York, age 18 months - 21 Jan. 1822

Harris, George, b. Olbury, Shropshire, age 24, migr. from Liverpool, whitesmith - 26 Dec. 1822

Harrington, John [report 4 Dec. 1821]: b. Co. Cork, Ire., age
40, migr. from Cove of Cork, cartman; wife Mary, b. Co. Cork,
age 40; dau. Catherine, b. Co. Cork, age 12 - 2 Jan. 1822

Henderson, Samuel [report 10 Apr. 1821]: b. Co. Tyrone, Ire.,
age 32, migr. from Londonderry, cartman - 28 Feb. 1822

Hardy, William H., b. Birmingham, Eng., age 34, migr. from Liverpool, merchant - 31 Jan. 1823

Hughes, John, b. Co. Down, Ire., migr. from London, tanner; wife
Catherine, b. Co. Monaghan, age 30; their son Edward, b. Philadelphia, age 3; Patrick McKernon, son of Catherine and stepson
to John Hughes, b. Ire., age 12 - 17 Mar. 1823

Hettrich, Conrad [report 30 July 1823]: b. village of Nidder-
germt [?], near Wetzlar in Germany, age 49, migr. from Bremen,
gardner, subj. of the Govt. of the Germanic Confederation - 31
July 1823

Hickey, William, b. Co. Wexford, Ire., age 25, migr. from Dublin,
labourer; wife Mary, b. Co. Waterford, age 26; son James, b.
New York, age 6; dau. Bridget, b. New York, age 5 - 10 Apr.
1823

Haviland, Bernard [report 10 Nov. 1823]: b. Londonderry Co., Ire.,
age 21, migr. from Londonderry, pedlar - 21 Nov. 1823

Haviland, Bartholomew, b. Co. Londonderry, age 25, migr. from
Londonderry, pedlar - 10 Nov. 1823

Henderson, James (by James Rooney, his guardian), b. Co. Monoghan,
age 13, migr. from Dublin - 14 Nov. 1823

Hodgins, James, b. Co. Tipperary, age 21, migr. from Neahan[?],
Ire., cartman - 27 Feb. 1824

Harries, John William [report 22 Apr. 1824]: b., as were all of
the family, at Carmarthen, Wales, age 23, migr. from Liverpool, farmer; wife Mary, age 34; son Thomas, age 11; son John,
age 9; son David, age 7; son William, age 5; dau. Ann, age 3
- 23 Apr. 1824

Higgs, William, b. Co. Middlesex, Eng., age 35, migr. from London, hatmaker; wife Mary Ann, b. Co. Middlesex, age 35; son
William, b. Co. Middlesex, age 3 - 28 June 1824

Hoyt, Cornelius [report 28 Feb. 1825]: b. Dublin, age 27, migr.
from Dublin, grocer; wife Ann, b. Co. Roscommon, age 25 - 2
Mar. 1825

Hughs, William [report 4 Apr. 1825]: b. Co. Monaghan, Ire., age
27, migr. from Belfast, ropemaker - 18 Apr. 1825

Hay, James, Jr., b. Scotland, age 34, migr. from New Brunswick,
Nova Scotia, merchant; wife Rebecca, b. New Brunswick, age 28;
son James, b. New Brunswick, age 11; son Thomas H., b. New
Brunswick, age 8; dau. Ann, b. NYC, age 10; dau. Mary W., b.
New Brunswick, age 3 - 27 Apr. 1825

Hencken, George [report 29 Apr. 1825]: b. Kingdom of Hanover,
age 30, migr. from Bremen, sugar baker - 30 Apr. 1825

Heaney, William [report 9 May 1825]: b., like all the family, Co.
Longford, Ire., age 28, migr. from Dublin, labourer; wife Mary,
age 28; son James, age 2 years and 6 months - 16 May 1825

Henckenn, Johann [report 8 July 1825]: b. village of Siven, Hanover, age 23, migr. from London, sugar baker - 27 Mar. 1826

Hutton, Robert [report 17 Oct. 1825]: b. St. Johns, Newfoundland,
age 30, migr. from St. Johns and Port Glasgow, Scotland,
merchant - 22 Oct. 1825

Healy, James [report 20 Dec. 1825]: b., as all the family, Co.
Leitrem, Ire., age 41, migr. from Sligo, grocer; wife Catharine,
age 35; dau. Anne, age 12; dau. Mary, age 10; son James, age 6
years and 10 months - 22 Dec. 1825

Harrison, John, b. Liverpool, age 42, migr. from Liverpool, ship-
carpenter; wife Mary, b. NYC, age 32 - 20 Feb. 1826

Haycock, Hamilton [report 10 Apr. 1826]: b. Co. Sligo, Ire., age
24, migr. from Sligo, labourer - 11 Apr. 1826

Harman, Joseph S. [report 17 Aug. 1826]: b. Grodno, Russian Poland, age 29, migr. from Liverpool, merchant, subj. of Emperor
of Russia - 25 Aug. 1826

Hunter, James, b. Londonderry, Ire., age 23, migr. from Londonderry, grocer - 15 Jan. 1827

Henriques, Joseph, b. Island of Jamaica, like all of family, age
48, migr. from Jamaica, merchant; wife Abigail, age 42; son
Moses Joseph, age 16; dau. Abigail, age 14; son Aaron Joseph,
age 9; dau. Leah Lemira, age 4; son Joseph Augustin, age about
2 - 19 Jan. 1826 - "oath not taken"

Henriques, Moses, b. London, Eng., age 42, migr. from Island of
Jamaica, merchant; wife Sarah, b., as all their children, at
Kingston, Jamaica, age 27; son Jacob M., 19; son George M.,
age 15; son David M., age 9; son Alexander M., age 8; dau.
Rachel M., age 6; dau. Julia M., age 2; son Joseph M., age 7
months - 19 Jan. 1826

Henriques, David, b. Kingston, like all of family, age 23, migr.
from Kingston, merchant; wife Esther, age 33; dau. Abigail,
age 11; son Moses, age 8; dau. Rebecca, age 7; son Aaron, age
5; son Alexander, age 4; dau. Eugenia, age 2 - 23 Jan. 1826

Henderson, Thomas, b. Co. Fermanagh, Ire., age 46, migr. from Belfast, dry good merchant - 10 Mar. 1827

Hillsburgh, Charles, b. town of Gottenburg, Sweden, age 24 on 2 Apr. 1826, migr. from Gottenburg, plumber - 20 Mar. 1827

Herbit, Michael (by his guardian, Zebediah Tucker), b. Bordeaux, France, mariner apprentice, intending to settle in town of Addison, Maine - 28 Mar. 1827

Hayes, James [report 23 Apr. 1827]: b. Co. Waterford, Ire., age 25, migr. from Waterford, porter - 24 Apr. 1827

Heilbronn, Adolph, b. Hanover, Lower Saxony, age 32, migr. from Hamburgh, via London, merchant - 30 May 1827

Healey, Patrick, b. Co. Roscommon, age 23, migr. from Liverpool, labourer; wife Bridget, b. Co. Roscommon, age 25; dau. Ann, b. Co. Roscommon, age 3 - 29 Dec. 1827

Hall, Thomas [report 10 Jan. 1828]: b. Co. Carlow, Ire., age 30, migr. from Dublin, cartman; wife Eliza, b. Co. Down, age 35 - 12 Jan. 1828

Horrocks, Richard, b. Bolton, Eng., age 26, migr. from Liverpool, mason; wife Betty, b. Bolton, age 25 - 22 Jan. 1828

Hacket, Mathew, b. Fantourra [?], Co. Tyrone, age 19 years and 8 months, migr. from Belfast, hack driver - 17 Mar. 1828

Holton, William, clerk, subj. of G.B. - 27 Sept. 1828

Harrison, Joseph, minister, subj. of G.B. - 21 Dec. 1829

Hyland, William, formerly of Kilbride, Queens Co., Ire., carriage driver - 23 Jan. 1830

Hope, John, late of Yorkshire, Eng., merchant - 25 Mar. 1830

Howrigan, Patrick, labourer, subj. of G.B. - 30 Sept. 1830

Harned, Patrick, subj. of G.B. - 15 Oct. 1838

Heerwagen, Elias G., late of Bavaria, cooper - 18 Apr. 1831

Haggart, James, accountant, subj. of G.B. - 17 Sept. 1832

Hilgard, Theodore, farmer, subj. of King of Bavaria - 29 Mar. 1833

Hagerthy, Timothy, distiller, subj. of G.B. - 24 June 1833

Heimberger, Carl Gustav, farmer, subj. of King of Bavaria - 29 Mar. 1833

Hale, Thomas, merchant, subj. of G.B. - 29 Apr. 1834

Hudson, Thomas, tailor, subj. of G.B. - 1 May 1834

Harrison, Andrew, tavern-keeper, subj. of G.B. - 3 Nov. 1834

Hollywood, Patrick, tailor, subj. of G.B. - 5 Nov. 1834

Hawkesworth, James, gentleman, subj. of G.B. - 19 Nov. 1834

Hamilton, James, subj. of G.B. - 16 Dec. 1834

Higgins, Hugh, subj. of G.B. - 20 Apr. 1835

Hislop, Andrew, gardner, subj. of G.B. - 22 July 1835

Hetzel, John Jacob, furrier, subj. of Grand Duke of Baden - 4 Nov. 1835

Hetzel, Charles Francis, furrier, subj. of Grand Duke of Baden - 4 Nov. 1835

Heinemann, Johann Adam, subj. of Prince of Hesse Cassel - 12 Apr. 1836

Harris, William, cabinetmaker, subj. of G.B. - 5 Aug. 1836

Hollis, Lawrence M., subj. of G.B. - 29 Aug. 1836

Hart, John, of Channingville, Dutchess Co., N.Y., subj. of G.B. - 26 Sept. 1836

Hirlemann, George, butcher, subj. of King of France - 24 Oct. 1836

Hepp, Jacob, baker, subj. of King of Bavaria - 13 Jan. 1837

Hesler, Peter, subj. of G.B. - 13 Apr. 1837

Hughes, Edward, subj. of G.B. - 15 May 1837

Hennessy, Philip, subj. of G.B. - 29 May 1837

Harrington, Patrick, subj. of G.B. - 29 May 1837

Hoffstrom, Alexander, of Thomastown, Maine, subj. of Emperor of Russia - 20 June 1837

Hasel, Frederick Augustus, subj. of King of Hanover - 7 Sept. 1837

Harkin, Michael, subj. of G.B. - 17 Oct. 1837

Herken, Edward, subj. of G.B. - 30 Dec. 1837

Hanker, John Henry, subj. of King of Hanover - 9 Apr. 1838

Herrmann, Christopher Frederick, subj. of King of Wurtemberg - 9 Apr. 1838

Henkel, Philipp, subj. of Prince of Hesse Cassel - 11 Apr. 1838

Hastett, Henry, subj. of King of Hanover - 12 Apr. 1838

Hutchinson, Alexander, subj. of G.B. - 12 May 1838

Hinrichs, Carl Ernst Louis, subj. of Republic of Hamburgh - 1 Oct. 1838

Henderson, Robert, subj. of G.B. - 5 Nov. 1838

Henderson, Joseph, subj. of G.B. - 5 Nov. 1838

Humphrey, John, subj. of G.B. - 5 Nov. 1838

Hurley, James, subj. of G.B. - 5 Nov. 1838

Hackett, John, subj. of G.B. - 7 Nov. 1838

Hill, James H., subj. of G.B. - 7 Nov. 1838

Hannah, Daniel, subj. of G.B. - 7 Nov. 1838

Horn, Charles E., subj. of G.B. - 12 Dec. 1838

Hampton, Joseph, subj. of G.B. - 24 Dec. 1838

Hauser, Emmanuel, subj. of King of France - 8 Apr. 1839

Hoffmann, Michael, subj. of King of Bavaria - 10 Apr. 1839

Hartmann, Jacob, subj. of King of Bavaria - 8 Apr. 1839

Henn, Peter, subj. of King of Bavaria - 1 Jan. 1839

Henn, Karel, subj. of King of Bavaria - 1 Jan. 1839

Herring, Honora Victorine (wife of William C. Herring), subj. of G.B. - 6 Mar. 1839

Harry, Philip, subj. of G.B. - 13 Mar. 1839

Hunt, Owen, subj. of G.B. - 15 Mar. 1839

Hindhaugh, William, subj. of G.B. - 16 Mar. 1839

Hill, James, subj. of G.B. - 5 Apr. 1839

Humphreys, Owen, subj. of G.B. - 6 Apr. 1839

Hamilton, Francis, subj. of G.B. - 9 Apr. 1839

Halliday, George, subj. of G.B. - 9 Apr. 1839

Hart, James, subj. of G.B. - 12 Apr. 1839

Hughes, James, subj. of G.B. - 12 Apr. 1839

Hart, John, subj. of G.B. - 12 Apr. 1839

Hewer, Benjamin, Jr., subj. of G.B. - 6 May 1839

Heber, Augustus J., subj. of Republic of Switzerland - 14 June 1839

Hendricksen, William, subj. of King of Denmark - 26 July 1839

Hamilton, John, subj. of G.B. - 5 Aug. 1839

Haase, John, subj. of G.B. - 8 Aug. 1839

Hemmerling, Etienne Philipp, subj. of the Free Cantons of Switzerland - 11 Oct. 1839

Harvey, James, subj. of G.B. - 31 Oct. 1839

Hinds, David, subj. of G.B. - 4 Nov. 1839

Hinds, James, subj. of G.B. - 4 Nov. 1839

Hunter, Henry J., subj. of G.B. - 4 Nov. 1839

Hammer, John Michael, subj. of King of Bavaria - 6 Nov. 1839

Henriken, Jacob, subj. of King of Bavaria - 9 Nov. 1839

Hughes, Edward, subj. of G.B. - 13 Feb. 1840

Harvey, William Harding, subj. of G.B. - 30 Mar. 1840

Hinrichs, Charles F.A., subj. of Grand Duke of Oldenburgh - 28 Mar. 1840

Hilliker, James, subj. of G.B. - 1 Apr. 1840

Hooker, Stephen, subj. of G.B. - 13 Apr. 1840

Hall, Edward, subj. of G.B. - 14 Apr. 1840

Hanlan, Michael, subj. of G.B. - 13 June 1840

Hoare, James, subj. of G.B. - 27 July 1840

Henderson, George, subj. of G.B. - 17 Aug. 1840

Hyde, John, subj. of G.B. - 16 Sept. 1840

Hulcen, Michael, subj. of King of Bavaria - 2 Oct. 1840

Hamilton, William, subj. of G.B. - 6 Oct. 1840

Horsin, Peter, subj. of G.B. - 13 Oct. 1840

Hiscox, Richard, subj. of G.B. - 16 Oct. 1840

Herbrich, Valentine, subj. of Grand Duke of Baden - 17 Oct. 1840

Hamill, Henry, subj. of G.B. - 17 Oct. 1840

Hudson, James, subj. of G.B. - 19 Oct. 1840

Hickman, James, subj. of G.B. - 19 Oct. 1840

Hayne, John, subj. of G.B. - 20 Oct. 1840

Height, William, subj. of G.B. - 21 Oct. 1840

Heley, Richard, subj. of G.B. - 26 Oct. 1840

Hunt, James, Sr., subj. of G.B. - 2 Nov. 1840

Hannigan, Terry, subj. of G.B. - 3 Nov. 1840

Hutchinson, William, subj. of G.B. - 31 Dec. 1840

Hurley, Thomas, subj. of G.B. - 31 Dec. 1840

Hurley, Michael, subj. of G.B. - 31 Dec. 1840

Hurley, Patrick, subj. of G.B. - 31 Dec. 1840

I

Irish, Charles, watchmaker, subj. of G.B. - 27 June 1812

Irish, William Augustus, b. Portsmouth, Hampshire, Eng., age 21, migr. from Portsmouth, mariner - 28 Apr. 1818

Ingham, Thomas [report 5 June 1819]: b. Betthurbed, Co. Cavan, Ire., sge 47, migr. from Dublin; wife Jane, b. Brtthurbed, age 40; son Thomas, b. Dublin, age 18; dau. Florence, b. Dublin, age 16; dau. Mary, b. Dublin, age 14; son Sidney, b. Dublin, age 13; son John W., b. Dublin, age 12; son Oscar, b. Dublin, age 10; dau. Augusta, b. Dublin, age 7; dau. Jane, b. Dublin, age 4 - 24 June 1819

Ingham, Thomas, Jr. [report 28 July 1819]: b. Dublin, age 22, migr. from Dublin, cabinetmaker - 18 June 1821

Irvine, Thomas Washington [report 15 Feb. 1825]: b. on board ship Mars of Liverpool in St. George's Channell, age 32, migr. from Belfast, bricklayer, intending to reside in NYC or Charleston, S.C. - 7 Mar. 1825

Isaac, James [report 3 Apr. 1827]: b. Co. of Hampshire, Eng., age 39, migr. from Liverpool, house-painter - 17 Apr. 1827

Ireland, William M., b. Devonshire, Eng., age 48, migr. from London, physician - 22 May 1828

Irvin, Richard, merchant, subj. of G.B. - 26 Oct. 1829

Ince, George, gentleman, subj. of G.B. - 18 Mar. 1830

Irvin, James, subj. of G.B. - 2 Mar. 1833

Inshaw, Joseph, subj. of G.B. - 1 May 1838

Isaacs, Moses, subj. of G.B. - 19 Dec. 1840

Irvin, James, subj. of G.B. - 27 May 1830

J

Johnston, William John, b. Dumfries, Scotland, age 30, migr. from Cork, arrived NYC in Nov. 1802 - 21 Dec. 1805

Jones, George, b. Kidderminster, Worcester Co., Eng., age 33, migr. from Liverpool, tallow chandler, intending to settle in State of New York or State of Ohio - 26 Sept. 1817

Jones, George, b. London, as rest of family, age 30, migr. from London, blacking manufacturer, intending to settle in Boston; wife Mary, age 35; son George, age 9; son Richard T., age 4; dau. Mary Ann, age 7 - 25 Feb. 1818

Jeffery, John, b. Dover, Eng., age 22, migr. from Bristol, mariner - 10 Oct. 1818

Jennings, Solomon [report 15 Feb. 1821]: b. Halifax, Nova Scotia, age 35, migr. from Halifax, mariner; wife Mary, b. NYC, age 30; dau. Mary Ann, b. Halifax, age 9; son James William, b. Halifax, age 7; son Solomon George, b. Halifax, age 5 - 31 Mar. 1821

Jefferys, Michael [report 4 Apr. 1821]: b. Yorkshire, Eng., age 28, migr. from Liverpool, tailor; wife Sarah, b. Yorkshire, age 27 years and 6 months - 18 Apr. 1821

Jouy, Peter Louis [report 11 Apr. 1821]: b. Carcassonne, Dept. of the Oder, France, age 39, migr. from Bordeaux, grocer - 19 Apr. 1821

Johnston, William, b. Co. Kirkcudbright, Scotland, age 21, migr. from Greenock, merchant - 27 Oct. 1821

Johnston, Robert (by William Johnston, his guardian) [report 27 Oct. 1821]: b. Co. Kirkcudbright, age 17, migr. from Liverpool, accountant - 29 Oct. 1821

Jacobs, John [report 15 Apr. 1822]: b. Co. Surrey, Eng., age 49, migr. from London, milkman; wife Catherine, b. London, age 38; dau. Rachel, b. London, age 18; dau. Mary, b. London, age 17 - 16 Apr. 1822

Jenkins, Richard, b. Shropshire, Eng., age 30, migr. from Bradford in Wiltshire, merchant - 21 Jan. 1823

Jackson, John, b. Warwickshire, Eng., age 48, migr. from Bristol, storekeeper; wife Ann, b. Staffordshire, age 40; dau. Sarah, b. Staffordshire, age 20 - 18 Feb. 1823

James, James [report 16 Apr. 1823]: b. Co. Carmarthen, South Wales, age 37, migr. from town of Carmarthen, grocer; wife Elizabeth, b. Co. Pembroke, South Wales, age 42 - 23 Apr. 1823

Jackson, John A., b. Otley, Yorkshire, Eng., age 28, migr. from Liverpool, ropemaker - 29 Oct. 1824

Jones, David, b. Co. of Gloucester, Eng., age 62, migr. from Bristol, mason - 2 Dec. 1825

Jonas, James [report 3 Apr. 1827]: b. Co. Sussex, Eng., age 36, migr. from Portsmouth, sawyer; wife Fanny, b. Co. Sussex, age 29; son James, Jr., b. Co. Sussex, age 11; son John, b. Co. Sussex, age 9; dau. Sarah Ann, b. Co. Sussex, age 6; dau. Mary Elizabeth, b. NYC, age 1 year and 6 months - 18 Apr. 1827

Joyce, David [report 30 May 1828]: b. Co. Cork, Ire., age 36, migr. from Waterford, boot- and shoemaker - 30 Dec. 1830

Jachimsen, Louis, bookseller, subj. King of the Belgians - 25 June 1832

Jackson, Francis Blower, student-at-law, subj. of G.B. - 29 Oct. 1833

Jaclard, Sebastien, wigmaker, subj. of King of France - 28 Jan. 1834

Jones, William, of Rockland Co., N.Y., late of Shropshire, Eng., engineer - 24 May 1834

Jarratt, Joseph, milkman, subj. of G.B. - 4 Nov. 1834

Jone, Francis Joseph, merchant, subj. of King of Wurtemburg - 6 Jan. 1836

Jeffers, William F., subj. of G.B. - 10 Nov. 1836

Jacob, Michael, subj. of King of France - 6 Nov. 1837

Jessop, Henry, subj. of G.B. - 3 Jan. 1838

Jacob, John, subj. of Duke of Brunswick - 9 Apr. 1838

Jacob, Augustus, subj. of Duke of Brunswick - 12 Apr. 1838

Jones, John R., subj. of G.B. - 11 Dec. 1838

Jacobs, Jacob, subj. of G.B. - 19 Dec. 1838

Jordan, Francis, subj. of G.B. - 21 Mar. 1839

Jacob, Frederick, subj. of King of Hanover - 9 Apr. 1839

Johnston, John Natross, lately from London, subj. of G.B. - 12 Dec. 1839

Jacon, Christian, subj. of King of Hanover - 9 Apr. 1839

Joseph, Adam, subj. of Emperor of Russia - 8 Oct. 1840

Jolliff, John, subj. of G.B. - 26 Oct. 1840

Jacomella, Peter, subj. of Republic of Switzerland - 5 Nov. 1840

Jones, John, subj. of G.B. - 26 Dec. 1840

K

Knight, Abram, subj. of G.B. - 27 June 1812

Kass, Ernest [report 28 Jan. 1813]: b. town of Uslor, Hanover, age 40, migr. from Hamburgh, baker, subj. of Emperor of France and King of Italy; wife Margaret, b. Umstadt, Hesse Darmstadt, age 34, migr. from Amsterdam - 29 Jan. 1813

Kearns, Charles, b. town of Straloghan, Co. Leitrim, Ire., age 31, migr. from Dublin, minister of the Gospel - 23 Apr. 1818

Keelan, James, b. Co. Louth, town of Ardee, Ire., age 23, migr. from Liverpool, mason - 21 Dec. 1818

Keating, Richard, b. town of Ardee, Co. of Louth, Ire., age 23, migr. from Waterford, tailor - 21 Dec. 1818

Keup, Christian [report 7 Apr. 1819]: b. town of Stolp, Prussia, age 23, migr. from Lisbon, Portugal, farmer - 20 Apr. 1819

Kane, John [report 13 Apr. 1819]: b. Dublin, Ire., age 24, migr. from Dublin, mechanic - 21 Apr. 1819

Kirton, Joseph, b. London, age 29, migr. from London, labourer; wife Elizabeth, b. Dublin, age 23 - 29 Apr. 1819

Kelly, Jeremiah, b. Co. Cork, Ire., age 23, migr. from Cork, grocer; wife Mary, b. city of Limerick, age 21; son Lawrence, b. Cove of Cork, age 4 - 11 Jan. 1820

Kearsing, John (by his guardian, John Kearsing), b. London, age 18, migr. from London, butcher - 16 Mar. 1820

Keefe, Michael [report 9 Apr. 1821]: b. Co. Waterford, Ire., age 41, migr. Cove of Cork, porter - 10 Apr. 1821

Kane, James, b. Co. Londonderry, Ire., age 32, migr. from Cork, grocer - 16 Apr. 1821

Kelly, William, b. Co. Sligo, Ire., age 35, migr. from Londonderry, labourer; wife Bridget, b. Co. Sligo, age 25 - 20 Apr. 1821

Kelly, Gregory, b. Co. Roscommon, Ire., as all of the family, age 75, migr. from Dublin, grocer; dau. Peggy, age 36; dau. Bridget, age 19; dau. Catherine, age 17 - 18 May 1821

Kenny, Michael [report 2 May 1821]: b. Co. Galway, Ire., age 30, migr. from London, grocer; wife Ellenor, b. London, age 28 - 22 May 1821

Killin, Patrick, b. Co. Fermanagh, Ire., age 23, migr. from Dublin, cartman - 24 May 1821

Killin, James [report 9 June 1821]: b., as all the family, in Co. Fermanagh, Ire., age 33, migr. from Belfast, farmer; wife Mary, age 30; son John, age 14; son James, age 6; dau. Ann, age 10; dau. Catherine, age 4; dau. Mary, age 2 - 18 Sept. 1821

Kearnan, Michael, b. Co. West Meath, Ire., age 30, migr. from Dublin, millstone maker; wife Catherine, b. Co. West Meath, age 30 - 30 June 1821

King, John [report 9 Oct. 1821]: b. Co. Essex, Eng., age 24, migr. from Dartmouth, musical instrument maker; wife Harriet, b. Co. Middlesex, Eng., age 21; son John, b. Co. Surrey, age 12 months - 15 Oct. 1821

Kerr, William [report 7 Jan. 1822]: b. Co. Tyrone, Ire., age 27, migr. from Londonderry, shoemaker - 21 Jan. 1822

Kirby, William, b. Lillerkenny, Ire., age 38, migr. from Ire., sadler; wife Eliza, b. Dublin, age 31; dau. Lydia, b. Dublin, age 8; son William, b. Dublin, age 6; dau. Eliza, b. at sea, age 5 - 26 Feb. 1822

Keys, Christopher [report 25 Sept. 1822]: b. Co. Fermanagh, Ire., age 22, migr. from Londonderry, cartman - 22 Oct. 1822

King, John [report 21 Mar. 1823]: b. Co. Essex, Eng., age 55, migr. from London, soap and candle manufacturer - 21 Apr. 1823

Keogh, Martin, b. Co. Wexford, Ire., Newtown Barry, age 25, migr. from Dublin, accountant - 15 Nov. 1824

Kearsing, John, subj. of G.B. - 2 July 1825

Karans, John, b. Co. Armagh, Ire., age 24, migr. from Newry, labourer - 29 Mar. 1826

Kevny, Patrick, b., as all the family, in Co. Leitrim, age 36, migr. from Sligo, dealer; wife Mary, age 22; son Thomas, age 5; dau. Eliza, age 3 - 18 Apr. 1826

King, Charles, b. Co. Dumfries, Scotland, age 26, migr. from Port Patrick, via Belfast, slater; wife Mary, b. Gallway, Scotland, age 28; dau. Elizabeth, b. Dumfries, Scotland, age 1 - 20 Oct. 1826

Kerr, John, b. Glasgow, Scotland, age 27, migr. from Greenock, cartman - 27 Jan. 1827

Keeler, George, b. Holstein, Denmark, age 38, migr. from Hamburgh, mariner - 18 June 1827

Kiernan, Francis [report 10 Aug. 1827]: b. Co. Cavan, Ire., age 26, migr. from Liverpool, labourer - 21 Nov. 1827

Kivlin, John, b. Co. Sligo, Ire., age 24, migr. from St. Johns, Newfoundland, cartman - 10 Dec. 1827

Knight, Daniel, b. Co. Hampshire, Eng., age 37, migr. from Portsmouth, blacksmith; son William, b. NYC, age 4; son Daniel, b. NYC, age 3; son James, b. NYC, age 3 months - 28 Jan. 1828

Kelly, Patrick [report 9 June 1828]: b. Co. Tyrone, age 28, migr. from Belfast, waiter - 17 June 1828

Kerrigen [clerk wrote "Kerrigan"], William subj. of G.B. - 31 Oct. 1828

Kneebel, Henrich, subj. of King of Hanover - 23 Jan. 1829

Knox, Mary, widow, b. Paisley, Scotland, age 61, migr. from Greenock, "no particular occupation" - 22 Dec. 1830

Kalbfleisch, Martin, painter, subj. of King of the Netherlands - 27 June 1831

Krag, Ludvig, carpenter, subj. of King of Denmark - 22 Oct. 1831

Kelly, William, soap boiler, subj. of G.B. - 2 Nov. 1833

Knöller [or Knölber?], Johan Philip, subj. of King of Wurtemberg - 1 Apr. 1836

Kellihan, John, subj. of G.B. - 31 Mar. 1837

Kavanagh, John, subj. of G.B. - 22 May 1837

Kunkelmann, Jacob Charles, merchant, subj. of Grand Duke of Baden - 26 July 1837

King, Edward P., subj. of G.B. - 3 Feb. 1838

Kelly, John, subj. of G.B. - 10 Apr. 1838

Kearsley, James, subj. of G.B. - 28 June 1838

Kealey, James, subj. of G.B. - 12 Sept. 1838

Kretzschmann, Henry, subj. of King of Saxony - 6 Nov. 1838

Kinloch, James, subj. of G.B. - 7 Nov. 1838

Klawser, Landerlin, subj. of Grand Duke of Baden - 9 Nov. 1838

Keller, George, subj. of Grand Duke of Baden - 21 Jan. 1839

Koehneken, John, subj. of King of Hanover - 6 Mar. 1839

Klais, Matthew, subj. of Grand Duke of Baden - 11 Apr. 1839

Keller, Aloys, subj. of Emperor of Austria - 11 Apr. 1839

Kattenhorn, John, subj. of King of Hanover - 11 Apr. 1839

Kratz, John, subj. of Grand Duke of Baden - 9 Apr. 1839

Kusick, James, subj. of G.B. - 12 Apr. 1839

Knight, Charles, subj. of G.B. - 1 Aug. 1839

Korn, Augustus, subj. of King of Prussia - 4 Oct. 1839

Kopf, George William, subj. of City of Hamburgh - 10 Sept. 1839

Kelly, James, subj. of G.B. - 5 Nov. 1839

Knapheade, Hermann, subj. of King of Hanover - 6 Nov. 1839

Kahn, Isaac, subj. of King of Bavaria - 11 Mar. 1840

Kech, Matthias, subj. of Grand Duke of Baden - 14 Mar. 1840

Kannengieser, George, subj. of King of Bavaria - 8 June 1840

Kelly, Owen, subj. of G.B. - 13 June 1840

Kruger, George William, subj. of Principality of Bremen - 23 Sept. 1840

Kite, James M., subj. of G.B. - 28 Sept. 1840

Kane, Barney, subj. of G.B. - 5 Oct. 1840

Kelly, John, subj. of G.B. - 14 Oct. 1840

Konrad, John, subj. of Grand Duke of Hesse Darmstadt - 17 Oct. 1840

Keenen, John, subj. of G.B - 28 Oct. 1840

Kyle, Matthew, subj. of G.B. - 2 Nov. 1840

Kane, John, subj. of G.B. - 2 Nov. 1840

Kaminski, Stanislaus, subj. of Emperor of Russia - 6 Nov. 1840

Kreiter, Philip, subj. of King of Bavaria - 7 Dec. 1840

Kreiter, George, subj. of King of Bavaria - 7 Dec. 1840

Kniebas, Christian, subj. of King of Prussia - 24 Dec. 1840

L

Lyon, Joseph [report 19 Oct. 1816]: b. London, age 36, migr. from Havre de Grace, merchant - 20 Nov. 1818

Lyon, Philip, b. Belgium, age 22, subj. of King of Holland, migr. from Havre de Grace, merchant - 19 Oct. 1816

Lee, Allen, b. parish of Paisley, Scotland, age 40, migr. from Greenock, gardner - 18 Feb. 1817

Leonard, Edward, b. Queens Co., Ire., age 46, migr. from Cock - 26 July 1817

Lavie, Joseph M., b. Passas [or Passase?], Spain, age 20, subj. of King of Spain, migr. from Passas [or Passase?], mariner - 19 Nov. 1817

Lorenberg, Bernard Ludwig [report 9 Dec. 1817]: b. Berlin, Germany, age 43, migr. from Rotterdam, subj. of King of Prussia, merchant; wife Ann, b. Gloucestershire, Eng., age 25, subj. of G.B.; dau. Ann, b. London, age 3; son Francis, b. London, age 18 months - 22 Dec. 1817

Lazenby, John Birks [report 8 Jan. 1818]: b. town of Pontefract, Yorkshire, Eng., age 25, migr. from London, gentleman - 19 Jan. 1818

Liddard, William, b., as all the family, in London, age 45, migr. from Liverpool, merchant, intending to settle in Illinois Territory; wife Susanah Matilda, age 40; dau. Susanah, age 17; dau. Ann, age 15, dau. Lucretia, age 12; dau. Virginia, age 8; son William, age 5 - 26 May 1818

Lawrence, Henry, b. Falmouth, Co. of Cornwall, age 29, migr. from Falmouth, mariner; wife Elizabeth, b. Falmouth, age 25; dau. Elizabeth, b. Falmouth, age 1 - 20 July 1818

Lovatt, Thomas [report 5 Aug. 1818]: b. Winster, Derbyshire, age 28, migr. from Liverpool, tallow chandler and farmer, intending to reside in State of Ohio or Indiana Territory - 17 Aug. 1818

Lovatt, Samuel [report 5 Aug. 1818]: b. Winster, Derbyshire, age 22, migr. from Liverpool, tallow chandler and farmer, intending to reside in State of Ohio or Indiana Territory - 17 Aug. 1818

Latham, Nathaniel, b. Hough, Co. of Cheshire, Eng., age 30, migr. from Liverpool, baker and farmer, intending to settle in Indiana Territory or Illinois Territory; wife Mary, age 26 - 1 Sept. 1818

Leddy, Michael, b. Co. Cavan, Ire., age 28, migr, from Dublin, weaver; family consists of wife, son Philip, and daus. Jane and Catharine - 9 Sept. 1818

Lender, Peter, b. Dantzig, Prussia, age 22, migr. from Dantzig, arrived NYC in Sept. 1815, seaman - 19 Jan. 1819

Ludby [or Ludly?], John, b. Petworth, Co. of Sussex, age 25, migr. from Portsmouth, tallow chandler; wife Ann, b. town of Leicester, Leicestershire, Eng., age 29; dau. Sophia, b. Portsmouth, Co. of Sussex, age 4; dau. Rachel, b. Portsmouth, age 3; son William, b. Portsmouth, age 15 months - 10 June 1819

Longfield, Thomas, b. Rotterdam, Holland, age 29, migr. from Rotterdam, mariner - 20 July 1819

Lambert, John, b. Yorkshire, Eng., age 40, migr. from Liverpool, merchant, intending to reside in Brooklyn, Kings Co., N.Y.; wife Elizabeth, age 26 - 31 July 1819

Lynar, Anthony [report 28 Sept. 1819]: b. parish of Maynooth, Co. Kildare, Ire., age 30, migr. from Dublin, smith - 8 Oct. 1819

Lowe, Samuel (by his father, Sager Lowe, his guardian), b. London, age 20, migr. from Havre de Grace, hairdresser - 25 Jan. 1820

Laidlaw, John [report 22 July 1820]: b. Co. Roxburgh, Scotland, age 26, migr. from Leith, teacher, intending to reside in Brooklyn, N.Y.; wife Agnes, b. Edinburgh, Scotland, age 26 - 24 July 1820

Larwill, Abraham [report 7 Nov. 1820]: b. Frome, Somersetshire, Eng., age 47, migr. from Brighton, tinplate worker; wife Elizabeth; dau. Eliza, age 17; son Abraham, age 14; son Ebenezer, age 12; son Edwin, age 10; son John, age 7; dau. Maria, age 6; dau. Sarah, age 4; dau. Henrietta, age 2 - 22 Nov. 1820

Leepe, William, born. Co. Fermanagh, Ire., age 30, migr. from Londonderry, cartman - 5 Apr. 1821

Laine, David, subj. of G.B. - 17 Apr. 1821

Lynar, David [report 10 Sept. 1819]: b. Co. Kildare, Ire., age 28, migr. from Dublin, grocer - 16 Apr. 1821

Lynch, Dennis [report 7 Apr. 1821]: b. Co. Waterford, Ire., age 45, migr. from Cork, porter - 19 Apr. 1821

Lodge, Philip [report 2 May 1821]: b. Gloucestershire, Eng., age 43, migr. from Liverpool, grocer - 21 May 1821

Ludby [or Ludley?], John, subj. of G.B. - 22 May 1821

Logue, Edward [report 7 May 1821]: b. Co. Tyrone, Ire., age 28, migr. from Londonderry, grocer - 23 May 1821

Leddy, John, b. Co. Cavan, Ore., age 40, migr. from Galway, cartman; wife Mary, b. Co. Cavan, age 30 - 24 May 1821

Loughlin, Michael, b. Co. Tyrone, age 30, migr. from Belfast, labourer - 28 May 1821

Leird, Andrew [report 6 July 1821]: b. Co. Monaghan, Ire., age 33, migr. from Dublin, farmer - 17 July 1821

Lowe, Samuel James, b. Co. Surrey, Eng., age 22, migr. from Havre de Grace, hairdresser - 19 Sept. 1821

Lowery, David, b. Co. Monaghan, Ire., age 23, migr. from Newry, weaver - 30 Mar. 1822

Laundre, Paul [report 11 May 1822]: b. town of Three Rivers, Canada, age 44, migr. from Three Rivers, ship-carpenter; son Paul, b. Three Rivers, age 18 - 28 May 1822

Logan, John [report 2 July 1822]: b. Co. Donegal, Ire., age 27, migr. from Greenock, Scotland, labourer - 15 July 1822

Le Cras, Peter, b. Island of Guernsey, age 37, migr. from Brazil, mariner - 29 July 1822

Lowry, Robert [report 10 Aug. 1822]: b., as all the family, Co. Down, Ire., age 29, migr. from Belfast, farmer; wife Anne, age 20; dau. Anne, age 6; dau. Elizabeth, age 4; son James, age 2 - 19 Aug. 1822

Ludby [or Ludley?], John [report 10 June 1819]: b Petworth, Co. Sussex, Eng., age 25, migr. from Portsmouth, tallow chandler; wife Ann, b. town and co. of Leicester, age 29; dau. Sophia, b. Petworth, age 4; dau. Rachel, b. Petworth, age 3; son William, b. Petworth, age 15 months - 14 Dec. 1822

Ludby [or Ludley?], John, subj. of G.B. - 14 Dec. 1822

Lyons, Cornelius, b. Co. Longford, Ire., age 26, migr. from Dublin, labourer - 23 Dec. 1822

Lohse, Frederick A., b. Leipsic, age 23, subj. of King of Saxony, migr. from Bremen, merchant - 17 Feb. 1823

Legal, Joseph [report 5 Mar. 1823], b. Lorient, France, age 36, migr. from Nantes, lookingglass plater; wife Jane Catherine, b. Lorient, age 30; dau. Francine, b. Lorient, age 10; son Eugene, b. Lorient - 17 Mar. 1823

Lamothe, John Bertrand [report 12 May 1823]: b. town of Tarbes, Dept. of High Pyrenees, France, age 32, migr. from Bordeaux, merchant - 19 May 1823

Logue, William [report 6 May 1823], b. Co. Tyrone, Ire., age 22, migr. from Londonderry, grocer - 19 May 1823

Lennon, Joseph, b. Co. Waterford, Ire., age 28, migr. from Waterford, leather dealer - 29 May 1823

Longet, Antoine, b. Geneva, Switzerland, age 29, migr. from Havre de Grace, merchant - 24 Nov. 1823

Lawler, Michael [report 5 Jan. 1824]: b. Co. Carlow, Ire., age 33, migr. from Dublin, waiter - 21 Jan. 1824

Langlois, Charles, b. Beauvais, France, age 31, migr. from Havre, merchant - 20 Jan. 1824

Lamb, Maria Ann (wife of John Lamb) [report 7 Dec. 1824]: b. Edinburgh, Scotland, age 26, migr. from London - 24 Dec. 1824

Landau, Christopher [report 12 Jan. 1825]: b. city of Spanenbergh in dominions of Prince of Hesse Cassel, age 29, migr. from Hamburgh and then to London, baker; wife Ann, b. Wetenstine, Prussia, age 20 - 20 Jan. 1825

Louther, Robert, b. parish of Baloston, Co. Antrim, Ire., age 28, migr. from Belfast, intending to settle in Brooklyn; wife Margaret, b. Co. Donegal, age 19, migr. from Londonderry, labourer - 25 Jan. 1825

Little, John [report 11 Apr. 1825]: b. Co. Tyrone, Ire., age 39, migr. from Belfast, cartman; wife Angee, b. Co. Tyrone, age 30 - 18 Apr. 1825

Lewis, Evan, b. Montgomeryshire, Wales, as all his family, age 37, migr. from London, hatter; wife Ann, age 38; dau. Mary, age 18; son William, age 13; dau. Jane, age 13; son Edward, age 9 - 23 May 1825

Lewin, John, b. Eng., age 48, migr. from Liverpool, seaman - 20 June 1825

Linn, Patrick [report 15 Nov. 1825]: b. Belfast, age 41, migr. from Belfast, livery stabler; wife Matilda, b. Co. Tyrone, age 36; dau. Catharine Ann, b. Belfast, age 13; dau. Hanna Maria, b. Belfast, age 9 - 21 Nov. 1825

Low, Thomas, b. Newry, age 25, migr. from Newry, labourer; wife Sarah, b. Sheffield, Eng., age 21 - 16 May 1825

Long, Oliver, b. Londonderry, age 27, migr. from Belfast, type founder - 29 Nov. 1825

Leaird, Alexander [report 6 Feb. 1826]: b. Co. Tyrone, Ire., age 27, migr. from Londonderry, labourer - 20 Feb. 1826

Leonard, John (by James McBride, his guardian) [report 10 Apr. 1826]: b. Co. Fermanagh, Ire., age 17 years and 6 months, migr. from Belfast, labourer - 11 Apr. 1826

Lynch, Thomas, b. Gillingham, Co. of Kent, age 37, migr. from Liverpool, labourer - 23 Feb. 1827

Lackie, John [report 16 Apr. 1827]: b. Co. Louth, Ire., age 39, migr. from Draghada, via Liverpool, shoemaker; wife Bridget, b. Co. Louth, age 28; son William, b. Co. Louth, age 3 - 18 Apr. 1827

Lorut, Louis, b. Cusset, France, age 26, migr. from Havre, merchant - 25 May 1827

Lynch, John [report 3 Oct. 1827]: b. Co. Cavan, Ire., age 25, migr. from Liverpool, labourer - 15 Oct. 1827

Logan, Thomas [report 14 Apr. 1828]: b. town of Garvagh, Co.
  Leitrim, as rest of family, age 34, migr. from Dublin, mason;
  wife Catharine, age 34; Francis, a son of Catharine, age 19;
  Julia, a dau. of Catharine, age 8 - 22 Apr. 1828

Lidgerwood, John, b. parish of Longside, Aberdeenshire, Scotland, age 33 years, 10 months and 21 days, migr. from Liverpool, formerly a mason but now a merchant -

Lestrade, M.A.L. Depeyre, physician, subj. of King of France -
  20 Mar. 1830

Ledwith, Richard F., clerk, subj. of G.B. - 28 Oct. 1830

Lentz, Henry F., surgeon, subj. of King of Wurtemberg - 20 June
  1831

Le Moyne, Adolph, subj. of King Phillipe of France - 20 Aug.
  1831

Lewis, John, coachman, subj. of G.B. - 31 Mar. 1832

Lewis, Dennis, mason, late of Co. Cork, subj. of G.B. - 24 May
  1832

Lewis, Alfred, subj. of G.B. - 17 Feb. 1834

Lowe, Joshua, engraver, subj. of G.B. - 26 Apr. 1834

Leahy, Patrick, clerk, subj. of G.B. - 17 Feb. 1834

Le Barbier, Adolphus, merchant, subj. of King of France - 26
  July 1834

Leep, William, subj. of G.B. - 5 Nov. 1834

Long, James Page, clerk, subj. of G.B. - 3 Dec. 1834

Legier, Antoine, baker, subj. of King of France - 23 Feb. 1835

Lowry, William, engineer, subj. of King of Sweden - 14 Mar. 1835

Lucas, John, of Belleville, N.J., subj. of G.B. - 8 Sept. 1835

Levin, Thomas C., subj. of G.B. - 11 Aug. 1835

Louden, James, Jr., of Vienna, Oneida Co., N.Y., farmer, subj.
  of G.B. - 28 Sept. 1836

Longman, Robert, gold refiner, subj. of G.B. - 24 Oct. 1835

Lewis, William, subj. of G.B. - 29 June 1837

Lux, Henry, subj. of King of France - 22 Mar. 1838

Lewis, Benjamin G., subj. of G.B. - 4 Apr. 1838

Lockwood, William, subj. of G.B. - 9 Apr. 1838

Leslie, Alexander, subj. of G.B. - 9 Apr. 1838

Lynch, Patrick, subj. of G.B. - 9 Apr. 1838

Lavin, Thomas, subj. of G.B. - 12 June 1838

Lynch, Dennis, subj. of G.B. - 5 May 1838

Lindley, James, of Rahway, N.J., subj. of G.B. - 8 Oct. 1838

Lessing, Meyer, subj. of King of Hanover - 15 Oct. 1838

Lambert, Charles A., subj. of King of France - 15 Oct. 1838

Logan, William, subj. of G.B. - 17 Oct. 1838

Levy, Joseph, subj. of G.B. - 18 Oct. 1838

Lloyd, Thomas, subj. of G.B. - 3 Nov. 1838

Lewis, John, subj. of G.B. - 2 Nov. 1838

Labatt, Edward, subj. of Hamburgh - 28 Nov. 1838

Langan, James, subj. of G.B. - 12 Jan. 1839

Leefe, Edward Benjamin, subj. of G.B. - 7 Mar. 1839

Lindon, Patrick, subj. of G.B. - 8 Apr. 1839

Loftus, Thomas, subj. of G.B. - 9 Apr. 1839

Loftus, David, subj. of G.B. - 9 Apr. 1839

Ledwith, James William, subj. of G.B. - 10 Apr. 1839

Lane, Thomas, subj. of G.B. - 7 June 1839

Lewenberg, Leon, subj. of King of Prussia - 20 June 1839

Lonergan, Patrick, subj. of G.B. - 10 Aug. 1839

Luue[?], Johan Georg, subj. of King of Wurtemberg - 5 Nov. 1839

Leclair, Charles, subj. of G.B. - 6 Nov. 1839

Lawlor, Michael, subj. of G.B. - 17 Feb. 1840

Luis, Ferdinand, subj. of Free City of Hamburgh - 23 Mar. 1840

Light, Christopher, subj. of King of Prussia - 6 Apr. 1840

Lannigan, Richard, subj. of G.B. - 13 Apr. 1840

Lawton, Timothy, subj. of G.B. - 14 Apr. 1840

Leahey, John, subj. of G.B. - 21 Apr. 1840

Large, Alfred, subj. of G.B. - 26 Sept. 1840

Lothimer, William, subj. of G.B. - 28 Sept. 1840

Lelli, Aaim, subj. of King of Prussia - 8 Oct. 1840

Lafferty, Dennis, subj. of G.B. - 13 Oct. 1840

Leydel, Joseph, subj. of King of France - 13 Oct. 1840

Lavender, William, subj. of G.B. - 19 Oct. 1840

Langstader, Bernard, subj. of King of Bavaria - 20 Oct. 1840

Lewin, Robin, subj. of G.B. - 2 Nov. 1840

Lange, Frederick, subj. of King of Hanover - 3 Nov. 1840

Lowdin, John, subj. of G.B. - 18 Dec. 1840

Longham, George, subj. of G.B. - 22 Dec. 1840

Mc

McKittrick, Thomas, late of Belfast, Co. Antrim - 12 Nov. 1802

McMahon, James, late of parish of Tully, Co. Donegal, grocer -
24 Dec. 1802

McNevin, William James, Doctor of Physic, subj. of G.B. - 25 June
1806

McClean, John, subj. of G.B. - 15 Jan. 1810

McGinnis, John, of New Utrecht, Kings Co., L.I., dealer, subj.
of G.B. - 20 Mar. 1815

McFarlane, Alexander, subj. of G.B. - 28 Apr. 1815

McDougall, Allen, subj. of G.B. - 28 Apr. 1815

McEnerny, Henry O'Neill, b. Co. Limerick, Ire., age 22 years and
9 months, migr. from Cork, merchant - 24 Oct. 1816

McDonnell, Michael John, b. town of Drogheda, Prov. of Leinster,
Ire., age 24, migr. from Dublin, paper manufacturer - 21 Nov.
1817

McDonough, Edward [report 1 Apr. 1819]: b. town of "Arbracen" [Ardbraccan], Co. Meath, Ire., age 27, migr. from Liverpool, labourer - 20 Apr. 1819

McLaughlin, Patrick, b. Co. Armagh, age 28, migr. from Newry & Warings Point, labourer - 30 Aug. 1819

McKee, Charles, b. Co. Donegal, Ire., age 35, migr. from Londonderry, stone cutter; wife Margaret, b. Belfast, age 34 - 13 Nov. 1819

McKeon, Robert, b. Dublin, age 40, migr. from Dublin, brass founder; wife Ann, b. Dublin, age 28 - 27 Apr. 1818

McCray, William, b. Co. Monaghan, age 29, migr. from Newry, farmer, intending to settle in Smith Vale, Chenango Co., N.Y.; wife Margaret, b. Co. Monaghan, age 24 - 6 Nov. 1818

McKayghney, age 24, born in and migrated from Glasgow, Scotland, late a shoemaker; wife Mary, b. parish of Blantyre [Co. of Lanark], Scotland, age 20 - 11 Nov. 1818

McDonnell, James J., subj. of G.B. - 16 Nov. 1818

McKenny, Lawrence, b. Co. Armagh, age 24, migr. from Belfast, wheelwright - 20 June 1820

McCann, Edward, b. Co. Tyrone, Ire., age 30, migr. from Londonderry, cartman - 26 Mar. 1821

McGinnis, Henry, b. Co. Monaghan, Ire., age 51, migr. from Londonderry, cartman - 27 Mar. 1821

McCune, Joseph, b. Co. Down, Ire., age 35, migr. from Belfast, cartman - 27 Mar. 1821

McKenny, Barney, b. Co. Monaghan, Ire., age 52, migr. from Newry, cartman; wife Rose, b. Co. Monaghan, age 43; son Thomas, b. Co. Monaghan, age 12; son Barney, b. Co. Monaghan, age 9 - 28 Mar. 1821

McEllister, James [report 29 Mar. 1821]: b. Co. Kerry, Ire., age 25, migr. from London, cartman - 30 Mar. 1821

McFadden, Richardson, b. Co. Tyrone, Ire., age 28, migr. from Dublin, bookseller; wife Mary, age 23 - 2 Apr. 1821

McDonnell, Mathew, b. Co. Tyrone, age 28, migr. from Londonderry, cartman - 2 Apr. 1821

McBride, Thomas, b. Co. Armagh, Ire., age 47, migr. from Londonderry, cartman; wife Ann, b. Co. Londonderry, age 46; dau. Jane, b. Co. Londonderry, age 18 - 3 Apr. 1821

McKenna, Andrew, subj. of G.B. - 16 Apr. 1821

McCummiskey, John, b. Co. Down, Ire., age 35, migr. from Newry, rigger; wife Mary, b. Co. Down, age 27 - 16 Apr. 1821

McLaughlin, Owen [report 2 Apr. 1821]: b. Co. Armagh, Ire., age 37, migr. from Newry, porter; wife Agnes, b. Co. Armagh, age 30; dau. Agnes, b. Co. Armagh, age 7 - 16 Apr. 1821

McKernan, Patrick, b. Co. Leitrim, Ire., age 42, migr. from Dublin, grocer - 16 Apr. 1821

McIntyre, Samuel [report 2 Apr. 1821]: b. Co. Donegal, age 30, migr. from Londonderry, cartman - 17 Apr. 1821

McMurray, Francis [report 4 Apr. 1821]: b. Co. Sligo, Ire., age 36, migr. from Sligo, grocer - 18 Apr. 1821

McLean, Alexander, b. Co. Londonderry, Ire., age 30, migr. from Londonderry, labourer - 18 Apr. 1821

McCarthy, John [report 14 Apr. 1821]: b. Co. Wexford, Ire.,age
   48, migr. from Dublin, grocer - 18 Apr. 1821

McDermot, Charles, b. Co. Leitrim, Ire., age 34, migr. from
   Sligo, grocer; wife Ann, b. Co. Cavan, age 40 - 18 Apr. 1821

McGill, Samuel [report 2 Apr. 1821]: b. Co. Monaghan, age 60,
   migr. from Newry, cartman - 18 Apr. 1821

McLeod, James [report 4 Apr. 1821]: b. Co. Donegal, Ire., age
   27, migr. from Londonderry, cartman - 18 Apr. 1821

McGowan, Michael [report 14 Apr. 1821]: b. Co. Leitrim, Ire.,
   age 40, migr. from Sligo, grocer; wife Barbary, b. Co. Leitrim,
   age 26; son Michael, b. Co. Leitrim, age 5 - 19 Apr. 1821

McDonnell, William [report 13 Apr. 1821]: b. Dublin, Ire., age
   38, migr. from Dublin, tailor - 20 Apr. 1821

McGowan, Peter [report 14 Apr. 1821]: b. Co. Leitrim, Ire., age
   24, migr. from Sligo, accountant - 21 Apr. 1821

McDonnell, Michael [report 26 Apr. 1821]: b. Co. Sligo, Ire.,
   age 34, migr. from Sligo, grocer and mason; wife Jane, b. Co.
   Leitrim, age 31 - 27 Apr. 1821

McKenna, John, b. Co. Monaghan, Ire., age 25, migr. from Londonderry, grocer - 1 May 1821

McCleery, James [report 14 May 1821]: b. Co. Down, Ire., age 43,
   migr. from Belfast, labourer - 15 May 1821

McKiggin, John, b. Co. Fermanagh, Ire. age 27, migr. from Belfast, cartman - 24 May 1821

McGovern, James, b. Co. Cavan, Ire., age 30, migr. from Belfast,
   labourer - 24 May 1821

McLaughlin, Patrick, subj. of G.B. - 25 May 1821

McGrath, John [report 4 June 1821]: b. Co. Carlow, Ire., age 27,
   migr. from Dublin, fruiterer and grocer; wife Catherine, b.
   Co. Kilkenny, age 23 - 18 June 1821

McKibbin, John S. (by John A. Slidell, his guardian), b. Co.
   Down, age 20, migr. from Belfast, grocer - 30 July 1821

McLaughlin, James, b. Co. Leitrim, Ire., age 31, migr. from Sligo, cartman; wife Mary, b. Co. Leitrim, age 23; son James, b.
   Co. Leitrim, age 8 - 18 July 1821

McWhorter, Alexander, b. Co. Meath, age 25, migr. from Newry or
   Warings Point, carpenter - 21 July 1821

McGeehan, Niel, b. Co. Donegal, age 29, migr. from Dublin, grocer - 20 Aug. 1821

McManus, Andrew, b. Co. Cavan, age 31, migr. from Newry, labourer; wife Bridget, b. Co. Cavan, age 26; dau. Mary, b. New York,
   age 2; dau. Susannah, b. New York, age 12 weeks - 19 Nov. 1821

McBurney, Thomas, b. Co. Down, age 27, migr. from Belfast, farmer - 1822

McCroskery, Michael, subj. of G.B. - 21 Feb. 1822

McGowan, Patrick, b. Co. Leitrim, age 27, migr. from Sligo, labourer - 23 Mar. 1822

McGowan, Michael [report 13 Apr. 1822]: b. Co. Leitrim, age 36,
   migr. from Sligo, pedlar; wife Margaret, b. Co. Sligo, age 27
   - 16 Apr. 1822

McGavern, Patrick [report 1 Apr. 1822]: b. Co. Cavan, age 30,
   migr. from Waterford, waiter - 22 Apr. 1822

McCartin, Charles, b. Co. Leitrim, Ire., age 45, migr. from Dublin, labourer; wife Sarah, b. Co. Fermanagh, age 30; son Michael, b. Co. Leitrim, age 14 - 24 Apr. 1822

McMullen, William, b. Co. Fermanagh, Ire., age 27, migr. from Londonderry, blacksmith; wife Elizabeth, b. Co. Fermanagh, age 21; dau. Mary Anne, b. Co. Fermanagh, age 10 - 31 Oct. 1822

McCracken, Joseph [report 3 Dec. 1822]: b. Co. Tyrone, Ire., age 42, migr. from St. Johns, Newfoundland, farmer - 17 Dec. 1822

McKie, John, b. Co. Donegal, Ire., age 34, migr. from Sligo, labourer - 31 Jan. 1823

McDonald, John, b. Co. Tyrone, Ire., age 26, migr. from Londonderry, labourer; wife Mary, b. Co. Tyrone, age 26 - 17 Feb. 1823

McMahon, John [report 12 Apr. 1823]: b. Co. Monaghan, Ire., age 28, migr. from parish of Glonas, Co. Monaghan, wheelwright - 21 Apr. 1823

McMullen, John, b. Co. West Meath, Ire., age 36, migr. from Dublin, wheelwright - 28 Apr. 1823

McGowan, James [report 4 Aug. 1823]: b. Co. Monaghan, Ire., age 36, migr. from Sligo, fruiterer; wife Bridget, b. Co. Leitrim, age 28; dau. Margaret, b. NYC, age 15 months - 23 Aug. 1823

McDonald, Mathew, subj. of G.B. - 18 Nov. 1823

McCavitt, John, b. Co. Down, Ire., age 27, migr. from Belfast, labourer - 31 Jan. 1824

McBride, Michael [report 13 Apr. 1824]: b. Co. Tyrone, Ire., age 28, migr. from Londonderry, sawyer - 19 Apr. 1824

McManus, James, b. Co. Cavan, age 28, migr. from Dublin, cotton manufacturer; wife Margaret, b. Co. Cavan, age 28, migr. from Belfast - 21 Sept. 1824

McLaughlin, John, b. Co. Down, age 26, migr. from Newry, porter - 20 Oct. 1824

McNeany, Patrick [report 14 Dec. 1824]: b. Co. Monaghan, Ire., as all of family, age 35, migr. from Liverpool, weaver; wife Anne, age 30; son John, age 10; dau. Catharine, age 12 - 20 Dec. 1824

McQuade, John [report 30 Nov. 1824]: b. Co. Fermanagh, Ire., age 23, migr. from Belfast, farmer; wife Mary, b. Co. Down, age 25; son Thomas, b. NYC, age 8 months - 20 Dec. 1824

McAwly, Peter [report 12 May 1825]: b. Co. Sligo, Ire., age 24, migr. from Sligo, cooper - 27 Aug. 1825

McCaffrey, Hugh, b. Co. Tyrone, Ire., age 24, migr. from Londonderry, labourer - 20 Aug. 1825

McDougall, John [report 9 Nov. 1825]: b. Co. Donegal, Ire., age 39, migr. from Londonderry, sawyer; wife Margaret, b. Co. Donegal, age 28 - 21 Nov. 1825

McCann, Hugh, b. Co. Cavan, Ire., age 24, migr. from Sligo, labourer; wife Rosannah, b. Co. Cavan, age 18; son Thomas, b. NYC, age 1 - 23 Jan. 1826

McMurray, Joseph, b. Co. Down, age 25, migr, from Belfast, clerk; wife Ellen, b. Co. Down, age 22 - 1 Mar. 1826

McManus, Philip (by Bernard McManus, his guardian), b. Co. Cavan, Ire., age 16, migr. from Belfast, labourer - 10 Apr. 1826

McBride, Hugh, b. Co. Fermanagh, Ire., age 33, migr. from Belfast, weaver - 10 Apr. 1826

McCall, Bryan, b. Co. Cavan, Ire., age 36, migr. from Newry, cartman - 15 May 1826

McGinnis, Hugh, b. Co. Monaghan, Ire., age 26, migr. from Liverpool, blacksmith; wife Catharine, b. Co. Wexford, age 25 - 19 May 1826

McDowell, Michael, b. Co. Cavan, Ire., age 21, migr. from Belfast, via Quebec, labourer - 19 Sept. 1826

McCann, Philip [report 2 Oct. 1826]: b. Co. Tyrone, Ire., age 25, migr. from Belfast, hack driver - 27 Oct. 1826

McCourt, James, b. Co. Tyrone, Ire., age 33, migr. from Belfast, mason; wife Bridget, b. Co. Tyrone, age 20 - 2 May 1827

McGovern, Hugh [report 5 May 1827]: b. Co. Longford, Ire., age 40, migr. from Belfast, labourer - 28 May 1827

McMullen, Daniel, b. Co. Donegal, Ire., age 33, migr. from Londonderry, boatman, intending to reside in Brooklyn - 24 July 1827

McNulty, Felix, b. Co. Tyrone, Ire., age 31, migr. from Londonderry, painter and glazier - 15 Oct. 1827

McDermott, Michael, b. Co. West Meath, Ire., age 25, migr. from Dublin, grocer; wife Bridget, b. Co. West Meath, age 25 - 1 Nov. 1827

McCort, Peter [report 29 Nov. 1827]: b. Co. Tyrone, Ire., age 23, migr. from Belfast, tinsmith - 30 Nov. 1827

McDonell, Thomas, b. Co. Roscommon, Ire., age 28, migr. from Liverpool, labourer - 18 Dec. 1827

McGuire, Andrew, b. Co. Fermanagh, Ire., age 27, migr. from Belfast, via New Brunswick, carpenter - 20 Dec. 1827

McManus, James [report 9 June 1828]: b. Co. Cavan, Ire., age 23, migr. from Dublin, labourer - 16 June 1828

McGrath, Stephen, b. parish of Carlingford, C. Louth, Ire., age 30, migr. from Newry, labourer; wife Mary, b. parish of Carlingford, age 25 - 23 Jan. 1828

McGuckin, William, b. Co. Antrim, Ire., age 32, migr. from Belfast, schoolteacher - 16 Feb. 1828

McGuire, Peter (by Francis McCabe, his guardian), b. Dublin, Ire., age 16, migr. from Belfast - 8 May 1828

McGarvey, James, b. Londonderry, Ire., age 25, migr. from Belfast, grocer - 13 May 1828

McGinnis, Henry (by his guardian, Henry McGinnis), b. Co. Monaghan, Ire., age 18, migr. from Belfast, labourer - 27 May 1828

McMurray, Thomas, b. Co. Tyrone, Ire., age 24, migr. from Londonderry, labourer - 16 June 1828

McBlain, Robert, weaver, subj. of G.B. - 19 Sept. 1828

McGuire, Patrick, subj. of G.B. - 18 Sept. 1828

McCarthy, Richard, subj. of G.B. - 17 Nov. 1828

McCormick, James, subj. of G.B. - 20 Nov. 1828

McManus, Redmond, subj. of G.B. - 29 Jan. 1829

McKeever, John, late of Co. Armagh, Ire., subj. of G.B. - 28 Nov. 1829

McCauley, John, labourer, subj. of G.B. - 18 Jan. 1830

McEnneriney, Patrick, late of Co. Limerick, Ire., coachman, subj. of G.B. - 23 June 1830

Mc Cabe, Patrick, formerly of Co. Cavan, Ire., labourer - 28 Jan. 1830

McBurney, Alexander, slater, subj. of G.B. - 26 Feb. 1830

McGuire, Timothy, subj. of G.B. - 30 Sept. 1830

McKee, James, weaver, subj. of G.B. - 28 May 1830

McDonagh, Francis, of Richmond Co., N.Y., farmer, subj. of G.B. - 27 Oct. 1832

McWhirter, Thomas, late of Co. Meath, Ire., subj. of G.B. - 21 Feb. 1833

McDermott, Michael, of Rocky Hill, N.J., labourer, subj. of G.B. - 16 Sept. 1833

McManus, Henry, morocco dresser, subj. of G.B. - 17 Mar. 1834

McGinty, Patrick, labourer, subj. of G.B. - 24 Nov. 1834

McHugh, Thomas, of Shrewsbury, N.J., subj. of G.B. - 22 Dec. 1834

McGregor, Fanny, of Kingston, Ulster Co., N.Y., subj. of G.B. - 5 Feb. 1835

McCarthy, John, carpenter, subj. of G.B. - 21 Sept. 1835

McGrath, Patrick, labourer, subj. of G.B. - 6 Oct. 1835

McLaughlin, Richard, labourer, subj. of G.B. - 6 Oct. 1835

McMenomy, Patrick, labourer, subj. of G.B. - 17 May 1836

McKeon, Michael, blacksmith, subj. of G.B. - 27 June 1836

McKune, James, of Richmond Co., N.Y., subj. of G.B. - 25 Oct. 1836

McShane, Terence, subj. of G.B. - 29 July 1837

McMahon, James, subj. of G.B. - 21 Sept. 1837

McGhee, William, subj. of G.B. - 7 Feb. 1838

McMahon, Charles, subj. of G.B. - 7 Apr. 1838

McManus, John, subj. of G.B. - 9 Apr. 1838

McCormick, James, subj. of G.B. - 12 Apr. 1838

McGowan, Thomas, subj. of G.B. - 12 Apr. 1838

McGowan, Patrick, subj. of G.B. - 12 Apr. 1838

McIndoe, William, subj. of G.B. - 28 Apr. 1838

McKellar, James Rogers, subj. of G.B. - 30 June 1838

McKenna, Charles, subj. of G.B. - 5 July 1838

McAdoo, John, subj. of G.B. - 8 Aug. 1838

McGuire, John, subj. of G.B. - 10 Oct. 1838

McGuire, Joseph, subj. of G.B. - 10 Oct. 1838

McDermott, Francis, subj. of G.B. - 1 Nov. 1838

McCullough, Andrew, subj. of G.B. - 3 Nov. 1838

McGloan, Patrick, subj. of G.B. - 5 Nov. 1838

McNamara, Patrick, subj. of G.B. - 5 Nov. 1838

McGinnis, James, subj. of G.B. - 5 Nov. 1838

McGough, John, subj. of G.B. - 5 Nov. 1838

McWilliams, James, subj. of G.B. - 28 Feb. 1839

McGloin, Patrick, subj. of G.B. - 25 Mar. 1839

McGeorge, William, subj. of G.B. - 29 Mar. 1839

McCauley, Owen, subj. of G.B. - 10 Apr. 1839

McCanna, John, subj. of G.B. - 11 Apr. 1839

McGowan, Michael, subj. of G.B. - 11 Apr. 1839

McDonough, William, subj. of G.B. - 24 Apr. 1839

McQuade, Hugh, subj. of G.B. - 24 June 1839

McCarthy, Daniel, subj. of G.B. - 16 July 1839

McCarthy, James, subj. of G.B. - 2 Aug. 1839

McQuin, Peter, subj. of G.B. - 10 Aug. 1839

McLeay, Thomas, subj. of G.B. - 6 Nov. 1839

McAuley, Thomas, subj. of G.B. - 26 Dec. 1839

McCoy, Joseph, subj. of G.B. - 14 Feb. 1840

McQuillen, Patrick, subj. of G.B. - 6 Mar. 1840

McGee, James, subj. of G.B. - 13 Apr. 1840

McKenzie, John, subj. of G.B. - 13 Apr. 1840

McClusky, Bernard, subj. of G.B. - 14 Apr. 1840

McQuigin, Christopher, subj. of G.B. - 28 May 1840

McCaffrey, Hugh, subj. of G.B. - 4 June 1840

McKeon, Robert, subj. of G.B. - 22 July 1840

McGrath, James, subj. of G.B. - 27 July 1840

McKee, Robert, subj. of G.B. - 25 Sept. 1840

McConologue, Daniel, subj. of G.B. - 29 Sept. 1840

McCue, Francis, of 6th Ave. & 25th St., NYC, subj. of G.B. - 6
    Oct. 1840

McConnil, John, subj. of G.B. - 7 Oct. 1840

McGowan, Bartley, subj. of G.B. - 10 Oct. 1840

McKernan, Peter, subj. of G.B. - 15 Oct. 1840

McKenzie, William, subj. of G.B. - 19 Oct. 1840

McLean, William, subj. of G.B. - 23 Oct. 1840

McMurray, Robert, subj. of G.B. - 6 Nov. 1840

McNulty, Charles, subj. of G.B. - 9 Nov. 1840

McKee, William, subj. of G.B. - 26 Dec. 1840

McGlinchey, William, subj. of G.B. - 26 Dec. 1840

M

Marshall, Benjamin, merchant, subj. of G.B. - 24 Aug. 1807

Magenis, Arthur, b. Co. Down, Ire., age 19, migr. from Belfast,
    merchant - 20 Jan. 1817

Montgomery, Samuel, b. Co. Armagh, Ire., age 50, migr. from
    Newry, physician - 19 Dec. 1817

Moore, James, b. Co. Derbyshire, Eng., age 38, migr. from Liver-
    pool, tailor - 16 Mar. 1818

Mortimer, George, b. Dublin, Ire., age 26, migr. from Ire., clerk;
    wife Sarah, b. London, age 28; son George, b. New York, age 9
    months - 9 May 1818

Murphy, John [report 16 Sept. 1818]: b. Co. Antrim, Ire., age 27, migr. from Belfast, labourer; wife Margaret, b. Co. Antrim, age 27; dau. Nancy, b. Co. Antrim, age 7; dau. Mary, b. Co. Antrim, age 2 - 27 Nov. 1818

Morey, John, b. Middlesex, Eng., age 52, migr. from Hull, teacher; wife Maria; dau. Maria, age 21; dau. Eleanor, age 20 - 31 Oct. 1818

Mullany, Hugh [report 1 Dec. 1818]: b. Co. Fermanagh, Ire., age 26, migr. from Londonderry, bricklayer and mason - 21 Dec. 1818

Maitland, David [report 15 Dec. 1818]: b. Co. Kirkcudbright, Scotland, age 22, migr. from Liverpool, merchant - 15 Mar. 1824

Maintain, Anthony D., b. Marseilles, France, age 32, migr. from Marseilles, arrived West Hampton, L.I. in Nov. 1806, merchant, intending to reside in NYC - 20 Apr. 1819

Matsell, George, b. Walsingham, Co. Norfolk, Eng., age 50, migr. from London, tailor; wife Elizabeth; son William, age 18; dau. Mary, age 20; dau. Susan, age 16; son George, age 7; son Augustus, age 5; dau. Elizabeth, age 2 - 2 Mar. 1819

Mortimer, John, b. Leeds, Eng., age 21, migr. from Leeds, woolen draper - 19 Apr. 1820

Mahony, Jeremiah, b. Co. Kerry, age 45, migr. from London, labourer; wife Margaret, b. Co. Kerry, age 44; son Owen, b. London, age 8; son Michael, b. London, age 6; dau. Peggy, b. in America, age 1 - 2 Sept. 1820

Marlow, Michael [report 9 Dec. 1820]: b. Co. Tyrone, Ire., age 24, migr. from Londonderry, sand cartman - 18 Dec. 1820

Murphy, James, b. Co. Tipperary, age 37, migr. from Cork, porter; wife Ellen, b. Co. Waterford, age 28; son William, b. at sea, age 12 - 26 Mar. 1821

Miller, James, b. Co. Cavan, Ire., age 29, migr. from Dublin, grocer - 27 Mar. 1821

Mingam [or Mingan?], Robert, b. Co. Tyrone, Ire., age 36, migr. from Londonderry, cartman - 28 Mar. 1821

Mould, Charles, b. Co. Sussex, Eng., age 41, migr. from Havre de Grace, grocer; wife Harriet, b. Co. of South Hampton, Eng., age 37; dau. Matilda Harriet, b. C. South Hampton, age 5; dau. Adeline Caroline, b. NYC, age 5 months - 29 Mar. 1821

Murphy, John, b. Co. Down, Ire., age 45, migr. from Belfast, cartman - 30 Mar. 1821

Miller, Hugh [report 13 Apr. 1821]: b. Co. Antrim, Ire., age 22, migr. from Newry, grocer - 16 Apr. 1821

Maginn, John, b. Co. Down, Ire., age 42, migr. from Liverpool, maltster; wife Margaret, b. Co. Down, age 26; son John, b. Co. Down, age 12 - 16 Apr. 1821

Martin, John, b. Leicestershire, Eng., age 32, migr. from Plymouth, grocer - 16 Apr. 1821

Mathews, Charles, b. Co. Tyrone, Ire., age 24, migr. from Londonderry, farmer - 18 Apr. 1821

Moore, James [report 4 Apr. 1821]: b., as all the family, Co. Tyrone, age 59, migr. from Belfast, cartman; wife Martha, age 55; son James, age 24; son William, age 15; son Robert, age 13 - 18 Apr. 1821

Murrell, Robert [report 9 Apr. 1821]: b. Co. Londonderry, Ire., age 26, migr. from Londonderry, grocer - 18 Apr. 1821

Murray, Robert [report 2 Apr. 1821]: b. Co. Donegal, Ire., age 29, migr. from Halifax, N.S., cartman - 19 Apr. 1821

Morton, George, b. Derbyshire, Eng., age 40, migr. from Liverpool, brewer and tavern-keeper; wife Jane, b. London, age 26; son John, b. Manchester, age 12; son Mathew, b. Manchester, age 8; dau. Jane, b. Manchester, age 4; son George, b. Upper Canada, age 2 - 19 Apr. 1821

Murdough, John [report 2 Apr. 1821]: b. Co. Down, Ire., age 28, migr. from Newry, cartman - 19 Apr. 1821

Murphy, Walter [report 6 Apr. 1821]: b. Co. Wexford, Ire., age 40, migr. from Halifax, N.S., house [?] cartman; wife Mary, b. Co. Cork, age 32; son Thomas Edward, b. Halifax, age 6; dau. Mary, b. NYC, age 2; son James, b. NYC, age 9 weeks - 19 Apr. 1821

Marshall, Joseph [report 9 Apr. 1821]: b. Co. of Derby, Eng., age 34, migr. from Liverpool, manufacturer of Britania metal; wife Mary, b. Nottinghamshire, age 22 - 20 Apr. 1821

Miller, William [report 10 Apr. 1821]: b. Co. Surrey, Eng., age 43, migr. from Havre de Grace, tavern-keeper; wife Maria, b. Co. of Cambridge, age 40 - 21 Apr. 1821

Miller, Christian, b. City of Haalburg, Denmark, age 29, migr. from Haalburg, milkman - 27 Apr. 1821

Morton, Thomas, b. Co. Cavan, Ire., age 37, migr. from Dublin, grocer; wife Catherine, b. Co. Cavan, age 37 - 7 May 1821

Morris, Robert [report 14 May 1821]: b. Lancashire, Eng., age 45, migr. from Bristol, grocer - 22 May 1821

Midy, Touissant [report 3 May 1821]: b. Rouen, Normandy, France, age 48, migr. from Havre de Grace, tavern-keeper; wife Catherine, b. town of Mans, France, age 45; Adrien Chandmanch [?], a stepson of Touissant Midy, b. in Mans, age 20 - 22 May 1821

Magouvran, Patrick, b. Co. Cavan, Ire., age 22, migr. from Nova Scotia, labourer - 31 May 1821

Malone, Francis, b. Co. Cavan, Ire., age 23, migr. from Liverpool, cartman - 23 June 1821

Mackin, Mathew, b. Co. Longford, Ire., age 31, migr. from Dublin, farmer, intending to reside in Warwarsing, Ulster Co., N.Y. - 25 June 1821

Martin, George [report 2 Oct. 1821]: b. Co. Cavan, Ire., age 50, migr. from Belfast, cartman; wife Jane, b. Co. Cavan, age 35 - 15 Oct. 1821

Morton, Joseph, b. Co. Fermanagh, Ire., age 36, migr. from Belfast, cartman; wife Alice, b. Co. Donegal, age 32; son William Henry, b. Co. Fermanagh, age 12; dau. Jane, b. New York, age 8 - 23 Oct. 1821

Mortimer, John, Jr., b. Leeds, Eng., age 22, migr. from Liverpool, woolen draper - 27 Oct. 1821

Mitchell, James, b. Killmarnock, Scotland, age 22, migr. from Greenock, carpet weaver - 18 Mar. 1822

Mahan, Patrick, b. Co. Fermanagh, Ire., age 31, migr. from Sligo, labourer - 23 Mar. 1822

Meert, Joseph Michael [report 8 Apr. 1822], b. Brussels, age 37, migr. from Antwerp, subj. of King of the Netherlands, merchant - 16 Apr. 1822

Mash, Thomas [report 14 Aug. 1822]: b. Co. Essex, Eng., age 50,
migr. from London, storekeeper; dau. Anne, b. London, age 21;
son Thomas, b. London, age 13 - 19 Aug. 1822

Moore, Thomas [report 11 Feb. 1823]: b. Co. Longford, Ire., age
26, migr. from Dublin, labourer, arrived NYC 20 Aug. 1819 -
17 Feb. 1823

Moughan, Michael, b. Co. Cavan, Ire., age 20, migr. from Newry,
labourer - 3 Apr. 1823

Marrin, Thomas [report 16 Apr. 1823]: b. Co. Monaghan, Ire., age
30, migr. from Newry, grocer - 21 Apr. 1823

Mooney, Patrick [report 16 Apr. 1827]: b. Co. Louth, Ire., age
28, migr. from Belfast, labourer - 24 Apr. 1827

Murphy, Thomas [report 5 Apr. 1827]: b. Co. Tipperary, Ire., age
28, migr. from Waterford, labourer - 5 Apr. 1827

Murray, John, b. Co. Sutherland, Scotland, age 30, migr. from
Greenock, carpenter - 29 Mar. 1827

Morrison, Hugh, b. Belfast, Ire., age 28, migr. from Belfast,
grocer - 21 Feb. 1827

Montgomery, John, b. Co. Donegal, Ire., age 26, migr. from Londonderry, labourer; wife Martha, b. Co. Londonderry, age 23;
son James, b. New York, age 9 months - 26 Feb. 1827

Morris, Robert, b. Co. Tipperary, Ire., age 48, migr. from Liverpool, merchant; wife Ellenor, b. Co. Kilkenny, age 44; son
Robert, Jr., b. Co. Tipperary, age 18; dau. Allice, b. Co.
Kilkenny, age 12; son Michael, b. Co. Kilkenny, age 7; son
Richard, b. Co. Tipperary, age 6; dau. Ellenor, b. Co. Tipperary, age 5; son John, b. Co. Tipperary, age 3 - 22 Feb.
1827

Montgomery, John, b. Co. Down, Ire., age 26, migr. from Belfast,
whitesmith - 20 Dec. 1826

Montgomery, James, subj. of G.B. - 30 Nov. 1826

Mullally, Richard, b. Co. Kilkenny, as were all of his family,
age 48, migr. from Waterford, labourer; wife Honor, age 48;
his son Richard, age 16; their son John, age 15; their son
Michael, age 13; their son Pierre, age 11; their son James,
age 7 - 20 July 1826

Murray, Patrick, b. Co. West Meath, age 28, migr. from Dublin,
labourer - 15 May 1826

Miller, John, b. in Bavaria, age 38, migr. from Amsterdam, tailor - 3 Dec. 1825

Murray, Samuel (by Robert Murray, his guardian), b. Co. Donegal,
Ire., age 20, migr. from Londonderry, cartman - 17 Oct. 1825

Montgomery, James R., b. Co. Down, Ire., age 31 years and 7 mos.,
migr. from Belfast, whitesmith; wife Johanna, b. Greenock,
Scotland, age 24 - 3 Nov. 1825

Mullin, John, b. Co. Fermanagh, Ire., age 30, migr. from Londonderry, mason; wife Bridget, b. Co. Fermanagh, age 30; dau.
Catharine, b. Co. Fermanagh, age 5; dau. Mary, b. Co. Fermanagh, age between 3 and 4 - 27 Sept. 1825

Mensch, Frederick Augustus [report 1 Sept. 1825]: b. Dresden,
Saxony, age 26, migr. from Havre, merchant - 19 Sept. 1825

Marr, Michael [report 4 Apr. 1825]: b. Co. Kilkenny, Ire., age
30, migr. from town of New Ross, Ire., tailor - 23 Sept. 1825

Morris, James [report 17 May 1825]: b. Co. Cavan, Ire., age 46, migr. from Dublin, labourer; son Andrew, b. Co. Cavan, age 17 - 18 May 1825

Mitchell, Alexander, b. Ire., age 27, migr. from Newry, gardener; wife Eliza, b. Ire., age 27 - 25 Feb. 1825

Martin, Patrick, b. Co. Leitrim, Ire., age 27, migr. from Dublin, shoemaker - 24 Nov. 1824

Miller, Benjamin G., b. Co. Cavan, Ire., age 37, migr. from Belfast, merchant - 15 Nov. 1824

Moore, Samson (by John Little, his guardian), b. Co. Antrim, age 17 years, 5 months and 23 days, migr. from Belfast, flour baker -

Mendia, Joseph, b. Cadiz, Spain, age 25 years and 2 months, migr. from Havana, Cuba, merchant - 21 July 1824

Maitland, Joseph, b. Kirkcudbright, Scotland, age 22, migr. from Liverpool, merchant, intending to reside in Norfolk, Va. - 15 Dec. 1823

Murray, Robert, subj. of G.B. - 18 Nov. 1823

Mullen, Michael [report 10 Nov. 1823]: b. Co. Londonderry, Ire., age 28, migr. from Londonderry, pedlar; wife Eliza, b. Co. Londonderry, age 28; son John, b. Londonderry, age 11 - 21 Nov. 1823

Mullen, Patrick [report 10 Nov. 1823]: b. Co. Londonderry, Ire., age 28, migr. from Londonderry, storekeeper - 21 Nov. 1823

Meehan, Thomas [report 14 May 1823]: b. Co. Sligo, Ire., age 30, migr. from Sligo, labourer - 21 May 1823

Mitchell, George [report 7 May 1823]: b. Co. Down, Ire., age 32, migr. from Belfast, farmer; wife Susan, b. Co. Down, age 22; dau. Margaret, b. Boston, Mass., age 7 months - 24 May 1823

Murphy, Thomas, subj. of G.B. - 17 Apr. 1827

Morrison, James, b. Co. Waterford, Ire., age 28, migr. from Waterford, porter; wife Ann, b. Co. Tipperary, age 34 - 24 July 1827

Moehring, Gotthilf, b. Dantzig, Prussia, age 25, migr. from Hamburgh, physician; wife Sophia, b. Hamburgh, age 22 - 16 Oct. 1827

Mali, Henry W. [report 15 Jan. 1828]: b. Verviers, Netherlands, age 23, migr. from Liverpool, merchant - 22 Jan. 1828

Midwood, James, Jr., b. Huddersfield, Co. of York, Eng., age 36, migr. from Huddersfield, merchant - 20 June 1828

Mackie, William, Jr., subj. of G.B. - 23 Aug. 1828

Marshall, Robert, seaman, subj. of G.B. - 20 Oct. 1828

Mahon, Con, subj. of G.B. - 17 Nov. 1828

Morse, John [report 11 June 1828]: b. Co. Tyrone, Ire., age between 14 and 15, migr. from Londonderry (by his guardian, Michael McBride) - 2 Dec. 1828

Maltman, William, subj. of G.B. - 30 Jan. 1830

Murphy, Michael, labourer, subj. of G.B. - 17 May 1830

Manigold, Peter, farmer, late of Sentheim, France, subj. of King of France - 21 June 1830

Muller, Peter, mariner, late of Copenhagen, subj. of King of Denmark - 24 June 1830

Meyer, Leopolt, late of the Duchy of Baden, painter, subj. of the Duke of Baden - 20 Apr. 1831

Mitchell, Henry, farmer, late of Westchester Co. and intending to reside in Oswego Co., N.Y., aubj. of G.B. - 26 Apr. 1832

Maag, John Baptiste, machinist, subj. of King of France - 24 Oct. 1832

Mel, John, merchant, subj. of King of France - 25 Feb. 1833

Mulligan, Michael, cooper, subj. of G.B. - 24 Mar. 1834

Magnusson, Levi Joseph, clerk, subj. of King of Sweden - 20 May 1834

Mortimer, Thomas, of Orange Co., spinner, subj. of G.B. - 12 July 1834

Manvell, John, late of Middlesex Co., Eng., brewer, subj. of G.B. -20 Oct. 1834

Monkhouse, John, late of London, tavern-keeper, subj. of G.B. - 20 Oct. 1834

Maganty, Patrick, labourer, subj. of G.B. - 4 Nov. 1834

Mahaffy, Francis, druggist, subj. of G.B. - 5 Nov. 1834

Moncrief, Alexander, subj. of G.B. - 8 June 1835

Metford, Francis, broker, subj. of G.B. - 27 Aug. 1835

Murphy, Patrick, shoemaker, subj. of G.B. - 21 Sept. 1835

Merian, John J., merchant, subj. of Republic of Switzerland - 5 Oct. 1835

Minerbi, Samuel, merchant, subj. of Emperor of Austria - 5 Nov. 1835

Malone, Richard, subj. of G.B. - 14 Jan. 1836

Menck, William, baker, subj. of King of Prussia - 4 Apr. 1836

Murphy, Owen, subj. of G.B. - 6 Apr. 1836

Megar, Patrick, grocer, subj. of G.B. - 24 May 1836

Milne, Alexander, stone cutter, subj. of G.B. - 21 June 1836

Marsi, Martin, labourer, subj. of G.B. - 21 June 1836

Morin, Andrew, subj. of G.B. - 12 Dec. 1836

Mulhallond, Richard, subj. of G.B. - 13 Dec. 1836

Montague, Henry, subj. of G.B. - 28 Feb. 1837

Morgan, James, residing in Phila., stone cutter, subj. of G.B. - 21 Mar. 1837

Murphy, James, subj. of G.B. - 31 Mar. 1837

Macklin, John, subj. of G.B. - 13 Apr. 1837

Macartney, William, subj. of G.B. - 4 May 1837

Mulligan, Matthew, subj. of G.B. - 29 July 1837

Mulligan, James, labourer, subj. of G.B. - 31 July 1837

Mullen, James, subj. of G.B. - 2 Jan. 1838

Mayor, Augustus Francis, subj. of King of Prussia - 5 Feb. 1838

Murtha, Patrick, subj. of G.B. - 3 Apr. 1838

Mackay, Francis, subj. of G.B. - 18 Apr. 1838

Murphy, John, subj. of G.B. - 6 June 1838

Mercer, James, of Rahway, N.J., subj. of G.B. - 8 Oct. 1838

Martin, Philip, subj. of G.B. - 8 Oct. 1838

Marsch, Charles, subj. of King of France - 15 Oct. 1838

Mackay, John, subj. of G.B. - 25 Oct. 1838

Manzanedo, Joseph, subj. of King of Spain - 2 Nov. 1838

Morgan, Edward, subj. of G.B. - 8 Nov. 1838

Mübert, Edward, subj. of King of Saxony - 16 Nov. 1838

Major, John, subj. of G.B. - 15 Jan. 1839

Matcovich, Antonio, subj. of Emperor of Austria - 30 Jan. 1839

Macully, James F., subj. of G.B. - 13 Mar. 1839

Martin, William, subj. of G.B. - 28 Feb. 1839

Murdock, Alexander, subj. of G.B. - 11 Mar. 1839

Mack, Francis, subj. of G.B. - 6 Mar. 1839

Machin, Owen, subj. of G.B. - 20 Mar. 1839

Millen, John Samuel, subj. of G.B. - 2 Apr. 1839

Maher, John, subj. of G.B. - 6 Apr. 1839

Martin, John, subj. of G.B. - 11 Apr. 1839

Motsch, Johannes, subj. of King of Bavaria - 11 Apr. 1839

Magher, Patrick, subj. of G.B. - 11 Apr. 1839

Molloy, Patrick J., subj. of G.B. - 12 Apr. 1839

May, Antoine, subj. of Free City of Hamburgh - 20 Apr. 1839

Martin, Conrad, subj. of King of Bavaria - 11 June 1839

Mahoney, Michael, subj. of G.B. - 16 July 1839

Morriss, Henry, subj. of G.B. - 25 July 1839

Macklin, Sarah, subj. of G.B. - 9 Aug. 1839

Morris, Peter, subj. of G.B. - 19 Aug. 1839

Morris, Bernard, subj. of G.B. - 19 Aug. 1839

Mulliner, Samuel, of Springfield, Illinois, subj. of G.B. - 27 Aug. 1839

May, Thomas P., subj. of G.B. - 25 Sept. 1839

Mier, Joseph Marquis, subj. of G.B. - 24 Oct. 1839

Morgan, Bernard, of Stapleton, Southfield, Richmond Co., N.Y., subj. of G.B. - 28 Oct. 1839

Mulligan, Samuel, subj. of G.B. - 4 Nov. 1839

Murray, John, subj. of G.B. - 5 Nov. 1839

Mahon, Patrick, subj. of G.B. - 6 Nov. 1839

Mansfield, Richard, subj. of G.B. - 30 Nov. 1839

Moran, Hugh, subj. of G.B. - 5 Mar. 1840

Meletta, Charles Conrad, subj. of Grand Duke of Hesse Darmstadt - 24 Mar. 1840

Mulcahy, Patrick, subj. of G.B. - 30 Mar. 1840

Mulcahy, Andrew, subj. of G.B. - 30 Mar. 1840

Mitchell, Thompson, subj. of G.B. - 6 Apr. 1840

Madden, James, subj. of G.B. - 17 June 1840

Molony, John, subj. of G.B. - 30 July 1840

Murphy, Stephen, of Hempstead, Queens Co., N.Y., subj. of G.B. -
   30 Sept. 1840

Murray, Robert, subj. of G.B. - 30 Sept. 1840

Meany, John, subj. of G.B. - 1 Oct. 1840

Mangan, John, subj. of G.B. - 1 Oct. 1840

Mangles, John, subj. of King of Hanover - 6 Oct. 1840

Moir, John, subj. of G.B. - 6 Oct. 1840

Miller, Balser, subj. of King of Wurtemberg - 12 Oct. 1840

Mallison, Charles, subj. of G.B. - 26 Oct. 1840

Moore, John B., subj. of G.B. - 26 Oct. 1840

Marriner, Joseph, subj. of G.B. - 27 Oct. 1840

Mullan, Michael, subj. of King of Bavaria - 30 Oct. 1840

Myer, Emanuel, subj. of Emperor of Germany - 30 Oct. 1840

Murphy, William, subj. of G.B. - 31 Oct. 1840

Migliore, Nicolo, subj. of King of Naples - 31 Oct. 1840

Murphy, John, subj. of G.B. - 2 Nov. 1840

Müller, Philip, subj. of King of Bavaria - 2 Nov. 1840

Mallen, Patrick, subj. of G.B. - 2 Nov. 1840

Mooney, Patrick, subj. of G.B. - 3 Nov. 1840

Margaritel, Giovan [clerk wrote "John"], subj. of Republic of
   Switzerland - 3 Nov. 1840

Mulane, Patrick, subj. of G.B. - 3 Nov. 1840

Maer, Francis, subj. of King of France - 3 Nov. 1840

Mathews, John W., subj. of G.B. - 6 Nov. 1840

Müller, John, subj. of Grand Duke of Baden - 13 Apr. 1840

Meyer, Ann Charlotte (wife of Lewis Henry Meyer), subj. of Free
   City of Bremen - 2 Dec. 1840

Meyer, Lewis Henry, subj., of Free City of Bremen - 2 Dec. 1840

Martin, James, subj. of G.B. - 31 Dec. 1840

Martin, Peter, subj. of G.B. - 31 Dec. 1840

                              N

Netterville, John Thomas, b. Swanlinbar, Co. Cavan, Ire., migr.
   from Londonderry - 27 Oct. 1804

Newport, George, b. Waterford, Ire., age 30, mihr. from Ire. -
   17 July 1812

Newman, John Pearse, late of London, merchant - 18 July 1808

Nixon, James, accountant, subj. of G.B. - 26 Apr. 1813

Nicholls, Anthony Edward, b. Plymouth, Eng.,, age 30, migr. from
   Bristol, ship-carpenter; wife Elizabeth, b. Charleston, S.C.,
   age 27; dau. Ann Maria, b. Washington City, age 5 - 16 Aug.
   1813

Nugent, William Henry, b. Dublin, Ire., age 31, migr. from Eng.
   - 1 Aug. 1817

Newbould, Samuel, b. Sheffield, Co. of York, Eng., age 30, migr.
   from Liverpool, merchant - 17 Nov. 1818

Nicholson, Charles [report 2 Apr. 1821]: b. Co. Armagh, Ire., age
   33, migr. from Belfast, cartman - 17 Apr. 1821

Nelson, Robert D., b. Co. Cavan, Ire., age 50, migr. from Dublin, grocer - 19 Apr. 1821

Nash, William [report 7 May 1821]: b. Kensington, Middlesex Co., Eng., age 39, migr. from Portsmouth, porterhouse or tavern-keeper; wife Hannah, b. Co. Sussex, Eng., age 35; dau. Hannah Eliza, b. Portsmouth, age 6 years and 5 months; dau. Mary Ann, b. Portsmouth, age 6 years - 22 May 1821

Nicol, James, b. Paisley, Scotland, age 24, migr. from Greenock, weaver - 27 Nov. 1822

Nepomuceno, Cesareo Isaac, b. Island of Teneriffe, age 30, migr. from Teneriffe, merchant - 27 Sept. 1825

Nepomuceno, Francisco de Paulo, b. Teneriffe, age 36, migr. from Teneriffe, merchant; wife Rita, b. Teneriffe, age 28 - 27 Sept. 1825

Nicholson, Samuel [report 21 June 1824]: b. Co. Down, Ire., age 22, migr. from Belfast, merchant - 18 Jan. 1826

Nealis, John, b. Co. Donegal, Ire., age 22, migr. from Belfast, waiter - 1 Mar. 1826

Newman, John, b. Co. Longford, Ire., age 29, migr. from Liverpool, cartman; wife Margam [?], b. Co. Longford, age 28 - 24 Jan. 1828

Newsom, Eli, subj. of G.B. - 17 Jan. 1834

Niebuhr, Edward, clerk, subj. of Republic of Hamburgh - 11 June 1834

Norton, William, of Governor's Island, N.Y., carpenter, subj. of G.B. - 6 Nov. 1834

Nelson, William, accountant, subj. of G.B. - 29 Nov. 1834

Naudin, Stephen Nicholas, physician, subj. of King of France - 20 Feb. 1835

Nunnenmacher, John, sergt. in U.S. Army, residing on Governor's Island, subj. of Republic of Switzerland - 20 July 1835

Nevilles, James, labourer, subj. of G.B. - 17 May 1836

Norris, Henry, subj. of G.B. - 10 Sept. 1836

Niederman, John, subj. of King of Bavaria - 20 May 1837

North, Francis Thomas, merchant, subj. of G.B. - 26 May 1838

Noonen, Cornelius, subj. of G.B. - 1 Oct. 1838

Nelson, Samuel, subj. of G.B. - 24 Oct. 1838

Nugent, John S., subj. of G.B. - 5 Nov. 1838

Neagle, Michael, subj. of G.B. - 13 Apr. 1840

Nichols, John, of Flushing, Queens Co., N.Y., subj. of G.B. - 24 Oct. 1840

Noble, William, subj. of G.B. - 29 Oct. 1840

Nunes, Jacinto Pedro, b. Madeira, age 15 (by his master, Richard Sears, to whom he is apprenticed), migr. from Medeira, seaman, subj. of King of Portugal - 20 Mar. 1826

Nelson, Andrew, subj. of King of Sweden - 19 Oct. 1839

Northeimer, Bernard, subj. of King of Bavaria - 19 Apr. 1839

O

Ogilby, Robert, late of parish of Dromcosain [?], Co. Londonderry, Ire. - 24 Dec. 1802

O'Neil, Hugh, b. Co. Derry, Ire., age 35, migr. from Ire. - 22
Mar. 1806

O'Connor, Dennis, b. City of Dublin, age 30, migr. from Ire. -
22 Mar. 1806

O'Donnell, James Delaney, b. Dublin, age 22, migr. from Ire. -
2 Apr. 1812

Okell, Joseph, b. Cheshire, Eng., age 42, migr. from Liverpool,
butcher; wife Freelove, b. Huntington, L.I., N.Y., age 22; son
William, b. Huntington, age 3 years and 11 months; son Moses,
b. Huntington, age 1 year and 10 months - 26 Dec. 1821

Overend, William, b. Co. Armagh, Ire., age 27, migr. from Belfast, grocer - 4 May 1821

O'Leary, Timothy [report 13 Apr. 1821]: b/ City of Cork, age 40,
migr. from Cove of Cork, soap boiler; wife Ann, b. City of
Cork, age 34; son Arthur, b. City of Cork, age 18; son Michael,
b. City of Cork, age 17; son Daniel, b. NYC, age 2; dau. Mary
Ann, b. City of Cork, age 19; dau. Joanna, b. City of Cork,
age 10; dau. Catherine, b. City of Cork, age 8; dau. Jane, b.
NYC, age 4 - 21 Apr. 1821

Ogden, John [report 12 Apr. 1821]: b. Lancashire, Eng., as all
his family, age 29, migr. from Liverpool, manufacturer; wife
Jane, age 29; dau. Julia Jane, age 9; dau. Caroline Matilda,
age 7 - 21 Apr. 1821

O'Connor, Patrick John [report 14 Apr. 1821]: b. Co. Galway, Ire.,
age 30, migr. from London, grocer; wife Mary, b. Co. Cork, age
30 - 16 Apr. 1821

O'Grady, Joseph D., b. Co. Kerry, Ire., age 54, migr. from London, grocer; wife Ellen, b. Co. Kerry, age 60 - 16 Apr. 1821

Ogilby, Leonard [report 22 Nov. 1820]: b. Londonderry, Ire., age
30, migr. from Bordeaux, merchant; wife Eliza, age 29; son
John David, age 10; son Robert, age 8; son Frederick, age 6;
son Arthur, age 4; dau. Elizabeth, age 2; dau. Olivia, age 6
weeks - 2 Aug. 1823

O'Connor, Joseph James [report 15 Nov. 1819]: b. Co. Roscommon,
Ire., age 24, migr. from Dublin, farmer - 16 Nov. 1819

Oakley, William Smith [report 12 Oct. 1818]: b. London, age 35,
migr. from Amsterdam, merchant - 19 Oct. 1818

O'Connell, John, b. Co. Kilkenny, Ire., age 30; migr. from Waterford, pedlar; wife Frances, b. Co. Wexford, age 26 - 21 Jan.
1822

O'Shiel, William, grocer, subj. of G.B.; rec. by Dennis Gillespie, cartman, and Philip Fulkerson, late sergeant at arms in
the Court of Chancery - 27 Apr. 1822

O'Bryen [clerk wrote "O'Brien"], Patrick, b. Co. West Meath, Ire.,
age 28, migr. from Dublin, farmer - 28 Apr. 1823

O'Neil, Owen [report 13 Apr. 1824]: b. Co. Monaghan, Ire., age
24, migr. from Newry, sawyer - 19 Apr. 1824

Owens, James, b. Co. Tyrone, Ire., age 24, migr. from Londonderry, porter - 15 Nov. 1824

O'Neil, John, b. Co. Longfrod, Ire., age 28, migr. from Dublin,
burr millstone manufacturer - 7 Jan. 1825

O'Mara, John, b. Co. Kilkenny, Ire., age 31, migr. from Waterford,
grocer; wife Margaret, b. Co. Kilkenny, age 25 - 21 Mar. 1825

O'Neil, James C. [report 27 Feb. 1826]: b. Co. Mayo, as all the family, age 28, migr. from Co. Mayo, cartman; son Connel, age 7; James, age 5; John, age 4 - 6 Mar. 1826

O'Neill, James, b. Ire., age 38, migr. from Ire., clerk - 13 Apr. 1826

O'Rourke, Bernard, b. Co. Leitrim, Ire., age 24, migr. from Sligo, brickmaker - 18 Apr. 1826

O'Brien, Thomas [report 1 May 1826]: b. Co. Carlow, Ire., age 29, migr. from Liverpool, labourer; wife Bridget, b. Co. Wicklow, age 22; son James, b. Co. Carlow, age 5 years and 4 months; son William, b. Co. Carlow, age 3 years and 7 months; dau. Maria, b. Co. Carlow, age 1 year and 7 months - 16 May 1826

O'Ferrall, James, b. Co. West Meath, Ire., age 35, migr. from Dublin, Professor of Humanity - 29 May 1826

Ott, Anthony [report 2 Aug. 1826]: b. Willgottheim, France, age 48, migr. from Rotterdam, merchant - 21 Aug. 1826

O'Connor, Patrick, b. Co. Roscommon, as all his family, age 37, migr. from Liverpool, labourer; wife Ann, age 28; dau. Bridget, age 10; son Thomas, age 7; dau. Maria, age 5; son James, age 3; son Michael, age 1 year and 3 months - 29 Dec. 1827

O'Neill, Thomas, b. Co. Wexford, Ire., age 33, migr. from Liverpool, cordwainer; wife Bridget, b. Co. Wexford, age 28; son Joseph, b. Dublin City, age 3 - 9 Mar. 1827

O'Hern, David, subj. of G.B. - 21 July 1828

O'Meara, James, subj. of G.B. - 1 Nov. 1828

Owen, David Dale, chemist, subj. of G.B. - 2 Oct. 1829

Nightengale, William, late of Co. of Kent, Eng., butcher - 27 July 1830

O'Connor, James William, merchant, subj. of G.B. - 28 May 1831

O'Maher, Timothy, subj. of G.B. - 4 June 1831

O'Neil, James, coachmaker, subj. of G.B. - 15 Aug. 1831

O'Shea, Patrick, cooper, subj. of G.B. - 21 Sept. 1835

O'Connor, Luke, subj. of G.B. - 12 Nov. 1836

Osbrey, Thomas, of Brooklyn, Kings Co., N.Y., subj. of G.B. - 22 Mar. 1833

Osbrey, Elizabeth, subj. of G.B. - 9 Apr. 1833

O'Neill, James, subj. of G.B. - 7 Nov. 1838

Owen, Edward W., subj. of G.B. - 12 Apr. 1838

Oldham, Thomas M., subj. of G.B. - 4 Feb. 1839

O'Rorke, Hugh, subj. of G.B. - 16 Apr. 1839

O'Brien, James, subj. of G.B. - 6 Nov. 1839

O'Connor, Daniel, subj. of G.B. - 13 Apr. 1840

O'Hara, Patrick, subj. of G.B. - 14 Apr. 1840

O'Grady, Hugh, subj. of G.B. - 17 June 1840

O'Brien, Patrick, subj. of G.B. - 10 Oct. 1840

Oneretti, Thomas, subj. of King of Naples - 2 Nov. 1840

Oepp, William, subj. of King of Wurtemberg - 3 Nov. 1840

P

Parks, John, merchant, age 30, subj. of G.B. - 29 July 1802

Pirson, Joseph P., b. Walworth, age 19, migr. from Eng. - 22 June 1811

Pindar, Charles, b. Cronstadt, Russia, age 27, migr. from Russia - 20 July 1812

Phillips, Thomas [report 28 Dec. 1813]: b. Birmingham, Eng., age 33, migr. from Dublin, joiner; wife Elizabeth, b. Ire., age 29; son William, b. NYC, age 5; dau. Mary, b. NYC, age 4; dau. Elizabeth, b. NYC, age 2 - 28 July 1813

Page, Edward Postlethwayt, b. Devizes, Wiltshire, Eng., age 33, migr. from London, teacher; wife Sarah, b. New York, age 39 - 23 Mar. 1815

Patterson, James, subj. of G.B. - 28 Apr. 1815

Pisani, Andrew, b. Genoa, age 27, migr. from Lisbon, merchant, subj. of King of Sardinia - 1 Dec, 1815

Pihlstrom, Adolphus Peter, b. Gottenburg, Sweden, age 43, migr. from Gottenburg, seaman; son Joseph, b. Dorchester, Eng., age 8 - 24 Aug. 1816

Phillips, Thomas, b. Co. Antrim, Ire., age 50, migr. from Belfast, farmer; wife Jane; dau. Grace, age 22; son Robert, age 19; gives status as "merchant" - 28 May 1817

Plaskitt, Joshua, Jr. [report 2 June 1818]: b. Grimsby, Co. Lincoln, Eng., age 23, migr. from Hull, mariner - 24 June 1818

Prest, James Abbey, b. Hendon, Middlesex Co., Eng., age 33, migr. from London, merchant; wife Jane; dau. Williamina, age 11; son James, age 7; dau. Jane, age 3 - 9 Nov. 1818

Patterson, James, b. Co. Donegal, Ire., age 25, migr. from Londonderry, cartman; wife Margaret, b. Co. Donegal, age 23 - 23 Mar. 1819

Pool, Samuel [report 25 Sept. 1819]: b. Belfast, age 26, migr. from Belfast, cartman - 2 Oct. 1819

Penna, Joseph Joaquim, b. Relvas, Portugal, age 21, migr. from Rio Janeiro, merchant - 20 Apr. 1819

Pirnie, John, b. Perthshire, Scotland, age 29, migr. from Greenock, distiller - 3 Mar. 1820

Pollard, John Dobey, b. London, age 25, migr. from London, attorney-at-law - 12 Mar. 1821

Passmore, William, b. Co. Armagh, Ire., age 40, migr. from Newry, cartman - 30 Mar. 1821

Pernie, Peter, b. Perthshire, Scotland, age 28, migr. from Belfast, accountant - 2 Apr. 1821

Palmer, John, b. Co. Antrim, Ire., age 50, migr. from Belfast, grocer - 16 Apr. 1821

Perry, William, b. Dorcestershire, Eng., age 45, migr. from Liverpool, mason; wife Ellen, b. Derbyshire, age 49 - 17 Apr. 1821

Parker, John, b. Co. Antrim, Ire., age 40, migr. from Belfast, stone cutter; wife Arabella, b. Co. Antrim, age 35; son Samuel, b. Co. Antrim, age 15; son Isaac, b. Co. Antrim, age 13 - 19 Apr. 1821

Pettit, James [report 21 Apr. 1821]: b. Co. Longford, age 27, migr. Dublin, milkman; wife Mary, age 22 - 23 Apr. 1821

Page, Louis [report 16 Apr. 1821]: b. Genoa, Italy, age 41, subj. of King of Sardinia, migr. from St. Bartholomews in the W.I., fruiterer; wife Eliza, b. St. Martins, W.I., age 25 - 27 Apr. 1821

Parker, James [report 5 May 1821]: b. City of Cork, Ire., age 23, migr. from Cork, tavern-keeper - 21 May 1821

Patterson, John [report 3 May 1821]: b. Hanover, Germany, age 32, migr. from Hamburg, subj. of authorities of Hanover, grocer - 22 May 1821

Parker, Robert [report 10 May 1821]: b. Co. Fermanagh, Ire., age 35, migr. from Bordeaux, France, grocer; wife Catherine, b. Co. Cavan, age 30 - 31 May 1821

Patterson, William, b. Co. Donegal, Ire., age 23, migr. from Londonderry, cartman - 10 July 1821

Patten, Dennis [report 12 Dec. 1821]: b. Co. Donegal, Ire., age 28, migr. from Greenock, Scotland, grocer - 17 Dec. 1821

Powers, Patrick, b. Co. Waterford, Ire., age 42, migr. from Watreford, labourer - 20 May 1822

Philary, Denis, b. France, age 27, migr. from Havre de Grace, merchant - 27 Nov. 1822

Prendergast, Mary, b. Co. Surrey, Eng., age 23, migr. from London, spinster, arrived NYC in Oct. 1820 - 2 May 1823

Porter, John [report 4 June 1823]: b. Kings Co., Ire., age 24, migr. from Dublin, farmer - 24 June 1823

Paterson, Isaac, b. Invernessshire, Scotland, age 25, migr. from Liverpool, farmer; wife Ann, b. Rosshire, Scotland, age 18 - 30 Oct. 1823

Poschinger, Joseph Jacob [report 9 Oct. 1824]: b. town of Pettau in Styria, Austria, age 21, subj. of Emperor of Austria, migr. from Trieste in Iliria, merchant - 18 Oct. 1824

Pattison, William [report 20 Apr. 1824]: b. Co. of Dublin, age 27, migr. from Dublin, fur manufacturer, residence Brooklyn, N.Y. - 24 Apr. 1824

Patterson, Alexander, b. Co. Donegal, Ire., age 25, migr. from Londonderry, cordwainer, res. of Brooklyn, N.Y. - 24 Jan. 1825

Patterson, James, b. Co. Donegal, Ire., age 29, migr. from Londonderry, labourer, res. of Brooklyn - 24 Jan. 1825

Pignolet, Louis, b. Rheims, France, age 30, migr. from Havre, dyer; wife Susan, b. NYC, age 22; dau. Charlotte, b. NYC, age 3; son Louis, b. NYC, age 3 months - 19 Sept. 1825

Petersen, George Christopher [report 1 Sept. 1825]: b. Elsinore, Denmark, age 22, migr. from Gottenburg, Sweden, merchant - 19 Sept. 1825

Petri, John William, b. Bavaria, age 52, migr. from Eng., clerk; son John Richard, b. London, age 16; son John William, b. London, age 12 - 27 June 1826

Powell, George W. (by his guardian, William H. Smith, of Mount Desert, Maine, shipmaster) [report 11 Mar. 1826]: b. Co. of Hampshire, Eng., age 14, migr. from Portsmouth, apprentice seaman to Wm. H. Smith - 19 July 1826

Peterson, Charles, b. Hamburgh, Germany, age 34, subj. of the Emperor of Austria, migr. from Hamburgh, mariner - 30 Sept. 1826

Pratesy, Maximilian [report 5 Oct. 1826]: b. Florence, Italy, age 33, subj. of Grand Duke of Tuscany, seaman - 16 Oct. 1826

Porter, William H., b. Cambridge, Eng., age 34, migr. London, clerk - 31 May 1827

Pate, McDowall [report 15 Apr. 1828]: b. town of Paisley, Co. Renfrew, age 39, migr. from Greenock, weaver; son Mathew, b. Glasgow, age 14; son William, b. Glasgow, age 13 - 23 Apr. 1828

Porteous, Robert, subj. of G.B. - 23 Dec. 1828

Phiquepal, William, physician, subj. of King of France - 2 Oct. 1829

Pearson, Joseph, gentleman, subj. of G.B. - 28 Apr. 1830

Pilling, James, of Bushwick, Kings Co., farmer, subj. of G.B. - 22 Dec. 1830

Povey, John, subj. of G.B. - 8 Feb. 1831

Perkins, John, late of Liverpool, Nova Scotia, merchant, now of Dover, N.J., clerk, subj. of G.B. - 23 July 1831

Pedersen, James, mariner, subj. of King of Sweden - 19 Oct. 1831

Pearson, Thomas, of Kings Co., N.Y., subj. of G.B. - 24 Nov. 1831

Pope, Charles, Jr., carpenter, subj. of G.B. - 19 Oct. 1832

Pfotrer, George, subj. of Grand Duke of Baden - 29 May 1832

Pettit, Patrick, distiller, subj. of G.B. - 23 Mar. 1833

Parker, William, dyer, subj. of G.B. - 3 June 1834

Paulus, Gustav Ludwig Henry, druggist, subj. of Elector of Hesse - 27 Sept. 1834

Penzer, Valentin, subj. of King of Bavaria - 1 Apr. 1836

Paisley, William J., cartman, subj. of G.B. - 18 Aug. 1836

Pascoe, Nicholas Jasper, chairmaker, late of Davenport, Co. of Devon, Eng. - 27 Sept. 1836

Pratt, Robert, tailor, subj. of G.B. - 28 Nov. 1836

Pritchard, Richard, carpenter, subj. of G.B. - 22 Dec. 1836

Polwarth, James, subj. of G.B. - 3 Nov. 1838

Pollock, Samuel, subj. of G.B. - 29 Oct. 1838

Peacock, William Robert, subj. of G.B. - 3 Apr. 1838

Panzer, Charles, subj. of King of France - 9 Apr. 1838

Picabia, John M., subj. of Queen of Spain - 27 Nov. 1838

Portilla, Ramon de la, subj. of Queen of Spain - 20 Dec. 1838

Pfrommer, Gottlieb Friedrich, subj. of Grand Duke of Baden - 9 Apr. 1839

Pfrommer, Philip, subj. of Grand Duke of Baden - 9 Apr. 1839

Pulte, Johan, subj. of King of Prussia - 9 Apr. 1839

Pyne, Thomas, subj. of G.B. - 12 Apr. 1839

Pearce, Charles, subj. of G.B. - 29 May 1839

Parish, George, subj. of Free City of Hamburgh - 8 June 1839

Padden, Michael, of New Brighton, Richmond Co., N.Y., carpenter, subj. of G.B. - 11 Sept. 1839

Pfeffel, Peter Charles, subj. of Free City of Frankfort a/M - 26 Sept. 1839

Pfluger, John Jacob, subj. of Prince of Hesse Cassel - 5 Nov. 1839

Peterkin, John, subj. of G.B. - 6 Nov. 1839

Pfirrmann, Charles, subj. of King of Bavaria - 3 Feb. 1840

Palmer, Francis, subj. of G.B. - 30 Mar. 1840

Porter, Frederick, farmer, subj. of G.B. - 28 May 1840

Patterson, Thomas, subj. of G.B. - 30 Sept. 1840

Picabia, Joseph M.M., subj. of King of Spain - 7 Oct. 1840

Panton, James, subj. of G.B. - 19 Oct. 1840

Paget, Charles, subj. of G.B. - 21 Oct. 1840

Pillory, Joseph, subj. of King of France - 30 Oct. 1840

Pettit, James, subj. of G.B. - 3 Nov. 1840

Paisley, John, subj. of G.B. - 4 Nov. 1840

Pedroita, Charles, subj. of Republic of Switzerland - 5 Nov. 1840

Prior, Hugh, subj. of G.B. - 21 Nov. 1840

Q

Quin, John, age 28, b. Newry, migr. from Ire. - 25 Sept. 1809

Quig, Michael [report 14 Apr. 1821]: b. Glasgow, Scotland, age 25, migr. from Londonderry, bleecher - 16 Apr. 1821

Queen, John, b. Co. Donegal, Ire., age 30, migr. from Londonderry, labourer; wife Fanny, b. Co. Donegal, age 25; son John, b. Co. Donegal, age 6; dau. Mary, b. NYC, age 2 - 27 Apr. 1821

Quinn, Thomas, b. Ire., age 23, residing in Phila., b. Sligo, migr. from Killybeggs, arrived Port of New York 30 July 1821 - 30 Mar. 1826

Quin, Daniel, baker, subj. of G.B. - 17 Mar. 1836

Quin, James, of New Brighton, Richmond Co., N.Y., mason, subj. of G.B. - 10 Aug. 1839

Quin, Patrick, of New Brighton, Richmond Co., N.Y., subj. of G.B. - 10 Aug. 1839

Quinley [clerk wrote "Quinlin"], Patrick, of New Brighton, Richmond Co., mason, subj. of G.B. - 10 Aug. 1839

R

Russell, James [report 16 July 1818]: b. Ire., age 25, migr. from Londonderry, carpenter; wife Pamela B., b. Newark, N.J., age 26; son Josiah, age 1 year and 5 months - 20 July 1818

Rodgers, Joseph [report 7 July 1818]: b. Eng., age 32, migr. from town of Sheffield, York Co. - 20 July 1818

Reiner, Augustus, b. Brackenheimer, Wurtemberg, age 31, migr. from Holland, via London, grocer - 20 Dec. 1813

Romanis, Robert, b. Scotland, age 52, merchant; wife Barbara, b. Scotland, age 40; dau. Elizabeth, b. London, age 13; son Robert, Jr., b. London, age 11; dau. Katharine, b. London, age 10; dau. Agnes, b. London, age 2 - 22 May 1818

Robbins, Edward [report 7 July 1818]: b. Eng., age 29, migr. from Birmingham, Warwickshire; wife Ann, age 28 - 20 July 1818

Rhodes, Samuel, subj. of G.B. - 15 Nov. 1819

Radcliffe, Edward, b. Dobcross, Yorkshire, Eng., age 29, migr. from Liverpool, cordwainer, intending to reside in Washington, Middlesex Co., N.J.; wife Ann; dau. Sarah, age 5; dau. Betsy, age 3 - 27 Nov. 1819

Robinson, Thomas [report 12 Nov. 1819]: b. Co. Derry, Ire., age 29, migr. from Londonderry, clerk; wife Priscilla, b. Co. Derry, age 27 - 27 Dec. 1824

Reilly, Myles [report 20 Apr. 1820]: b. Bullinlough [?], Co. of West Meath, Ire., age 27, migr. from Liverpool, grocer - 21 Apr. 1820

Rielly, Patrick, b. Bally James Duff, Ire., age 31, migr. from Dublin, farmer and gardner: wife Mary, b. Bally James Duff, age 31; son Peter, b. New York, age 1; dau. Ellenor, b. Bally James Duff, age 4 - 24 Feb. 1821

Rooney, Hugh, b. Co. Leitrim, Ire., as were all his family, age 46, migr. from Belfast, grocer; wife Mary, age 42; son Hugh, age 18 years and 3 months; son Patrick, age 10; son James, age 6; son Niel, age 5; dau. Catherine, age 16 - 29 Mar. 1821

Rooney, James [report 9 Apr. 1821]: b. Co. Cavan, Ire., age 30, migr. from Belfast, grocer; wife Ann, b. Co. Monaghan, age 30 - 16 Apr. 1821

Reddy, Patrick [report 6 Apr. 1821]: b. Co. Tippersry, Ire., age 34, migr. from Halifax, N.S., accountant - 16 Apr. 1821

Robertson, Hugh [report 2 Apr. 1821]: b. Perthshire, Scotland, age 30, migr. from Greenock, grocer - 17 Apr. 1821

Robinson, Peter, subj. of King of Prussia - 17 Apr. 1821

Rees, John, b. Cardiganshire, Wales, age 27, migr. from London, grocer - 19 Apr. 1821

Richers, Hinrich, b. Hanover, Germany, age 30, migr. from London, grocer - 21 Apr. 1821

Rotchford, William, b. Dublin, Ire., age 25, migr. from Belfast, grocer; wife Margaret, b. Co. Wicklow, age 28 - 23 Apr. 1821

Reynolds, William [report 1 May 1821]: b. Staffordshire, Eng., age 28, migr. from London, tavern- and boarding house keeper - 21 May 1821

Rea, James [report 1 May 1821]: b. Co. Down, Ire., age 33, migr. from Belfast, boarding house keeper; wife Jane, b. Co. Down, age 30 - 22 May 1821

Rorke, Thomas [report 7 May 1821]: b. Co. Down, Ire., age 31, migr. from Newry, cartman; wife Barbery, b. Co. Down, age 21; dau. Margaret, b. Co. Down, age 1 - 22 May 1821

Roes, John Joseph, b. Palermo, Sicily, age 32, subj. of King of Naples, migr. from London, seaman - 28 May 1821

Ryan, George, b. Co. Limerick, Ire., age 25, migr. from Cork, accountant; wife Mary, b. Co. Limerick, age 22; dau. Mary, b. NYC, age 3 months - 28 May 1821

Ramsey, John [report 20 June 1821]: b. Co. Antrim, Ire., age 37, migr. from Londonderry, sawyer; wife Mary Ann, b. Co. Armagh, age 26 - 22 June 1821

Ryan, William, b. Co. Tipperary, age 30, migr. from Dublin, a teacher; wife Amelia, b. Dublin, age 22; son Maurice, b. Montreal, Lower Canada, age 3; son William, b. Montreal, age 1 - 2 Jan. 1822

Ray, James H., b. Digby, N.S., age 22 years and 17 days, migr. from Digby, druggist - 29 Mar. 1822

Robey, George [report 19 Apr. 1822]: b. Nottinghamshire, Eng., age 33, migr. from Dundee, Scotland, dyer; wife Janet, b. Perthshire, Scotland, age 43 - 20 Apr. 1822

Reilly, Michael, b. Co. Meath, Ire., age 26, migr. from Dublin, cartman; wife Mary, b. Co. Meath, age 25; dau. Ellen, b. Co. Meath, age 5; son James, b. New York, age 3; dau. Catharine, b. New York, age 10 months - 19 Sept. 1822

Reilly, Thomas, b. Co. Leitrim, Ire., age 25, migr. from Belfast, farmer - 30 Jan. 1823

Rogers, Joseph, b. Paisley, Scotland, age 29, migr. from Greenock, stone cutter - 19 Feb. 1823

Robertson, James, b. Edinburgh, Scotland, as were all of family, age 46, migr. from Greenock, confectioner; wife Margaret, age 42; dau. Margaret, age 19; dau. Mary, age 17; dau. Jean, age 10; son James, age 7; son John, age 4 - 31 May 1823

Reily, John P., b. Drum, Co. Monaghan, Ire., age 22, migr. from Dublin, accountant - 21 June 1823

Rooney, John [report 4 Aug. 1823]: b. Co. Sligo, Ire., age 36, migr. from Sligo, fruiterer; wife Sarah, b. Co. Sligo, age 29; dau. Margaret, b. Co. Sligo, age 8 - 20 Aug. 1823

Ripamonti, Andrea, b. Leghorn, age 25, migr. from Liverpool, a merchant, subj. of Emperor of Austria - 19 Aug. 1823

Rayner, James, b. Manchester, Eng., age 24, migr. from London, merchant - 22 Nov. 1823

Roberts, Hugh J. [report 13 Nov. 1823]: b. Cadiz, Spain, age 24, migr. from Cadiz, merchant, subj. of King of Spain - 27 Nov. 1823

Robinson, Thomas, subj. of G.B. - 27 Dec. 1834

Rafferty, Barney [report 4 Apr. 1825]: b. Co. Cavan, Ire., age 26, migr. from Dublin, mason - 18 Apr. 1825

Reilly, Michael, subj. of G.B. - 16 May 1825

Ronalds, Robert [report 11 June 1825]: b. London, Eng., age 24, migr. from Island of Grenada, W.I., labourer - 20 June 1825

Reinhold, Casper [report 9 Aug. 1825]: b. Marburg, Hesse Cassel, age 33, migr. from Bremen, die sinker - 19 Sept. 1825

Robinson, William, b. Londonderry, Ire., age 24, migr. from Londonderry, type founder - 29 Nov. 1825

Roper, James [report 2 Dec. 1825]: b. Eng., age 37, migr. from Bristol, carpenter; son William, b. Tiverton, age 16; son Abraham, b. Taunton, age 14; dau. Betsey, b. Bristol, age 12; son James, b. Bristol, age 11; son John, b. Bristol, age 9 - 20 Dec. 1825

Rottiers, John Nepomucene, b. Antwerp, age 25 years, 9 months & 13 days, migr. from Antwerp, subj. of King of the Netherlands, formerly in military service of Emperor of Russia, to be an agent or factor in N.Y. State, intending to reside in town of Le Rayville, Jefferson Co., N.Y. - 21 June 1824

Roche, Stephen, b. Co. Cork, Ire., age 23, migr. from Waterford, labourer - 22 June 1826

Richers, Carsten, b. Kingdom of Hanover, age 25, migr. from Bremen, sugar baker - 19 Apr. 1826

Richardson, Jeremiah, b. Cumberland Co., Eng., age 21 years and 2 months, migr. from Liverpool, blacksmith - 20 May 1826

Richard, Frederick, b. Strasburg, Dept. of the Lower Rhine, France, age 40, migr. from Havre, merchant; wife Aglai, b. Paris, age 29 - 22 Sept. 1826

Robb, William, b. Co. Armagh, Ire., age 30, migr, from Belfast, grocer - 21 Dec. 1826

Ryan, James [report 31 Aug. 1826]: b. Co. Tipperary, Ire., age 35, migr. from London, labourer - 27 Dec. 1826

Rose, George, b. London, age 34, migr. from Liverpool, gentleman - 17 Jan. 1827

Roberts, John, b. Co. Suffolk, Eng., age 49, migr. from Liverpool, gardner - 19 Feb. 1827

Rogan, John [report 19 Mar. 1827]: b. Co. Tyrone, Ire., age 27, migr. from Liverpool, coachman - 29 Mar. 1827

Reily, William, b. Co. Tyrone, Ire., age 36, migr. from Belfast, accountant; wife Elizabeth, b. Co. Monaghan, age 34; son James, b. Co. Tyrone, age 5 years and 6 months; dau. Margaret, b. N.Y., age 4; dau. Mary, b. New York, age 2 - 26 May 1827

Rhodes, James, b. Yorkshire, Eng., age 22, migr. from Liverpool, merchant - 19 Nov. 1827

Rankin, John [report 9 Nov. 1827]: b. Co. Longford, Ire., age 26, migr. from Liverpool, mason; wife Catherine, b. Co. West Meath, age 28; son John, b. New York, age 4 months - 22 Jan. 1827

Rea, Arthur [report 22 Mar. 1828]: b. Co. Cavan, Ire., age 34, migr. from Belfast, grocer; son Edward, b. Co. Cavan, age 12 years and 6 months - 24 Mar. 1828

Randall, William, late of London, subj. of G.B. - 23 May 1829

Reilly, John, barkeeper, subj. of G.B. - 28 Sept. 1829

Robb, Mary Antoinette, widow, subj. of G.B. - 30 June 1830

Reilly, Farrel, late of Co. Longford, Ire., labourer - 21 Aug. 1830

Reed, James, weaver, subj. of G.B. - 22 Nov. 1831

Reed, John, broadcloth finisher, subj. of G.B. - 22 Nov. 1831

Reilly, Michael, labourer, subj. of G.B. - 23 Feb. 1832

Rogers, Thomas, jeweller, subj. of G.B. - 18 Dec. 1832

Ruby, Anthelme, subj. of King of France - 22 Feb. 1834

Roach, Patrick, labourer, subj. of G.B. - 25 Feb. 1834

Rankin, George Nicholas, gentleman, subj. of G.B. - 22 July 1834

Russell, Matthew, druggist, subj. of G.B. - 2 Feb. 1835

Roth, Johan Georg, butcher, subj. of King of Wurtemberg - 30 Mar. 1835

Reid, John, physician, subj. of G.B. - 3 June 1835

Reid, Alexander, physician, subj. of G.B. - 3 June 1835

Read, John, tailor, subj. of G.B. - 22 Oct. 1835

Rohr, Augustus William, subj. of Republic of Hamburgh - 24 Feb. 1836

Rawlins, Thomas C., subj. of G.B. - 2 Apr. 1836

Rabadan, Carlos, subj. of King of Spain - 26 Aug. 1836

Ratheram, Edward, bricklayer, subj. of G.B. - 22 Dec. 1836

Ratheram, James, mason, subj. of G.B. - 22 Dec. 1836

Richardson, John Morgan, of Newtown, Queens Co., N.Y., subj. of G.B. - 14 Mar. 1837

Riley, James, subj. of G.B. - 7 Mar. 1837

Roach, David, of Westchester Co., N.Y., subj. of G.B. - 20 Nov. 1837

Rittergerod, Heinrich, subj. of King of Hanover - 9 Apr. 1838

Robertson, Robert, subj. of G.B. - 9 Apr. 1838

Riley, James, subj. of G.B. - 11 Apr. 1838

Russell, William, subj. of G.B. - 12 Apr. 1838

Rittergerod, Friedrich, subj. of King of Hanover - 12 Apr. 1838

Ready, John, subj. of G.B. - 1 June 1838

Roe, Edward, subj. of G.B. - 28 June 1838

Ryan, James, subj. of G.B. - 5 July 1838

Reid, George, subj. of G.B. - 2 Aug. 1838

Riese, Rudolph, subj. of King of Prussia - 29 Oct. 1838

Roche [clerk wrote "Roach"], John, subj. of G.B. - 5 Nov. 1838

Rourke, Patrick, subj. of G.B. - 8 Mar. 1839

Ruben, Christian, subj. of Republic of Switzerland - 25 Mar. 1839

Reid, John, subj. of G.B. - 6 Apr. 1839

Richmond, John, subj. of G.B. - 6 Apr. 1839

Regan, James, subj. of G.B. - 8 Apr. 1839

Rorrie, Justus, subj. of King of Hanover - 11 Apr. 1839

Ramsey, Alexander, subj. of G.B. - 13 Apr. 1840

Rosenbaum, Frederick, subj. of King of Bavaria - 19 Apr. 1839

Raistrick, George, subj. of G.B. - 11 June 1839

Reilly, John, subj. of G.B. - 24 June 1839

Reichard, Frederick, subj. of Free City of Hamburgh - 3 July 1839

Reuning, Louis, subj. of Grand Duke of Hesse Darmstadt - 26 July 1839

Rapp, Friedrich, subj. of King of Bavaria - 22 Oct. 1839

Raworth, Morris, subj. of G.B. - 22 Oct. 1839

Rice, Bernard, subj. of G.B. - 14 Apr. 1840

Robb, Isaac, subj. of G.B. - 9 May 1840

Ryan, John, subj. of G.B. - 20 May 1840

Renchen, Mathew, subj. of G.B. - 3 June 1840

Robinson, Thomas, subj. of G.B. - 13 July 1840

Rodrigues, Bernardo Jose, subj. of Queen of Portugal - 15 July 1840

Rapp, Martin, subj. of Grand Duke of Baden - 13 Aug. 1840

Reynaud, Nicholas Joseph, subj. of King of France - 25 Sept. 1840

Robins, William, subj. of G.B. - 30 Sept. 1840

Ryan, Thomas, subj. of G.B. - 29 Sept. 1840

Rogers, Daniel, subj. of G.B. - 5 Oct. 1840

Roda, Zachariah, subj. of King of Prussia - 8 Oct. 1840

Riley, Richard, subj. of G.B. - 10 Oct. 1840

Reich, Solomon, subj. of King of Prussia - 12 Oct. 1840

Robertson, John, subj. of G.B. - 19 Oct. 1840

Russ, Sidney George, subj. of G.B. - 20 Oct. 1840

Russell, Thomas, subj. of G.B. - 22 Oct. 1840

Robinson, George, subj. of G.B. - 26 Oct. 1840

Ryan, Andrew, subj. of G.B. - 27 Oct. 1840

Roe, Thomas, subj. of G.B. - 4 Nov. 1840

Rieder, Henry, subj. of G.B. - 5 Nov. 1840

Rogers, James, subj. of G.B. - 5 Nov. 1840

Rosweiler, Jakob, subj. of King of Bavaria - 7 Dec. 1840

Robinson, Thomas, subj. of G.B. - 14 Dec. 1840

S

Sproull. Joseph, b. Co. Tyrone, Ire., age 46, migr. from Hust-
lend [?], Co. Donegal - 8 Feb. 1804

Sampson, William, b. Londonderry, age 41, migr. from Ire. - 12
July 1806

Sweney, John, b. Cork, Ire., age 29, migr. from France - 18 Dec.
1805

Swiney, John, merchant, subj. of G.B. - 27 June 1806

Sweetman, John, b. Dublin, age 50, migr. from Ire. - 25 June
1807

Swan, William, b. Co. Armagh, Ire., age 22, migr. from Ire. - 10
July 1807

Smyth, John, of Newbirgh, Orange Co., N.Y., merchant, subj. of
G.B. - 24 Nov. 1807

Stubbs, William, b. Whitewood, Co. Meath, Ire., age 50, migr.
from Ire. - 31 Dec. 1807

Stubbs, Edward, b. Dublin, Ire., age 22, migr. from Ire. - 31
Dec. 1807

Sampson, William, counsellor-at-law, subj. of G.B. - 20 Aug. 1808

Smith, Thomas, of Mount Pleasant, Westchester Co., N.Y., subj. of
G.B. [report 26 Dec. 1809]: b. Scotland, age 33, migr. from
Scotland - 27 Dec. 1809

Stephens, Edward [report 9 Nov. 1809]: b. Dublin, age 26, migr.
from Ire. - 9 Nov. 1809

Schmidt, John William [report 3 Jan. 1810]: b. Wunsiedel, Prussia, age 28 - 15 Jan. 1810

Simpson, Edmund, age 24, subj. of G.B. - 19 Jan. 1810

Swanton, John, age 35, b. Co. Cork, Ire., migr. from France - 1
Sept. 1810

Sampson, William [report 29 Oct. 1810]: wife Grace, b. Co. Antrim, Ire., age 40; son John Curran, b. Co. Antrim, age 16;
dau. Catherine Anne Sampson, b. Co. Antrim, age 14

Smissaert, Gilbert, b. Utrecht, Holland, age 32, migr. from Holland - 26 June 1812

Sieveking, John Henry, subj. of Emperor of France - 15 June 1812

Shields, William, b. Ire., age 26, migr. from Newry, mariner - 21 Dec. 1815

Speyer, Christian Frederick, subj. of King of Bavaria [report 9 Dec. 1817]: b. Windsheim, Franconia, age 41, migr. from Rotterdam, merchant; wife Eliza Henrietta, b. London, age 29; dau. Eliza, b. London, age 12; dau. Maria, b. London, age 8; son George William, b. London, age 6 - 22 Dec. 1817

Syme, Andrew, b. Borness, Linlithgow, Scotland, age 29, migr. from Liverpool, merchant, intending to reside in New Orleans - 14 Oct. 1817

St. Marie, Alexis, b. Bordeaux, France, age 24, migr. from Havre, counsellor-at-law - 29 Nov. 1817

Sloan, John, b. Co. Antrim, sge 30, migr. from Belfast, cartman; wife Jane, b. Co. Antrim, age 30; dau. Jane, b. NYC, age 8; dau. Eliza, b. NYC, age 6; dau. Mary, b. NYC, age 4; dau. Marittia, b. NYC, age 2 - 2 May 1818

Snip, John [report 15 May 1818]: b. Wurtemberg, age 41, migr. from Antigua, sausage maker and Gardner; wife Dorothy, b. Belleburgh, Germany, age 31; dau. Susannah, b. NYC, age 7; dau. Catharina, b. NYC, age 4; dau. Maria, b. NYC, age 2; Sally Ann, b. NYC, age 1 - 18 May 1818

Spinolla, John L., b. Madeira, age 35, migr. from Madeira, subj. of King of Portugal; wife Eliza, b. N.Y. State; son John L., Jr., b. NYC, age 8 - 20 July 1818

Simpson, Robert [report 5 June 1819]: b. Ire., age 29, migr. from Belfast, manufacturer; wife Sarah; dau. Mary Jane, age 6; son John, age 4; son Samuel Martin, age 2 [said children all born in U.S.] - 28 Aug. 1819

Sinclair, George (by his guardian, Thomas S. Walsh), b. Co. of Dublin, age 17, migr. from Ire. - 25 Feb. 1829

Strippel, Nicholas, b. Hesse Cassel, age 37, migr. from London, colour manufacturer, subj. of Elector of Hesse Cassel - 30 June 1819

Salborg, Jonas M., b. Stockholm, Sweden, age 33, migr. from Gottenbord, shipmaster - 16 July 1819

Smith, Edward [report 19 July 1819]: b. Salisbury, Eng., age 33, migr. from London; wife Fanny; son Henry Roome Smith, age 2 months - 22 July 1819

Somerville, William H., b. Glasgow, Scotland, age 25, migr. from Liverpool, butcher - 30 Sept. 1819

Stewart, Charles [report 30 Sept. 1819]: b. Co. Forfar, Scotland, age 36, migr. from Greenock, farmer, intending to settle in the State of N.Y.; wife Isabella; son John, age 9 - 2 Oct. 1819

Snook, John, b. town of Wellington, Co. of Somerset, Eng., age 25, migr. from London, carpenter - 16 Dec. 1819

Skeen, John [report 11 Feb. 1820]: b. Forfarshire, Scotland, age 25, migr. from Dundee, tailor - 22 Feb. 1820

Steffenson, Erick, b. Sweden, age 36, migr. from London, seaman [report 18 Mar. 1820] - 21 Mar. 1820

Smith, Nicholas Winter [report 2 May 1820]: b. Co. Durham, Eng., age 25, migr. from Co. Durham - 2 May 1820

Shorland, Thomas, subj. of G.B. - 26 Aug. 1820

Schlieman, Hinrich, b. Neuschanebeek [?], Hanover, Germany, age 20, migr. from Bremen, butcher, subj. of King of Hanover - 26 June 1820

Smith, Robert [report 17 Jan. 1821]: b. Co. Tyrone, Ire., age 32, migr. from Londonderry, cartman; wife Ann, age 32 - 27 Jan. 1821

Smith, Bernard [report 16 Feb. 1821]: b. Co. Cavan, Ire., as all his family, age 36, migr. from Dublin, cartman; wife Catharine, age 30; dau. Mary, age 9; dau. Bridget, age 6 - 19 Feb. 1821

Steuart, William, b. Co. Cavan, Ire., age 53, migr. from Dublin, cartman; wife Jane, b. Co. Cavan, age 54 - 19 Mar. 1821

Seidel, John [report 30 Mar. 1821]: b. town of Lauterbach, Germany, age 35, migr. from Vienna, merchant, subj. of Germany, Emperor of Austria, King of Bohemia and Hungary - 31 Mar. 1821

Shields, Richard, b. Co. Cavan, Ire., age 31, migr. from Galway, cartman; son Patrick, b. Co. Cavan, age 5 - 31 Mar. 1821

Schofield, John, b. Sheffield, Eng., age 39, migr. from Liverpool, cartman - 31 Mar. 1821

Sheridan, Mathew [report 9 Apr. 1821]: b. Co. Cavan, Ire., age 35, migr. from Newry, grocer and brewer; wife Bridget, b. Co. Cavan, age 26; son Patrick, b. Co. Cavan, age 8; son John, b. NYC, age 5; son Thomas, b. NYC, age 3; dau. Ann, b. NYC, age 2 - 10 Apr. 1821

Sheehy, William, b. Co. Cork, Ire., age 59, migr. from Dublin, grocer; wife Ann, b. Staffordshire, Eng., age 45 - 13 Apr. 1821

Simister, Joseph [report 6 Apr. 1821]: b. Lancashire, Eng., age 30, migr. from Liverpool, grocer; wife Trulove, b. Dudley, Worcestershire, Eng., age 33 - 16 Apr. 1821

Strong, Duncan, b. Perthshire, Scotland, age 45, migr. from Greenock, grocer - 18 Apr. 1821

Shields, Andrew [report 7 Apr. 1821]: b. Co. Monaghan, Ire., as all his family, age 45, migr. from Newry, porter; son Owen, age 20; son Andrew, age 14; son Henry, age 10; dau. Mary, age 18 - 19 Apr. 1821

Sweeny, Myles [report 7 Apr. 1821]: b. Co. Mayo, Ire., age 36, migr. from Sligo, porter - 19 Apr. 1821

Schmidt, Detlof Henry [report 19 Apr. 1821]: b. Hamburgh, Germany, age 36, migr. from Hamburgh, merchant; wife Ann Ulricka Christiana, b. Straesen, Germany, age 35; son William Frederick, b. village of Velgast, age 5 - 20 Apr. 1821

Sinnott, John [report 19 Apr. 1821]: b. Co. Wexford, Ire., age 34, migr. from Dublin, grocer - 20 Apr. 1821

Stafford, Nicholas, b. Co. Wexford, Ire., age 25, migr. from Liverpool, blacksmith - 23 Apr. 1821

Smith, William, b. Wiltshire, Eng., age 35, migr. from Calcutta, E.I., grocer; wife Martha, b. Co. Mayde [sic!], Ire., age 32 - 23 Apr. 1821

Speight, Henry [report 24 Apr. 1821]: b. Staffordshire, Eng., as all his family except son Henry, age 39, migr. from Sunderland, brewer; wife Mary, age 41; dau. Elizabeth, age 18; dau. Mary, age 14; son Alexander Nicholson, age 9; son Francis Cartwright, age 7; son Alfred Cockran, age 3; son Henry, b. NYC, age 1 - 27 Apr. 1821

Smith, Gerret [report 25 Apr. 1821]: b. town of Wesel, Circle
of Westphalia, Germany, age 31, migr. from Amsterdam, gardner
- 27 Apr. 1821

Shee, Richard, b. Co. Kilkenny, Ire., age 60, migr. from Dublin,
grocer; wife Elizabeth, b. Co. Sligo, age 32 - 27 Apr. 1821

Stephenson, Thomas [report 13 Apr. 1821]: b. Co. York, Eng., age
38, migr. from Liverpool, grocer; wife Christiana, b. Co. York,
age 38; son James, b. Huntingtonshire, Eng., age 7 - 28 Apr.
1821

Sullivan, Michael [report 26 Aug. 1820]: b. Co. Kilkenny, Ire.,
age 32, migr. from London, labourer, residing in Brooklyn, N.Y.;
wife Mary, b. Killany, Co "Kary" [Kerry], Ire., age 22 - 21
May 1821

Snyder, Joseph [report 30 Apr. 1821]: b. Strasburg, Dept. of the
Lower Rhine, France, age 30, migr. from Portsmouth, tavern-
keeper; wife Mary, b. near Montreal, Lower Canada, age 23; son
Joseph, b. Plattsburg, N.Y., age 10 years and 6 months - 21
May 1821

Steinbrenner, Frederick W., b. Weissenburg, age 34, migr. from
Lyons, merchant, subj. of King of France; [son] Philip Pister,
b. Bergzabern, age 14; [son] Paul Boell, b. Lyons, age 12 -
29 Aug. 1821

Snook, James, subj. of G.B. - 18 Dec. 1821

Scannell, Daniel [report 9 Apr. 1822]: b. Co. Kerry, Ire., age
36, migr. from Waterford, grocer; wife Mary, b. Co. Cork, age
29; dau. Julia, b. Co. Cork, age 8; dau. Catherine, b. Co.
Cork, age 6; son Daniel, b. Co. Cork, age 4; son Dennis, b.
NYC, age 1 - 16 Apr. 1822

Smith, James, b. Rawdon, Yorkshire, Eng., age 22, migr. from
Yorkshire, merchant - 20 Apr. 1822

Sheridan, Mathew, subj. of G.B. - 23 Apr. 1822

Stitt, David [report 25 Apr. 1822]: b. Co. Armagh, Ire., age 25,
migr. from Belfast, cartman; wife Ann, b. Co. Armagh, age 20;
son Alexander, b. NYC, age 7 months - 27 Apr. 1822

Scott, George Penman, b. Newcastle upon Tyne, Eng., age 27, migr.
from Liverpool, printer - 20 May 1822

Sharp, Alexander, b. Scotland, age 50, migr. from London, gentleman - 1 June 1822

Scanlin, Barney, b. Co. Sligo, age 24, migr. from Sligo, cooper
- 17 June 1822

Stansbie, Luke, b. Birmingham, Eng., age 33, migr. from Liverpool, merchant - 19 Dec. 1822

Schwab, Christopher, b. Germany, age 25, migr. from Lisbon, Portugal, baker, subj. of King of Wittenburgh or Emperor of Prussia; wife Maria, b. Germany, age 28; son John, b. NYC, age 6;
son Frederick, b. NYC, age 3 months - 30 Jan. 1823

Stapleton, John [report 24 Jan. 1823]: b. Co. Kilkenny, Ire.,
age 35, migr. from Waterford, mason - 25 Jan. 1823

Sharp, Henry David, b. Alloa, Scotland, age 21, migr. from Greenock, merchant - 20 Mar. 1823

Shirley, William W. [report 21 Sept. 1818]: b. Staffordshire,
Eng., age 21, migr. from Liverpool, merchant - 20 Mar. 1823

Souillard, Bernard [report 22 Mar. 1823]: b. Vie, France, age 27,
migr. from Bordeaux, druggist, arrived NYC Jan, 1819 - 23 Mar.
1823

Sadleir, Hugh B., b. town of Tipperary, Prov. of Munster, Ire.,
    age 28, migr. from Ire., druggist and apothecary 24 July 1823

Sturcken, Henry, b. town of Debsteat [?], near Bremen, Kingdon
    of Hanover, age 27, migr. from Bremen, sugar refiner - 24 July
    1823

Shields, Thomas, b. Co. Monaghan, Ire., age 21, migr. from London-
    derry, labourer - 19 Apr. 1824

Shields, John (by his father, Richard Shields), b. Co. Cavan,
    Ire., age 19, migr. from Ire., cartman - 23 Aug. 1824

Shanahan, John, b. Co. Kilkenny, Ire., age 31, migr. from Water-
    ford, clergyman - 27 Oct. 1824

Shaves [?], Isaac [report 4 Nov. 1824], b. Co. Kent, Eng., age
    31, migr. from London, cooper - 15 Nov. 1824

Shaves [?], William [report 4 Nov. 1824]: b. Co. Kent, Eng., age
    26, migr. from London, grocer and boarding house keeper; wife
    Ellen, b. Newry, Co. Down, Ire., age 30; dau. Elizabeth Sarah,
    b. NYC, age 3; son William Isaac, b. NYC, age 1 - 15 Nov. 1824

Sands, Thomas, b. Leeds, Eng., age 36, migr. from Liverpool,
    merchant; wife Sarah, b. Yorkshire, Eng., age 33; son Thomas
    Branson, b. Brooklyn, N.Y., age 10; dau. Susannah, b. Liver-
    pool, age 7; dau. Sarah Elizabeth, b. NYC, age 4; son Hugh
    Spooner, b. NYC, age 6 months - 31 Dec. 1824

Steitz, Ludwig [report 12 Jan. 1825]: b. town of Trandelburgh,
    Hesse Cassel, age 41, migr. from London, baker - 15 Jan. 1825

Souza, John, b. Portugal, age 25, migr. from Madeira, labourer;
    wife Julia, b. Ire., age 21 - 26 Apr. 1825

Smith, James, b. Scotland, age 28, migr. from Selkirk, Scotland,
    teacher; wife Isabella, b. Eng., age 30; dau. Margaret Ann, b.
    New York, age 3; dau. Isabella, b. New York, age 18 months -
    16 May 1825

Shirley, Cephas, b. Staffordshire, Eng., age 31, migr. from Liver-
    pool, merchant - 21 June 1825

Shields, Patrick [report 8 Aug. 1825]: b. Co. Armagh, Ire., age
    22, migr. from Belfast, dirt cartman - 15 Aug. 1825

Saynish, Lewis [report 29 Aug. 1825]: b. Duchy of Nassau, age 29,
    migr. from Havre, physician - 24 Sept. 1825

Smith, Joseph [report 24 July 1820]: b. Co. of Wiltshire, Eng.,
    age 30, migr. from London, umbrella maker; wife Mary Ann, b.
    London, age 31; dau. Eliza, b. NYC, age 7 months - 21 Nov. 1825

Smith, James T., subj. of G.B. - 21 Nov. 1825

Shoals, John, b. Co. Londonderry, Ire., age 28, migr. from Lon-
    donderry, type founder; wife Elizabeth, b. Co. Antrim, age 26
    - 29 Nov. 1825

Scanlon, Thomas [report 17 Feb. 1826]: b. Co. Sligo, Ire., age
    24, migr. from Sligo, labourer - 20 Feb. 1826

Scanlan, William John [report 30 Mar. 1826]: b. Co. Sligo, Ire.,
    age 24, migr. from Ire., gentleman - Apr. 1826

Stanton, James, b. Co. Londonderry, Ire., age 25, migr. from Bel-
    fast, labourer - 10 Apr. 1826

Sarjeant, Thomas [report 1 May 1826]: b. Bristol, Eng., age 32,
    migr. from London, merchant - 1 May 1826

Simmonite, George, b. Sheffield, Eng., age 58, migr. from Liver-
    pool, tailor, residing in State of Conn.; wife Elizabeth, b.
    Derby, age 56; son Thomas, age 17 and dau. Elizabeth, age 13,
    both b. Sheffield - 22 June 1826

Sawyer, Charles Henry, b. Devonshire, Eng., age 19, migr. from Eng., farmer - 27 June 1826

Schreyer, John, b. Vienna, Austria, age 32, migr. from Hamburgh, turner - 25 July 1826

Swan, Samuel [report 10 Apr. 1826]: b. Co. Londonderry, Ire., age 39, migr. from Londonderry, labourer; wife Esther, b. Co. Donegal, age 32; dau. Margaret, b. Co. Londonderry, age 14; son Joseph, b. Co. Londonderry, age 12; son James, b. Co. Londonderry, age 9 - 26 Aug. 1826

Selmes, Tilden, b. Co. Sussex, Eng., age 22, migr. from London, carpenter - 18 Dec. 1826

Stewart, Peter, of Perthshire, Scotland, age 40, migr. from Is. of Guernsey, mason - 25 Jan. 1827

Smith, William, b. Devonshire, Eng., age 40, migr. from Eng., gentleman; son Thomas, b. Devonshire, age 15 - 8 Mar. 1827

Steinbrenner, Frederick William [report 25 Sept. 1821]: b. Wissemburg, France, age 33 in Feb. 1821, migr. from Lyons, France, merchant - 19 Feb. 1827

Stevenson, George Goude, b. Stamford, Lincolnshire, Eng., age 25, migr. from Gravesend, via South America, gentleman; wife Mary, b. Gosport, Eng., age 25 - 17 Apr. 1827

Scanlin, Barney [report 16 Apr. 1827]: b. Co. Donegal, Ire., age 26, migr. from Londonderry, hack driver - 21 May 1827

Sherryd, Patrick [report 16 June 1827]: b. Co. Fermanagh, Ire., age 35, migr. from Sligo, mason and grocer - 18 June 1827

Sievers, John Frederick, b. Bremen, age 31, migr. from Bremen, mariner - 28 June 1827

Schaeffer, Herman [report 15 Jan. 1828]: b. Frankfurt, age 29, migr. from Havre, merchant - 22 Jan. 1828

Stein, John Frederick [report 11 Feb. 1828]: b. Stralsund, Prussia, age 23, subj. of King of Prussia, migr. from Hamburgh, mariner - 20 Feb. 1828

Short, John , b. Co. Tipperary, Ire., age 46, migr. from Limerick, labourer, residing in town of Bedford, Westchester Co., N.Y. - 1 Apr. 1828

Schufzler, Frederick [report 7 Apr. 1828]: b. Bremen, age 26, migr. from Bremen, sugar baker - 21 Apr. 1828

Sneath, John, subj. of G.B., house-carpenter - 17 June 1828

Samuel, David, merchant, subj. of G.B. - 29 Nov. 1828

Schlesinger, Philipp, merchant, subj. of Hamburgh - 31 July 1829

Scallin, Andrew, glass packer, subj. of G.B. - 18 Jan. 1830

Shaw, Joseph, b. Chesterfield, Eng., age 48, migr. from England, gardener - 22 Feb. 1830

Shaw, Joseph, Jr., b. Eng., age 22, migr. from Eng., gardener - 22 Feb. 1830

Sheehey, John, grocer, subj. of G.B. - 26 May 1830

Smith, Daniel, late of London, subj. of G.B. - 21 Aug. 1830

Shea, Bartholomew, boarding house keeper, age 32, subj. of G.B. - 24 Dec. 1830

Scantlebury, Joseph, subj. of G.B. - 17 Feb. 1831

Stead, Edward, merchant, subj. of G.B. - 21 Mar. 1831

Soulier, Achille, subj. of King of France - 23 Mar. 1831

Swanton, Thomas, student of medecine, subj. of G.B. -14 May 1831

Smith, Martin, mariner, subj. of King of Denmark - 22 June 1831

Stewart, William, mariner, subj. of King of Sweden - 19 Oct. 1831

Stunt, William Henry, subj. of G.B. - 24 Oct. 1831

Stewart, Charles, subj. of G.B. - 9 June 1832

Sparr, John Henry Godfrey, farmer, subj. of King of Denmark - 25 June 1832

Senff, Henry, subj. of Prince of Schaumburgh - 8 Oct. 1832

Sheedy, Michael, labourer, subj. of G.B. - 16 Sept. 1833

Smith, James, labourer, subj. of G.B. - 28 Aug. 1833

Santini, John, native of Corsica, confectioner, subj. of King of France - 21 May 1833

Shelton, James, painter, subj. of G.B. - 21 May 1833

Sullivan, James, subj. of G.B. - 11 Feb. 1833

Simmons, Michael, late of Co. Carlow, cartman, subj. of G.B. - 28 May 1833

Slack, James W., subj. of G.B. - 18 Feb. 1834

Stevens, David, cabinetmaker, subj. of G.B. - 24 Feb. 1834

Seaton, Henry, ship chandler, subj. of G.B. - 30 Sept. 1834

Saunders, William Edward, late of London, student-at-law, subj. of G.B. - 21 Oct. 1834

Shephard, Samuel, subj. of G.B. - 4 Nov. 1834

Simms, Robert B., Sr., gunmaker, subj. of G.B. - 5 Nov. 1834

Spencer, Frederick, mariner, subj. of G.B. - 12 June 1835

Scarth, Thomas, subj. of G.B. - 22 Apr. 1835

Scheitlin, Anthony, merchant, subj. of Republic of Switzerland - 29 Aug. 1835

Stengel, David, smelter, subj. of Grand Duke of Baden - 3 June 1835

Sweeny, Michael, labourer, subj. of G.B. - 21 Sept. 1835

Scho, George, merchant, subj. of Emperor of Austria - 8 Oct. 1835

Schott, Florence, shoemaker, subj. of King of France - 23 Sept. 1835

Smith, George, carpenter, subj. of G.B. - 14 Nov. 1835

Sole, John T., architect, subj. of G.B. - 23 Dec. 1835

Sevin, David Frederick, subj. of King of Bavaria - 3 Aug. 1835

Sheppard, George G., merchant, subj. of G.B. - 18 Feb. 1836

Spencer, John S., merchant, subj. of G.B. - 25 Apr. 1836

Stultz, George, of Williamsburgh, ropemaker, subj. of Grand Duke of Baden - 6 July 1836

Sthamer, William, subj. of Republic of Hamburg - 19 Dec. 1836

Santwaik, Johanis, mariner, subj. of King of Holland - 13 Aug. 1836

Smith, Thomas, bricklayer, subj. of G.B. - 23 Dec. 1836

Sunderland, John, subj. of G.B. - 12 Apr. 1837

Simpson, William, cabinetmaker, subj. of G.B. - 10 Apr. 1837

Shearer, Archibald, of Westchester Co., farmer, subj. of G.B. - 4 Nov. 1837

Schuler, George Frederick, shoemaker, subj. of Grand Duke Leopold of Baden - 16 Aug. 1837

Schäfer, Meyer, subj. of King of Bavaria - 8 Nov. 1838

Stirling, William, subj. of G.B. - 19 Jan. 1838

Sherrerd, Jane G. (widow of Archibald Sherrerd), subj. of G.B. - 23 Jan. 1838

Shannessy, Patrick, blacksmith, subj. of G.B. - 28 Feb. 1838

Schoeffberger, Anthony, subj. of Emperor of Austria - 22 Mar. 1838

Simpson, Robert, subj. of G.B. - 9 Apr. 1838

Smith, Arthur A., subj. of G.B. - 12 Apr. 1838

Spier, Frederick Albert, subj. of King of Prussia - 21 June 1838

Slavin, James, subj. of G.B. - 2 July 1835

Sargeant, Thomas, subj. of G.B. - 9 July 1838

Shelly, William, labourer, subj. of G.B. - 20 Sept. 1838

Schmeltz, Francis A., subj. of King of France - 15 Oct. 1838

Spence, George, subj. of G.B. - 15 Oct. 1838

Shaughnessy, John, subj. of G.B. - 5 Nov. 1838

Simpson, John, subj. of G.B. - 6 Nov. 1838

Singleton, George, subj. of G.B. - 7 Nov. 1838

Stothard, George, subj. of G.B. - 9 Nov. 1838

Sandaver, John, subj. of G.B. - 9 Nov. 1838

Shedel, John J., subj. of G.B. - 10 Nov. 1838

Schiesser, John, subj. of King of Bavaria - 12 Nov. 1838

Sumfleth, Jacob, subj. of King of Hanover - 30 Nov. 1838

Stodart, Daniel, subj. of G.B. - 30 Nov. 1838

Sturges, Robert, subj. of G.B. - 10 Dec. 1838

Sturcke, Carl Joh. Quintus Friedrich, subj. of Republic of Hamburgh - 8 Mar. 1839

Schmidt, Balthasar Daniel, subj. of Republic of Switzerland - 11 Feb. 1839

Schwartz, Jacob, subj. of King of Bavaria - 1 Jan. 1839

Schäfer, Lewis, subj. of King of Hanover - 6 Feb. 1839

Sullivan, John, subj. of G.B. - 1 Apr. 1839

Sommer, Philip, subj. of King of Bavaria - 9 Apr. 1839

Schnakenberg, Claus, subj. of King of Hanover - 9 Apr. 1839

Sweeny, Owen, subj. of G.B. - 11 Apr. 1839

Schilling, Hermann, subj. of King of Hanover - 11 Apr. 1839

Such, James, subj. of G.B. - 18 Apr. 1839

Sullivan, William, subj. of G.B. - 22 Apr. 1839

Smith, James, subj. of G.B. - 17 June 1839

Seyler, Charles, subj. of King of Prussia - 26 July 1839

Selter, Andrew, subj. of King of Bavaria - 29 July 1839

Shortis, Edward, subj. of G.B. - 30 July 1839

Sinclair, John, subj. of G.B. - 10 Aug. 1839

Sullivan, James, of Richmond Co., N.Y., mason, subj. of G.B. - 13 Aug. 1839

Sholl, John, silk manufacturer, subj. of G.B. - 14 Aug. 1839

Stoler, Jacob, subj. of Grand Duke of Baden - 27 Aug. 1839

Seligmann, Samuel, subj. of King of Prussia - 30 Sept. 1839

Seligmann, David, subj. of King of Prussia - 30 Sept. 1839

Siebert, Silvester, subj. of Prince of Hesse Cassel - 5 Nov. 1839

Stief, Frederick H., subj. of Grand Duke of Saxe Weimar - 6 Nov. 1839

Shelley, John, subj. of G.B. - 9 Nov. 1839

Sander, William, subj. of King of Prussia - 7 Dec. 1839

Seligmann, Michael, subj. of King of Prussia - 12 Dec. 1839

Seligmann, Henry, subj. of King of Prussia - 12 Dec. 1839

Sutton, William, subj. of G.B. - 14 Dec. 1839

Smith, John Preston, subj. of G.B. - 30 Dec. 1839

Seller, Emanuel, subj. of Free City of Bremen - 13 Apr. 1840

Speyer, Philip, subj. of Free City of Frankfort a/M - 11 May 1840

Silva, Joaquim Jose Duarte, subj. of Queen of Portugal - 31 July 1840

Stebil, Abraham, subj. of King of Prussia - 30 Sept. 1840

Schauffer, Friedrich, subj. of King of Wurtemberg - 12 Oct. 1840

Schneider, Gottfried Jacob, subj. of King of France - 14 Jan. 1840

Smith, Hugh, of Westchester Co., N.Y., subj. of G.B. - 29 Jan. 1840

Sifert, Ludwig, subj. of King of Bavaria - 1 Apr. 1840

Scott, Thomas, subj. of G.B. - 3 Apr. 1840

Sauer, John, subj. of King of Bavaria - 13 Apr. 1840

Steers, Benjamin, subj. of G.B. - 13 Apr. 1840

Smith, Charles C., subj. of G.B. - 14 Apr. 1840

Southwell, John, subj. of G.B. - 16 Apr. 1840

Schlumpf, John P., subj. of Switzerland - 19 May 1840

Schmults, John, subj. of King of Hanover - 30 May 1840

Sproul, David, subj. of G.B. - 4 June 1840

Staunton, John, subj. of G.B. - 4 June 1840

Stewart, William, subj. of G.B. - 9 June 1840

Schnyder, Charles, subj. of Switzerland - 25 Aug. 1840

Schertsen, John, subj. of Grand Duke of Baden - 28 Sept. 1840

Sullivan, Jeramiah, subj. of G.B. - 30 Sept. 1840

Smith, Anton, subj. of King of Prussia - 2 Oct. 1840

Scott, William, subj. of G.B. - 8 Oct. 1840

Sands, Joseph, subj. of Queen of Spain - 19 Oct. 1840

Stoupp, Johan Peter, subj. of King of Prussia - 26 Oct. 1840

Stoupp, Peter, subj. of King of Prussia - 26 Oct. 1840

Shaughnassy, John, subj. of G.B. - 2 Nov. 1840

Schober, Christopher, subj. of King of Bavaria - 4 Nov. 1840

Sawyer, Henry R., subj. of G.B. - 22 Dec. 1840

Schultz, Heinrich, subj. of King of Hanover - 22 Dec. 1840

Thomson, Andrew, late of Strathaven, Scotland - 31 Dec. 1803

Thompson, George, subj. of G.B. - 21 Oct. 1811

Tomes, Francis [report 16 May 1816]: b. Campden, Co. of Gloucester, Eng. age 36, migr. from Birmingham and Liverpool, merchant;
wife Maria, b. Dolgelly, North Wales, age 26; son Francis, b.
Birmingham, age 3; son Charles, b. Birmingham - 23 May 1816

Tone, William Theobald Wolfe, subj. of King of France, age 25 -
31 Oct. 1816

Thomas, Pierre, a professor at West Point, b. Berne, Switzerland,
age 26, prof. of the sword, migr. from St. Malo, France - 31
July 1817

Turner, William [report 6 Aug. 1818]: b. Yorkshire, Eng., age 52,
shoemaker, migr. from Liverpool, intends to reside in Ohio or
Indiana Territory; wife Sarah; son William, age 7; dau. Mary
Ann, age 2 - 17 Aug. 1818

Tiernan, Julius William, b. Hesse Cassel, age 49, migr. from London, chair manufacturer - 30 June 1819

Thoms, Christian [report 5 June 1820]: b. Hanover, Germany, age
27, migr. from London, laborer - 20 June 1820

Ternen, James, b. Co. Tyrone, Ire., as were all of family,, age
35, migr. from Londonderry, cartman; wife Maria, age 35, son
John, age 11; dau. Eliza, age 8 - 3 Apr. 1821

Topham [he signs "Tepham"], Thomas, b. Co. Cavan, Ire., age 29,
migr. from Dublin, grocer - 16 Apr. 1821

Turner, Joseph Prentiss [report 14 Apr. 1821]: b. Horton, Kings
Co., Nova Scotia, age 34, migr. from Windsor, N.S., grocer -
17 Apr. 1821

Tally, Michael, b. Co. Tyrone, Ire., age 21, migr. from Belfast,
grocer - 17 Apr. 1821

Toohey, Michael J. [report 10 Apr. 1821]: b. Co. Tipperary, Ire.,
age 35, migr. from London, grocer; wife Mary, b. Co. Tipperary,
age 26; dau. Mary Ann, b. Co. Tipperary, age 8; dau. Eliza, b.
Co. Tipperary, age 5 - 19 Apr. 1821

Thompson, Robert, b. Co. Armagh, Ire., age 30, migr. from Newry,
grocer; wife Sarah, b. Co. Armagh, age 30 - 28 Apr. 1821

Toner, Bryan [report 16 May 1821]: b. Co. Armagh, Ire., age 30,
migr. from Newry, grocer - 2 June 1821

Thornton, Patrick, b. Co. Monaghan, Ire., age 25, migr. from Belfast, milkman; wife Mary, b. Co. Monaghan, age 19 - 26 June
1821

Taylor, Abraham [report 2 Aug. 1822]: b., as all the family, at
Hampshire, Isle of Wight, age 32, migr. from Cowes, Isle of
Wight, farmer; wife Sarah, age 24; son Robert, age 5; son Leonard Abraham, age 3; dau. Sarah, age between 1 and 2 - 24 Aug.
1822

Thompson, Samuel, b. Rawden, Eng., age 25, migr. from Rawden,
merchant - 18 Dec. 1821

Truelove, James, b. Nottinghamshire, Eng., age 32, migr. from
London, engineer; wife Hannah, b. Staffordshire, age 38; son
George, b. London, age 6; son John b. London, age 3 - 27 Jan.
1823

Tucker, George, b. Island of St. Thomas, age 26, migr. from Liverpool, merchant, subj. of G.B. - 19 Aug. 1823

Thériat, Augustus R., b. Paris, age 34, migr. from Bordeaux, merchant - 22 Oct. 1823

Thomas, William, b. Liverpool. Nova Scotia, age 36, migr. from Liverpool, N.S., shipmaster - 23 Sept. 1824

Tiffanan, Patrick, b. Co. Sligo, Ire., age 35, migr. from Sligo, cartman - 20 Feb. 1826

Timmoney, James, b. Co. Tyrone, Ire., age 20, migr. from Londonderry, waiter - 27 July 1826

Taber, Henry [report 16 Sept. 1826]: b. Saulwert, Prussia, age 58, migr. from Hamburgh, porter - 18 Sept. 1826

Traner, Thomas, b. Co. Galway, Ire., age 27, migr. from Galway, domestic servant; wife Anne, b. Co. Tyrone, age 25 - 1 Dec. 1826

Timmins, Patrick, b. Queens Co., Ire., age 36, migr. from Dublin, stone cutter - 22 Dec. 1826

Travers, James [report 20 Jan. 1827]: b. New Brunswick, Nova Scotia, age 35, migr. from N.S., tobacconist - 26 Jan. 1827

Thally, Charles, b. Ire., age 37, migr. from Belfast, hatter; wife Sarah, b. Ire., age 27 - 28 June 1827

Taylor, George [report 16 Apr. 1823]: b. Temple Port Parish, Co. of Cavan, Ire., age 28, migr. from Dublin, labourer - 17 July 1827

Trotter, Jonathan, b. Disbrow, Eng., age 30, migr. from New Castle upon Tyne, morocco manufacturer - 7 Mar. 1828

Toumine, Lucas [report 19 May 1828]: b. Island of Guernsey, age 36, migr. from Guernsey, shoemaker; wife Pamela, b. Yonkers, Westchester Co., N.Y., age 34; son Edward, b. NYC, age 13; dau. Clarissa, b. Yonkers, age 11; son John, b. NYC, age 8; dau. Harriet, b. NYC, age 6; dau. Sarah, b. NYC, age 2 - 20 May 1828

Thompson, Ralph, b. Berwick upon Tweed, Eng., age 46, migr. from Jamaica, W.I., planter - 20 June 1828

Tobin, Richard, subj. of G.B. - 14 Sept. 1828

Tully, Philip C., subj. of G.B. - 17 Nov. 1828

Tool, Jeremiah, subj. of G.B. - 18 Nov. 1828

Tyson, Isaac, clerk, subj. of G.B. - 20 Nov. 1828

Todd, Samuel, distiller, subj. of G.B. - 20 July 1829

Tunbridge, John, house-painter, subj. of G.B. - 17 Mar. 1829

Thomson, William, web manufacturer, subj. of G.B. - 25 Oct. 1830

Thurston, Joshua, subj. of G.B. - 5 Mar. 1830

Tomlinson, Joseph Hale, merchant, subj. of G.B. - 27 June 1831

Tomlinson, George, gentleman, subj. of G.B. - 27 June 1831

Tool, Martin, late of Co. Tipperary, Ire., cartman - 22 Nov. 1831

Thomson, John, subj. of G.B. - 23 Jan. 1832

Thode, William Denton, builder, subj. of Republic of Hamburgh - 24 Apr. 1832

Tardif, William, house-carpenter, subj. of G.B. - 1 Sept. 1832

Tomlinson, Henry, of Huntington, L.I., subj. of G.B. - 28 Jan. 1833

Taylor, Thomas, builder, subj. of G.B. - 21 May 1833

Toomy, Daniel, labourer, subj. of G.B. - 6 Oct. 1835

Tittermann, Charles Edward, subj. of King of Saxony - 14 Dec. 1836

Turnbull, James, subj. of G.B. - 6 Nov. 1837

Tooley, John, subj. of G.B. - 9 Apr. 1838

Thatcher, Thomas, subj. of G.B. - 3 Nov. 1838

Talbot, Joseph, subj. of G.B. - 7 Nov. 1838

Taylor, George, M.D., subj. of G.B. - 7 Mar. 1839

Twaddle, James, subj. of G.B. - 13 Mar. 1839

Twaddle, Robert, subj. of G.B. - 13 Mar. 1839

Thomson, John W., subj. of G.B. - 23 Mar. 1839

Thomson, William, subj. of G.B. - 3 Apr. 1839

Tate, Calhoun, subj. of G.B. - 11 Apr. 1839

Tregent, Henry Wakeman, subj. of G.B. - 30 May 1839

Tracy, Martin, subj. of G.B. - 7 June 1839

Taylor, Henry, subj. of G.B. - 16 Sept. 1839

Terra, Kaspar, subj. of King of Bavaria - 7 Oct. 1839

Topinard, Antoine, subj. of King of France - 4 Nov. 1839

Toole, Edward, subj. of G.B. - 4 Nov. 1839

Thompson, Michael, subj. of G.B. - 5 Nov. 1839

Timlin, Edward, subj. of G.B. - 9 Nov. 1839

Talbot, Whitton, subj. of G.B. - 30 Mar. 1840

Taylor, Andrew, subj. of G.B. - 25 Apr. 1840

Townsend, Andrew James, subj. of G.B. - 16 Oct. 1840

Twaddle, Alexander, subj. of G.B. - 21 Oct. 1840

Tobin, Patrick, subj. of G.B. - 29 Oct. 1840

Tennent, W., formerly of Belfast, subj. of G.B. - 16 Jan. 1810

U

Usher, Luke, b. Dublin, Ire., age 36, migr. from Dublin, mineral water manufacturer; wife Mary B.; son William, age 11; dau. Ann, age 8; son Francis W., age 7; son Luke, age 5; dau. Caroline, age 3; dau. Emma, age 16 months; dau. Rebecca, age 1 month - 30 Jan. 1819

Uren, John, b. parish of Pweness, age 45, migr. from Liverpool, husbandman, resident of North Castle, Westchester Co., N.Y.; wife Grace, b. Co. of Cornwall, age 51; son John, b. parish of Masnon [?], age 19; son William, b. parish of Masnon, age 16; son Richard, b. parish of Perrain, age 13; son Thomas, b. parish of Perrain, age 11; dau. Christiana, b. Maoren [or Maoven], age 17; dau. Grace, b. Perrain, age 14; dau. Mary, b. Perrain, age 9 - 5 May 1819

Ulrich, August L. [report 14 June 1819]: b. Jena in Duchy of Saxon Weimar, age 30, migr. from Liverpool, merchant; wife Henrietta; dau. Mary, age 4; dau. Jenny, age 3; dau. Louise, age 2 - 23 Nov. 1819

Ungemach, Seibert, subj. of Duke of Hesse Cassel - 11 Nov. 1840

Unger, Jacob, subj. of King of Prussia - 12 Nov. 1838

V

Van Duisburg, Henry Anthony Charles, b. Danzig in Prussia, age 42, migr. from Hamburgh, merchant - 22 Nov. 1815

Varey, Joseph [report 15 July 1818]: b. West Ardsley, Yorkshire, Eng., age 29, migr. from Falmouth, merchant - 20 July 1818

Vallier, Joseph [report 28 June 1820]: b. Quebec, Canada, grocer, migr. from Quebec, age 28 - 29 June 1820

Vaissiere, Victor, b. town of Millau, Dept. of Aveyron, France, age 44, migr. from Bordeaux, jeweller - 20 Apr. 1822

Van Salzen, Cordt, b. Kingdon of Hanover, age 25, migr. from London, sugar baker - 22 Mar. 1826

Van Seggern, Christian [report 22 June 1827]: b. village of Schiffdorf, Amt Stootel, Kingdon of Hanover, migr. from town of Bremen, Hanover, gardner - 23 June 1827

Verren, Antoine Francois, clergyman, subj. of King of France - 22 Feb. 1831

Veith, John Adam, subj. of King of Bavaria - 1 Apr. 1836

Veith, Friedrich, subj. of King of Bavaria - 1 Apr. 1836

Veith, Jacob, subj. of King of Bavaria - 1 Apr. 1836

Vyse, William, subj. of G.B. - 3 Jan. 1838

Von Brause, John Robert, subj. of King of Saxony - 16 Nov. 1838

Veale, John, subj. of G.B. - 6 Apr. 1840

Von Baur, Gustavus, subj. of King of Prussia - 27 Aug. 1840

Von Seht, Adolphus William, subj. of King of Hanover - 26 Nov. 1840

Valentine, Richard, subj. of G.B. - 3 Dec. 1840

Veille, Isaac, b. Hatstate, France, age 44, migr. from Bordeaux, merchant - 20 Jan. 1824

Wilson, Robert, late of parish of Belfast, Co. Antrim, Ire.,
   merchant - 27 Dec. 1800

Wilson, William, late of city of Londonderry, Ire., merchant -
   28 July 1807

Wallace, James, subj. of G.B. - 24 July 1809

Wall, Stephen, subj. of G.B. - 15 Jan. 1810

White, John, sawyer - 26 Jan. 1813

Wetzel, Ludwig Daniel [report 7 Oct. 1817]: b. Frankfort a/M,
   age 38, merchant, migr. from London Graves End, subj. of Emperor of Austria - 22 Oct. 1817

Wood, George [report 1 May 1817]: b. town of Port Glasgow, Co.
   of Renfrew, Scotland, age 23, migr. from Greenock, merchant -
   3 May 1817

Woodhead, John [report 8 Jan. 1817]: b. Hopton, Yorkshire, Eng.,
   age 27, migr. from Liverpool, accountant - 28 Apr. 1817

Watts, William [report 2 Mar. 1818]: b. parish of Raetan [?],
   Co. of Sussex, Eng., age 40, migr. from Liverpool, morocco
   leather manufacturer; wife Mary, b. Co. of Sommersetshire,
   Eng., age 38; son George, b. parish of St. Savour, Southwark,
   near London, age 15; son William Henry, b. parish of St. Savour, age 11; son Arthur, b. parish of Bermondsey, age 9; dau.
   Hannah, b. parish of St. Savour, near London - 16 Mar. 1818

Wadsworth, Henry, b. Co. Monaghan, Ire., age 31, migr. from Dublin, grocer; wife Elizabeth, b. Co. Monaghan, age 30; dau.
   Elizabeth, b. Co. Monaghan, age 11; dau. Abigail, b. Co. Monaghan, age 8; dau. Phoebe - 23 July 1818

Woodhead, Thomas [report 15 July 1818]: b. town of Heckmondwike,
   Yorkshire, Eng., age 20, migr. from Liverpool, accountant - 24
   Sept. 1818

Wilson, Edward [report 17 Oct. 1818]: b. Co. Donegal, Ire., age
   28, migr. from Londonderry, grocer - 19 Oct. 1818

Wilson, Thomas [report 13 Nov. 1818]: b. Edinburgh, Scotland,
   age 60, migr. from Greenock, gentleman; wife Matilda, b. Dublin, age 49 - 16 Nov. 1818

Wright, Camilla Elizabeth C. [report 13 Nov. 1818]: b. Dundee,
   Scotland, age 21, migr. from Liverpool - 16 Nov. 1818

Wright, Frances [report 13 Nov. 1818]: b. Dundee, Scotland, age
   33, migr. from Liverpool - 16 Nov. 1818

Whyte, James, b. Kirkcaldy, Scotland, age 42, migr. from Liverpool, merchant, intending to reside in Mississippi Territory -
   6 Jan. 1819

Windmuller/Windmiller, Solomon [report 15 May 1819]: b. Warren-
   dorff, Co. of Westphalia, Prussia, age 35, migr. from Bremen,
   tavern-keeper; wife Julianna, b. Leignitz, Silesia, Prussia,
   age 28 -: 17 Apr. 1820

Wittrock, Hans Christopher [report 29 Apr. 1819]: b. town of
   Pritz, Holstein, Denmark, age 28, migr. from Hamburgh, sea-
   farer - 30 Apr. 1819

Wheelock, Charles, b. Co. Wexford, Ire., age 30, migr. from Dublin, farmer - 2 July 1819

Wallworth, John [report 25 Nov. 1819]: b. Isle of Man, age 30,
   migr. from Russia, merchant, intending to settle in St. Louis,
   Missouri Territory - 26 Nov. 1819

Williamson, Richard, age 37, migr. from Londonderry, grocer - 8
   Dec. 1819

Wadsworth, James, b. Howden, Yorkshire, Eng., age 39, migr. from Liverpool, gentleman - 10 Dec. 1819

Willcox, Richard, b. Bristol, Eng., age 45, migr. from Havre de Grace, engineer; wife Elezabeth Jeriass [?] - 18 Jan. 1820

Woltmann, Nicolaus Matthias, b. Kingdom of Hanover, age 22, migr. from London, farmer - 1 Apr. 1826

Winson [or Winsel?], Peter, b. Schualbach [or Schiralbach?], Prussia, age 44, migr. from Hamburgh, cartman - 26 Mar. 1821

Wood, John, b. Leicester, Eng., age 42, migr. from Dublin, grocer; wife Lucy, b. Co. of Derby, Eng., age 42; his stepdau. Caroline. Matilda Shipley, b. London, age 16; his stepson Frederick William Shipley, b. London, age 14; his stepson Alfred Loraine Shipley, b. London, age 13; his stepson, Sylvenus Hy. Shipley, b. Bristol, age 10; gis stepdau. Selina Penepole Shipley, b. Bristol, age 8 - 29 Mar. 1821

Wilson, John [report 30 Mar. 1821]: b. town of Leith, Scotland, age 54, migr. from Portsmouth, cartman - 31 Mar. 1821

Waddell, James [report 10 Apr. 1821]: b. Co Armagh, Ire., age 21, migr. from Belfast, grocer - 18 Apr. 1821

Wadsworth, Henry [report 11 Apr. 1821]: b. Co. Monaghan, Ire., as all his family, age 33, migr. from Dublin, grocer; wife Eliza, age 32; dau. Eliza, age 13; dau. Abigail, age 10; dau. Phoebe, age 9 - 11 Apr. 1821

West, James [report 10 Apr. 1821]: b. London, age 46, migr. from London, tavern-keeper; wife Ann, b. Liverpool, age 37 - 20 Apr. 1821

Walsh, Edward C. [report 20 Apr. 1821]: b. Dublin, age 55, migr. from Cork, grocer; wife Elizabeth, b. London, age 60 - 20 Apr. 1821

Williams, Roger [report 13 Apr. 1821]: b. town of Mundall, Norway, age 38, migr. from Liverpool, grocer - 21 Apr. 1821

Williams, Thomas [report 21 Apr. 1821]: b. town of Wakefield, Yorkshire, as all his family, age 45; dau. Ann, age 20; dau. Sarah, age 18; son George, age 16; dau. Elizabeth, age 14; dau. Emma, age 11; dau. Mary, age 8; dau. Hannah, age 4; he migr. from Liverpool;trade of woolstapler - 21 Apr. 1821

Wignall, Samuel [report 10 Apr. 1821]: b. Warwickshire, Eng.,age 28, migr. from Dublin, tavern-keeper - 23 Apr. 1821

Wilson, Thomas [report 24 Apr. 1821]: b. Co. Armagh, Ire., age 40, migr. from Belfast, cartman; wife Ann, b. Co. Armagh, age 30 - 24 Apr. 1821

Willey, John [report 23 Apr. 1821]: b. Co. Armagh, Ire., age 23, migr. from Dublin, grocer - 23 Apr. 1821

Warneker, Anthony, b. Westphalia, Germany, age 55, migr. from Mambel [?], Prussia, grocer - 3 May 1821

Williamson, Thomas, b. Co. Down, Ire., age 33, migr. from Belfast, weaver; wife Jane, b. Co. Down, age 33 - 22 May 1821

Winning, William [report 29 May 1821]: b. Lanarkshire, Scotland, age 31, migr. from London, pocketbook maker; wife Abishag, b. Berkshire, Eng., age 26; dau. Julia, b. London, age 6; son Samuel, b. London, age 3; son Joseph, b. London, age 1 - 29 May 1821

Whalers, George, b. Hanover, Germany, age 30, migr. from Hamburgh, grocer - 2 June 1821

Wright, John W., subj. of G.B. - 2 June 1821

Wlasak, Francis , b. Prague, Bohemia, age 23, migr. from Liverpool, furrier - 22 Oct. 1821

Wallach, Samuel, b. Cologne, Dept. of the Lower Rhine, age 44,
migr. from Rotterdam, grocer, subj. of Emperor of Germany - 20
Apr. 1821

Woods, Peter [report 8 Feb. 1822]: b. Co. Armagh, Ire., age 30,
migr. from London, pedlar - 18 Feb. 1822

Watson, Hugh, b. parish of Mearns, Scotland, age 44, migr. from
Greenock, carpet weaver; wife Elizabeth, b. Kilwinning, Scotland, age 37; son Robert, b. Paisley, age 17; dau. Jennet, b.
Paisley, age 17; son Matthew, b. Paisley, age 15 years and 10
months; son George, b. Paisley, age 13; son William, b. Paisley, age 11 - 18 Mar. 1822

Walker, Joseph, b. Leeds, Yorkshire, Eng., age 23, migr. from
Leeds, merchant - 20 Apr. 1822

West, Bartholomew, b. Co. of Dublin, age 34, migr. from Dublin,
cartman - 22 Oct. 1822

Wichelhausen, Francis [report 7 May 1823]: b. Bremen, age 41,
migr. from Haesum, Holstein, merchant - 19 May 1823

Wolf, Elias, b. Frankfort a/M, age 27, migr. from Amsterdam, physician - 20 Aug. 1824

Wobbe, John Bernard, b. Minster [Munster] in Westphalen, age 38,
migr. from London, tailor, subj. of King of Prussia - 20 Sept.
1824

Wilkens, Wilco Peter, b. Surinam, age 24, migr. from Surinam,
merchant, subj. of King of Holland - 15 Nov. 1824

Wallace, Andrew J.B., b. Co. Down, Ire., age 19 years and 8
months, migr. from Dublin, student-at-law - 16 Nov. 1824

Welsh, James, b. Athlone, Co. Roscommon, age 32, migr. from Cove
of Cork, accountant - 22 Dec. 1824

Welsh, Jeremiah, b. Co. Cork, Ire., age 26, migr. from Cork, labourer - 17 Oct. 1825

Watson, Thomas George [report 10 Dec. 1825]: b. London, age 26,
migr. from Bristol, merchant - 19 Dec. 1826

Williams, Joseph [report 6 Apr. 1826]: b. Co. Donegal, Ire., age
25, migr. from Londonderry, accountant; wife Eliza, b. Co.
Monoghan, age 21 - 17 Apr. 1826

Walsh, Peter [report 13 Apr. 1826]: b. Co. Cork, Ire., age 33,
migr. from Liverpool, labourer - 19 Apr. 1826

Wattyen, Conrad, b. Kingdom of Hanover, age 31, migr. from London,
grocer; wife Catherine, b. Kingdom of Hanover, age 24 - 25 Apr.
1826

Wilson, Joseph (by Andrew Caldwell, his guardian) [report 15 May
1826]: b. Co. Monaghan, Ire., age 19, migr. from Newry, baker -
29 Dec. 1827

Walsh, Patrick [report 9 Sept. 1826]: b. Co. Kilkenny, Ire., age
28, migr. from Waterford, via Newfoundland, labourer; wife
Alice, b. Kilkenny, age 30 - 19 Sept. 1826

Winter, James, b. Northumberland, Eng., age 38, migr. from Leith,
mason and plaisterer - 23 Oct. 1826

Wilson, John, b. Mondel, Norway, age 24, migr. from Antwerp, seaman, subj. of King of Sweden - 25 Aug. 1827

Ward, James [report 12 Sept. 1827]: b. Co. of West Meath, Ire.,
age 28, migr. from Liverpool, collier - 19 Sept. 1827

Williams, Frederick, b. Oxford, Eng., age 41, migr. from Falmouth, gentleman - 23 Nov. 1827

Weatherby, Peter, b. Cheshire, Eng., age 39, migr. from Cheshire, tailor and corset maker - 24 Nov. 1827

Wilson, William, b. Co. Monaghan, Ire., age 26, migr. from Belfast, carpenter; wife Jane, b. Co. Monaghan, age 24; son Henry, b. Co. Monaghan, age 6; son James, b. Co. Monaghan, age 4; son William, b. Co. Monaghan, age 2 - 20 Dec. 1827

Weber, Frederick, gentleman, subj. of King of Prussia - 19 Apr. 1830

Wood, John F., late of Island of Barbadoes, W.I., subj. of G.B. - 30 Sept. 1830

Walsh, John, boarding house keeper, subj. of G.B. - 24 Nov. 1830

Warburg, Israel Marcus, farmer, subj. of King of Denmark - 27 Aug. 1831

Wilson, Samuel D., subj. of G.B. - 25 Feb. 1831

Wilson, Stafford, late of London - 18 June 1831

Wilson, Hugh, of Sullivan Co., N.Y., farmer, subj. of G.B. - 18 Oct. 1831

Williams, Caroline [report 3 Oct. 1826]: b. Wiltshire, Eng., age 27, migr. from Bristol, equestrien - 24 Oct. 1826

Wright, John Tennent, b. town of Darlington, Co. of Durham, Eng., age 23, migr. from London, via Boston, in 1818, mariner - 30 Oct. 1826

Westhorp, Richard [report 18 Mar. 1825]: b. Yarmouth, Eng., age 24, migr. from London, mariner - 21 Feb. 1828

Welsh, James, merchant, subj. of G.B. - 22 Sept. 1828

Whybrew, Thomas, subj. of G.B. - 16 Dec. 1828

Welsh, John, baker, subj. of G.B. - 29 Jan. 1829

Waring, James, weaver, subj. of G.B. - 16 Mar. 1829

Whiteside, Edward, mariner, subj. of G.B. - 17 Mar. 1829

Wagener, Henry, subj. of Elector of Hesse Cassel - 24 July 1829

Leo-Wolf, William, physician, subj. of Republic of Hamburgh - 28 Sept. 1829

Leo-Wolf, Morris, physician, subj. of Republic of Hamburgh - 28 Sept. 1829

Walker, Robert, b. Glasgow, Scotland, as all his family, age 32, migr. from Greenock, boot- and shoemaker; wife Christian, age 32; dau. Mary, age 9 - 19 Mar. 1827

Waklam, William [report 1 Nov. 1826]: b. Co. Leitrem, Ire., age 26, migr. from Port of Sligo, coachman - 25 Aug. 1827

Williams, John, mariner, subj. of King of Sweden - 19 Oct. 1831

Waters, William, porter, subj. of G.B. - 20 Oct. 1831

Westerman, Joseph, of Brooklyn, L.I., merchant, subj. of G.B. - 23 Oct. 1832

West, William B., of Queens Co., manufacturer, subj. of G.B. - 22 Nov. 1832

Westerman, James, of Kings Co., N.Y., draftsman, subj. of G.B. - 1 Dec. 1832

Wenham, Thomas Smith, of Brooklyn, Kings Co., N.Y., subj. of G.B. - 17 July 1833

Watt, James, Jr., merchant, subj. of G.B. - 28 Nov. 1833

Weiss, Christian Ernest, clerk, subj. of King of Prussia - 10 May 1834

Wyett, George Philip, gentleman, subj. of G.B. - 11 Oct. 1834

Whitfield, George T., of Queens Co., N.Y., subj. of G.B. - 10 Nov. 1834

Winkler, John Frederick, classical teacher, subj. of King of Prussia - 25 Nov. 1834

Warburg, Adolph Rudolph, merchant, subj. of Republic of Hamburgh - 22 Apr. 1835

Warburg, John, merchant, subj. of Republic of Hamburgh - 30 July 1835

Windeat, James, subj. of G.B. - 7 Sept. 1836

Watson, Walter, of Richmond Co., subj. of G.B. - 25 Oct. 1836

Wassermann, Heindrick, cabinetmaker, subj. of King of Prussia - 21 Nov. 1836

Wedekind, Henry, subj. of King of Hanover - 9 Nov. 1837

Wuller, Hermann, subj. of King of Hanover - 9 Apr. 1838

Weidner, Peter, subj. of King of France - 9 Apr. 1838

Witte, Henre, subj. of Duke of Brunswick - 10 Apr. 1838

Wilson, Samuel, subj. of G.B. - 13 Apr. 1838

Watt, William, subj. of G.B. - 28 Apr. 1838

Watson, John, subj. of G.B. - 28 Apr. 1838

Wagner, John Frederick, subj. of King of Prussia - 7 May 1838

Walker, Daniel, subj. of G.B. - 21 July 1837

Walsh, Owen, subj. of G.B. - 18 July 1838

Wilson, Robert, subj. of G.B. - 24 Aug. 1838

Williams, William, subj. of G.B. - 10 Sept. 1838

Wark, Isaac, subj. of G.B. - 24 Oct. 1838

Wallace, Edward, subj. of G.B. - 25 Oct. 1838

Watts, John, subj. of G.B. - 6 Nov. 1838

Wittsien, Johes., subj. of King of Hanover - 7 Nov. 1838

Wolfe, Abraham, subj. of G.B. - 27 Nov. 1838

Wortmann, Henry, subj. of King of Denmark - 2 Nov. 1838

Waters, Timothy, subj. of G.B. - 2 Mar. 1839

Wilkinson, William Denison, subj. of G.B. - 12 Mar. 1839

Wheatley, John, subj. of G,B. - 27 Mar. 1839

Whitwell, John, subj. of G.B. - 1 Apr. 1839

Welch, Anthony, subj. of G.B. - 6 Apr. 1839

Webber, Charles, subj. of Prince of Hesse Cassel - 9 Apr. 1839

Walter, Jacob, subj. of Grand Duke of Baden - 13 May 1839

Walters, Abel N., subj. of G.B. - 6 Nov. 1839

Weisgerber, Jacob, subj. of King of Bavaria - 9 Dec. 1840

Ward, Thomas, subj. of G.B. - 13 Feb. 1840

Wright, Peter, subj. of G.B. - 6 Apr. 1840

Williamson, William, subj. of G.B. - 14 Apr. 1840

White, John, subj. of G.B. - 29 May 1840

Walpole, Henry, subj. of G.B. - 24 June 1840

Woods, James, subj. of G.B. - 21 Sept. 1840

Warden, Daniel, subj. of G.B. - 6 Oct. 1840

Williams, Ezekiel, subj. of G.B. - 10 Oct. 1840

Welwood, Thomas, subj. of G.B. - 10 Oct. 1840

Winn, Thomas, subj. of G.B. - 2 Nov. 1840

Wright, Joseph Farrell, subj. of G.B. - 3 Nov. 1840

Wilbiy, George, subj. of King of Bavaria - 4 Nov. 1840

Westley, Henry J., subj. of G.B. - 7 Nov. 1840

Wulff, John, subj. of Free City of Hamburgh - 10 Nov. 1840

Y

Young, George, b. Cortachy, Co. of Forfar, Scotland, age 28,
    migr. from London, merchant, residing in Alabama Territory -
    10 Nov. 1817

Young, Joseph [report 15 Apr. 1822]: b. London, age 24, migr.
    from London, grocer - 16 Apr. 1822

Young, Robert, weaver, subj. of G.B. - 20 July 1829

Young, Mary, late Knox, b. Paisley, Scotland, age 61, migr. from
    Greenock, widow - 23 Dec. 1830

Z

Zoeller, Christian E. [report 6 Aug. 1817]: b. Emmendingen,
    Germany, age 34, migr. from Amsterdam, residing at West Point,
    professor of military drawings and surveyor, subj. of Grand
    Duke of Baden - 18 Aug. 1817

Zelkin, Nicholas, b. village of Yurtenich, Duchy of the Lower
    Rhine, Prussia, age 33, migr. from Lunnenburg, N.S., store-
    keeper - 23 Nov. 1824

Zweck, Christian, subj. of Grand Duke of Baden - 1 Jan. 1839

Zuller, Misschell, subj. of King of Wertemburgh - 8 Oct. 1840

Smith, John N., merchant; rec. by Charles McLean and James Kinmouth - 4 May 1824 [4]

Scrugham, Warburton, hosier, born Dublin, Ire., age 38, migrated from Dublin; wife Ellenor, age 28; son George, age 5; son Edward, age 2; rec. by Christopher Chester and Richard Ellis - 11 Oct. 1824 [4A & 5]

Smedberg, Charles Gustavus, merchant, born Stockholm, Sweden, age 32, migrated from Portsmouth, Eng.; rec. by John B. Miller and William Renwick - 21 Nov. 1824 [6]

Harley, Thomas, cabinetmaker; report 16 Mar. 1818: born Co. of Leister, G.B., age 30, migrated from Liverpool; wife Elizabeth, age 22; son Frederick, age 2; rec. by John Bartine - 8 Dec. 1824 [7]

Potts, Ralph Henry, merchant; report 15 May 1829: born Birmingham, Eng., age 25, migrated from Liverpool; rec. by Joseph Hudson and William Hutchinson - 15 Jan. 1825 [8]

Daly, Bryan, shoemaker; report 29 Dec. 1819: born Queens Co., Ire., age 44; wife Elenor, born Co. Kilkenny, Ire., age 35; son Patrick, born Co. Kilkenny, age 17; son Andrew, born Co. Kilkenny, age 11; son John, born Co. Kilkenny, age 9; son Edward, born Co. Kilkenny, age 5; dau. Sarah, born Co. Kilkenny, age 6; rec. by Jeremiah L. Pierce - 1 Feb. 1825 [9]

Dunlop, William, druggist; report 26 Jan. 1820: born Manchester, Lancashire, age 30, migrated from Liverpool; rec. by Frederick Seely - 3 Feb. 1825 [10]

Thom, Christian, laborer; report 5 June 1820: born Hanover, Germany, age 27, migrated from London; rec. by John Smith - 6 June 1825 [11]

Fratebas, Jerome, farmer; report in Phila. Co. 9 Oct. 1817: born Marseilles, France, age 40, migrated from Marseilles, arrived Phila. 30 Sept. 1815; rec. by Thomas Morris - 17 June 1825 [12]

Mitchell, William, merchant; report 11 May 1811: born Eng., age 26, migrated from England; rec. by Jeremiah Cooper - 11 July 1825 [13]

Basse, John, speculator; report 30 Dec. 1818: born Bordeaux, France, age 39, migrated from Cape Francois; rec. by Antony Bonnesset - 18 July 1825 [14]

Byrne, Richard, cabinetmaker; report 25 July 1820: born Ire., age 31, migrated from Dublin; wife Ellen, born Ire., age 25; dau. Ellen, born Ire., age 6; son Richard, born Ire., age 5; rec. by William G. Miller - 2 Aug. 1825 [15]

Hüpeden, Augustus William, merchant; report 8 Oct. 1819: born Hoya, Hanover, age 21; rec. by George Meyer - 5 Dec. 1825 [16]

Stephens, James Wilson, cotton manufacturer; report 20 Dec. 1819: born Aberdeen, Scotland, age 35, migrated from Liverpool; rec. by Charles Bouton - 12 Dec. 1825 [17]

Reid, John, baker; report 20 May 1818: born Ire., age 24, migrated from Newry; rec. by Thomas Miller - 4 Feb. 1826 [18]

Robinson, Peter, merchant; report 11 Feb. 1821: born Westphalia, Prussia, age 42, migrated from Hamburgh; wife Sarah, born Shelburne, N.S., age 31, migrated from Shelburne; rec. by John Connor - 22 Feb. 1826 [19]

Rees, John, cartman; report 19 Apr. 1821: born Cardiganshire, Wales, age 27, migrated from London; rec. by David F. Lawrence - 19 Apr. 1826 [20]

Wall, John, baker; report Phila. Co. 6 Nov. 1813: born Co. Meath, Ire., in 1780, age now 30, migrated from Newry, arrived Port of Amboy 16 July 1806; rec. by Robert Speir - 2 May 1826 [21]

Ramsay, John, grocer; report 20 June 1821: born Co. Antrim, Ire., age 37, was a sawyer in Ire., migrated from Londonderry; wife Mary Ann, born Co. Armagh, age 26; rec. by Adam Patterson - 7 Aug. 1826 [22]

O'Connor, Joseph, mason; report 11 Dec. 1819: born Tullymore, age 25, migrated from Galloway; rec. by Thomas Sandford - 8 Nov. 1826 [23]

Blood, Harris, merchant; report 5 Apr. 1819: born Dublin, age 31, migrated from Liverpool; wife Harriet, born Dublin, age 25; dau. Mary Sarah, age 3; rec. by Joseph F. Carroll - 7 May 1827 [24]

Daly, Patrick, labourer; report 29 Dec. 1819: born Queens Co., Ire., age 44; wife Elenor, born Co. Kilkenny, as were all the children, age 35; son Patrick, age 17; son Andrew, age 11; son John, age 9; son Edward, age 5; dau. Sarah, age 6; rec. by Bryan Daly - 10 May 1827 [25]

Castro, Henri, merchant; report 13 Mar. 1821: born France, age 35, migrated from London; rec. by Louis B. Henriques - 7 Aug. 1827 [26]

Henriques, Louis B., distiller; report 25 Jan. 1819: born France, age 32, migrated from Bordeaux; rec. by Jaques Ruden - 3 Sept. 1827 [27]

Parrott, Richard, merchant; report 17 June 1811: born Ire., age 46, grocer, migrated from Ire.; wife Judith, age 36; son Richard, age 20; son John, age 18; dau. Catherine, age 19; dau. Winnifred, age 19; son William, age 14; dau. Mary, age 11; rec. by John Hurley - 31 Oct. 1827

McNeish, John, merchant; report [no date]: born Largo, age 43, migrated from Scotland; wife Janet, born Glendeven, Scotland, age 49; dau. Jane, age 20; dau. Elizabeth, age 18; dau. Janet, age 16; son John, age 14; son James, age 12 (all children born in Falkirk); rec. by John Phyfe - 5 Feb. 1828 [29]

Rode, William, labourer; report 18 May 1822: born Pillau, Prussia, age 28, migrated from Pillau; wife Sophia, age 33; rec. by George N. Devries - 1 Apr. 1828 [30]

Brodie, James, distiller; report 6 Nov. 1821: born Selkirkshire, Scotland, age 24, migrated from Greenock; rec. by Henry Raymond - 14 May 1828 [31]

Madigan, John, laborer, subj. of G.B. - 27 May 1828 [32] - not completed

Montgomery, James, milkman; report 19 May 1821: born Scotland, age 28, migrated from Greenock; rec. by William McGill - 10 June 1828 [33]

Martin, Charles, distiller, subj. of G.B.; certificate 20 Sept. 1816: age 19; rec. by Andrew Foster and George Sewell - 10 Oct. 1828 [34]

Paulmier, Francis, merchant, French subj.; certif. of intent 5 Dec. 1825; rec. by Ward Higgins and Jeremiah Horton - 29 Oct. 1828 [35]

Wright, Samuel, merchant; report 14 Oct. 1816: born Lononghmoore, Co. Down, Ire., age 22, migrated from Belfast; rec. by Saul Allen [or Alley?] - 28 Oct. 1828 [36]

O'Connor, John, clothier; report 9 May 1822: born Tipperary, age 35, migrated from Dublin; rec. by Patrick Byrne and Charles Mahon - 29 Oct. 1828 [37]

Loud, Thomas, piano forte maker, subj. of G.B.; declar. intent Court of Nisi Prius in Phila. 19Apr. 1813; rec. by James Love and John Cumberland - 1 Nov. 1828 [38]

Talbot, Samuel White, merchant; report 30 Oct. 1812 made by his guardian, Thomas H. Merry: Samuel White Talbot, "yet in college," born Ire., age 13, migrated from Ire., and Thomas Talbot, mariner, born Ire., age 12 - Samuel White Talbot rec. by James M. Cummings and William R. Talbot - 25 Mar. 1829 [39]

Harvey, Jacob, merchant; report 20 Feb. 1822: born Limerick, age 24, migrated from Belfast; rec. by Charles Graham and Jacob Morton - 6 Aug. 1829 [40]

Armstrong, Thomas, gardener, subj. of G.B.; declar. of intent 9 Oct. 1826; rec. by Robert N. Waite and Robert Waite, Jr. - 4 Aug. 1829 [41]

Schmidt, Frederick William, merchant; report 24 Mar. 1823: born Wuntul [or Wuntal?], Bavaria, age 21, migrated from Liverpool; declar. of intent 10 May 1824; rec. by Charles McEvers, Jr., and John W. Schmidt - 9 Oct. 1829 [42]

Becar, Noel J., merchant; report 16 Oct. 1824: born Montrecourt, France, age 21, migrated from Havre; rec. by Ira Smith and Thomas W. Wells - 2 Nov. 1829 [43]

Day, John, carpenter, subj. of G.B.; rec. by Edward J. Webb and Benjamin Pike - 13 Nov. 1829 [44]

Fusier, John Peter, boarding house keeper, subj. of France; rec. by John H. Metzler and Hilaire Pelerin - 9 July 1830 [45]

[No. 46 is blank]

Wintringham, Thomas, cider and porter dealer, subj. of G.B.; rec. by David S. Brown and Isaac Brown - 17 Dec. 1830 [47]

Lentithon, Anthony, merchant; report 13 May 1825: born Lyons, France, age 28, migrated from Havre; rec. by Jotham S. Fountain and Francis B. Cutting - 4 Jan. 1831 [48]

McFarlane, John, teacher; report 26 Apr. 1809: born Scotland, age 40, migrated from Glasgow; wife Catharine, born Scotland, age 36; rec. by John Boyd, Esq., and Alexander Martin - 15 Mar. 1831 [49]

Sanderson, Edward Fisher, merchant, subj. of G.B.; has copy of declaration of intent dated 2 Mar. 1829; rec. by Isaac Carow and Henry F. Waring - 4 Nov. 1831 [50]

Muller, John U., merchant, subj. of Swiss Confederation; declaration of intent dated 4 Aug. 1829; rec. by Samuel Downer, Jr., and John Crumby - 19 Jan. 1832 [51]

Ford, John, laborer; report 7 May 1825: born Kilkenny, Ire., age 24, migrated from Co. Kilkenny; rec. by Peter Dempsey and John O'Brien - 11 Apr. 1832 [52]

O'Brien, John, laborer; report 5 May 1825: born Kilkenny, Ire., age 24, migrated from Co. Kilkenny; rec. by Peter Dempsey and John Ford - 11 Apr. 1832 [53]

Lyon, Aaron, coal merchant; report 5 June 1827: born London, age 51, migrated from Hamburgh [?]; rec. by Joseph Davis and Ransom Crosby - 8 Oct. 1832 [54]

Reid, John Hope, merchant; report 5 Oct. 1830: born Scotland, age 30, migrated from Scotland for Savannah; rec. by Alexander Thompson & James S. Shapter - 5 Oct. 1833 [55]

Belcher, Charles, rule maker; report 17 Nov. 1824: born Sheffield, Eng., age 21, migrated from Liverpool; rec. by Richard Patten and William Halsey - 3 Dec. 1833 [56]

Belcher, William, rule maker; report 17 Nov. 1824: born Sheffield, Eng., age 26, migrated from Liverpool; rec. by Richard Patten and William Halsey - 3 Dec. 1833 [57]

Matthews, John, clerk; declar. of intent 14 Nov. 1831; subj. of G.B.; rec. by Peter Perine and John H. Cornell - 15 Feb. 1834 [58]

Sylvester, Sylvester Joseph, broker; report Phila. Co. 18 Sept. 1826: born Liverpool on 28 Dec. 1801, age now 25, arrived in Phila. 27 Aug. 1826; rec. by John Blake and James E. Betts - 19 May 1836 [59]

Hunter, Alfred, cutler, subj. of G.B.; declar. of intent 26 Nov. 1833; rec. by William Belcher and John Phyfe - 5 Nov. 1836 [60]

Vitty, John A., tavern-keeper, subj. of G.B.; declar. of intent 19 Dec. 1834; rec. by Henry McGill and George Braden - 8 Apr. 1837 [61]

Percival, Pearce, subj. of G.B.; declar. of intent 12 Nov. 1829; rec. by John Day and George Menett - 12 Oct. 1837 [62]

Leatham, Robert H., merchant, subj. of G.B.; declar. of intent 8 July 1835; rec. by James Hunter and Samuel Osborne - 3 Nov. 1838 [63]

Bishop, Edward W., attorney-at-law; declar of intent 7 Sept. 1836 in Albany: born London, age 34, migrated from Hull, arrived NYC in 1833; rec. by Charles G. Griffin and Theophilus Bridges - 3 Nov. 1838 [64]

Schuchardt, John Jacob, gentleman, subj. of Grand Duke of Baden; declar. of intent 18 Nov. 1836; rec. by Frederick Gebhard and John Reinicke - 12 Dec. 1838 [65]

Welsh, Robert, gardner, subj. of G.B.; declar. of intent 7 Sept. 1836; rec. by Francis C. Sanneborn - 11 Sept. 1840 [66]

Murray, Michael, stone cutter, subj. of G.B.; rec. by John Hurley - 11 Sept. 1840 [67]

O'Dougherty, Patrick, cooper, subj. of G.B.; declar. intent 16 Apr. 1838; rec. by Constantine Dougherty - 11 Sept. 1840 [68]

Dougherty, Constantine, cooper, subj. of G.B.; declar. intent 16 Apr. 1838; rec. by Patrick O'Dougherty - 11 Sept. 1840 [69]

Sheridan, James, laborer, subj. of G.B.; declar. intent 25 May 1837; rec. by Francis Riley - 11 Sept. 1840 [70]

Gibney, Patrick, laborer, subj. of G.B.; declar. intent 23 Apr. 1828; rec. by James Tuite - 11 Sept. 1840 [71]

Denzi, Louis Anthony, musician, subj. of the Pope of Rome; declaration of intent 1 Apr. 1836; rec. by William A. Vultee - 11 Sept. 1840 [72]

Cober, George, butcher, subj. of King of Wuertemberg; declar. of intent 16 Apr. 1838; rec. by Philip Bender - 12 Sept. 1840 [73]

Maul, George, musical instrument maker, late of Germany; declar. of intent in Marine Court 3 Mar. 1834; subj. of Prince of Hesse Cassel; rec. by Philip Bender - 12 Sept. 1840 [74]

Schmidt, Louis, musical instrument maker, subj. of King of Saxony; declar. of intent in Marine Court 12 Nov. 1836; rec. by Philip Bender - 12 Sept. 1840 [75]

Walsh, Edward, porter, subj. of G.B.; decl. of intent in Marine
Court 29 June 1837; rec. by Peter Stuyvesant, Sr. - 12 Sept.
1840 [76]

Goldsmith, Joseph, laborer, subj. of G.B.; decl. of intent in
Marine Court 5 Sept. 1838; rec. by Henry E. Riell - 12 Sept.
1840 [77]

Miles, John, blacksmith, subj. of G.B.; rec. by Dominick Faany
- 12 Sept. 1840 [78]

Bowden, George, laborer, subj. of G.B.; decl. of intent 30 June
1835 in Marine Court; rec. by John Ward - 12 Sept. 1840 [79]

Ward, John, laborer, subj. of G.B.; decl. of intent 23 Aug.
1836 in Marine Court; rec. by George Bowden - 12 Sept. 1840
[80]

Dennan, Michael, laborer, subj. of G.B.; decl. of intent 6 Aug.
1838 in Marine Court; rec. by Francis O'Reiley - 12 Sept. 1840
[81]

McGuire, Patrick, fireman, subj. of G.B.; decl. of intent 3 July
1838 in Marine Court; rec. by Mathew Hart - 12 Sept. 1840 [82]

Hart, Mathew, Jr., pattern maker, subj. of G.B.; rec. by Mathew
Hart - 12 Sept. 1840 [83]

Kiernan, John, laborer, subj. of G.B.; decl. of intent 9 May
1838 in Marine Court; rec. by Bartley Magee - 12 Sept. 1840
[84]

Corken, James, stage driver, subj. of G.B.; rec. by Silvanus M.
Gautier - 12 Sept. 1840 [85]

Sullivan, John B., machinist, subj. of G.B.; rec. by James Brady
and Henry Pullis - 12 Sept. 1840 [86]

Murray, Patrick, waiter, subj. of G.B.; rec. by George McCluskey
- 12 Sept. 1840 [87]

Gallagher, Patrick, flagger, late of Co. Donegal, Ire., subj. of
G.B.; decl. of intent 5 Apr. 1838; rec. by James Wallace - 12
Sept. 1840 [88]

Henning, Ludwig, baker, subj. of King of Prussia; decl. of intent 11 Apr. 1838 in Marine Court; rec. by Enoch Fessing - 12
Sept. 1840 [89]

Mehegan, John, fireman, subj. of G.B.; rec. by John McCarty -
12 Sept. 1840 [90] - incomplete

Dougherty, Edward, fireman, subj. of G.B.; rec. by John Dougherty
- 12 Sept. 1840 [91]

McCarthy, Florence, waiter, subj. of G.B., born Co. Kerry, Ire.,
on 1 Jan. 1802 and arrived Boston 15 Oct. 1827; decl. of intent in Municipal Court of Boston 24 May 1834; rec. by John
Henly - 12 Sept. 1840 [92]

Conroy, Patrick, porter, subj. of G.B.; decl. of intent 5 May
1838 in Court of Common Pleas; rec. by John Conroy - 12 Sept.
1840 [93]

Sulivan, Martin, laborer, subj. of G.B.; decl. of intent 13 July
1836 in Marine Court; rec. by Michael O'Connor - 12 Sept. 1840
[94]

Clarke, Joshua, plasterer, subj. of G.B.; decl. of intent 9 Sept.
1833 in Marine Court; rec. by Patrick Foley - 12 Sept. 1840
[95]

Offerman, Carsten, brass founder, subj. of King of Hanover; rec.
by Thomas Wallace - 12 Sept. 1840 [96]

Ryder, Bartholomew, porter, subj. of G.B.; decl. of intent 28 Oct. 1836 in Marine Court; rec. by Augustine Smith - 12 Sept. 1840 [97]

Murray, John, flax dresser, subj. of G.B., migrated from Aberdeen; decl. of intent 6 July 1824 in Marine Court; rec. by Alexander Murray - 12 Sept. 1840 [98]

Garraty, James, bookmaker, subj. of G.B.; rec. by Andrew Brackin - 12 Sept. 1840 [99]

Keane, Patrick A., jeweller, subj. of G.B.; rec. by John Brennan - 17 Sept. 1840 [100]

Staunton, Patrick, coachman, subj. of G.B.; decl. of intent 17 May 1836 in Marine Court; rec. by James Quarry - 18 Sept. 1840 [101]

Gibney, Patrick S., manufacturer, subj. of G.B.; decl. of intent 26 Dec. 1836 in Marine Court; rec. by Edward Sherlock - 18 Sept. 1840 [102]

Stott, Alexander, merchant, subj. of G.B.; decl. of intent 17 Jan. 1837 in Marine Court; rec. by John Murray - 18 Sept. 1840 [103]

Miller, Cortt, clerk, subj. of King of Prussia; rec. by John Brown - 18 Sept. 1840 [104] - incomplete

Rantzum, Ferdinand, blacksmith, subj. of King of Prussia; rec. by John Brown - 24 Sept. 1840 [105] - incomplete

Norman, John Moore, merchant, subj. of G.B.; decl. of intent 8 Sept. 1835; rec. by James McBride - 24 Sept. 1840 [106]

McMenomy, Edward, paver, subj. of G.B.; decl. of intent 3 Aug. 1838 in Marine Court; rec. by Thomas Finigan - 24 Sept. 1840 [107]

Miles, Jacob, clerk, subj. of G.B.; rec. by Benjamin Miles - 7 Oct. 1840 [108]

Tims, Richard, of Orange Co., N.Y., farmer, subj. of G.B; decl. of intent 18 Nov. 1837; rec. by William Stobbs Newham - 9 Oct. 1840 [109]

Hall, Adam, engineer, subj. of G.B.; decl. of intent 29 May 1837 in Marine Court; rec. by Maelzer Howel - 9 Oct. 1840 [110]

Roach, Patrick, hostler, subj. of G.B.; decl. of intent 8 Oct. 1838 in Marine Court; rec. by James Quarry - 9 Oct. 1840 [111]

McCredie, William, mariner, subj. of G.B., nephew of Elizabeth Donald, arrived in U.S. in 1809; rec. by Robert Donald, James Furey and Elizabeth Donald - 3 Oct. 1840 [112] - incomplete

Nathan, James, merchant, subj. of City of Hamburg; rec. by Franklin Brown - 3 Nov. 1840 [113]

Mitchell, John, clerk, subj. of G.B.; decl. of intent 19 Sept. 1836; rec. by William Mitchell - 3 Nov. 1840 [114]

Colter, Benjamin, of Orange Co., N.Y., farmer; rec. by Nathaniel Ketchum and Peter Cannon - 3 Nov. 1840 [115 and 116]

Bundle 1

Tyson, William, mariner, subj. of G.B.; rec. by Henry Tyson, ship-carpenter, & Isaac P. Tuckerman, sailmaker - 6 Nov. 1828 [1]

Melleous, George, labourer, subj. of Duke of Brunswick; rec. by Ernest Kass, baker - 26 Feb. 1829 [2]

O'Connell, John, pedlar; report 21 Jan. 1822: born Co. Kilkenny, Ire., age 30, pedlar, migrated from Waterford; wife Frances, born Co. Wexford, Ire., age 26; rec. by John R. Roberts, cartman - 3 Mar. 1829 [3]

Powis, Henry, merchant; rec. by William Israel, merchant - 18 Nov. 1829 [4] - paper not entered as "incomplete"

Ulrick, Henry, gardner, late of Baden, Germany; rec. by John Sidell - 14 Dec. 1829 [5]

McGuckin, William M., student-at-law, subj. of G.B.; rec. by James Hora, merchant - 12 Feb. 1831 [6]

Cumberland, Elizabeth (wife of John Cumberland), subj. of G.B.; rec. by John Sidell, fuse [?] marshal, William Hadley, cordwainer, and Ann Hadley - 7 Sept. 1830 [7]

Hunter, William, milkman, late of Co. Sligo, Ire.; rec. by Robert Thompson, grocer - 6 Oct. 1830 [8]

Douglas, John C., of Whitestown, Oneida Co., brewer & distiller, born parish of Dunfermline, Co. of Fife, Scotland, age 46, migrated from Greenock, Scotland; rec. by Josiah Converse, of Troy - 11 Oct. 1830 [9]

Leahy, Dennis, fruiterer, subj. of G.B.; rec. by John Hurly, stone mason - 13 Apr. 1831 [10]

Keirnin, Bernard, subj. of G.B.; rec. by Edward Colgan, grocer - 16 Apr. 1831 [11]

Melleous, George, labourer; rec. by Allen Gardener, public porter - 26 Feb. 1829 [12]

Whybrew, Thomas, bookseller, subj. of G.B.; rec. by Charles Carrill, bookseller, and William R. Cazlet, hatter - 6 Nov. 1832 [13]

McDermott, Peter, formerly of Co. Longford, Ire.; rec. by Michael McDermott - 6 Nov. 1832 [14]

Shaw, Joseph, gardener, formerly of Chesterfield, Eng.; rec. by Thomas Kain and Robert Morris - 7 Nov. 1832 [15]

O'Farrell, James, teacher, subj. of G.B.; rec. by William Duff, tailor, and Hugh Duggan, clerk - 7 Nov. 1832 [16]

Ardley, Mary; rec. by Thomas Morton and Mrs. Mary Hattrick - 20 Dec. 1832 - not entered and later a duplicate certificate was issued [17]

Wills, William, stage driver, late of Co. of Kent, Eng., entered the U.S. in Aug. 1827; rec. by James Van Beuren - 9 Apr. 1833 [18]

Keasey/Kasey, John, late of Co. Tyrone, Ire.; rec. by Barney Kurnin - 24 Apr. 1833 [19]

Chinery, William, lapidary, late of Primigham, Warwick, Eng.; rec. by Ezra Dodge - 20 May 1833 [20]

Finley, James, waiter, arrived U.S. about 1 Sept. 1827; rec. by Peter Shillear - 6 June 1833 [21]

Kennedy, John, weaver, subj. of G.B. - 11 Aug. 1831 [21A]

McEwen, Edward, arrived U.S. 3 Aug. 1825 - 6 June 1833 [22]

Canady, Cornelius, labourer, subj. of G.B., arrived U.S. before
1 May 1828; rec. by William Shaw, cartman - 24 July 1833 [23]

Mann, Francis, merchant, arrived U.S. 1 Aug. 1821, subj. of G.B.;
rec. by Andrew Bacchus - 5 Sept. 1833 [24]

Rea, James, boarding house keeper; report 1 May 1821: born Co.
Down, Ire., age 33, migrated from Belfast; wife Jane, born
Co. Down, age 30; rec. by Daniel Peoples - 14 Nov. 1833

Ackerman, Charles F., subj. of G.B., arrived U.S. 18 June 1812 -
9 Apr. 1834 [26]

Buist, John, subj. of G.B., arrived U.S. 1818 - 9 Apr. 1834 [27]

Carpenter, Jacob, subj. of Prince of Hesse Cassel, arrived U.S.
1 Jan. 1816; rec. by George B. King, Jr., and John Dougherty -
9 Apr. 1834 [28]

Flanagan, Robert, subj. of G.B., arrived U.S. June 1815; rec.
by Thomas Quinn - 9 Apr. 1834 [29]

Garesche, Paul, subj. of France, merchant; rec. by Benjamin
Canenge and Henry Paillet, merchants - 9 Apr. 1834 [30]

Heyney, Dennis, coachman, subj. of G.B.; declaration of intent
in Marine Court 24 Nov. 1829; rec. by Thomas Quin - 9 Apr.
1834 [31]

Healy, Edward, arrived U.S. 31 May 1828, subj. of G.B.; rec. by
John Jordan - 9 Apr. 1834 [32]

Hart/Heart, Patrick, labourer, subj. of G.B., first papers in
Marine Court 5 Nov. 1828, arrived U.S. 11 July 1825; rec. by
Patrick Golden - 9 Apr. 1834 [33]

King, John, arrived U.S. 1 Sept. 1821; rec. by William King -
9 Apr. 1834 [34]

Lester, George, subj. of G.B., arrived U.S. before May 1811; rec.
by John Corgan - 9 Apr. 1834 [35]

Martin, John B., subj. of G.B., arrived U.S. in 1819; rec. by
Martin M. Turrell & Samuel Waterbury - 9 Apr. 1834 [36]

Moran, Patrick, subj. of G.B., arrived U.S. Sept. 1826; rec. by
Miles Moran - 9 Apr. 1834 [37]

Mee, Thomas, subj. of G.B., arrived U.S. 5 May 1828; declaration
of intent in Marine Court 2 March 1832; rec. by Edward Reynolds - 9 Apr. 1834 [38]

McGonagle, James, Jr., born Ire. 1 Apr. 1797, migrated from Londonderry, arrived U.S. 14 Nov. 1815; declaration of intent in
Philadelphia 16 Jan. 1818; rec. by Bartholomew Rooney - 9 Apr.
1834 [39]

McCrea, Robert, stone cutter, arrived U.S. 16 June 1825; declaration of intent Marine Court 20 June 1831; arrived U.S.
16 June 1825; rec. by Jery Dores - 9 Apr. 1834 [40]

McCormick, Thomas; report 2 Dec. 1823 in Berks Co., Pa.: born
Co. Galway, Ire., age 26, migrated from Galway 14 May 1822,
arrived NYC 22 June 1822; rec. by John Wall - 9 Apr. 1834 [41]

McDonald, James, turner; report 10 May 1820: born Edinburgh, age
31, migrated from Greenock, arrived U.S. 1 May 1820; rec. by
Ebenezer Byram - 9 Apr. 1834 [42]

Mel, John, arrived U.S. before Sept. 1815; rec. by William W.
Shirley - 9 Apr. 1834 [43]

Nally, Owen, subj. of G.B., arrived U.S. July 1828; rec. by John
Jordan - 9 Apr. 1834 [44]

Norman, Thomas, subj. of G.B., arrived U.S. 23 June 1826; rec. by William Phillips - 9 Apr. 1834 [45]

Nicholson, Francis, subj. of G.B., arrived U.S. 1 Jan. 1819; rec. by James B. Murray - 9 Apr. 1834 [46]

O'Brien, John, labourer, subj. of G.B., arrived U.S. 1 June 1827; declaration of intent Marine Court 11 Nov. 1831; rec. by Eduard Aldworth - 9 Apr. 1834 [47]

O'Brien, Thomas, subj. of G.B., arrived U.S. 1 June 1824; declaration of intent Marine Court 9 July 1829; rec. by John O'Donohue - 9 Apr. 1834 [48]

O'Connell, George D., arrived U.S. 1 May 1828; rec. by Edward Thurston - 9 Apr. 1834 [49]

Parks, Frederick, subj. of G.B., arrived U.S. June 1822; rec. by James G. Moffet - 9 Apr. 1834 [50]

Rooney, Daniel, subj. of G.B., arrived U.S. April 1822; rec. by Cornelius Courtwright - 9 Apr. 1834 [51]

Reed, John, aubj. of G.B., arrived U.S. 25 Dec. 1820; rec. by Ira Smith - 9 Apr. 1834 [52]

Sleman, James, arrived U.S. by May 1815, aubj. of G.B.; rec. by Margaret Slemen - 9 Apr. 1834 [53]

Wallis, Hammond, subj. of G.B., arrived U.S. 23 July 1817; rec. by Thomas B. Smith - 9 Apr. 1834 [54]

Kelly, Patrick, late of Co. Cavan, Ire., arrived U.S. 12 June 1825; rec. by Owen Smith, cartman - 21 May 1834 [55]

McLourley, Hugh, formerly of Fermanagh, Ire., arrived U.S. 16 May 1828; rec. by Barnet Kiernan - 2 June 1834 [56]

Ireland, William M., physician, subj. of G.B., arrived U.S. 11 Aug. 1826; rec. by Charles O'Connor, counsellor-at-law - 17 July 1834 [57]

Dupant, Sicame, subj. of France, arrived U.S. 1812; rec. by Wm. S. Hart - 27 Sept. 1834 [57A]

Hows, John William Stanhope, late of London, merchant, arrived U.S. 3 March 1828; declaration of intent 9 Oct. 1830; rec. by George B. Butler, attorney-at-law - 8 Oct. 1834 [58]

Carey, Patrick M., subj. of G.B., arrived U.S. by Oct. 1828; rec. by James Mullen - 21 Oct. 1834 [59]

Le Moyne, Adolphe, subj. of France, arrived NYC 4 May 1828 from Le Havre; declaration of intent 20 Aug. 1831; rec. by Francis Depau - 9 Dec. 1834 [60]

Denniston, James, subj. of G.B.; rec. by William Adams - 16 Dec. 1834 [61]

Cochran, William Johnson, subj. of G.B.; report 4 June 1829: born Dundee, Angusshire, Scotland, age 32, tailor, migrated from Dundee, arrived U.S. 1 May 1820; rec. by Samuel Blanchard - 27 Mar. 1834 [62]

Criswell, Alan/Allen, stone cutter, subj. of G.B., arrived U.S. 4 July 1827; rec. by William Dunlop, morocco dresser - 7 Apr. 1834 [63]

Gravillon, Jean Claude Auguste, subj. of King of France, arrived U.S. 10 June 1826; rec. by John Michael Jacquelin - 7 Apr. 1834 [64]

Heerwagen, Elias G., cooper, subj. of King of Bavaria, arrived U.S. 27 June 1827; rec. by Nicholas Rosse - 7 Apr. 1834 [65]

Mali, Henry W.T., merchant, subj. of King of the Netherlands, arrived U.S. 1 Apr. 1826; rec. by Thatcher Tucker - 7 Apr. 1834 [66]

Artiguenave, Jean Francois, subj. of King of France, arrived U.S. 7 Sept. 1826; rec. by Alphonse P. Garesché - 8 Apr. 1834 [67]

Breese, Thomas, subj. of G.B.; rec. by Robert Breese - 8 Apr. 1834 [68]

Betts, Jabez, subj. of G.B., arrived U.S. 5 Oct. 1820; rec. by George Cox and James Seymour - 8 Apr. 1834 [69]

Bielle, John Baptiste Joseph, manufacturer, subj. of King of France, arrived U.S. before 1 Sept. 1820; rec. by Marshall B. Blake - 8 Apr. 1834 [70]

Bedson, Thomas, mariner, late of Co. of Middlesex, Eng., subj. of G.B., arrived U.S. March 1807; rec. by Wm. H. Bell - 8 Apr. 1834 [71]

Brady, James, late of Co. Caven, Ire., subj. of G.B., arrived U.S. Aug. 1827; rec. by Matthew Coyle - 8 Apr. 1834 [72]

Cox, Joseph, merchant, subj. of G.B.; report 9 Mar. in Marine Court: born England, age 33, migrated from Liverpool; rec. by William L. Rushton - 8 Apr. 1834 [73]

Cox, John, merchant, subj. of G.B.; report 9 Mar. 1827: born Eng., age 31, migrated from Liverpool; rec. by William L. Rushton - 8 Apr. 1834 [74]

Edwards, Charles Henry, subj. of G.B., arrived U.S. Sept. 1819; rec. by George B. Browne - 8 Apr. 1834 [75]

Garesché, Alphonse P., subj. of King of France, arrived U.S. before 1 May 1828 (when under age of 18); rec. by Jean Francois Artiguenave - 8 Apr. 1834 [76]

Metcalf, Samuel W., subj. of G.B., arrived U.S. 17 July 1822; rec. by William C. Baldwin - 8 Apr. 1834 [77]

Metcalf, Cyrus, printer, subj. of G.B., arrived U.S. about 1819; rec. by Justus L. Redfield - 8 Apr. 1834 [78]

McGuire, Patrick, labourer, subj. of G.B., arrived U.S. 1 May 1826; rec. by William Lynd - 8 Apr. 1834 [79]

Newcomb, John, subj. of G.B., arrived U.S. 1802; rec. by Daniel Herrick - 8 Apr. 1834 [80]

Rushton, William L., subj. of G.B., arrived U.S. 12 Mar. 1817 (when under age 18); rec. by Joseph Cox - 8 Apr. 1834 [81]

Simon, Henry, subj. of King of France, arrived U.S. Nov. 1815; rec. by Daniel J. Hauxhurst - 8 Apr. 1834 [82]

Sharp, Edward, "horsler," subj. of G.B., arrived U.S. 4 March 1828; rec. by Robert Sharp - 8 Apr. 1834 [83]

Woodhead, John, merchant, subj. of G.B., arrived U.S. before 1812; rec. by Martin Habershaw [or Habershan?] - 8 Apr. 1834 [84]

Yates, Sidney, subj. of G.B., arrived U.S. 13 May 1827; rec. by Samuel J. Smith - 8 Apr. 1834 [85]

Ashley, Robert, subj. of G.B., arrived U.S. Oct. 1822; rec. by James Horn - 10 Apr. 1834 [86]

Archibald, Robert, subj. of G.B., arrived U.S. May 1812; rec. by Joseph Finnemore - 10 Apr. 1834 [87]

Bowden, Thomas, subj. of G.B., arrived U.S. 2 Dec. 1821 (under age 21); rec. by Matthew Bowden - 10 Apr. 1834 [88]

Batrsbee, Francis, subj. of G.B., arrived U.S. 12 May 1825 (under age of 18); rec. by John Riley - 10 Apr. 1834 [89]

Bennet, James, subj. of G.B., arrived U.S. 24 May 1824 (under age of 18); rec. by William Johnson - 10 Apr. 1834 [90]

Brown, Thomas, shoemaker, subj. of G.B., arrived U.S. 20 Oct. 1828; decl. of intent Marine Court 15 Feb. 1830; rec. by Philip Daly - 10 Apr. 1834 [90A]

Bowden, Matthew, subj. of G.B., arrived U.S. 2 Dec. 1821 (under age of 18); rec. by Thomas Bowden - 10 Apr. 1834 [91 & 91B]

Bellemere, Louis, subj. of King of France, arrived U.S. Nov. 1816 (under age of 18); rec. by Francis Bellemere - 10 Apr. 1834 [92]

Cowan, John, subj. of G.B., arrived U.S. 18 June 1822; rec. by Robert Ferguson - 10 Apr. 1834 [93]

Cummins, John, subj. of G.B., arrived U.S. June 1819; report at decl. of intent in Marine Court 10 Apr. 1827: born Ire., age 31, farmer, migrated from Belfast, intends to settle in West Chester, Westchester Co.; wife Mary, born Ire., age 31; rec. by George Cummins - 10 Apr. 1834 [94]

Coggay, William J., carpenter, subj. of G.B., arrived U.S. Apr. 1828; decl. of intent in Marine Court 29 Mar. 1832; rec. by George McAleer [?] - 10 Apr. 1834 [95]

Christie, Alexander, stone cutter, subj. of G.B., arrived U.S. Jan. 1815; decl. of intent in Marine Court 5 Dec. 1831; rec. by Abraham Starns, Jr. - 10 Apr. 1834 [96]

Costigan, William, subj. of G.B., arrived U.S. Oct. 1828; decl. of intent in Marine Court 3 Dec. 1830; rec. by James Kelly - 10 Apr. 1834 [97]

Costigan, James, late of Ire., subj. of G.B., arrived U.S. 20 Sept. 1827 (under age of 18); rec. by William Costigan - 10 Apr. 1834 [98]

Cantrell, John, subj. of G.B., arrived U.S. 1819 (under age of 18); rec. by Gilbert Radan - 10 Apr. 1834 [99]

Cantrell, Joseph, subj. of G.B., arrived U.S. Feb. 1819 (under age of 18); rec. by Gilbert Radan - 10 Apr. 1834 [100]

Cain, John, subj. of G.B., arrived U.S. May 1820 (under age of 18); rec. by Jotham Peabody - 10 Apr. 1834 [101]

Cleary, James, subj. of G.B., arrived U.S. May 1826 (under age of 18); rec. by Jotham Peabody - 10 Apr. 1834 [102]

Campbell, Barney, subj. of G.B., arrived U.S. July 1825; rec. by Bernard O'Donnel - 10 Apr. 1834 [103]

Dodd, John B., druggist, subj. of G.B., arrived U.S. 11 Nov. 1818; report of 3 Oct. 1825: born Northumberland, Eng., age 31, migrated from Liverpool; rec. by John Woodhead - 10 Apr. 1834 [104]

Donnellon, Edward, labourer, subj. of G.B., arrived U.S. June 1825; decl. of intent in Marine Court 28 Jan. 1831; rec. by Thomas O'Connor - 10 Apr. 1834 [105]

Emerson, James, subj. of G.B, arrived U.S. last of June 1810 (under age of 18); rec. by John Rea - 10 Apr. 1834 [106]

Fletcher, Joseph, late of Eng., arrived U.S. May 1804; rec. by Alexander Andrews - 10 Apr. 1834 [107]

Greason, George, subj. of G.B., arrived U.S. 1 Oct. 1828; rec. by George Machine - 10 Apr. 1834 [108]

Graham, Alexander, subj. of G.B., arrived U.S. June 1826 (under age of 18); rec. by William Graham - 10 Apr. 1834 [109]

Gregg, Thomas, subj. of G.B., arrived U.S. Sept. 1825 (under age of 18); rec. by William Graham - 10 Apr. 1834 [110]

George, Robert, subj. of G.B., arrived U.S. 1 Dec. 1825; rec. by William Hornby - 10 Apr. 1834 [111]

Grant, Daniel, subj. of G.B.; decl. of intent in Court of Common Pleas in Philadelphia and report on 9 Oct. 1826: born Co. Armagh, Ire., 15 Dec. 1808, migrated from Warren Point, arrived U.S. Aug. 1823; rec. by Charles Drake - 10 Apr. 1834 [112]

Gasquet, Joseph, subj. of King of France, arrived U.S. 1827; report in Marine Court 14 Mar. 1827: born Marseilles, France, age 33, accountant, migrated from Havre de Grace; wife Elizabeth, born Eng., age 28; rec. by Manuel Godquin - 10 Apr. 1834 [113]

Gornly, Bernard, subj. of G.B., arrived U.S. 2 June 1828; rec. by Peter Smith - 10 Apr. 1834 [114]

Hofer, Victor, subj. of Republic of Berne, arrived U.S. 15 Aug. 1825 (under age of 18); rec. by Francis J. Berier - 10 Apr. 1834 [115]

Harms, Claus, subj. of G.B., arrived U.S. Jan. 1828 (under age of 18); rec. by John J. Brincklee - 10 Apr. 1834 [116]

Hickey, John, labourer, subj. of G.B., arrived U.S. 4 July 1826; decl. of intent in Marine Court 18 June 1829; rec. by John Murphy - 10 Apr. 1834 [117]

Hamilton, James, subj. of G.B., arrived U.S. 1818; rec. by Robert Smith - 10 Apr. 1834 [118]

Hornby, William, subj. of G.B., arrived U.S. 1 Dec. 1828 (under age of 18); rec. by Robert George - 10 Apr. 1834 [119]

Hughes, Daniel, stone cutter, subj. of G.B., arrived U.S. 15 Nov. 1828; decl. of intent in Marine Court 23 Jan. 1832; rec. by John Kelly - 10 Apr. 1834 [120]

Hagan, Francis, subj. of G.B., arrived U.S. 6 May 1827 (under age of 18); rec. by John Hagan - 10 Apr. 1834 [121]

Jackson, Samuel, late of Ire., subj. of G.B., arrived U.S. 16 Apr. 1825 (under age of 18); rec. by John Richardson - 10 Apr. 1834 [122]

Jackson, Robert, subj. of G.B., arrived U.S. 29 Mar. 1829 (under age of 18); rec. by John Jackson, tavern-keeper - 10 Apr. 1834 [123]

Johnson, James, subj. of G.B., arrived U.S. 11 June 1824; decl. of intent in Marine Court 3 Oct. 1832; rec. by Thomas Mc Cormick, of Brooklyn - 10 Apr. 1834 [124]

Kennedy, John, subj. of G.B., arrived U.S. June 1828; rec. by John Cotter - 10 Apr. 1834 [125]

Keogan, Bartholomew, subj. of G.B., arrived U.S. 31 July 1825; report at time of decl. of intent in Marine Court 21 May 1828: born Ire., age 30, labourer, migrated from Belfast - 10 Apr. 1834 [126]

King, George B., Jr., subj. of G.B., arrived U.S. May 1817 (under age of 18); rec. by Lois Wilkes - 10 Apr. 1834 [127]

King, John, of Eng., subj. of G.B., arrived U.S. 21 Sept. 1828 (under age of 18); decl. of intent in Marine Court 3 May 1833; rec. by George W. Miller - 10 Apr. 1834 [128]

Lee, Christopher, subj. of G.B., arrived U.S. 3 Nov. 1810; rec. by Henry Kind - 10 Apr. 1834 [129]

Merrick, Patrick, subj. of G.B., arrived U.S. 18 Sept. 1828; rec. by Richard M. Burke; decl. of intent in Marine Court 9 Nov. 1831 - 10 Apr. 1834 [130]

Macklin, Edward, subj. of G.B., arrived U.S. 20 Aug. 1828; rec. by Edward Blair - 10 Apr. 1834 [131]

Martin, Samuel, subj. of G.B., arrived U.S. 29 July 1824; decl. of intent in Marine Court 4 Mar. 1828; rec. by David Clark - 10 Apr. 1834 [132]

Maniates, Nicholas, subj. of King of Greece, arrived U.S. 2 July 1828 (under age of 18); rec. by William E. Sanford - 10 Apr. 1834 [133]

Moran, John, cabinetmaker and upholsterer, subj. of G.B., arrived U.S. 22 Aug. 1827; decl. of intent in Marine Court 13 May 1829; rec. by Morgan Doherty - 10 Apr. 1834 [134]

Murtha, Thomas, subj. of G.B., arrived U.S. June 1817 (under age of 18); rec. by Joshua Gilbert - 10 Apr. 1834 [135]

Murphy, John, labourer, subj. of G.B., arrived U.S. July 1827; decl. of intent in Marine Court 14 Apr. 1831; rec. by John Hickey - 10 Apr. 1834 [136]

McNamara, Michael, subj. of G.B., arrived U.S. May 1820; rec. by Jotham Peabody - 10 Apr. 1834 [137]

McKenny, John, cartman, subj. of G.B., arr. U.S. 8 Dec. 1829; decl. of intent in Marine Court 5 July 1831; rec. by Lawrence Mount - 10 Apr. 1834 [138]

McCallum, Archibald, mariner, subj. of G.B., arrived U.S. Mar. 1823; report at decl. of intent in Marine Court on 23 Aug. 1824: born Scotland, age 28, migrated from Greenock; wife Elizabeth, born Scotland, age 24; son Dugall, born Scotland, age 18 months; rec. by James Maguire - 10 Apr. 1834 [139]

McKee, Thomas, subj. of G.B., arrived U.S. Dec. 1827; rec. by Peter Hues - 10 Apr. 1834 [140]

McCollough, Patrick, labourer, subj. of G.B., arrived U.S. July 1824; report 24 July 1827 in Marine Court at decl. of intent: born Ire., age 21, migrated from Belfast; rec. by Patrick Cahill - 10 Apr. 1834 [141]

McFarland, Bernard, labourer, subj. of G.B., arrived U.S. 13 Sept. 1828; decl. of intent in Marine Court 12 July 1821; rec. by William Kennedy - 10 Apr. 1834 [142]

McKowan, James, aubj. of G.B., arrived U.S. 10 June 1818 (under age of 180; rec. by John Smith - 10 Apr. 1834 [143]

O'Brien, Daniel, subj. of G.B., arrived U.S. 5 May 1827 (under age of 18); rec. by William Farrell - 10 Apr. 1834 [144]

Perry, William Henry, subj. of G.B., arrived U.S. 1 June 1812 (under age of 18); rec. by John Moony - 10 Apr. 1834 [145]

Power, John, subj. of G.B., arrived U.S. 1818 (under age of 18); rec. by Henry Harvey - 10 Apr. 1834 [146]

Reilly, Edward, carpenter, arrived U.S. 2 May 1827; decl. of intent 16 May 1828: born Ire., age 19 years & 9 mos., migrated from Belfast; rec. by John Carney - 10 Apr. 1834 [147]

Riley, John, subj. of G.B., arrived U.S. 5 June 1827 (under age of 18); rec. by Francis Batresbee - 10 Apr. 1834 [148]

Richards, William, Jr., subj. of G.B., arrived U.S. March 1825 (under age of 18); rec. by Wm. Richards - 10 Apr. 1834 [149]

Richardson, John, subj. of G.B., arrived U.S. 16 Apr. 1825 (under age of 18); rec. by Samuel Jackson - 10 Apr. 1834 [150]

Roe, Thomas, subj. of G.B., arrived U.S. Oct. 1827 (under age of 18); rec. by Edward Roe - 10 Apr. 1834 [151]

Still, Adam, subj. of G.B., arrived U.S. 1815 (under age of 18); rec. by John Orser - 10 Apr. 1834 [152]

Slater, William, subj. of G.B., arrived U.S. 1821 (under age of 18); rec. by Washington Woodward - 10 Apr. 1834 [152]

Troy, Philip, subj. of G.B., arrived U.S. 2 Oct. 1828; decl. of intent 5 Dec. 1831; rec. by John Murphy - 10 Apr. 1834 [153]

Thompson, William H., subj. of G.B., arrived U.S. June 1820 (under age of 18); rec. by Randolph White - 10 Apr. 1834 [154]

Walker, William, subj. of G.B., arrived U.S. Aug. 1805 (under age of 18); rec. by Andrew Bleakley, Jr. - 10 Apr. 1834 [155]

Samuel, David, subj. of G.B., arrived U.S. 19 Nov. 1828; rec. by Gerard Hopkins - 4 Feb. 1835 [156]

Peuscher, George, subj. of Grand Duke of Hessia; rec. by John Schnaufer - 9 Apr. 1835 [157]

Schnaufer, John, subj. of Drand Duke of Hessia; rec. by George Peuscher - 9 Apr. 1835 [158]

Krammer, Joseph, subj. of Grand Duke of Baden; rec. by Andrew Bennett - 15 Apr. 1835 [159]

Ekel, John, subj. of King of Bavaria; rec. by Herman Kothe - 15 Apr. 1835 [160]

Balestier, Joseph Nérée, subj. of King of France, arrived U.S. 1817; rec. by William C. Baldwin - 25 Apr. 1835 [161]

Burnett, Jonathan, subj. of G.B., arrived U.S. 4 Aug. 1827; rec. by Wm. Maccartney - 16 May 1835 [162]

Jung, John, subj. of Grand Duke of Baden; rec. by Franz Staat - 27 May 1835 [163]

Staat, Franz, subj. of King of France; rec. by John Jung - 27 May 1835 [164]

Acoste, Dominick, subj. of King of Sardinia, arrived U.S. 1826; rec. by John Galloway - 27 June 1835 [165]

Woodhead, Matthew, subj. of G.B., arrived U.S. Feb. 1822; rec. by John Woodhead - 18 Nov. 1835 [166]

Tyson, John, mariner, formerly of Liverpool, subj. of G.B., arrived U.S. May 1830; decl. of intent 15 June 1830; rec. by James L. Roberts - 19 Mar. 1836 [167]

Hyatt, James, engraver, subj. of G.B., arrived U.S. before Apr. 1831; rec. by William H. Goodday - 15 May 1836 [168]

Bryan, Frederick Henry Barker, subj. of G.B., arrived U.S. Nov. 1823 (according to evidence of Henry Bolland, of Phila.); rec. by Christopher C. Marsh - 8 Dec. 1836 [169]

Chinery, James, engraver, late of Birmingham, Warwickshire, Eng., arrived U.S. 23 Oct. 1826; decl. of intent 29 Mar. 1834, when rec. by William Chinery - 29 Mar. 1836 [170]

Devlin, Thomas; decl. of intent Court of Common Pleas of Rensselaer Co. on 11 June 1834: born Granard, Co. of Longford, Ire., age 30, migrated from Dublin , arrived U.S. 1826 and now resides in Troy; rec. by John Hasey - 31 Jan. 1837 [171]

Godry, Frederick, subj. of King of France; decl. of intent 15 Apr. 1833; rec. by Joseph Bailey - 15 Mar. 1837 [172]

Van Arx, Samuel James, late of Canton Berne, Switzerland; rec. by Henry Kurtzemeyer - 25 Mar. 1837 [173]

Dimond, Denis, late of Ire., arrived U.S. Oct. 1831; decl. of intent 14 June 1834; rec. by William McCluskey - 11 Apr. 1837 [174]

Kennedy, Pearce, subj. of G.B., arrived U.S. 6 May 1831; decl. of intent 7 Oct. 1834; rec. by Robert Clark - 12 Apr. 1837 [175]

Caldwell, George, born Co. Antrim, Ire., arrived U.S. Mar. 1832; decl. of intent Inferior Court of Common Pleas, Bergen Co., N.J., 11 Oct. 1834; rec. by Silas Henry Dunning - 12 Apr. 1837 [176]

Barnsdall, John, subj. of G.B., arrived U.S. 1 Dec. 1836; decl. of intent Court of Common Pleas, NYC, 19 Dec. 1836: born Bedfordshire, Eng., age 21, tailor, migrated from London; rec. by George W. White - 13 Apr. 1837 [177]

Betts, William, of Brooklyn, subj. of G.B.; rec. by Gerard W. Morris - 21 June 1837 [178]

Marion, Amedèe Jean, subj. of King of France; decl. of intent 23 Nov. 1832; rec. by John Delmonico - 13 Sept. 1837 [179]

Warburg, Ludwig, merchant, late of Hamburg; decl. of intent 7 May 1831; rec. by Elijah Boardman - 23 Sept. 1837 [180]

McGinley, John; rec. by Patrick Moore - 7 Nov. 1837 [181]

Bundle 2

Morrison, Francis, late of Edinburgh, Scotland; decl. of intent 13 Mar. 1833; rec. by Jesse Grant - 5 Apr. 1838 [1]

Stiff, Henry, late of Eng.; rec. by George Fraser - 9 Apr. 1838 [2]

Hoyer, Joseph F., subj. of King of the Netherlands; rec. by Joseph Foulke, Jr. - 14 May 1838 [3]

Heeney, John, subj. of G.B.; decl. of intent Justices Court of Albany 29 Oct. 1833: born Co. Antrim, Ire., age 24, migrated from Belfast; rec. by Delancey Kane - 17 May 1838 [4]

Arnold, John, subj. of G.B.; rec. by Alexander Arnold - 5 Nov. 1838 [5]

Brady, Patrick, subj. of G.B., arrived U.S. 26 Oct. 1833; decl. of intent 11 Aug. 1835; rec. by James McGuire - 5 Nov. 1838 [6]

Baird, William, subj. of G.B.; rec. by William Beechley - 5 Nov. 1838 [7]

Birmingham, Patrick, subj. of G.B., arrived U.S. 1 Aug. 1832; decl. of intent 2 Apr. 1836; rec. by Patrick Callahan - 5 Nov. 1838 [8]

Benz [clerk wrote "Baus"], Mathias, subj. of Grand Duke of Baden, arrived U.S. 27 July 1833; decl. of intent 3 Nov. 1834; rec. by Henry Sailer - 5 Nov. 1838 [9]

Byrnes, Patrick, subj. of G.B., arrived U.S. 27 May 1829; decl. of intent 13 Apr. 1836; rec. by Robert Stinson - 5 Nov. 1838 [10]

Carroll, Paul, subj. of G.B., arrived U.S. Aug. 1833; decl. of intent 9 Nov. 1835; rec. by James McAuley - 5 Nov. 1838 [11]

Crumlisk, John, subj. of G.B., arrived U.S. 23 June 1833; decl. of intent 5 Nov. 1834; rec. by Edward Lynch - 5 Nov. 1838 [12]

Curran, Joseph, subj. of G.B.; rec. by William Rider - 5 Nov. 1838 [13]

Balestier, Joseph Nereus (by his guardian, Joseph Balestier, of Boston), b. Island of Guadaloupe, W.I., age 7, subj. of King of France - report 8 Aug. 1821

Hutcheson, John, late of Lincolnshire, Eng., leather dealer, subj. of G.B. - 9 Sept. 1829

Keernin, Bernard, subj. of G.B. - 14 Nov. 1828

McCosker, Bernard, subj. of G.B. - 6 Nov. 1828

Toumy, John, subj. of G.B. - 6 Nov. 1828

Leahy, Dennis, subj. of G.B. - 6 Nov. 1828

Ulrick, Henry, b. Baden, age 42, subj. of King of Wurtemberg , gardner, migr. from Amsterdam - 27 Nov. 1824

Cochran, Alexander, of Newburgh, Orange Co., N.Y., cotton manufacturer, late of Co. Antrim, Ire. - 16 Dec. 1829

Muir, William, baker, subj. of G.B. - 5 Jan. 1829

Mitteregger, Jacob, waiter, subj. of King of Bavaria - 7 Feb. 1829

Geay, Peter, subj. of King of France - 3 Feb. 1829

Whelan, John, subj. of G.B. - 10 Mar. 1829

Brown, Audley, blacksmith, subj. of G.B. - 4 May 1829

Wharton, Thomas, late of Yorkshire, Eng., merchant - 7 May 1829

Cochrane, William Johnson, b Dundee, Angusshire, Scotland, age 32, migr. from Dundee, tailor - 4 June 1829

Ledlie, John, late of Co. Armagh, Ire., farmer - 2 June 1829

Sullivan, Daniel, late of Co. Cork, Ire., subj. of G.B. - 11 June 1829

Birmingham, Henry, late of Co. Armagh, Ire., subj. of G.B. - 6 July 1829

Fokkes, Itje, late of Hamburgh, mariner, subj. of City of Hamburgh - 6 Oct. 1829

Düsterkötter, Henrich, late of Osnabruck, Kingdom of Hanover, labourer - 15 Feb. 1830

Parsonson, John, late of Dorcaster, Yorkshire, Eng., subj. of G.B. - 10 Feb. 1830

Real, Thomas, formerly of Dublin, Ire., labourer - 3 Feb. 1830

Woodhead, Mathew, late of Yorkshire, Eng., manufacturer - 4 May 1830

Bedicker, Herman, late of Weisebeck [?], Kingdon of Hanover, sugar baker, subj. of King of Hanover - 5 Apr. 1830

Boschen, Harman, late of Tarmstadt [?], Kingdom of Hanover, subj. of King of Hanover - 5 Apr. 1830

Machlin, Edward, labourer, subj. of G.B. - 28 Apr. 1830

Stever [or Steuer?], John, late of Ninehausen, Kingdom of Hanover, tailor - 5 Apr. 1830

Sands, Joseph, formerly of Leeds, Eng., merchant - 10 Apr. 1830

Bedson, Thomas, mariner, late of Middlesex Co., Eng. - 22 May 1830

Hobday, Edward, fishmonger, late of Co. of Kent, Eng. - 8 May 1830

McDonald, Patrick, late of Co. Monaghan, Ire., labourer - 24 May 1830

Ricard, John B., grocer, late of Dept. of the Meuse, France - 3 My 1830

Wohlgehagen, Jacob, late of Amsterdam the Netherlands, seaman - 4 May 1830

Burnett, Jonathan, late of Bannockburn, Scotland, grocer - 18 June 1830

Hamilton, John, late of Co. Tyrone, Ire., wheelwright - 16 June 1830

Jaffords, Michael, late of Co. Cork, Ire. labourer 21 June 1830

Jaffords, Maurice, late of Co. Cork, Ire. - 21 June 1830

Tyson, John, mariner, late of Liverpool - 15 June 1830

Cops, Frederick, late of London, Eng., collector of natural curiosities - 7 July 1830

Adams, Joseph, late of London - 20 Sept. 1830

Dunderdale, John, gentleman, late of Leeds, Yorkshire, Eng. - 30 Sept. 1830

Hunter, William, b. Ire., age 41, migr. from Sligo, milkman; wife Ann, b. Ire., age 40 - 6 Oct. 1830

Hows, John William Stanhope, late of London, merchant - 9 Oct. 1830

Prebble, John, late of Co. of Kent, Eng., parish of Higham, a merchant - 15 Oct. 1830

Marron, Patrick, late of Dublin, reporter - 29 Oct. 1830

Chinery, William, late of Birmingham, Warwickshire, Eng., lapidary - 11 Nov. 1830

Chinery, James, late of Birmingham, Warwickshire, Eng., engraver - 11 Nov. 1830

Parts, Francis, labourer, late of town of Sarrebruck, Germany, subj. of King of Prussia - 4 Nov. 1830

Wood, Thomas James, late of Co. of Northumberland, Eng., general salesman - 10 Nov. 1830

McCourt, Michael, late of Co. Tyrone, subj. of G.B. - 11 Dec. 1830

Milby, Benjamin, late of Shelburn, N.S. - 18 Dec. 1830

Ursin, Francis, late of Co. Monaghan, Ire., labourer - 29 Jan. 1831

Cohen, Mayer, merchant, late of Putlanche, France, subj. of King of France - 21 Jan. 1831

Warburg, Ludwig, merchant, late of Hamburgh, subj. of City of Hamburgh - 7 May 1831

Mann, Francis, late of Kings Co., Ire., subj. of G.B. - 17 Feb. 1831

Wreaks, Henry, merchant, late of Sheffield, Yorkshire, Eng. - 12 Feb. 1831

Angel, Charles, late of Prussia, sugar baker - 18 Mar. 1831

Farr, Robert, late of Beccles, Suffolk, Eng. - 14 Mar. 1831

Wreaks, Charles, merchant, late of Sheffield, Eng. - 9 Mar. 1831

Bent, William, merchant, late of Yorkshire, Eng. - 7 Apr. 1831

Hurly, John, stone mason, late of Co. Cork, Ire. - 13 Apr. 1831

Keernin, Bernard, subj. of G.B. - 14 Nov. 1828

Keasey, John, coach driver, late of Co. Tyrone, Ire. - 18 Apr. 1831

Platt, Thomas, merchant, late of Yorkshire, Eng. - 7 Apr. 1831

Wills, William, stage driver, late of Co. of Kent, Eng. - 9 Apr. 1831

Finlay, James, waiter, late of Co. Monaghan, Ire. - 10 May 1831

Arnold, William, dentist, late of Dublin, Ire. - 7 June 1831

O'Hara, Michael, labourer, late of Co. Limerick, Ire. - 25 July 1831

Herlihy, Cornelius, late of Co. Kerry, Ire., at present of the town of Flushing, Queens Co., N.Y. - 4 Aug. 1831

Bielle, John Baptiste Joseph, box-maker, formerly of Havre de Grace, France - 8 Sept. 1831

Hyatt, James, mariner, late of Turks Island, Bahamas, subj. of G.B. - 8 Dec. 1831

Lewis, Seth E., currier, late of Cardiff, South Wales - 21 Sept. 1831

Collan, Peter, late of Co. Monaghan, Ire., labourer - 9 Sept. 1831

Reid, James, late of Co. Down, Ire., weaver - 13 Sept. 1831

Wright, James, late of Co. Down, Ire., cartman - 13 Sept. 1831

Boothman, John, b. Manchester, Eng., age 27, migr. from Liverpool, baker - 24 Oct. 1825

McCombs, James, type caster, late of Londonderry, Ire. - 17 Nov. 1831

Williams, Thomas, of Poughkeepsie, Dutchess Co., N.Y., woolstapler, arrived NYC 15 May 1820, age 25 years and 9 months - 11 July 1831

McDermott, Peter, b. Co. Longford, Ire., age 23, migr. from Ire., labourer - 29 May 1827

O'Ferrall, James, subj. of G.B. - 29 May 1826

Smith, John, subj. of G.B. - 6 Nov. 1832

Whybrew, Thomas, subj. of G.B. - 16 Dec. 1828

Shaw, Joseph, b. Chesterfield, Eng., age 48, migr. from Eng., gardener - 22 Feb. 1830

Campbell, Berney, labourer, subj. of G.B. - 5 Mar. 1832

Neenan, Michael, card manufacturer, formerly of Co. Cork, Ire. - 5 Mar. 1832

Hawes, Sidney, late of Co. of Norfolk, Eng., farmer - 17 May 1832

Moore, James, labourer, formerly of Ballymana, Ire. - 22 May 1832

McSourley, Hugh, waiter, formerly of Co. Fermanagh, Ire. - 22 May 1832

McCarey, Patrick, waiter, formerly of Colebrook, Co. Fermanagh, Ire. - 4 June 1832

Perkins, John, late of Northamptonshire, Eng., now of Brooklyn, Kings Co., N.Y. - 11 June 1832

White, William, late of Co. Armagh, grocer - 2 June 1832

Busvine, Edward John, late of London, physician and surgeon - 21 Dec. 1833

Mann, Francis, merchant, late of Kings Co., Ire. - 17 Feb. 1831

Murray, James, formerly of Drougherty, Co. Co. Louth, Ire. - 4 Sept. 1833

Cowley, Thomas, late of Wiltshire, Eng., house-carpenter - 4 Sept. 1833

Finlay, James, waiter, late of Co. Monaghan, Ire. 10 May 1831

Morrison, Francis, formerly of Edinburgh, Scotland - 13 Mar. 1833

Monehen, John, late of Co. Louth, Ire. - 23 Feb. 1833

Monaghan, John, subj. of G.B. - 14 Jan. 1834

Eck, John Daniel, tailor, native of Strasburg, subj. of King of France - 21 Sept. 1829

Hannigan, Thomas, late of Co. Waterford, Ire. - 5 Feb. 1834

Wohning, Carl, of Swambeg [or Swamberg?], Kingdom of Hanover, subj. of G.B. - 11 Feb. 1834

Flood, John, labourer, late of Co. Meath, Ire. - 25 Mar. 1834

Artiquenave, Jean Francois, native of France, residing in Boston, Mass.[report 1 Jan. 1827]: b. Commune of Alereilhan [?] in arrondissement in District of Tarbes, France; on 23 Mar. 1825 age was 20; migr. from Havre, arrived Boston 7 Sept. 1826 - 25 Apr. 1829

Coyle, Matthew, late of Co. Cavan, Ire. - 9 Apr. 1834

Cole, William, late of London, subj. of G.B. - 9 Apr. 1834

Black, Patrick, late of Co. Cavan, Ire. - 9 Apr. 1834

Blair, Edward, late of Co. Antrim, Ire. - 8 Apr. 1834

Reilly, Hugh, late of town of Ballanamore, Co. Leitrim, Ire. - 4 Aug. 1834

Dunlap, William, formerly of Co. Donegal, Ire. - 7 Apr. 1834

Doyle, James, late of Co. Longford, Ire. - 8 Apr. 1834

Espie, James, late of Scotland - 10 Apr. 1834

Fanell, Francis, late of Co. Cavan, Ire. - 9 Apr. 1834

Faulkner, Thomas, late of Co. Tyrone, Ire. - 9 Apr. 1834

Fleming, James, late of town of Clemell [?], Ire. - 9 Apr. 1834

Lockwood, William, late of Eng. - 9 Apr. 1834

McBride, John, late of Co. Down, Ire. - 8 Apr. 1834

McFaul, Andrew, late of Ire. - 9 Apr. 1834

Mills, William, late of London, Eng. - 10 Apr. 1834

McCarty, Michael, labourer, late of Ire. - 24 Apr. 1834

Neeson, James, late of Co. Antrim, Ire. - 8 Apr. 1834

Nesbett, James, late of Co. Down, Ire. - 8 Apr. 1834

Neeson, Dennis, late of Co. Antrim - 8 Apr. 1834

Owens, William, late of Co. Cavan, Ire. - 7 Apr. 1834

Salmon, Thomas, late of Co. Longford, Ire. - 7 Apr. 1834

Tuita, Peter, late of Co. Longford, Ire. - 8 Apr. 1834

Welsh, William, late of Co. Waterford, Ire. - 8 Apr. 1834

Williamson, John, late of Ire. - 9 Apr. 1834

Burge, Edward, late of Bristol, Eng. - 5 May 1834

Dubois, Francis Blake, late of Island of Tortola, planter, subj. of G.B. - 23 June 1834

Boizard, Eustache Napoleon, late of Paris, France, merchant - 10 May 1834

Silva, Manuel, formerly of Oporto, Portugal, confectioner - 28 May 1834

Bell, John, late of Lancaster, Eng., block- and pump maker - 10 June 1834

Delaney, John, late of Co. Cavan, Ire., farmer - 7 June 1834

Garigan, Philip, late of Co. Meath, Ire. - 21 June 1834

Zum Hagen, Louis, formerly of Hanover, miner - 20 June 1834

Maclean, Henry Clinton, late of Island of Tortola, planter, subj. of G.B. - 23 June 1834

Staggemeyer, Philip Henry, subj. of King of Prussia - 20 June 1834

Weimer, Joseph, late of Prussia, farmer, subj. of King of Prussia - 20 June 1834

Holmes, James, late of Co. Down, Ire., labourer - 9 July 1834

Gilbride, John, late of town of Ballimagrurin [Ballymagauran], Co. Cavan, Ire. - 4 Aug. 1834

Brannan, Michael, late of Co. Longford, Ire. - 21 Oct. 1834

McCarey, Patrick, waiter, formerly of Colebrook, Co. Fermanagh, Ire. - 4 June 1832

Delle Piane, Bernardino, subj. of Grand Duke of Tuscany - 13 Dec. 1834

De Covarrubias, Gabriel, late of Havana, Cuba, subj. of Queen of Spain - 1 Nov. 1834

Magee, Matthias, subj. of Duke of Baden - 31 Oct. 1834

Kahn, Charles, late of Stockholm, Sweden, merchant - 20 Sept. 1832

Yackoby, Woolf J., late of London, subj. of G.B. - 27 May 1835

Levy, Bernd, formerly of Hohensolsus [?], Prussia - 26 Nov. 1835

Stoltz, Peter, of Bavaria, Germany, subj. of King of Bavaria - 31 Jan. 1835

Adamson, Thomas, late of Selby, Yorkshire, Eng. - 2 Feb. 1835

Rupp, Martin, subj. of King of France - 5 Feb. 1835

Frith, Edward, merchant, subj. of G.B - 28 Feb. 1835

Kniff [clerk wrote "Seith"], Michael, subj. of Grand Duke of Baden - 5 Feb. 1835

Van Arx, Samuel Jacob, of Canton Berne, Switzerland - 13 Feb. 1835

Hempel, John William, subj. of King of Prussia - 9 Feb. 1835

Bonsall, Thomas, late of Cardiganshire, Wales - 14 Mar. 1835

Greig, Alexander Mount, formerly of London - 26 Mar. 1835

Hettinger, John, subj. of King of Wirtemberg - 31 Mar. 1835

Richter, Frederick, subj. of King of Prussia - 23 Mar. 1835

Rigler, John Andrew, subj. of King of Wirtemberg - 31 Mar. 1835

Wagner, Francis, subj. of Grand Duke of Baden - 12 Mar. 1835

Bechstein, Friedrich, subj. of King of Wurtemburg - 5 May 1835

Schuh, Johann Georg, subj. of King of Wurtemberg - 11 May 1835

Williams, Hutchins Thomas, native of London, Eng., late of Dublin, Ire. - 8 May 1835

Aubry, Charles, formerly of Paris, France, subj. of King of France - 26 June 1835

Simpson, Andrew, late of Ire. - 11 June 1835

Maigrot, Lewis, subj. of King of France - 6 July 1835

Pappi [or Pappis?], John, glazier, subj. of Canton of Ticino, Switzerland - 16 July 1835

Scolari, Giobani, glazier, subj. of Canton of Ticino, Switzerland - 16 July 1835

Cuendet, Eugene, subj. of Republic of Switzerland - 3 Aug. 1835

Wilding, James Leo Horace, subj. of G.B. - 26 Sept. 1835

Cousins, Robert, late of Wales - 8 Oct. 1835

Julius, George Henry, subj. of King of Prussia - 21 Oct. 1835

Haslan, George, late of London - 16 Nov. 1835

McAdam, Owen, formerly of Co. Longford, Ire. - 26 Dec. 1835

Collins, Patrick, formerly of Co. Cavan, Ire. - 20 Jan. 1836

Legay, Louis André, of Samanche [?], France - 12 Jan. 1836

McLarney, Michael, formerly of Co. Cavan, Ire. - 6 Jan. 1836

Masterson, Patrick, formerly of Co. Fermanagh, Ire. - 20 Jan. 1836

Moran, John, formerly of Co. Longford, Ire. - 22 Jan. 1836

Strybing, Henry, subj. of Grand Duke of Mecklenburg - 7 Jan. 1836

Welsh, John, formerly of Co. Cork, Ire. - 6 Jan. 1836

Winckles, Thomas, late of Northamptonshire, Eng. - 20 Jan. 1836

Buckley, Lawrence, formerly of Cork, Ire. - 15 Mar. 1836

Canning, Christopher, late of Ire. - 29 Mar. 1836

Daily, Michael, formerly of Co. Cork, Ire. - 25 Mar. 1836

Metzger, John Joachim, formerly of Neustadt on the Aisch, Bavarai, subj. of King of Bavaria - 16 Mar. 1836

Morris, Charles Hughes, formerly of Oswestry, Eng. - 31 Mar. 1836

Ogs, Georg, subj. of Grand Duke of Baden - 15 Mar. 1836

Roberts, James, formerly of Island of Tortola, subj. of G.B. - 11 Mar. 1836

Schukt, Edward, late of Northausen, Germany, subj. of King of Prussia - 2 Mar. 1836

Carey, Patrick, formerly of Tipperary, Ire. - 2 Apr. 1836

Campion, Catharine (widow of Patrick Campion), formerly of Queens Co., Ire. - 4 Apr. 1836

Dougherty, Patrick, formerly of Co. Cavan, Ire. - 2 Apr. 1836

Tully, James, formerly of Co. Cavan, Ire. - 2 Apr. 1836

Miley, Ambrose, late of Dublin, Ire. - 17 Mar. 1837

Nelson, Robert, late of Scotland - 10 Mar. 1837

Allanson, John, subj. of G.B. - 27 May 1837

Agan, Dennis, late of Limerick C., Ire. - 12 June 1837

Evans, Daniel M., late of Carmarthen, Wales - 1 June 1837

McCarty, Michael, subj. of G.B. - 14 June 1837

Matfeld, Gustavus A., subj. of Hamburgh - 15 June 1837

Phillip, John, subj. of G.B. - 17 June 1837

Phillip, Caleb, subj. of G.B. - 17 June 1837

Roach, Cornelius, subj. of G.B. - 27 June 1837

Richards, William S., Jr., late of Co. Glamorganshire, Wales - 5 Aug. 1837

Elliott, Samuel M., late of Inverness, Scotland - 12 Sept. 1837

Jones, John, subj. of G.B. - 28 Sept. 1837

Martin, Philip, late of Co. Cavan, Ire. - 19 Dec. 1837

Dempsey, Daniel, subj. of G.B. - 14 Mar. 1838

Vugener, Charles E. [clerk wrote "Augener"], subj. of King of Prussia - 3 Jan. 1838

Goldschmidt, Ludwig, subj. of Free City of Hamburgh - 2 Apr. 1838

Gooding, Stephen, subj. of G.B. - 5 Apr. 1838

Hyndes, Michael, late of Co. of West Meath, Ire. - 23 Apr. 1838

O'Reilly, Robert, late of Co. Cavan, Ire. - 12 Apr. 1838

Stephens, Alexander, subj. of Grand Duke of Oldenburgh - 12 Apr. 1838

Alexander, Sarah, subj. of G.B. - 8 May 1838

Connelly, John, late of Co. Galway, Ire. - 30 May 1838

Finke, John Frederick, late of Bremen, subj. of Elector of Ha- nover - 31 May 1838

Pillin, Dan, late of Lancashire, Eng. - 7 May 1838

Hayden, Laughlin, subj. of G.B. - 20 Sept. 1838

Hueson, Edward Henzell, late of Dublin, Ire. - 29 Sept. 1838

Martin, Catharine, late of Co. Donegal, Ire. - 3 Sept. 1838

Sims, David, subj. of G.B. - 19 Sept. 1838

Riley, Miles, subj. of G.B. - 3 Oct. 1838

Bour, Nicholas, subj. of King of France - 6 Nov. 1838

Dolan, Michael, subj. of G.B. - 8 Nov. 1838

Bernhard, Henry, subj. of King of Bavaria - 7 Nov. 1838

Wohlleben, Jacob, subj. of King of Bavaria - 7 Nov. 1838

Trautmann, Adam, subj. of Duke of Bavaria - 7 Nov. 1838

Foersch, John Augustus, subj. of Elector of Hesse Cassel - 7 Nov. 1838

Golden, Michael, subj. of G.B. - 7 Nov. 1838

Hala, Thomas, subj. of G.B. - 7 Nov. 1838

Lambert, D., subj. of King of Prussia - 7 Nov. 1838

Cumiskey, John, formerly of Co. Cavan, Ire. - 25 May 1836

Beales, John Charles, subj. of G.B. - 6 May 1836

Smith, William, formerly of Co. Antrim, Ire. - 30 June 1836

Tudor, Thomas, formerly of Staffordshire, Eng. - 9 June 1836

Cheesman, Maurice, subj. of G.B. - 22 July 1836

Leffers, Anthony, formerly of Papenburgh, Hanover, subj. of G.B. - 11 July 1836

Vaughan, Henry P., formerly of Montreal, Lower Canada - 13 July 1836

Bonner, John, late of Londonderry, Ire. - 9 Aug. 1836

Jones, Robert M., late of Co. Armagh, Ire. - 22 Aug. 1836

Highet, Robert, subj. of G.B. - 30 Aug. 1836

Boylan, John, subj. of G.B. - 12 Sept. 1836

Jones, William, subj. of G.B. - 19 Sept. 1836

Shrott, Joseph, subj. of Emperor of Germany - 17 Oct. 1836

Clarke, Daniel, subj. of G.B. - 1 Nov. 1836

Duffy, Edward, subj. of G.B. - 5 Nov. 1836

Gaspart, Jean, late of town of Sharlouis, Prussia, subj. of King of Prussia - 7 Nov. 1836

Conroy, John, subj. of G.B. - 5 Nov. 1836

Davock, Michael E., late of Ire. - 5 Nov. 1836

Grischele, John, subj. of Duke of Baden - 3 Nov. 1836

Hawkins, Charles, subj. of King of Denmark - 14 Nov. 1836

Johnson, William, late of Eng., merchant - 6 Nov. 1834

Koelln, Ernest, late of Hanover, subj. of G.B. - 3 Nov. 1834

Miller, John, late of Scotland, subj. of G.B. - 3 Nov. 1834

Maag, George Adam, subj. of King of France - 3 Nov. 1834

Pfoersch, Henrich, subj. of King of France - 3 Nov. 1834

Sarbach, John, subj. of King of France - 3 Nov. 1834

Sackmeister, Bernhard, subj. of King of Bavaria - 3 Nov. 1834

Scarborough, John, subj. of G.B. - 5 Nov. 1834

Wall, Johann, Heinrich, subj. of King of France - 3 Nov. 1834

Haverty, Michael, late of Dublin, Ire. - 23 Dec. 1834

Jurgens, Henry, late of Hamburg, Germany, subj. of Emperor of Germany - 7 Nov. 1836

Sullivan, Patrick, late of Co. Cork, Ire. - 7 Nov. 1836

Weaver, Meinrad, subj. of Emperor of Germany - 12 Dec. 1836

Ryan, Michael, subj. of G.B. - 20 Jan. 1837

Phealan, Michael, subj. of G.B. - 20 Jan. 1837

O'Brien, Charles, late of Co. Tyrone, Ire. - 3 Feb. 1837

Stuart, James, late of Co. Tyrone, Ire. - 3 Feb. 1837

French, Nathan, subj. of G.B. - 30 Mar. 1837

Harrop, Thomas, late of Yorkshire, Eng. - 29 Mar. 1837

Kelly, Michael C., late of Kings Co., Ire. - 20 Mar. 1837

McCuley, Patrick, subj. of G.B. - 7 Nov. 1838

Wiley, Robert, late of Co. Cork, Ire - 8 Nov. 1838

Neumann, Gustavus Adolphus, subj. of King of Prussia - 7 Nov. 1838

Riley, Patrick, subj. of G.B. - 8 Nov. 1838

Ritter, Philipp, subj. of King of Bavaria - 20 Nov. 1838

Ringshausen, Georg, subj. of Emperor of Germany - 30 Nov. 1838

Seinsoth, Henry Jacob, subj. of King of Bavaria - 7 Nov. 1838

Schmidt, Philipp W., subj. of King of Bavaria - 20 Nov. 1838

Talin, Wladimir Appollonius, subj. of King of Sweden - 7 Nov. 1838

Uhl, John, subj. of Duke of Bavaria - 7 Nov. 1838

Curtin, Dennis, subj. of G.B. - 19 Dec. 1838

Rittner, Johannes, subj. of King of France - 10 Dec. 1838

Schrorfner, Valentin, subj. of King of Germany - 10 Dec. 1838

Fogarty, Edward, late of Queens Co., Ire. - 11 Jan. 1839

Larkin, Neil, late of Co. Derry, Ire. - 31 Jan. 1839

Fitzgerald, Patrick, subj. of G.B. - 27 Feb. 1839

Hahn, Heymann, subj. of King of Prussia - 18 Mar. 1839

Dignan, Patrick, subj. of G.B. - 3 Apr. 1839

McFardan, James, subj. of G.B. - 11 Apr. 1839

McBrearty, James, subj. of G.B. - 11 Apr. 1839

Mirandoli, Edward, subj. of Grand Duke of Tuscany - 27 Apr. 1839

Parker, Joseph, late of Ire. - 13 Apr. 1839

Parker, John, late of Ire. - 13 Apr. 1839

Schminki, Francis C., subj. of Elector of Hessia - 10 Apr. 1839

Larney, James, late of Ire. - 3 May 1839

Shadgett, William Henry, subj. of G.B. - 19 June 1839

Keefe, George L., subj. of G.B. - 18 Sept. 1839

Karck, Ferdinand, subj. of City of Hamburgh - 23 Sept. 1839

Roberts, James, formerly of Island of Tortola, a subj. of G.B. - 17 Mar. 1836

O'Leary, Dennis, subj. of G.B. - 14 Apr. 1840

McDermott, Cornelius, subj. of G.B. - 13 Apr. 1840

Brour, Jacob, subj. of Duke of Hesse Cassel - 14 Apr. 1840

Cecil, William, subj. of G.B. - 14 Mar. 1840

Hanna, John, subj. of G.B. - 15 Nov. 1839

Harris, Richard, late of Lincolnshire, Eng. - 4 Nov. 1839

Brian, John, late of Co. Cork, Ire. - 7 Nov. 1839

Buyer, Joseph, subj. of King of Bavaria - 2 Oct. 1839

Gans [or Gaus?], Meyer, subj. of King of Hanover - 10 June 1839

Kolb, Henry, subj. of King of Bavaria - 2 Oct. 1839

Buyer, Andrew, subj. of King of Bavaria - 2 Oct. 1839

Smith, Edward S., subj. of G.B. - 23 Apr. 1840

Willmott, Robert, subj. of G.B. - 24 June 1840

Levy, Emanuel, subj. of Grand Duke of Tuscany - 3 July 1840

Boylan, Michael, late of Co. Cavan, Ire. - 6 Sept. 1840

Costley, Patrick, late of Kings Co., Ire. - 15 Sept. 1840

Cuyler, Edward, late of Chatham, Co. of Kent, Eng. - 18 Sept. 1840

Doschen, Claus, subj. of King of Hanover - 16 Sept. 1840

Duffy, Daniel, subj. of King of Hanover - 18 Sept. 1840

Hulle, Christian, subj. of King of Hanover - 16 Sept. 1840

Jackson, James, subj. of G.B. - 15 Sept. 1840

Kissack, Daniel, subj. of G.B. - 16 Sept. 1840

Lalley, Michael, subj. of G.B. - 14 Sept. 1840

McCaulay, Robert, subj. of G.B. - 16 Sept. 1840

McCadam, Owen, subj. of G.B. - 26 Sept. 1840

Scanlan, William, subj. of G.B. - 19 Sept. 1840

Smith, Thomas, subj. of G.B. - 23 Sept. 1840

Urbani, Francis, subj. of Duke of Lucca - 15 Sept. 1840

Carr, William, subj. of G.B. - 5 Oct. 1840

Lulsfelder, Solomon Lob, subj. of King of Bavaria - 14 Oct. 1840

Darby, Jabez, subj. of G.B. - 5 Oct. 1840

Duffy, Patrick, subj. of G.B. - 22 Oct. 1840

Fribiss, Johann, subj. of King of Bavaria - 10 Oct. 1840

Gron, John, subj. of Duke of Baden - 10 Oct. 1840

Johnston, Thomas, subj. of G.B. - 12 Oct. 1840

Logue, James, subj. of G.B. - 10 Oct. 1840

McDonnald, Andrew, subj. of G.B. - 5 Oct. 1840

Muldoon, Patrick, subj. of G.B. - 8 Oct. 1840

Russ, Horace, subj. of G.B. - 19 Oct. 1840

Savage, John, subj. of G.B. - 5 Oct. 1840

Sweeney, Alexander, subj. of G.B. - 10 Oct. 1840

Stephenson, Isaac, late of Ire. - 29 Oct. 1840

Tomes, James, late of Eng. - 30 Oct. 1840

Grace, Piere B., late of Ire. - 2 Nov. 1840

Gentle, James, late of Scotland - 30 Nov. 1840

Hazlett, Matthew, late of Ire. - 3 Nov. 1840

Klähr, Jacob, subj. of Grand Duke of Baden - 2 Nov. 1840

Knox, Richard, late of Eng. - 3 Nov. 1840

Laddauer, Rudolph, subj. of Prince of Hesse Cassel - 2 Nov. 1840

Manion, Thomas, late of Ire. - 5 Nov. 1840

World, Joshua, late of Co. of Oxford, Eng. - 2 Nov. 1840

Wessau, Konrad, subj. of King of Bavaria - 4 Nov. 1840

Vol. 1

Phillips, Robert (resident of U.S. between 18 June 1798 and 14 Apr. 1802), grocer, subj. of G.B.; rec. by John Annett, tobacconist - 2 Apr. 1807 [1A]

McIsaac, Angus, mariner, subj. of G.B.; rec. by Thomas Lane, house-carpenter - 4 Mar. 1806 [1]

Currie, John, subj. of G.B.; rec. by Thomas Lane, house-carpenter - 4 Mar. 1806 [2]

Longhurst, William, mariner, subj. of G.B.; rec. by James C. [?] Miller - 4 Dec. 1805 [3]

Thompson, Archibald, mariner, subj. of G.B.; rec. by Thomas Lane, house-carpenter - 4 Mar. 1806 [5]

Ford, John, subj. of G.B.; rec. by Henry Hyde, innkeeper - 28 Apr. 1806 [6]

Clark, Thomas B., shipwright, subj. of G.B.; rec. by Asa Gage, grocer - 28 Apr. 1806 [7]

Wymes, Thomas, grocer, subj. of G.B.; rec. by Michael Wyms, grocer - 28 Apr. 1806 [8]

Forrest, James, rigger, subj. of G.B.; rec. by William Inkester, rigger - 29 Apr. 1806 [9]

Gibson, John, gentleman, subj. of G.B.; rec. by John G. Taylor, grocer - 29 Apr. 1806 [10]

Macfaull, John, gentleman, subj. of G.B.; rec. by Evan Lewis, grocer - 29 Apr. 1806 [11]

White, George, gentleman, subj. of G.B.; rec. by Philip Phoenix, tailor [11A]

Brown, John, labourer, subj. of G.B.; rec. by Michael Roach, gentleman - 29 Apr. 1806 [12]

Phillips, John, fruiterer, subj. of France; rec. by James Drake, merchant - 30 Apr. 1806 [13]

Gilbert, Edward, tobacconist, subj. of G.B.; rec. by Isaac Luufborray, teacher - 30 Apr. 1806 [14]

Chalk, James, gentleman, subj. of G.B.; rec. by Henry Miller, storekeeper - 30 Apr. 1806 [15]

Moore, William, butcher, subj. of G.B.; rec. by Andrew Paff, butcher - 30 Apr. 1806 [16]

Horner, James, well digger, subj. of G.B.; rec. by Richard Jennings, innkeeper - 30 Apr. 1806 [17]

Baird, Matthew, stone cutter, subj. of G.B.; rec. by James Hay, stone cutter - 30 Apr. 1806 [18]

McCready, Wm., late of Donnegal, age 39, tanner, subj. of G.B., and William McCready, tanner, subj. of G.B.; rec. by John Wark, innkeeper - 8 July 1800 [19 & 20]

Ferguson, Robert, sawyer, subj. of G.B.; rec. by John Dana, sawyer - 30 Apr. 1806[21]

Rice, John, subj. of G.B.; rec. by John Wiley, baker - 30 Apr. 1806 [22]

Turlock, Joseph, grocer, subj. of G.B.; rec. by David J. Daniels, merchant - 30 Apr. 1806 [23]

Langley, James, grocer, subj. of G.B.; rec. by David J. Daniels, merchant - 30 Apr. 1806 [24]

Jefferies, John, carpenter, subj. of G.B.; rec. by David Sherwood, ropemaker - 1 May 1806 [25]

Standerwick, William, grocer, subj. of G.B.; rec. by Burnell
Brown, ship chandler - 1 May 1806 [26]

Hammond, Judah, student-at-law, subj. of G.B.; rec. by Joshua
Secor, physician - 1 May 1806 [27]

Ostrand, Carls, shipwright, subj. of Sweden; rec. by Robert
Brown, shipwright - 1 May 1806 [28]

Reinold, Charles, sexton of the Lutheran Church, subj. of Hesse
Cassel; rec. by John Christopher Kunze - 1 May 1806 [29]

Ghoghotty, John B., grocer, subj. of Emperor of France & King of
Italy; rec. by Peter Dieterich, merchant - 1 May 1806 [30]

Bellamy, Thomas, innkeeper, subj. of G.B.; rec. by Andrew Inder-
wick, grocer - 1 May 1806 [31]

Farren, Hugh, lamplighter, subj. of G.B.; rec. by Philip Dougherty, stevedore - 1 May 1806 [32]

Pfaltzgraf, Peter, gardener, subj. of France; rec. by Richard
Amos, gentleman - 1 May 1806 [33]

Haffee, John, laborer, subj. of G.B.; rec. by Cornelius Haffee,
coffee manufacturer - 1 May 1806 [34]

Gowdey, William, cartman, subj. of G.B.; rec. by John Wilson,
mason - 1 May 1806 [35]

Chambers, James, rigger, subj. of G.B.; rec. by Joseph Chadwick,
rigger - 1 May 1806 [36]

Burns, Patrick, laborer, subj. of G.B.; rec. by Cornelius Haffee,
coffee manufacturer - 1 May 1806 [37]

Henry, Edward, carpenter, subj. of G.B.; rec. by Andrew Gilchrist, grocer - 1 May 1806 [39]

Barron, John, shipwright, subj. of G.B.; rec. by William Ball,
shipwright - 1 May 1806 [40]

Starkey, Charles P., tobacconist, subj. of G.B.; rec. by Abraham
Casey, cordwainer - 1 May 1806 [41]

Bush, Henry, mariner, subj. of Hamburg; rec. by Thomas Hasam,
grocer -13 May 1806 [42]

Amenta, Emanuel, segar maker, subj. of Spain; rec. by John B.
Ghigliotty, grocer & fruiterer - 16 May 1806 [43]

Williams, Jacob, tailor, subj. of France; rec. by Christian Bur-
gurs, merchant - 20 May 1806 [44]

Nonn, Emer, mariner, subj. of Elector of Hanover; rec. by Thomas
Hasam, grocer - 26 May 1806 [45]

Marot, John, merchant, subj. of France; rec. by Robert Guedeon,
innkeeper - 26 May 1806 [46]

Plunkett, Patrick C., house-carpenter, subj. of G.B.; rec. by
Andrew Lott, conveyancer - 18 June 1806 [47]

Gilmor, Mathew, upholsterer, subj. of G.B.; rec. by Henry Hyde,
innkeeper - 27 June 1806 [48]

Feek, Charles, mariner, subj. of King of Prussia; rec. by Elizabeth Johnson - 9 July 1806 [49]

McCullagh, Alexander, tailor, subj. of G.B.; rec. by William
Cuppels, grocer - 29 July 1806 [50]

Heyl, Francis William, tanner & currier, subj. of Prince of
Ysenberg; rec. by Jacob Warner, innkeeper - 12 Sept. 1806 [51]

Bachelle, David, grocer, subj. of Elector of Hanover; rec. by
John Warner, innkeeper - 12 Sept. 1806 [52]

Kille, Karl, gentleman, subj. of Prince of Hesse Cassel; rec. by
Francis Child, conveyancer - 25 Oct. 1806 [53]

Esplin, Michael, mariner, subj. of G.B.; rec. by Thomas Hasam,
grocer - 16 Oct. 1806 [54]

Bell, John, hostler, subj. of G.B.; rec. by William Fitzsimmons,
grocer - 4 Nov. 1806 [55]

Dunning, Thomas, butcher, subj. of G.B.; rec. by James Marsh,
butcher - 7 Nov. 1806 [56]

Love, John, mariner, subj. of G.B.; rec. by Joseph Chadwick,
grocer - 17 Nov. 1806 [57]

McBrierty, Patrick, cartman, subj. of G.B.; rec. by Patrick
Burns, laborer - 17 Nov. 1806 [58]

Burns, John, tailor, subj. of G.B.; rec. by Patrick Burns,
laborer - 17 Nov. 1806 [59]

Dougherty, Dennis, distiller, subj. of G.B.; rec. by Hugh Cassidy, grocer - 18 Nov. 1806 [60]

McNalty, Terrence, mason, subj. of G.B.; rec. by Bryan Conally,
grocer - 18 Nov. 1806 [61]

Main, John, cordwainer, subj. of G.B.; rec. by John K. Leaycraft, shoemaker - 18 Nov. 1806 [62]

Hore, Matthew, rigger, subj. of G.B.; rec. by Thomas Hasam,
grocer - 19 Nov. 1806 [63]

Marmion, Richard, tobacconist, subj. of G.B.; rec. by John Cummings, grocer - 19 Nov. 1806 [64]

Doran, James, grocer, subj. of G.B.; rec. by Richard Marmion,
tobacconist - 19 Nov. 1806 [65]

Cunningham, Phelix, grocer, subj. of G.B.; rec. by Richard Marmion, tobacconist - 19 Nov. 1806 [66]

Craig, Alexander, carpenter, subj. of G.B.; rec. by George Cliland, merchant - 19 Nov. 1806 [67]

White, Archibald, carpenter, subj. of G.B.; rec. by George Cliland, merchant - 19 Nov. 1806 [68]

Zimmerman, Godfrey, tobacconist, subj. of King of Prussia; rec.
by Richbell Mott, tobacconist - 19 Nov. 1806 [69]

Grayson, Anthony, mariner, subj. of G.B.; rec. by William Ridge,
mariner - 19 Nov. 1806 [70]

Denoyelle, Paul, carpenter, subj. of France; rec. by Peter Bock-
over, blacksmith - 19 Nov. 1806 [71]

McGowan, James, subj. of G.B.; rec. by Bryan Conelly, grocer -
19 Nov. 1806 [73]

Edwards, John, Jr., seal beam maker, subj. of G.B.; rec. by
Charles Hunt, cartman - 19 Nov. 1806 [74]

Barr, Philip, subj. of G.B.; rec. by Peter Balen, gentleman - 19
Nov. 1806 [75]

Annet, John, grocer, subj. of G.B.; rec. by Richard Marmion,
tobacconist - 19 Nov. 1806 [78]

Dyck, Daniel, subj. of King of Prussia; rec. by Charles Valentine, grocer - 19 Nov. 1806 [77]

Brown, John, mariner, subj. of King of Portugal; rec. by Robert
Guedron, innkeeper - 19 Nov. [78]

McDonald, James, house-carpenter, subj. of G.B.; rec. by Edward
Henry, house-carpenter - 24 Dec. 1806 [79]

Murdoch, John, merchant, subj. of G.B.; rec. by John McPhie,
grocer - 24 Dec. 1806 [80]

Burges, Francis, mariner; rec. by David Crone, auctioneer - 5
Feb. 1807 [81] - naturalization not completed.

Williamson, David, subj. of G.B.; rec. by Charles J. Richardson,
counsellor-at-law - 21 Mar. 1807 [82]

Cooke, George, of Westchester Co., baker, subj. of G.B.; rec.
by Jonathan Thompson, merchant - 28 Mar. 1807 [83]

Sexton, James, of Westchester Co., whitesmith, subj. of G.B.;
rec. by Jonathan Thompson, merchant - 28 Mar. 1807 [84]

Blaney, Charles, cartman, subj. of G.B.; rec. by Garrit Byrne,
mason - 30 Mar. 1807 _85]

Edgar, Samuel, cartman, subj. of G.B.; rec. by Alexander Mc
Cullagh, tailor - 30 Mar. 1807 [86]

Sleeth, James, cartman, subj. of G.B.; rec. by Alexander Mc
Cullagh, tailor - 30 Mar. 1807 [87]

Jones, Peter, of New Rochelle, Westchester Co., subj. of G.B.;
rec. by James James, blacksmith -31 Mar. 1807 [88]

Bruns, Henry, cartman, subj. of Elector of Hanover; rec. by
David Bachelle, grocer - 31 Mar. 1807 [89]

Barry, Patrick, cartman, subj. of G.B.; rec. by Patrick Crawley,
cartman - 31 Mar. 1807 [90]

Meighan, Andrew, cartman, subj. of G.B.; rec. by William Burns,
shoemaker - 31 Mar. 1807 [91]

Clark, John, cartman, subj. of G.B.; rec. by Lawrence Courtney,
grocer - 31 Mar. 1807 [92]

Carney, Patrick, cartman, subj. of G.B.; rec. by William Gaynor,
grocer - 31 Mar. 1807 [93]

McMahon, Patrick, cartman, subj. of G.B.; rec. by Lawrence
Courtney, grocer - 31 Mar. 1807 [94]

Harrison, John, cartman, subj. of G.B.; rec. by William Little,
physician - 31 Mar. 1807 [95]

Bannan, Robert, cartman, subj. of G.B.; rec. by Thomas Brown,
grocer - 31 Mar. 1807 [96]

Brown, John, cartman, subj. of G.B.; rec. by Robert Brown,
grocer - 31 Mar. 1807 [97]

Johnston, John, subj. of G.B.; rec. by John Benson, a marshal
of NYC - 31 Mar. 1807 [98]

McCale, John, cartman, subj. of G.B.; rec. by John Mathews,
mason - 31 Mar. 1807 [99]

Long, Samuel, cartman, subj. of G.B.; rec. by Peter Switzer,
brass founder - 1 Apr. 1807 [100]

Virtue, David, cartman, subj. of G.B.; rec. by Thomas Anderson,
grocer - 1 Apr. 1807 _101]

Dougherty, Thomas, cartman, subj. of G.B.; rec. by Henry Maloy,
cartman - 1 Apr. 1807 [102]

Wilson, Francis, subj. of G.B.; rec. by Joseph Brotherton, a
marshal of NYC - 1 Apr. 1807 [103]

Nelson, William, grocer, subj. of G.B.; rec. by James Braiden,
grocer - 1 Apr. 1807 [104]

Quigley, Daniel, cartman, subj. of G.B.; rec. by George Dooremus - 1 Apr. 1807 [105]

Connor, Patrick, sawyer, subj. of G.B.; rec. by Andrew Meighan, cartman - 1 Apr. 1807 [106]

Devoy, Michael, cartman, subj. of G.B.; rec. by Charles Gillerd, cartman - 1 Apr. 1807 [107]

Whitty, Nicholas, cartman, subj. of G.B.; rec. by John Webster, cartman - 1 Apr. 1807 [108]

Dillon, John, cartman, subj. of G.B.; rec. by Walter Fisher, mason - 1 Apr. 1807 [109]

Ashley, Robert, cartman, subj. of G.B.; rec. by Morris Oakley - 2 Apr. 1807 [110]

McGinn, Edward, cartman, subj. of G.B.; rec. by William Fitzsimons, grocer - 2 Apr. 1807 [111]

Griffiths, John, blacksmith, subj. of G.B.; rec. by James James, blacksmith - 1 Apr. 1807 [112]

Cunningham, James, grocer, subj. of G.B.; rec. by Hugh Clark, grocer - 2 Apr. 1807 [113]

Walker, Ralph, cartman, subj. of G.B.; rec. by Peter Van Cott, cartman - 2 Apr. 1807 [114]

Phillips, Robert, grocer, subj. of G.B.; rec. by John Annet, tobacconist - 2 Apr. 1807 [115]

Donaldson, Robert, cartman, subj. of G.B.; rec. by George Walton, mason - 2 Apr. 1807 [116]

James, Jacob, labourer, subj. of G.B.; rec. by Robert Wallace, grocer - 2 Apr. 1807 [117]

McGregor, Charles, cartman, subj. of G.B.; rec. by William Smith, innkeeper - 2 Apr. 1807 [118]

Bulwinkle, Henry, cartman, subj. of Elector of Hanover; rec. by John Becker, a constable of NYC - 2 Apr. 1807 [119]

Price, Timothy, grocer, subj. of G.B.; rec. by William Gray, house-carpenter - 2 Apr. 1807 [120]

McGarvey, John, cartman, subj. of G.B.; rec. by Dennis Hanaty, cartman - 2 Apr. 1807 [121]

McKee, Robert, cartman, subj. of G.B.; rec. by John Gowan, grocer - 3 Apr. 1807 [122]

Carr, James, cartman, subj. of G.B.; rec. by Hugh Clark, grocer - 3 Apr. 1807 [123]

Grant, James, cartman, subj. of G.B.; rec. by Patrick Mackrill, cartman - 3 Apr. 1807 [124]

Adair, Robert, subj. of G.B.; rec. by Hugh Clark, grocer - 3 Apr. 1807 [125]

Pierson, Thomas, cartman, subj. of G.B.; rec. by George Walton, mason - 3 Apr. 1807 [126]

Caffry, Barnard, cartman, subj. of G.B.; rec. by Francis Raymond, cooper - 3 Apr. 1807 [127]

McCowan, John, cartman, subj. of G.B.; rec. by Francis Raymond, cooper - 3 Apr. 1807 [128]

Aikens, William, cartman, subj. of G.B.; rec. by James Braiden, grocer - 1 Apr. 1807 [129]

McCown/McCowan, James, cartman, subj. of G.B.; rec. by James Braiden, grocer - 3 Apr. 1807 [130]

Thompson, Alexander, grocer, subj. of G.B.; rec. by Daniel Carmichael, grocer - 4 Apr. 1807 [131]

Volckman, Charles F., baker, subj. of King of Prussia; rec. by John Becker - 4 Apr. 1807 [132]

McDonogh, Patrick, cartman, subj. of G.B.; rec. by John Spratt, laborer - 4 Apr. 1807 [133]

Ward, Dennis, tanner, subj. of G.B.; rec. by Hugh Ward, hairdresser - 6 Apr. 1807 [134]

Drennon, Andrew, iron founder, subj. of G.B.; rec. by Dennis Ward, tanner - 6 Apr. 1807 [135]

Dermot, Patrick, grocer, subj. of G.B.; rec. by Hugh Farren, lamplighter - 6 Apr. 1807 [136]

Currey, John, cartman, subj. of G.B.; rec. by William Thompson, cartman - 6 Apr. 1807 [137]

Mahony, John, cartman, subj. of G.B.; rec. by John O'Neale, grocer - 6 Apr. 1807 [138]

Wilson, James, grocer, subj. of G.B.; rec. by Patrick Carney, cartman - 6 Apr. 1807 [139]

Bringes, John, grocer, subj. of Elector of Hanover; rec. by Friedrick Meyer, grocer - 6 Apr. 1807 [140]

McNemara, Patrick, grocer, subj. of G.B.; rec. by James Mc Laughlin, lamplighter - 6 Apr. 1807 [141]

Rogers, John, grocer, subj. of G.B.; rec. by John Burger - 7 Apr. 1807 [142]

Gallaugher, Patrick, laborer, subj. of G.B.; rec. by Patrick Waters, grocer - 7 Apr. 1807 [143]

Olson, Lear, groder, subj. of Elector of Hanover; rec. by John Koster, sugar refiner - 7 Apr. 1807 [144]

Gercken, Christian, grocer, subj. of Elector of Hanover; rec. by Friedrich Meyer, grocer - 7 Apr. 1807 [145]

Meyer/Myer, Henry, grocer, subj. of Elector of Hanover; rec. by Friedrich Meyer, grocer - 7 Apr. 1807 [146]

Johnsen, John, cartman, subj. of Denmark; rec. by John McMannus - 8 Apr. 1807 [147]

Ryan, Cornelius, cartman, subj. of G.B.; rec. by John Correy, cartman - 8 Apr. 1807 [148]

Gourlie, Robert, watchmaker, subj. of G.B.; rec. by Archibald Davie, letter-carrier - 8 Apr. 1807 [149]

Mischott, Friedrich, innkeeper, subj. of France; rec. by Lororent Weber, baker - 9 Apr. 1807 [150]

Fogarty, Michael, bricklayer, subj. of G.B.; rec. by William Butler, cartman - 9 Apr. 1807 [151]

Deininger, Christoph, cartman, subj. of King of Wirtemberg; rec. by George Straethoof, gardener - 9 Apr. 1807 [152]

Gaynor, William, grocer, subj. of G.B.; rec. by Patrick Carney, cartman - 9 Apr. 1807 [153]

Dealy, Charles, grocer, subj. of G.B.; rec. by Thomas Dealy, grocer - 9 Apr. 1807 [154]

Glennan, Peter, grocer, subj. of G.B.; rec. by Charles Dealy, grocer - 10 Apr. 1807 [155]

Camblin, Robert, grocer, subj. of G.B.; rec. by John Clark, cartman - 15 Apr. 1807 [156]

Lunny, Edward, merchant, subj. of G.B.; rec. by James Mullany, merchant - 11 Apr. 1807 [157]

O'Brien, Patrick, grocer, subj. of G.B.; rec. by Edward Lummy, merchant - 11 Apr. 1807 [158]

McKenny, John, pedlar, subj. of G.B.; rec. by James Mullany, merchant - 11 Apr. 1807 [159]

Jamieson, James, cartman, subj. of G.B.; rec. by Abraham Pettit, mason - 11 Apr. 1807 [160]

Lunny, Patrick, merchant, subj. of G.B.; rec. by Gad Taylor, merchant - Apr. 1807 [161]

Moore, Samuel, shoemaker, subj. of G.B.; rec. by James Doran, grocer - 10 Apr. 1807 [162]

Monaghan, Patrick, ferryman, subj. of G.B.; rec, by Patrick Gallagher, cartman - 13 Apr. 1807 [163]

Moon, Cornelius, gardener, subj. of G.B.; rec. by Hugh Clark, grocer - 13 Apr. 1807 [164]

Matthews, John, gentleman, subj. of G.B.; rec. by Garrit Byrne, grocer - 13 Apr. 1807 [165]

Rose, John, cartman, subj. of Elector of Hanover; rec. by John Becker - 13 Apr. 1807 [166]

Buck, Daniel, ship-carpenter, subj. of G.B.; rec. by John Brown, surgeon-barber - 13 Apr. 1807 [167]

Nugent, John M., bricklayer, subj. of G.B.; rec. by John Corbitt, grocer - 13 Apr. 1807 [168]

Dunn, Edward, farmer, subj. of G.B.; rec. by Peter Glennan, grocer - 13 Apr. 1807 [169]

Kine, Darby, cartman, subj. of G.B.; rec. by Thomas Duggan - 14 Apr. 1807 [170]

McCarty, Patrick, grocer, subj. of G.B.; rec. by Patrick Manon, cartman - 14 Apr. 1807 [171]

Emlach, James, butcher, subj. of G.B.; rec. by Cornelius Schuyler, butcher - 14 Apr. 1807 [172]

Kidson, Joseph, shoemaker, subj. of G.B.; rec. by Robert Coe, shoemaker - 14 Apr. 1807 [173]

Reynolds, John, grocer, subj. of G.B.; rec. by Matthias Carvey, cartman - 14 Apr. 1807 [174]

McBride, Andrew, grocer, subj. of G.B.; rec. by Alexander McKibbin - 15 Apr. 1807 [175]

Conroy, William, grocer, subj. of G.B.; rec. by Edward Maloy, grocer - 15 Apr. 1807 [176]

Coulter, Samuel, teacher, subj. of G.B.; rec. by Joseph Brotherton - 15 Apr. 1807 [177]

Megson, Robert, rigger, subj. of G.B.; rec. by Jesse Legoine, shoemaker - 15 Apr. 1807 [178]

Enever, John, cartman, subj. of G.B.; rec. by Thomas Mooney, grocer - 15 Apr. 1807 [179]

Palmer, Sebastian, storekeeper, subj. of Spain; rec. by James B. Cheveé, storekeeper - 15 Apr. 1807 [180]

Dinan, Peter, baker, subj. of G.B.; rec. by John Smith, baker - 15 Apr. 1807 [181]

Peterson, John, subj. of King of Swedem; rec. by James Nott, rigger - 15 Apr. 1807 [182]

Dalyell, James, grocer, subj. of G.B.; rec. by George Cliland, merchant - 16 Apr. 1807 [183]

McGowan, John, grocer, subj. of G.B.; rec. by Bryan Connally, grocer - 16 Apr. 1807 [184]

Carroll, Patrick, carpenter, subj. of G.B.; rec. by Richard Nugent, grocer - 16 Apr. 1807 [185]

McCrea, Archibald, rigger, subj. of G.B.; rec. by Matthew Collier, cartman - 16 Apr. 1807 [186]

Hailshorn, John, cartman, subj. of Elector of Hanover; rec. by John Becker - 16 Apr. 1807 [187]

Constable, James, sadler, subj. of G.B.; rec. by Alexander Hutchinson, grocer - 17 Apr. 1807 [188]

Moore, James, grocer, subj. of G.B.; rec. by David J. Craig, grocer - 17 Apr. 1807 [189]

McNickle, Arthur, grocer, subj. of G.B.; rec. by Joseph Brotherton - 17 Apr. 1807 [190]

Fullmer, Jacob, sausage-maker, subj. of King of Wirtemberg; rec. by Peter Cook, cartman - 17 Apr. 1807 [191]

Rosbach, Joseph, subj. of France; rec. by Peter Cook, cartman - 17 Apr. 1807 [192]

Reynolds, Alexander, grocer, subj. of G.B.; rec. by William Spencer, nailor - 17 Apr. 1807 [193]

Phillips, George, cartman, subj. of France; rec. by Samuel Marks, grocer - 17 Apr. 1807 [194]

Agnew, James, laborer, subj. of G.B.; rec. by David Bryson, currier - 17 Apr. 1807 [195]

McCreery, David, bricklayer, subj. of G.B.; rec. by David Bryson, currier - 17 Apr. 1807 [186]

Taxbold, William, ship-painter, subj. of King of Denmark; rec. by Richard Sawyer, ship-painter - 17 Apr. 1807 [197]

Frazer, Alexander, cartman, subj. of G.B.; rec. by George Phillips, cartman - 20 Apr. 1807 [198]

Baird, Robert, teacher, subj. of G.B.; rec. by William Ambrose - 20 Apr. 1807 [199]

Scott, Archibald, grocer, subj. of G.B.; rec. by Mary McAuley (wife of James McAuley, house-carpenter) - 21 Apr. 1807 [200]

Campbell, John, gardener, subj. of G.B.; rec. by George Gordon, cartman - 21 Apr. 1807 [201]

Burke, Thomas, grocer, subj. of G.B.; rec. by William Smith, grocer - 21 Apr. 1807 [202]

Shannon, James, grocer, subj. of G.B.; rec. by James Dobbin, grocer - 21 Apr. 1807 [203]

Johnston, Andrew, subj. of G.B.; rec. by John Davis, mariner - 22 Apr. 1807 [204]

Plane, Bartholomew, shopkeeper, subj. of France; rec. by Joseph Lamette, fruiterer - 22 Apr. 1807 [205]

Daly, John, grocer, subj. of G.B.; rec. by William Smith, grocer - 22 Apr. 1807 [206]

McGowin, John, grocer, subj. of G.B.; rec. by James Wilson, farmer - 22 Apr. 1807 [207]

Hall, Thomas, shipwright, subj. of G.B.; rec. by William Johnson, grocer - 22 Apr. 1807 [208]

Renouf, Charles, shipwright, subj. of G.B.; rec. by John Hazleton, shipwright - 22 Apr. 1807 [209]

Clendenen, Alexander, bricklayer, subj. of G.B.; rec. by Matthew Collier, cartman - 22 Apr. 1807 [210]

Harwood, Edward, broker, subj. of G.B.; rec. by Matthew Collier, cartman - 22 Apr. 1807 [211]

Hopkins, Job, wheelwright, subj. of G.B.; rec. by James James, blacksmith - 23 Apr. 1807 [212]

Connoley, Patrick, grocer, subj. of G.B.; rec. by Dennis Herraty, cartman - 23 Apr. 1807 [213]

Slipper, Thomas M., cordwainer, subj. of G.B.; rec. by Joseph F. Slipper, cordwainer - 23 Apr. 1807 [214]

Sharp, Nicholas, shipwright, subj. of G.B.; rec. by John Hazleton, shipwright - 23 Apr. 1807 [215]

Ricard, John, house-carpenter, subj. of France; rec. by William Peterson, cordwainer - 23 Apr. 1807 [216]

Woodrow, James, shipwright, subj. of G.B.; rec. by Charles Renout, shipwright - 23 Apr. 1807 [217]

Pickering, Robert, tailor, subj. of G.B.; rec. by Robert Cannell, tailor - 23 Apr. 1807 [218]

Glinck, Christian, grocer, subj. of King of Wirtemberg; rec. by John Koster, sugar refiner - 23 Apr. 1807 [219]

Fenton, Samuel, leatherdresser, subj. of G.B.; rec. by Ephraim Place, shoemaker - 23 Apr. 1807 [220]

Adams, Peter, rigger, subj. of King of Denmark; rec. by James Swan, ropemaker - 23 Apr. 1807 [221]

Ervin, James, grocer, subj. of G.B.; rec. by John Benson - 24 Apr. 1807 [222]

Labawan, Martin, grocer, subj. of France; rec. by Michael Cashman, grocer - 24 Apr. 1807 [223]

Grice, John, carpenter, subj. of G.B.; rec. by Andrew J. McLaughlin, trunk maker - 24 Apr. 1807 [224]

Elsden, Benjamin, carpenter, subj. of G.B.; rec. by John Grice, carpenter - 24 Apr. 1807 [225]

Kenny, Dennis, subj. of G.B.; rec. by Asa Gage, grocer - 24 Apr. 1807 [226]

Oliver, John, subj. of G.B.; rec. by Archibald Ball, mason - 24 Apr. 1807 [227]

Harrison, William, carpenter, subj. of G.B.; rec. by Archibald Ball, mason - 24 Apr. 1807 [228]

Kellett, Harris, subj. of G.B.; rec. by George Harwood, cartman - 24 Apr. 1807 [230]

Lawrence, Stephen, milkman, subj. of France; rec. by John Phillips, fruiterer - 24 Apr. 1807 [231]

Kennedy, Patrick, cartman, subj. of G.B.; rec. by George Harwood, cartman - 24 Apr. 1807 [232]

Kellett, Robert, cartman, subj. of G.B.; rec. by George Harwood, cartman - 24 Apr. 1807 [233]

Nevin, Robert, sawyer, subj. of G.B.; rec. by Joseph McKibbin, grocer - 24 Apr. 1807 [234]

Noble, Francis, bricklayer, subj. of G.B.; rec. by Joseph Mc Kibbun, grocer - 24 Apr. 1807 [235]

Barr, Hugh, labourer, subj. of G.B.; rec. by John McGuvay, cartman - 24 Apr. 1807 [236]

Donnelly, Patrick, mason, subj. of G.B.; rec. by John Regan,
physician - 24 Apr. 1807 [237]

Thomas, James, drayman, subj. of G.B.; rec. by John Withington,
brewer - 24 Apr. 1807 [238]

Anthony, John, labourer, subj. of G.B.; rec. by John Withington,
brewer - 24 Apr. 1807 [239]

Warren, James, rigger, subj. of G.B.; rec. by Aspinwall Cornwell, grocer - 24 Apr. 1807 [240]

McDonald. John, rigger, subj. of G.B.; rec. by Aspinwall Cornwell, grocer - 24 Apr. 1807 [241]

Lunny, Edward, grocer, subj. of G.B.; rec. by Patrick O'Brien,
grocer - 24 Apr. 1807 [242]

Anderson, James, cork-cutter, subj. of G.B.; rec. by Asa Gage,
grocer - 24 Apr. 1807 [243]

Anderson, Peter, subj. of G.B.; rec. by Asa Gage, grocer - 24
Apr. 1807 [244]

Tausius, John, cabinetmaker, subj. of Spain; rec. by Peter V.
Tilyou, gentleman - 24 Apr. 1807 [245]

Pye, George, locksmith, subj. of G.B.; rec. ny Thomas Pye, locksmith - 24 Apr. 1807 [246]

Niven, George, grocer, subj. of G.B.; rec. by Gavin Spence,
watchmaker - 24 Apr. 1807 [247]

Campbell, John, teacher, subj. of G.B.; rec. by Peter V. Tilyou,
gentleman - 24 Apr. 1807 [248]

Taggert, John, house-carpenter, subj. of G.B.; rec. by Arthur
McNickle, grocer - 24 Apr. 1807 [249]

Lacostte, John, cooper, subj. of France; rec. by Rivey Morrell,
shipwright - 24 Apr. 1807 [250]

Davies, Thomas, gardener, subj. of G.B.; rec. by John Rees,
blacksmith - 24 Apr. 1807 [251]

Evans, David, labourer, subj. of G.B.; rec. by John Rees,black-
smith - 24 Apr. 1807 [252]

Adams, George, shipwright, subj. of G.B.; rec. by William Johnston - 24 Apr. 1807 [253]

Noble, Archibald, bricklayer, subj. of G.B.; rec. by Henry Hyde,
innkeeper - 24 Apr. 1807 [254]

Mitchell, Henry, rigger, subj. of Denmark; rec. by Aspinwall
Cornwell, grocer - 25 Apr. 1807 [255]

Snyder, Jacob, laborer, subj. of Emperor of Germany; rec. by
Peter Cisco, cordwainer - 25 Apr. 1807 [256]

Thomas, Benjamin, brass founder, subj. of G.B.; rec. by David
Evans, laborer - 25 Apr. 1807 [257]

Austin, William, carpenter, subj. of G.B.; rec. by Peter Cisco,
cordwainer - 25 Apr. 1807 [258]

Nelson, Patrick, laborer, subj. of G.B.; rec. by James Kelly,
cartman - 25 Apr. 1807 [259]

Fortier, Louis Henry, gardener, subj. of France; rec. by Jacob
H. Varian, butcher - 25 Apr. 1807 [260]

Gallaher, Charles, subj. of G.B.; rec. by Charles Haffey, coffee
manufacturer - 25 Apr. 1807 [261]

Miler, Edward, laborer, subj. of G.B.; rec. by Michael Smallen [or Smaller?], grocer - 25 Apr. 1807 [262]

Stantial, Jacob, subj. of G.B.; rec. by James Davis, laborer - 25 Apr. 1807 [263]

McLaughlin, Mark, subj. of G.B.; rec. by David Wilheran, laborer - 25 Apr. 1807 [264]

Bruno, Agostino Maria, subj. of France; rec. by Joseph Anasstassi, storekeeper - 25 Apr. 1807 [265]

Sharp, Alexander, labourer, subj. of G.B.; rec. by Thomas Smith - 25 Apr. 1807 [266]

Rea, William, stone cutter, subj. of G.B.; rec. by Thomas Smith - 25 Apr. 1807 [267]

Boyd, John, subj. of G.B.; rec. by Robert McLee, cartman - 25 Apr. 1807 [268]

Brant, Jacob, pot-baker, subj. of Emperor of Germany; rec. by Issachar Cozzens, baker - 27 Apr. 1807 [269]

Hill, Charles, rigger, subj. of G.B.; rec. by Nicholas A. Hanson, boarding house keeper - 27 Apr. 1807 [270]

Oliver, John, subj. of G.B.; rec. by William Lockarty, cartman - 27 Apr. 1807 [271]

Dougherty, John, subj. of G.B.; rec. by Charles Dougherty, laborer - 27 Apr. 1807 [272]

Glen, Daniel, subj. of G.B.; rec. by William Norris - 27 Apr. 1807 [273]

McCartan, James, subj. of G.B.; rec. by Moses Pingree, a marshal - 27 Apr. 1807 [274]

Stevens, Richard, subj. of G.B.; rec. by Robert Cannell - 27 Apr. 1807 [275]

Shields, Terrence, subj. of G.B.; rec. by Andrew McBride - 27 Apr. 1807 [276]

McFadden, Robert, subj. of G.B.; rec. by Andrew McBride - 27 Apr. 1807 [277]

Volume 2

McClusky, William, grocer, subj. of G.B.; report of 10 Aug. 1819: born town of Keels, Co. of Meigh [Kells, Co. of Meath], Ire.; migrated from Dublin; rec. by John W. Wright, brewer - 26 Sept. 1826 [1]

Robinson, Henry, late of Baltimore but now in NYC, merchant, subj. of G.B.; rec. by Hugh Maxwell, counsillor-at-law, and Robert Waite, Jr. - 2 July 1828 [2]

Dickinson, George, late clerk byt now merchant, born Wigan, Eng., age 43, and wife Alice, born Wigan, age 37; rec. by Joseph Lloyd, reed maker - 29 Sept. 1826 [3]

Shannon, Samuel, mariner, born Ire., age 26, migrated from Newry; rec. by Elisha Letts, pump- and blockmaker - 2 Oct. 1826 [4]

Pittaluga, Luigi, merchant, subj. of King of Sardinia, born Genoa, age 25; wife Maria, born Port Mahon, Minorca, age 25; dau. Rosa, born Port Mahon, age 8; Bastiano, son, born Port Mahon, age 7; Jacomo, son, born Port Mahon, age 6; family migrated from Gibraltar; rec. by Anthony Meucci, painter - 3 Oct. 1826 [5]

Meucci, Anthonio, painter, born Rome, Italy, age 24, subj. of
the Pope, migrated from Gibraltar; wife Nina, born Rome, age
24; dau. Sabina, born Rome, age 12; rec. by Luigi Pittaluga,
merchant - 3 Oct. 1826 [6]

Blackhurst, James, tailor, born Liverpool, Eng., age 22, migrated from Liverpool; rec. by John Blackhurst, bootmaker -
6 Oct. 1826 [7]

Bond, Henry, merchant, formerly of NYC but now of Tallahasie,
Fla.; report 17 Apr. 1815: born Dublin, Ire., age 22, migrated from Londonderry, Ire.; rec. by Thomas J. Bond, merchant - 9 Oct. 1826 [8]

Lewis, Robert, storekeeper, born Ire., age 36; wife Margaret,
born Ire., age 30; migrated from Galway; rec. by William
Darcy, accountant - 11 Oct. 1826 [9]

Pinchot, Constantine Cirile, Jr., trader; report 7 Nov. 1818:
born Dept. of Loire, France, age 22, migrated from Havre de
Grace; rec. by Benoist Bonifon, merchant - 11 Oct. 1826 [10]

Maginnis, Edward, surrier; report 21 Apr. 1821: born Newry, Ire.,
age 39, migrated from Newry; rec. by Lewis Cronly, gentleman -
13 Oct. 1826 [11]

Garner, John, teacher, of Southampton, subj. of G.B.; rec. by
Micah Jackson, of Flatbush, Kings Co., and Benjamin C. Jackson, of South Hempstead, Queens Co. - 14 Oct. 1826 [12]

Bolton, Francis, gentleman, born Ire., age 28, migrated from
Cork; rec. by Silvanus Miller, counsellor-at-law - 16 Oct.
1826 [13]

Cameron, Frederick Gavin, mariner; report 4 Mar. 1824: born
London, Eng., age 22, migrated from Calcutta; wife Ester, born
N.Y. State, age 25; rec. by Wm. Bishop, grocer - 17 Oct. '26[14]

Biggam, Hamilton, merchant; report 7 Apr. 1810: born Downe [Dou-
ne, Scotland], age 27, migrated from Scotland; rec. by James
Montgomery, merchant - 19 Oct. 1826 [15]

Lowe, Samuel J., hairdresser; report 19 Sept. 1821: born Surrey,
Eng., age 22, migrated from Havre de Grace, France; rec. by
James Duncan, lumber merchant - 19 Oct. 1826 [16]

Taylor, Patrick H., musician; report 1 May 1820: born Ire., age
35, migrated from Dublin; rec. by Peter Dempsey, attorney-at-
law - 21 Oct. 1826 [17]

Blondel, Peter, storekeeper; report 20 June 1821: born Dublin,
Ire., age 44, migrated from Dublin; wife Elizabeth, born Dublin, age 40; son William, born Dublin, age 16; son Joshua, born
Dublin, age 10; son Charles, born Dublin, age 7; son Jacob,
born Dublin, age 4; son Joseph, born Dublin, age 1; dau. Susannah, born Dublin, age 15; dau. Jane, born Dublin, age 13;
in Ire. Peter was a farmer; rec. by John Hewitt, cabinetmaker -
23 Oct. 1826

Karr, Andrew, seaman; report 15 May 1821: born Swinemund, Prussia, age 28, migrated from Swinemund; rec. by Jacob Albrecht,
grocer - 24 Oct. 1826 [19]

Best, John, mariner, born Ire., age 23, migrated from Newry; rec.
by John Quin, grocer - 24 Oct. 1826 [20]

Sheails, Matthew, cartman, born Ire., age 27, migrated from Dublin; rec. by Patrick Bunner, labourer - 26 Oct. 1826 [21]

Levée, Francis, brushmaker; report 25 Oct. 1821: born Nantes,
France, age 31, migrated from Nantes; wife Ann, born Rochelle,
age 40; rec. by Henry Crevolin, tavern-keeper - 26 Oct. 1826
[22]

Kinch, William, grocer; report 15 Mar. 1807: born in Ire., age
32, migrated from Ire.; wife Rebecca, born Eng., age 32; son
William, born Ire., age 6; rec. by Alexander McWhorter, carpenter - 27 Oct. 1826 [23]

McWhorter, Alexander, carpenter; report 21 July 1821: born Co.
Meath, Ire., age 25, migrated from Newry or Warings Point,
Ire.; rec. by William Kinch, grocer - 27 Oct. 1826 [24]

Saluza, Christobal Garcia, merchant, subj. of King of Spain;
rec. by Francis J. Berier, teacher, and Peter F. Fontaine,
fruiterer - 28 Oct. 1826 [25]

Friel, William, grocer; report 3 Apr. 1821: born Ire., age 32,
migrated from Londonderry; rec. by Joseph C. Cooper, attorney-
at-law - 30 Oct. 1826 [26]

Kusel, Christopher H., carpenter; report 11 July 1821: born
Hamburgh, age 34, migrated from Hamburgh; rec. by James S.
Meredith, mariner - 30 Oct. 1826 [27]

Davies, John Mayer, merchant; report 11 Apr. 1821: born Gorcum,
age 22, migrated from Liverpool, subj. of the Netherlands;
rec. by Rowland Davies, merchant - 31 Oct. 1826 [28]

Pettigrew, Robert, labourer; report 16 Apr. 1821: born East
Lothian, Scotland, age 38, migrated from Leith; wife Eleanor,
age 39; son John, age 16; dau. Margaret, age 14; dau. Jane,
age 13; dau. Ann, age 6; dau. Ellen, age 9; wife and all of
children born in East Lothian; rec. by William M. Wilson,
pump maker - 1 Nov. 1826 [29]

Hamill, Patrick, tailor; report 29 Oct. 1821: born Co. Tyrone,
Ire., age 32, migrated from Greenock; wife Mary, born Ire.,
age 32; children, Mary Ann, age 5, and Edward, age 4, both
born in Scotland, and Patrick, age 2, born in Montreal; rec.
by Hugh McCaffrey, tailor - 1 Nov. 1826 [30]

Chitry, Peter, silversmith; report 23 July 1821: born Santo
Domingo, age 37, subj. of King of France & Navarre, migrated
from Port au Poeme [?]; rec. by Daniel Adams, blacksmith - 2
Nov. 1826 [31]

Rohr, John G., tailor; report 8 Jan. 1821: born Baden, Germany,
age 25; rec. by Joseph Heim, shoemaker - 3 Nov. 1826 [32]

Thompson, Thomas M., mariner; report 4 Nov. 1821: born Liverpool, Eng., age 24, migrated from Liverpool; rec. by Rebecca
Jefferson, widow - 3 Nov. 1826 [33]

McGowan, John P., leather dresser; report 4 Nov. 1821: born Ire.,
age 22, migrated from Londonderry - rec. by William McAlpine,
leather dresser - 4 Nov. 1826 [34]

Hesketh, John, formerly of Phila., now of Brooklyn, distiller;
report 9 Apr. 1821: born Liverpool, Eng., age 29, migrated
from Liverpool; rec. by John Kurtz, of Brooklyn, silver plater - 4 Nov. 1826 [35]

Lyon, Samuel, painter & glazier; report 6 Nov. 1821 in Phila.:
born Ire., age 28, migrated from Londerry; wife Margaret, born
Ire., age 24; rec. by John Boyd, tallow chandler - 6 Nov. 1826
[36]

Barclay, George, merchant; report 6 Nov. 1821: born Nova Scotia,
age 36, migrated from Nova Scotia; wife Matilda, born Germany,
age 33; rec. by Thomas Barclay, commissioner of his Britanic
Majesty - 6 Nov. 1826 [37]

Connolly, James, shoemaker; report 6 Nov. 1821: born Ire., age
21, migrated from Sligo; rec. by Matthew Lane, accountant -
6 Nov. 1826 [38]

Prendergast, Michael, grocer; report 7 Mar. 1820: born Ire.,
   age 25, migrated from Dublin; rec. by William McLaughlin,
   grocer - 6 Nov. 1826 [39]

McLaughlin, William, grocer; report 4 May 1821: born Londonderry, Ire., age 31, distiller; rec. by Michael Prendergast,
   grocer - 6 Nov. 1826 [40]

Harbinson, John, grocer; report 6 Apr. 1821: born Ire., age 31,
   migrated from Liverpool; wife Sarah, age 30; dau. Ann, age 12;
   son Arthur, age 10; son James, age 7; dau. Ellen, age 6; dau.
   Martha, age 4; wife and children all born in Ire.; rec. by
   James Carroll, grocer - 6 Nov. 1826 [41]

Keelan, Michael, teacher; report 10 Dec. 1823: born Ire., age
   21, migrated from Liverpool; rec. by Thomas Mooney, Jr.,
   grocer - 7 Nov. 1826 [42]

West, James, formerly of Washington, D.C., but now of Brooklyn,
   painter & glazier; report 28 June 1819 in District Court of
   D.C.: born Ire., age 32, migrated from Co. Wexford and arr.
   NYC 10 Dec. 1817; rec. by Ebenezer Jones, of Brooklyn, painter & glazier - 7 Nov. 1826 [43]

McCormick, Robert, merchant; report 27 Mar. 1821: born Co. Tyrone, Ire., age 45, migrated from Londonderry; rec. by Peter B.
   Van Beuren, grocer - 7 Nov. 1826 [44]

Hamilton, Robert, grocer; report 12 Apr. 1821: born Co. Donegal,
   Ire., age 23, migrated from Londonderry; rec. by John Wark, a
   marshal of NYC - 7 Nov. 1826 [45]

Delatour, Louis Antoine Jousseaum, feather-maker; report 2 Apr.
   1821: born Paris, France, age 44, migrated from Brest; rec.
   by Peter Cotte, confectioner - 7 Nov. 1826 [46]

Pye, David, brewer; report 2 Apr. 1821: born, as all of family,
   in Eng., age 35; wife Elizabeth, age 32; son David, age 10;
   dau. Elenor, age 12; dau. Maria, age 8; son Joseph, age 7;
   son William, age 5; rec. by John Barberie, a marshal of NYC -
   7 Nov. 1826 [47]

Mathews, Charles, late a farmer byt now a merchant; report 18
   Apr. 1821: born Co. Tyrone, Ire., age 24, migrated from Londonderry; rec. by William Hill, merchant - 7 Nov. 1826 [48]

Angus, William, formerly of NYC but now of Brooklyn, carpenter;
   report 25 Apr. 1821: born Stirling, Scotland, age 42, migrated
   from Greenock; rec. by Alexander Birkbeck, of Brooklyn, blacksmith - 7 Nov. 1826 [49]

Waters, Patrick, grocer; report 8 Nov. 1821: born Ire., age 38,
   migrated from Sligo; rec. by George Gardner, grocer - 8 Nov.
   1826 [50]

Hall, George, of Brooklyn, merchant; report 8 Nov. 1826: born
   Ire., age 23, migrated from Belfast; rec. by John E.W. Stevenson, of Brooklyn, merchant - 8 Nov. 1826 [51]

Montgomery, James, grocer; report 30 Mar. 1821: born Co. Donegal,
   Ire., age 28, migrated from Londonderry; rec. by Edward Maginnis, currier - 8 Nov. 1826 [52]

Stewart, John, heretofore shipwright but now grocer; report 18
   Feb. 1819: born Scotland, age 28, migrated from Greenock; rec.
   by Daniel Stewart, grocer - 8 Nov. 1826 [53]

Ash, Michael, labourer; report 14 Apr. 1802: born Co. Kerry, Ire.,
   age 45; wife Catherine, age 40, born Co. Kerry; daus. Mary, age
   15, and Honor, age 13, both born Co. Kerry; sons John, age 7,
   Michael, age 4, Simeon, age 2, born Deptford, Eng., all migrated
   Limerick; rec. by Walter Coppinger, grocer - 8 Nov. 1826 [54]

Fagan, Francis, stone cutter; report 23 Mar. 1821: born Ire.,
age 28, migrated from Newry; wife Catherine, born Ire., age
25; dau. Elenor, born NYC, age 3; rec. by John Wark, a marshal of NYC - 8 Nov. 1826 [55]

McLaughlin, Peter, grocer; report 2 Apr. 1821: born Ire., age
24, migrated from Londonderry; rec. by George Goodheart,
butcher - 8 Nov. 1826 [56]

Burnet, Martin, of Brooklyn, coachmaker; report 24 Apr. 1817:
born Dublin, age 42, migrated from Dublin; rec. by Thomas A.
Lynch, of Brooklyn, coachmaker - 8 Nov. 1826 [57]

Murdough, John, cartman; report 2 Apr. 1821: born Co. Down,
Ire., age 28, migrated from Newry; rec. by Richard Sneeden,
of Brooklyn, contractor - 8 Nov. 1826 [58]

Kennedy, John, heretofore of Washington, D.C., but now of NYC,
gentleman; certificate in Washington 1 Nov. 1821: born Co. of
Tipperary, Ire., age 25, migrated from London, arrived NYC
1 Nov. 1818; rec. by Peter Laporte, farmer - 10 Nov. 1826 [59]

Newman, John, cartman; report 10 Nov. 1826: born Ire., age 30,
migrated from Belfast; wife Rosa, born Ire., age 32 - 10 Nov.
1826 [60]

Murphy, John, cartman; report 24 Sept. 1821: born Co. Caven,
Ire., age 33, migrated from Dublin; rec. by Patrick Murphy,
cartman - 13 Nov. 1826 [61]

Baret, Christopher, grocer; report 15 Nov. 1826: born Ire., age
22, migrated from Cork; rec. by Peter McLaughlin, grocer - 15
Nov. 1826 [62]

McManus, Andrew, labourer; report 19 Nov. 1821: born Co. Caven,
Ire., age 31; wife Bridget, born Co. Caven, age 26; dau. Mary,
born NYC, age 2; dau. Susannah, born NYC, age 12 weeks; migrated from Newry; rec. by Thomas Doyle, grocer - 20 Nov.
1826 [63]

Sadgebury, James, drayman; report 19 June 1821: born Eng., age
34, migrated from Bristol; rec. by Daniel D. Jones, mason -
27 Nov. 1826 [64]

Chance, George, merchant; report 23 Nov. 1815: born Birmingham,
Eng., age 25, migrated from Liverpool; rec. by John Timmins,
merchant - 30 Nov. 1826 [65]

Krook, August, mariner; report 30 Oct. 1821: born Stockholm,
Sweden, age 25, migrated from Stockholm; rec. by John Peterson, ship-carpenter - 1 Dec. 1826 [66]

Schmidt, Detlof Henry, merchant; report 19 Apr. 1821: born Hamburg, Germany, age 36, migrated from Hamburg; wife Ann Ulricka Christian, born Stralsen, Germany, age 25; son William
Frederick, born village of Velgast, Germany, age 5; rec. by
Joseph L. Lewis, engraver - 8 Dec. 1826 [67]

McCosker, Bernard, weaver; report 9 Feb. 1821: born Ire., age
38, migrated from Londonderry; rec. by John McCosker, bootmaker - 8 Dec. 1826 [68]

Loughrin, Michael, labourer; report 28 May 1821: born Co. Tyrone,
Ire., age 30, migrated from Belfast; rec. by John O'Neil,
grocer - 11 Dec. 1826 [69]

Hill, Samuel, gardner; report 14 Apr. 1802: born Axminster, Co.
Devon, Eng., age 27; rec. by Grant Thorburn, seedman - 12 Dec.
1826 [70]

McEllister, James, cartman; report 29 Mar. 1821: born Co. Kerry,
Ire., age 25, migrated from London; rec. by John Boulger, man
milliner - 13 Dec. 1826 [71]

Barry, John, gentleman, subj. of G.B.; rec. by Richard Burk, public porter, and James Flanagan, justice of the 9th Ward - 14 Dec. 1826 [72]

Rockett, John, mariner; report 15 Dec. 1826: born Eng., age 26, migrated from Liverpool; rec. by Marcus Belford, mariner - 15 Dec. 1826 [73]

Brown, William, dyer, born Eng., age 26, migrated from London; rec. by Thomas Bryan, dyer - 18 Dec. 1826 [74]

Hanigan, Hugh, cartman, born Ire., age 23, migrated from London-derry; wife Eunice, born Ire., age 23; rec. by Bernard Hani-gan, labourer - 21 Dec. 1826 [75]

O'Neil, John, wheelwright, born Ire., age 27, migrated from Harrington, Eng.; rec. by Bernard O'Neil, weaver - 22 Dec. 1826 [76]

Dougherty, Thomas, cartman; report 27 July 1821: born Co. Ros-common, Ire., age 24, migrated from Liverpool; wife Mary, born Eng., age 24; son William, born Eng., age 6; dau. Catherine, born Eng., age 4; rec. by James Congdoun, cartman - 26 Dec. 1826 [77]

Fitzgerald, John, labourer; report 3 Dec. 1821: born Ire., age 36; wife Biddy, born Ire., age 30; dau. Mary, born Ire., age 4; all migrated from Dublin; rec. by John Wark, a marshal of NYC - Dec. 1826 [78]

Harrison, James, tavern-keeper; report 1 May 1820: born Ire., age 28; wife Isabella, born Ire., age 20; family migrated from Co. Monaghan; rec. by William Harrison, barkeeper - 27 Dec. 1826 [79]

Foley, William, heretofore pedlar byt now merchant; report 2 Aug. 1821: born Co. Sligo, Ire., age 35, migrated from Sligo; rec. by John Wymbs, gentleman - 29 Dec. 1826 [80]

Connor, Edward, butcher, born Ire., age 24, migrated from Dublin; rec. by Daniel Everett, sadler - 29 Dec. 1826 [81]

Petersen, Eric Eiegod, merchant, born Elsenore, Denmark, age 26, migrated from Elsinore; rec. by Francis J. Berier, teacher - 2 Jan. 1827 [82]

Petersen, George Christopher, merchant, born Elsinore, Denmark, age 23, migrated from Gottenburgh, Sweden; rec. by Francis J. Berier, teacher - 2 Jan. 1827 [83]

Serra, Bartholomew, merchant, born Port Mahon, Spain, age 26, migrated from Port Mahon; rec. by Francis J. Berier, teacher - 12 Jan. 1827 [84]

Midgley, Edward J., painter & glazier, born Eng., age 24; rec. by Joseph Marsh, painter & glazier - 12 Jan. 1827 [85]

Fearnley, John, of Brooklyn, butcher; report 18 Dec. 1821: born Eng., age 29, migrated from Liverpool; wife Martha, born Eng., age 23; dau. Mary Ann, born Eng., age 6; dau. Priscilla, born Eng., age 4; rec. by Samuel Smith, watchmaker - 15 Jan. 1827 [86]

Ramppan, Francis Joseph, sugar baker; report 2 Nov. 1821: born Westphalia, Prussia, age 51, migrated from London; rec. by George Jacobs, sexton of St. Patrick Cathedral - 15 Jan. 1827 [87]

Tully, Bartholomew, tavern-keeper; report 2 May 1820: born Co. Caven, Ire., age 21, migrated from Co. Caven; rec. by Peter Dempsey, attorney-at-law - 18 Jan. 1827 [88]

Cronly, John, grocer, born Ire., age 21, migrated from Dublin;
rec. by James D.M. Martin, miniature painter - 18 Jan. 1827
[89]

Grason, James, cooper; report 26 Mar. 1825: born Ire., age 28,
migrated from Newry; wife Sarah, born Ire., age 26; rec. by
Samuel Storer, ship-carpenter - 20 Jan. 1827 [90]

Davey, Tighe, carpenter, born Ire., age 33, migrated from Dublin;
rec. by Jacob Van Nostrand, carpenter - 23 Jan. 1827 [91]

Blanchard, George, comedian, born London, Eng., age 23, migrated
from Havre de Grace, France; rec. by Peter McIntire, keeper of
Washington Hall - 26 Jan. 1827 [92]

Farrell, Peter, born Ire., age 30, migrated from Belfast; wife
Mary, born Ire., age 27; rec. by George More, rigger - 27
Jan. 1827 [93]

Smith, Owen, weaver; report 19 Jan. 1822: born Co. Caven, Ire.,
age 22, migrated from Dublin; rec. by Samuel McIntire, cartman - 27 Jan. 1827 [94]

Bridle, John, butcher; report 1 June 1821: born Devonshire, Eng.,
age 31, migrated from Island of Guernsey; wife Mary, born
Dorsetshire, age about 27; dau. Mary Ann, born Guernsey, age
6; rec. by Isaac A. Isaacs, street inspector - 29 Jan. 1827
[95]

Travers, James, tobacconist, subj. of G.B.; rec. by William H.
Sparks, grocer, and Lucas Strites, fisherman - 27 Jan. 1827
[96]

Grimshaw, John, merchant; report 18 Dec. 1821: born Harton, Eng.,
age 21, migrated from Harton; rec. by William Paxton Hallett,
counsellor-at-law - 31 Jan. 1827 [97]

Baggott, Joseph, glass cutter; report 23 Apr. 1821: born Worcestershire, Eng., age 28, migrated from London; wife Ester, born
Worcestershire, age 25; dau. Eliza, born Worcestershire; dau.
Ester, born Worcestershire, age 5; rec. by Stephen Kingsland,
builder - 5 Feb. 1827 [98]

Evans, David, labourer; rec. by Caleb Briggs, of North Castle,
Westchester Co., farmer, and Thomas Marshall, of NYC, cartman
- 5 Feb. 1827 [99]

Smith, John W., distiller, subj. of Duke of Mecklenburgh; report
26 May 1815: born Pollnetz, Germany, age 34, migrated from
Hamburgh; wife Ann, born Peekskill, N.Y., age 38; rec. by
Jacob Bylandt, gentleman - 6 Feb. 1827 [100]

Orr, Robert, farmer; report 7 Feb. 1822: born Ire., age 24, migrated from Londonderry; rec. by James Russell, of NYC, builder - 7 Feb. 1827 [101]

Bowman, Samuel W.L., painter, subj. of G.B.; rec. by George
Bampton, shipwright, and James Avery, grocer - 8 Feb. 1827
[102]

Morrison, Matthew, labourer; report 13 Nov. 1826: born Ire., age
26, migrated from Belfast; rec. by John Hamilton, coachman -
8 Feb. 1827 [103]

Casares, Manuel, merchant, born Bilboa, Spain, age 25, migrated
from Bilboa; rec. by Francis J. Berier, teacher - 9 Feb. 1827
[104]

Henningson, Christian August, mariner; report 19 Oct. 1821: born
Denmark, age 36, migrated from Gibraltar; rec. by John Meyer,
boarding house keeper - Feb. 1827 [105]

Attwell, James, baker; report 2 Feb. 1822: born, as wife & his children, in Eng., age 41; wife Jane, age 30; son William. age 10; son James, age 8; son John, age 3; migrated from London; rec. by Samuel Ruckle, grocer - 12 Feb. 1827 [106]

Cantarali, Gregory, fruiterer, born Rome, Italy, age 30, migrated from Canada; rec. by Justus Hardick, tobacconist - 12 Feb. 1827 [107]

Graebe, Charles, merchant; report 8 Feb. 1822: born Germany, age 25, migrated from Bremen; rec. by William Allen, attorney-at-law - Feb. 1827 [108]

Braine, James H., heretofore mariner but now merchant; report 27 Dec. 1820: born Nova Scotia, age 25, migrated from Nova Scotia; rec. by Cyrus Barber, attorney-at-law - 22 Feb. 1827 [109]

Windle, William B., carpenter; report 28 Jan. 1822: born Eng., age 30, emigrated from Hull; rec. by Edward Smith, tavern-keeper - 23 Feb. 1827 [110]

Clarke, William, merchant; report 22 Sept. 1821: born Co. Worcester, Eng., age 40, migrated from Liverpool; wife Ann, born Co. of Kent, Eng., age 40; children, all born in London, Elizabeth, age 14; William B., age 12; Richard J., age 10; Thomas E., age 4; rec. by John Fellows, merchant - Feb. 1827 [111]

Duncan, Alexander, Jr., at present of NYC but residing in Canandaigua, Ontario Co., student-at-law - report 8 Apr. 1822: born Park Hill, Scotland, age 16, arrived at NYC on 31 Jan. 1822 from Liverpool in the ship _Amity_; John Greig, of Ontario Co., counsellor-at-law, is his guardian; Alexander Duncan, late of Scotland but now of New Haven, took cut first papers in New Haven on 1 Mar. 1825 - naturalized 2 Mar. 1827 [112]

Consalvi, Camillo, mariner, born Island of Corsica, age 32, subj. of King of France, migrated from Gibraltar; rec. by Stephen Mealio, boarding house keeper - 9 Mar. 1827 [113]

Sanis, James, merchant, born Barcelona, Spain, age 22, migrated from Barcelona; rec. by Charles Del Vecchio, merchant - 9 Mar. 1827 [114]

Wallis, Alfred, cordwainer, subj. of G.B.; rec. by William Tompkins, printer, and Matthew Vanderhoof, cordwainer - 21 Feb. 1827 [115]

Searle, Luke, baker; report 12 Apr. 1821: born Co. Surrey, Eng., age 42, emigrated from London; rec. by John F. Hurley, gold-beater - 10 Mar. 1827 [116]

Donnelly, Thomas, hatter; report 9 Mar. 1822: born, as all the family, in Ire., age 42, migrated from Limerick; wife Anastia, age 40; dau. Eliza, age 15; Mary, age 12; James, age 9, Catherine, age 7; Winny, age 4; rec. by Patrick Hamill, clothing store keeper - 12 Mar. 1827 [117]

Gibson, Wood, Jr., merchant; report 25 Feb. 1822: born Ire., age 24, migrated from Liverpool; rec. by Walter McFarlane, merchant - 13 Mar. 1827 [118]

Mead, William, of town of Fallsburgh, Sullivan Co., N.Y., farmer, born Eng., age 29, migrated from Portsmouth; rec. by James Dickinson, livery stable keeper - 15 Mar. 1827 [119]

Bello, Anthony M., mariner, subj. of Spain; report 16 July 1821: born Teneriffe, age 28, migrated from Matanzas; rec. by Joseph Collet, boarding house keeper - 16 Mar. 1827 [120]

Glancy, John, grocer, born Co. Sligo, Ire., age 35, migrated from Sligo; wife Bridget, born Co. Sligo, age 25; rec. by Patrick Casey, marshal of NYC - 23 Mar. 1827 [121]

Ryan, Michael, shipwright, born Ire., age 24, migrated from
Dublin; rec. by Thomas W. Jackson, upholsterer - 24 Mar. 1827
[122]

McGowan, Bartholomy, labourer; report 20 Nov. 1821: born Ire.,
age 23, migrated from Sligo; rec. by Patrick Flynn, blacksmith - 26 Mar. 1827 [123]

McGowan, Patrick, labourer; report 23 Mar. 1822: born Co. Leitrim, Ire., age 27, migrated from Sligo; rec. by Alexander
Scott, gentleman - 26 Mar. 1827 [124]

Gilmore, John, Jr., morocco dresser, born Ire., age 26, migrated
from Newry; wife Hannah, born Ire., age 20; rec. by John Gilmore, labourer - 27 Mar. 1827 [125]

Mead, Henry, of Fallsburgh, Sullivan Co., subj. of G.B.; rec. by
John Tice, grocer, and James Dickinson, livery stable keeper -
28 Mar. 1827 [126]

Thompson, Peter, rigger & stevedore, born Sweden, age 34, migrated from Stockholm; rec. by James Weldon, shipmaster - 30
Mar. 1827 [127]

Finigan, Patrick, grocer, born Ire., age 28, migrated from Newry;
rec. by William Moneypenny, dyer - 2 Apr. 1827 [128]

Jones, Richard, waiter; report 2 Mar. 1822: born Wales, age 26,
migrated from Liverpool; rec. by Joseph Bonsor, brewer - 2
Apr. 1827 [129]

McCullum, John, mariner, born Ire., age 22, migrated from Londonderry; rec. by Andrew Lishman [or Liskman?], rigger - 4
Apr. 1827 [130]

Adair, Henry, engineer, born Ire., age 22 years & 8 mos., migrated from Belfast - 6 Apr. 1827 [131]

McGinnis, Stewart, planter, born Ire., age 26, migrated from
Londonderry; rec. by James McGinnis, accountant - 7 Apr. 1827
[132]

Stackpole, Joseph, seaman; report 4 June 1821: born Co. Clare,
Ire., age 20, migrated from Limerick; rec. by Francis Stackpole, grocer - 10 Apr. 1827 [133]

Foster, George, labourer; report 10 Apr. 1822: born Ire., age 30,
migrated from Newry; rec. by Hugh Acheson, cartman - 10 Apr.
1827 [134]

Bleakley, Adam, dyer, born Ire., age 26, migrated from Londonderry - 11 Apr. 1827 [135]

Healy, Owen, cartman, born Ire., age 21, migrated from Sligo;
rec. by Owen Healy, soap-boiler - 11 Apr. 1827 [136]

Preia, Anthony, mariner, born Island of Madeira, age 21, subj.
of Portugal, migrated from Madeira; rec. by R.M. Blatchford,
counsellor-at-law - 12 Apr. 1827 [137]

Cowhey, Michael, coachman; report 10 Apr. 1822: born Ire., age
28, migrated from Dublin; wife Margaret, born Ire., age 22;
son William, born Ire., age 4; rec. by James Sweeny, tavern-
keeper - 19 Apr. 1827 [138]

Cudlipp, David, hatter; report 25 Jan. 1820: born Portsmouth,
Eng., age 29, migrated from Portsmouth; wife Sarah, born Portsmouth, age 26; dau. [Le?]na, age 5; rec. by Thomas Knight,
glass-cutter - 21 Apr. 1827 [139]

McGowan, Michael, pedlar; report 15 Apr. 1822: born Co. Leitrim,
Ire., age 36; wife Margaret, born Sligo, age 27; rec. by James
Ballagh, grocer - 23 Apr. 1827 [140]

Stafford, Mary (widow of Martin Stafford); report 24 July 1822:
Martin, servant, born Ire., age 26; wife Mary, born Ire., age
23; dau. Margaret, born NYC, age 3; dau. [Em]ily, born NYC,
age 7 mos.; migrated from St. Johns, Newfoundland; rec. by
Thomas Ryan, labourer - 23 Apr. 1827 [141]

McKee, Samuel, mariner; report 15 Nov. 1817: born Co, Down, Ire.,
age 27, migrated from Belfast; rec. by Elijah Letts, baker -
27 Apr. 1827 [142]

Mahony, Jeremiah, of Long Island, labourer; report 24 Aug.
1820: born Co. Kerry, Ire., age 45; wife Margaret, born Co.
Kerry, age 44; son Owen, born London, age 8; son Michael,
born London, age 6; dau. Peggy, born America, age 1; family
migrated from London; rec. by John Shea, shoemaker - 28 Apr.
1827 [143]

Kelly, Patrick, pedlar, born Ire., age 23, migrated from Londonderry; rec. by Hugh Reilly, accountant - 1 May 1827 [144]

Kelly, Felix, pedlar, born Ire., age 27, migrated from Londonderry; rec. by Patrick Kelly - 1 May 1827 [145]

Smith, John, mariner, born Bordeaux, France, age 22, migrated
from Cadiz, Spain; rec. by James Wilson, mariner - 1 May 1827
[146]

Walsh, George, labourer; report 18 Apr. 1822: born Ire., age
28, migrated from Waterford; rec. by James Sweeny, tavern-
keeper - 2 May 1827 [147]

Gilfillan, James, baker, born Ire., age 23, migrated from Londonderry; rec. by Samuel Swan, farmer - 3 May 1827 [148]

Bergen, Daniel, labourer; report 26 Apr. 1819: born Ire., age
30, migrated from Dublin; rec. by William Foley, labourer -
3 May 1827 [149]

Broyer, Claudius, confectioner, subj. of King of France & Navarre; rec. by Francis J. Berier, teacher, & John Gruez,
cabinetmaker- 3 May 1827 [150]

McCaffry, James, labourer; report 25 Aug. 1820: born Ire., age
20, migrated from Dublin; rec. by James Sweeny, tavern-keeper
- 3 May 1827 [151]

Hylen, Nicholas, sawyer; report 27 Apr. 1821: born Co. Tipperary,
Ire., age 37, migrated from Waterford; wife Elizabeth, born
Co. Down, Ire., age 30; rec. by Elisha Morrill, justice of
the 6th Ward Court of NYC - 3 May 1827 [152].

Althouse, Conrad, druggist; report 18 Dec. 1821: born town of
Althousen, Prussia, age 28, migrated from Antwerp; rec. by
Engel Friend, cloak maker - 4 May 1827 [153]

Kent, John, butcher; report 1 May 1821: born Co. Tipperary, Ire.,
age 25, migrated from Waterford; rec. by Michael Cowhy, waterman - 5 May 1827 [154]

McLoughlin, Peter, grocer; report 9 Feb. 1822: born Ire., age
27, sawyer, migrated from Londonderry; rec. by James Moran,
currier - 7 May 1827 [155]

Meghan, Henry, paver, born Ire., age 22, migrated from Londonderry; rec. by Patrick McCafferty, paver - 7 May 1827 [156]

Mullan, William, morocco dresser; report 16 June 1823: born Ire.,
migrated from Belfast - 7 May 1827 [157]

Weightman, Thomas, clerk, born Eng., age 28, migrated from
Liverpool; rec. by Joseph Weightman, sawyer - 8 May 1827 [158]

Blackburn, George B., mariner, born Eng., age 21, migrated from Liverpool; rec. by John Blackburn, merchant - 9 May 1827 [159]

Cooper, James, baker, born Ire., age 28, migrated from Newry; rec. by Hugh Cooper, gentleman - 9 May 1827 [160]

Glasier, Elias, baker; report 22 Apr. 1822: born Germany, age 43, sugar baker, subj. of King of Wirtemburg, migrated from London; rec. by Uriah Rider, tavern-keeper - 9 May 1827 [161]

Moubray, Ralph, formerly of NYC but now of Brooklyn, labourer; report 23 Aug. 1820: born Ire., age 30, migrated from Londonderry; rec. by Thomas Harran, coachman - 9 May 1827 [162]

Carrick, Robert, merchant; report 5 May 1820: born Glasgow, age 25, migrated from Liverpool; rec. by Thomas Hutchison, merchant - 9 May 1827 [163]

Beatty, James, innkeeper; report 1 Feb. 1822: born Co. Tyrone, Ire., age 27, storekeeper, migrated from Belfast; wife Ann, born Co. Fermanagh, age 20; rec. by William Purvis, carpenter - 10 May 1827 [164]

Sherlock, Edward, slater; declaration of intent in Superior Court of Chatham Co., Georgia, 6 May 1822: born Ire., age now 27, embarked Dublin 21 Aug. 1819 on ship Hope, Capt. Newman, arrived NYC 10 Oct. 1819 and came to Savannah 15 Jan. 1820; rec. by Thomas Sheridan - 10 May 1827 [165]

Artechea, Anthony J., merchant, born Spain, age 26, migrated from Cadiz; rec. by Francis J. Berier, teacher - 10 May 1827 [166]

St. Paul, Bries, gentleman, born Dyon, France, age 25, migrated from Havre de Grace; rec. by Francis J. Berier, teacher - 10 May 1827 [167]

O'Rourke, Owen, stone cutter, born Ire., age 21, migrated from Sligo; rec. by William Clancy, grocer - 14 May 1827 [168]

Maguire, Michael, cabinetmaker, born Ire., age 26, migrated from Belfast; rec. by Patrick Slowey, grocer - 14 May 1827 [169]

Hillsburgh, Charles, plumber & pewterer, born Gottemburgh, age 26, subj. of King of Sweden & Norway, migrated from London; rec. by John J. Rogers, plumberer & pewterer - 14 May 1827 [170]

Gerken, John, sugar baker; report 23 June 1821: born Hanover, age 21, migrated from Bremen; rec. by Conrad Brinkman, sausage maker - 12 May 1827 [171]

Gallies, Joseph, hairdresser & perfumer; report 14 Jan. 1822: born Antwerp, Holland, age 27, migrated from Antwerp; rec. by Charles F. Cummings, painter & glazier - 14 May 1827 [172]

Hunt, Mathew, waterman; report 21 Jan. 1822: born Co. Kilkenny, Ire., age 36, migrated from Waterford; wife Margaret, born Co. Wexford, age 33; son John, born NYC, age 10; dau. Mary, age 8, born NYC; dau. Emily Cornelia, born NYC, age 6; Ann Henrietta, born NYC, age 18 mos.; rec. by John McCosker, shoemaker - 15 May 1827 [173]

Schofield, John, cartman; report 31 Mar. 1821: born Sheffield, Eng., age 39, migrated from Liverpool; rec. by Uriah Ryder, tavern-keeper - 16 May 1827 [175]

Nevill, James, rigger; report 16 May 1822: born Ire., age 40, migrated from Dublin; wife Mary, born Ire., age 40; son John, born Ire., age 11; son Edward, born Ire., age 8; rec. by John Murphy, mariner - 16 May 1827 [176]

McLeod, James, cartman; report 4 Apr. 1821: born Co. Donegal, Ire., age 27, migrated from Londonderry; rec. by James McGuire, grocer - 16 May 1827 [177]

Mulligan, Charles, grocer; report 13 Apr. 1821: born Co. Longford, Ire., age 25, migrated from Dublin; rec. by Kames Kain, hackmaster - 17 May 1827 [178]

Duffy, James, grocer; report 15 Apr. 1822: born Ire., age 30, migrated from Liverpool; rec. by Michael McColgan, accountant - 17 May 1827 [179]

Boudren, John, shoemaker, born Ire., age 23, migrated from Cork; rec. by Michael Boudren, shoemaker - 18 May 1827 [180]

Tully, Patrick, mason; report 7 May 1821: born Ire., age 20, migrated from Dublin; rec. by Bartholomew Tully, tavern-keeper - 22 May 1827 [181]

Nisbet, William, mariner, born Scotland, age 32, migrated from Kirkwell, Scotland; rec. by William Ireland, mariner - 22 May 1827 [182]

Russell, Samuel, carpenter, born Ire., age 25, migrated from Londonderry; rec. by James Russell, builder - 23 May 1827 [183]

Story, William, previously mariner but now grocer; report 23 May 1822: born Ire., age 36, migrated from London; rec. by Edward Inglish - 23 May 1827 [184]

Farrelly, Bernard, cartman; report 29 June 1821: born Co. Cavan, Ire., age 23, migrated from Dublin; rec. by Peter Smith, paver - 24 May 1827 [185]

Burke, John, tavern-keeper; report 27 May 1822: born Ire., age 79, migrated from Warings Point; children, all born in Ire.: Winifred, age 30; Alexander, age 23; Thomas, age 19; John, age 18; rec. by Abraham M. Griffin, attorney-at-law - 28 May 1827 [186]

Bullinger, Henry, mariner, born London, age 24, migrated from Liverpool; rec. by Charles Bullinger, cartman - 28 May 1827 [187]

Britton, John, mariner; report 26 Apr. 1822: born Ire., age 19, migr. from Dublin; rec. by John Wark, a marshal of NYC - 30 May 1827 [188]

McClosky, Daniel, sawyer; report 25 Aug. 1820: born Ire., age 21, migrated from Londonderry, labourer; rec. by Robert King, sawyer - 30 May 1827 [189]

Pile, John, mariner, born Eng., age 29, migrated from Liverpool; rec. by Thomas Ridder, rigger - 1 June 1827 [190]

Wetherel, Charles, of Brooklyn, born Sweden, age 35, migrated from Stockholm; rec. by Thomas Armstrong - 1 June 1827 [191]

Peon, Jose Maria, merchant, born Merida, State of Yucatan, Mexico, age 26, migrated from Merida - 2 June 1827 [192]

Largery, John, baker; report 28 June 1820: born Ire., age 27, migrated from Newry; rec. by James G. Finn, constable - 2 June 1827 [193]

Power, Edmund, merchant, formerly of NYC but now of Milford, Pike Co., Pa.; report 11 Nov. 1818: born Eng., age 28, migrated from London; rec. by Daniel Gassner, gentleman - 5 June 1827 [194]

Williams, Owen Perry, grocer; report 9 Feb. 1822: born Wales, age 30, migrated from Liverpool; wife Margaret, born Wales, age 30; dau. Elizabeth, born Wales, age 3; rec. by John Eldridge, farmer - 6 June 1827 [195]

Eldridge, John, farmer; report 4 May 1822: born Eng., age 38,
   migrated from Liverpool; rec. by Owen Williams, grocer - 6
   June 1827 [196]

Mackey, Thomas, mason; report 17 Apr. 1821: born Cork, Ire.,
   age 49, migrated from Cork; wife Ellen, born Cork, age 42;
   dau. Margaret, born Cork, age 11; rec. by Patrick Casey, a
   marshal of NYC - 8 June 1827 [197]

Mullony, William, labourer, born Ire., age 40, migrated from
   Halifax; rec. by Samuel Storer, ship-carpenter - 8 June 1827
   [198]

McDermit, John, labourer, born Ire., age 26, migrated from Londonderry; rec. by Hugh Dougherty and Ruth Falkner - 9 June
   1827 [199]

Smith, Benjamin, heretofore of NYC but now of Eastport, Maine,
   late mariner but now merchant; report 27 Oct. 1821: born New
   Brunswick, age 34, migrated from St. Johns; wife Jane, born
   New Brunswick, age 22; rec. by William Jessup, boarding house
   keeper - 11 June 1827 [200]

Greniker, Thomas, at present of NYC but inhabitant of city of
   Charleston, S.C., mariner, born Eng., age 28, migrated from
   Liverpool; rec. by John Jamison, mariner - 12 June 1827 [201]

Currie, William, innkeeper; report 11 Feb. 1822: born Ire., age
   32, migrated from Liverpool; rec. by John Fegan, grocer - 13
   June 1827 [202]

Lockhart, William, gardner; report 6 June 1822: born Ire., age
   38, migrated from Londonderry; wife Isabella, born Ire., age
   32; son Francis, born Ire., age 7; dau. Catherine, born NYC,
   age 1; rec. by William Lord, carpenter - 13 June 1827 [203]

Martin, Daniel, grocer; report 17 May 1822: born Ire., age 38,
   migrated from Londonderry; rec. by John Barberie, marshal -
   13 June 1827 [204]

Graham, William, cartman; report 4 Apr. 1821: born Co. Tyrone,
   Ire., age 27, migrated from Londonderry; rec. by John Wark, a
   marshal of NYC - 14 June 1827 [205]

Powers, Patrick, labourer; report 20 May 1822: born Co. Wexford,
   Ire., age 42, migrated from Waterford; rec. by John Quincy,
   labourer - 14 June 1827 [206]

Bergin, Patrick, porter, born Ire., age 25, migrated from Dublin;
   rec. by Ceasar Hall, labourer - 15 June 1827 [207]

Victor, Theodore, merchant, born Ruiteln, Hesse Cassel, age 25,
   migrated from Bremen; rec. by Francis J. Berier, teacher - 16
   June 1827 [208]

Laws, John, of Brookhaven, Suffolk Co., farmer, born Eng., age
   46, migrated from London; rec. by Azur Raynor, of Brookhaven -
   16 June 1827 [209]

Laws, Simmons, of Brookhaven, farmer, born Eng., age 44, migrated
   from London; rec. by Azur Raynor, of Brookhaven - 16 June 1827
   [210]

Ducasse, James, merchant, born Bordeaux, France, age 27, migrated
   from Bordeaux; rec. by Francis J. Berier, teacher - 18 June
   1827 [211]

Cairon, John, merchant, born Bezier, France, age 27, migrated
   from Marseilles; rec. by Francis J. Berier, teacher - 18 June
   1827 [212]

Jaclson, David, mariner, born Eng., age 27, migrated from Liverpool; rec. by F.W.S. Shaeffer, boarding house keeper -20 June [213

Wright, John Tenant, at present of NYC but late of Boston,
   mariner, born Eng., age 24, migrated from London; rec. by
   Ebenezer Harwood, of NYC but late of Boston, mariner - 22
   June 1827 [214]

Martin, Robert, distiller, subj. of G.B.; rec. by Dominick
   Shields, labourer, and Alexander Devvici [?], distiller -
   22 June 1827 [215]

Toohey, Michael J., grocer; report 10 Apr. 1821: born Co. Tipperary, Ire., age 35, migrated from London; wife Mary, born
   Co. Tipperary, age 26; dau. Mary Ann, born Co. Tipperary, age
   8; dau. Eliza, born Co. Tipperary, age 5; rec. by Samuel L.
   White, chairmaker - 26 June 1827 [216]

Rice, Gilbert Cuthbert, gentleman, born Ire., age 28, migrated
   from Cork; rec. by Christopher C. Rice, of Brooklyn, gentleman - 26 June 1827 [217]

Macfarlan, Frederick, Jr., painter & glazier, born Scotland,
   age 32, migrated from Leith; rec. by Jonathan Seymour, printer
   - 27 June 1827 [218]

Macfarlan, Thomas, painter & glazier, born Scotland, age 34,
   migrated from Leith; rec. by Jonathan Seymour, printer - 27
   June 1827 [219]

Giesz, Anthony, cooper; report 5 Dec. 1821: born Dept. of Lower
   Rhine, France, age 34, migrated from Amsterdam; rec. by Jacob
   Wardell, grocer -27 June 1827 [220]

Dermit, John, of Brooklyn, boatman, subj. of G.B., was in U.S. by
   18 June 1798; rec. by James Sutton, of Brooklyn - 28 June 1827
   [221]

Fitzpatrick, Owen, cartman; report 3 July 1827: born Ire., age
   27, migrated from Liverpool; rec. by Nicholas Anderson, silver
   plater - 3 July 1827 [222]

Del Hoyo, Francis, merchant, born Santander, Spain, age 26, migrated from Santander; rec. by Francis J. Berier, teacher - 3
   July 1827 [223]

Parker, Samuel, cabinetmaker; report made by his late father
   John on 19 Apr. 1821: John, born Co. Antrim, Ire., age 40, migrated from Belfast; wife Arrabella, born Co. Antrim, age 35;
   son Samuel, born Co. Antrim, age 15; son Isaac, born Co. Antrim, age 13; John was rec. by William Turner, shoemaker, on
   19 Apr. 1821; Samuel rec. by Anthony Robinson, shoemaker - 2
   July 1827 [224]

News, Edward, heretofore of the town of Courtlandt, Westchester
   Co., but now of York Town in sd. county, weaver; report 3 May
   1822: born Ire., age 40, migrated from Belfast; wife Mary, age
   39, and sons, William, age 20, and James, age 17, all born in
   Ire.; rec. by Garrit Williams, shoemaker - 5 July 1827 [225]

Wiseman, Michael, mariner, born Ire., age 21, migrated from Dublin; rec. by John Robertson, mariner - 7 July 1827 [226]

Brady, Owen, cartman, born Ire., age 26. migrated from Cork; rec.
   by Catherine Brady, spinster - 11 July 1827 [227]

O'Neill, Cornelius, labourer; report 15 Sept. 1824: born Ire.,
   age 26, migrated from Limerick; wife Catherine, born Ire., age
   27; rec. by James Westerfield, milkman - 11 July 1827 [228]

Kierans, Thomas, carpenter & joiner, subj. of G.B.; rec. by Aaron
   Crigier & Henry Neil, each a carpenter & joiner - 13 July 1827
   [229]

Wardle, Thomas, mariner, born Eng., age 27, migrated from London; rec. by Julia Ann Davis, boarding house keeper - 17 July 1827 [230]

Bussinger, Charles Ferdinand, coachman, born Stantz, Switzerland, subj. of Canton Underwalden, age 26, migrated from Havre de Grace - 20 July 1827 [231]

O'Donnell, James, porter; report 2 Apr. 1821: born Ire., age 28, migrated from Belfast; rec. by James McKeon, porter - 20 July 1827 [232]

Devereux, James, labourer; report 20 Mar. 1822: born Ire., age 34, migrated from London; rec. by Hugh Duffin, coachman - 21 July 1827 [233]

Hanley, Henry, porter; report 2 Apr. 1821: born Co. Roscommon, Ire., age 28, migrated from Cork; rec. by Henry Hagan, public porter - 23 July 1827 [234]

Henery, Louis, confectioner; report 2 May 1811: subj. of Emperor of France and King of Spain, was residing in U.S. by 18 June 1798; rec. by Peter La Chaise, jeweller - 30 July 1827 [235]

O'Connors, Andrew, labourer, born Ire., age 22, migrated from Liverpool; rec. by Bridget O'Connors, of Hoboken, Bergen Co., N.J. - 25 July 1827 [236]

Nicholson, Meadows Taylor, manufacturer, born Ire., age 21, migrated from London; rec. by Joshua Clibborn, merchant - 26 July 1827 [237]

Gaudin, Louis Frederick, labourer, born Monner, Canton de Vaud, Switzerland, age 24, migrated from Havre de Grace; rec. by David Briant, shoemaker - 1 Aug. 1827 [238]

Shortland, Thomas, cooper, born Eng., age 24, migrated from Liverpool; rec. by Samuel Rudolph, carpenter - 1 Aug. 1827 [239]

Peterson, Hans, mariner; report 29 Apr. 1822: born Sweden, age 38, migrated from East Stadt; rec. by John Thompson, rigger - 8 Aug. 1827 [240]

Jones, James, cabinetmaker; report 27 Apr. 1820: born London, age 38, migrated from Bristol; rec. by Samuel Orrell, reedmaker - 9 Aug. 1827 [241]

Fegan, Patrick, labourer, born Ire., age 28, migrated from Belfast; rec. by Daniel Everitt, shoemaker - 10 Aug. 1827 [242]

Toner, Timothy, labourer, born Ire., age 26, migrated from Newry; rec. by Daniel Everitt, shoemaker - 11 Aug. 1827 [243]

Le Carron, Charles, merchant, born Rouen, France, age 27, migrated from Havre de Grace; rec. by Francis J. Berier, teacher - 15 Aug. 1827 [244]

McLaughlin, Patrick, labourer; report 30 Aug. 1819: born Ire., age 28, migrated from Newry; rec. by Thomas M. Collins, a marshal of NYC - 16 Aug. 1827 [245]

Gray, Andrew, merchant; report 24 Jan. 1820: born Ire., age 23, migrated from Dublin; rec. by William Van Hook, counsellor-at-law - 21 Aug. 1827 [246]

Ryan, James, heretofore teacher but now bookseller; report 17 Apr. 1822: born Ire., age 28, migrated from Limerick- 23 Aug. 1827 [247]

Robert, John, tailor; report 13 May 1822: born Eng., age 39, migrated from London; rec. by James Matthews, whip-maker - 24 Aug. 1827 [248]

Harrison, William, bookkeeper, born Ire., age 28, migrated from Newry; rec. by William W. Cox, of Patterson, N.J. - 24 Aug. 1827 [249]

Pelly, John, merchant; report 3 Jan. 1821: born Ire., age 28, migrated from Dublin; rec. by Patrick Casey, a marshal of NYC - 28 Aug. 1827 [250]

Abeille, Francis, physician, born Bordeaux, France, age 27, migrated from Bordeaux; rec. by Guillaume Rozat, merchant - 30 Aug. 1827 [251]

De Gerate, Eugenio Roque, merchant, born Oguindi, Spain, age 25, migrated from Santander; rec. by Francis J. Berier, teacher - 3 Sept. 1827 [252]

Quirk, Patrick, morocco dresser; report 24 Aug. 1822: born Ire., age 33, migrated from Dublin; rec. by Thomas Quirk, leather dresser - 6 Sept. 1827 [253]

Bergin, William, labourer, born Ire., age 23, migrated from Dublin; rec. by Patrick Bergin, labourer - 14 Sept. 1827 [254]

Roach, Benjamin H., guager, born Island of St. Croix, age 31, migrated from St. Croix, subj. of King of Denmark - 15 Sept. 1827 [255]

Bruce, Alexander, grocer; report 18 Apr. 1821: born Aberdeen, Scotland, age 32, migrated from Greensmouth, Scotland; rec. by Duncan Strong, grocer - 20 Sept. 1827 [256]

Anderson, James, grocer; report 26 Aug. 1820: born Ire., age 40, migrated from Belfast; rec. by Duncan Strong, grocer - 20 Sept. 1827 [257]

Carson, John, gentleman, born Ire., age 23, migrated from Londonderry; rec. by David Beatty, cartman - 21 Sept. 1827 [258]

Furman, John, labourer, born Ire., age 26, migrated from Sligo; rec. by Daniel Everitt, shoemaker - 22 Sept. 1827 [259]

Simms, John C., carpenter, born Eng., age 26, migrated from Havre de Grace; rec. by Elizabeth Simms - 24 Sept. 1827 [260]

Muldoon, John, heretofore of Fayette Co., Pa., but now of NYC, labourer; according to certificate from Pa. of 18 Nov. 1817 was born Co. Meath, Ire., age 30, migrated from Ire. in June 1815 and arrived U.S. in July 1815 and then resided about five months in Fayette Co.; rec. by Peter McLaughlin, grocer - 24 Sept. 1827 [261]

McNally, Terrence, mason, subj. of G.B., was in U.S. by 18 June 1798; rec. by Bryan Connally, grocer - 24 Sept. 1827 [262]

Cunningham, Phelix, grocer, subj. of G.B.; rec. by Richard Marmion, tobacconist; made declaration of intent on 19 Nov. 1806 - Sept. 1827 [263]

Jouan, Auguste, merchant, born France, age 21, migrated from Calais; rec. by Francis J. Berier, teacher - 25 Sept. 1827 [264]

James, William, merchant; report 17 Oct. 1816: born Bailieborou, Ire., age 27, migrated from Dublin; rec. by John James, merchant - 26 Sept. 1827 [265]

Very, Joseph, porter; report 3 Sept. 1825: born Teneriffe, age 20, migrated from Teneriffe; rec. by Abraham Lefoy, merchant - 26 Sept. 1827 [266]

Vol. 3

Duncan, Alexander, tailor, subj. of G.B.; rec. by William Marshall & John McIntyre - 30 June 1828 [1]

Hitchcock, William G., late innkeeper but now mariner; report 30 June 1821: born London, Eng., age 45, migrated from Liverpool; wife Elizabeth, born London, age 36; son James, born London, age 17; rec. by James Vincent, cartman - 28 Sept. 1826 [2]

McCormick, Charles, weaver, subj. of G.B.; rec. by Hugh Read, weaver, and Murtagh Gilmor, labourer - 2 July 1828 [3]

Wood, James, Jr., of Haverstraw, Rockland Co., brickmaker, subj. of G.B.; rec. by Daniel Delavan, gentleman - 2 July 1828 [4]

Lammer, Joseph, merchant, subj. of Emperor of Austria; rec. by John A. Snyder, gentleman, and John G. Wendel, gentleman - 3 July 1828 [5]

Doran, Edward, cooper, subj. of G.B.; rec. by William McGinnis and James Patterson - 7 July 1828 [6]

McCready, Nancy, grocer, subj. of G.B.; rec. by Thomas Cahill, mariner, and John Pernie, distiller - 22 July 1828 [7 & 8]

Bragos, Anthony, merchant, subj. of King of Portugal; rec. by Domingos Pereira, mariner, and Thomas Brooks, merchant - 2 Aug. 1828 [9]

Powley, John, farmer, subj. of G.B.; rec. by John Dougherty, livery stable keeper, and Miln Parker, coachmaker - 2 Aug. 1828 [10]

Baker, Thomas, cordwainer, subj. of G.B.; rec. by Henry Venn, cordwainer, and James Lennon, cordwainer - 19 Aug. 1828 [11]

Baker, Richard, cordwainer, subj. of G.B.; rec. by Thomas Baker, cordwainer, and Daniel Morgan, grocer - 21 Aug. 1828 [12]

Wardell, Christopher, fisherman, subj. of King of Denmark; rec. by Jonas Beekman, rigger, and Peter Mansfield, fisherman - 23 Aug. 1828 [13]

Haskell, William, mariner, subj. of G.B.; rec. by Helm Jenkins and Thomas Fargo, carpenter - 2 Sept. 1828 [14] - whole item was deleted.

Brackett, William H., merchant, subj. of G.B.; rec. by Thomas Gender, fruiterer, and Christian Burdett, blacksmith - 4 Sept. 1828 [15]

Vasques, Joaquim Jose, merchant, subj. of King of Portugal; rec. by John C. Zimmerman, merchant, and Charles L. Fontaine, auctioneer - 4 Sept. 1828 [16]

Waters, Thomas, cartman, subj. of G.B.; rec. by John Rice, mason, and John Heffernen, grocer - 8 Sept. 1828 [17]

McDonald, Archibald, of Westfield, N.J., woolen manufacturer, subj. of G.B.; rec. by William Marshall, shoemaker, and James Marshall, shoemaker - 13 Sept. 1828 [18]

Dickey, John, ship-carpenter, subj. of G.B.; rec. by James Leakman, block- and pump maker, and Thomas L. Watson, block- and pump maker - 16 Sept. 1828 [19]

Philip, William, of Brooklyn, Kings Co., baker, subj. of King of Prussia; rec. by Edward McGaraghan, counsellor-at-law, and Peter V. Remsen, attorney-at-law - 22 Sept. 1828 [20]

Rice, Patrick, rigger, subj. of G.B.; rec. by Henry Turley, cartman, & John Rice, mason - 22 Sept. 1828 [21]

Petter, Robert, boatbuilder, subj. of G.B.; rec. by John Robbins, grocer, and John Dickie, of Brooklyn, shipwright - 24 Sept. 1828 [22 & 23]

Canter, Rachel, subj. of King of Denmark; rec. by Charlotte Saaportas and David G. Seixas, merchant - 3 Oct. 1828 [24]

McGown, John, labourer, subj. of G.B.; rec. by Charles Fanning, grocer, and John O'Connor, grocer - 11 Oct. 1828 [25]

McGlade, Thomas, gardner, subj. of G.B.; rec. by Garrit Byrne, grocer, and David Atkins, tobacconist - 15 Oct. 1828 [26]

Quin, Edward C., of Essex Co., N.J., teacher, subj. of G.B.; rec. by James R. Mullany, of Bergen Co., N.J., and Peter Higgins, of NYC, grocer - 15 Oct. 1828 [26A]

Alexander, Matthew, of Essex Co., N.J., leather dresser, subj. of G.B.; rec. by Robert McCormick, grocer, and Benjamin Marshall, gentleman - 15 Oct. 1828 [27]

Tyson, Henry, ship-carpenter, subj. of G.B.; rec. by Stephen Wright, ship-carpenter, and John Casilear, ship-carpenter - 24 Oct. 1828 [28]

Tapper, John, teacher, subj. of G.B.; rec. by Frederick Wheatley, jeweller, and Richard Ellis, constable - 25 Oct. 1828 [29]

Morrell, Thomas, matts maker, subj. of G.B.; rec. by Reuben Knapp, fisherman, and Lyman Clark, rigger - 27 Oct. 1828 [30]

Sexton, Michael, livery stable keeper, subj. of G.B.; rec. by Micajah Reynolds, grocer, & William Ryan, labourer - 28 Oct. 1828 [31]

McCausland, William, mariner, subj. of G.B.; rec. by Samuel Lyon, constable, and James McCausland, accountant - 28 Oct. 1828 [32]

Da Ponte, Lorenzo, professor of languages, subj. of Emperor of Austria; rec. by Richard Ellis, a constable of NYC, and Lorenzo Da Ponte, Jr., professor of languages - 31 Oct. 1828 [33]

Davey, Peter, grocer, subj. of G.B.; rec. by Tighe Davey, carpenter, and Charles O'Connor, counsellor-at-law - 31 Oct. 1828 [34]

Gilligan, William, pedlar, subj. of G.B.; rec. by William Knapp, tailor, and Peter Davey, grocer - 1 Nov. 1828 [35]

Portley, John, cooper, subj. of G.B.; rec. by William Friel, grocer, and Hugh McGinnis, cooper - 1 Nov. 1828 [36]

Culbert/Colbert, John, paver, subj. of G.B.; rec. by Samuel Waddell, grocer, and James Anderson, grocer - 1 Nov. 1828 [37]

McKee, Henry, printer, subj. of G.B.; rec. by Samuel Waddell, grocer, and James Anderson, grocer - 1 Nov. 1828 [38]

Fraherty, William, fruiterer, subj. of G.B.; rec. by Luke Corrigan and Martin Waters, fruiterers, and John Gilmartin, grocer - 3 Nov. 1828 [39]

Ring, Zebedee, shipwright, subj. of G.B.; rec. by James De Baun, merchant, and Abraham De Baun, gentleman - 4 Nov. 1828 [40]

Mulheran, Peter, grocer, subj. of G.B.; rec. by Thomas Dougherty, cartman, and Philip Campbell, labourer - 4 Nov. 1828 [41]

Gallagher, John, cartman, subj. of G.B.; rec. by Bernard McCasker and William McCluskey, grocers - 4 Nov. 1828 [42]

Clinton, Bartholomew, fruiterer, subj. of G.B.; rec. by Luke
Corrigan, fruiterer, and John Gilmartin, grocer - 4 Nov. 1828
[43]

Bass, George, cartman, subj. of G.B.; rec. by Richard Robbins,
grocer, and Daniel Morgan, grocer - 4 Nov. 1828 [44]

Swan, Thomas, paver, subj. of G.B.; rec. by James Clyde, cartman, and Daniel Kennedy, cartman - 4 Nov. 1828 [45]

Morton, Robert, stone cutter, subj. of G.B.; rec. by John D.
Campbell and John Brower [?] - 4 Nov. 1828 - incomplete [46]

McAleer, George, of Jersey City, N.J., porter, subj. of G.B.;
rec. by George Dummer, of Jersey City, merchant, and William
Glaze, of Jersey City, glass-maker - 5 Nov. 1828 [47]

McMahon, Patrick, labourer, subj. of G.B.; rec. by James Cope-
land, grocer, and Andrew Hart, labourer - 5 Nov. 1828 [48]

Glaze, William, glass-maker, subj. of G.B.; rec. by George Dummer, of Jersey City, merchant, and George McAleer, of Jersey
City, porter - 5 Nov. 1828 [49]

Armstrong, Thomas, of Brooklyn, waterman, subj. of G.B.; rec.
by Charles Cole, cartman, and John Martin, storekeeper - 5 Nov.
1828 [50]

Paton, George, dyer, subj. of G.B.; rec. by William Buchanan,
tavern-keeper, and George H. Cooper, merchant - 5 Nov. 1828
[51]

Richards, George, engineer, subj. of G.B.; rec. by Michael Post,
shoemaker, and Asa C. Rainetaux, accountant - 5 Nov. 1828 [52]

Roy, William, merchant, subj. of G.B.; rec. by John Boyd, minister of the Gospel, and Mathew Vanderhoff, shoemaker - 5 Nov.
1828 [53]

McGown, Farrel, labourer, subj. of G.B.; rec. by Terence Feighan,
grocer, and Peter Clarey, grocer - 5 Nov. 1828 [54]

Brawley, Thomas, weaver, subj. of G.B.; rec. by Henry Drake,
storekeeper, and Lambert Faron, mason - 5 Nov. 1828 [55]

McNulty, James, of Brooklyn, labourer, subj. of G.B.; rec. by
Darby Dawson, of Brooklyn, labourer, and John Striker, of
Brooklyn, labourer - 5 Nov. 1828 [56]

Welling, Henry F.; rec. by Samuel Storm, commission merchant -
incomplete [57]

Code, Patrick, morocco dresser, subj. of G.B.; rec. by Robert
Anderson and Joseph Church, morocco dressers - 5 Nov. 1828 [58]

Dougherty, William, shoe-and bootmaker, subj. of G.B.; rec. by
Alfred M. Ryder, hatter, and Alexander J. Henderson, grocer -
5 Nov. 1828 [59]

Cummins, Patrick, labourer, subj. of G.B.; rec. by Jacob Acker-
son, of Jersey City, butcher, and William Kerrigan, of Jersey
City, labourer - 5 Nov. 1828 [60]

Hart, Joseph, merchant, subj. of King of Prussia; rec. by Tobias
Ezekiel, quil manufacturer, and George Lyon, merchant - 5 Nov.
1828 [61]

Little, Michael, gutter maker, subj. of G.B.; rec. by John Bruce,
baker, and Theodore Fowler, grocer - 18 Nov. 1828 - incomplete
[62]

Smith, John Ravenscraft, mariner, subj. of G.B.; rec. by William
Cullen, cooper, and James Anderson, grocer - 6 Dec. 1828 [63]

Durando, Paul M. Piccard, merchant tailor, subj. of King of
France; rec. by Charles G. Wille, tailor, and Xavier Bill,
tailor - 9 Dec. 1828 [64]

Anderson, Andrew, rigger & stevedore, subj. of King of Denmark;
rec. by Samuel Mitchell, coach lamp maker, and Peter Seely,
rigger and Stevedore - 8 Jan. 1829 [65]

Dowie, Henry, of Delaware Co., N.Y., farmer, subj. of G.B.; rec.
by Robert Stoddard, carpenter, and William Thomson, silversmith - 12 Jan. 1829 [66]

Leger, Claudius, mariner, subj. of France; rec. by John B. Martin, grocer, and George Ledermann, shoemaker - 13 Jan. 1829
[67]

Barry, Lawrence, gardner, subj. of G.B.; rec. by Joseph Hill,
and Frederick Evenen, gardner - 19 Jan. 1829 [68]

Dickers, Henry, milkman, subj. of G.B.; rec. by Francis Feitner,
gardner, and William A. Hardenbrook, a marshal of NYC - 26
Jan. 1829 [69]

Taylor, John L., boatman, subj. of France; rec. by Lewis Smith,
grain measurer, and Francis Smith, waterman - 2 Feb. 1829 [70]

Trupell, Eleanor (widow of Richard Trupell), subj. of G.B.; rec.
by Daniel N. Jucker, blacksmith, and Peter McLaughlin, grocer
- 9 Feb. 1829 [71]

Miller, William, grocer, subj. of G.B.; rec. by James Miller,
grocer, and Hugh Miller, grocer - 13 Feb. 1829 [72]

Jones, Susanna (widow of William Jones), subj. of G.B.; rec. by
William Rollinson, engraver, and Abraham R. Luyster, merchant
- 25 Feb. 1829 [73]

Mary Luyster (wife of Abraham R. Luyster), subj. of G.B.; rec.
by William Rollinson, engraver, and Susanna Jones - 25 Feb.
1829 [74]

Greer, George, weaver, subj. of G.B.; rec. by John Gukin, carpenter, and William Shaw, storekeeper - 12 Mar. 1829 [75]

Hancock, John, mechanic, subj. of G.B.; rec. by Henry Hinsdale,
merchant, and David Thompson, merchant - 20 Mar. 1829 [76]

Del Noce, Gennaro, sadler, subj. of King of Naples; rec. by
Charles D. New, grocer, and Pietro Pastronick, porter house
keeper - 24 Mar. 1829 [77]

Bunning, Nicholas R., of Newark, N.J., sadler, subj. of City of
Hamburgh; rec. by Margarete Schmidt and Stephen Hooper, hatter
- 7 Apr. 1829 [78]

McCullagh, Patrick, porter, subj. of G.B.; rec. by William Cal-
len, cooper, and George Jacobs, sugar baker - 11 Apr. 1829
[79]

Savage, Robert, accountant, subj. of G.B.; rec. by John Wintringham, a constable of NYC, and Thomas Franklin, register of
NYC - 25 Apr. 1829 [80]

Corrigan, Luke, fruiterer, subj. of G.B.; rec. by Bartholomew
Clinton, fruiterer, and John Laughlin, cartman - 19 Apr. 1829
[81]

Burns, Andrew, of village of Geneva, Ontario Co., brewer, subj.
of G.B.; rec. by Peter McIntyre, boarding house keeper, and
William W. Cowan, counsellor-at-law - 11 May 1829 [82]

Dalton, Jane, spinster, subj. of G.B.; rec. by Anna Dalton, a
widow, and Eldad Holmes, merchant - 12 May 1829 [83]

Smith, William, cartman, subj. of G.B; rec. by Patrick McEvoy,
coachman, and James Stafford, porter - 1 June 1829 [84]

Steeple, George, of St. Lawrence, N.Y., farmer, subj. of G.B.;
rec. by Alexander Cuthill, gentleman, and John Steeple, hatter
- 2 June 1829 [85]

Thomson, David, distiller, subj. of G.B.; rec. by Gavin Spence,
watchmaker, and William Welch, watchmaker - 6 June 1829 [86]

Wilson, William, shipwright, subj. of G.B.; rec. by John Lozier,
shipwright, and Peter Martin, watchmaker - 13 June 1829 [87]

Riley, Bartholomew, labourer, subj. of G.B.; rec. by Patrick
Hamilton, paver, and Barney Slaman, labourer - 15 June 1829
[88]

Kerassy, Thomas, gardner, subj. of G.B.; rec. by Thomas McKay,
mason, and Edmund Fitz Gerald, accountant - 29 July 1829 [89]

Martin, James, manufacturer, subj. of G.B.; rec. by William Patterson, grocer, and Alexander McKee, shipwright - 14 Sept.
1829 [90]

Buchanan, Thomas, undertaker, subj. of G.B.; rec. by Anthony
Lynn, locksmith, and James McAndrews, grocer - 17 Sept. 1829
[91]

Stoddart, Walter G., of Brooklyn, millwright, subj. of G.B.;
rec. by Malcolm McGregor, distiller, and James C. Leal, accountant - 13 Oct. 1829 [92]

Portal, Juan Antonio, merchant, subj. of King of Spain; rec. by
Francis J. Berrier, teacher, and Thomas Gentil - 16 Oct. 1829
[93]

Vogt, Henry, collector, subj. of Prince of Hesse Cassell; rec.
by Gertrude Vultee, grocer, and George D. Strong, grocer - 21
Oct. 1829 [94]

Anderson, William, subj. of G.B.; rec. by Frederic Groshon, merchant , and John Barberie, a marshal - 22 Oct. 1829 [95]

Lindsay, George, Jr., morocco leather dresser, subj. of G.B.;
rec. by George Lindsay, morocco leather dresser, and Joseph
Watson, morocco leather dresser - 2 Nov. 1829 [96]

Campbell, Robert, blacksmith, subj. of G.B.; rec. by James Wallace, blacksmith, and John Barberie, a marshal - 3 Nov. 1829
[97]

Fisher, Andrew, butcher, subj. of G.B.; rec. by Jacob Wiggins,
butcher, and Thomas Harrison, butcher - 3 Nov. 1829 [98]

Williamson, Alfred, hack keeper, subj. of King of the Netherlands; rec. by Luke Gillin, painter and glazier, and Augustus
C. Rametaux, accountant - 4 Nov. 1829 [99]

Lavin, Lawrence, drayman, subj. of G.B.; rec. by Charles Fanning,
locksmith, and William Bannan - 4 Nov. 1829 [100]

Waters, James, tailor, subj. of G.B.; rec. by Edward McGaraghan,
attorney-at-law, and James McAndrew, grocer - 4 Nov. 1829 [101]

Hart, Andrew, labourer, subj. of G.B.; rec. by Luke Gillen, painter and glazier, and James Waters, tailor - 4 Nov. 1829 [102]

O'Rourke, Bernard, fruiterer, subj. of G.B.; rec. by Luke Gillen,
painter and glazier, and James McAndrew, grocer - 4 Nov. 1829
[103]

Corrigan, James, laborer, subj. of G.B.; rec. by James Farrell,
mason, and Charles Fanning, locksmith - 4 Nov. 1829 [104]

Nalis, Matthew, laborer, subj. of G.B.; rec. by Dennis Cornan,
cartman, and James McAndrews, grocer - 4 Nov. 1829 [105]

McGowan, John, labourer, subj. of G.B.; rec. by Dennis Cornan,
cartman, and Bernard O'Rourke, fruiterer - 4 Nov. 1829 [106]

Monahan, Richard, gardner, subj. of G.B.; rec. by John McCabe
and Thomas McCabe - 4 Nov. 1829 [107]

McGloan, Farrel, laborer, subj. of G.B.; rec. by James McCand-
row and Thomas Costello - 4 Nov. 1829 [108]

Crooks, Ramsey, merchant, subj. of G.B.; rec. by Benjamin Clapp,
merchant, and George Cheninger, merchant - 26 Jan. 1830 [109]

Evans, James, mariner, subj. of G.B.; rec. by John M. Blood, Jr.,
and John Wark - 28 Jan. 1830 [110]

Morrison, John, merchant, subj. of G.B.; rec. by Harvey Bates,
merchant, and John Smith, upholsterer - 29 Jan. 1830 [111]

Babaud, Auguste, merchant, subj. of King of France; rec. by
Eugene Farrard, tavern-keeper, and Peter Douglas, seaman - 4
Feb. 1830 [112]

Green, Patrick, boatman, subj. of G.B.; rec. by Thomas Mooney,
grocer, and George McGowan - 10 Feb. 1830 [113]

Coffie, Eleanor, subj. of G.B.; rec. by George Dupleix, mariner,
and John Chambers, gentleman - 19 Feb. 1830 [114]_

Sutton, George, merchant, subj. of G.B.; rec. by Ralph Bulkley,
merchant, and William Clark, mariner - 5 Mar. 1830 [115]

Molony, Patrick, of town of Pelham, Westchester Co., N.Y., farmer, subj. of G.B.; rec. by John Ryan, sealer, and Garret
Fitzgerald, porter house keeper - 3 Apr. 1830 [116]

Brossard, Claudius Francis Ferdinand. merchant, subj. of King
of France; rec. by Francis J. Berier , teacher, and Thomas Gentil - 10 May 1830 [117]

Wright, Joseph, of New Haven, Conn., rigger, subj. of G.B.; rec.
by John F. Davis, shipmaster, and John Munson, boarding house
keeper - 14 May 1830 [118]

Pattison, Robert, shoemaker, subj. of G.B.; rec. by Hamilton
Biggand [clerk wrote "Bigham"], and Edward Maginnis, paver -
20 May 1830 [119]

Boker, John G., merchant, subj. of King of Prussia; rec. by John
G. Zimmermann, merchant, and John F. Delaplaine - 21 May 1830
[120]

Christy, Joseph, fruiterer, subj. of G.B.; rec. by George Wooldridge, merchant, and Charles Delvecchio - 25 May 1830 [121]

Powell, William, minister of the Gospel, subj. of G.B.; rec. by
Thomas Addis Emmet, councellor-at-law, and William C. Emmet,
councellor-at-law - 5 Aug. 1830 [122]

No. 123 is crossed out.

Garner, Thomas, tavern-keeper, subj. of G.B.; rec. by Thomas
Garner, Jr., umbrella manufacturer, and Henry Garner, merchant
- 27 Aug. 1830 [124]

Gaterau, Cesar, merchant, subj. of King of France; rec. by Francis J. Berier, teacher, and Thomas Gentil - 6 Sept. 1830 [125]

There is no record of Nos. 126-129.

Zubia, Juan Miguel, merchant, subj. of Spain; rec. by Francis
J. Berier, teacher, and Thomas Gentil, gentleman - 17 Sept.
1830 [130]

Bosque, Cayetano, merchant, subj. of Spain; rec. by Francis J.
Berier, teacher, and Thomas Gentil, gentleman - 21 Sept. 1830
[131]

Quinder, Antonio, merchant, subj. of Spain; rec. by John Sylvie,
cabinetmaker, and Francis Stopping, merchant - 24 Sept. 1830
[132]

Corbley, Thomas, paver, subj. of G.B.; rec. by Garret Byrne,
grocer, and Francis McCabe, distiller - 11 Oct. 1830 [133]

Kirk, Robert, grocer, subj. of G.B.; rec. by Eli C. Blake, a
teacher, and Henry Anderson, shoemaker - 16 Oct. 1830 [134]

Marshall, Alexander, engineer, subj. of G.B.; rec. by William
Marshall, shoemaker, and John Miller, tavern-keeper - 27 Oct.
1830 [135]

McQueen, Peter, carpenter, subj. of G.B.; rec. by William Elder,
grocer, and William Morgan, millwright - 2 Nov. 1830 [136]

Park, James, weaver, subj. of G.B.; rec. by Smyth Clark, gentleman, and Robert Simpson, grocer - 3 Nov. 1830 [137]

Curr, William, gardner, subj. of G.B.; rec. by William Elder,
grocer, and Joshua McLaughlin, blacksmith - 3 Nov. 1830 [138]

McPherson, Adam, blacksmith, subj. of G.B.; rec. by Joshua Mc
Laughlin, blacksmith, and William Elder, grocer - 3 Nov. 1830
[139]

Smith, William, watchmaker, subj. of G.B.; rec. by Alfred Lockwood, watchmaker, and William Smith, mariner - 23 Nov. 1830
[140]

Wilson, William, merchant, subj. of G.B.; rec. by Joshua Mc
Laughlin, blacksmith, and Stephen Tuttle, blacksmith - 11 Jan.
1831 [141]

McCarthy, Eliza (wife of Dennis McCarthy, merchant), subj. of
G.B.; rec. by Elisha W. King, counsellor-at-law, and Ellen
Cofe, of Brooklyn - 29 Jan. 1831 [142]

Hawkes, Petty, grocer, subj. of G.B.; rec. by Charles Hyslop,
baker, and Alexander McKenzie, gentleman - 31 Jan. 1831 [143]

Manson, Thomas, rigger, subj. of King of Spain; rec. by Charles
Roden, rigger, and Augustus Oliver, rigger - 29 Feb. 1831 [144]

Hunt, Benjamin, of Queens Co., N.Y., farmer, subj. of G.B.; rec.
by John Perrot, grocer, and William E. Dunscomb, councellor-at-
law - 25 Feb. 1831 [145]

Racey, Eliza (widow of Charles Racey), subj. of G.B.; rec. by
Tyzack Hodges, accountant, and James Donaldson, baker - 5 Mar.
1831 [146]

De Ruyter, John C., merchant, subj. of government of Belgium;
rec. by Francis J. Berier, teacher, and Thomas Gentil, gentleman - 17 Mar. 1831 [147]

Boyd, Andrew, of Pittsfield, Mass., wool stappler, subj. of G.B.;
rec. by Joshua McLaughlin, blacksmith, and William Elder, grocer - 31 Mar. 1831 [148]

Moro, Gaetano, engineer, subj. of Emperor of Austria; rec. by
Francis J. Berier, teacher, and Thomas Gentil, gentleman - 7
Apr. 1831 [149]

Brown, Manuel, confectioner, subj. of King of Sardinia; rec. by
John Brown, confectioner, and Maria Brown - 7 Apr. 1831 [150]

Owens, Thomas, painter, subj. of G.B.; rec. by William Inslee,
painter, and John Lynn, tavern-keeper - 9 Apr. 1831 [151]

McKinley, John, teacher, subj. of G.B.; rec. by Edward Hamilton, grocer, and James Sweeny, tavern-keeper - 11 Apr. 1831 [152]

Osborn, Michael, public porter, subj. of G.B.; rec. by Thomas Hopper, cooper, and James Simpson, rigger - 12 Apr. 1831 [153]

Watson, John, morocco dresser, subj. of G.B.; rec. by Joseph Church and Patrick Rode, morocco dressers - 13 Apr. 1831 [154]

Cunningham, Michael, labourer, subj. of G.B.; rec. by Paul Haly, labourer, and Martin Waters - 14 Apr. 1831 [155]

McGowan, Martin, labourer, subj. of G.B.; rec. by Paul Haly, labourer, and Martin Waters, fruiterer - 14 Apr. 1831 [156]

Raper, Barney, labourer, subj. of G.B.; rec. by Rose Gilmartin and Peter Smith, fruiterer - 14 Apr. 1831 [157]

Murtlend, William, shoemaker, subj. of G.B.; rec. by Daniel Boyd, shoemaker, and Timothy Gorham, grocer - 14 Apr. 1831 [158]

Charlton, William, labourer, subj. of G.B.; rec. by Bartholomew Clinton, fruiterer, and Martin Waters, fruiterer - 14 Apr. 1831 [159]

Etienne, Denis Germain, professor of music, subj. of France; rec. by Francis J. Berier, teacher, and Thomas Gentil, gentleman - 25 Apr. 1831 [160]

Rickers, Hannah, subj. of King of Bavaria; rec. by Ephraim Conrad, printer, and Christopher Goost, grocer - 25 Apr. 1831 [161]

Fontaine, Frances Antoinette (widow of Claudius G. Fontaine), subj. of King of France; rec. by John G. Tazey [?], merchant, and Archibald Moore, merchant - 26 Apr. 1831 [162]

Robinson, Henry G., gilder, subj. of G.B.; rec. by John Rogers, tobacconist, and William Bailey, physician - 18 May 1831 [163]

Peters, James, of Newark, N.J., furniture broker, subj. of G.B.; rec. by John Rogers, tobacconist, and William Bailey, physician - 18 May 1831 [164]

Greer, Joseph, grocer, subj. of G.B.; rec. by and William Shaw, cartman - 7 June 1831 [165]

Taylor, John, mariner, subj. of G.B.; rec. by Richard Robbins, grocer, and George Bass, cartman - 8 June 1831 [166]

Humbert, Charles Henri, watchmaker, subj. of Canton of Neuchatel, Switzerland; rec. by Francis J. Berier, teacher, and Thomas Gentil, gentleman - 15 June 1831 [167]

Divin, John, baker, subj. of G.B.; rec. by Thomas Mooney, clothier, and Thomas Mead, grocer - 11 July 1831 [168]

Christie, Alexander, farmer, subj. of G.B.; rec. by Archibald Davie, gentleman, and Robert McCrea, merchant - 27 July 1831 [169]

Sarony, Adolphus, merchant, subj. of King of Prussia; rec. by Francis J. Berier, teacher, and Thomas Gentil, gentleman - 29 July 1831 [170]

Cohu, William, wooden ware storekeeper, subj. of G.B.; rec. by James Rouget, mariner, and William Ketcham, attorney-at-law - 5 Sept. 1831 [171]

Arnaud, John Lewis, of New Orleans but at present of NYC, a merchant, subj. of King of France; rec. by Peter E. Frevall, broker, and Francis Caille, tinman - 27 Sept. 1831 [172]

De Barcaiztequi, Joseph Michael, merchant, subj. of King of
Spain; rec. by Francis J. Berier, teacher, and Thomas Gentil,
gentleman - 14 Oct. 1831 [173]

Hulsenbeck, Christopher, merchant, subj. of St. Gall in Switzerland; rec. by Francis J. Berier, teacher, and Thomas Gentil,
gentleman - 14 Oct. 1831 [174]

Martin, Margaret (widow of Morris Martin), subj. of G.B.; rec.
by Robert Phillips, constable, and James Scott - 29 Nov. 1831
[175]

Uban, John, rigger and stevedore, subj. of King of Prussia; rec.
by Daniel Ley and Eliza Sassenberg - 5 Dec. 1831 [176]

Lacoste, Anne Mary (widow of John Peter Lacoste), subj. of King
of France; rec. by Pierre Maury, grocer, and Antoine Bouyee,
umbrella manufacturer - 20 Dec. 1831 [177]

Baxter, John Henry, subj. of Prince of Hesse Cassel; rec. by
Jeremiah Bennett and Lucas Toumine - 10 Jan. 1832 [178]

Marshall, Robert, gas fitter, subj. of G.B.; rec. by Alexander
Marshall, engineer, and James Witherspoon, comb manufacturer
- 9 Mar. 1832 [179]

Gledhill, William, dyer, subj. of G.B.; rec. by John Barrow,
merchant, and Lawrence Barrow - 21 Mar. 1832 [180]

Wiseman, James, of Conn., shoemaker, subj. of G.B.; rec. by
Timothy W. Van Derbilt, shoedealer, and Daniel Allen, shoedealer - 26 Mar. 1832 [181]

Judah, Elizabeth (widow of Benjamin J. Judah), subj. of G.B.;
rec. by Cary Judah, merchant, and Samuel B.H. Judah, counsellor-at-law - 27 Mar. 1832 [182]

Boyle, Michael, pedlar, subj. of G.B.; rec. by Thomas Boyle,
dealer, and Thomas McSurley, weaver - 9 Apr. 1832 [183]

Reed, Thor, labourer, subj. of King of Debmark; rec. by George
Higday and James H. Brizier - 10 Apr. 1832 [184]

McMurtrie, William, subj. of G.B.; rec. by Robert Ferguson and
William Elder, grocer - 11 Apr. 1832 [185]

Currie, Michael, subj. of G.B.; rec. by William Currie and Martin Waters, grocer - 12 Apr. 1832 [186]

Hunt, Joseph, subj. of G.B.; rec. by James Finn, constable, and
William McDonnell - 12 Apr. 1832 [187]

Uban, George, rigger, subj. of King of Prussia; rec. by Christian Peterson, rigger, and Nelson Berry, rigger - 24 Apr.
1832 [188]

Cochrane, James, engineer, subj. of G.B.; rec. by Thomas Cochran and William Thompson, silversmith - 12 May 1832 [189]

Duffy, Patrick, subj. of G.B.; rec. by Patrick Morris and William Dougherty - 16 May 1832 [190]

Davis, Solomon, subj. of G.B.; rec. by Frederic Seely and Michael Davis - 11 June 1832 [191]

Blight, John, subj. of G.B.; rec. by Samuel G. City, in the U.S.
service, and Robert Petten, of Brooklyn - 16 June 1832 [192]

City, Samuel G., subj. of G.B.; rec. by John Blight and Robert
Petten, of Brooklyn - 16 June 1832 [193]

Smith, Thomas, subj. of G.B.; rec. by Elizabeth Malone and James
G. Finn - 18 June 1832 [194]

Butler, Francis, mariner, subj. of G.B.; rec. by Edward Smith
and Samuel Thompson - 25 Sept. 1832 [195]

Bathgate, Carles, subj. of G.B.; rec. by William Elder, grocer, and William Curr, gardner - 6 Oct. 1832 [196]

Morison, James, Sr., of Haesemus, N.J., subj. of G.B.; rec. by James Thorburn, of NYC, and Andrew Anderson, of Haesemus - 10 Oct. 1832 [197]

Partridge, William, subj. of G.B.; rec. by Stephen Dando and Wood Gibbs - 20 Oct. 1832 [198]

Armstrong, Matthew, subj. of G.B.; rec. by Andrew Bleakley and Mark Moore - 1 Nov. 1832 [199]

Andrews, John, subj. of G.B.; rec. by Andrew Bleakley and James Camerson - 2 Nov. 1832 [200]

Hanna, Matthew, subj. of G.B.; rec. by Adam Patterson and Peter Booth - 2 Nov. 1832 [201]

Hall, William, subj. of G.B.; rec. by William Hall, Jr., and Daniel E. Tylee - 2 Nov. 1832 [202]

Robertson, James, subj. of G.B.; rec. by Thomas Cochran and William Elder - 3 Nov. 1832 [203]

Cochran, Nathan, subj. of G.B.; rec. by Thomas Cochran and William Elder - 3 Nov. 1832 [204]

Sylvester, Christian, subj. of King of Holland; rec. by John H. King and William Cook - 3 Nov. 1832 [205]

Lucky, Theophilus, subj. of G.B.; rec. by Matthew Armstrong and Robert Morris - 3 Nov. 1832 [206]

Stephens, Henry, subj. of G.B.; rec. by James B. Patterson and Robert Breese - 3 Nov. 1832 [207]

McGraw, Michael, subj. of G.B.; rec. by James McAndrew and Martin Waters - 5 Nov. 1832 [208]

McCall, George, subj. of G.B.; rec. by James Mechan and Daniel Green - 5 Nov. 1832 [209]

Lewis, Alexander, subj. of G.B.; rec. by James Addamson and Henry Addamson - 5 Nov. 1832 [210]

Argall, William, subj. of G.B.; rec. by Henry Johnson and David Argall - 6 Nov. 1832 [211]

Bartram, Andrew, subj. of G.B.; rec. by John Pernie and Joel G. Clayton - 6 Nov. 1832 [212]

Kent, John D., subj. of G.B.; rec. by Cornelius Schenck and Hugh Duggan - 6 Nov. 1832 [213]

Sadlo, Samuel, subject of King of the United [Provinces]; rec. by Alexander Ritchie and Robert Smith - 6 Nov. 1832 [214]

McCausland, James, Sr., subj. of G.B.; rec. by James McCausland, Jr., and William McCartney - 7 Nov. 1832 [215]

Machrie, James, subj. of G.B.; rec. by James Seuguien - 7 Nov. 1832 [216]

Taaffe, James, subj. of G.B.; rec. by Thomas M. Collins and William Kerr - 7 Nov. 1832 [217]

Smith, John, subj. of King of the United [Provinces]; rec. by Stephen Conover and Martin Waters - 7 Nov. 1832 [218]

Cowan, George, subj. of G.B.; rec. by Albert Wannenberg and Charles W. Reinold - 13 Nov. 1832 [219]

Carter, Joseph, subj. of G.B.; rec. by Elizabeth Jolly and Thomas Carter - 13 Dec. 1832 [220]

Smith, Isaac, subj. of G.B.; rec. by Charles Smith and Thomas Beadle/Bedle - 21 Dec. 1832 [221]

Halsted, Ann B., subj. of G.B.; rec. by Smith Barker and Edward
   Hilton - 24 Dec. 1832 [222]

Brown, Thomas, subj. of G.B.; rec. by John Honeywell and John
   V. Tilyou/Tillou - 5 Jan. 1833 [223]

Martin, Narciso de Francisco, subj. of Republic of Columbia;
   rec. by Francis J. Berier, teacher, and Thomas Gentil, gentleman - 23 Jan. 1833 [224]

Hays, Jane (wife of Thomas Hays), subj. of G.B.; rec. by James
   Shaw and John Wintringham - 25 Jan. 1833 [225]

Hilton, John, subj. of G.B.; rec. by William Hilton and Joseph
   G. Durell - 8 Feb. 1833 [226]

Hoyt, Azor, subj. of G.B.; rec. by John Hilton - item incomplete and crossed out [227]

Caffry, Patrick, subj. of G.B.; rec. by Elias Dixon and Samuel
   Dixon - 23 Mar. 1833 [228]

Ureck, John, subj. of Canton Argau, Switzerland; rec. by Gottlieb Apffelbach, baker, and John F. Wolf - 27 Mar. 1833 [229]

Smart, Joseph, subj. of G.B.; rec. by John Shannon and Daniel
   Comstock - 8 Apr. 1833 [230]

Price, Ellis, subj. of G.B.; rec. by Christian Covenhowen - 11
   Apr. 1833 [231]

Davis, Aaron, subj. of G.B.; rec. by Isaac Kipp and John Nixon
   - 6 May 1833 [232]

Swanton, Ann (wife of Robert Swanton, attorney and counsellor-
   at-law), subj. of G.B.; rec. by William Sampson, Esq., counsellor-at-law, and Henry Eagle, gentleman - 8 June 1833 [233]

Pirsson, William, subj. of G.B.; rec. by Jeremiah Cooper and
   Alexander F. Pirsson - 12 July 1833 [234]

Dick, James, subj. of G.B.; rec. by William Curr and William
   Elder, grocer - 12 Sept. 1833 [235]

Murphy, Michael, subj. of G.B.; rec. by Timothy Desmond, labourer, and John Crow - 20 Sept. 1833 [236]

Simon, Nicholas, subj. of G.B.; rec. by William Cohn and Henry
   Querepel [clerk wrote "Queripen"] - 18 Oct. 1833 [237]

De Pedro, Joseph, subj. of King of Portugal; rec. by Samuel T.
   Hildreth and Michael C. Wiggins - 21 Oct. 1833 [238]

Hanlin, Catharine, subj. of G.B.; rec. by Mary Gillen and Matthew Meghan, labourer - 4 Nov. 1833 [239]

Ottignon, Catherine, widow, subj. of G.B.; rec. by Ann Martinot
   and William Barnes, Sr. - 24 Dec. 1833 [240]

Gillender, Ann (wife of James Gillender), subj. of City of Hamburgh; rec. by James Gillender, gentleman, and Ann King (wife
   of Aaron O. King) - 27 Dec. 1833 [241]

Christman, Daniel William, subj. of King of Prussia; rec. by
   John Good, baker, and Charles G. Christman - 15 Jan. 1834
   [242]

Baggot, Louis, subj. of King of France; rec. by John B. Grivet,
   confectioner, and Francis Cook, victualler - 16 Jan. 1834 [243]

Price, Constantine (alias John Price), subj. of King of France;
   rec. by Richard Blanchan, rigger and stevedore, and John Jacobs
   - 17 Mar. 1834 [244]

Cascaden, William, subj. of G.B.; rec. by Joshua S. Place, baker,
   and Thomas Cooper, baker - 20 Mar. 1834 [245]

Guischard, Henry, subj. of King of France; rec. by Elijah Y.
Pinckney, counsellor-at-law, and Louis Benoit - 31 Mar. 1834
[246]

Rosenquest, John, subj. of King of Sweden; rec. by John Jacobs
and Lawrence Green - 2 Apr. 1834 [247]

Witherspoon, James, subj. of G.B.; rec. by John Hagadorn and
Elias O. Taylor - 2 Apr. 1834 [248]

Myers, Cornelius, subj. of King of Denmark; rec. by Constantine
Price and Richard Totten - 3 Apr. 1834 [249]

Walsh, William H., subj. of G.B.; rec. by Jacob Van Winkle and
Lawrence Lavin - 3 Apr. 1834 [250]

Elgren, Alexander, subj. of King of Sweden; rec. by Michael
Emanuel, grocer, and William Rhodes, a marshal of NYC - 3
Apr. 1834 [251]

Clark, Joseph, subj. of G.B.; rec. by Jannet Clark, widow, and
Cornelius C. Jacobus - 4 Apr. 1834 [252]

Jamieson, William, subj. of G.B.; rec. by John McIntire and
James Michael - 4 Apr. 1834 [253]

Montgomery, Alexander, subj. of G.B.; rec. by Basel Dykes and
William Elder, grocer - 5 Apr. 1834 [254]

Mathews, Samuel, subj. of G.B.; rec. by Moses C. Humphreys and
James Ballagh, grocer - 5 Apr. 1834 [255]

Dobbs, Ambrose; rec. by Thomas Dobbs and Jacob F. Hagadorn - 8
Apr. 1834 [256]

Book 4

Caldwell, Andrew, baker, subj. of G.B.; rec. by William Rider
grocer - 4 Nov. 1829 [1]

Rourke, Thomas, grocer, subj. of G.B.; rec. by Daniel Rourke,
grocer - 4 Nov. 1829 [2]

Foley, John, labourer, subj. of G.B.; rec. by Stephen McInroy,
cartman - 10 Nov. 1829 [3]

Frugoni, Matthew, confectioner, subj. of King of Sardinia; rec.
by Charles Del Vecchio, merchant - 12 Nov. 1829 [4]

Birmingham, Michael, labourer, subj. of G.B.; rec. by Walter F.
Osgood, attorney-at-law - 12 Nov. 1829 [5]

Holden, John, of Montgomery, Orange Co., miller, subj. of G.B.;
rec. by William Walsh, malster - 14 Nov. 1829 [6]

McKenny, Patrick, coachman, subj. of G.B.; rec. by Mary Mc Gin-
nis - 26 Nov. 1829 [7]

Mullender, Samuel, mariner, subj. of G.B.; rec. by James Doran,
tavern-keeper - 30 Nov. 1829 [8]

Antonio, Joseph, boarding house keeper, subj. of King of Portugal; rec. by Henry Buffy, waiter - 6 Feb. 1830 [9]

Murray, James, carpenter, subj. of G.B.; rec. by Henry McCaddin,
undertaker - 4 Nov. 1829 [10]

Thomas, John, Jr., tanner, subj. of G.B.; rec. by John Thomas,
shipbuilder - 27 Nov. 1829 [11]

Wood, George, butcher, subj. of G.B.; rec. by George M. Hartell,
butcher - 12 Dec. 1829 [12]

Schonher, Henry, cartman, subj. of G.B.; rec. by George D.
Schonher, cabinetmaker - 8 Jan. 1830 [13]

Hoffman, John, confectioner, subj. of King of Wirtemberg; rec.
by Michael Boyer, tavern-keeper - 11 Jan. 1830 [14]

Grousset, Alexandre Eugene, merchant, subj. of King of France;
rec. by Francis J. Berier, teacher - 20 Jan. 1830 [15]_

Treacy, Patrick, coachdriver, subj. of G.B.; rec. by James Morris, labourer - 20 Jan. 1830 [16]

Pierson, John, mariner, subj. of G.B.; rec. by Alexander McCracken, cooper - 4 Feb. 1830 [17]

D'Ozeville, Lewis, merchant, subj. of King of France; rec. by
Francis J. Berier, teacher - 13 Feb. 1830 [18]

Redmond, Charles F., seaman, subj. of G.B.; rec. by Charles
Rourke, seaman - 18 Feb. 1830 [19]

Brodie, James, slater, subj. of G.B.; rec. by John Brodie, slater - 20 Feb. 1830 [20]

O'Donnell, John, cordwainer, subj. of G.B.; rec. by John Bates,
cordwainer - 23 Feb. 1830 [21]

Brady, Edward, cartman, subj. of G.B.; rec. by John Martin, cartman - 24 Feb. 1830 [22]

McIntyre, James, labourer, subj. of G.B.; rec. by John Boyd,
labourer - 2 Mar. 1830 [23]

Rouhier, Alphonse, merchant, subj. of King of France; rec. by
Francis J. Berier, teacher - 13 Mar. 1830 [23A]

Alexander, William S., accountant, subj. of G.B.; rec. by John
Alexander, merchant - 31 Mar. 1830 [24]

Kirk, William, rigger, subj. of G.B.; rec. by John Killings-
worth, rigger - 8 Apr. [25]

McCoy, William, tailor, subj. of G.B.; rec. by Walter F. Osgood,
attorney-at-law - 5 Apr. 1830 [26]

McPeke, John, weaver, subj. of G.B.; rec. by Walter F. Osgood,
attorney-at-law - 7 Apr. 1830 [27]

Fenwick, John, grocer, subj. of G.B.; rec. by James Inness - 19
Apr. 1830 [28]

Freeman, William Y., mariner, subj. of G.B.; rec. by William
Booth, mariner - 24 Apr. 1830 [29]

Thompson, James, confectioner, subj. of G.B.; rec. by Thomas
Thompson, of "Suskeamea" Co., Pa., farmer - 1 May 1830 [30]

Duggan, Michael, of Flushing, Queens Co., labourer, subj. of
G.B.; rec. by John Desmond, labourer - 3 May 1830 [31]

Colgan, Owen, tailor, subj. of G.B.; rec. by Daniel Cramsey, upholsterer - 5 May 1830 [32]

Dawson, Thomas C., accountant, subj. of G.B.; rec. by John Carney, grocer - 7 May 1830 [33]

Collins, William, grocer, subj. of G.B.; rec. by James Ennis,
marshal - 8 May 1830 [34]

Shiells, James, tinman, subj. of G.B.; rec. by John Mount,
gentleman - 8 May 1830 [35]

Jolly, Walter, farmer, subj. of G.B.; rec. by Walter F. Osgood,
attorney-at-law - 11 May 1830 [36]

Weldon, Thomas, of Jersey City, N.J., subj. of G.B.; rec. by
Charles Martin, of Jersey City - 13 May 1830 [37]

Solomon, Solomon B., clothing store keeper, subj. of King of the
Netherlands; rec. by Jacob Levy, dealer - 15 May 1830 [38]

Dougherty, John, labourer, subj. of G.B.; rec. by Daniel Everett, shoemaker - 19 May 1830 [39]

Fennell, Arthur, farmer, subj. of G.B.; rec. by Walter F. Osgood, Counselor-at-law - 20 May 1830 [40]

De la Quintana, Manuel, merchant, subj. of King of Spain; rec. by Francis J. Berier, teacher - 24 May 1830 [41]

De la Quintana, Pedro, merchant, subj. of King of Spain; rec. by Francis J. Berier, teacher - 24 May 1830 [42]

Riba, Jacinto, merchant, subj. of King of Spain; rec. by Francis J. Berier, teacher - 25 May 1830 [43]

Field, Patrick, farmer, subj. of G.B.; rec. by Walter F. Osgood, counselor-at-law - 27 May 1830 [44]

Martin, Thomas, labourer, subj. of G.B.; rec. by John Martin, cartman - 29 May 1830 [45]

Jolly, Thomas, milkman, subj. of G.B.; rec. by Pattison Jolly, grocer - 2 June 1830 [46]

Jacobs, William H., tavern-keeper, subj. of G.B.; rec. by George Cockman, jeweller - 2 June 1830 [47]

Braden, John, coachmaker, subj. of G.B.; rec. by Thomas Murray, cooper - 2 June 1830 [48]

Parker, William, cooper, subj. of G.B.; rec. by Stephen Collins, saddler - 7 June 1830 [49]

Oram, William, grocer, subj. of G.B.; rec. by Samuel Dennison, rigger - 8 June 1830 [50]

Giles, Robert, labourer, subj. of G.B.; rec. by John Giles, fruiterer - 9 June 1830 [51]

Tomey, John, farmer, subj. of G.B.; rec. by W.F. Osgood, attorney-at-law - 11 June 1830 [52]

Kelly, Arthur, farmer, subj. of G.B.; rec. by Walter F. Osgood, attorney-at-law - 11 June 1830 [53]

Gray, Henry, cartman, subj. of G.B.; rec. by Matthew Rowe - 14 June 1830 [54]

Koch [clerk wrote "Proch"], Ludwig, merchant, subj. of King of Prussia; rec. by Francis J. Berier. teacher - 16 June 1830 [55]

McMenomin, Michael, tavern-keeper, subj. of G.B.; rec. by Elizabeth McMenomin - 19 June 1830 [56]

O'Donnell, Jeremiah, milkman, subj. of G.B.; rec. by Michael Connolly, gardner - 24 June 1830 [57]

Stainton, William, seaman, subj. of G.B.; rec. by John G. Spicer, of town of Preston, New London Co., Conn., mariner - 29 June 1830 [58]

McGivney, Thomas, farmer, subj. of G.B.; rec. by Walter F. Osgood, attorney-at-law - 6 July 1830 [59]

Finingan, Thomas, labourer, subj. of G.B.; rec. by Daniel Everett, shoemaker - 13 July 1830 [60]

Braden, John, stone cutter, subj. of G.B.; rec. by Henry Fulton, stone cutter - 14 July 1830 [61]

Baird, Hugh, clerk, subj. of G.B.; rec. by Edward Silk, weaver - 16 July 1830 [62]

Tullock, Alexander, plane maker, subj. of G.B.; rec. by William H. Jacobs, patee [?] store keeper - 21 July 1830 [63]

Gandolfo, Joseph, merchant, subj. of King of Sardinia; rec. by
  Charles Delvecchio, merchant - 28 July 1830 [64]

Kleffler, John Michael, merchant, subj. of King of Bavaria; rec.
  by Charles Delvecchio, merchant - 4 Aug. 1830; on 27 June 1832
  Francis Blondeau, merchant, that John Michael Kleffler was
  naturalized as Michael Kleffler [65]

Saret, John B., merchant, subj. of King of France; rec. by John
  Millo, labourer - 9 Aug. 1830 [66]

McColgan, James, farmer, subj. of G.B.; rec. by Walter F. Osgood, attorney-at-law - 9 Aug. 1830 [67]

Wileman, William N.C., mariner, subj. of G.B.; rec. by Horatio
  Colter, cabinetmaker - 12 Aug. 1830 [68]

Crassen, Joaquin M., merchant, subj. of King of Spain; rec. by
  Charles Delvecchio, merchant - 12 Aug. 1830 [69]

Cormier, Lewis, mariner, subj. of King of France; rec. by Angela
  Heyer, spinster - 14 Aug. 1830 [70]

Scott, John, labourer, subj. of G.B.; rec. by Samuel Storer,
  shipwright - 16 Aug. 1830 [71]

Tobias, Tobias J., merchant, subj. of G.B.; rec. by Samuel M.
  Judah, merchant - 19 Aug. 1830 [72]

Garner, Thomas, Jr., umbrella manufacturer, subj. of G.B.; rec.
  by Thomas Garner, tavern-keeper - 24 Aug. 1830 [73]

Garner, Henry, merchant, subj. of G.B.; rec. by Thomas Garner,
  tavern-keeper - 24 Aug. 1830 [74]

Nixon, John B., merchant, at present in NYC but inhabitant of
  Mobile, Alabama, subj. of G.B.; rec. by James Flanagan, assis-
  tant justice of the 12th Ward - 26 Aug. 1830 [75]

Dupré, Julius A., merchant, subj. of King of France; rec. by
  Francis J. Berier, teacher - 4 Sept. 1830 [76]

Cook, John, grocer, subj. of G.B.; rec. by Neil Morrison, grocer
  - 11 Sept. 1830 [77]

Beascoecher, Francis, merchant, subj. of Republic of Mexico; rec.
  by Charles Delvecchio, merchant - 14 Sept. 1830 [78]

Michaletti, Luigi, storekeeper, subj. of King of Naples; rec. by
  Charles Delvecchio, merchant - 14 Sept. 1830 [79]

Raberg, Charles Henry, accountant, subj. of King of the Netherlands; rec. by Anthony Chardon, merchant - 28 Sept. 1830 [80]

Thouvenin, John C., merchant, subj. of King of France; rec. by
  Francis J. Berier, teacher - 29 Sept. 1830 [81]

Portal, John A., merchant, subj. of King of Spain; rec. by Charles Delvecchio, merchant - 7 Oct. 1830 [82]

Clark, James, labourer, subj. of G.B.; rec. by Daniel Everitt,
  shoemaker - 9 Oct. 1830 [83]

Campbell, John T., moulder, of Newark, Essex Co., N.J., subj. of
  G.B.; rec. by Thomas Campbell, tavern-keeper - 12 Oct. 1830
  [84]

Donnelly, Charles, coachman, subj. of G.B.; rec. by Walter F.
  Osgood, attorney-at-law - 11 Dec. [error for Oct.?] 1830 [85]

Swedman, George Douglas, mariner, subj. of King of Sweden and
  Norway; rec. by Charles Harrington, mariner - 12 Oct. 1830
  [85A]

Perrot, Anthony Savimin, merchant, subj. of King of France; rec.
  by Francis J. Berier, teacher - 15 Oct. 1830 [86]

Gisbert, Augustus, mariner, subj. of King of France; rec. by
Francis J. Berier, teacher - 16 Oct. 1830 [87]

Agal, William Marius, mariner, subj. of King of Sardinia; rec.
by Suchet Mauran, of Rhode Island, mariner - 19 Oct. 1830 [88]

Ashton, Emanuel, of town of Warwasing, Ulster Co., farmer, subj.
of G.B.; rec. by Morris Ashton, hack owner - 20 Oct. 1830 [89]

Doyle, Anna (wife of Patrick Doyle), subj. of G.B.; rec. by Susan Drake (wife of Aaron Drake) - 20 Oct. 1830 [90]

Eyguen, Gervaise, cartman, subj. of King of France; rec. by Joseph Le Gal, grocer - 21 Oct. 1830 [91]

Fetnam, Robert, mariner, subj. of G.B.; rec. by Elisha Sawyer,
at present of NYC, mariner - 22 Oct. 1830 [92]

McAnally, Daniel, weaver, subj. of G.B.; rec. by Walter F. Osgood, attorney-at-law - 26 Oct. 1830 [93]

Williams, Thomas, mariner, subj. of G.B.; rec. by Stafford
Brownell, of town of Rochester, Plymouth Co., Mass., mariner
- 29 Oct. 1830 [94]

Glass, John, shoemaker, subj. of G.B.; rec. by James Glass, shoemaker - 2 Nov. 1830 [95]

Kervick, John, stone cutter, subj. of G.B.; rec. by James Cahill,
stone cutter - 3 Nov. 1830 [96]

Bustamante, Jose, merchant, subj. of King of Spain; rec. by
Francis J. Berier, teacher - 10 Nov. 1830 [97]

Corr, David, grocer, subj. of G.B.; rec. by Walter F. Osgood,
attorney-at-law - 10 Nov. 1830 [98]

Curtis, Richard, at present of NYC, mariner, subj. of G.B.; rec.
by James McAllister, at present of NYC, mariner - 10 Nov. 1830
[99]

McCleary, Archibald, servant, subj. of G.B.; rec. by Walter F.
Osgood, attorney-at-law - 22 Nov. 1830 [100]

Althouse, Jacob, baker, subj. of King of Prussia; rec. by Jacob
Escher, brass founder - 29 Nov. 1830 [101]

Lister, Joseph, accountant, subj. of G.B.; rec. by Daniel Dieterich, currier - 4 Dec. 1830 [102]

Goll, George, Frederic, farmer, subj. of King of France; rec.
by Francis J. Berier, teacher - 18 Dec. 1830 [103]

Parry, William Henry, steam engineer, subj. of G.B.; rec. by
Joseph Morgan, carpenter - 22 Dec. 1830 [104]

Shaw, Joseph, butcher, subj. of G.B.; rec. by William C. Shaw,
cartman - 7 Jan. 1831 [105]

Hasch, Peter, at present of NYC, mariner, subj. of City of Hamburgh; rec. by Elisha Sawyer, of Brooklyn, mariner - 8 Jan.
1831 [106]

Gaudard, John Francis Rodolphus, merchant, subj. of King of
France; rec. by Francis J. Berier, teacher - 10 Jan. 1831 [107]

Whalley, James, silversmith, subj. of G.B.; rec. by Ann Whalley
- 11 Jan. 1831 [108]

Leconte, Alphonso Michael, merchant, subj. of King of France;
rec. by Francis J. Berier, teacher - 20 Jan. 1831 [109]

Gleeson, Michael, accountant, subj. of G.B.; rec. by John Gleeson, accountant - 5 Feb. 1831 [110]

Riley, Edward Cat, professor of music, subj. of G.B.; rec. by
Joseph Jacobson, accountant - 17 Feb. 1831 [111]

Riley, Henry, music instrument maker, subj. of G.B.; rec. by
    Joseph Jacobson, accountant - 17 Feb. 1831 [112]

Leakey, Alexander, blacksmith, subj. of G.B.; rec. by John Mc
    Gowan, a marshal of NYC - 24 Feb. 1831 [113]

Ryan, John, farmer, subj. of G.B.; rec. by Walter F. Osgood,
    attorney-at-law - 1 Mar. 1831 [114]

Pichet, Claude, merchant, subj. of King of France; rec. by Peter
    Johnson, boarding house keeper - 2 Mar. 1831 [115]

Gilmore, George, cartman, subj. of G.B.; rec. by Alva Gifford,
    grocer - 7 Mar. 1831 [116]

Carrull, John Frederick, seaman, subj. of City of Hamburgh; rec.
    by Samuel B. Rudolph, ship-carpenter - 10 Mar. 1831 [117]

DeLacey, Matthew P., house-carpenter, subj. of G.B.; rec. by
    James Dempsey, carpenter - 14 Mar. 1831 [118]

Morlot, Robert, merchant, subj. of King of France; rec. by Fran-
    cis J. Berier, teacher - 16 Mar. 1831 [119]

Schultz, Daniel John, chemist, subj. of King of Hanover; rec. by
    Adriel Pease, chemist - 16 Mar. 1831 [120]

Darramon, James, merchant, subj. of King of France; rec. by John
    Richard, merchant - 21 Mar. 1831 [121]

Smith, Henry K., student-at-law, subj. of King of Denmark; rec.
    by Edmund D. Barry, clergyman - 23 Mar. 1831 [122]

Richards, John Henry, mariner, subj. of King of Prussia; rec. by
    John Munson, boarding house keeper - 23 Mar. 1831 [123]

Ridden, Bernard, of Brooklyn, grocer, subj. of G.B.; rec. by
    John Ridden, distiller - 24 Mar. 1831 [124]

Hart, Michael, butcher, subj. of G.B.; rec. by James Ryan, moro-
    cco dresser - 30 Mar. 1831 [125]

Feusier, Joseph, blacksmith, subj. of King of France; rec. by
    Peter Johnson, boarding house keeper - 2 Apr. 1831 [126]

No. 127 is crossed out.

Costa, John B., fruiterer and confectioner, subj. of King of Sar-
    dinia; rec. by Peter Guli, confectioner - 7 Apr. 1831 [128]

Mantona, Bernard, fruiterer, subj. of Emperor of Austria; rec.
    by Laurent Mantona, fruiterer - 9 Apr. 1831 [129]

McGuire, John, labourer, subj. of G.B.; rec. by Stephen McInroy,
    grocer - 11 Apr. 1831 [130]

Wakalin, John, labourer, subj. of G.B.; rec. by James Feely,
    speculator - 12 Apr. 1831 [131]

Davies, Sutherton R., musician, subj. of G.B.; rec. by James Pir-
    ssen, piano forte maker - 12 Apr. 1831 [132]

McKenzie, Allan, gardner, subj. of G.B.; rec. by William Curr,
    gardner - 12 Apr. 1831 [133]

Vaillant, Anthony, tinman, subj. of King of France; rec. by
    Nicholas Decamp, tinman - 12 Apr. 1831 [134]

Rooney, Thomas, coachman, subj. of G.B.; rec. by John Foley,
    labourer - 12 Apr. 1831 [135]

Coyle, Patrick, labourer, subj. of G.B.; rec. by Patrick O'Con-
    nor, baker - 13 Apr. 1831 [136]

Adrian, John, shoemaker, subj. of G.B.; rec. by John Glass, shoe-
    maker - 13 Apr. 1831 [137]

Fearnhead, William, block cutter, subj. of G.B.; rec. by William
Simpson - 13 Apr. 1831 [138]

Keelan, Thomas, hatter, subj. of G.B.; rec. by Thomas Phelan,
hatter - 13 Apr. 1831 [139]

Stoppani, Charles G., gentleman, subj. of King of Sardinia; rec.
by Charles Delvecchio, merchant - 13 Apr. 1831 [140]

Mahony, John, carver, subj. of G.B.; rec. by John Glass, shoemaker - 13 Apr. 1831 [141]

Logan, Francis, ship-carpenter, subj. of G.B.; rec. by Thomas
Logan, mason - 14 Apr. 1831 [142]

Delany, Thomas, grocer, subj. of G.B.; rec. by Walter F. Osgood,
counselor-at-law - 14 Apr. 1831 [143]

Vernon, Robert, brass founder, subj. of G.B.; rec. by James Mc
Farran, cartman - 14 Apr. 1831 [144]

Ross, Samuel, weaver, subj. of G.B.;rec. by John McGee, mason -
14 Apr. 1831 [145]

Frame, Robert, weaver, subj. of G.B.; rec. by John Frame, weaver
- 14 Apr. 1831 [146]

McLeester, John, type founder [trade also given as "cartman"],
subj. of G.B.; rec. by Nicholas Dumond, tavern-keeper - 14
Apr. 1831 [147]

Smith, John, cartman, subj. of G.B.; rec. by William Cunningham,
tavern-keeper - 14 Apr. 1831 [148]

Mulveny, James, painter, subj. of G.B.; rec. by Mary Piggot,
widow - 14 Apr. 1831 [149]

Vidal, Jean Baptiste, glass blower, subj. of King of France; rec.
by William Thompson, glass blower - 16 Apr. 1831 [150]

Delius, Henry, merchant, subj. of City of Bremen; rec. by Francis J. Berier, teacher - 18 Apr. 1831 [151]

Jung, Theobald, merchant, subj. of King of Prussia; rec. by Francis J. Berier, teacher - 18 Apr. 1831 [152]

Hennesy, Patrick, weaver, subj. of G.B.; rec. by Walter F. Osgood, counselor-at-law - 19 Apr. 1831 [153]

Carson, John, labourer, subj. of G.B.; rec. by Daniel Everitt,
shoemaker - 21 Apr. 1831 [154]

Olwell, James, grocer, subj. of G.B.; rec. by Michael Olwell,
labourer - 25 Apr. 1831 [155]

Gray, Thomas, grocer, subj. of G.B.; rec. by William Elder, grocer - 30 Apr. 1831 [156]

Herren, Mary (widow of John Herren), subj. of G.B.; rec. by John
Corgan, grocer - 2 May 1831 [157]

McVaney, John, labourer, subj. of G.B.; rec. by Daniel Everett,
shoemaker - 25 May 1831 [158]

Healy, Patrick, ship chandler storekeeper, subj. of G.B.; rec.
by Luke Feeny, accountant - 3 May 1831 [159]

Mathyas, Joseph, merchant, subj. of Emperor of Brazil; rec. by
Charles Delvecchio, merchant - 5 May 1831 [160]

Collings, Samuel R., seaman, subj. of G.B.; rec. by John Munson,
boarding house keeper - 7 May 1831 [161]

Escher, George, baker, subj. of King of Saxony; rec. by George
Wolff, merchant - 9 May 1831 [162]

Shea, Bartholomew, grocer, subj. of G.B.; rec. by Walter F. Osgood, counselor-at-law - 13 May 1831 [163]

Magnin, John, watchmaker, subject of Geneva, Switzerland; rec.
by Nicholas Casthelas, merchant - 13 May 1831 [164]

Walsh, John, boarding house keeper, subj. of G.B.; rec. by Walter F. Osgood, counselor-at-law - 14 May 1831 [165]

Langdon, James, grocer, subj. of G.B.; rec. by Michael Hanlon,
patee [?] -26 May 1831 [166]

Logan, William, shoemaker, subj. of G.B.; rec. by William Orr,
grocer - 16 May 1831 [167]

Mangles, Fabian, mariner, subj. of King of Hanover; rec. by Frederick Friend, brass founder, and John Brommer, blacksmith -
17 May 1831 [168]

O'Sullivan, Dennis, of Dutchess Co., clothier, subj. of G.B.;
rec. by Jeremiah O'Sullivan, locksmith - 18 May 1831 [169]

Corcoran, Thomas, labourer, subj. of G.B.; rec. by Walter F. Osgood, sounselor-at-law - 19 May 1831 [170]

Truden, Patrick, gardner, subj. of G.B.; rec. by William Wesland,
porter house keeper - 20 May 1831 [171]

O'Meara, Jeremiah, accountant, subj. of G.B.; rec. by James O'
Meara, cordwainer - 20 May 1831 [172]

Powers, Patrick, grocer, subj. of G.B.; rec. by Walter F. Osgood,
counselor-at-law - 23 May 1831 [173]

O'Connor, Jeremiah, porter, subj. of G.B.; rec. by Walter F. Osgood, counselor-at-law - 23 May 1831 [174]

Home, Francis, merchant, subj. of G.B.; rec. by William H. Scrym-
ser, accountant - 26 May 1831 [175]

McKenna, Vincent, labourer, subj. of G.B.; rec. by Patrick Truden, gardner - 30 May 1831 [176]

Richard, John F., grocer, subj. of King of France; rec. by John
R. Weldin, sausage-maker - 31 May 1831 [177]

McCaddin, Henry, cabinetmaker, subj. of G.B.; rec. by Catherine
Murray - 10 June 1831 [178]

Murray, James, porter, subj. of G.B.; rec. by Owen Murray, labourer - 27 June 1831 [179]

Murray, Michael, cabinetmaker, subj. of G.B.; rec. by Owen Murray, labourer - 27 June 1831 [180]

Taylor, Robert B., of Poughkeepsie, Dutchess Co., student-at-law,
subj. of G.B.; rec. by Philip S. Crooke, attorney-at-law - 30
June 1831 [181]

Mulson, Edward, of Utica, N.Y., labourer, subj. of G.B.; rec. by
Samuel Storer [clerk wrote "Story"], shipwright - 6 July 1831
[182]

Tone, Richard, gardner, subj. of G.B.; rec. by Thomas Stevens,
grocer - 11 July 1831 [183]

184 is blank.

Brodie, John, Jr., slater, subj. of G.B.; rec. by James Brodie,
slater - 14 July 1831 [185]

Ferguson, Robert, copper plate printer, subj. of G.B.; rec. by
William Elder, grocer - 15 Aug. 1831 [186]

Kehoe, Michael, labourer, subj. of G.B.; rec. by Samuel Storer,
shipwright - 19 Aug. 1831 [187]

Gillespie, William J., bookseller, subj. of G.B.; rec. by Wm.
Wood, mariner - 30 Aug. 1831 [188]

Macken, James, painter, subj. of G.B.; rec. by Ann Macken - 2
Sept. 1831 [189]

Bunel, Damas Napoleon, cook, subj. of France; rec. by Peter Johnson, boarding house keeper - 12 Sept. 1831 [190]

Coghlan, John, weigher, subj. of G.B.; rec. by Catherine Coghlan
- 14 Sept. 1831 [191]

Scott, John, mariner, subj. of G.B.; rec. by Thomas Taylor, rigger - 15 Sept. 1831 [192]

McGovern, Hugh, coachman, subj. of G.B.; rec. by Mary McGovern,
widow - 21 Sept. 1831 [193]

McFarland, Bernard, farmer, subj. of G.B.;rec. by Walter F. Osgood, counselor-at-law - 1 Oct. 1831 [194]

Gandolfo, Jerolamo, fruiterer and confectioner, subj. of King of
Sardinia; rec. by John Baptiste Coslo [?], confectioner - 7
Oct. 1831 [195]

McKenna, James, refiner of liquors, subj. of G.B.; rec. by
Michael O'Hagan, tailor - 10 Oct. 1831 [196]

Miege, Pierre Auguste, merchant, subj. of King of France; rec. by
Francis J. Berier, teacher - 13 Oct. 1831 [197]

Hoodless, William R., mariner, subj. of G.B.; rec. by William
Britton, mariner - 13 Oct. 1831 [198]

Forest, Peter A., mariner, subj. of King of France; rec. by Augustus Raymond, boot and shoe store keeper - 13 Oct. 1831 [188]

Trumpy, John Jacob, ship-carpenter, subj. of King of Sweden; rec.
by Jacob S. Bogert, printer - 14 Oct. 1831 [200]

Tracy, Patrick, cartman, subj. of G.B.; rec. by Margaret Tracy -
28 Oct. 1831 [201]

Giraud, Francis Theodore, merchant, subj. of King of France; rec.
by Francis J. Berier, teacher - 31 Oct. 1831 [202]

Robert, William, of Dutchess Co., hairdresser, subj. of G.B.; rec.
by Joseph Gunn, of Dutchess Co., inspector - 4 Nov. 1831 [203]

Salomon, Jonas, sexton, subj. of King of Holland; rec. by Moses
Spyers, merchant - 7 Nov. 1831 [204]

Londe, Adolphe, mariner, subj. of King of France; rec. by Henry
H. Stevens, merchant - 9 Nov. 1831 [205]

Reimer, Fridrick, mariner, subj. of King of Denmark; rec. by En-
sign Studley, mariner - 9 Nov. 1831 [206]

McComb, Alexander, type caster, subj. of G.B.; rec. by Thomas Mc
Comb, tailor - 15 Nov. 1831 [207]

Scouller, John, butcher, subj. of G.B.; rec. by William Curr,
gardner - 16 Nov. 1831 [208]

Aitken, Alexander, grocer, subj. of G.B.; rec. by William Curr,
gardner - 16 Nov. 1831 [209]

Testard, Ernest, merchant, subj. of King of France; rec. by Francis J. Berier, teacher - 19 Nov. 1831 [210]

Faherty, Patrick, teamster, subj. of G.B.; rec. by Thomas Stephens, grocer - 21 Nov. 1831 [211]

Ashton, James, of Ulster Co., farmer, subj. of G.B.; rec. by Robert Jones, painter - 30 Nov. 1831 [212]

Rush, Patrick, tavern-keeper, subj. of G.B.; rec. by Lawrence
Rush, labourer - 3 Dec. 1831 [213]

Valpey, John, mariner, subj. of G.B.; rec. by Thomas Pierce, mariner - 5 Dec. 1831 [214]

Parsons, Daniel, rigger, subj. of G.B.; rec. by James Cox, grocer - 9 Dec. 1831 [215]

Mieregaes, Otto Heinrich, merchant, subj. of Duke of Oldenburgh; rec. by Francis J. Berier, teacher - 31 Dec. 1831 [216]

Leeper, James, labourer, subj. of G.B.; rec. by William Leeper, labourer - 3 Jan. 1832 [217]

Meyer, Leopolt, subj. of canton of Berne, Switzerland; rec. by Thomas Taylor, rigger - 17 Jan. 1832 [218]

Lühring, Henry, mariner, subj. of Senate of Hamburgh; rec. by John Heeney - 20 Jan. 1832 [219]

Gotthilff, August Philip Jurdes, subj. of City of Lubeck; rec. by Peter Kum - 26 Jan. 1832 [219A]

Tilley, John, shoemaker, subj. of G.B.; rec. by Edward Mills, tailor - 10 Feb. 1832 [220]

Lawrence, Mark, painter, subj. of King of Portugal; rec. by Joseph Deseomas - 15 Feb. 1832 [221]

White, William, carpet weaver, subj. of G.B.; rec. by James White, carpet weaver - 15 Feb. 1832 [222]

Slater, Samuel, cooper, subj. of G.B.; rec. by Adam Gamble, shoemaker - 21 Feb. 1832 [223]

Pinol, Emanuel J., subj. of Govt. of Central America; rec. by Francis J. Berier, teacher - 23 Feb. 1832 [224]

Gafney, Michael, merchant, subj. of G.B.; rec. by John Rider - 29 Feb. 1832 [225]

Malone, John, waiter, subj. of G.B.; rec. by Walter F. Osgood, counselor-at-law - 6 Mar. 1832 [226]

King, John, of Queensburgh, boatman, subj. of G.B.; rec. by John Fyte, furniture merchant - 15 Mar. 1832 [227]

No. 228 is blank.

Pembroke, Nicholas, porter, subj. of G.B.; rec. by Walter F. Osgood, counselor-at-law - 15 Mar. 1832 [229]

Ross, Francis A., rigger and stevedore, subj. of G.B.; rec. by John Ridder, grocer - 21 Mar. 1832 [230]

O'Neill, Hugh, labourer, subj. of G.B.; rec. by Walter F. Osgood, counselor-at-law - 23 Mar. 1832 [231]

Spinola, Francisco, carpenter, subj. of King of Portugal; rec. by James Meldrum, ship-joiner - 24 Mar. 1832 [232]

Willersdorff, Israel, confectioner, subj. of Prince of Hesse Casel; rec. by Peter Willersdorff - 24 Mar. 1832 [233]

Decker, Augustus, mariner, subj. of King of Sweden; rec. by Thomas Taylor, rigger - 31 Mar. 1832 [234]

Roach, James, brass founder, subj. of G.B.; rec. by Adam Gamble, shoemaker - 3 Apr. 1832 [235]

Sandham, Andrew, physician, subj. of G.B.; rec. by George W. Sandham - 9 Apr. 1832 [236]

Hart, Patrick, subj. of G.B.; rec. by Bridget Devine - 10 Apr. 1832 [237]

Lennon, John, subj. of G.B.; rec. by John Teig - 10 Apr. 1832 [238]

Woodhead, John, carpenter, subj. of G.B.; rec. by William Haigh - 10 Apr. 1832 [239]

Megram, Edward, subj. of G.B.; rec. by James Harbinson - 10 Apr.
1832 [240]

Cahill, James, carpenter, subj. of G.B.; rec. by Edward Cahill
- 11 Apr. 1832 [241]

Vol. 5

McGuire, Patrick, mason, subj. of G.B.; decl. of intent 11 Aug.
1827; rec. by William Quin, locksmith - 14 Apr. 1831 [1]

Corry, Patrick, cartman, subj. of G.B.; decl. of intent 4 Nov.
1828; rec. by Michael Flanagan - 14 Apr. 1831 [2]

Masterson, Michael, labourer, subj. of G.B.; decl. of intent 18
June 1825 in Court of Common Pleas in Philadelphia: native of
Ire., age 27; rec. by James Dawson, labourer - 14 Apr. 1831
[3]

McGown, William, milkman, subj. of G.B.; decl. of intent 5 Nov.
1828; rec. by Oliver O'Neil, labourer - 14 Apr. 1831 [4]

O'Mara, Maurice, sawyer, subj. of G.B.; decl. of intent 9 Jan.
1828; rec. by John Blake, sawyer - 14 Apr. 1831 [5]

Turner, William, shoemaker, subj. of G.B.; decl. of intent 3
Oct. 1825; rec. by William Reid, shoe dealer - 14 Apr. 1831
[6]

Jacobs, Angel, watchmaker, subj. of G.B.; decl. of intent 5 May
1824; rec. by Nathaniel T. Weeks, tavern-keeper - 14 Apr. 1834
[7]

Lenox, Anthony, labourer, subj. of G.B.; decl. of intent 6 Dec.
1828; rec. by Samuel Carson, porter - 14 Apr. 1831 [8]

Reid, William, accountant, subj. of G.B.; decl. of intent 21
Oct. 1823; rec. by William Turner, shoemaker - 14 Apr. 1831
[9]

McKinney, Edward, soapboiler, subj. of G.B.; decl. of intent 5
Nov. 1828; rec. by Patrick Sweeny, shoemaker - 14 Apr. 1831
[10]

McGown, Bartly, milkman, subj. of G.B.; decl. of intent 5 Dec.
1828; rec. by Henry Burden, cartman - 14 Apr. 1831 [11]

Kelly, James, cooper, subj. of G.B.; decl. of intent 20 Apr.
1820; rec. by James Caulfield, merchant - 14 Apr. 1831 [12]

Dunn, Bernard, merchant, subj. of G.B.; decl. of intent 4 Dec.
1826; rec. by John P. Gotts - 14 Apr. 1831 [13]

Vidal, John B., glass blower, subj. of King of France; rec. by
William Thompson, glass blower - 16 Apr. 1831 [14]

Delius, Henry, merchant, subj. of City of Bremen; rec. by Francis J. Berier, teacher - 18 Apr. 1831 [15]

Jung, Theobald, merchant, subj. of King of Prussia; rec. by Francis J. Berier, teacher - 18 Apr. 1831 [16]

Kennesy, Patrick, weaver, subj. of G.B.; rec. by Walter F. Osgood, attorney-at-law - 19 Apr. 1831 [17]

Marshall, John, shoemaker, subj. of G.B.; decl. of intent 16
Apr. 1829; rec. by John Simpson, grocer - 19 Apr. 1831 [18]

Boyle, John, labourer, subj. of G.B.; decl. of intent 10 Apr.
1827; rec. by John Donohue, shoemaker - 19 Apr. 1831 [19]

Little, Michael, gutter maker, subj. of G.B.; decl. of intent
18 Nov. 1828; rec. by John Samuel, cabinetmaker - 21 Apr. 1831
[20]

Carson, John, labourer, subj. of G.B.; rec. by Daniel Everitt, shoemaker - 21 Apr. 1831 [21]

Crisfield, John, merchant, subj. of G.B.; decl. of intent 28 Nov. 1825; rec. by Henry Simmons, merchant - 23 Apr. 1831 [22]

Daucé, Benjamin, mariner, subj. of King of France; decl. of intent 29 Aug. 1825; rec. by John F. Rowling, seaman - 25 Apr. 1831 [23]

Olwell, James, grocer, subj. of G.B.; rec. by Michael Olwell, labourer - 25 Apr. 1831 [24]

Gray, Thomas, grocer, subj. of G.B.; rec. by William Elder, grocer - 30 Apr. 1831 [25]

Etienne, Denis Germaine, professor of music, subj. of King of France; rec. by Francis J. Berier, tacher, and Thomas Gentil, gentleman - 25 Apr. 1831 [26]

Richers, Hannah, subj. of King of Prussia; rec. by Ephraim Conrad, printer, and Christopher Goost, grocer - 25 Apr. 1831 [27]

Fontaine, Francis Antoinette, subj. of King of France; rec. by John G. Tardy, merchant, and Archibald D. Moore, merchant - 25 Apr. 1831 [28]

Callaghan, Patrick, coachman, subj. of G.B.; decl. of intent 23 Nov. 1827; rec. by Daniel McCarthy, surgeon - 26 Apr. 1831 [29]

Rooney, Patrick, labourer, subj. of G.B.; decl. of intent 6 Mar. 1826; rec. by Thomas Rooney, coachman - 27 Apr. 1831 [30]

Richers, Henry, late a grocer but now a cartman, subj. of King of Hanover; decl. of intent 21 Apr. 1821; rec. by Henry Volckman, cartman - 27 Apr. 1831 [31]

McKenney, Paul, subj. of G.B.; decl. of intent 6 Oct. 1825; rec. by John Bennett, varnish maker - 29 Apr. 1831 [32]

Gilmore, Francis, carpenter, subj. of G.B.; decl. of intent 3 Nov. 1828; rec. by Patrick Quirk, grocer - 29 Apr. 1831 [33]

Cummings, John, labourer, subj. of G.B.; decl. of intent 9 Jan. 1827; rec. by David O'Hara, cartman - 2 May 1831 [34]

Kinney, John, labourer, subj. of G.B.; decl. of intent 18 Apr. 1827 in Superior Court, Chatham Co., Georgia: born Ire., age 26, embarked 14 Aug. 1822 at Quebec and arrived at Fort Niagara, N.Y., 3 Sept. 1822; arrived Savannah, Ga., 10 Oct. 1826; rec. by Andrew Moore, labourer - 4 May 1831 [35]

Dalton, Richard, gentleman, subj. of G.B.; decl. of intent 21 Apr. 1829; rec. by James Sweeny, tavern-keeper - 5 May 1831 [36]

Corgan, Mary (widow of John Corgan), subj. of G.B.; rec. by John Corgan, grocer - 2 May 1831 [37]

Healy, Patrick, ship chandler, subj. of G.B.; rec. by Luke Feeny, accountant - 3 May 1831 [38]

Mathyas, Joseph, merchant, subj. of Emperor of Brazil; rec. by Charles Delvecchio, merchant - 5 May 1831 [39]

Newton, James S., miniature painter, subj. of G.B.; decl. of intent 18 Aug. 1828; rec. by Humphrey Thacker. gentleman - 6 May 1831 [40]

Daggett, George, carpenter, subj. of G.B.; decl. of intent 3 Nov. 1828; rec. by John Divin, baker - 6 May 1831 [41]

Collings, Samuel R., seaman, subj. of G.B.; rec. by John Munson, boarding house keeper - 7 May 1831 [42]

Bundle 1

Borduzat, Anthony M., merchant, subj. of Republic of France - 18 June 1799 [1]

Andrews, Samuel, of North Hempstead, Queens Co., subj. of G.B.; rec. by Daniel Francis, of North Hempstead - 2 June 1812 [2]

Iveson, John, of North Hempstead, Queens Co. [report 15 Oct. 1828]: b. town of Haslimgden, Co. of Lancaster, Eng., age 37, migr. from Blackburn, Co. of Lancaster, cabinetmaker; renounced allegiance to G.B. on 15 Oct. 1828; rec. by Daniel Bogart and Samuel Sherman, both of North Hempstead - 9 Nov. 1830 [3]

Beatty, James, subj. of G.B.; rec. by John Simonson - 28 Oct. 1834 [4]

Beaty, William, subj. of G.B.; rec. by Rem Remsen - 28 Oct. 1834 [5]

Shore, Thomas, of Hempstead, Queens Co., subj. of G.B.; rec. by Israel Wright, of Hempstead - 4 June 1834 [6]

Thompson, William, subj. of G.B.; rec. by John Simonson - 28 Oct. 1834 [7]

Crampton, Thomas, of Hempstead, Queens Co., subj. of G.B.; rec. by Gideon N. Searing, of Hempstead - 4 June 1835 [8]

Freel, Hugh, of North Hempstead, Queens Co., subj. of G.B.; rec. by Charles Denton - 3 June 1835 [9]

Freel, James, of North Hempstead, Queens Co., subj. of G.B.; rec. by Charles Denton - 3 June 1835 [10]

Manwaring, John, of Jamaica, Queens Co., subj. of G.B.; rec. by Daniel Rider - 8 June 1836 [11]

McGalughlin, Barney, formerly of Co. Donegal, Ire., now of North Hempstead, Queens Co., subj. of G.B.; rec. by Samuel Armstrong, of North Hempstead - 8 June 1836 [12]

Kiles, Richard, subj. of G.B., age 27, resident of U.S. 22 years and of State of New York last 8 years; rec. by Samuel Thompson (age about 50, a native of U.S.), of North Hempstead, Queens Co. - 2 Nov. 1839 [13]

COURT OF RICHMOND COUNTY

Bundle 1

Root, William S. - 12 Apr. 1820 [1]

Byrdsall, Fitz William, subj. of G.B.; rec. by James Hora - 14 Apr. 1840 [2]

Vol. 1

Graham, John B., subj. of G.B.; rec. John A. Cross - 21 Sept. 1834 [1]

Hunt, James, subj. of G.B.; rec. by James McFarlan - 10 Oct. 1834 [2]

Merrick, Philip M., subj. of G.B.; rec. by Philip Riley - 11 Oct. 1834 [3]

Rolfe, John P., subj. of G.B.; rec. by John Johnson - 11 Oct. 1834 [4]

Shanley, Edward, subj. of G.B.; rec. by Owen Flood - 15 Oct. 1834 [5]

McColgan, Michael, subj. of G.B.; rec. by William Kearney - 20 Oct. 1834 [6]

Sullivan, Patrick, subj. of G.B.; rec. by Joseph Ward - 27 Oct. 1834 [7]

Davis, David, subj. of G.B.; rec. by John Lott, Jr. - 31 Oct. 1834 [8]

Davis, Evan, subj. of G.B.; rec. by David Davis - 31 Oct. 1834 [9]

Lowe, John, subj. of G.B.; rec. by John Johnson - 1 Nov. 1834 [10]

Reitz, Francis Joseph, subj. of G.B.; rec. by Francis A. Reitz - 1 Nov. 1834 [11]

Kinney, John, subj. of G.B.; rec. by Evan M. Johnson - 2 Nov. 1834 [12]

Hegan, Martin, subj. of G.B.; rec. by Michael Kearney - 2 Nov. 1834 [13]

Barry, Edmund, subj. of G.B.; rec. by John Kerrigan - 2 Nov. 1834 [14]

Sheeran, William, subj. of G.B.; rec. by John Kerrigan - 4 Nov. 1834 [15]

Ryan, Patrick, subj. of G.B.; rec. by John Quigley - 2 Nov. 1834 [16]

Lavett, Manuel, subj. of King of Spain; rec. by John George Fries - 2 Nov. 1834 [17]

King, James, subj. of G.B.; rec. by Francis Gallagher - 3 Nov. 1834 [18]

Donnahey, Timothy, subj. of G.B.; rec. by James King - 3 Nov. 1834 [19]

Keliher, John, subj. of G.B.; rec. by John Kerrigan - 3 Nov. 1834 [20]

McGrath, Thomas, subj. of G.B.; rec. by Patrick Powell - 3 Nov. 1834 [21]

Stack, Garret, subj. of G.B.; rec. by Thomas McGrath - 3 Nov. 1834 [22]

Morton, Patrick, subj. of G.B.; rec. by Hugh Mallon - 3 Nov. 1834 [23]

Brady, James, subj. of G.B.; rec. by Charles Brady - 4 Nov. 1834 [24]

Brogan, Mathew, subj. of G.B.; rec. by Charles Brady - 4 Nov. 1834 [25]

McNamee, James, subj. of G.B.; rec. by Owen Flood - 4 Nov. 1834 [26]

Hanly, John, subj. of G.B.; rec. by James O'Farrell - 4 Nov. 1834 [27]

Kennedy, John, subj. of G.B.; rec. by John Kerrigan - 4 Nov. 1834 [28]

Finney, Patrick, subj. of G.B.; rec. by Thomas McGrath - 4 Nov. 1834 [29]

Magranel, Hugh, subj. of G.B.; rec. by Thomas Deinke - 5 Nov. 1834 [30]

Sneider, Jacob, subj. of King of France; rec. by John Murray - 5 Nov. 1834 [31]

Carty, James, subj. of G.B.; rec. by Michael Clark - 5 Nov. 1834 [32]

Levy, Daniel, subj. of G.B.; rec. by Owen Flood - 5 Nov. 1834 [33]

Doherty, James, subj. of G.B.; rec. by Hugh Magranel - 5 Nov. 1834 [34]

Cunningham, Thomas, subj. of G.B.; rec. by James O'Farrell - 5 Nov. 1834 [35]

McLaughlin, Dennis, subj. of G.B.; rec. by Thomas Reynolds - 5 Nov. 1834 [36]

Heafford, Samuel, subj. of G.B.; rec. by Issachar G.W. Reed - 5 Nov. 1834 [37]

Dougherty, George, subj. of G.B.; rec. by Hugh Magranel - 5 Nov. 1834 [38]

Cooke, John, subj. of G.B.; rec. by James Raynor - 5 Nov. 1834 [39]

Colgan, Neil, subj. of G.B.; rec. by Michael McColgan - 5 Nov. 1834 [40]

Colgan, Edward, subj. of G.B.; rec. by Neil Colgan - 5 Nov. 1834 [41]

Kelagher, Terrence, subj. of G.B.; rec. by James Harper - 5 Nov. 1834 [42]

McGuire, Francis, subj. of G.B.; rec. by James McNamee - 5 Nov. 1834 [43]

McLaughlin, Barney, subj. of G.B.; rec. by James Hicks - 5 Nov. 1834 [44]

Gillas, Charles, subj. of G.B.; rec. by Hugh Docherty - 5 Nov. 1834 [45]

Lear, Thomas, subj. of G.B.; rec. by Samuel Mitchell - 5 Nov. 1834 [46]

Lear, John, subj. of G.B.; rec. by Samuel Mitchell - 5 Nov. 1834 [47]

Lear, James, subj. of G.B.; rec. by Samuel Mitchell - 5 Nov. 1834 [48]

Mortimer, Mary, subj. of G.B.; rec. by Peter Morton - 18 Nov. 1834 [49]

Farhan, Daniel, subj. of G.B.; rec. by Gilbert Baylis - 1 Dec. 1834 [50]

Arbona, Francis, subj. of King of Spain; rec. by Joseph Quevedo - 1 Feb. 1837 [51]

Brice, John, subj. of G.B.; rec. by James Hilliard - 21 March 1837 [52]

Collins, John, subj. of G.B.; rec. by Henry Russell - 21 Mar. 1837 [53]

Hamilton, James, subj. of G.B.; rec. by John Gilfiland - 28 Mar. 1837 [54]

Webb, George, subj. of G.B.; rec. by Joseph Ward - 29 Mar. 1837 [55]

Friganza, Romeo, subj. of King of Spain; rec. by Joseph Quevedo - 1 Apr. 1837 [56]

Westwater, John, subj. of G.B.; rec. by Henry Morrison - 4 Apr. 1837 [57]

Turner, Thomas, subj. of G.B.; rec. by John A. Reilly - 6 Apr. 1837 [58]

Coggin, Thomas P., subj. of G.B.; rec. by Moses Montgomery - 8 Apr. 1837 [59]

Thompson, Thomas, subj. of G.B.; rec. by John Teasdale - 10 Apr. 1837 [60]

Armstrong, James, subj. of G.B.; rec. by John Teasdale - 10 Apr. 1837 [61]

Dobbins, James, subj. of G.B.; rec. by Samuel Dorsey - 10 Apr. 1837 [62]

Patterson, Robert, subj. of G.B.; rec. by Alanson Ackerly - 10 Apr. 1837 [63]

Patterson, David, subj. of G.B.; rec. by Alanson Ackerly - 10 Apr. 1837 [64]

Turnbull, James, subj. of G.B.; rec. by Elijah Lewis - 10 Apr. 1837 [65]

Faulkner, George, subj. of G.B.; rec. by Henry Cadley - 10 Apr. 1837 [66]

McCabe, John, subj. of G.B.; rec. by William M. Udall - 12 Apr. 1837 [67]

Welsh, Terrence, subj. of G.B.; rec. by Thomas Bryan - 3 June 1837 [68]

Gregory, John, subj. of G.B.; rec. by Martin Higgins - 8 June 1837 [69]

Filnor, William, subj. of G.B.; rec. by John N. Robins - 8 June 1837 [70]

Avila, John, subj. of G.B.; rec. by James H. Wright - 12 June 1837 [71]

Avila, Samuel, subj. of G.B.; rec. by James H. Wright - 12 June 1837 [72]

Newble, Thomas, subj. of G.B.; rec. by William Filmer - 16 June 1837 [73]

Westrop, Philip, subj. of G.B.; rec. by Thaddeus Willson - 27 June 1837 [74]

Stammers, Joseph, subj. of G.B.; rec. by William Stammers, Jr. - 15 Aug. 1837 [75]

Woodward, George, subj. of G.B.; rec. by William H. Hale - 16 Aug. 1837 [76]

Hall, William, subj. of G.B.; rec. by Nathan B. Morse - 6 Sept. 1837 [77]

Stewart, David, subj. of G.B.; rec. by Thomas Stewart - 30 Sept. 1837 [78]

McCarty, Henry, subj. of G.B.; rec. by Ferdinand Boyle - 7 Oct. 1837 [79]

Faggett, Robert, subj. of G.B.; rec. by Nathaniel Hempsted, Jr.; item void because of mistake in declaration paper [80]

Bibrim, Joseph, subj. of G.B.; rec. by Nathaniel Hempsted, Jr. - 2 Nov. 1837 [81]

McCormick, John F., subj. of G.B.; rec. by Patrick Cain - 3 Nov. 1837 [82]

Woodcock, Thomas S., subj. of G.B.; rec. by Stephen Crowell - 4 Nov. 1837 [83]

Woodcock, Frederick, subj. of G.B.; rec. by Stephen Crowell - 4 Nov. 1837 [84]

Parker, Joshua, subj. of G.B.; rec. by Stephen Crowell - 4 Nov. 1837 [85]

Ryan, Patrick, subj. of G.B.; rec. by John Beatty - 4 Nov. 1837 [86]

Fisher, John, Jr., subj. of G.B.; rec. by John Beatty - 4 Nov. 1837 [87]

McKinney,

Dougherty, Daniel, subj. of G.B.; rec. by Lodawick Weller - 4 Nov. 1837 [89]

Dougherty, William, subj. of G.B.; rec. by Lodawick Weller - 4 Nov. 1837 [90]

Brice, Israel Bertram, subj. of G.B.; rec. by Owen Colgan - 4 Nov. 1837 [91]

McDonald, John S., subj. of G.B.; rec. by Joseph Dean - 21 Nov. 1837 [92]

Doyle, Barney M., subj. of G.B.; rec. by Lodawick Weller - 29 Nov. 1837 [93]

Bounar, William, subj. of G.B.; rec. by William McGivney - 14 Dec. 1837 [94]

Dobson, Henry, subj. of G.B.; rec. by John Beatty- 29 Dec. 1837 [95]

Farrall, Patrick, subj. of G.B.; rec. by Patrick Farrall, Jr. - 8 Jan. 1838 [96]

Dwyer, John, subj. of G.B.; rec. by Patrick John McNamara - 9 Feb. 1838 [97]

Knox, Joseph, subj. of G.B.; rec. by John Evans - 26 Feb. 1838 [98]

Lewis, Alexander C., subj. of G.B.; rec. by John Davis - 28 Feb. 1838 [99]

Kennedy, William, subj. of G.B.; rec. by Cyrus P. Smith - 14 Mar. 1838 [100]

Stephens, John C., subj. of G.B.; rec. by Charles W. Pittman - 24 Mar. 1838 [101]

Jones, John, subj. of G.B.; rec. by Henry Cadley - 27 Mar. 1838 [102]

Davies, John D., subj. of G.B.; rec. by Rowland Story - 3 Apr. 1838 [103]

Crummey, Michael, subj. of G.B.; rec. by Edward Crummey - 5 Apr. 1838 [104]

Mulvihill, John, subj. of G.B.: rec. by James Hughes - 6 Apr. 1838 [105]

McIntosh, Robert, subj. of G.B.; rec. by Jeremiah Mundell - 7 Apr. 1838 [106]

Clayton, John, subj. of G.B.; rec. by Samuel Carman - 7 Apr. 1838 [107]

Campbell, John, subj. of G.B.;rec. by Andrew J.F. Tombs - 9 Apr. 1838 [108]

Doorley, John, subj. of G.B.; rec. by Owen Flood - 9 Apr. 1838 [109]

McMahon, Edward, subj. of G.B.; rec. by John McCabe - 9 Apr. 1838 [110]

Wallace, John, subj. of G.B.; rec. by David Halliard - 9 Apr. 1838 [111]

Gillespey, Martin, subj. of G.B.; rec. by William Higbee - 9 Apr. 1838 [112]

McIvry, James, subj. of G.B.; rec. by Robert McDermott - 9 Apr. 1838 [113]

Sweeny, George, subj. of G.B.; rec. by John McCabe - 9 Apr. 1838 [114]

McMahon, John, subj. of G.B.; rec. by Thomas Hunt - 9 Apr. 1838 [115]

McGahey, James, subj. of G.B.; rec. by Charles Brady - 9 Apr. 1838 [116]

McCormick, John, subj. of G.B.; rec. by Gilbert C. Baylis - 9 Apr. 1838 [117]

Mackay, Peter, subj. of G.B.; rec. by Patrick Mackay - 9 Apr. 1838 [118]

Lanagan, John, subj. of G.B.; rec. by Henry Cadley - 9 Apr. 1838 [119]

Ford, William, subj. of G.B.; rec. by Samuel Frisbee - 9 Apr. 1838 [120]

Glannon, William, subj. of G.B.; rec. by George Sweeny - 9 Apr. 1838 [121]

McLaughlin, Daniel, subj. of G.B.; rec. by George Sweeny - 9 Apr. 1838 [122]

Cunningham, Richard, subj. of G.B.; rec. by Joseph McCloud - 9 Apr. 1838 [123]

Cooke, Thomas, subj. of G.B.; rec. by Nathaniel Waring - 9 Apr. 1838 [124]

Mahony, Cornelius, subj. of G.B.; rec. by Thomas Cooke - 9 Apr. 1838 [125]

McCann, Patrick, subj. of G.B.; rec. by Henry McCann - 9 Apr. 1838 [126]

McCann, Arthur, subj. of G.B.; rec. by Henry McCann - 9 Apr. 1838 [127]

McCann, David, subj. of G.B.; rec. by Henry McCann - 9 Apr. 1838 [128]

Darmfelser, Adam, subj. of Duke of Hessen; rec. by James Walters - 7 May 1838 [129]

Conlin, John, subj. of G.B.;rec. by Patrick Bridge - 9 May 1838
    [130]

Davis, Edmund, subj. of G.B.; rec. by John Taylor - 12 May 1838
    [131]

Curow, Thomas, subj. of G.B.; rec. by George Wood - 30 May 1838
    [132]

Vollmer, John Andrew, subj. of King of Wuertemberg; rec. by
    William Bennit - 1 June 1838 [133]

Thomas, John, subj. of G.B.; rec. by John Davis - 9 July 1838
    [134]

Brady, John, subj. of G.B.; rec. by Francis Langley - 1 Aug.
    1838 [135]

Jaffers, Hugh, subj. of G.B.; rec. by John Lanagan - 14 Sept.
    1838 [136]

Mullen, Thomas, subj. of G.B.; rec. by James McGrath - 25 Sept.
    1838 [137]

Draper, William, subj. of G.B.; rec. by John Gildersleve - 12
    Oct. 1838 [138]

Donlon, John, subj. of G.B.; rec. by Patrick McCoy - 19 Oct.
    1838 [139]

Dodd, William, Jr., subj. of G.B.; rec. by William Kennedy - 20
    Oct. 1838 [140]

Feinnan, Joseph, subj. of G.B.; rec. by Peter Gregory - 22 Oct.
    1838 [141]

Donoly, Peter, subj. of G.B.; rec. by Terrence Brady - 23 Oct.
    1838 [142]

Gannon, Michael, subj. of G.B.; rec. by Peter Donoly - 23 Oct.
    1838 [143]

Mullvihill, Dominic, subj. of G.B.; rec. by Michael Gannon - 23
    Oct. 1838 [144]

Lyon, John, subj. of G.B.; rec. by Robert Lyon - 24 Oct. 1838
    [145]

Quevedo, John, subj. of Queen of Spain; rec. by Joseph Quevedo
    - 25 Oct. 1838 [146]

White Michael, subj. of G.B.; rec. by Terrence Brady - 27 Oct.
    1838 [147]

Horn, John [not completed]; rec. by Robert Lowther - 27 Oct.
    1838 [148]

McConway, Hugh, subj. of G.B.; rec. by William Glennan - 30 Oct.
    1838 [149]

Jirry, William, subj. of G.B.; rec. by James Dunning - 29 Oct.
    1838 [150]

Dalton, Michael, subj. of G.B.; rec. by Peter Donoly - 29 Oct.
    1838 [151]

Kelly, Hugh, subj. of G.B.; rec. by William Serrey - 29 Oct.
    1838 [152]

Callihan, James, subj. of G.B.; rec. by David Halliard - 30 Oct.
    1838 [153]

McCoy, James, subj. of G.B.; rec. by John Donlan - 31 Oct. 1838
    [154]

McGranaghan, James, subj. of G.B.; rec. by James Dunning - 1 Nov.
    1838 [155]

Johnson, Edward, subj. of G.B.; rec. by James Dunning 1 Nov. 1838 [156]

Miller, Joseph, subj. of G.B.; rec. by William Thornton - 2 Nov. 1838 [157]

Shanley, John, subj. of G.B.; rec. by John Kerrigan - 2 Nov. 1838 [158]

Haiston, Francis, subj. of G.B.; rec. by Philip Rily - 2 Nov. 1838 [159]

Brady, John, subj. of G.B.; rec. by Philip Rily - 2 Nov. 1838 [160]

Wilson, Richard, subj. of G.B.; rec. by Barnard Boyle - 2 Nov. 1838 [161]

Boyle, Patrick, subj. of G.B.; rec. by Barnard Boyle - 2 Nov. 1838 [162]

Williams, Richard, subj. of G.B.; rec. by Barnard Boyle - 2 Nov. 1838 [163]

McGroety. John, subj. of G.B.; rec. by Barnard Boyle - 2 Nov. 1838 [164]

Dickson, James Stewart, subj. of G.B.; rec. by Thomas McCormick - 2 Nov. 1838 [165]

Gallagher, Niel, subj. of G.B.; rec. by Edward Diver - 2 Nov. 1838 [166]

Shields, John, subj. of G.B,; rec. by Terrence Holaher - 3 Nov. 1838 [167]

O'Donnell, Bryan, subj. of G.B.; rec. by Patrick Cunningham - 3 Nov. 1838 [168]

Murdock, Thomas, subj. of G.B.; rec. by William Prince - 3 Nov. 1838 [169]

McNiell, Thomas, subj. of G.B.; rec. by George Jamison - 3 Nov. 1838 [170]

Boyle, James, subj. of G.B.; rec. by John Murray - 3 Nov. 1838 [171]

Casey, Patrick, subj. of G.B.; rec. by Terrence Brady - 3 Nov. 1838 [172]

McGuire, Patrick, subj. of G.B.; rec. by Patrick Casey - 3 Nov. 1838 [173]

Simpson, James, subj. of G.B.; rec. by Patrick Casey - 3 Nov. 1838 [174]

Faroll, William, subj. of G.B.; rec. by Patrick Casey - 3 Nov. 1838 [175]

Flintoft, Francis, subj. of G.B.; rec. by Israel Brice - 3 Nov. 1838 [176]

Harvey, John Quilliam, subj. of G.B.; rec. by Thomas Woodcock - 3 Nov. 1838 [177]

Harvey, Joseph, subj. of G.B.; rec. by Thomas Woodcock - 3 Nov. 1838 [178]

Conlon, Patrick, subj. of G.B.; rec. by Patrick Finney - 3 Nov. 1838 [179]

Brannan, James, subj. of G.B.; rec. by Barney Flood - 3 Nov. 1838 [180]

Dunn, Michael, subj. of G.B.; rec. by Edward Butler - 3 Nov. 1838 [181]

Mooney, John, subj. of G.B.; rec. by Francis Keenan - 3 Nov.
1838 [182]

Stuart, John, subj. of G.B.; rec. by John Mooney - 3 Nov. 1838
[183]

Roark, Patrick, subj. of G.B.; rec. by James McGrath - 3 Nov.
1838 [184]

Partridge, Daniel, subj. of G.B.; rec. by David Fithian - 3 Nov.
1838 [185]

Smith, Joseph, subj. of G.B.; rec. by William M. Udall - 3 Nov.
1838 [186]

Mulligan, Thomas, subj. of G.B.; rec. by Patrick Conroy - 3 Nov.
1838 [187]

Kidd, Whitten, subj. of G.B.; rec. by Israel Brice - 3 Nov.
1838 [188]

Granger, John, subj. of G.B.; rec. by John Granger, Jr. - 9
Nov. 1838 [189]

McBurney, Thomas, subj. of G.B.; rec. by Robert Malcom - 10
Jan. 1839 [190]

Alvey, Samuel, subj. of G.B.; rec. by William Bennet - 9 Mar.
1839 [191]

McMahon, Phillip, subj. of G.B.; rec. by Michael Colgan - 15
Mar. 1839 [192]

Wrinkle, Christopher, subj. of G.B.; rec. by Peter Howlin - 18
Mar. 1839 [193]

Connell, John, subj. of G.B.; rec. by Christopher Wrinkle - 18
Mar. 1839 [194]

McCabe, Bernard, subj. of G.B.; rec. by Phillip McMahon - 26
Mar. 1839 [195]

Bannon, John, subj. of G.B.; rec. by Owen Flood - 29 Mar. 1839
[196]

Griffin, Patrick, subj. of G.B.; rec. by Owen Flood - 29 Mar.
1839 [197]

Keenan, James, subj. of G.B.; rec. by James Victory - 29 Mar.
1839 [198]

Cunningham, John, subj. of G.B.; rec. by Alexander Stewart - 29
Mar. 1839 [199]

Connor, John, subj. of G.B.; rec. by John Lott, Jr. - 30 Mar.
1839 [200]

Campbell, Robert, subj. of G.B.; rec. by Barney Boyle - 1 Apr.
1839 [201]

Cloonan, Patrick, subj. of G.B.; rec. by Patrick Bagley - 1 Apr.
1839 [202]

Donoho, William, subj. of G.B.; rec. by Patrick Bagley - 1 Apr.
1839 [203]

McCall, Hugh, subj. of G.B.; rec. by John McCabe - 3 Apr. 1839
[204]

Campbell, John, subj. of G.B.; rec. by Hugh McCabe - 4 Apr. 1839
[205]

Phillips, John, subj. of G.B.; rec. by William Jenkins - 4 Apr.
1839 [206]

McGinley, Robert, subj. of G.B.; rec. by John McCabe - 4 Apr.
1839 [207]

Pearson, John S., subj. of G.B.; rec. by Stephen Crowell - 5 Apr. 1839 [208]

McManus, Philip, subj. of G.B.; rec. by Hugh McConway - 5 Apr. 1839 [209]

Dougherty, Barney, subj. of G.B.; rec. by Hugh McConway - 5 Apr. 1839 [210]

McFall, Dennis, subj. of G.B.; rec. by Patrick Flaherty - 5 Apr. 1839 [211]

Gillen, Anthony, subj. of G.B.; rec. by Bernard Gillen - 5 Apr. 1839 [212]

Lynch, Barney, subj. of G.B.; rec. by James Drum - 5 Apr. 1839 [213]

Reddin, Niel, subj. of G.B.; rec. by John Robinson - 5 Apr. 1839 [214]

Cloon, John, subj. of G.B.; rec. by Michael Egan - 6 Apr. 1839 [215]

Kearnan, Miles, subj. of G.B.; rec. by John Gregory - 6 Apr. 1839 [216]

McKnight, Robert, subj. of G.B.; rec. by John Gregory - 6 Apr. 1839 [217]

Mackinson, Thomas, subj. of G.B.; rec. by Terrance Brady - 6 Apr. 1839 [218]

McLaughlin, Barney, subj. of G.B.; rec. by John McLaughlin - 8 Apr. 1839 [219]

Bagley, John, subj. of G.B.; rec. by William Donoho - 8 Apr. 1839 [220]

Divine, James, subj. of G.B.; rec. by John Gilfilland - 8 Apr. 1839 [221]

Hughes, Daniel, subj. of G.B.; rec. by Thomas Braine - 8 Apr. 1839 [222]

Gibson, John, subj. of G.B.; rec. by John Fisher - 8 Apr. 1839 [223]

Quigley, Hugh, subj. of G.B.; rec. by Thomas Braine - 8 Apr. 1839 [224]

Reed, James, subj. of G.B.; rec. by James Freel - 8 Apr. 1839 [225]

Day, Joseph, subj. of G.B.; rec. by William Jenkins - 8 Apr. 1839 [226]

Davis, Thomas, subj. of G.B.; rec. by Enock Davis - 8 Apr. 1839 [227]

Pollock, James, subj. of G.B.; rec. by John P. Cummings - 8 Apr. 1839 [228]

Davis, David, subj. of G.B.; rec. by Enock Davis - 8 Apr. 1839 [229]

Dailey, Patrick, subj. of G.B.; rec. by William McGivney - 8 Apr. 1839 [230]

Williams, Patrick, subj. of G.B.; rec. by Joseph Lott - 8 Apr. 1839 [231]

Dougherty, Patrick, subj. of G.B.; rec. by James Keenan - 8 Apr. [232]

Monahan, Owen, subj. of G.B.; rec. by Thomas Fullom - 8 Apr. 1839 [233]

McGinty, Patrick, subj. of G.B.; rec. by John Teasdale - 8 Apr. 1839 [234]

Judge, Thomas, subj. of G.B.; rec. by Thomas Carmody - 8 Apr. 1839 [235]

White, Thomas, subj. of G.B.; rec. by Samuel Mitchell - 8 Apr. 1839 [236]

Withers, Henry, subj. of G.B.; rec. by Samuel Mitchell - 8 Apr. 1839 [237]

Claffey, John, subj. of G.B.; rec. by John Cunningham - 8 Apr. 1839 [238]

Nowlan, Patrick, subj. of G.B.; rec. by William McGivney - 22 Apr. 1839 [239]

Messenger, Thomas, subj. of G.B.; rec. by Nathaniel F. Waring - 25 Apr. 1839 [240]

McGee, John, subj. of G.B.; rec. by William Lee - 4 June 1839 [241]

Bazing, William Hamilton, subj. of G.B.; rec. by John C. Bach - 4 June 1839 [242]

Atchison, Robert, subj. of G.B.; rec. by Charles Dougherty - 5 June 1839 [243]

Thompson, James, subj. of G.B.; rec. by John Stoddart - 5 Sept. 1839 [244]

Denny, James, subj. of G.B.; rec. by Patrick Dougherty - 6 June 1839 [244A]

Carroll, Patrick, subj. of G.B.; rec. by Francis Gallagher - 3 Aug. 1839 [245]

Dunn, Helen (formerly Helen Hayes), subj. of G.B.; rec. by Eliza Margaret Hayes - 17 Aug. 1839 [245A]

Lennon, John, subj. of G.B.; rec. by Michael Dunn - 14 Sept. 1839 [246]

McHugh, Thomas, subj. of G.B.; rec. by James Grogan - 17 Sept. 1839 [247]

Kelly, Peter, subj. of G.B.; rec. by James Boyle - 7 Oct. 1839 [248]

McLaughlin, Margaret, subj. of G.B.; rec. by John Kerrigan - 16 Oct. 1839 [249]

McGeorge, John, subj. of G.B.; rec. by John C. Harvey - 17 Oct. 1839 [250]

Cologan, Patrick, subj. of G.B.; rec. by John Gardner - 24 Oct. 1839 [251]

Burnett, William M., subj. of G.B.; rec. by Thomas Burnett - 21 Oct. 1839 [252]

Sweeney, Michael, subj. of G.B.; rec. by George Sweeney - 24 Oct. 1839 [253]

Kenan, Michael, subj. of G.B.; rec. by George Sweenny - 24 Oct. 1839 [254]

Lynch, Bernard, subj. of G.B.; rec. by John Sweeney - 26 Oct. 1839 [255]

Dougherty, Michael, subj. of G.B.; rec. by Patrick Powell - 29 Oct. 1839 [256]

Dennison, James, subj. of G.B.; rec. by Patrick Cologan - 29 Oct. 1839 [257]

Gray, John, subj. of G.B.; rec. by Daniel Bowie - 29 Oct. 1839 [258]

Rose, John, subj. of G.B.; rec. by Francis Obry - 30 Oct. 1839 [259]

Wright, Wesley, subj. of G.B.; rec. by Robert E. Dinan - 30 Oct. 1839 [260]

Bohnirt, George, subj. of Prince of Hesse Cassel; rec. by Garret Bergen - 30 Oct. 1839 [261]

Bohnerd, Conrad, subj. of Prince of Hesse Cassel; rec. by Garret Bergen - 30 Oct. 1839 [262]

Connell, John, subj. of G.B.; rec. by Daniel Dennison - 30 Oct. 1839 [263]

Davies, David, subj. of G.B.; rec. by Henry Birdsall - 30 Oct. 1839 [264]

Reynolds, Christopher, subj. of G.B.; rec. by Patrick Nowlan - 30 Oct. 1839 [265]

Clark, William, subj. of G.B.; rec. by Owen Flood - 30 Oct. 1839 [266]

Murray, John, subj. of G.B.; rec. by Thomas Daltin - 31 Oct. 1839 [267]

Fox, Patrick, subj. of G.B.; rec. by Nathaniel Gove - 31 Oct. 1839 [268]

Vol. 2

No. 1 is missing.

Rice, Patrick, subj. of G.B.; rec. by William McGivney - 31 Oct. 1839 [2]

Goodwin, Thomas, subj. of G.B.; rec. by John Reily - 31 Oct. 1839 [3]

Mundell, William A., subj. of G.B.; rec. by Francis B. Stryker - 1 Nov. 1839 [4]

Booth, Samuel, subj. of G.B.; rec. by Isaac M. Folk - 1 Nov. 1839 [5]

Lawler, Patrick, subj. of G.B.; rec. by James Lawry - 1 Nov. 1839 [6]

Hayden, James, subj. of G.B.; rec. by John Milay - 1 Nov. 1839 [7]

Milay, John, subj. of G.B.; rec. by Augustus Williams - 1 Nov. 1839 [8]

Tirrey, Daniel, subj. of G.B.; rec. by William Tirrey - 1 Nov. 1839 [9]

Cain, Patrick, subj. of G.B.; rec. by Owen Flood - 1 Nov. 1839 [10]

Tirrey, John, subj. of G.B.; rec. by William Tirrey - 1 Nov. 1839 [11]

Farrell, John, subj. of G.B.; rec. by Owen Flood - 1 Nov. 1839 [12]

Corcoran, Michael, subj. of G.B.; rec. by Owen Flood - 1 Nov. 1839 [13]

Nolen, James, subj. of G.B.; rec. by Abraham Wright - 1 Nov. 1839 [14]

Withers, John, subj. of G.B.; rec. by William Withers - 31 Oct. 1839 [14A]

McDonough, James, subj. of G.B.; rec. by James Nolen - 1 Nov. 1839 [15]

Mulrooney, Michael, subj. of G.B.; rec. by Owen Flood - 1 Nov. 1839 [16]

Wright, George, subj. of G.B.; rec. by Henry A.C. Heins - 1 Nov. 1839 [17]

Fox, Thomas, subj. of G.B.; rec. by James Doherty - 2 Nov. 1839 [18]

St. George, William, subj. of G.B.; rec. by Hiram Wilson - 2 Nov. 1839 [19]

Walters, Michael, subj. of G.B.; rec. by Joshua R. Holden - 2 Nov. 1839 [20]

McMasters, Stephen B., subj. of G.B.; rec. by Terrence Riley - 2 Nov. 1839 [21]

Jones, David, subj. of G.B.; rec. by Herbert Wiley - 2 Nov. 1839 [22]

Duffy, John, subj. of G.B.; rec. by John Shields - 2 Nov. 1839 [23]

Boylan, Patrick, subj. of G.B.; rec. by Charles W. Pittman - 2 Nov. 1839 [24]

Boylan, Matthew, subj. of G.B.; rec. by Patrick Boylan - 2 Nov. 1839 [25]

Murray, Peter, subj. of G.B.; rec. by James Carty - 2 Nov. 1839 [26]

Carly, Owen, subj. of G.B.; rec. by Barney Campbell - 2 Nov. 1839 [27]

Kielty, Thomas, subj. of G.B.; rec. by Peter Murray - 2 Nov. 1839 [28]

Close, John, subj. of G.B.; rec. by Thomas Higbee - 2 Nov. 1839 [29]

Fay, David, subj. of G.B.; rec. by Jacob C. Blackly - 30 Nov. 1839 [30]

Duffey, James, subj. of G.B.; rec. by Edward Colgan - 12 Dec. 1839 [31]

Garnin, John, subj. of Grand Duke of Baden; rec. by Francis A. Reitz - 15 Jan. 1840 [32]

No. 33 is blank.

Gray, John, subj. of G.B.; rec. by John Lowe - 6 Mar. 1840 [34]

Hesler, Peter, subj. of G.B.; rec. by John Bannon - 6 Mar. 1840 [35]

Rainey, John, subj. of G.B.; rec. by Patrick Rorke - 14 Mar. 1840 [36]

Chatelle, Francis, subj. of G.B.; rec. by John Rendells - 31 Mar. 1840 [37]

Owen, William, subj. of G.B.; rec. by John Burroughs - 2 Apr. 1840 [38]

Masterton, John, subj. of G.B.; rec. by Andrew G. Dalton - 3 Apr. 1840 [39]

Teitler, Jacob, subj. of King of Bavaria; rec. by John Paulsen - 3 Apr. 1840 [40]

Mullen, Patrick, subj. of G.B.; rec. by Evander Berry - 3 Apr. 1840 [41]

Middole, Samuel, subj. of G.B.; rec. by Evander Berry - 3 Apr. 1840 [42]

O'Hare, John, subj. of G.B.; rec. by Evander Berry - 3 Apr. 1840 [43]

Quin, Matthew, subj. of G.B.; rec. by Evander Berry - 3 Apr. 1840 [44]

Owen, Patrick, subj. of G.B.; rec. by Nicholas Owen - 4 Apr. 1840 [45]

Smith, William, subj. of G.B.; rec. by John O'Hare - 6 Apr. 1840 [46]

Weston, Job, subj. of G.B.; rec. by Samuel Baseley - 7 Apr. 1840 [47]

Tuill, William, subj. of G.B.; rec. by Alexander D. Berry - 7 Apr. 1840 [48]

Hutton, Joseph, subj. of G.B.; rec. by Francis B. Stryker - 8 Apr. 1840 [49]

Ross, James, subj. of G.B.; rec. by Christopher R. McClellan - 11 Apr. 1840 [50]

Herald, Lawrence, subj. of G,B.; rec. by Peter Herald - 9 Apr. 1840 [51]

Donnelly, Thomas, subj. of G.B.; rec. by William Glennen - 9 Apr. 1840 [52]

Philps, John M., subj. of G.B.; rec. by Jacob B. Boerum - 9 Apr. 1840 [53]

Fitzgibbon, Michael, subj. of G.B.; rec. by William Fitzgibbon - 10 Apr. 1840 [54]

Shields, Samuel, subj. of G.B.; rec. by John A. Stager - 11 Apr. 1840 [55]

Mason, Samuel, subj. of G.B.; rec. by Abraham Van Nostrand - 13 Apr. 1840 [56]

Wilson, Edward, subj. of G.B.; rec. by Johnson Leake - 13 Apr. 1840 [57]

McLaughlin, James, subj. of G.B.; rec. by John McLaughlin - 13 Apr. 1840 [58]

Jones, David, subj. of G.B.; rec. by William H. Kenney - 13 Apr. 1840 [59]

Coombs, Richard, subj. of G.B.; rec. by Francis B. Stryker - 13 Apr. 1840 [60]

Mullen, Thomas, subj. of G.B.; rec. by Paul Diver - 13 Apr. 1840 [61]

Lane, Richard S., subj. of G.B.; rec. by Lawrence Van Cott - 13 Apr. 1840 [62]

Wilson, Hugh W., subj. of G.B.; rec. by William Kenmore - 13 Apr. 1840 [63]

Cummisky, Patrick, subj. of G.B.; rec. by John Kelty - 13 Apr. 1840 [64]

Meighan, Philip, subj. of G.B.; rec. by John Farnan - 13 Apr. 1840 [65]

Smith, William, subj. of G.B.; rec. by Alexander Birbeck - 13 Apr. 1840 [66]

Connelly, James, subj. of G.B.; rec. by William Rady - 13 Apr. 1840 [67]

Wilson, Leatham, subj. of G.B.; rec. by Edward Wilson - 13 Apr. 1840 [68]

Potts, William J., subj. of G.B.; rec. by John Brown - 13 Apr. 1840 [69]

Newman, Michael, subj. of G.B.; rec. by James McCoy - 13 Apr. 1840 [70]

Maitland, John, subj. of G.B.; rec. by Charles J. Taylor - 20 Apr. 1840 [71]

Collins, John, subj. of G.B.; rec. by John L. Farrington - 28 Apr. 1840 [72]

Hester, William, subj. of G.B.; rec. by Samuel Grisson - 27 May 1840 [73]

Hawker, John, subj. of G.B.; rec. by Elijah Lewis - 29 May 1840 [74]

Kirkner, Kaspar, subj. of King of Bavaria; rec. by John Paulson - 13 June 1840 [75]

Ward, Patrick, subj. of G.B.; rec. by Pierce Kennedy - 13 Aug. 1840 [76]

Crummey, Thomas, subj. of G.B.; rec. by Edward Crummey - 13 Aug. 1840 [77]

Gray, William, Jr., subj. of G.B.; rec. by William Gray - 25 Aug. 1840 [78]

Craven, Patrick, subj. of G.B.; rec. by Thomas Fitzsimons - 5 Sept. 1840 [79]

Simpson, William, subj. of G.B.; rec. by Archibald Wallace - 7 Sept. 1840 [80]

Wallace, Archibald, subj. of G.B.; rec. by John Kerr - 7 Sept. 1840 [81]

Lewis, John, subj. of Queen of Spain; rec. by Richard D. Berry - 12 Sept. 1840 [82]

Cosgrove, Patrick, subj. of G.B.; rec. by Patrick Masterson - 15 Sept. 1840 [83]

Mullaly, Patrick, subj. of G.B.; rec. by Samuel E. Johnson - 18 Sept. 1840 [84]

Harkins, Patrick, subj. of G.B.; rec. by William Harper] 18 Sept. 1840 [85]

Schaeffer, Konrad, subj. of King of France; rec. by Johannes Ledermann - 18 Sept. 1840 [86]

Lange, Maria Margaretha, subj. of City of Bremen; rec. by Peter Henry Dreyer - 19 Sept. 1840 [87]

Thompson, Joseph, subj. of Queen of Portugal; rec. by Emanuel Joseph - 24 Sept. 1840 [88]

McGaffigan, Dennis, subj. of G.B.; rec. by Robert McDermott - 30 Sept. 1840 [89]

Puser, George, subj. of Republic of Switzerland; rec. by William Powers - 6 Oct. 1840 [90]

Willson, Thomas, subj. of G.B.; rec. by Robert Pattison - 9 Oct. 1840 [91]

Dixon, Horatio, subj. of G.B.; rec. by George Birkbeck - 13 Oct. 1840 [92]

Matthews, Patrick, subj. of G.B.; rec. by Patrick Carroll - 14 Oct. 1840 [93]

Mullen, James, subj. of G.B.; rec. by Thomas Mullen - 16 Oct.
1840 [94]

Wynn, Peter, subj. of G.B.; rec. by John Dooley - 17 Oct. 1840
[95]

Buchanan, Robert, subj. of G.B.; rec. by Robert T. Shannon - 19
Oct. 1840 [96]

Orr, Robert, subj. of G.B.; rec. by Robert T. Shannon - 19 Oct.
1840 [97]

Piper, William, subj. of G.B.; rec. by Thomas Paggott - 19 Oct.
1840 [98]

McFarlen, Joseph, subj. of G.B.; rec. by John Macfarlane - 21
Oct. 1840 [99]

Pringle, James, subj. of G.B.; rec. by John Teasdale - 21 Oct.
1840 [100]

Thompson, George, subj. of G.B.; rec. by Nicholas Wyckoff - 23
Oct. 1840 [101]

Hall, Daniel, subj. of G.B.; rec. by Richard Spragg - 23 Oct.
1840 [102]

Hall, Isaac, subj. of G.B.; rec. by Richard Spragg - 23 Oct.
1840 [103]

Orr, Joseph, subj. of G.B.; rec. by Samuel Orr - 24 Oct. 1840
[104]

Hardy, Thomas, subj. of G.B.; rec. by Alexander Underhill - 26
Oct. 1840 [105]

McDonald, Reynolds, subj. of G.B.; rec. by Lawrence Van Cott -
27 Oct. 1840 [106]

Goin, Charles, subj. of G.B.; rec. by Michael Trappal - 28 Oct.
1840 [107]

Friend, John, subj. of Duke of Hessen Cassel; rec. by John Emmons - 28 Oct. 1840 [108]

Piper, Edward, subj. of G.B.; rec. by Samuel Jarvis - 28 Oct.
1840 [109]

Jewkes, James, subj. of G.B.; rec. by Edward Piper - 28 Oct.
1840 [110]

Luhrs, Berend, subj. of King of Hanover; rec. by Peter Madden -
29 Oct. 1840 [111]

Wrigley, Joseph, subj. of G.B.; rec. by Wyman Johnson - 29 Oct.
1840 [112]

McMillan, John, subj. of G.B.; rec. by James McFarlan - 29 Oct.
1840 [113]

Haffy, Edward, subj. of G.B.; rec. by Ebenezer H. Gould - 29
Oct. 1840 [114]

McCloskey, Francis, subj. of G.B.; rec. by Dennis McCloskey -
30 Oct. 1840 [115]

Taggert, Robert, subj. of G.B.; rec. by James Dobbins - 30 Oct.
1840 [116]

Dobbins, Nicholas, subj. of G.B.; rec. by James Dobbins - 30
Oct. 1840 [117]

Jackson, James, subj. of G.B.; rec. by Frederick Gatkins - 30
Oct. 1840 [118]

Pearson, James, subj. of G.B.; rec. by George Russell - 30 Oct.
1840 [119]

Chiverton, Thomas, subj. of G.B.; rec. by William Covert - 30
   Oct. 1840 [120]

Williams, John, subj. of G.B.; rec. by Orvil Bissell - 31 Oct.
   1840 [121]

Tomsey, Alexander, subj. of G.B.; rec. by Joseph Dean - 31 Oct.
   1840 [122]

Taylor, David, subj. of G.B.; rec. by Benjamin Cole - 31 Oct.
   1840 [123]

Earp, William, subj. of G.B.; rec. by Charles Dougherty - 31
   Oct. 1840 [124]

Morris, John, subj. of G.B.; rec. by Orvil Bissell - 31 Oct.
   1840 [125]

Griffin, Job, subj. of G.B.; rec. by Rem Lefferts, Jr. - 31
   Oct. 1840 [126]

Satchell, Richard, subj. of G.B.; rec. by Thomas Baylis - 31
   Oct. 1840 [127]

Patterson, Ephraim, subj. of G.B.; rec. by William Patterson -
   9 Nov. 1840 [128]

McGuire, Philip, subj. of G.B.; rec. by Thomas McGuire - 16 Nov.
   1840 [129]

Grimshaw, Edwin S. 70; John 170, 232, 338

Grinnell, Moses H. 141

Grisch, Anthony 169

Grischele, Hypolite 88; John 88, 91, 319

Grisson, Samuel 385

Grist, David 115

Griswald, Calvin 78

Grivet, John B. 358

Grocer, Thomas W. 169

Groff, Stephen 115

Grogen/Grogan, Bernard 232; Bridget 232; Ellenor 232; James 164, 232, 381

Groh, Johann 142

Grojean, Alexander 233

Gron, John 321

Grosclaude, Frederick 168

Groshon, Frederic 352; John Pier 35

Gross, Lewis 235

Groundwell, John 39, 51

Grousset, Alexandre Eugene 360

Grubb, George 225; Janet 225

Gruez, John 341

Grunenthal, William Theodore 234

Grusemeyer, Georg/ George 148, 235

Guedron/Gudeon, Robert 323, 324

Guental, Charles 171

Guerin, John 73; Peter 73

Guest, Edwin 171; John 63; William 37

Guier, John 169

Guillot, Joseph 55

Guinan, Lack 234

Guischard, Henry 167, 359

Gukin, John 351

Gulden, Jacob 168

Guli, Peter 364

Gunn, James 168; John 87; Joseph 367

Gunner, Robert 52

Gunther, Adam 89

Gunton, Mark 21

Gurnee, Jonas 137, 140

Guthrie, William 4

Gutman, Joseph 188, 203, 234

Guy, George 163; Thomas 115

Guischard/Guyschard, Henry 127, 131, 137, 138; William H. 134

Gwinner, John A. 235

Haag, Johan Adam 108, 117

Haarstrich, Carl/Charles 114, 131

Haas/Haase, David, 165, 173, 187; Gottlob 131; John 140, 171, 242; Martin 118; Michael 174

Habershaw, Martin 306

Hacke, Christian 171

Hackett/Hacket, James 236; John 26, 241; Mathew 240; Richard 90; William 90

Haddaway, Henry 108

Hadden, Patrick 171

Hadike, Friederich 178

Hadley, Ann 303; William 303

Haeffile, Moritz 131

Haescher, Jacob 91; Samuel 91

Haeselbarth, Adam C. 75

Hafard, Anthony 171

Haffey/Haffy/ Haffee, Charles 331; Cornelius 323; Edward 386; John 323

Hagadorn, Jacob F. 359; John 359

Hagen/Hagan, Archibald 117; Francis 308; Henry 346; John 103, 172, 191, 308; Michael 172; William 154

Hageman, Nelson 40

Haggart, James 240

Haggerty/Hagerty/ Hagarty/Hagerthy, Barney 117; John 173; Joseph 174; Ogden 136; Robert 70; Timothy 240; William 91

Haghue, Patrick 90

Hahn, Godfrey 95; Heymann 320; Jacob 195

Haigh, William 368

Haight, Gilbert 40, 46

Hailshorn, John 329

Hains, Cassen 40

Haiston, Francis 378

Hala, Thomas 318

Halbert, Augustus 68, 171; Louis 171; Rene 171

Haldane, John 172

Hale, Thomas 240; William H. 374

Haley/Halley/ Haly, Paul 355; Robert 131; Thomas 90

Hall/Holl, Adam 302; Archibald 39, 40, 52; Ceasar 344; Charles 26; Daniel 386; David 116; Edward 162, 242; Eliza 240; Ellen 188; Frederick 237; George 116, 335; Henry Long 237; Isaac 172, 386; James 116; John 41, 116; Joseph 40; Nye 149; Peter 54; Richard 237; Richard Y. 116; Thomas 116, 237, 240, 329; William 357, 374; William, Jr. 357

Hallebread, Daniel 171

Hallerin, F.O. 117

Hallett, Richard S. 8; William Paxton 338

Halliard, David 376, 377

Halliday/Hallyday, Henry 5; George 242

Halligan, James 79

Hallock, Allen C. 128

Halloran, Patrick 171; Timothy 124

Halsey, Henry J. 20; William 300

Halsm, Godfrey 181

Halsted/Halstead, Ann B. 357; James 91; N. Norris 129

Halton, Joseph 91

Hamill/Hamel, Baltazar 164; Edward 334; Henry 242; Mary 334; Mary Ann 334; Patrick 334; Peter 90

Hamilton, Edward 355; Francis 242; Henry 238; James 172, 240; 308, 374; John 242, 313, 338; John L. 66; Joseph 172; Owen 116; Patrick 352; Robert 158, 335; William 31, 33, 40, 117, 242

Hammer/Hamer, Johann/ Johan 117, 198; John Michael 242; Joseph 117; Michael 165

Hammond, Judah 323

Hammons, La Fayette 138

Hampton, Joseph 241

Hanan, Henry 238; Joseph 90

Hanaty, Dennis 326

Herman/Herrman/Hermans/
  Herrmann (cont'd),
  Jacob 117

Herne, Patrick 238

Herraty, Dennis 19, 29

Herrick, Daniel 306;
  John J. 109

Herring, Honora Victo-
  rine 241; William C.
  241

Herrlich, Engelhard 91

Herttell, Cornelius 2

Hervig, John 27

Herzog, Christian 117

Heschar, Jacob 107

Hesh, Jacob 34, 50, 53

Hesketh, John 334

Hesler, Peter 241, 383

Hess, John H. 141

Hesser, Adam 91

Hester, William 385

Hettinger, John 88, 91,
  128, 142, 316

Hettrich, Conrad 238

Hetzel, Charles Francis
  91, 240; Francis 106;
  John Jacob 240

Heugham, William 172

Heuratty, John 179

Heuser, Peter 91

Heuston, Alexander 174;
  William 174

Hewer, Benjamin, Jr.
  242

Hewitt/Hewett, John 333;
  Josephus 236; Thomas
  13, 69

Heyde, Albert 82, 91

Heydecker, Joachim 75

Heydinger, Nicholas 158

Heyer, Angela 362

Heyl, Francis William
  323

Heyman, Mark/Marks 180;
  189

Heyney, Dennis 304

Hibberd/Hibberd,
  Cornelius W. 144, 157

Hibert, Louis 40, 53,
  59

Hickenbottom/Hicking-
  bottom, David 172;
  Robert 172; William
  59

Hickey, Bernard 174;
  Bridget 238; James
  118, 238; John 308,
  309; Mary 238;
  William 238

Hickman, James 242

Hicks, James 373;
  Nathaniel T. 164

Hickton, John George 174

Higbee, Thomas 383;
  William 376

Higday, George 356

Higgins, David 137, 171;
  Edward 66; Hugh 240;
  John 31, 178; Martin
  374; Michael 69, 90;
  Obadiah 182; Peter 349;
  Thomas 116; Ward 298;
  William 31, 85

Higginson, John Henry 237

Higgs, Mary Ann 239;
  Robert W. 162; William
  239

Higham, John 61

Highet, Robert 319

Hilber, George 118, 150

Hildreth, John 75, 76;
  Samuel P. 58; Samuel
  T. 358

Hildwein, John Christoph
  116

Hilgard, Theodore 240

Hill, Charles 332; Isaac
  236; James 241; James
  H. 241; John 40, 116,
  125; Joseph 29, 351;
  Peter 174; Samuel 336;
  William 6, 335

Hiller, Johannes 90

Hilliard, James 374

Hilliker, James 242

Hillsburgh, Charles 240,
  342

Hilton, Edward 358; John
  358; Joseph 53;
  William 174, 358

Hinbeck, John 39

Hinchman, George H. 174

Hindaugh, William 241

Hinds/Hindes/Hind, David
  242; James 242;
  Joseph 107; Thomas 116

Hinrichs, Carl Ernst
  Louis 241; Charles F.A.
  242

Hinritz, John 117

Hinsdale, Henry 351

Hinton, John 13

Hintz, Alexander 117

Hipper, John 40; Joseph
  F. 39

Hipwell, Abraham 56

Hirlemann, George 241

Hiscox, Richard 242

Hitchens, Philip 31

Hitchcock, Elizabeth
  348; James 174, 348;
  Myrtel B. 132;

William G. 348

Hobday, Edward 312

Hobson, Jonathan 5

Hoch, John 117

Hochkin/Hotchkin,
  Charles H. 158

Hodder/Hoddes, Charles
  91, 104

Hodges/Hodge, Andrew B.
  116, 123; Tyzack 354;
  William 115

Hodgetts, Charles 183,
  199

Hodgins, James 238

Hodgson, George 66, 237;
  Thomas 117

Hoefle, Johannes 91

Hoes, John 19

Hofarer, Jacob 197

Hofer, Victor 308

Hoffman, Charles
  Frederick 173;
  Cornelius 36; John
  360; Josiah Ogden/
  Joseph 1, 2, 7;
  Michael 75, 241;
  Tobias 35, 39, 42, 52

Hoffmire, Peter 38

Hoffstrom, Alexander
  241

Hogan/Hegan, Daniel 72;
  Martin 372; Matthew
  27; Michael 57, 236;
  Thomas 171, 174, 190;
  William 13

Hogg, George 70; Thomas
  131

Hoguet, Anthony 118

Hojier, Peter C. 39, 50

Holahan/Holohan, Thomas
  116, 143

Holaher, Terrence 378

Holbarg, Reyer 116

Holbrook, Jonathan 133

Holden, Ann Margaret 116;
  Edward Henry Strange
  116; Horace 65, 67;
  John 359; Joshua R.
  383; Patrick 90;
  Thomas B. 151

Holder, John 173;
  William 173

Holford, James 117, 131

Holland/Hollands,
  Cornelius 173; Walter
  131; William P. 174

Holliday, Arthur 40

Hollidge, Eli 131;
  Thomas 131

Hollis, John, Jr. 173;
  John, Sr. 173; Law-
  rence M. 241;
  Nathaniel 73